NEWCOMER'S
HANDBOOK®

FOR MOVING TO AND LIVING IN

NEW YORK CITY

Including Manhattan, Broooklyn, The Bronx,
Queens, Staten Island, and Northern New Jersey

22nd Edition

503-968-6777
www.firstbooks.com

22nd Edition

Newcomer's Handbook® and First Books® are registered trademarks of First Books.

Authors: Stewart Lee Allen (22nd edition); Jennifer Cecil, Jack Finnegan, and Belden Merims (previous editions)
Editors: Linda Franklin, Matthew Korfhage
Cover design and layout: Erin Johnson Design and Masha Shubin
Cover Images: Chrysler Building, Brooklyn Bridge, Moon/Stars by Erin Johnson; Statue of Liberty © 2009 susaro (iStockPhoto.com); Taxi by Masha Shubin
Interior design: Erin Johnson Design
Interior layout and composition: Masha Shubin
Maps provided by Scott Lockheed and Jim Miller/fennana design

ISBN-13: 978-0-912301-96-9
ISBN-10: 0-912301-96-1

Printed in the USA on recycled paper.

Published by First Books®, 503-968-6777, www.firstbooks.com.

What readers are saying about Newcomer's Handbooks:

I recently got a copy of your Newcomer's Handbook for Chicago, and wanted to let you know how invaluable it was for my move. I must have consulted it a dozen times a day preparing for my move. It helped me find my way around town, find a place to live, and so many other things. Thanks.

– Mike L.
Chicago, Illinois

Excellent reading (Newcomer's Handbook for San Francisco and the Bay Area) … balanced and trustworthy. One of the very best guides if you are considering moving/relocation. Way above the usual tourist crap.

– Gunnar E.
Stockholm, Sweden

I was very impressed with the latest edition of the Newcomer's Handbook for Los Angeles. It is well organized, concise and up-to-date. I would recommend this book to anyone considering a move to Los Angeles.

– Jannette L.
Attorney Recruiting Administrator for a large Los Angeles law firm

I recently moved to Atlanta from San Francisco, and LOVE the Newcomer's Handbook for Atlanta. It has been an invaluable resource—it's helped me find everything from a neighborhood in which to live to the local hardware store. I look something up in it everyday, and know I will continue to use it to find things long after I'm no longer a newcomer. And if I ever decide to move again, your book will be the first thing I buy for my next destination.

– Courtney R.
Atlanta, Georgia

In looking to move to the Boston area, a potential employer in that area gave me a copy of the Newcomer's Handbook for Boston. It's a great book that's very comprehensive, outlining good and bad points about each neighborhood in the Boston area. Very helpful in helping me decide where to move.

– no name given (online submit form)

Upon moving to Chicago from Portland, Oregon, I found myself shocked by more differences than a sales tax. Newcomer's has been amazing! I continue to use my copy years later. Newcomer's gave me contacts, confidence, and street smart tips even my native Chicago friends use. Thank you!

– Dusty W.
Chicago

TABLE OF CONTENTS

CONTENTS

CONTENTS

THIS BOOK IS DEDICATED TO THE PROPOSITION THAT LIVING IN NEW York City is something extraordinary and wonderful. However, the transition from newcomer to New Yorker isn't necessarily achieved without some discomfort. To minimize the difficulties involved in moving to the Big Apple, we have written the *Newcomer's Handbook® for Moving to and Living in New York City*, which has been continually updated since its 1980 inception, in order to keep up with change in this fastest-paced of cities.

This is the fourth edition of this book since the tragedy of September 11th, 2001, shook the city and the world. Since then the focus has shifted significantly from the darkness of that day to the promise of tomorrow. Though scars remain and sorrow lingers, New York and New Yorkers push ever-forward. These pages will help you navigate this magnificent city and set you on the path to becoming a New Yorker yourself. Whether you are looking for the right neighborhood, the right health club, the right synagogue, or simply a quiet, green oasis, these chapters will guide you in your search.

As we go to press the entire world is being shaken by the credit crisis and the realization that the economy is possibly entering the worst recession in decades. New York will be particularly affected because one of the worst hit sectors is the banking and financial area, which pays approximately a third of all New York taxes. Mayor Bloomberg has already ordered $2.5 billion in cuts in the city budget, an approximately 15% cut—by one estimate 225,000 people will be laid off because of the meltdown on Wall Street, with the tax losses from the securities sector alone totaling $6.5 billion. On the positive side, for newcomers, all this means that apartment prices (if not necessarily rents) will be going down, particularly in the outlying areas that catered to Wall Street workers, where decreases are already being reported.

Then again, New York has a way of bouncing back with remarkable speed. In addition to regular updating, this 22nd edition includes new information on finding a home to rent or buy in the **Finding a Place to Live** chapter, as well as new activities for the active in **Sports and Recreation**, some direction for those seeking a brief respite from the city in **Day Trips**, and the most current information on everything from phone lines to satellite radio in **Getting Settled**. We've added a brand-new chapter, **Green Living**, devoted to greening your home, environmentally friendly services and products, greener transportation, and green resources. Throughout the book, wherever available, we've included web sites for institutions and establishments that are mentioned. There is information on getting around the city by subway, bus, bike, and by car in the **Transportation** chapter. For the outdoorsy and nature loving, you'll find the **Greenspaces** chapter helpful, and for the erudite and inquisitive, see the **Cultural Life** chapter.

As usual, we welcome readers' suggestions and comments on the tear-out page at the back of the book.

We hope that the information presented on the following pages will help you establish a New York City residence smoothly and speedily. We also hope that once you select your neighborhood and settle in, the book will help you get on with the pleasure part: enjoyment of the city's myriad and unrivaled resources. Should you have any city-specific queries, from questions about parking, trash pick-up, or upcoming neighborhood festivals, dial the city's call center at 311 (outside New York City, 212-639-9675). Operators are on 24/7 and will work to answer your questions or will direct you to the appropriate New York City agency. Or go to www.nyc.gov.

F ROM THE WIND-WHIPPED CORNER OF EAST END AVENUE ON AN ICY
January evening, Greenwich Village seems as accessible as Alaska. So,
you cancel plans to meet a Village acquaintance downtown, call a friend
on East 67th and get together at an uptown bistro instead. Clearly, the neighborhood in which you live affects what you do and whom you see in New York
City. It takes time, exploration, and a certain street-honed sophistication to feel
at home in any new area, but the fact that New York is a walking city will benefit you tremendously as you get to know it. Unless money is no object, today's
rental market often requires compromises, not only in the way you live but also
in the neighborhood you choose. But wherever you settle, once established
you're likely to become rooted in your own part of town.

More than just an address or a source of necessary services, neighborhoods
provide residents with identification and a sense of belonging, which in turn
provides sufficient sustenance and heart for daily confrontations with the city's
size and pace. Most New Yorkers feel fairly chauvinistic about their area and delight in extolling its virtues—and detailing its faults. As large as New York City is,
individual neighborhoods are often as tight-knit as small towns.

In the following profiles, Manhattan neighborhoods are listed clockwise
(picture an exceedingly elongated clock) starting with Yorkville, continuing
south along the East River downtown around the tip of the island and then uptown along the Hudson ending with Washington Heights/Inwood. Descriptions
of communities in The Bronx, Brooklyn, Queens, and Staten Island—as well as
five in New Jersey—follow Manhattan. No description, however, can substitute
for your own experience. You are strongly encouraged to visit the neighborhoods that interest you and talk to residents before signing a lease. (Among other
things, it is an excellent way to get leads on apartments that might otherwise escape your attention.) Resources and city services within each neighborhood are
included in order to facilitate orientation once you're settled.

For newcomers who might wish to look further afield, to the suburbs for example, we have listed additional communities worth investigating in Brooklyn, Queens, and Staten Island, as well as suburban towns in New Jersey, Connecticut, Westchester County, NY, and Long Island, none more than an hour's commute from Manhattan. Your choice of location will depend largely on where you will be working, your life situation (single, married, family, gay, etc.), your economic situation, what you enjoy doing, and what neighborhood ambiance appeals to you. Suggestions on how to go about finding an apartment or house and how best to enjoy the city come after **Neighborhoods**, in **Finding a Place to Live** and in other sections.

FORMULAS FOR FINDING STREET AND AVENUE ADDRESSES ABOVE 14th Street are described below. Crosstown street numbers follow a more-or-less set pattern; not so, avenue street numbers. In a town where 950 Amsterdam Avenue is at 107th Street, 950 Broadway at 23rd, 950 Fifth at 76th, and 950 Third at 57th, the somewhat elaborate system used to discover the location of an avenue address is worth knowing.

EAST AND WEST SIDE AVENUES

To determine the cross street for an address on an avenue, proceed as follows: first, take off the last digit of the building number; second, divide the remainder by two; third, add or subtract the number given in the column below.*

Avenues A,B,C,D	+3
1st Ave.	+3
2nd Ave.	+3
3rd Ave.	+10
4th Ave.	+8
5th Ave.	
Up to 200	+13
Up to 400	+16
Up to 600	+18
Up to 775	+20
From 775 to 1286	
(cancel last figure)	−18
6th Ave.	
(Ave. of the Americas)	−12
7th Ave.	
Below 110th St.	+12
Above 110th St.	+20
8th Ave.	+10
9th Ave.	+13
10th Ave.	+14
Amsterdam Ave.	+60
Broadway	
Above 23rd St.	−30
Columbus Ave.	+60
Convent Ave.	+127
Lenox Ave.	+110
Lexington Ave.	+22
Madison Ave.	+26
Manhattan Ave.	+100
Park Ave.	+35
West End Ave.	+60

EAST SIDE CROSSTOWN STREETS

5th to Madison & Park	1-99
Park to Lexington	100-139
Lexington to 3rd	140-199
3rd to 2nd	200-299
2nd to 1st	300-399
1st to York	400-499

WEST SIDE CROSSTOWN BELOW 58TH

5th to Ave. of Americas	1-99
Ave. of Americas to 7th	100-199
7th to 8th	200-299
8th to 9th	300-399
9th to 10th	400-499
10th to 11th 5.	00-599

WEST SIDE CROSSTOWN ABOVE 58TH

Central Park West	
to Columbus	100-199
Columbus to Amsterdam	200-299
Amsterdam to West End	300-399
West End to Riverside	400-499

*Central Park West and Riverside Drive do not fit into this formula. Divide the house number by 10 and add 60 to find the cross street on Central Park West; for Riverside Drive, divide the house number by 10 and add 72.

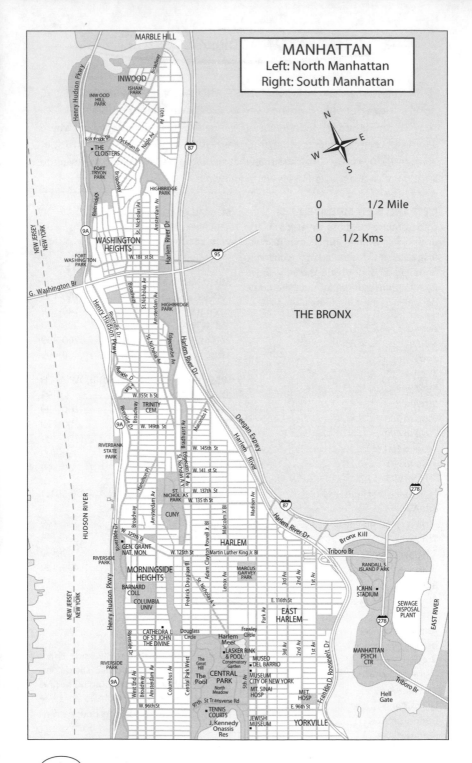

MARBLE HILL

MANHATTAN
Left: North Manhattan
Right: South Manhattan

INWOOD

INWOOD HILL PARK

ISHAM PARK

THE CLOISTERS

FORT TRYON PARK

HIGHBRIDGE PARK

WASHINGTON HEIGHTS

FORT WASHINGTON PARK

W. 181 st St

G. Washington Br

NEW JERSEY
NEW YORK

HIGHBRIDGE PARK

THE BRONX

0   1/2 Mile

0   1/2 Kms

W. 155t h St

TRINITY CEM.

W. 149th St

RIVERBANK STATE PARK

W. 145th St

W. 141 st St

W. 137th St

ST. NICHOLAS PARK

W. 135th St

CUNY

HUDSON RIVER

W. 125th St

GEN. GRANT NAT. MON.

W. 125th St

HARLEM

Martin Luther King Jr. Bl

Triboro Br

Bronx Kill

RANDALL S ISLAND P ARK

RIVERSIDE PARK

MORNINGSIDE HEIGHTS

BARNARD COLL

COLUMBIA UNIV

MARCUS GARVEY PARK

ICAHN STADIUM

NEW JERSEY
NEW YORK

E. 116th St

EAST HARLEM

SEWAGE DISPOSAL PLANT

CATHEDRA L OF ST JOHN THE DIVINE

Douglass Circle

Frawley Circle

Harlem Meer

MUSEO DEL BARRIO

EAST RIVER

RIVERSIDE PARK

LASKER RINK & POOL

Conservatory Garden

MUSEUM CITY OF NEW YORK

MANHATTAN PSYCH CTR

The Great Hill

The Pool

CENTRAL PARK

MT. SINAI HOSP

MET. HOSP

North Meadow

97th St Transverse Rd

Hell Gate

W. 96th St

TENNIS COURTS

J. Kennedy Onassis Res

JEWISH MUSEUM

E. 96th St

YORKVILLE

Triboro Br

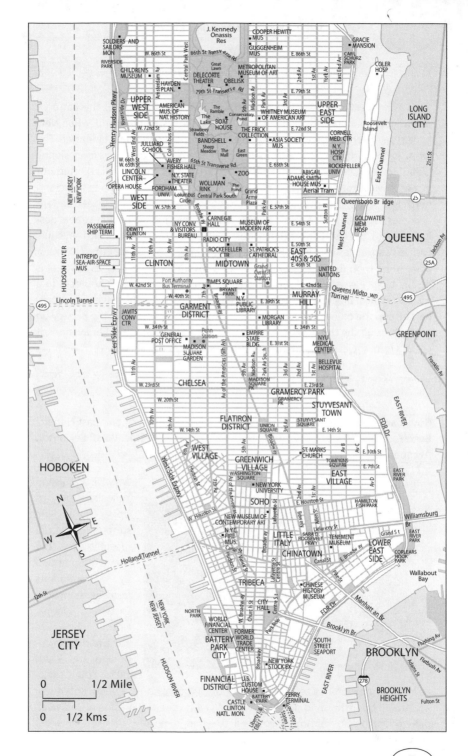

MANHATTAN

"New York, New York, it's a wonderful town, The Bronx is up and the Battery's down," goes the song. That'll do for a start. Like the rest of the world, when New Yorkers say New York they generally mean Manhattan. And from Manhattan, The Bronx is up (north), and the Battery is the southern-most tip of this long, skinny island. To navigate Manhattan you need to know that the island is plotted out in a grid, with crosstown streets running east and west, and avenues stretching north and south, except below 14th Street, where much of the street pattern becomes irregular. Fifth Avenue bisects most of this grid, with cross streets designated east or west. For example, West 25th Street runs west of Fifth Avenue, East 25th stretches east from Fifth. Building numbers begin at Fifth, so 15 West 25th Street is on the first block west of Fifth Avenue and 15 East 25th Street is on the block east of Fifth Avenue. North to south there are 20 city blocks to a mile; crosstown blocks are longer, but not uniformly. The longest avenue in Manhattan, and the oldest, Broadway follows an old Indian trail from the Battery up north through the top of the island into The Bronx. Unlike the other avenues, it crosses from the east side to the west side as it winds its way along.

YORKVILLE

Boundaries and Contiguous Areas: North: East 96th Street and East Harlem; **East**: East River; **South**: East 79th Street and Upper East Side; **West**: Lexington Avenue and Upper East Side

What distinguished Yorkville from its Upper East Side surroundings until recently was the character imbued by immigrants from Germany and Eastern Europe. Now, however, you'll find more co-op signs and health clubs than residents of Hungarian or Czech ancestry. In the 1980s, a co-op, condo, and rental apartment boom finished off what World War II started: the erosion of Yorkville's old-world ethnicity. Although you will still find some old walk-ups on cross streets in the east 80s, most of these pre-war buildings were leveled, beginning in the late 1940s, to make way for new apartment buildings attractive to profes-sionals who, once drawn to the neighborhood, began replacing the immigrants in the remaining railroad flats. Only traces of Yorkville's European heritage re-main, and while Yorkville is still the most accessible part of the Upper East Side, what began as a scattering of stolid brick apartment buildings in mid-century is now an area chockablock with a range of high-rises.

Eighty-sixth Street, from Lexington to First avenues, has been attempting to redefine itself into a pricier shopping strip. However, the hoped-for stability has not entirely materialized. Most of the shopping choices along the well-traveled 86th Street are currently of the chain store variety, with well-known fast food eateries and popular electronics retailers turning the area into a kind of open-air mall. Several multiplex cinemas also have sprung up and draw the younger set for the latest hit films.

Yorkville was a pleasant rural community when the first wave of German and Irish immigrants arrived on these shores in the 1850s. Tranquil pastures surrounded river estates owned by wealthy merchants, many of whom were of German origin. In the 1880s the completion of the Second and Third Avenue elevated lines opened the area to settlement, and German immigrants, many attracted by jobs in the developing breweries, moved north from the Lower East Side. Irish immigrants followed and then, as they grew more prosperous, Hungarians, Czechs, and Slovaks. Today, the second and third generations are more likely to be found in Queens and Westchester than in Yorkville, and it is a dwindling, elderly Middle European population that patronizes the few remain-ing ethnic bakeries, butcher shops, and restaurants. Not that these stores are empty; customer ranks have been swelled by appreciative young professionals who now dominate the area.

The inviting mix of buildings, old and new, that characterizes Yorkville, as well as the community's relatively low crime rate, upper middle class status, and good public schools, makes it an attractive destination for the determined apart-ment seeker. After a slow-down in the early 1990s, housing construction is again active, with luxury rentals rising between East 86th and 96th streets. Variations in pricing for housing will be determined by proximity to the only Upper East Side subway that runs up and down Lexington Avenue; the closer you are the higher your rent will be, although this could all change if the city ever succeeds in con-structing its long-planned East Side subway line. According to a recent article from the *New York Times*, good deals on housing can be found on First, Second, and York avenues, perhaps because of the many bars lining those streets, espe-cially First and Second.

For a refreshing pause, explore Carl Schurz Park bordering the East River at 86th Street and East End Avenue, where you can also spy the mayor's residence, graceful Gracie Mansion built in 1799. Jutting over FDR Drive, this relatively green oasis recalls Yorkville of yore and affords a spectacular view of the East River, its is-lands, boats, and barges. The charm of this park is that other than neighborhood residents, most New Yorkers don't know it's there, allowing for more elbow-room in an often-crowded city. Astors, Rhinelanders, and Schermerhorns once had their estates here, and this quiet neighborhood is still Yorkville's most coveted roost and home to two of the city's best private girls' schools, not to mention the Asphalt Green sports/community center and adjacent AquaCenter.

While the upscale new apartment towers continue to attract a tide of young professionals to the upper northeast reaches of Yorkville, many of the older, six-story redbrick buildings and the more affordable tall towers are now also attracting families. It's not uncommon to see parents or nannies pushing strollers and kids pointing to the child-inspired goods displayed in store windows. The gentrification of so many other parts of the city combined with the vast number of buildings that have been built here over the past twenty years has made it considerably easier to find apartments in Yorkville and the adjacent Upper East Side.

Web Site: www.nyc.gov, www.yorkvillenyc.blogspot.com

Area Codes: 212, 646, 917

Post Offices: Yorkville Station, 1617 Third Ave at 91st St; Gracie Station, 229 E 85th St; Cherokee Station, 1483 York Ave

Zip Codes: 10128, 10028, 10021

Police Precinct: Nineteenth, 153 E 67th St, 212-452-0600, www.nyc.gov/nypd

Emergency Hospitals: Mt. Sinai Hospital, 1190 Fifth Ave at 100th St, 212-241-6500; Metropolitan Hospital Center, 1901 First Ave, 212-423-6262

Libraries: 96th St Branch, 112 E 96th St, 212-289-0908, Yorkville Branch, 222 E 79th St, 212-744-5824; www.nypl.org

Public School Education: School District #2 in region 9 at 333 Seventh Ave, 12th floor, 212-356-3700, http://schools.nyc.gov

Community Resources: 92nd St Y (Young Men and Young Women's Hebrew Association), 1395 Lexington Ave, 212-415-5500, www.92y.org

Transportation—Subway: #6: 77 St, 86 St, 96 St; #4/#5 (Express): 86 St, www.mta.info

Transportation—Bus: Crosstown 96th St (M96); Crosstown 86th St (M86); Crosstown 79th St (M79); Uptown First Ave - Downtown Second Ave (M15); Uptown Third Ave - Downtown Lexington Ave (M98, M101, M102, M103); www.mta.info

UPPER EAST SIDE

Boundaries and Contiguous Areas: North: East 96th Street; **East**: the East River; **South**: 59th Street; **West**: Fifth Avenue

The affluent heart of the Upper East Side—that quadrant caught between Fifth, 79th, Lexington, and 59th Street and the panhandle stretching from 79th along

Fifth to 96th Street—has landmark status. But this does not mean that Manhattan's most popular neighborhood for the wealthy and the upwardly mobile is completely homogeneous. Each avenue that traverses the area, from Fifth east to York, has a distinctive character all its own.

Fifth Avenue, flanking Central Park, glitters with some of the city's most magnificent museums, most exclusive cooperatives, and some of its most glamorous relics, those wonderfully ornate mansions that so clearly reflect the

tastes and fortunes of our turn-of-the-20th-century millionaires. Fricks, Dukes, Carnegies, Whitneys—their versions of palaces, chateaux, and Gothic castles established the avenue as highly fashionable. Dominating Fifth physically and artistically in the East 80s, the Metropolitan Museum is also the site of one of the liveliest street scenes in town. Its sprawling stone steps, while providing access to the museum, offer seats and a meeting place from which to watch the mimes, musicians, and street vendors who use the sidewalk around the entrance as performing space.

Madison Avenue between 60th and 86th streets is a veritable gauntlet of classy international boutiques and fine arts galleries. This solid wall of chic includes The Limited, Ralph Lauren, Timberland, and Barneys. Around 81st Street and P.S. 6 (Public School #6), the premier elementary school on the Upper East Side, a number of trendy designers have set up shop. Above 86th Street, where Andrew Carnegie built the elaborate mansion that now houses the Cooper-Hewitt Museum, most of the other palatial beaux-arts residences constructed in the early 1900s have been acquired by schools, consulates, and cultural institutions. Today these grand buildings, interspersed with bow-fronted, brick Georgian homes and solid pre–World War II apartment buildings, form an exceedingly harmonious neighborhood.

On Park, the handsome center strip of year-round greenery and seasonal plantings makes the stately square cooperative buildings that proceed shoulder to elegant shoulder up the avenue more gracious still.

Lexington Avenue has largely taken over from Madison as purveyor of quality produce to Upper East Siders. Immaculate and imaginative shops harboring fishmongers and florists, greengrocers and bakers, are crowded into the ruddy, rustic brick buildings that line the street.

The area from Third Avenue east to the river, once the province of the "el" train and tenements, has been "Trumped up." Today, sleek glass and granite shafts intersperse postwar brick apartment blocks that loom over the once characteristic, and now disappearing, five-story walk-ups. Popular eateries featuring ethnic fare—Chinese, Thai, Greek, Italian, Indian—line the avenues, and turn-of-the-20th-century buildings once aimed at young professional singles are now home to many young professional parents. The multitude of strollers and busy youngsters cramming into St. Catherine's Park (playground), between 67th and 68th streets on First Avenue, is testimony to the baby boom that is in full swing on the Upper East Side. The proliferation of apartments and gentrification of other neighborhoods, plus an increase in what are considered "safe" parts of town, have made living in this area more accessible than in previous years. As realtors explain it, the Upper East Side is still a terrific neighborhood and has not changed much in the past two decades. However, unlike 20 years ago, there are now other excellent neighborhoods to be found throughout Manhattan, so the waiting lists to get into apartments in the Upper East Side have shortened. That said, however, the Upper East Side's luxury co-ops and condominiums are some of the most expensive in the city, and with the persistently steady climb in prices, records are being broken. According to Trulia.com, in 2008 the average price for one square foot of Upper East Side real estate reached $1700 by the end of 2008, with no noticeable drop due to the economic mayhem that characterized the end of the year. Co-ops average just below two million dollars, and prices overall have doubled in the last five years. There are less expensive options, to be sure, but a strong relationship with a trusted broker is the best means to finding it.

Web Sites: www.uppereast.com, www.cb8m.com, www.friends-ues.org, www.nyc.gov

Area Codes: 212, 646, 917

Post Offices: Lenox Hill Station, 217 E 70th St; Gracie Station, 229 E 85th St; Cherokee Station, 1483 York Ave

Zip Codes: 10128, 10028, 10021, 10022

Police Precinct: Nineteenth, 153 E 67th St, 212-452-0613, www.nyc.gov/nypd

Emergency Hospitals: Lenox Hill Hospital, 100 E 77th St, 212-434-2000, www.lenoxhillhospital.org; New York Presbyterian Hospital–Cornell Medical Center, 525 E 68th St, 212-746-5454, www.nyp.org; Manhattan Eye, Ear and Throat Hospital, 210 E 64th St, 212-838-9200, www.nymeeth.org; nearby: Mt. Sinai Hospital, 1190 Fifth Ave at 100th St, 212-241-6500

Libraries: 96th St Branch, 112 E 96th St, 212-289-0908; Webster Branch, 1465 York Ave at 78th St, 212-288-5049; 67th St Branch, 321 E 67th St, 212-734-1717; www.nypl.org; The New York Society Library, 53 E 79th St, 212-288-6900, www.nysoclib.org, a private institution, with membership dues of $200 per year and 250,000 volumes, is an outstanding resource; its reference room is open to non-members.

Public School Education: School District #2 in region 9 at 333 Seventh Ave, 12th floor, 212-356-3700, http://schools.nyc.gov

Adult Education: Marymount Manhattan College, 221 E 71st St, 212-517-0400, www.mmm.edu; Hunter College, 695 Park Ave at 68th St, 212-772-4000, www.hunter.cuny.edu

Community Resources: 92nd St Y (Young Men's and Women's Hebrew Association), 1395 Lexington Ave, 212-415-5500, www.92y.org; the Cooper-Hewitt Museum, 2 E 91st St, 212-849-8400, www.cooperhewitt.org; the Jewish Museum, 1109 Fifth Ave at 92nd St, 212-423-3200, www.jewishmuseum.org; the Solomon R. Guggenheim Museum, 1071 Fifth Ave at 89th St, 212-423-3500, www.guggenheim.org; the Whitney Museum of American Art, 945 Madison Ave at 75th St, 212-570-3600, www.whitney.org; the Metropolitan Museum of Art, 1000 Fifth Ave at 82nd St, 212-535-7710, www.metmuseum.org; the Frick Collection, 1 E 70th St, 212-288-0700, www.frick.org; The Asia Society, 725 Park Ave, 212-288-6400, www.asiasociety.org; the China Institute, 125 E 65th St, 212-744-8181, www.chinainstitute.org; Society of Illustrators, 128 E 63rd St, 212-838-2560, www.societyillustrators.org; Mount Vernon Hotel Museum & Garden, 421 E 61st St, 212-838-6878, www.mvhm.org, Viennese Neuegalerie, 104 5th Ave at 86th, 212-628-6200, neuegalerie.org; and numerous other societies, museums, galleries and auction houses

Transportation—Subway: #6: 96 St, 86 St, 77 St, 68 St, 59 St/Lexington Ave; #4/#5 (Express): 86 St, 59 St/Lexington Ave; F: 63 St at Lexington Ave; N/R/W: 59 St/Lexington Ave; www.mta.info

Transportation—Bus: Crosstown 96th St (M96); Crosstown 86th St (M86); Crosstown 79th St (M79); Crosstown 72nd St (M72); Crosstown 66th/67th St (M66); Crosstown 57th St (M57); Crosstown 57th & 72nd (M30); Crosstown 57th & Uptown/Downtown on York Ave (M31), Uptown Madison Ave - Downtown Fifth Ave (M1, M2, M3, M4); www.mta.info

ROOSEVELT ISLAND

Located off of 59th Street in the East River

Roosevelt Islanders have always had an unusual commute: a silent aerial ride to and from 59th Street and Second Avenue in Manhattan (every 5 to 15 minutes for $2.00) up and over the East River with the city's skyline first at eye level and then, incredibly, beneath your feet. Small wonder that the tram finds favor with tourists and day-trippers. Residents used to be reduced to taking cabs or a roundabout bus ride through Queens to Manhattan when the tram occasionally faltered. Now, however, the city's Transit Authority has a subway line (the F train) connecting the island with Queens (at 21st Street and 41st Avenue) and Manhattan (at 63rd and Lexington Avenue).

An appealing small-town quality pervades this island community of under 15,000 with its modern apartment buildings. It's quiet. Automobile access is limited, and a red bus (25¢) provides regular service between the tram terminal and high-rises lining relatively spotless streets where strolls with baby carriages and street corner chats are ritual—a sort of time zip back to the 1940s. There's even a fortnightly publication called *The Main Street Wire*. Several spacious parks, six historical landmarks, a waterfront Promenade, and unparalleled views of the Manhattan skyline highlight life on this 147-acre island. Roosevelt Island has extensive recreational facilities and shops that supply the basic needs, if not the exotic or ethnic ones. Built by early farmers in 1796, the Manor House is preserved at the foot of Main Street. The Octagon Lighthouse is now restored. Schools go up to the eighth grade and are part of District #2 (information in the **Chelsea** section).

Inauguration of the long-awaited subway line in 1989 was accompanied by Manhattan Park's five-building development on an eight-acre site, which added 1,100 units to the housing stock and some 2,500 inhabitants to the island's population, which is now over 9,000 people. Manhattan Park attracts upper middle class families (no studios) with stunning views and concierge service at prices about 25% below comparable Manhattan rents. Northtown, Island House, Westview, Eastwood, and Rivercross are all housing developments providing a wide array of apartments for middle- to upper-income families. Southtown is the newest series of high-rises, with two buildings completed and five more planned. Contact the Roosevelt Island Development Corporation for more information (212-832-4540, www.rioc.com). While residents enjoy the peaceful, low-crime character of this narrow two-and-a-half-mile island, some are concerned that the island is beginning to get too crowded. Drawbacks? Despite the marvelous views of Manhattan, which sits just a stone's throw away, there is still limited access when commuting back and forth. And not everyone finds the uber-groomed ambiance to their liking.

Manhattan Park buildings are managed by Grenadier Realty Corporation (212-759-8660, www.manhattanpark.com). The Roosevelt Island Housing Management Corporation (552 Main Street, 212-838-4747) manages the rental units and subsidized apartments (for which there are specified income limits) in Westview, Eastwood, and Island House; Rivercross Tenants Corporation, the island's only co-ops, can be reached at 212-308-7271.

There is a long-standing rumor that dogs are not permitted on Roosevelt Island, and this is simply not true. Dogs are perfectly welcome; it's finding a lease that allows your companion to come inside that is virtually impossible.

Web Sites: www.rooseveltisland.us, www.rioc.com, www.cb8m.com, www.nyc10044.com, www.nyc.gov

Area Codes: 212, 646, 917

Post Office: Island Post Office, 694 Main St

Zip Code: 10044

Police Precinct: One Hundred and Fourteenth, 34-16 Astoria Boulevard, Queens, 718-626-9311, www.nyc.gov/nypd

Emergency Hospital: Coler-Goldwater Hospital, 1 Main St, 212-318-8000

Library: Roosevelt Island Community Library, 524 Main St, 212-308-6243, www.nypl.org

Public School Education: School District #2 in region 9, 333 Seventh Ave, 12th floor, 212 356 3700, http://schools.nyc.gov

Community Resources: The Chapel of the Good Shepherd Community Center, 555 Main St, 212-832-6778, built in 1888, this old chapel now serves the island as an active community center; Youth Programs Inc., 506 Main St, 212-935-3645, offers various classes for children; Main St Theatre & Dance Alliance, 548 Main St, 212-371-4449, features performances and offers classes in theater, dance, yoga, and aerobics for kids and adults.

Transportation—Tramway: 59th St and Second Ave (scheduled to be shut down for renovation during the latter half of 2009)

Transportation—Subway: Roosevelt Island (F)

Transportation—Bus: Manhattan-Queens (Q101, 60, 32); Queens (Q102); Red Bus, Main St (25¢)

EAST FORTIES AND FIFTIES

Boundaries and Contiguous Areas: North: 59th Street and the Upper East Side; **East**: East River; **South**: 42nd Street and Murray Hill; **West**: Lexington Avenue

In 1763, when James Beekman built a summer home called Mount Pleasant on the rural landscape that is now the bustling corner of 51st Street and First Avenue, it's unlikely he could have imagined the value this property would eventually command. With steady growth and development, by the late 18th century this urbane neighborhood was known as Turtle Bay Farm. The mid-19th century brought industrialization and the "el," or elevated subway trains, rumbling over tenements built along the East River. A construction boom in the 1920s left the heart of

Turtle Bay much as you see it today: handsome, tree-shaded blocks of carefully maintained brownstones interspersed with relatively small apartment buildings. But not until the 1940s, when the squalid slaughterhouses that had replaced the riverside slums were razed to make room for the United Nations, and the 1950s, when the "el" came tumbling down, did Turtle Bay become eminently respectable from Lexington Avenue clear to the East River. Today the neighborhood is one of the most prestigious—and one of the safest—in town; a self-assured place with charming culs-de-sac such as Amster Yard on 49th Street, Greenacre Park on 51st, and the private, somewhat secret, garden enclosed by twenty Italianate town-houses in which Katharine Hepburn and E.B. White once lived.

Apartment prices, as befits a neighborhood embracing exclusive Sutton Place, Beekman Place, the two glass towers at United Nations Plaza, and the latest and tallest Trump tower, are among the highest around. For the least rarefied rates, look along First and Second avenues and the side streets in between. The 3,000-unit Tudor City (which lies on what used to be called Goat Hill (for its slaughterhouses) is just southwest of Sutton Place. Bounded by 40th and 43rd streets, this huge complex of Tudor-style buildings between First and Second avenues was built to revitalize a slum area and includes a hotel, church, and private parking area. Unfortunately for would-be tenants, eleven of the twelve buildings completed in 1930 have been converted to cooperatives.

The 1999 opening of the long-awaited Bridgemarket in the extraordinary Guastavino tile-vaulted hall beneath the Queensborough Bridge at 59th Street, between First and York avenues, is probably the most exciting development in this otherwise sedate neighborhood since the building of the UN. Designed originally in 1914 as an open-sided marketplace, but left dormant for many years,

the 24- to 44-foot-high domed ceilings house a market-style food emporium, two restaurants, and a high-end Conran home furnishings store. Predictably, the completion of this project has stimulated new residential development in the neighborhood. A half-mile to the south, Donald Trump's 72-story Trump World Tower is making its own waves—not to mention casting a long shadow—throughout the area. Home Depot has opened a second store in the city, at 980 Third Avenue, near 59th Street, offering a virtually endless array of do-it-yourself options, hardware selection, instructional seminars, tool rental, and home decorating supplies.

Web Sites: www.nyc.gov, www.tudorcity.com

Area Codes: 212, 646, 917

Post Offices: Tudor City Station, 5 Tudor City Place; FDR Station, 909 Third Ave; Dag Hammerskjold Station, 884 Second Ave; UN Station, 405 E 42nd St

Zip Codes: 10022, 10017, 10016

Police Precinct: Seventeenth, 167 E 51st St, 212-826-3211, www.nyc.gov/nypd

Emergency Hospitals: New York Presbyterian Hospital–Cornell Medical Center, 525 E 68th St, 212-746-5454, www.nyp.org; New York–Langone Medical Center, 550 First Ave at 33rd St, 212-263-7300, www.med.nyu.edu

Libraries (nearest): 58th St Branch, 127 E 58th St, 212-759-7358; Mid-Manhattan, 455 Fifth Ave, 212-340-0863; Terence Cardinal Cooke-Cathedral, 560 Lexington Ave, 212-752-3824; www.nypl.org

Public School Education: School District #2 in region 9 at 333 Seventh Ave, 12th floor, 212-356-3700, http://schools.nyc.gov

Adult Education: Turtle Bay Music School, 244 E 52nd St, 212-753-8811, www.tbms.org

Community Resources: YMCA of Greater New York, Vanderbilt Branch, 224 E 47th St, 212-912-2500, www.ymcanyc.org; YWCA of the City of New York, 50 Broadway, 212-755-4500, www.ywcanyc.org; Japan Society, 333 E 47th St, 212-832-1115, www.japansociety.org; Phillip Morris branch of the Whitney Museum of American Art at Altria, 120 Park Ave, 917-663-2453, www.whitney.org

Transportation—Subway: #6: 59 St/Lexington Ave, 51 St, 42 St/Grand Central; #4/#5 (Express): 59 St/Lexington Ave, 42 St/Grand Central; N/R/W: 59 St/Lexington Ave; E/V: 53 St/Lexington Ave, 53 St/Fifth Ave; S (Crosstown shuttle)/#7 Crosstown to Queens): 42 St/Grand Central

Transportation—Bus: Crosstown 49th/50th Sts (M27, M50); Crosstown 42nd St (M42); Crosstown 42nd St - Downtown Broadway (M104); Uptown Madison Ave - Downtown 5th Ave (M1, M2, M3, M4); Uptown Third Ave - Downtown Lexington Ave (M98, M101, M102, M103); Uptown First Ave - Downtown Second Ave (M15)

MURRAY HILL

Boundaries and Contiguous Areas: North: 42nd Street and the East Forties and Fifties; **East**: East River; **South**: 34th Street and the Gramercy Park Area; **West**: Fifth Avenue

Murray Hill is the kind of neighborhood where you can walk into a compact, ground-floor apartment, open a back door, and have access to a garden larger than the flat. Time was when the great mansions of Fifth and Madison avenues— lastingly elegant buildings such as J.P. Morgan's magnificent McKim, Mead, and

White–designed library—conferred social status on the houses highest on the hill. Below these were the stables and carriage houses serving them, and in the shadow of the old Third Avenue "el," tenements. The tenements are gone now, and as Fifth Avenue became more commercial, residential Murray Hill shifted east and the carriage houses proved to be fashionable—indeed, charming—homes. The streets are a mix of tranquil landmarks such as Sniffen Court, a private mews at 150–158 East 36th Street, nondescript brick apartment buildings, postmodern fantasies such as the undulating, 57-story Corinthian, and brownstones: solid and unpretentious turn-of-the-20th-century buildings that are nonetheless elegant and lend a particularly substantial quality to city life.

The neighborhood takes its name from a Quaker merchant, Robert Murray, who built a farmhouse at what is now the corner of 37th Street and Park Avenue.

Grand Central Station stands on what was his cornfield. Murray's wife and daughters played a minor role in the Revolutionary War by detaining General Howe and his officers at tea while Washington and his troops escaped their pursuit. Among the historic buildings in the area is the slender brownstone at 125 East 36th Street where Franklin and Eleanor Roosevelt first lived. An active neighborhood association guards the quiet residential character of Murray Hill.

University and Bellevue Hospitals and related New York University medical facilities are a major presence just to the south, and the casual, inviting shops and restaurants crowding Second and Third avenues play to a youthful audience, where the bar scene can get quite raucous on a weekend. Housing possibilities include proliferating high-rises on the flatlands east of Third as well as brownstones and carriage houses on Murray Hill itself. Although it is less expensive than other areas, prices have at least doubled in the last decade.

Web Sites: www.murrayhillnyc.org, www.nyc.gov
Area Codes: 212, 646, 917
Post Offices: Murray Hill Finance Station, 115 E 34th St; Murray Hill Annex, 205 E 36th St
Zip Code: 10016
Police Precinct: Seventeenth, 167 E 51st St, 212-826-3211, www.nyc.gov/nypd

Emergency Hospitals (nearest): New York University -Langdon Medical Center, 550 First Ave at 33rd St, 212-263-7300, www.med.nyu.edu; Bellevue Hospital Center, 462 First Ave at 27th St, 212-562-3015, www.nyc.gov/hhc

Libraries: Kips Bay Branch, 446 Third Ave, 212-683-2520, www.nypl.org; New York Public Library's Science, Industry, and Business Library (SIBL), 188 Madison Ave at 34th St, 212-592-7000; The Morgan Library and Museum, 225 Madison Ave, 212-685-0008, www.morganlibrary.org, an exquisite edifice housing an extraordinary collection of rare books, including three Gutenberg Bibles, manuscripts, and works of art.

Public School Education: School District #2 in region 9 at 333 Seventh Ave, 12th floor, 212-356-3700, http://schools.nyc.gov

Adult Education: American Academy of Dramatic Arts, 120 Madison Ave, 800-463-8890, www.aada.org; Stern College for Women, Yeshiva University, 245 Lexington Ave at 35th St, 212-60-5400, www.yu.edu

Community Resources: Murray Hill Neighborhood Association, 212-886-5867, www.murrayhill.org

Transportation—Subway: S (Crosstown shuttle): 42 St/Grand Central; #7 (Crosstown to Queens): Fifth Ave, 42 St/Grand Central; #6: 33 St, 42 St/Grand Central; #4/#5 (Express): 42 St/Grand Central

Transportation—Bus: Crosstown 34th St (M16, M34); Uptown Madison Ave - Downtown Fifth Ave (M1, M2, M3, M4); Uptown Third Ave - Downtown Lexington Ave (M98, M101, M102); Uptown First Ave - Downtown Second Ave (M15)

GRAMERCY PARK AREA

Boundaries and Contiguous Areas: North: 34th Street and Murray Hill; **East**: First Avenue and Stuyvesant Area; **South**: East 14th Street; **West**: Park Avenue South/Chelsea and the Flatiron District

The actual park (and namesake of the neighborhood), Gramercy Park, is a verdant, block-square, fenced and locked enclave to which only residents of the surrounding buildings hold keys. With its lovely old trees, squirrels, flowering spring plantings, and the occasional nanny, the park is reminiscent of a quiet London square. But it wasn't the work of a homesick Brit; a real estate developer wanting to increase the value of his 66 lots laid out the private park in 1831. That this strategy was successful is evidenced by the quality of the ornate, later-19th-century buildings that still surround the square—elaborate structures such as The Players Club (Edwin Booth's former home) and the National Arts Club (designed in a Gothic Revival style by Calvert Vaux).

The air of dignified elegance that permeates Gramercy Park and sets such a pleasant tone for the neighborhood as a whole is reinforced by historic

Stuyvesant Square (located four blocks to the southeast at 15th Street), with its lovely brick Friends Meeting House and brownstone St. George's Church, where J.P. Morgan worshiped. In general, this is an enclave of small townhouses and rows of trim brickfronts interspersed with renovated tenements, modest apartment houses, and an occasional high-rise.

North of the park, the Kips Bay neighborhood, stretching from Lexington Avenue to the East River, houses a fairly middle-class populace, including medical personnel from the hospitals along First Avenue, in corner high-rises and side street brownstones. Subsidized rental complexes include the highly desirable Waterside between 23rd and 28th streets, overlooking the East River, and Henry Phipps Plaza along Second Avenue in the 20s.

To the west, Lexington Avenue in the 20s, redolent with the spices of the Indian restaurant strip known locally as "Curry Hill" (a play on adjacent Murray Hill), is recently gentrified. Apartment buildings there have been upgraded, making the area worth a look. Convenient take-out is a bonus.

Renovation of the once-again handsome Madison Square Park and Union Square Park has coincided with the resurgence of Park Avenue South as a commercial market and a dining destination, attracting residents—many from the fashion and publishing fields—to newly available housing. On Second Avenue, and in the 20s and low 30s, new condos have sprouted like field mushrooms after a fall rain. The newly renovated Union Square Park is filled with business types lunching on warm days.

As this area increases in popularity, available apartments become scarcer although several recent towers on Third Ave have opened up some space and contributed to a more youthful presence. The most desirable, overlooking Gramercy Park, are expensive and vacancies are rare. You will have a better chance in one of the newer high-rises in the east 20s. In any event, the Gramercy area is neigh-

borly, although busy, with a healthy community presence. Area safety is assisted by the presence of young police cadets in training, and by the police station itself on 21st Street. As is the case throughout the city, it's a good idea to walk through the community talking with doormen, building superintendents, and, if possible, residents when searching for an apartment here.

Web Site: www.nyc.gov

Area Codes: 212, 646, 917

Post Offices: Murray Hill Finance Station, 115 E 34th St; Madison Square Station, 149 E 23rd St

Zip Codes: 10016, 10010, 10003

Police Precincts: Seventeenth (above 30th St), 167 E 51st St, 212-826-3211; Thirteenth, 230 E 21st St, 212-477-7411, www.nyc.gov/nypd

Emergency Hospitals (nearest): New York University–Langdon Medical Center, 550 First Ave at 33rd St, 212-263-7300; Bellevue Hospital Center, First Ave at 27th St, 212-562-3015, www.nyc.gov/hhc; Beth Israel Medical Center, 16th St at First Ave, 212-420-2000, www.wehealny.org

Libraries: Kips Bay Branch, 446 Third Ave, 212-683-2520; Epiphany Branch, 228 E 23rd St, 212-679-2645; www.nypl.org

Public School Education: School District #2 in region 9 at 333 Seventh Ave, 12th floor, 212-356-3700, http://schools.nyc.gov

Adult Education: School of Visual Arts, 601 W. 26th St, 646-638-2079, www.schoolofvisualarts.edu; Baruch College of Adult and Continuing and Professional Studies, 55 Lexington Ave at 25th St, Room D1-110, 646-312-5000, www.baruched.com

Community Resources: Theodore Roosevelt House, 28 E 20th St, between Broadway and Park Ave South, 212-260-1616, www.nps.gov; Roosevelt's exuberantly Victorian birthplace contains letters, books, and objects collected from his many trips contained in this two-house gallery and museum.

Transportation—Subway: L (Crosstown to Brooklyn): 14 St/Union Sq, Third Ave, First Ave; #6: 33 St, 28 St, 23 St, 14th St/Union Sq; N/W/#4/#5 (Express): 14 St/Union Sq

Transportation—Bus: Crosstown 34th St (M16, M34); Crosstown 23rd St (M23); Crosstown 14th St (M14); Uptown Madison Ave - Downtown Fifth Ave (M1, M2, M3, M4); Uptown Third Ave - Downtown Lexington Ave (M101, M102); Uptown First Ave - Downtown Second Ave (M15)

STUYVESANT TOWN AND PETER COOPER VILLAGE

Boundaries and Contiguous Areas: North: 23rd Street; **East**: FDR Drive; **South**: 14th Street and the East Village; **West**: First Avenue and Gramercy Park Area

Today, two of the oldest and best known properties in New York City, Stuyvesant Town, 14th to 20th streets, and its upscale (larger apartments and rents) little brother, Peter Cooper Village, 20th to 23rd streets, are easier to penetrate. Major renovation of many formerly rent-regulated apartments has opened the door to new tenants. While, with over 11,000 apartments in the two enclaves, the process of complete deregulation is expected to take a couple of decades, market-rate apartments are now available for those who meet the income requirements. What makes these developments so desirable is their resolutely middle-class, family-ori-ented population, along with 15 playgrounds and grassy areas tucked away within. Both developments, with their full-time security force, remain safe, and—after 50 years' growth of trees, flowers, ivy and climbing hydrangea against the red brick walls—they are unpretentious and attractive. Apply at the renting office for both developments at the Peter Cooper Management Office, at 332 First Avenue (between 19th and 20th streets), or visit www.pcvst.com and www.stuytown.com.

Eyebrows have been raised and heartbeats quickened by the sale of these complexes by MetLife, the insurance giant, to Tishman Speyer, in a joint venture with BlackRock Realty, a real estate firm, for 5.4 billion dollars. The sense of community is made evident by the bidding war that preceded the sale: tenants assembled a 4.5 billion dollar bid of their own, and are fired up about protecting their neighborhoods. Tishman Speyer has no stated plans for development, and claims "stewardship" of the property, assuring residents they will work alongside them on plans for the future. Of late, however, papers have been featuring stories in which tenants report they are being forced out to make room for higher paying occupants, so stay tuned.

The community surrounding Peter Cooper and Stuyvesant includes luxury buildings as well as owner-occupied brownstones and upgraded tenements. When scouting the area (First Avenue west to Lexington), try the side streets. The neighborhood is a comparison shopper's dream, with major supermarkets and many ethnic food stores (especially south on First Avenue), clothing shops, and decorating showrooms along First and Second avenues vying for your dollars. The nearby 14th Street and Union Square area covers you for electronics, books (Barnes & Noble), bargains (Filene's Basement), and Whole Foods. There are large, quiet, tree-shaded parks for breaks between apartment visits, and in warm weather the renovated public swimming pool at 23rd Street and Asser Levy Place is available for a cooling few laps. (In fact, look for this turn-of-the-20th-century stone Roman bath even if you can't swim; it's a beauty.) And if you are, like so many people, concerned about available health care, this neighborhood, with five top hospitals within walking distance, merits serious consideration.

Web Sites: www.nyc.gov, www.pcvst.com

Area Codes: 212, 646, 917

Post Offices: Peter Stuyvesant Station, 432 E 14th St; Madison Square Station, 149 E 23rd St

Zip Codes: 10010, 10009

Police Precinct: Thirteenth, 230 E 21st St, 212-477-7411, www.nyc.gov/nypd

Emergency Hospitals: New York University–Langdon Medical Center, 5350 First Ave at 33rd St, 212-263-7300, www.med.nyu.edu; Bellevue Hospital Center, First Ave at 27th St, 212-562-3015, www.nyc.gov/hhc; Cabrini Medical Center, 227 E 19th St, 212-995-6000, www.cabrininy.org; Beth Israel Hospital Medical Center, First Ave and 16th St, 212-420-2000, www.wehealny.org

Libraries: Epiphany Branch, 228 E 23rd St, 212-679-2645; Kips Bay Branch, 446 Third Ave, 212-683-2520; www.nypl.org

Public School Education: School District #2 in region 9 at 333 Seventh Ave, 12th floor, 212-356-3700, http://schools.nyc.gov

Adult Education: School of Visual Arts, 601 W 26th St, 212-592-2000, www.schoolofvisualarts.edu; Baruch College of Continuing & Professional Education, 55 Lexington Ave, Room B1-113, 646-312-5000, www.caps.baruch.cuny.edu

Transportation—Subway: L (Crosstown to Brooklyn): 14 St/Union Sq, Third Ave, First Ave; #6: 23 St, 14 St/Union Sq; N/Q/R/W#4/#5: 14 St/Union Sq

Transportation—Bus: Crosstown 34th St (M16) goes across 34th St and down Second Ave, then east across 23rd St and uptown to 34th St along FDR Drive; Crosstown 23rd St (M23); Crosstown 14th St - Downtown Avenue A/Avenue D(M14A/M14D); Uptown First Ave - Downtown Second Ave (M15); Uptown/ Downtown Avenue C - Crosstown Houston St (M21)

EAST VILLAGE

Boundaries and Contiguous Areas: North: 14th Street and the Stuyvesant Town area; **East**: East River; **South**: Houston Street and the Lower East Side; **West**: Broadway and Greenwich Village

More than most Manhattan neighborhoods, the East Village has been a reliable mirror for the social changes of the last 50 years. Once a Puerto Rican and Ukrainian enclave, it became the epicenter of the beatnik/hippie movement in the 1950s and '60s, only to decline into the infamous homeless and drug wars of the 1980s. While remnants of these eras enrich the area and give it an unusually rich social fabric, the East Village today is dominated by younger professionals and upmarket alternative types who throng its bars, cafés, health food stores, boutiques, and restaurants late into the night. The latest wave of immigrants has arrived in baby strollers, with a noticeable number of young families moving into the area (or perhaps they're just the artists and thespians of yore growing up).

The most obvious gentrification is happening west of First Avenue. Old-school grunge-punk cafés have added playrooms and public schools have set up innovative teaching programs. P.S. 363, at 121 East 3rd Street, places an emphasis on learning in a non-competitive environment, and P.S. 364 at 600 East 6th Street, known as the Earth School, offers studies with an ecological bent. Rents in this area can be as high as almost anywhere in the city. Cheaper digs can be found for the moment in the Puerto Rican/young singles area east of First Avenue known as Alphabet City (so named because that's where the numbered avenues give way to alphabetized ones). But until the endlessly delayed Second Avenue subway line is finished, ostensibly in 2020, Alphabet City remains cut off from any convenient mass transit.

There are two distinct centers to the East Village. The eastern part is focused on the bucolic dollop of Tompkins Square Park, where the notorious homeless camp of the 1980s has given way to dog runs, fairs, farmers' markets, and shady benches. On the western edge the tone is set by the distinctly urban Astor Place, with its metal sculpture popularly known as the "Cube." This recently restored spinning steel cube sculpture by Tony Rosenthal continues to be the hangout for adolescent punks and skaters, but the wave of the future is the green glass tower behind it that—it'll cost you $2 million for any of forty apartments in the newly constructed "Sculpture for Living." This high-rise is typical of the buildings transforming the area's traditional low-rise, brick-and-leaf ambiance, from the controversial "Blue Building" on Delancey, to the glass cube the private arts school Cooper Union is throwing up on Astor Place. The area to the south between the Bowery and Broadway (called NoHo, for North of Houston) remains notable for its elegant old loft buildings recalling the era of the millionaire Astor, although that too is being undermined by some of the new buildings and chains like K-Mart.

Connecting Astor Place with the Second Avenue heart of the East Village is St. Mark's Place. Actually part of 8th Street, this lively little block was once home to W.H. Auden (and later a huge methadone clinic) but now runs to cheap Japanese taverns, t-shirt stands, and rowdy teen tourists. There's also a small ethnic enclave known as Little India on 6th Street between First and Second avenues. Urban lore holds that the dozens of Indian restaurants here share a single kitchen, but this has never actually been proven.

Housing comes in two main forms: old walk-ups and converted lofts. Many walk-ups are rent stabilized. If you think you're being offered a rent-stabilized apartment at market prices, you can find out at the New York State Division of Housing and Community Renewal (DHCR), 718-739-6400 or 212-961-8930. In addition, much of NoHo is legally reserved for certified artists. Check with the City Loft Board, 100 Gold Street #2 (212-788-7610), to determine their eligibility and to be sure the particular building is in compliance with city loft laws.

Since much of the East Village housing consists of minimally rehabbed tenements you should be prepared for the lack of elevators. Start your apartment search by studying ads in the *Village Voice*, check Cooper Union and NYU bulletin boards, or walk the streets and talk to people who live there. Numerous web sites will also be helpful; craigslist.com continues to lead the way, with rent.com not far behind. Finding reasonable rent is a challenge and many people find a permanent apartment by first subletting—check out sublet.com if this idea appeals to you. Several subscription sites are also available.

Web Site: www.nyc.gov, east-village.com

Area Codes: 212, 646, 917

Post Offices: Cooper Station, 93 Fourth Ave; Peter Stuyvesant Station, 432 E 14th St; Tompkins Square Station, 244 E 3rd St

Zip Codes: 10003, 10009

Police Precinct: Ninth, 130 Ave C, 212-477-7811

Emergency Hospitals: Beth Israel Medical Center, 281 First Ave at 16th St, 212-420-2000, www.wehealny.org; New York Eye and Ear Infirmary, 310 E 14th St, 212-979-4000, www.nyee.edu

Libraries: Ottendorfer Branch, 135 Second Ave near St. Mark's Place, 212-674-0947; Tompkins Square Branch, 331 E 10th St, 212-228-4747; www.nypl.org

Public School Education: School District #1 in region 9 at 333 Seventh Ave, 12th floor, 212-356-3700, http://schools.nyc.gov

Adult Education: New York University's School of Continuing and Professional Studies, 145 Fourth Ave, 212-998-7200, scps.nyu.edu, offers a huge range of classes; Third Street Music School Settlement, 235 E 11th St, 212-777-3240, www.thirdstreetmusicschool.org; The Cooper Union for the Advancement of Science and Art, Third Ave and 7th St, 212-353-4195, www.cooper.edu

Community Resources: La Mama Experimental Theater Club, 74A E 4th St, 212-475-7710, www.lamama.org, on the cutting edge of avant-garde theater for over two decades; PS 122, 150 First Ave, 212-477-5288, www.ps122.org, is a reclaimed public school turned cutting edge performance space (hence its PS pun); The Nuyorican Poets Café, 230 E 3rd St, 212-505-8183, nuyorican.org, has been home to bilingual NYC Puerto Rican poets, writers, musicians, and performers for 35 years; Joseph Papp Public Theater, 425 Lafayette St,

212-539-8500, www.publictheater.org, founded in 1954 and home to plays, musicals, and Shakespeare; the Classic Stage Company has been successfully producing classics for more than 35 years at 136 E 13th St, 212-677-4210 (ext. 10), www.classicstage.org; Third Street Music School (see above) offers concerts and recitals; Cooper Union, 51 Astor Place, 212-353-4100, www.cooper. edu, has frequent exhibits, concerts, and lectures; theater and opera thrive even on the Bowery: classics at the Jean Cocteau Repertory at 330 Bowery, 212-677-0060, www.jeancocteaurep.org; and Italian opera at The Amato Opera Theater at 319 Bowery, 212-228-8200, www.amato.org

Transportation—Subway: L (Crosstown to Brooklyn): 14th St/Union Sq, Third Ave, First Ave; N/R/W: 14 St/Union Sq, 8th St/NYU; 4/5/Q: 14th St/Union Sq; #6: 14 St/Union Sq, Astor Pl, Bleecker St; B/D: Broadway-Lafayette; F/V: Broadway-Lafayette, Second Ave

Transportation—Bus: Crosstown 14th St (M14); Crosstown East-West 8th/9th Sts (M8) Uptown Third Ave/Lexington - Downtown Lexington/Third Ave (M101, M102); Uptown First Ave - Downtown Second Ave (M15); Crosstown East-West Houston St (M21); Downtown Bowery to City Hall (M103); Union Sq to Battery Park via Ave B (M9)

LOWER EAST SIDE, LITTLE ITALY, CHINATOWN

Boundaries and Contiguous Areas: North: Houston Street and the East Village; **East**: East River; **South**: Downtown; **West**: Broadway and SoHo

"Give me your tired, your poor..." wrote Emma Lazarus, and when they arrived, many of them settled on the Lower East Side. Between 1870 and 1920, wave upon wave of immigrants from Italy, China, and the ghettos of Eastern Europe poured into the warren of then fetid tenements on Mulberry, Elizabeth, Hester, and Division streets. Here many lived and worked until able to move up and out to the suburbs or more spacious quarters in other boroughs, leaving room for the next wave. Others remained, and many generations have grown up in this neighborhood that defined what coming to America was all about.

Public housing, especially along the easternmost strip of the Lower East Side, alleviated some of the crowding and let in some light and air, and along Grand Street, from Essex to the river, 28 co-op buildings provided affordable housing for the middle class. The Grand Street co-ops now sell at market rates their previous owners could not have imagined. Renewal began along the fringes, where the young and impecunious—artists, students, and the like—established beachheads. Formerly vacant tenements have been renovated, attracting a more affluent crowd. Along East Houston (pronounced "how-ston") and grungy Ludlow Street, clubs, trendy restaurants, and boutiques have now become virtual tidal waves of gentrification where weekend evenings resemble a gargantuan frat party with hordes of drunken revelers. The area still has lots of appeal but regular complaints from long-term residents about noise levels, along with the number of bars, represent unmistakable signs of gentrification. Nonetheless, an

old-fashioned community spirit pervades the Lower East Side, and many long-time tenants still pay much lower rents than newcomers to this area.

There are actually a number of Lower East Side neighborhoods, each very distinctive but all featuring scarce parking and crowded with shops and restaurants lining narrow streets. To the east is the old Jewish Lower East Side, now largely Latino and Chinese; Chinatown is in the southwest portion, which continues to expand inexorably northward into the third area, Little Italy. Colorful Orchard Street still has a few Yiddish-speaking shopkeepers, many of them Hasidim, but much of the once vibrant Jewish community is gone, and forlorn old synagogues have been converted into churches or are used for other purposes. Some of the buildings above the shops, formerly vacant, now house young professionals in $3,000-a-month studios, and antique shops and young designer boutiques have crept in among the dusty menswear shops.

A wave of recent arrivals has burst Chinatown's traditional seams past East Broadway into the old Jewish enclave and north over Canal Street into Little Italy, which is now two-thirds Asian. Housing is impossibly crowded, and sweatshops can still be found. But walking the almost impassable sidewalks of Chinatown on a Saturday, one would think this area existed solely to satisfy the city's insatiable appetite for Chinese food. The northern edge of Chinatown east of Bowery has recently been "discovered" by younger professionals, making for an interesting mix with the older Chinese residents as well as the potential for an area that seems likely to be become the next Nolita or some other imaginative name.

Little Italy, between Canal and Houston streets, has a vanishing Italian population but an expanding selection of Italian restaurants and cafés. Along Mulberry Street on a warm spring evening, the combined hisses of uncountable cappuccino machines sound like a locomotive gathering steam. The neighborhood has become a restaurant district. And although frozen dim sum take the place of frozen ravioli in innumerable small stores, a bit of the old Southern Italian character remains, as does the community's reputation as a don't-mess-with-us, low-crime neighborhood with strong ethnic ties around the old, original St. Patrick's on

Mulberry Street. On the northern edge of Little Italy, galleries, boutiques, and cafés are filling the once-vacant storefronts, and the neighborhood has acquired the name Nolita (for North of Little Italy).

Infiltration of the Lower East Side by the middle class is no longer news. Construction is rampant on The Bowery; the New Museum is now up and running and surrounded by high-rise luxury condos working their way down the strip from the Village and uptown from SoHo, as well as overdesigned boutique hotels and restaurants featuring lobster in cherry butter. CBGB's, the legendary punk club, is now gone and in its place (if not literally) is the 712-unit mixed-use residential and commercial complex called Avalon Chrystie Place, which features a three-story Whole Foods with three full-on cafés, a cheese cellar, a specialty beer shop, and lots of space for groups to meet. See www.avaloncommunities. com for details.

Those considering a rental here would do best to talk to someone who lives in the neighborhood and to walk around, looking, block by block, as one can be quite different from the next in tone and character. The typical real estate web sites tend to have more broker listings than no-fee listings for this area.

Web Site: www.nyc.gov, www.lowereastside.nyc
Area Codes: 212, 646, 917
Post Offices: Knickerbocker Station, 128 E Broadway; Pitt Station, 185 Clinton St; Chinatown Station, 6 Doyers St
Zip Codes: 10012, 10013, 10002
Police Precincts: Fifth, 19 Elizabeth St, 212-334-0711; Seventh, 19 1/2 Pitt St, 212-477-7311, www.nyc.gov/nypd
Emergency Hospital (nearest): New York Downtown Hospital, 170 William St, 212-312-5000, www.downtownhospital.org
Libraries: Hamilton Fish Park Branch, 415 E Houston St, 212-673-2290; Seward Park Branch, 192 E Broadway, 212-477-6770; www.nypl.org
Public School Education: School District #2 in region 9 at 333 Seventh Ave, 12th floor, 212-356-3700, http://schools.nyc.gov
Community Resources: The Henry Street Settlement offers a variety of resources, including its Abrons Arts Center at 265 Henry St, 212-766-9206, www. henrystreet.org. The New Federal Theatre, at 466 Grand St, 212-353-1176, www.newfederaltheatre.org, specializes in minority dramas and has been a staple of the neighborhood for nearly 35 years. The Lower East Side Tenement Museum, 108 Orchard St, 212-431-0233, www.tenement.org, includes exhibits in three buildings (one of which has been "unrestored" to illustrate life as it was) as well as neighborhood walking tours. The Museum of Chinese in America, 70 Mulberry St, 212-619-4785, www.mocanyc.org, offers historical walking tours as well as exhibits and video documentaries.
Transportation—Subway: F: Broadway-Lafayette, Second Ave, Delancey-Essex St, East Broadway; V: Broadway-Lafayette, Second Ave; B/D: Broadway-Lafay-

ette, Second Ave; #6: Bleecker St, Spring St, Canal St; N/R/W: Prince St, Canal St; Q: Canal St; J/M/Z: Chambers St, Canal St, Bowery, Delancey-Essex St

Transportation—Bus: Crosstown Houston St (M21); Uptown First Ave - Downtown Second Ave (M15); Uptown Bowery/Third Ave - Downtown Third Ave/Bowery M103); Crosstown Delancey St (M39); Uptown Grand St/Essex St/Avenue A - Crosstown 14th St to Union Sq (M14A)

DOWNTOWN

Boundaries and Contiguous Areas: North: Chambers Street and Tribeca; **East**: East River; **South**: Upper New York Bay; **West**: Hudson River

Lower Manhattan has some of the most vocally optimistic leaders and proponents of any New York City neighborhood. For good reason—the area seems to teeter precariously between its enormous potential and the still-raw wounds of the devastation wrought here in September, 2001. The scales are tipping: there is tremendous growth and rapid change taking place despite the fact that seven years after the Twin Towers came down their replacement remains essentially unstarted. And though some of the bustle that once defined the area has returned, it is tinged with solemnity, especially near the vast, fenced-in scar beneath Vesey Street.

Slow and confused progress at Ground Zero has become a source of major frustration not only for locals but for the city as a whole. Meanwhile, there are major developments elsewhere. A wide variety of initiatives have been under-

taken: an esplanade is taking shape along the East River, high-fashion retailers and restaurants are courting wealthy residents in the Wall Street area, and newly rebuilt 7 World Trade is already taking in tenants.

The Fulton Fish Market, after 183 years of continuous operation by the South Street Seaport, has moved to the Bronx, and the hundreds of thousands of square feet it occupied are being eyed hungrily by developers, with plans ranging from museums to shopping complexes to condos. One serious proposal under consideration is for a year-round, indoor, agrarian public market, which at this point remains merely a series of open markets held two or three times a year; the local planning commission recently gave tentative go-ahead to a plan to tear down or remove the century-old structures and turn the area into a mall and boutique hotel. Time will tell, but for now the market spaces sit empty.

The historic Seaport is chock full of shops and restaurants, as well as several museums and a satellite TKTS booth for discounted Broadway tickets. The lines are usually shorter here than in Times Square, and on Wednesdays and Saturdays offer tickets for evening performances and matinees simultaneously.

Battery Park City continues to evolve and is considered an exemplary model of urban planning, with such forward-thinking measures as The Solaire, at 20 River Terrace, the first of several environmentally friendly buildings in the neighborhood. Nine thousand residents enjoy 35 acres of parks that join up with a series of beautifully done lawn area right on the river where you can watch boats and joggers sail past. There are also public works such as the Skyscraper Museum and the Irish Hunger Memorial. BPC's connection to the World Trade Center is more than geographic; built on land excavated to make way for the Towers, it is nearly complete after forty-plus years of development.

The World Financial Center, a four-building complex of businesses, shops, and restaurants, is still adjusting to its role as an active centerpiece in the neighborhood. The Cesar Pelli–designed buildings with their copper tops and glass panels magnificently reflect sunsets, clouds, and city lights. The slightly antiseptic buildings are offset by the dramatic sweep of the Winter Garden, a soaring glass and polished-steel public atrium between buildings 2 and 3. The Winter Garden faces the WFC Plaza and the North Cove Marina, where one can take in views of the Statue of Liberty and the Jersey City skyline across the river. Also facing the marina are WFC 4 and 1 North End Avenue, the new home of the New York Mercantile Exchange, which lost its trading floor in the attacks of September 11th. PJ Clarke's, the venerated saloon on the Upper East Side, has recently opened a sister restaurant in the space formerly occupied by the beloved and much-missed Moran's, restoring the legendary outdoor beer garden on the marina.

What has long been one of the loudest complaints for people who live and work in the area is the absence of a thriving night life or a sense of "neighborhood." The Winter Garden has frequent concerts and performances, many free, and in the summertime there are many events in the community's parks and along the waterfront, but overall the area empties out in the evening. Most of the restaurants close early, and many are not open on the weekends. Bars tend to close well before New York's bar time of 4 a.m., and there is only one movie theatre in the immediate vicinity. The Wall Street area is particularly underserved, and though the South Street Seaport thrives, it is constantly trafficked by tourists, and many of the shops and eateries there are priced accordingly.

Renewal is the theme downtown, and among its strongest supporters is the Lower Manhattan Development Corporation, a state-chartered organization founded in the aftermath of September 11th for the express purpose of revitalizing this part of the city. The Downtown Alliance manages the Downtown–Lower Manhattan Business Improvement District and aims to improve everything from quality of life to business opportunities. All changes fall under the intense scrutiny of Community Board 1, an active and vocal board made up of fifty local volunteers.

Developers have succeeded in drawing young professionals and families to the area, and there are a great number of baby boomers living comfortably between the parks and the construction. These groups and the young families eagerly seize upon new developments with fervor and strong community pride. Though frustrated by the lack of core development at the World Trade Center site, they give the populace of Lower Manhattan an infectious, determined charm that bodes well for the future. Nowhere else in the city is there such meticulous and passionate planning for what is yet to come.

Web Sites: www.lowermanhattan.info, www.cb1.org, www.downtownny.com, www.batteryparkcity.org, www.worldfinancialcenter.com, www.nyc.gov, www.downtownexpress.com

Area Codes. 212, 646, 917

Post Offices: Peck Slip Station, 1 Peck Slip; Federal Plaza Station, 26 Federal Plaza, Bldg 1; Church Street Station, 90 Church St

Zip Codes: 10004, 10005, 10006, 10007, 10038, 10041, 10280, 10281, 10282

Police Precinct: First, 16 Ericsson Place, 212-334-0611, www.nyc.gov/nypd

Emergency Hospital: New York Downtown Hospital, 170 William St, 212-312-5063, www.downtownhospital.org

Library: New Amsterdam Branch, 9 Murray St, 212-732- 8186; www.nypl.org

Public School Education: School District #2 in region 9 at 333 Seventh Ave, 12th floor, 212-356-3700, http://schools.nyc.gov

Adult Education: Pace University, 1 Pace Plaza, 212-346-1200, www.pace.edu; Borough of Manhattan Community College, 199 Chambers St, 212-220-8000, www.bmcc.cuny.edu

Community Resources: South Street Seaport, 19 Fulton St, 212-732-8257, www.southstreetseaport.com; South Street Seaport Museum, 12 Fulton St at Water St, 212-748-8600, www.southstseaport.org; Federal Reserve Bank, 33 Liberty St, 212-720-6130, www.newyorkfed.org; American Numismatic Society, 1 Hudson Sq, 212-571-4470, www.numismatics.org; Museum of Jewish Heritage, 36 Battery Place, 646-437-4200, www.mjhnyc.org; Trinity Church, Broadway at Trinity Place, 212-602-0800, www.trinitywallstreet.org, houses a museum and offers frequent concerts, as does St. Paul's Chapel, Broadway at Fulton St, 212-233-4164, www.saintpaulschapel.org; One Bowling Green is the address of the Alexander Hamilton US Customs House, which is also home to the National Museum of the American Indian, 212-514-3700, www.nmai.si.edu

Transportation—Subway: #1: Chambers St, Rector St, South Ferry; #2/#3 (Express): Chambers St, Park Pl, Fulton-Broadway-Nassau, Wall St; E: World Trade Center; A/C: Chambers St, Fulton-Broadway-Nassau; R/W: City Hall, Rector St, Whitehall-South Ferry; #6: Brooklyn Bridge-City Hall; #4/#5: Brooklyn Bridge-City Hall, Fulton-Broadway-Nassau, Wall St, Bowling Green; J/M/Z: Chambers St, Fulton-Broadway-Nassau, Broad St; **PATH**: Station beneath World Trade Center site, connections to Hoboken, Jersey City, and Newark

Transportation—Bus: Crosstown Chambers/West/Vesey/Park Row to Madison St (M22); Uptown Church/Centre/Lafayette - Downtown Broadway (M1); Uptown Church/Sixth Ave - Downtown Broadway (M6); Battery Park to LES/Alphabet City/Union Sq (M9); Wall St to Uptown First Ave - Downtown Second Ave (M15); Uptown and Downtown Grand Central Terminal - Wall St Express (M25x) weekdays only, Uptown Lincoln Center, Downtown Battery Park City (M20)

TRIBECA

Boundaries and Contiguous Areas: North: Canal Street and SoHo; **East**: Broadway; **South**: Chambers Street and Downtown; **West**: Hudson River

South of Canal Street, where the island of Manhattan narrows toward its tip, Greenwich Street angles toward West Broadway, leaving in its wake not only the loft district dubbed TriBeCa (**Tri**angle **Be**low **Ca**nal, but no one ever capitalizes the initials anymore) but triangular blocks and crossroad parks unique in the city.

Felicitous little Duane Park, the most charming of the lot, breathes into an area composed of 19th-century brick and cast iron structures, sprawling warehouses, and commercial space, an air of peace and tranquility that is rare in the Big Apple.

Before becoming "Tribeca-fied," the area consisted of a warren of scruffy walk-ups that housed the city's wholesale fruit, vegetable, and flower district, the Washington Market, as well as the butter and egg district. Most of the market was razed and sent packing to The Bronx in the late 1960s, to be replaced in part by the ponderous brick Independence Plaza project at 40 Harrison Street, but a few vestiges of the produce district remain, including a row of Federal houses tucked under Independence Plaza's angular wing, and the two-block Staple Street—an alley actually. There are no staples there.

Tribeca is also home to a number of elegantly sculptural cast-iron buildings—the first built not far from Duane Park by James Bogardus in 1849. The noticeably cleaner of the arched and colonnaded facades front residential lofts and cooperatives skillfully adapted from commercial space, as well as the galleries and offices of the avant-garde establishment (the pioneering fringe has moved to the Lower East Side and across the East River into Williamsburg, Brooklyn). Loft living with amenities is now an accepted urban lifestyle, and Tribeca has changed radically from the quiet backwater it remained throughout the 1970s. It is a prime destination for those who like their buildings wide and their spaces open. Catering to such tastes, antique and design stores cluster along Franklin and Duane streets.

The vaunted, often vaulted warehouses just south of the Holland Tunnel housed the clubs responsible for Tribeca's once-famous nightlife scene. Restaurants that the area's early disco devotees haunted now feed a more staid clientele. Tribeca hosts a kaleidoscopic range of dining with its 300 restaurants—including some of the best three- and four-star restaurants in Manhattan—frequented by the hip, the chic, and the up-and-coming; midday these eateries nourish Wall Street suits and rumpled denizens of city hall. In 2006 it had the dubious distinction of being ranked the 12th most expensive zip code in the US by *Forbes* magazine and you should expect to pay between $2,000 and 4,000 (and up) for a one-bedroom or studio.

Competing pressures—southbound from booming SoHo, from 10,000 students at Manhattan Community College in its midst, and most insistently from the ever-expanding Battery Park City—have transformed Tribeca into a thriving, cohesive, mixed-use community. The conversion of former warehouses and factories to handsome, upscale residential lofts continues, many now selling at seven-digit prices hitherto associated with the Upper East Side. A growing population of children where once there were none, an attractive neighborhood school (P.S. 234), and now a small-town newspaper, the *Tribeca Trib*, along with unimpeded bike riding on weekends, the architecture and night life, are among the attractions of living in Tribeca. Drawbacks? Few grocery stores.

Web Sites: www.cb1.org, www.tribeca.org, www.nyc.gov, www.tribecatrib.com
Area Codes: 212, 646, 917
Post Offices: Canal St Station, 350 Canal St; Federal Plaza, 26 Federal Plaza
Zip Code: 10013
Police Precinct: First, 16 Ericsson Place, 212-334-0611, www.nyc.gov/nypd
Emergency Hospitals (nearest): New York Downtown Hospital, 170 William St, 212-312-5000, www.downtownhospital.org; St. Vincent's Hospital and Medical Center, 170 W 12th St, 212-604-7000, www.svcmc.org

Library (nearest): New Amsterdam Branch, 9 Murray St, 212-732-8186; www. nypl.org

Public School Education: School District #2 in region 9 at 333 Seventh Ave, 12th floor, 212-356-3700, http://schools.nyc.gov

Adult Education: Borough of Manhattan Community College, Office of Continuing Education, 70 Murray St, 212-346-8420, www.bmcc.cuny.edu, offers a variety of inexpensive evening and weekend courses ranging from computer to business to self-improvement. Concerts and theater are also presented regularly in the College's Triplex Theater.

Community Resources: The ongoing reinvention of the riverside into the Hudson River Park from Battery City up to midtown has turned the stretch near Tribeca into a small paradise, although certain areas have lost some of their derelict charm—joggers can even "rent" high-end sneakers for a run on the riverside before deciding on a purchase. Visit the Friends of the Hudson River Park, www.fohrp.org, for information as to what is planned or available and how to get involved. Tribeca houses alternative spaces displaying works for and by the avant-garde, much as upper Madison Avenue houses deluxe galleries catering to the establishment. One such gallery is the Artists Space at 38 Greene St, 3rd Floor, 212-226-3970, www.artistsspace.org, but most open and close every few years. The tours by professional artists, however, remain; New York Gallery Tours, 212-946-1548, www.nygallerytours.com. Tribeca also has pictures that move at its annual Tribeca Film Center at 375 Greenwich St, 212-941-2400, host of the Tribeca Film Festival, www.tribecafilmfestival.org.

Transportation—Subway: #1: Canal St, Franklin St, Chambers St; #2/#3 (Express): Chambers St; A/C: Canal St, Chambers St; E: Canal St; J/M/N/Q/R/W/Z/#6: Canal St

Transportation—Bus: Crosstown Madison & Chambers St/West St & Grand St (M22); Uptown Hudson St/Eighth Ave - Downtown Seventh Ave/Varick St (M20); Uptown Sixth Ave - Downtown Seventh Ave/Broadway (M6); Uptown and Downtown Grand Central Terminal - Wall St Express (X25) weekdays only

SOHO

Boundaries and Contiguous Areas: North: West Houston Street and Greenwich Village; **East:** Broadway and Lower East Side; **South:** Canal Street and Tribeca; **West:** Sixth Avenue

SoHo's cast iron buildings are justifiably famous and a visual delight. Look up to appreciate the beauty of the patterns—columnar shapes, Greek Revival capitals, and other architectural embellishments—pressed into the cast iron facades. Windowsill house plants, paintings, and some of the city's most colorful walls reveal the loft residences, which now occupy most of what was manufacturing space. Behind these slightly grimy fronts live some of New York's trendiest trendsetters, often in 4,000-square-foot spreads. The structures are based on a technique perfected by James Bogardus around 1850. Fore-runners of today's  "curtain wall" skyscrapers, these cast iron buildings are supported by interior columns, obviating the need for thick walls and allowing the use of much more glass than was previously possible. As a result, the graceful windows, many of them arched, nicely complement the strong, solid buildings, and the whole is extremely harmonious. The buildings are also exceedingly attractive to the city's artists, ever on the lookout for good light and space. In the early 1960s they began to move into the area, just as industry had previously moved into what had been the city's red light district a century before; loft living became legal in 1971. With the subsequent discovery of SoHo by the affluent, high prices have driven many of the original artists to less costly neighborhoods although laws help protect some of the older artist residents and art galleries and audacious boutiques remain to prosper and proliferate.

The popularity of SoHo has in no way diminished. On the contrary, monied arrivistes commingle with painters and sculptors on the upper floors of the converted cast iron structures while at street level, hard-edged, minimalist (whatever the fashion-of-the-moment) showrooms spread their plate glass windows far and wide. "An international marketplace for style and design," the *New York Times* calls it, attracting shoppers from Jersey to Germany. "This feels like the world's greatest shopping mall," exclaims a merchant of upscale linens. Just so. You can buy the latest in wearable art, Japanese designer clothes, French prêt-à-porter, exquisite antique blouses and accessories, antique or art deco furniture, and more. Take a shopping break in a chic eatery along West Broadway's restaurant row. Bring money. And if you live here, don't venture out on the weekend. It's packed.

What has changed in recent years is the eastern edge of SoHo. Galleries, clothing shops, and even offices have spread east from West Broadway past Wooster, Greene, and Mercer to Broadway and beyond. Once drab and lifeless, Broadway has undergone a personality change as faux marble and hand-grained surfaces replace the tatty showrooms of fabric wholesalers. The relocation of Dean and DeLuca's extraordinary food emporium to a vast, white space resembling an edible art gallery was a sure sign of the Broadway revival. The replacement of landmark rag emporium Canal Jeans on Broadway by Bloomingdale's, along with the establishment of the very chic Prada store in the former SoHo Guggenheim space, pretty much defines the new emphasis, making this strip a shopper's dream. As SoHo crawls ever eastward, the boundary between it and Little Italy is blurring.

While loft living is legal in many buildings, and you need not necessarily qualify as an artist to rent or sublet SoHo space, caution is advised in taking over a lease or paying key money for a loft or apartment. Check with the New York City Loft Board (100 Gold St #2, 212-788-7610) for the status of legal rents and living situations (see **Lofts** in **Finding a Place to Live**). Many artists sublet when they go on sabbatical or receive grants that take them out of town. If you're not in the market for a condo in one of controversial high-rises going up on Soho's western edge (like the Soho Trump), the best line on housing availability down here is by word-of-mouth (and conversation is lively at the local art galleries and show openings, which anyone can attend) and by browsing community bulletin boards.

Web Sites: www.artseensoho.com, www. sohonyc.com, www.nyc.gov
Area Codes: 212, 646, 917
Post Offices: Prince St Station, 103 Prince St; Village Station, 201 Varick St; Canal Street Station, 350 Canal St
Zip Codes: 10012, 10013
Police Precinct: First, 16 Ericsson Place, 212-334-0611, www.nyc.gov/nypd
Emergency Hospitals (nearest): St. Vincent's Hospital and Medical Center, 170 W 12th St, 212-604-7000, www.svcmc.org; New York Downtown Hospital, 170 William St, 212-312-5000, www.downtownhospital.org
Libraries (nearest): Jefferson Market Branch, 425 Sixth Ave, 212-243-4334; Hudson Park Branch, 66 Leroy St, 212-243-6876, has an excellent film program for children; www.nypl.org.
Public School Education: School District #2 in region 9 at 333 Seventh Ave, 12th floor, 212-356-3700, http://schools.nyc.gov
Adult Education: The French Culinary Institute, 462 Broadway, 7th Floor, 212-219-8890, www.frenchculinary.com; offers a variety of professional and non-professional cooking courses (lunch and dinner, too, at their restaurant, L'Ecole; dial 212-219-3300 for reservations).
Community Resources: New Museum of Contemporary Art, 235 Bowery, 212-219-1222, www.newmuseum.org; the Museum of Comic and Cartoon Art, 594 Broadway, near Prince St, 212-254-3511, www.moccany.org; the Fire Museum, 278 Spring St, 212-691-1303, www.nycfiremuseum.org. The district is crammed with great and small gallery spaces—investigate them at leisure. Most are closed Sunday and Monday. A scan of *Art Now's Gallery Guide*, available in galleries throughout the city, gives a total picture of the area's re-

sources and current shows. For weekly guides to arts events in SoHo see the *Village Voice*, the "Weekend" section on Friday and "Arts and Leisure" section of the Sunday *New York Times*, *Time Out New York*, and the *New Yorker*'s "Goings on About Town" section or *New York Magazine*'s "Cue" section. Nearby Tribeca also offers opportunities to explore the more avant-garde side of the arts, as does the East Village, from which, amoeba-like, galleries have spread throughout the Lower East Side.

Transportation—Subway: B/D/F/V: Broadway-Lafayette; A: Canal St; C/E: Spring St, Canal St; N/R/W: Prince St, Canal St; J/M/Q/Z: Canal St; #6: Canal St, Bleecker St; #1: Houston St, Canal St

Transportation—Bus: Crosstown Houston St (M21); Downtown Fifth Ave - Uptown Sixth Ave (M5); Downtown Seventh Ave/Broadway (M20); Uptown Sixth Ave - Downtown Seventh Ave/Broadway (M6)

GREENWICH/WEST VILLAGE

Boundaries and Contiguous Areas: North: 14th Street, Chelsea, and Flatiron District; **East**: Broadway and the East Village; **South**: West Houston Street and SoHo; **West**: Hudson River

Greenwich Village is the kind of community where neighbors look after each other's plants and pets and where people do call the police or fire department if they notice something amiss. Residents still tend to be arts-oriented, and more liberal and politically active than most, particularly when it comes to incursions, real or threatened, on the free-wheeling lifestyle adopted by some or on the neighborhood's cherished landmarks and signature style. It was the Village's great good fortune to have its 18th-century farm lane streets in place before city planners superimposed the grid pattern on most of Manhattan. The crooked streets that intersect major arteries at skew angles are a refreshing change although navigating the streets may take time and determination.

Since the 19th century, the brick, Federal-style structures along these crooked streets have housed more than their share of the city's talented and creative. Writers came first: Edgar Allan Poe in 1837, later Mark

Twain, Henry James, and Walt Whitman. Artists and intellectuals followed. A handful of people and institutions played key roles in the evolution of the Village as a magnet for those in the vanguard of the arts and letters. Gertrude Vander-bilt Whitney opened her first studio here, exhibiting and encouraging the artists who subsequently became the nucleus of the "Ashcan school" of social realist painters. Mabel Dodge's famed literary salon was on Washington Square, and the Provincetown Players established an early experimental theater on Macdou-gal Street in 1916. New York University was founded on Washington Square in the 1830s, the New School on West 12th Street in the 1920s. By then the local populace included John Dos Passos, e.e. cummings, Willa Cather, Henry Miller, and Edna St. Vincent Millay, making Greenwich Village the avant-garde capital of the nation.

After WW II, abstract expressionists, method actors, controversial novelists, and muckraking journalists all coexisted, bringing creative vitality to the area. The written word was set to music in the fifties and sixties as folk legends per-formed anti-war hymns in small coffee houses. Hippies, yippies, and the latest in fashionable cultural trends and lifestyles have always been part of the Village's attraction, with only the spiraling rents setting in during the 1970s softening the neighborhood's appeal for artists and writers. These days there are probably more art appreciators around than artists, but the charm of the Village, with its pleasing proportions and special kind of peacefulness, remains. An annual art show on the streets around Washington Square Park and the city's foremost (and most outrageous, or at least gargantuan) Halloween Parade are among the fes-tivities that make this neighborhood special. The park itself, with its famed arch gleaming and free from the scaffolding that clung to it for years, was recently redone at great expense, although the difference is almost invisible to the naked eye—the new NYU mini-towers now lining the park's southern edge create a much greater impact.

Greenwich Village contains a balanced mix of high-rise elevator buildings, older, rent-stabilized apartments, lofts, renovated tenements, and brownstones (a harmonious ensemble threatened, in the West Village at least, by the emer-gence of several buildings above the prescribed height limit to obtain Hudson River views). New, pricey rental apartments and condos in the handsome con-versions in the wholesale antiques district bordering University Place and in the now-fashionable converted warehouses lining West and Washington streets are widely advertised.

The meatpacking district in the far-West Village, south of 14th Street, has experienced a complete makeover, with film studios, trendy restaurants, night-clubs, galleries, upscale-clothing stores, boutique hotels and now luxury housing completely overtaking the old transvestite hooker hangouts and butcher shops. The evening crowds here are huge and will soon be floating overhead as well, when the new High Line Park has finished converting the rusted elevated train rails into a "park in the sky." Recent additions to Village housing stock can be found on lower Hudson Street and along the river on West Street, where new rentals and condos continue to rise, offering upscale living options outside the landmarked district.

Because the area is essentially an assembly of small communities—the predominantly Italian **South Village**, the central **Washington Square** neighborhood, and the **West Village**, bounded by Seventh Avenue and the Hudson River—searching for rentals is best done on foot and through reliable real estate agents.

Web Sites: www.nycgv.com, www.nyc.gov, www.villagealliance.org

Area Codes: 212, 646, 917

Post Offices: Patchin Station, 70 W 10th St; West Village Station, 527 Hudson St; Cooper Station, 93 Fourth Ave; Prince Station, 124 Greene St; Village Station, 201 Varick St

Zip Codes: 10014, 10011, 10012, 10003

Police Precinct: Sixth, 233 W 10th St, 212-741-4811, www.nyc.gov/nypd

Emergency Hospital: St. Vincent's Hospital and Medical Center, 170 W 12th St, 212-604-7000, www.svcmc.orq

Libraries: Jefferson Market Branch, 425 Sixth Ave, 212-243-4334; Hudson Park Branch, 66 Leroy St, 212-243-6876, has an excellent film program for children; www.nypl.org.

Public School Education: School District #2 in region 9 at 333 Seventh Ave, 12th floor, 212-356-3700, http://schools.nyc.gov . Greenwich Village has two elementary schools. Public School 41 offers "traditional" public school education, while P.S. 3, with an "open corridor" program, is more experimental. Go to http://schools.nyc.gov for more information.

Adult Education: Parsons School of Design (part of the New School University), 66 Fifth Ave, 212-229-8900, www.parsonsnewschool.edu; New School University, 66 W 12th St, 212-229-5600, www.newschool.edu; The Cooper Union for the Advancement of Science and Art, Third Ave and 7th St, 212-353-4195, www.cooper.edu; Greenwich House Music School, 46 Barrow St, 212-242-4770, www.gharts.org; Greenwich House Pottery, 16 Jones St, 212-242-4106, www.greenwichhousepottery.org; New York University, 50 W 4th St, 212-998-1212, www.nyu.edu; Pratt Manhattan, the local branch of Brooklyn's Pratt Institute, 144 W 14th St, 212-647-7199, www.pratt.edu, has extensive evening and weekend course offerings in the arts and professional areas.

Community Resources: Yeshiva University Museum, 15 W 16th St, 212-294-8330, www.yumuseum.org; Cherry Lane Theatre, 38 Commerce St, 212-989-2020, www.cherrylanetheatre.com; Actor's Playhouse, 100 Seventh Ave South, 212-741-8189; Lesbian, Gay, Bisexual and Transgender Community Center, 208 W. 13th St, 212-620-7310, wwwgaycenter.org

Transportation—Subway: L (Crosstown to Brooklyn): Eighth Ave, Sixth Ave, 14 St/Union Sq; A/C/E: 14 St, W 4 St; #1: 14 St, Christopher St, Houston St;

#2/#3 (Express): 14 St; F/V: 14 St, W 4 St; N/R/W: 14 St/Union Sq, 8 St/NYU; Q/#4/#5/#6: 14 St/Union Sq

Transportation—Bus: Crosstown 14th St (M14A/M14D); Crosstown 8th/9th Sts (M8); Crosstown Houston to Ave C (M21), Uptown Greenwich St/Tenth Ave - Downtown Ninth Ave/Hudson St (M11); Uptown Hudson St/Eighth Ave - Downtown Seventh Ave (M20); Uptown Sixth Ave - Downtown Fifth Ave (M5) Uptown Sixth Ave - Downtown Broadway (M6), Uptown University Place/ Madison Ave - Downtown Fifth Ave (M2, M3)

FLATIRON DISTRICT/UNION SQUARE

Boundaries and Contiguous Areas: North: 23rd Street and Madison Square; **East**: Park Avenue South and Gramercy Park Area; **South**: 14th Street; **West**: Sixth Avenue and Chelsea

Thanks to the famous wintry photograph by Edward Steichen, the thrusting nose of the Flatiron Building is familiar, even to out-of-towners. The triangular structure at the convergence of Broadway and Fifth Avenue at 23rd Street was a wonder, a skyscraper, when completed in 1902. The 21-story steel-frame edifice was also at the apex of the Ladies' Mile, New York's elegant shopping district. Macy's, Tiffany, Lord & Taylor, and other now forgotten luxurious emporiums cut a fashionable swath down Broadway, Fifth, and Sixth avenues in the late 19th century.

But just as the rumbling Sixth Avenue elevated subway had stimulated the

development of the Ladies' Mile, so the city's booming economy caused the great stores to move uptown. The elegant buildings with rhythmic cast iron fronts, elaborate mansard roofs, Byzantine columns, and Gothic finials were abandoned to a dim and sooty half-life as manufacturing lofts and warehouses. The 1990s saw a reawakening south of 23rd Street, and the wedge-shaped Flatiron Building has lent its name to the neighborhood. Andy Warhol was, perhaps, among the first to make a mark in the Flatiron District when he established his notorious Factory on **Union Square**. Professional photographers began moving bed-and-tripod into the neighborhood's vast manufacturing lofts in the 1970s.

Photo supply houses and model agencies came next, followed by publishing houses, advertising agencies, and, most recently, internet and media startups. Of late a large Whole Foods and slew of discount clothing stores has opened at one end, with a four-story Barnes & Noble at the other, and a new upscale al fresco restaurant in the park now under construction (and of course being vigorously protested). Once a hang-out for drug dealers and such, the park has become a community center where political rallies are held almost every day amidst arts and crafts stalls. Immediately after the 2001 attacks, it was turned into an acre-wide shrine of flowers and candles.

Nearby on lower Fifth Avenue fashion heavyweights as Armani, Paul Smith, and Matsuda have taken root and the abandoned palaces of the Ladies Mile on Sixth Avenue have re-opened as mega-stores selling books, housewares, office supplies, and clothes. On Broadway, home furnishing stores cluster around the feet of ABC Carpet and Home.

There are rare rentals in the handsome Zeckendorf Towers, set back from Union Square with airy, teal pyramid points atop the brick towers and a 24-hour supermarket downstairs. Madison Green, overlooking restful **Madison Square Park**, is among the notable modern condominiums. And a sleek apartment tower, 1 Union Square South, rises above the new Circuit City. Building and renovation along the 14th Street corridor between Third and Seventh avenues is adding housing stock to the area, much of it for NYU, as well as a much improved streetscape. More typical of the Flatiron District, however, are the elegant, converted living lofts hidden away in the stolid manufacturing buildings that darken the side streets. Consult a real estate broker for the occasional sublet that comes on the market. Besides a prime location with good public transportation, you'll have the graceful, green breathing space that is now the completely refurbished Union Square for a front yard. The four-day-a-week greenmarket (see **Greenmarkets** in the **Shopping for the Home** chapter) is the Square's *pièce de résistance*. Manhattanites trek year round to the northwest corner at East 16th and Broadway for fresh produce, fish, sausages, cheese, pretzels, breads, honey—oh, endless edibles—and colorful armloads of cut flowers.

Web Sites: www.cb1.org, www.unionsquarenyc.org, www.nyc.gov, www.cenyc. org

Area Codes: 212, 646, 917

Post Offices (nearest): Cooper Station, 93 Fourth Ave; Madison Square Station, 149 E 23rd St; Old Chelsea Station, 217 W 18th St

Zip Codes: 10003, 10010, 10011

Police Precinct: Thirteenth, 230 E 21st St, 212-477-7411, www.nyc.gov/nypd

Emergency Hospitals (nearest): St. Vincent's Hospital and Medical Center, 170 W 12th St, 212-604-7000, www.svcmc.org

Libraries (nearest): Muhlenberg Library, 209 W 23rd St, 212-924-1585; Andrew Heiskell Braille & Talking Book Library, 40 W 20th St, 212-206-5400, TTY 212-

206-5458, a full-service library with large circulating collections of special format materials, audio playback equipment, and a variety of electronic reading aids; www.nypl.org.

Public School Education: School District #2 in region 9, 333 Seventh Ave, 12th floor, 212-356-3700, http://schools.nyc.gov

Adult Education: School of Visual Arts, 209 E 23rd St, 212-592-2000, www.schoolofvisualarts.edu; Baruch College of Continuing and Professional Studies, 55 Lexington Ave, Room B1-113, 212-312-5000, www.caps.baruched.com

Community Resources: Tibet House, 22 W 15th St, www.tibethouse.org, 212-807-0563; Theodore Roosevelt House, 28 E 20th St, between Broadway and Park Ave South, 212-260-1616, www.nps.gov; Roosevelt's exuberantly Victorian birthplace contains letters, books, and objects collected from his many trips contained in this two-house gallery and museum. The recently opened Rubin Museum of Art, 150 West 17th Street, 212-620-5000, rmanyc.org is an excellent addition with its quiet café—which features an interesting assortment of live Eastern music on the weekend—and exceptionally fine collection of Himalayan art.

Transportation—Subway: L (Crosstown to Brooklyn): Sixth Ave, 14 St/Union Sq; #6: 23 St, 14 St/Union Sq; N/R/W: 23 St, 14 St/Union Sq; Q/#4/#5: 14 St/Union Sq; F/V: 23 St, 14 St; #1: 23 St, 18 St, 14 St; #2/#3 (Express): 14 St

Transportation—Bus: Crosstown 23rd St (M23); Crosstown 14th St (M14A/M14D); Uptown Madison Ave - Downtown Fifth Ave South (M1, M2, M3), Uptown Sixth Ave - Downtown Fifth Ave (M5), Uptown Sixth Ave - Downtown Broadway (M6), Uptown Sixth Ave - Downtown Seventh Ave (M7); Uptown Eighth Ave – Downtown Seventh Ave (M20)

CHELSEA

Boundaries and Contiguous Areas: North: 34th Street and Clinton; **East**: Sixth Avenue and Flatiron District; **South**: 14th Street and Greenwich Village; **West**: Hudson River

Residential Chelsea is a sunny community renowned for peace, quiet, and four- and five-story brownstone row houses, but its origins date back to 1750, when Capt. Thomas Clarke's farm encompassed the area. In the 1830s, Clarke's grandson, Clement Clarke Moore, began developing Chelsea as a highly desirable suburb. Moore donated land for the block-square General Theological Seminary just down the street from the Gothic Revival style St. Peter's Episcopal Church, where he read his "A Visit from Saint Nicholas" to family and parishioners. The tree-shaded Seminary Close is still a neighborhood oasis.

To the west, the Hudson River Railroad attracted slaughterhouses, breweries, and shanties, and in 1871, Chelsea was darkened by the city's first elevated railroad, on Ninth Avenue. Successive decades saw the brief emergence of West 23rd Street as the city's theater district; the raising of vast cast iron structures on Sixth Avenue to house fashionable emporiums such as the original B. Altman's; and in the 1920s and 1930s a thriving vice district; the beginning of the nation's movie industry; and the opening of one of the city's first cooperative apartment houses, now the Hotel Chelsea (aka the Chelsea Hotel), home over the years to artists and writers. Urban renewal in the 1950s and 1960s spurred the restoration of many fine townhouses and made way for two low-income housing projects and the middle-income International Ladies Garment Workers cooperative between Eighth and Ninth avenues.

Sharing the side streets with restored one- and two-family houses is the occasional apartment house and tenement, not to mention formidable **London Terrace**, 405 West 23rd Street, with 14 buildings. The lofts in the photography, flower, fur, and fashion districts (roughly 15th to 30th streets between Fifth and Eighth avenues, which includes the Flatiron District) were discovered by artists in the 1950s and some now attract young families and professionals.

In 1982 the down-at-the-heels Elgin, a 1930s movie house on Eighth Avenue, was transformed into the exuberantly art deco Joyce Theater, the first theater in the dance capital of the world to be specifically designed for small and medium-sized dance troupes. Since then, Chelsea has become something of a dance and performance district. Way west, nightclubs offer do-it-yourself dance in between auto-repair shops and factories.

Eighth Avenue, between 14th and 23rd streets, is Main Street, Chelsea. With a lively restaurant scene and boutiques punctuating the relatively unobtrusive condos and co-ops, the once entirely gay Eighth Avenue strip is becoming a bit more sedate. Chelsea-ites and Villagers shop for quality foods in the imaginatively recycled Nabisco factories on Ninth Avenue and 15th Street called Chelsea Market (which has the best fish and produce in the city). The block-long Whole Foods Market on 24th Street and Seventh Avenue is a magnificent addition to the area, featuring 30,000 square feet of organic foods, fine cheeses, and free range meats. Along with great food shopping, the other recent wave to hit

Chelsea is the art scene: more than 100 trendy galleries cluster near the pioneering Dia Center for the Arts on 22nd Street and along the western corridor between 17th and 27th streets. Ninth and Tenth Avenue eateries feed the gallery crowd. A new Frank Gehry building, at Tenth and 18th Street, aims to spur more development in the area, and 37 Arts, a $23 million Off Broadway complex, with three theaters, state-of-the-art technology, and free parking, aims to draw both locals and tourists.

Simultaneously anchoring the western edge of Chelsea is the extraordinary 1.7-million-square-foot Chelsea Piers Sports and Entertainment complex in four piers over the Hudson River, stretching between 17th and 23rd streets. The movie industry returned to Chelsea in the new film and television studios housed in the pier-head, through which once streamed passengers from some of the world's great ocean liners. In fact, in 1912, this was to be the destination of the ill-fated Titanic. In the handsome complex stretched out behind the studios, workout devotees strain and sweat on state-of-the-art equipment while others (especially youngsters from all over the city) run; ice skate; in-line pirouette; play league hockey, soccer, lacrosse, and basketball; scale a climbing wall; bowl; refine gymnastic skills; or drive balls to target greens on a 200-foot Astroturf fairway under night lights. Others watch and hang out at one of several restaurants. For those who enjoy watching sports, you can take in the professionals at Madison Square Garden, which draws crowds to the west 30s to see the Knicks (basketball), Rangers (hockey), and The Liberty (women's basketball), along with the circus and other events.

North of the piers and looming over the Hudson, the vast industrial Starrett-Lehigh Building, long semi-vacant, attracts high-profile tenants now, including art galleries, film studios, and new media groups. And much of that industrial neighborhood is becoming luxury lofts. It's the new SoHo, and the impending completion of the riverside revitalization, with parks and kayaking galore, will only make it more so. Some of the piers still house older boats and draw an almost salty sea dog clientele.

Chelsea's hot; housing here is expensive and much in demand, and living spaces are often small. The new frontier, less attractive but accessible, is Sixth, Seventh, and Eighth avenues, from 23rd to 31st streets, where a zoning change now allows construction of apartment buildings in a previously industrial zone. Tenth Avenue has become home to a number of clubs, bars, and galleries, but there are few desirable apartments that far west. Home Depot opened their flagship Manhattan store at 40 West 23rd Street in 2005, and offers a virtually endless array of do-it-yourself options, hardware selection, instructional seminars, tool rental, and home decorating supplies. All this gentrification, however, has a price—the neighborly flea markets that filled the vacant lots around the west 20s have now vanished save for one smaller flea held in an old parking lot (which itself is set to go under in 2009) and a smaller on 25th Street between 6th and Broadway. The old fleas, much diminished, have moved to 39th and 9th

Avenue and a tiny lot at 6th Avenue and 18th. And the fabulous Chelsea Flower District in the upper 20s along 6th Avenue, while still a wonderful place to wander in the early morning, is greatly diminished.

Web Sites: www.chelseamarket.com, www.manhattancb4.org, www.nyc.gov, www.fohrp.org

Area Codes: 212, 646, 917

Post Offices: General Post Office, James Farley Station, 421 Eighth Ave at 33rd St, open 24 hours; London Terrace Station, 234 Tenth Ave, near 24th St; Old Chelsea Station, 217 W 18th St

Zip Codes: 10001, 10011

Police Precincts: Midtown South, 357 W 35th St, 212-239-9811; Tenth, 230 W 20th St, 212-741-8211, www.nyc.gov/nypd

Emergency Hospitals (nearest): St. Vincent's Hospital and Medical Center, 170 W 12th St, 212-604-7000, www.svcmc.org

Libraries: Muhlenberg Branch, 209 W 23rd St, 212-924-1585; Andrew Heiskell Braille & Talking Book Library, 40 W 20th St, 212-206-5400; www.nypl.org

Public School Education: School District #2 in region 9, 333 Seventh Ave, 12th floor, 212-356-3700, http://schools.nyc.gov ; Bayard Rustin High School for the Humanities, 351 W 18th St, 212-675-5350, is the city's newest college preparatory high school. http://schools.nyc.gov

Adult Education: Fashion Institute of Technology, 227 W 27th St, 212-912-2300, classes plus art gallery open to the public, www.fitnyc.edu

Community Resources: McBurney YMCA, 125 W 14th St, 212-741-9210, www.ymcanyc.org; the Joyce Theater, 175 Eighth Ave at 19th St, 212-691-9740, www.joyce.org; Dance Theatre Workshop, 219 W 19th St, 212-924-0077, www.dancetheaterworkshop.org; The Kitchen, 512 W 19th St, 212-255-5793, www.thekitchen.org; Dia Art Foundation, 535 W 22nd St, 212-989-5566, www.diaart.org; Atlantic Theater Company, 336 W 20th St, 212-645-1242, www.atlantictheater.org; Chelsea Art Museum, 556 W 22nd St, 212-255-0719, www.chelseaartmuseum.org; and galleries galore. The revamping of Chelsea's riverside area should be done in 2010, offering all sorts of outdoor activities. Visit Friends of the Hudson River Project for more info.

Transportation—Subway: L (Crosstown to Brooklyn): Eighth Ave, Sixth Ave; A: 34 St/Penn Station, 14 St; C/E: 34 St/Penn Station, 23 St, 14 St; #1: 34 St/Penn Station, 28 St, 23 St, 18 St, 14 St; #2/#3 (Express): 34 St/Penn Station, 14 St; B/D: 34 St/Herald Sq; F/V: 34 St/Herald Sq, 23 St, 14 St; N/Q/R/W: 34 St/Herald Sq

Transportation—Bus: Crosstown 34th St/Ninth Ave (M16) Twelfth Ave (M34); Crosstown 23rd St (M23); Crosstown 14th St (M14) also down Ave A and Ave D; Uptown Tenth Ave - Downtown Ninth Ave (M11); Uptown Eighth Ave - Downtown Seventh Ave (M20)

MIDTOWN/GARMENT DISTRICT

Boundaries and Contiguous Areas: North: 59th Street (Central Park South) and Central Park; **East**: Lexington Avenue and East 40s and 50s, Fifth Avenue (south of 42nd Street) and Murray Hill; **South**: 34th Street and Chelsea; **West**: Eighth Avenue and Clinton

For all that it contains within its bounds, Midtown is not a neighborhood. Some 700,000 people work here, but few call it home. Not since the mansions of the mighty—the Rockefellers, the Havemeyers, the Vanderbilts—were left to the wrecker's ball and commercial development around the turn of the 20th century has Midtown felt like a neighborhood. This core of the core of the city throbs and bustles daily with industry in the garment district, commerce between Lexington and Sixth Avenue (or Avenue of the Americas, its official name rarely used by New Yorkers), with shoppers from Macy's to Bergdorf Goodman to Bloomingdale's, and tourists everywhere. Except for the theater district, and the 40s and 50s west of Sixth Avenue, Midtown is quiet at night, all but deserted in some areas.

There are few supermarkets here, no children's playgrounds, and only one city park, the elegantly renovated Bryant Park behind the New York Public Library at 42nd Street, with its free ice skating rink, elegant restaurants, carousel and free outdoor reading area and summer movies—just one block square and a little bit of Europe. What *is* here is almost all of the city's legitimate theater, ballet at City Center Theater, music at Carnegie Hall, and smaller venues, museums, restaurants of every conceivable persuasion, Rockefeller Center, major art galleries along 57th Street, and shopping until you're dropping. Not to mention that perhaps your job is here.

You can live in Midtown. On the high side in Trump and other glassy towers along Fifth and Park avenues and Central Park South, in some fine pre-war (WW II, that is) apartment buildings between Sixth and Eighth avenues in the 50s, and just a bit more modestly in modern doorman buildings. The occasional brownstone is a side street surprise west of Fifth. Affordable apartments may be found in the 40s between Broadway and Eighth Avenue; explore the area first and talk to residents in order to be sure about location. The Times Square Alliance is working hard to attract more retailers for the residents here: hardware stores, dry cleaners, pharmacies. The lofty commercial rents have been prohibitive for independent owners, and progress is slight. Tourists overrun the area, and are the focal point of most businesses here.

The ongoing transformation of Times Square and West 42nd Street has attracted major law firms, publishing houses, investment firms, and family-friendly entertainment to the glassy new towers and renovated theaters in this throbbing, neon-lit "crossroads of the world." Tourists and New Yorkers use a comprehensive array of services at the Times Square Visitor's Center and at the city's official Visitor Information Center. This transformation is driving the development of a formerly shabby Eighth Avenue in the 50s as a new frontier of upscale modern apartment living. Where once the peep shows and XXX theaters huddled, gleaming apartment towers rise, offering marble baths and health clubs at East Side prices. Between these towering newcomers, housing will continue to be spotty but increasingly less shabby as the area continues to transform. Keep in mind, this is a busy, often noisy area and no place for a car. If you're working in the area, enjoy nightlife, theater, and dining out, this may be for you. If you like a more neighborhood feel or particularly if you're moving with kids in tow, look elsewhere.

The search here is best made with the help of reliable real estate agents. Watch the ads in the Sunday Times and the Village Voice to find agents handling properties in the area.

Web Sites: www.nyc.gov, www.timessquare.com, www.timessquarenyc.org, fashioncenter.com

Area Codes: 212, 646, 917

Post Offices: Grand Central Station, 450 Lexington Ave; Midtown Station, 223 W 38th St; Rockefeller Center Station, 610 Fifth Ave; Bryant Station, 23 W 43rd St; Murray Hill Station, 115 E 34th St; Macy's Finance Station, 151 W 34th St; Times Square Station, 340 W 42nd St

Zip Codes: 10016, 10017, 10018, 10019, 10020, 10022, 10036

Police Precincts: Midtown North, 306 W 54th St, 212-767-8447; Midtown South, 357 W 35th St, 212-239-9811, www.nyc.gov/nypd

Emergency Hospitals: St. Luke's–Roosevelt Hospital Center, 1000 Tenth Ave at 59th St, 212-523-4000, www.wehealny.org;

Libraries: The Mercantile Library, 17 E 47th St, 212-755-6710, www.mercantile library.org, a membership library; General Society Library, 20 W 44th St, 212-921-1767, www.generalsociety.org, a membership library; The Donnell Library Center, 20 W 53rd St, 212-621-0618, is closed until 2011; Fifty-Eighth St Branch, 127 E 58th St, 212-759-7358; Mid-Manhattan Branch, 455 Fifth Ave, 212-340-0833; New York Public Library (Humanities and Social Sciences), Fifth Ave and 42nd St, 917-275-6975; www.nypl.org; the Science, Industry and Business Branch (SIBL) in the former B. Altman building, 188 Madison Ave at 34th St, 212-592-7000

Public School Education: School District #2 in region 9 at 333 Seventh Ave, 12th floor, 212-356-3700, http://schools.nyc.gov

Adult Education: Pace University, 551 Fifth Ave, 212-346-1700, www.pace.edu; The Graduate Center, City University of New York (CUNY), 365 Fifth Ave, 212-817-7000, www.gc.cuny.edu

Community Resources: International Center of Photography (ICP) Midtown, 1133 Sixth Ave at 43rd St, 212-857-0000, www.icp.org; American Folk Art Museum, 45 W 53rd St, 212-265-1040, www.folkartmuseum.org; Museum of Modern Art, 11 W 53rd St, 212-708-9400, www.moma.org; Paley Center for Media (formerly Museum of Television and Radio), 25 W 52nd St, 212-621-6800, www.mtr.org; Museum of Arts & Design, 2 Columbus Circle, www.madmuseum.org; City Center Theater, 130 W 56th St, 212-581-1212, www.citycenter.org; Carnegie Hall and Weill Recital Hall, 154 W 57th St, 212-247-7800, www.carnegiehall.org; NYC's Official Visitor Information Center, 810 Seventh Ave, 212-484-1200, www.nycvisit.com; Times Square Visitors Center, 1560 Broadway at 46th St, 212-768-1560, www.timessquarenyc.org. Not to mention Ripley's Believe it or Not! Odditorium, 234 W. 42nd St, 212-398-3133, ripleysnewyork.com.

Transportation—Subway: S (Crosstown shuttle): 42 St/Times Sq, 42 St/Grand Central; #1: 59 St/Columbus Circle, 50 St, 42 St/Times Sq, 34 St/Penn Station; #2/#3: 42 St/Times Sq; B/D: 59 St/Columbus Circle, Seventh Ave, 47-50 Sts Rockefeller Center, 42 St, 34 St/Herald Sq; F: 57 St, 47-50 Sts/Rockefeller Center, 42 St, 34 St/Herald Sq; V: 53 St/Fifth Ave, 47-50 Sts/Rockefeller Center, 42 St, 34 St/Herald Sq; N/R/W: 59 St/Lexington Ave, 59 St/Fifth Ave, 57 St, 49 St, 42 St/Times Sq, 34 St/Herald Sq; Q: 57 St, 42 St/Times Sq, 34 St/Herald Sq; A: 59 St/Columbus Circle, 42 St/Port Authority, 34 St/Penn Station; C: 59 St/Columbus Circle, 50 St, 42 St/Port Authority, 34 St/Penn Station; E: 53 St/Lexington Ave, 53 St/Fifth Ave, Seventh Ave, 50 St, 42 St/Port Authority, 34 St/Penn Station; #7 (Crosstown to Queens): 42 St/Times Sq, Fifth Ave, 42 St/Grand Central; #6: 59 St/Lexington Ave, 51 St, 42 St/Grand Central, 33 St; #4/#5 (Express): 59 St/Lexington Ave, 42 St/Grand Central

Transportation—Bus: Crosstown 34th St (M34); Crosstown 42nd St (M42) Downtown Broadway - Crosstown 42nd St, (M104); Crosstown 49/50th Sts (M27, M50); Crosstown 57th St (M31, M57) Crosstown 57th St - Uptown York Ave (M31); Uptown Eighth Ave - Downtown Seventh Ave (MI0); Uptown Sixth Ave - Downtown Fifth Ave (M5); Uptown Sixth Ave - Downtown/Seventh Ave and Broadway (M6, M7); Uptown Madison Ave - Downtown Fifth Ave (M1, M2, M3, M4); Uptown Lexington Ave - Downtown Third Ave (M98, M101, M102, M103)

CLINTON/HELL'S KITCHEN

Boundaries and Contiguous Areas: North: 59th Street and Lincoln Center; **East**: Eighth Avenue and the Theater District; **South**: 34th Street and Chelsea; **West**: Hudson River

Despite efforts by the city and proponents of the neighborhood, most people still know Clinton as "Hell's Kitchen." The neighborhood—which produced gangster Owney Madden and inspired *West Side Story*—was for a long time a poor workingman's district with often-squalid tenements and rooming houses; it is still home to some rough and tumble types, and has some raunchy blocks catering to transients. But the spillover from Times Square, which continues, remarkably, to out-Times-Square itself, is bleeding into this area.

Upgrading began in the 1970s when Manhattan Plaza, 400 West 43rd Street, with its two towers, pool and tennis courts, was built. People with enough money to pay the high rents originally charged for the apartments were disinclined to live here because of the neighborhood, so the buildings were converted to subsidized housing for the long-time residents that were displaced by the complex and for people in the performing arts. This new population helped found and now supports the thriving off-Broadway Theater Row on the south side of 42nd Street, a bonanza for New York's theater-going public, not to mention the theater world. The new respectability is firmly anchored on far-west 42nd Street by 1 River Place, a vast luxury rental building zigzagging across a whole block on the city's western edge. Now in an area once characterized by sleaze and depression, there are good restaurants, theaters featuring more "cutting edge" off-Broadway shows, blocks of spiffed-up townhouses, and handsome co-op renovations such as the Piano Factory. Clinton's new frontier is Tenth Avenue, where The Foundry, a 222-apartment mixed-income rental complex, rose over a parking lot and taxi garage in 2000. The transformation of **West 42nd Street** from the tawdry "Deuce" that it once was to a safer, family-oriented entertainment/business center continues, especially apparent with a Disney Store and Disney-owned theaters in the midst of the hustle and bustle.

One Worldwide Plaza, a 49-story tower capped by a nouveau mansard roof, is both a symbol and a powerful instrument of change in Clinton.

Prestigious law firms and ad agencies now occupy space at Eighth Avenue and 50th Street, where the shabby old Madison Square Garden once squatted, and winos, hookers, and drug pushers roamed. A plaza separates the office spire in the mixed-use Zeckendorf development from the residential area, which is located to the west in the block-square complex. Public seating is available year-round on the open plaza, a pleasant respite from the noise that surrounds. Live bands often play near the fountain on the plaza in the summer, and five Off-Broadway theaters are tucked underneath in a space originally planned as a subterranean parking garage. Eighth Avenue is showing robust signs of growth, with condominiums beginning to replace long-standing dives and disused distribution warehouses, and Ninth Avenue and its adjoining side streets are starting to move up as well. Remnants of the bad old days remain in the form of run-down theaters and several adult video stores—and yes, there is still a shady element found on some of the streets after dark. Perhaps the biggest concern when considering this neighborhood is congestion—too many buildings, too many residents, and too many visitors, not to mention traffic heading for the tunnel to New Jersey. However, for the young trendsetter, theatergoer, or thespian, this may be the "hottest" place to settle. For a family with kids or those seeking a quiet refuge, Clinton would be an unlikely option.

One mammoth presence that has profoundly affected Clinton is the Jacob K. Javits Convention Center, 655 West 34th Street. Now, where there had been a nondescript patch of garages, warehouses, and parking lots, a mini-neighborhood springs forth, dubbed **TunJav** (for Lincoln Tunnel, which empties here, and Javits Center, which it adjoins) by the *New York Times*. A few artists, designers, architects, and others have carved homes out of these industrial buildings. The ethnic food shops and tantalizing fruits and vegetables along Ninth Avenue feed them. Talk of expanding the center has given way to action: 1.7 billion dollars have been spent to increase exhibition and meeting space in the center from 790,000 square feet to more than 1.3 million square feet. There's also a bevy of plans for reinventing the still desolate area by the old train tracks. With Mayor Bloomberg's plan for a New York Jets Stadium dead, the likeliest outcome will be a large planned mixed-use area of shops and homes. Because the neighborhood is in the midst of radical transformation, any apartment hunting here should be done block by block, on foot, and at different hours of the day. Besides the possibility of lucking into a reasonable rental, it will give you a good idea about the feel of an area and if it changes at night. Consult the weekly *Chelsea Clinton News* as an informative neighborhood reference, 212-268-0454.

Web Sites: www.hellskitchen.net, www.clintoncommunitygarden.org, www. nyc.gov

Area Codes: 212, 646, 917

Post Offices: Midtown Station, 223 W 38th St; Times Square Station, 340 W 42nd St; Radio City Station, 322 W 52nd St

Zip Codes: 10019, 10036, 10018

Police Precincts: Midtown North, 306 W 54th St, 212-767-8300; Midtown South, 357 W 35th St, 212-239-9811, www.nyc.gov/nypd

Emergency Hospitals: St. Luke's–Roosevelt Hospital Center, 1000 Tenth Ave at W 59th St, 212-523-4000, www.wehealny.org

Library: Columbus Branch, 742 10th Ave, 212-586-5098, www.nypl.org

Public School Education: School District #2 in region 9 at 333 Seventh Ave, 12th floor, 212-356-3700, http://schools.nyc.gov

Adult Education: John Jay College of Criminal Justice, 899 10th Ave, 212-237-8000, www.jjay.cuny.edu

Community Resources: In 2005 the Alvin Ailey American Dance Theatre, one of America's greatest dance companies and a true gem in New York's treasure chest, moved to a new space, 405 W 55th St at Ninth Ave, 212-405-9000, www.alvinailey.org; St. Clement's Episcopal Church, 423 W 46th St, 212-246-7277, www.stclementsnyc.org, has a special mission to the arts community, and its services are as likely to consist of theatrical performances as liturgy. New World Stages, 50th St between Eighth and Ninth avenues, 212-239-6200, www.newworldstages.com, a slick set of five modern theatres, draw tourists from nearby Times Square; the Intrepid Sea-Air-Space Museum, Pier 86 at W 46th St and 12th Ave, 212-245-0072, www.intrepidmuseum.org, is housed in and around the aircraft carrier *Intrepid* and contains, among other permanent and changing exhibits, the USS *Growler* submarine and the decommissioned supersonic transporter, the Concorde.

Transportation—Subway: A: 59 St/Columbus Circle; E: Seventh Ave; C/E: 50 St, 42 St/Port Authority, 34 St/Penn Station; #1: 59 St/Columbus Circle, 50 St, 42 St/Times Sq; #2/#3: 42 St Times Sq; N/R/W: 57 St/Seventh Ave, 49 St, 42 St/ Times Sq; Q: 57 St, 42 St/Times Sq; B/D: 59 St/Columbus Circle, Seventh Ave; #7/S (Crosstown shuttles): 42 St/Times Sq

Transportation—Bus: Crosstown 57th St (M57, M31); Crosstown 49th/50th Sts (M27, M50); Crosstown 42nd St (M42); Crosstown 34th St (M16, M34); Uptown Tenth Ave - Downtown Ninth Ave (M11); Uptown Eighth Ave - Downtown Seventh Ave (M10, M20); Downtown Broadway (M104) to 42nd St and then crossing to the East Side along 42nd St.

LINCOLN CENTER AREA

Boundaries and Contiguous Areas: North: 72nd Street and the Upper West Side; **East**: Central Park West; **South**: 59th Street and Clinton; **West**: Hudson River

This neighborhood, dubbed **Lincoln Square**, is a prime example of how a major cultural facility can improve a marginal New York location. Construction in 1960 of the glass and travertine Lincoln Center complex with theaters, opera and ballet houses, concert halls, library, and the Juilliard School transformed a dreary stretch of rundown tenements and warehouses. Limousines now queue up

where once trucks double-parked, and it seems as if every other pedestrian carries a musical instrument or moves with the marked grace of a ballet dancer. The Columbus Circle development, a 2.1-million-square-foot mixed-use facility, opened in 2003 and now includes the Time Warner Center, a number of retailers, a massive Whole Foods, and fine dining, as well as the Jazz at Lincoln Center concert hall and some of the most expensive restaurants in the U.S. See www.shopsatcolumbuscircle.com for details.

Columnar apartment and office buildings rise above the cafés, restaurants, and boutiques lining Broadway, Columbus, and Amsterdam avenues. Fordham University's West Side Campus and ABC are also firmly planted in the neighborhood, adding a boost to the renaissance of Columbus and Amsterdam avenues, which cater to the food, drink, and clothing needs of West Side residents.

Condo spires and columns have shot up south and west of the culture complex, even on barren Tenth Avenue, which may be the new frontier of Lincoln Square. Tall, white-brick luxury buildings compose most of Lincoln Square's housing. Breaking that mold, 35-story twin towers on a stone base, designed to appeal to families with dogs, opened to renters on West End Avenue between 64th and 65th streets in 2000. The builder was quoted in the *Times* as saying he chose that neighborhood because "it's young, vibrant, and cultural, blends the old New York with the new…and appeals to a broad range of people."

And now we have **Trump Place**, the much-heralded riverfront project known in the planning stages as Trump City. When "The Donald" purchased the site of the now-defunct railroad yards fronting the Hudson River between 59th and 72nd streets, plans for the development of an enormous housing, shopping, and business complex to the west of Lincoln Center received a boost. But resistance to the "Trumping of Lincoln Square" solidified among residents and community planners, and future development is likely to be less dense and less grandiose than the original Trump model. For now, three structures housing condos and luxury rentals tower alone over the Hudson River, not to mention (and the ads don't) the noisy West Side Highway. Nonetheless, the area surrounding

Lincoln Center remains a vibrant location, wonderful for walking, or sitting out-side in warm weather at one of the many cafés. A wide range of popular stores including a Barnes & Noble superstore can be found, and best of all, it's near Central Park and of course, Lincoln Center.

Web Sites: www.nyc.gov, www.trumpplace.com, www.lincolncenter.org

Area Codes: 212, 646, 917

Post Offices: Columbus Circle Station, 27 W 60th St; Ansonia Station, 178 Columbus Ave

Zip Codes: 10023, 10019

Police Precincts: Midtown North, 306 W 54th St, 212-767-8400; Twentieth, 120 W 82nd St, 212-580-6411, www.nyc.gov/nypd

Emergency Hospital (nearest): St. Luke's–Roosevelt Hospital Center, 1000 Tenth Ave at 59th St, 212-523-4000, www.wehealny.org

Libraries: Library of the Performing Arts at Lincoln Center, 40 Lincoln Center Plaza, 212-870-1630, marvelous for researching the arts; Riverside Branch, 127 Amsterdam Ave at 65th St, 212-870-1810; www.nypl.org

Public School Education; School District #3, 88 W 125th St, 212-342-8300; Committee on Special Education, 52 Chambers St, 212-374-6085; http://schools.nyc.gov

Adult Education: Fordham University, 113 W 60th St, 212-636-6000, www.fordham.edu; The Juilliard School, 60 Lincoln Center Plaza, 212-799-5000, www.juilliard.edu; Art Students League of New York, 215 W 57th St, 212-247-4510, www.theartstudentsleague.org; The Elaine Kaufman Cultural Arts Center at the Goodman House, 129 W 67th St, 212-501-3303, www.kaufman-center.org, offers courses in music, dance, art, and the theater.

Community Resources: for the plethora of cultural events, theaters, library, shops, restaurants, exhibits, and tours at Lincoln Center, call their customer service department at 212-875-5456 or go to www.lincolncenter.org. Merkin Concert Hall at the Elaine Kaufman Cultural Arts Center, 129 W 67th St, 212-501-3330, www.kaufman-center.org, presents a variety of concerts, primarily ethnic and chamber music; American Folk Art Museum, 2 Lincoln Square, 212-595-9533, www.folkartmuseum.org.

Transportation—Subway: #1: 72 St, 66 St, 59 St/Columbus Circle; #2/#3 (Express): 72 St; A: 59 St/Columbus Circle; B/C: 72 St, 59 St/Columbus Circle; D: 59 St/Columbus Circle

Transportation—Bus: Crosstown 72nd St (M72); Crosstown 66th/67th Sts (M66); Crosstown 57th St (M57, M31););Uptown Tenth/Amsterdam Ave - Downtown Ninth/Columbus Ave (M11); Uptown Eighth Ave - Downtown Central Park West/Seventh Ave (M10)

THE UPPER WEST SIDE

Boundaries and Contiguous Areas: North: 110th Street and Morningside Heights; **East**: Central Park West; **South**: 72nd Street and Lincoln Center; **West**: Hudson River

For decades, large sprawling apartments and an active community life have been luring writers, musicians, intellectuals—in general, those seeking an alternative to the Upper East Side's more constrained lifestyle—to the West Side. Indeed, the city's first large apartment buildings, with lofty ceilings, thick walls, and space to waste, were built here around the turn of the century. Grand structures rose first along Central Park West (note the famed Dakota at 72nd Street), claimed by some aficionados to be the most architecturally elegant avenue in New York; next on Broadway (the neoclassical Ansonia between 73rd and 74th streets and the block-square Apthorp between 78th and 79th are particularly grand), which was to be Park Avenue West but isn't; and then on West End Avenue and Riverside Drive. Many of these historic apartment buildings have been converted to condos or are in the conversion process.

Most buildings along the apartment-lined avenues—with the notable exception of **Columbus** and **Amsterdam**, which have only recently emerged from the Dickensian 19th to enter the trendiest century—managed to remain sufficiently attractive to hold the middle class. But the rows of brick, limestone, and brownstone townhouses built for the newly affluent on the cross streets during the early 1900s declined into squalid tenements and SRO (single room

occupancy) rooming houses. Not until the late 1960s, when an ambitious urban renewal plan spurred building and renovation, did this veritable architectural museum again become an address for affluent achievers. Today, the typical brownstone houses the owner's family on the garden or parlor floors and tenants on the original bedroom floors above. Ranks of condo towers have shot up along Columbus and, more recently, Amsterdam between 87th and 97th streets—just outside the boundaries of the Central Park West Historic District. These svelte and pricey (though less expensive than Lincoln Square) condominiums provide residents with plenty of play space: health clubs, pools, rooftop gardens, party rooms, and in-house parking are standard. Meanwhile, **Upper Broadway** is being transformed as high-rises are slotted among the wearier old-timers between 97th Street and Columbia University. A short-term rental in one of these buildings offers the undecided newcomer an opportunity to try out the neighborhood before making a long-term commitment.

Most of the handsome pre-war stone buildings fronting Central Park—the San Remo, the Beresford, the Majestic, etc.—are cooperatives now, and as sought after and as pricey as those on Fifth Avenue across the park. Just south of 96th Street, a few condos and rentals are to be found, and north of 96th to 110th, in the area known as **Manhattan Valley**, a mix of condos, co-ops, and rentals makes Central Park West more accessible for those with slimmer pocketbooks. The vast apartment co-ops lining West End Avenue and curving along Riverside Drive have enduring appeal. Pioneers stake their claims in Manhattan Valley east of Broadway in the upper 90s and 100s, and west of Broadway between 96th and 110th streets. For the less adventurous and thicker of purse, existing rental apartments are well worth pursuing, if only to live between Manhattan's greenest playgrounds, Central and Riverside parks, and near one of its cultural stalwarts, the massive Museum of Natural History, which devotes almost 25 acres of floor space to some of the finest scientific collections in the world.

Residents of the Upper West Side are privy to Central Park, the city's premier playground, and Riverside Drive, which stretches quietly from 72nd Street to 165th Street, looking west over Riverside Park, the Hudson River, and stunning sunsets over the Jersey Palisades. Market rate rental apartments are mostly between 92nd and 96th streets, the rest being largely co-ops whose boards tend to be less snobbish than in some other neighborhoods. Broadway is two blocks away, with its addictive gourmet food markets. It is Riverside Park, however, that gives the neighborhood its sense of community. Residents raise their children there, walk their dogs, play, and dream there. Says one, "With its many levels it is a wonderful place to walk and stroll, sit and read, and have a sandwich—even in the colder months."

Web Site: www.nyc.gov, www.nysite.com

Area Codes: 212, 646, 917

Post Offices: Cathedral Station, 215 W 104th St; Planetarium Station, 127 W 83rd St, 212-873-3701; Ansonia Station, 178 Columbus Ave; Park West Finance, 693 Columbus Ave

Zip Codes: 10025, 10024, 10023

Police Precincts: Twenty-fourth, 151 W 100th St, 212-678-1811; Twentieth, 120 W 82nd St, 212-580-6411, www.nyc.gov/nypd

Emergency Hospitals (nearest): Both branches of the St. Luke's–Roosevelt Hospital Center: The Roosevelt Hospital at 1000 Tenth Ave at 59th St, and St. Luke's Hospital at 1111 Amsterdam Ave at 114th St, both 212-523-4000, www.wehealny.org

Libraries: Bloomingdale Branch, 150 W 100th St, 212-222-8030; St. Agnes Branch, 444 Amsterdam Ave, 212-877-4380; Riverside Branch, 127 Amsterdam Ave, 212-870-1810; www.nypl.org

Public School Education: School District #3 in region 10 at 388 W 125th St, 212-342-8300, http://schools.nyc.gov

Adult Education: Bank Street College of Education, 610 W 112th St, 212-875-4400, www.bnkst.edu

Community Resources: Central Park, stretching from 59th St over 840 acres up to 110th St is the city's playground, rich with athletic activities, playgrounds, sunbathing sections, a zoo, restaurants and food vendors, street entertainers, a skating rink, summer concert series, and more; www.centralparknyc.org. The Beacon Theater, 2124 Broadway, between 74th and 75th Sts, 212-496-7070, www.beacontheater.com; American Museum of Natural History and the Rose Center for Earth and Space, Central Park West from 79th St to 81st St, including a recently opened skating rink, museum information: 212-769-5100, www.amnh.org; the Bard Graduate Center for Studies in the Decorative Arts, 18 W 86th St, 212-501-3000, www. bard.edu/bgc; Children's Museum of Manhattan, 212 W 83rd St, 212-721-1234, www.cmom.org; Nicholas Roerich Museum, 319 W 107th St, 212-864-7752, www.roerich.org

Transportation—Subway: #1: 110 St/Cathedral Pkwy, 103 St, 96 St, 86 St, 79 St, 82 St; #2/#3 (Express): 96 St, 72 St; B/C: 110 St/Cathedral Pkwy, 103 St, 96 St, 86 St, 81 St, 72 St

Transportation—Bus: Crosstown 96th St (M96); Crosstown 96th/106th Sts (M106) Crosstown 86th St (M86); Crosstown 79th St (M79); Crosstown 72nd St (M72); Crosstown 66th/67th Sts (M66) ending at Central Park West and 72nd St; Uptown Riverside Drive - Downtown Riverside Drive (M5); Uptown Amsterdam (Ninth) Ave - Downtown Columbus (Tenth) Ave (M7, M11); Uptown Broadway - Downtown Broadway (M104)

MORNINGSIDE HEIGHTS

Boundaries and Contiguous Areas: North: 125th Street and Harlem; **East**: Morningside Drive; **South**: 110th Street and Upper West Side; **West**: Hudson River

Academia amidst a gritty urbanscape, this lively community occupying the formerly rocky slopes of northern Manhattan is dominated—physically, economically, and socially—by Columbia University, one of the nation's oldest, richest, and largest educational institutions. In addition, Barnard College as well as two important religious seminaries, the Manhattan School of Music, a large teaching hospital, and two major churches share the Heights with a mixture of students, professors, professionals, and urban poor. Up here next to the granite bulk of Ulysses S. Grant's pompous tomb, Upper West Side gray is relieved by Riverside Park, used extensively by residents as a front yard, and by Morningside Park, until recently avoided as unsafe. Spear-headed by the Morningside Area Alliance, efforts to clean up the park have involved the Parks Department, Columbia students, and the "Friends of Morningside Park." Daytime strollers, dog-walkers, and

joggers now use the park. Safe at night? Maybe not.

Work on its massive towers remains halted indefinitely, but if they are ever completed, the Episcopal Cathedral Church of St. John the Divine will literally tower over the community; now spireless, the world's largest Gothic cathedral just looms. (The tall Gothic church tower you do see rising northwest of Columbia belongs to Riverside Church, the Rockefellers' nondenominational gift to the city.) Part of St. John's was destroyed by a five-alarm fire in late 2001, but the church reopened quickly and by 2005 was completely repaired. St. John's caters to cultural as well as spiritual needs, sponsoring a particularly rich and wide-ranging series of concerts from chamber music through liturgical works to jazz and other events including poetry readings, craft fairs, and dance programs.

Broadway, Morningside Heights' main street, showcases bookstores, coffee shops, all-night fruit stands, student bars/jazz joints, boutiques, and restaurants ranging from fast food to ethnic and elegant. The area ten blocks south of Columbia was recently rezoned for a major expansion of the university and there are lots of boarded-up buildings, but it will eventually become a major thoroughfare, appealing to a more sophisticated crowd. The lively street life that continues late at night makes the neighborhood relatively safer than in the past and certainly interesting.

As owners of one-third of the community's housing stock, over half of which is occupied by tenants affiliated with the college, Columbia University is the Heights' biggest landlord. However, an occasional rental does hit the open market, and sometimes space becomes available when Columbia-connected roommates separate (graduate, marry, or move), leaving behind an empty room and half the monthly rent bill. Co-ops, keenly sought now, escalated steeply in price during the 1990s, but still represent good value, if not a bargain, when compared to Upper West Side prices.

Web Sites: www.morningside-heights.net, www.nyc.gov, www.morningside-park.org

Area Codes: 212, 646, 917

Post Offices: Columbia University Station, 534 W 112th St; Morningside Station, 232 W 116th St

Zip Codes: 10027, 10026, 10025

Police Precinct: Twenty-sixth, 520 W 126th St, 212-678-1311, www.nyc.gov/nypd

Emergency Hospital: St. Luke's–Roosevelt Hospital Center: St. Luke's Hospital, 1111 Amsterdam Ave at 114th St, 212-523-4000, www.wehealny.org

Libraries: 115th St Branch, 203 W 115th St, 212-666-9393; Morningside Heights Library, 2900 Broadway, 212-864-2530; George Bruce Station, 518 W 125th St, 212-662-9727; www.nypl.org

Public School Education: School District #3 in region 10, 88 W 125th St, 212-342-8300, http://schools.nyc.gov

Adult Education: Barnard College, 3009 Broadway, 212-854-5262, www.barnard.edu; Columbia University, 2960 Broadway at 116th St, 212-854-1754, www.columbia.edu; Union Theological Seminary, 3041 Broadway at 120th St, 212-662-7100, www.utsnyc.edu; Bank St College of Education, 610 W 112th St, 212-875-4400, www.bankstreet.edu; Jewish Theological Seminary, 3080 Broadway, 212-678-8000, www.jtsa.edu; Manhattan School of Music, 120 Claremont Ave, 212-749-2802, www.msmnyc.edu

Community Resources: Cathedral Church of St. John the Divine, 1047 Amsterdam Ave at 112th St, 212-316-7490, www.stjohndivine.org, also has on its large grounds a Biblical Garden with plantings inspired by the Old Testament. Riverside Church, 490 Riverside Dr at 121st St, 212-316-7540, www.theriversidechurchny.org, offers educational and cultural programs in addition to religious services.

Transportation—Subway: #1: 125 St, 116 St/Columbia, 110 St/Cathedral Pkwy; B/C: 125 St, 116 St, 110 St/Cathedral Pkwy; A/D: 125 St

Transportation—Bus: Crosstown 116th St (M116); Uptown Amsterdam Ave - Downtown Columbus Ave (M7, M11); Uptown Broadway - Downtown Broadway (M104); La Guardia Airport via 125th St (M60)

THE HARLEMS

Boundaries and Contiguous Areas: *East Harlem:* **North** and **East**: Harlem River; **South**: 96th Street, Upper East Side and Yorkville; **West**: Central Park; *Harlem:* **North**: 155th Street and Washington Heights; **East**: Harlem River; **West**: Hudson River; **South**: 125th Street and Morningside Heights

This neighborhood, rich in culture, remains the spiritual focus of black America. Although Harlem pockets some of the worst poverty and crime in New York City, many of its high-stooped, row-house-lined streets are perfectly safe. A strong economy in the 1990s into the new millennium stimulated renovation of

Harlem's brownstones and abandoned apartment buildings, increased national chain retailers in its business district, and ignited the rebirth of restaurants and nightlife. The result has been an influx of middle-class professionals, black and white. Younger families and artists, too, have been filtering into Harlem for the past few years. This has caused some consternation among long-time residents, but many are pleased to see the streets cleaner, the crime rates lower, and their own property values rising.

Originally settled in 1636 by Dutch tobacco farmers, Harlem blossomed into a prosperous suburb in the 1800s. Around 1900, black New Yorkers began settling into an abundance of apartment buildings left empty when real estate developers' plans for a white middle-class neighborhood failed to materialize. In addition to brand new housing stock, Harlem offered its first black residents a less racially hostile environment than other parts of the city.

Harlem of the 1920s, home to the largest black community in the US, is synonymous with the Harlem Renaissance. Musicians, playwrights, and novelists flocked to the neighborhood, which was bursting with jazz clubs and casinos. For several decades beginning in the 1940s, the area fell on hard times, and by the 1960s, the racial tension and overall poor economy of the city caused Harlem to decline further. A revitalized Harlem greets visitors and newcomers today.

Since the 1930s, prominent African-American Harlemites have lived on Striver's Row, on West 138th and 139th streets, between Seventh and Eighth avenues. Dominated by brownstones that are now part of the **St. Nicholas Historic District**, Abyssinian Baptist Church, New York's oldest black church, is located at 132 West 138th Street. Equally appealing to professionals, and to City College professors, is the **Hamilton Heights** area just north of the college, in particular Hamilton Terrace, with its handsome landmarked brownstones. The central area around the **Mount Morris Park Historic District**, between 116th and 125th streets, has become a highly desirable location. The western strip along the water continues to be the site of forthcoming redevelopment with a waterside plaza, shopping, a hotel, and housing in the planning stages.

To the south, just above Central Park, in the area known as **West Central Harlem** or **Manhattanville**, between 110th and 116th streets, are rentals and co-ops in a redeveloped and now popular area. Some rentals here, particularly those north of 116th Street to 125th, are priced below

market (although not for long, with the new Columbia campus being given the green light). City-sponsored renovation of abandoned apartment buildings has recently created affordable condos across from Morningside Park. Thorough exploration and the help of a good realtor are essential here. Further north, **Sugar Hill**, with its mixture of high-rise and pleasing brownstone apartments in the 140s and 150s between St. Nicholas and Edgecombe avenues, has an enduring appeal, as does **Riverside Drive**, a racially mixed area housing professionals, as well as middle- and low-income residents.

Cultural and educational institutions and welcoming green spaces abound in Harlem. In its heart, at Lenox Avenue (Malcolm X Boulevard) and West 135th Street, is the Schomburg Center for Research in Black Culture, which houses the world's largest collection of black history. On West 135th Street is the facility's outdoor sculpture garden; the outdoor amphitheater is on West 136th. Another neighborhood treasure is the splendid Riverbank State Park—28 acres of landscaped greenery with spectacular sunset views over the Hudson at 145th Street. Completed in 1993 atop a waste treatment plant, the recreational complex comprises indoor and outdoor swimming pools, a gym and fitness room, softball fields, basketball, tennis and handball courts outdoors, an indoor theater and amphitheater, and an ice and roller skating rink. Admission is free, open daily from 6 a.m. to 11 p.m., with a fee for the use of tennis courts and a nominal fee for the pool (see **Sports and Recreation**). In the long-term, a big change is coming to the more industrial area between W. 129th and W. 133rd, west of Broadway, with Columbia University now being given the go-ahead (via eminent domain in some cases) to create a huge new and controversial campus over the next 25 years.

Harlem's east side is known as **Spanish Harlem** or **El Barrio**. Here you'll find mostly tenements and housing projects. Above 100th Street, newcomers should take care and know where they're going. La Marqueta, a Latino produce, meat, and housewares market, keeps things bustling along El Barrio's busiest street, East 116th to Park Avenue. Some of the tenements in Spanish Harlem are being renovated, but the area has not seen great progress yet. A small section of El Barrio is benefiting from some new apartments and townhouses, a result of $605 million designated to the area by the New York City Housing Authority. The revamped housing has brought in trendy cafés and art galleries. The Boricua Gallery and El Museo del Barrio are poised to be the epicenter for future development that is expected around East 106th Street.

Indeed, with new families restoring many of Harlem's brownstone buildings and a thriving cultural scene (see **Community Resources** below), this neighborhood is pumping with life around the clock now. Tourism has increased, restaurants and jazz clubs have proliferated, and if the good life is defined by jazz clubs, all-night dancing, authentic soul food, urban poetry, and the return of the Apollo Theater, then Harlem is indeed providing all the necessary elements. The highly touted Dance Theater of Harlem, productions by the award-winning Classical Theatre of Harlem, the annual Harlem Book Fair, the Urban World Film

Festival, numerous jazz venues, and the home purchases by African-American celebrities, including Maya Angelou and Roberta Flack, have generated great interest here. Visitors, who for years did not venture past 96th street, are now beating down a path to check out this revitalized neighborhood. Even former president Bill Clinton has set up shop with an office on 125th Street.

Over the next few years condominium projects are expected to emerge throughout Harlem. The recently built, and already filled, Sugar Hill Condominiums at 146th street are a prime example of what's to come. A converted six-story building, Sugar Hill Condos feature two- and three-bedroom units at slightly lower rates than Chelsea. A $300 million shopping complex anchored by Home Depot is rising on the site of a long-vacant East Harlem wire factory. In late 2008 the city rezoned Harlem artery 125th St to allow high-rises and over 2,000 market-rate condos, with expectations that some 70 small business will be displaced. Market rate today in Harlem means around $900,000, although the average household income still hovers around $25,000.

Start your search for Harlem housing in the real estate section of the *Amsterdam News* (212-932-7400).

Web Sites: www.hometoharlem.com, www.east-harlem.com, www.harlem discover.com, www.nyc.gov

Area Codes: 212, 646, 917

Post Offices: Hamilton Grange Station, 521 W 146th St; Manhattanville Station, 365 W 125th St; Oscar Garcia Rivera Station, 153 E 110th St; Triborough Station, 167 E 124th St; College Station, 217 W 140th St; Lincolnton Station, 2266 Fifth Ave

Zip Codes: 10026, 10027, 10029, 10030, 10035, 10039

Police Precincts: Twenty-third, 162 E 102nd St, 212-860-6411; Twenty-fifth, 120 E 119th St, 212-860-6511; Twenty-eighth, 2271 Eighth Ave, 212-678-1611; Thirtieth, 451 W 151st St, 212-690-8811; Thirty-second, 250 W 135th St, 212-690-6311; www.nyc.gov/nypd

Emergency Hospitals: Harlem Hospital Center, 506 Lenox Ave at 135th St, 212-939-1406, www.nyc.gov; Mount Sinai Medical Center, 1468 Madison Ave, 212-241-6500, www.mountsinai.org

Libraries: Countee Cullen Branch, 104 W 136th St, 212-491-2070; Hamilton Grange Branch, 503 W 145th St, 212-926-2147; www.nypl.org; The Schomburg Center for Research in Black Culture, 515 Malcolm X Boulevard (135th St at Lenox Ave), 212-491-2200, houses the city's African-American archives and presents local artists' works.

Public School Education: East Harlem schools fall in district 2, region 9, 333 7th Ave, 212-356-7500, http://schools.nyc.gov; high schools include the Manhattan Center for Science and Mathematics, 208 Pleasant Ave, at FDR Dr and 116th St, 212-876-4639, www.mcsm.net

Adult Education: City College, City University of New York (CUNY), 136th St and Convent Ave, 212-650-7000, www.ccny.cuny.edu; Boricua College, a private Hispanic liberal arts college, 3755 Broadway at 155th St, 212-694-1000, www. boricuacollege.edu

Community Resources: Harlem celebrates its past and present history each summer by hosting a season-long series of events, www.harlemweek. harlemdiscover.com. Also here: the Apollo Theater, 253 W 125th St, 212-531-5300, an institution and the hub for Harlem-based entertainment since 1914, www.apollotheater.com; Studio Museum in Harlem, 144 W 125th St, 212-864-4500, www.studiomuseum.org; The Museum of the City of New York, 1220 Fifth Ave at 103rd St, 212-534-1672, www.mcny.org; El Museo del Barrio, 1230 Fifth Ave and 104th St, 212-831-7272, www.elmuseo.org (art, culture, heritage of Puerto Rico and Latin America); Dance Theatre of Harlem, 466 W 152nd St, 212-690-2800, www.dancetheatreofharlem.com; Harlem School of the Arts, 645 St. Nicholas Ave between 141st and 145th Sts, 212-926-4100, www.harlemschoolofthearts.org; The Classical Theatre of Harlem, 520 Eighth Ave, 212-868-4444, www.classicaltheatreofharlem.org; Museum of African Art, 1280 Fifth Ave, 718-784-7700, www.africanart.org (scheduled opening 2010)

Transportation—Subway: #1: 157 St, 137 St, 125 St; #3: 148 St, 145 St; #2/#3: 135 St, 125 St, 116 St, 110 St/Central Park North; A: 145 St, 125 St; B/C: 155 St, 145 St, 135 St, 125 St, 116 St, 110 St/Cathedral Pkwy; D: 155 St, 145 St, 125 St; #4/#5/#6: 125 St; #6: 116 St, 110 St, 103 St, 96 St

Transportation—Bus: Crosstown 96th St (M96); Crosstown 116th St (M116); Uptown/Downtown Riverside Dr (M5); Uptown/Downtown Broadway (M100, M104, M4); Uptown/Downtown Powell Ave (M2) Uptown/Downtown St. Nicholas Ave (M3); Uptown/Downtown Third, Lexington, Amsterdam Ave (M101, M100); Third, Lexington, Lennox Ave (M98, M102, M103)

WASHINGTON HEIGHTS-INWOOD

Boundaries and Contiguous Areas: North: Harlem River and Riverdale; **East**: Harlem River; **South**: 155th Street and Harlem; **West**: Hudson River

Up here, where outcroppings from the Hudson riverbed rise to form Manhattan's highest ground, the tawny stone arches rhythmically lining the central courtyard at The Cloisters are echoed by the exceptionally graceful curve of the steel suspension cables of the silvery two-level George Washington Bridge. Long before John D. Rockefeller, Jr., gave the city the magnificent medieval Cloisters Museum as well as Fort Tryon Park, George Washington headquartered Revolutionary forces on the strategic terrain now called Washington Heights.

Six hundred acres of parkland, almost all of it in Fort Tryon Park and rocky, wooded Inwood Hill Park, refresh and beautify one of the most densely populated, and narrowest, sections of New York. On the map, the top of Manhattan

looks like a knobby finger pointing across the Harlem River at The Bronx from the elongated fist of Manhattan. Washington Heights and Inwood are all "West Side" on both sides of the island as the Harlem River lops off the "East Side" at 138th Street. It was here in 1776 that the new American Army built Fort Washington, only to suffer a whopping defeat and have 3,000 men killed or taken prisoner by the British. The progress of the battle is commemorated in plaques down Broadway.

Narrow as it is, this finger of Manhattan contains many neighborhoods, only two of which, along the western edge, we describe here. Commercial Broadway cuts through the area on a north-south bias, dividing the almost solidly Hispanic, mostly low-income Harlem River (eastern) half from the more middle-income (western) half overlooking the Hudson River. The western section contains the most coveted housing—solidly constructed pre–WW II one- and two-bedroom apartments, many with marvelous pleasing river views—situated in square, five- to ten-story buildings. The clusters of yellow, buff, and occasionally red brick art deco buildings clumped along a rocky spine above the river in the Hudson Heights section of Washington Heights have special appeal. Two of the most desirable complexes, half-timbered Hudson View Gardens, between 183rd and 185th streets, and Castle Village, with its gardens and panoramic Hudson River views nearby, are cooperatives, as are many of the neighborhood buildings. Sublets, where you can get them, are still priced well below rentals farther downtown, as are the co-ops.

In previous years, a violent drug trade made parts of **Washington Heights**, the West 150s and 160s in particular, a dicey neighborhood despite its solidly middle class population and the presence of prestigious New York Presbyterian Hospital. Most recently, however, crime is way down, and though rentals and co-op prices are up, they are significantly less than what comparable properties cost farther downtown. Brownstones and large apartments in pre-war buildings are well worth a look, especially along Riverside Drive West, Fort Washington Avenue, and the connecting streets.

For another dimension, travel up to **Inwood** and stroll the grassy fields of Inwood Hill Park near 218th Street and Indian Road. Ahead of you, to the north, the Harlem River sweeps under the Henry Hudson Bridge, beyond which you can see the Jersey Palisades. To your immediate right are Columbia University's Baker Field, the only college stadium in Manhattan, and the college boathouse and tennis bubble. Straight ahead is one of the city's loveliest and least-known parks, Inwood Hill Park, with wetlands, rolling greens, and six miles of footpaths rising into rocky woods where there are Indian caves to be seen. It's quiet, except for an astonishing variety of birds. The man jogging past is as likely to be an opera singer or an artist as he is to be a broker or a police officer. A farmers' market takes place on Isham Street on Saturdays, year-round.

If you find the friendly unassuming neighborhood attractive, plan to search, and search hard, on foot, questioning supers and building managers. Inwood is a small neighborhood of pleasing pre-war brick apartment buildings located between the park and Broadway, north of 207th Street, which are the two main streets. There are no trendy restaurants, lively after-hours clubs, or art film houses here. But the cost of a sunny one-bedroom (or two or three) on the park, if you can find one to rent, will make you giggle if you've been looking downtown, although prices are on the rise. With developments like the $3 million condo Noma 175 popping up—not to mention the planned rezoning of nearly 30 blocks near West 207th Street to allow 21-story towers—Inwood's village-type ambiance might be changing. Prices for upscale digs here have been doubling but the crash of 2008 seems to have caused a sudden drop. Consult a reputable local real estate agent when pursuing housing here

Web Site: www.nyc.gov, www.washington-heights.us, www.poopcity.typepad. com/inwoodite

Area Codes: 212, 646, 917

Post Offices: Audubon Station, 511 W 165th St; Sgt. Riayan A. Tejeda Station, 555 W 180th St; Fort George Station, 4558 Broadway; Inwood Station, 90 Vermilyea Ave; Fort Washington Station, 556 W 158th St

Zip Codes: 10031, 10032, 10033, 10034, 10040

Police Precincts: Thirty-fourth, 4295 Broadway, 212-927-9711; Thirty-third, 2207 Amsterdam Ave, 212-927-3200, www.nyc.gov/nypd

Emergency Hospital: Columbia-Presbyterian Medical Center, 630 W 168th St, 212-305-2500, www.cumc.columbia.edu

Libraries: Fort Washington Branch, 535 W 179th St, 212-927-3533; Washington Heights Branch, 1000 St. Nicholas Ave, 212-923-6054; Inwood Branch, 4790 Broadway, 212-942-2445; www.nypl.org

Public School Education: School District #6 in region 10, 388 W. 125th St, 212-342-8300, http://schools.nyc.gov

Adult Education: Yeshiva University, 500 W 185th St, 212-960-5400, www. yu.edu; Inwood Community Services, 651 Academy St (just north of Dyckman St), 212-942-0043, www.inwoodcommunityservices.org

Community Resources: The Cloisters, division of the Metropolitan Museum of Art, Fort Tryon Park (193rd St and Fort Washington Ave), 212-923-3700, www. metmuseum.org, devoted to the art and architecture of Medieval Europe; Audubon Terrace Museum complex, Broadway between W 155th and 156th Sts, including the American Academy of Arts and Letters, 633 W 155th St, 212-368-5900, www.artsandletters.org; The Hispanic Society of America, 613 W 155th St, 212-926-2234, www.hispanicsociety.org, includes a library and museum; Morris-Jumel Mansion and Museum, 65 Jumel Terrace, 212-923-8008, www.morrisjumel.org, a colonial home in garden surroundings used by Washington during the Revolution and later redecorated by Eliza Jumel; Dyckman Farmhouse Museum, 4881 Broadway at 204th St, 212-304-9422, www.dyckman farmhouse.org, the last 18th-century Dutch farmhouse-museum in New York and well worth a visit; with children's crafts on selected Saturdays.

Transportation—Subway: A: 207 St, Dyckman St, 190 St, 181 St, 175 St, 168 St; C: 168 St, 163 St, 155 St; #1: 215 St, 207 St, Dyckman St, 191 St, 181 St, 168 St, 157 St; B/D: 155 St

Transportation—Bus: Crosstown 181st St (Bx3, Bx11, Bx13, Bx36); Uptown/Downtown Fort Washington Ave to Broadway (M4); Uptown/Downtown Broadway (Bx7, M100); Uptown/Downtown St. Nicholas Ave (M3); Uptown/Downtown Lexington Ave to 193rd St (M101); Uptown/Downtown Third Ave, Adam Clayton Powell Blvd. (M102); Washington Heights/Midtown - limited service between 179 St and 34th St, via Harlem River Drive and Third Ave (M 98)

THE BRONX

When Swedish sailor Jonas Bronck purchased 500 acres of farmland north of Manhattan in the seventeenth century, he staked a claim to the Aquahung River, which bordered his property to the east. The river became known as the Bronck's River, and his farm known simply as the Bronck's. Thus began the modern development of what is now the fourth most populous of New York's five boroughs, though it is the smallest.

In spite of containing some of New York City's greatest gems like Wave Hill and the New York Botanical Garden, the Bronx has a tarnished reputation. Urban sprawl practically ruined the borough in the 1960s, and a wave of crime and unemployment ravaged many of the low- to middle-income neighborhoods in the '60s and '70s. A widespread pandemic of landlord arson destroyed much of the south Bronx in the '70s and early '80s, and made the phrase "The Bronx is burning!" synonymous with urban decay. But things are changing, particularly in

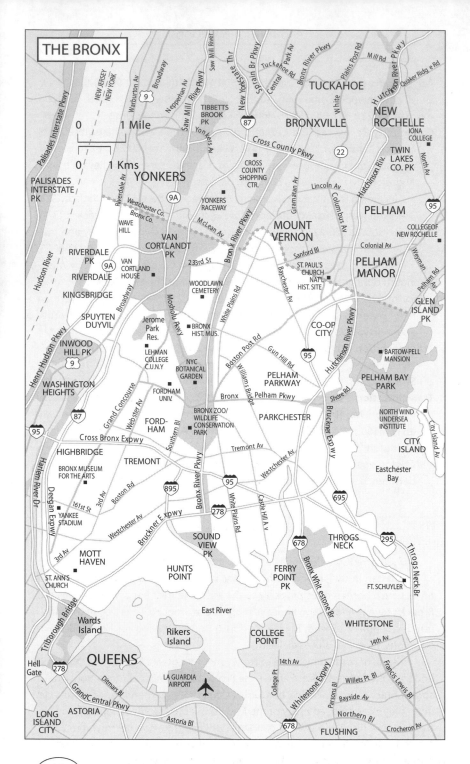

THE BRONX

0 — 1 Mile

0 — 1 Kms

NEW JERSEY / NEW YORK

Palisades Interstate Pkwy

Warburton Av

Broadway

9

Neperhan Av

Saw Mill River Pkwy

Saw Mill River Thr

Yonkers Av

TIBBETTS BROOK PK

New York State Thr

87

Central Park Av

Tuckahoe Rd

Bronx River Pkwy

White Plains Post Rd

Mill Rd

Hutchinson River Pkwy

Quaker Ridge Rd

TUCKAHOE

BRONXVILLE

NEW ROCHELLE

IONA COLLEGE

Cross County Pkwy

22

CROSS COUNTY SHOPPING CTR.

Gramatan Av

Lincoln Av

Columbus Av

TWIN LAKES CO. PK

North Av

PALISADES INTERSTATE PK

Riverdale Av

YONKERS

9A

YONKERS RACEWAY

PELHAM

95

COLLEGE OF NEW ROCHELLE

Werman Rd

Westchester Co. / Bronx Co.

McLean Av

MOUNT VERNON

Sanford Bl

Baychester Av

ST. PAUL'S CHURCH NAT'L HIST. SITE

Colonial Av

PELHAM MANOR

Pelham Rd

Pelham Av

WAVE HILL

VAN CORTLANDT PK

233rd St

Bronx River Pkwy

White Plains Rd

GLEN ISLAND PK

RIVERDALE PK

9A

VAN CORTLAND HOUSE

WOODLAWN CEMETERY

RIVERDALE

Hudson River

KINGSBRIDGE

Broadway

Mosholu Pkwy

Jerome Park Res.

BRONX HIST. MUS.

CO-OP CITY

SPUYTEN DUYVIL

LEHMAN COLLEGE C.U.N.Y

95

Boston Post Rd

Gun Hill Rd

BARTOW-PELL MANSION

Henry Hudson Pkwy

INWOOD HILL PK

9

NYC BOTANICAL GARDEN

Williams Bridge

PELHAM PARKWAY

Pelham Pkwy

Hutchinson River Pkwy

Shore Rd

PELHAM BAY PARK

WASHINGTON HEIGHTS

Grand Concourse

FORDHAM UNIV.

Bronx

NORTH WIND UNDERSEA INSTITUTE

City Island Av

87

Webster Av

Southern Bl

FORD-HAM

BRONX ZOO/ WILDLIFE CONSERVATION PARK

PARKCHESTER

Bruckner Expwy

CITY ISLAND

95

Cross Bronx Expwy

Tremont Av

Westchester Av

HIGHBRIDGE

TREMONT

Tremont Av

Eastchester Bay

Harlem River Dr

BRONX MUSEUM FOR THE ARTS

Boston Rd

3rd Av

895

95

White Plains Rd

Castle Hill Av

695

295

161st St

Westchester Av

278

Throgs Neck Br

Deegan Expwy

YANKEE STADIUM

Bruckner Expwy

SOUND VIEW PK

FERRY POINT PK

678

THROGS NECK

3rd Av

MOTT HAVEN

HUNTS POINT

Bronx Whitestone Br

FT. SCHUYLER

ST. ANN'S CHURCH

WHITESTONE

Triborough Bridge

Wards Island

Rikers Island

East River

COLLEGE POINT

14th Av

Hell Gate

278

QUEENS

LA GUARDIA AIRPORT

College Pt

14th Av

Whitestone Expwy

Parsons Bl

Willets Pt Bl

Francis Lewis Bl

LONG ISLAND CITY

Ditmars Bl

Grand Central Pkwy

ASTORIA

Astoria Bl

Bayside Av

Northern Bl

678

FLUSHING

Crocheron Av

Mott Haven, where the Bronck's farm was originally situated. The neighborhoods featured below are genuinely beautiful.

The Bronx was once home to Edgar Allan Poe and Mark Twain, and is currently home to the most successful sports franchise in American history, the beloved New York Yankees, whose new stadium, across the street from the original, opens on April 3, 2009. The Fulton Fish Market, after nearly two hundred years in Lower Manhattan, has found a new home in Hunts Point. Four of the city's finest high schools are situated in the Bronx: the prestigious public Bronx High School of Science, from which many Intel (formerly Westinghouse) Science Award winners graduate, as well as the private Fieldston, Horace Mann, and Riverdale Country Day schools. Eight universities and colleges enhance the borough's scholastic character.

A wealth of public land is probably the Bronx's greatest asset; parkland accounts for almost a quarter of the 43-square-mile borough. Partially forested Van Cortlandt Park, a mecca for cross country skiers in the winter, is the spot for soccer, rugby, and football in the summer, along with the city's oldest public golf course. Even larger Pelham Bay Park, from which little City Island dangles, harbors Orchard Beach along its sandy shore. But the star is Bronx Park with 500 acres about equally divided between two of the city's most enjoyable institutions: the Bronx Zoo (officially the New York Zoological Society's International Wildlife Conservation Park) and the New York Botanical Garden. The Haupt Conservatory, a sparkling crystal greenhouse complex, displays thousands of plant varieties in natural micro-climates and must be seen. Kids of all ages, naturalists, and explorers, too, frequent the zoo, using the tramlike Skyfari for an overview of the African exhibit as well as to commute between pavilions that include the World of Darkness and World of Birds.

Just south of Westchester County, City Island floats rather quaintly in placid Long Island Sound, providing a New Englandesque escape from city life, not to mention the finest seafood around. And over on the Hudson shore, Riverdale shelters some estates and sylvan lanes worthy of suburban Scarsdale, although more densely packed. In between these two neighborhoods, apartment buildings embellished with art deco motifs line the once-elegant Grand Concourse.

While chunks of the Bronx do flourish, the majority of residential sections continue to struggle toward economic recovery with low- to middle-income housing in pre-war buildings. Cooperatives and condominiums continue to slowly replace rental apartments, but the Bronx has yet to create a "happening" neighborhood like Brooklyn's Williamsburg or Queens' LIC. Web-based listing services, such as craigslist.com and rent.com, make a strong showing here, but the champion of Bronx rentals can be found at www.rentthebronx.com, with photos and no-fee listings as a priority.

RIVERDALE

Boundaries and Contiguous Areas: North: 263rd Street and Yonkers; **East**: Broadway and Van Cortlandt Park; **South**: West 239th Street and West 242nd Street, Spuyten Duyvil and Kingsbridge; **West**: Hudson River

Riverdale seems more like Westchester than New York and is certainly a departure from the rest of the Bronx. Call it a suburb in the city. It was mostly farmland, in fact, until the mid-19th century, when a few wealthy souls fled Manhattan's cholera epidemics, and carved estates overlooking the river. Among these was Wave Hill (see below). In 1853, with the completion of a railroad bridge across Spuyten Duyvil Creek (now known as the Harlem River), Riverdale soon became a prosperous suburb, desirable for possessing the best of both rural and urban life. When Riverdale was appended to New York City in 1874, it took the objections of Frederick Law Olmsted, co-designer of Central Park, to prevent the re-mapping of the winding, wooded roads that make Riverdale so beguiling today. But no one could prevent Robert Moses from bisecting both Riverdale and Spuyten

Duyvil with a clean slash of the Henry Hudson Parkway in the 1930s.

Many of the original mansions survive along the winding roads, often invisible behind ivy-crusted stone fences. Prospective purchasers can sometimes buy part of one, as many have been "condoed." Posh private schools attract kids who drive in from New Jersey and the suburbs as well as those who arrive by subway and bus from the boroughs. Shops are discreetly confined to a few zones of mom-and-pop businesses; supermarket complexes are built elsewhere. Riverdale's low, tree-shaded profile appeals to both affluent New York professionals and resident foreigners.

Tall, red-brick apartment towers cluster in clumps along the potholed lanes in south Riverdale, built mostly in the 1960s and '70s, and now almost all co-ops and condos. Spacious apartments, many with enviable views, can occasionally be had at prices slightly below Manhattan standards, but are increasingly harder to find as the area has become dense with ex-Manhattanites.

In north Riverdale, along the Yonkers border, brick and stucco houses on smallish lots can be had in a quiet neighborhood, but again the prices are rising.

There are plenty of mini-mansions in Riverdale, but there is a recent new explo-sion of less expensive high-rise condos in the southern area near the exclusive (and landmarked) community of **Fieldston**. The urban grid and bustle so typical of New York is found on the flats below in **Kingsbridge**. If you're looking here, pick up a copy of the *Riverdale Review* or the *Riverdale Press*, available in stores, lobbies, and libraries.

For a great day in this neighborhood, visit Wave Hill, West 249th Street and Independence Avenue (call 718-549-3200 or go to www.wavehill.org for direc-tions; the MTA runs shuttle buses from both its Riverdale and W 242 St stations). The Hudson-side complex at 249th Street and Independence Avenue consists of two stone manor houses offering occasional chamber music, a café, a green-house, and 28 acres of perfectly gorgeous gardens, wherein summer outdoor sculpture exhibits compete for your attention with lovely river views.

Web Sites: www.ilovethebronx.com, www.bronx.com, www.ssbx.org, www. riverdalepress.com, www.nyc.gov

Area Codes: 718, 347

Post Offices: Riverdale Station, 5951 Riverdale Ave; Fieldston Station, 444 W 238th St; Kingsbridge Station, 5517 Broadway

Zip Codes: 10463, 10471

Police Precinct: Fiftieth, 3450 Kingsbridge Ave, 718-543-5700

Emergency Hospital (nearest): Montefiore Medical Center West Campus, 210th St and Bainbridge Ave, 718-920-4321, the medical center has several leading hospital facilities throughout the Bronx including the University Hospital for Albert Einstein Medical University. There are two ERs: Child Medical Emer-gencies, 3415 Bainbridge Ave at Gunhill, 718-741-2150, and general ER at 845 Eastchrist, 718-904-3333.

Library: Riverdale Public Library, 5540 Mosholu Ave at 256th St, 718-549-1212, www.nypl.org

Public School Education: School District #10 in region 1, 1 Fordham Plaza, 718-741-5852/718-741-7644

Adult Education: Manhattan College, Manhattan College Parkway and W 242nd St, 718-862-8000, www.manhattan.edu; College of Mt. St. Vincent, 6301 Riv-erdale Ave and W 263rd St, 718-405-3267, www.cmsv.edu; Bronx Community College, University Ave & W 181st St, www.bcc.cuny.edu

Community Resources: Wave Hill, 675 W 252nd St, 718-549-3200, www. wavehill.org; Riverdale YM-YWHA, 5625 Arlington Ave, 718-548-8200, www. riverdaley.org

Transportation—Subway: #1 at 242nd and 238th streets (in Kingsbridge)

Transportation—Bus: commuters in Fieldston and Riverdale tend to use MTA buses, 718-652-8400, express buses to mid-Manhattan and Wall Street, 45 minutes, $7 one way. Local buses include the BX7 or BX10. Get a Bronx bus map for local MTA routes or go to www.mta.info.

Transportation—Train: Metro-North Hudson line, 212-532-4900, Riverdale Station at 200 W 254th St by the Hudson River, 25 minutes from Grand Central. Note: tickets cost significantly more if you buy them on the train. Purchase tickets at station ticket windows or online at www.mta.info.

SPUYTEN DUYVIL

Boundaries and Contiguous Areas: North: 239th Street and 242nd Street and Riverdale; **East**: Waldo and Johnson avenues and Kingsbridge; **South**: Harlem River and Washington Heights-Inwood; **West**: Hudson River

Henry Hudson gazes off at his river from atop a 100-foot Doric column in Henry Hudson Memorial Park. Spuyten Duyvil (pronounced SPY-ten DIE-vul, supposedly from "Spitting Devil") has a southward pitch, so it seems to look back at Manhattan, but if you live here you're sure to look west to the spectacular sunsets, which blaze and bleed over the river.

There's little to distinguish Spuyten Duyvil from Riverdale, which abuts it to the north. Both are bisected by the Henry Hudson Parkway and they share a rocky perch high over the Hudson River. But little Spuyten Duyvil, which has its own zip code and post office, feels like a village, despite being sliced and dotted with co-ops and condos. Perhaps it's charming little Edgehill Church, a country church, or the 19th-century wood frame houses on a winding street below in the shadow of the Henry Hudson Bridge. The narrow streets are all jammed and tangled down here, wiggling around Spuyten Duyvil Shorefront Park, where strollers meander along a gravel path that wanders down to the railroad station. Back up the hill joggers run along scenic Palisade Avenue above Riverdale Park and the Metro-North tracks.

Housing here is mostly in apartments, though there are houses occasionally on the market, especially east of the parkway. Both rentals and co-ops are considerably below Manhattan price levels, with the most expensive being

those west of the highway with river views. Shopping is available along Johnson Avenue, east of the parkway, from 235th to 236th streets, and along Riverdale Avenue between 235th and 238th streets. There's also a shopping area conveniently located around the 231st Street subway stop. In any of these places you can pick up a copy of the *Riverdale Review* to get a sense of the community.

You'll have fun living in Spuyten Duyvil, if for no other reason than listening to your friends trying to pronounce it.

Web Sites: www.nyc.gov
Area Codes: 718, 347
Post Office: Spuyten Duyvil Station, 562 Kapock St
Zip Code: 10463
Police Precinct: Fiftieth, 3450 Kingsbridge Ave, 718-543-5700
Emergency Hospital (nearest): Montefiore Medical Center West Campus, 210th St and Bainbridge Ave, 718-920-4321
Libraries: Riverdale Spuyten Duyvil Branch, 650 W 235th St at Independence Ave, 718-796-1202; Kingsbridge Branch, 280 W 231st St, 718-548-5656; www.nypl.org
Public School Education: see **Riverdale**
Adult Education: see **Riverdale**
Community Resources: see **Riverdale**
Transportation—Subway: #l at 238th, 231st and 225th streets (all in Kingsbridge)
Transportation—Bus: commuters tend to use MTA Buses, 718-652-8400, www.mta.info, for express bus service to mid-Manhattan and Wall Street. For local bus routes, use an MTA map or look at www.mta.info.
Transportation—Train: Metro-North Hudson Line, 212-532-4900, same pricing as Riverdale (see above)

YOU MIGHT ALSO WANT TO CONSIDER...

- **City Island, www.cityisland.com**; no, it's not Nantucket, but this unselfconscious little island dangling off Pelham Bay Park provides boat fanciers and aquaphiles with salty air, technicolor sunsets, and the scruffy charm of a watery small town…not to mention fresh seafood. It's fairly cheap though not altogether convenient living here, but you can park your sailboat out back. Housing on this tiny island is limited.
- **Crotona Park East (AKA East Morrisania)**; once the background for Jimmy Carter's pronouncement that the Bronx was America's "worst slum," little Crotona Park East has become what realtors call a "transition neighborhood." There's still lots of graffiti but crime has dropped almost 100% in the last decade and housing values are climbing—but still very affordable, considering it's only a 35-minute commute to mid-town. Bronx Community Board 3, 718-378-8054.
- **Mott Haven/Port Morris**; the southernmost neighborhood in the storied South Bronx has begun to show signs of new life in its southernmost area, with

artists and young professionals moving into newly refurbished tenements and historic brownstones and the chic new loft dwellings in The Watch Tower. New restaurants are opening, and an antiques district has cropped up along Bruckner Boulevard. Low prices, around a dollar a square foot per month, and the proximity to Manhattan are the biggest draws, and realtors are optimistically calling the area SoBro, but surrounding areas are still rather dicey.

- **Pelham Parkway/Bay**; straddling the leafy parkway that stretches between Bronx Park and Pelham Bay Park in the central Bronx, this area's ethnically and economically diverse populace lives in shady streets with lots of older two-story houses that go for around $500,000 (one-room co-ops go for under $100,000). Count on an hour to get to downtown Manhattan, but at least you don't have to change lines. "If you can't afford Riverdale, then you buy here," says one realtor.

BROOKLYN

"I too lived—Brooklyn, of ample hills, was mine," so wrote Walt Whitman, and so too can you live. New York is frequently described as a vertical city, but that sort of top-down crowding is not the domain in expansive Brooklyn. Though inextricably tied with neighboring Manhattan, Brooklyn is very much a city of its own. It has a strong spirit, a unique character, a spirited sense of community, and rich too is its history. There is no city like New York, and no borough quite like Brooklyn.

Formerly home to "The Honeymooners" and "The Cosbys," to the Dodgers at Ebbets Field, and still home to Coney Island's infamous roller coaster the Cyclone, Brooklyn has played no small hand in defining America's cultural landscape. It is also one of the nation's ten most populous communities. Brooklyn remains a viable option for anyone looking to move to New York City.

Boosters boast about excellent subway transportation, the quality of the public schools in District 15, and the lively cultural climate engendered by the culture scene's "big three": the Brooklyn Museum, Brooklyn Botanic Garden, and Brooklyn Academy of Music (BAM). Brooklyn, it is said, is a state of mind. To explore that state of mind, visit a site called 1010 President's Street at www.brooklyn.net, which has links to other Brooklyn sites worth meandering. For more about the history of the area check with the Brooklyn Historical Society, online at www.brooklynhistory.org.

The borough has been humming with change for several years now. As Manhattan's real estate market has swollen, artists, commuters, and the middle class have made their way to Brooklyn's pleasant neighborhoods. Immigrants, most recently from Asia and especially China, have flocked to Brooklyn, which is increasingly perceived as the chic alternative to crowded, expensive Manhattan.

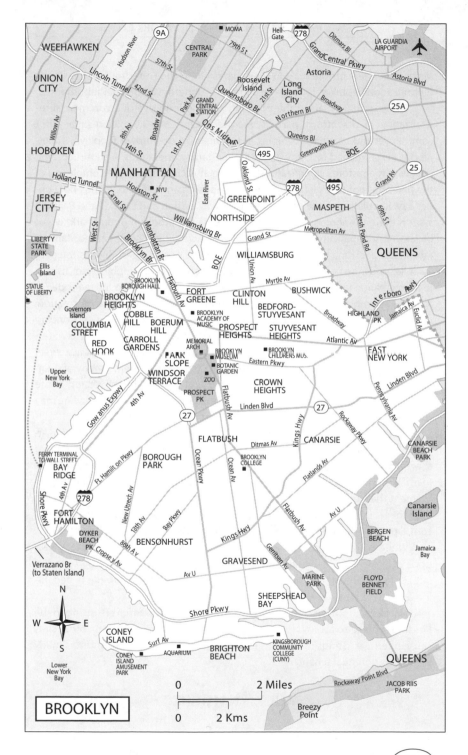

BROOKLYN

Major developments are making their marks along the waterfront, and a steady gentrification has taken hold of many formerly underdeveloped neighborhoods.

The year 1987 marked the beginning of the long-overdue commercial revitalization of downtown; part of Metrotech Center, a 7.6-million-square-foot commercial and academic complex in the heart of downtown Brooklyn, 1 Pierrepont Plaza opened first, housing Morgan Stanley operations. A suburban-type mall with megastores along Flatbush Avenue at Atlantic marks the completion of the first phase of the Atlantic Center, with housing and office buildings now underway. Rebuilding of the combination subway station and Long Island Railroad station there is ongoing. Tying it all together is the Brooklyn Bridge Park (www. brooklynbridgepark.org) is a done deal. This 67-acre project begins at the Manhattan Bridge and runs south past Brooklyn Bridge along the East River, stretching 1.3 miles and introducing playing fields and playgrounds, an amphitheater, fishing piers, recreation facilities, a new hotel, and a conference center to the riverside.

In fact, most of Brooklyn's western shore is undergoing a transformation: riverfront areas of **Greenpoint** and Northside (see **Williamsburg**) waterfront are sprouting high-rises up to 32 stories high and the beginnings of a 28-acre waterfront park and a two-mile esplanade. Although many projects have now slowed, it is estimated that this area will see up to 40,000 new apartments, many of them going from up to a million dollars, as well as a ultra-modern conversion of the old Domino sugar factory into a W hotel. Brooklyn's traditionally low skyline may soon be accentuated by buildings topping out at thirty or forty stories.

Further inland, proposed developments in Prospect Heights are called Atlantic Yards, with plans for a business and residential complex, as well as a major sports arena, all wrapped up in a Frank Gehry package. They aim to bring pro sports (namely, basketball) back to Brooklyn for the first time in half a century but for the moment the credit crisis, not to mention huge neighborhood opposition, has put this scheme in limbo. The developer's web site for the project is www.atlanticyards. com. Opposition to the project is large and organized; see www.dddb.net.

While some neighborhoods are still in need of revitalization, many sections of Brooklyn are indeed family friendly and affordable, though with the influx of newcomers and developments to the borough, affordable is becoming a relative term.

Names of Brooklyn realtors can be found under **Apartment Hunting** in the **Finding a Place to Live** chapter. Craigslist.com, rent.com, and many other sites carry extensive listings for the entire borough, and are a first stop for as many realtors as potential tenants.

BROOKLYN HEIGHTS

Boundaries and Contiguous Areas: North: Fulton Ferry Landing and Cadman Plaza West; **East**: Cadman Plaza and Court Street; **South**: Atlantic Avenue

and Cobble Hill; **West**: The Esplanade overlooking the East River and Brooklyn-
Queens Expressway (BQE)

A *New York Times* article described two young lawyers walking home along
Henry Street in the Heights one summer evening discussing cooperative apartments they had just bought. Not only did they estimate the purchase prices to
be about 20% lower than comparable real estate in Manhattan, but they also
believed the location couldn't be topped professionally. And as generalizations
go, that is a fair one. A large percentage of Heights residents have arrived, are
established, and will continue to lead the good life in carefully restored 19th and
early 20th century townhouses built by earlier generations of successful Manhattan professionals.

Robert Fulton's steamboat ferry service, inaugurated in 1814, spurred the
development of the rural Brooklyn settlement. Newly accessible to lower Manhattan, and cooled by East River breezes, the Heights attracted merchants and
lawyers, who built the substantial homes and noteworthy churches that characterize the community today. Brooklyn Heights boasts 684 pre–Civil War era
houses alone, and more than a dozen mostly-Gothic Revival churches.

The opening of the Brooklyn Bridge in 1883 brought the Heights that much
closer to Wall Street and provided its most spectacular landmark, the gossamer
span flung from Gothic tower to Gothic tower over the busy East River. Wealth
crossed the bridge to Brooklyn Heights and created one of the richest communities in the nation by the turn of the century. But the Depression wiped out many
residents, the bankers and businessmen who worked on Wall Street, and blight
came to the Heights.

In the 1950s and early 1960s,
Brooklyn's first "brownstoners," attracted by the innate quality of the
rundown housing stock, discovered
Brooklyn Heights. These pioneers began a wave of renovation that, in the
ensuing decades, has swept over row
upon row of dilapidated Brooklyn
townhouses. Today, the Heights' relatively cohesive population resides in
stolid pre-war apartment buildings and
lovingly restored brownstones, as well
as in striking warehouse conversions
down at Fulton Ferry Landing. Besides
the obvious—a five-minute subway
zip to Manhattan—other commuting
modes include the feet: hearty resi-

dents stride briskly along the soaring raised center walkway of the Brooklyn Bridge to their jobs in Lower Manhattan.

From the start, accessibility to Wall Street attracted residents to the Heights, and the exceptional view of Manhattan and the harbor kept them there. The magnificent panorama of the sweeping East River beneath the soaring bridges and lower Manhattan beyond brings a steady stream of day-trippers. Strolling the wide and gracious Esplanade and visiting the quiet, historic district with its informal restaurants and pleasant shops are popular pastimes.

From the north end of the Esplanade, continue down the hill past the pristine Watchtower complex to the foot of the hill and the great stone base of the Brooklyn Bridge. There along the water to the underbelly of the Manhattan Bridge, you are in Brooklyn's newest neighborhood, **DUMBO** (for **D**own **U**nder **M**anhattan **B**ridge **O**verpass). Artists, ever in search of affordable space, started moving into this somewhat spooky industrial area in the 1970s, despite the lack of services or other people, but its become more like another SoHo, albeit as SoHo was in the early 1980s. There are lots of open green spaces, restaurants, retail shops, an art gallery, and performance space in an area now occupied by an old warehouse. There are excellent local art events on a constant basis, but the artists themselves are being crowded out of the area and replaced with well-heeled Wall Street types.

Web Sites: www.southbrooklyn.net, www.brooklynonline.com, www.brooklyn. net, www.ibrooklyn.com, www.dumbonyc.com, www.nyc.gov

Area Codes: 718, 347

Post Offices: General Post Office, 271 Cadman Plaza East; Municipal Building Station, Municipal Bldg, 210 Joralemon St

Zip Code: 11201

Police Precinct: Eighty-fourth, 301 Gold St between Tillary St and Johnson St, 718-875-6811

Emergency Hospital (nearest): Long Island College Hospital, 340 Henry St at Amity St, 718-780-1000

Libraries: The Business Library, 718-623-7000, www.biz.brooklynpubliclibrary. org and the Brooklyn Heights Branch of the Brooklyn Public Library, 718-623-7100, www.brooklynpubliclibrary.org, share the same address: 280 Cadman Plaza West.

Public School Education: School District #13, 335 Park Place, 718-935-3234 www.schools.nyc.gov

Adult Education: Long Island University, 1 University Plaza, 718-488-1011 www. brooklyn.liu.edu; New York City Technical College, 300 Jay St, 718-260-5500, www.citytech.cuny.edu; St. Francis College, 180 Remsen St, 718-522-2300, www.stfranciscollege.edu

Community Resources: Arts at St. Ann's, formerly housed in St. Ann's Church, now at St. Ann's Warehouse, 38 Water St, 718-254-8779, www.artsatstanns.

org, sponsors numerous concerts and other cultural events. The Brooklyn Arts & Culture Association, Inc. (BACA), 195 Cadman Plaza West, 718-625-0080, coordinates and supports the efforts of a wide range of cultural programs within the borough; call or go to the web site to receive BACA's monthly Calendar of Cultural Events, www.brooklynartscouncil.org; New York Transit Museum (located in a former subway station), Boerum Pl and Schermerhorn St, 718-694-1600, www.mta.info; DUMBO Neighborhood Association, 45 Washington St, www.dumbo-dna.org.

Transportation—Subway: #2, #3, Clark St, Borough Hall; #4, #5, Borough Hall; A, C High St/Brooklyn Bridge; N, M, R at Court St

Transportation—Bus: for a Brooklyn bus map and schedule call 718-330-3322, Monday through Friday from 9 a.m. to 5 p.m., or go to www.mta.info.

COBBLE HILL

Boundaries and Contiguous Areas: North: Atlantic Avenue and Brooklyn Heights; **East**: Court Street and Boerum Hill; **South**: DeGraw Street and Carroll Gardens; **West**: Hicks Street

If it were possible to walk across the Mediterranean, a stroll starting at Atlantic Avenue down Court, Cobble Hill's main shopping street, to Carroll Gardens could be compared to a walk from the Middle East to Italy. Atlantic's famed Near East and Middle Eastern spice and grocery stores and restaurants filter along Court south for a couple of blocks before meeting up with the pizzerias, Neapolitan bakeries, and shops selling Italian housewares, near the heavily Italian Carroll Gardens on Cobble Hill's southern boundary. This intriguing ethnic mix results in top-notch food sources that attract shoppers from all over Brooklyn.

The row upon row of landmarked brownstones that cluster around the main streets of Court and Smith are less expensive and not quite as grand as those in Brooklyn Heights but beautifully shaded by large, leafy trees (note particularly the sycamore trees that completely cover Clinton Street as it crosses Baltic, Veranda, and Congress streets on the way to the Heights). They attract a young professional crowd and

Cobble Hill is probably the most homogeneous of all the Brooklyn brownstone communities. Award-winning Cobble Hill Park is a monument to neighborhood cohesiveness here. Apartment buildings and converted industrial properties have been established in Cobble Hill, notably The Henry Street Mews condos and One Tiffany Place, just west of the Brooklyn-Queens Expressway. Other conversions include Cobble Hill Towers, the city's first low-income housing project when it was built in 1878, and the P.S. 78 condominiums, lodged in a late-19th-century public school on Pacific Street.

It is not necessary to leave the neighborhood to find a good movie, a chic new sweater, or a bistro meal. The Cobble Hill Cinema boasts five screens. And along Smith Street, where it moves down into Carroll Gardens, boutiques and restaurants cater to a young and prosperous clientele from the neighborhood and beyond. Local P.S. 29 is said to have the most extracurricular activities of any public school in NYC.

Web Sites: www.southbrooklyn.net, www.brooklyncb6.org, www.brooklyn online.com, www.ibrooklyn.com, www.nyc.gov
Area Codes: 718, 347
Post Offices: Municipal Building Station, Municipal Bldg, 210 Joralemon St; CPU 386, 257 Columbia St
Zip Codes: 11201, 11231
Police Precinct: Seventy-sixth, 191 Union St between Hicks St and Henry St, 718-834-3211
Emergency Hospital: Long Island College Hospital, 340 Henry St at Amity St, 718-780-1000
Library (nearest): Carroll Gardens Branch, 396 Clinton St at Union St, 718-237-7996, www.brooklynpubliclibrary.org
Public School Education: School District #15 in region 8, 131 Livingston St., 718-935-4317, www.schools.nyc.gov
Adult Education: see **Brooklyn Heights** and **Boerum Hill**
Community Resources: see **Brooklyn Heights** and **Boerum Hill**
Transportation—Subway: #2, #3, #4, #5, Borough Hall; F, G, Bergen St
Transportation—Bus: for a Brooklyn bus map and schedule call 718-330-3322, Monday through Friday from 9 a.m. to 5 p.m., or go to www.mta.info.

CARROLL GARDENS

Boundaries and Contiguous Areas: North: DeGraw Street and Cobble Hill; **East**: Gowanus Canal; **South**: Hamilton Avenue; **West**: Brooklyn-Queens Expressway

In Carroll Gardens, singularly deep and lushly planted gardens front the four- and five-story row houses so characteristic of Brooklyn's brownstone neighborhoods.

These splendid yards, with trees as tall as the high-stooped townhouses, form part of an eleven-block tract laid out in the 1850s. Verdant block fronts are, however, only part of the reason urban homesteaders began moving to Carroll Gardens in the 1970s. This predominantly Italian community has a lower crime rate than many other areas in Brooklyn. And furthermore, just like Cobble Hill, another "tight" neighborhood to the north, Carroll Gardens boasts better-than-average public elementary and secondary schools.

Other pluses? Great food shopping. You'll find plenty of vegetable stands lining Court Street, where bulbous pecorino cheeses, salamis, and whole prosciuttos hang from grocery store ceilings. And subway transportation to Manhattan by Γ Train is fast and direct.

Less expensive, and less gentrified than the Heights and Cobble Hill, Carroll Gardens has long had limited housing stock although there are more and less expensive units in the southern section where conversions in industrial buildings have accelerated recently. On the eastern edge, an area in revival, the former St. Agnes School has become the School House in Carroll Gardens, a 90-unit middle-income rental on DeGraw Street. The occasional low-rise condo appears.

Walk along Court and you'll still hear Italian spoken. Bocce is still the game of choice among the senior set in sweet little Carroll Park, where handsome brownstones on the park's north side and graceful old trees make it feel like Washington Square in Greenwich Village. Heading north along Smith Street you can buy designer clothes in chic boutiques and eat Vietnamese, French, or nouveau Italian in smart eateries. Use a real estate agent to find an apartment here, if, after a stroll on the park-like streets, you find it appealing.

Another area to consider is the more affordable Columbia Street Waterfront District, adjacent to but separated from Carroll Gardens and Cobble Hill by the Gowanus Expressway. Its modest brick row houses were once the homes of the longshoremen who worked the docks here, but the neighborhood declined when the expressway isolated it from its loftier neighbors. Revival began in the 1980s with the construction of the Columbia Terrace condominiums and the conversion of a former Tiffany lamp factory into condos on cobblestoned Tiffany Place. There are no subway stations, schools, banks, or supermarkets here, but on-street parking is easy and the view from its quiet streets across Buttermilk

Channel to the Statue of Liberty and Lower Manhattan is stunning. For the truly adventuresome, there is the possibility of houseboats on Gowanus Canal. Long celebrated for its stench and as a dumping ground for mob hits—the book Motherless Brooklyn calls it "the only body of water in the world that is 90 percent guns"—recent improvement has led to a few houseboat dwellers during the winter. There's also kayaking trips regularly made by Gowanus Dredgers Canoe Club (www.waterfrontmuseum.org)

Web Sites: www.southbrooklyn.net, www.brooklyncb6.org, www.brooklynonline.com, www.ibrooklyn.com, www.nyc.gov
Area Codes: 718, 347
Post Offices: Red Hook Station, 615 Clinton St; CPU 386, 257 Columbia St
Zip Code: 11231
Police Precinct: Seventy-sixth, 191 Union St, 718-834-3211
Emergency Hospitals: Long Island College Hospital, 340 Henry St at Amity St, 718-780-1000;
Library: Carroll Gardens Branch, 396 Clinton St at Union St, 718-596-6972, www.brooklynpubliclibrary.org
Public School Education: School District #15 in region 8, 131 Livingston St., 718-935-4317, www.schools.nyc.gov
Adult Education: see **Brooklyn Heights** and **Boerum Hill**
Community Resources: see **Brooklyn Heights** and **Boerum Hill**
Transportation—Subway: F, Carroll St, Smith St; G, Carroll St, Smith St
Transportation—Bus: for a Brooklyn bus map and schedule call 718-330-3322, Monday through Friday from 9 a.m. to 5 p.m., or go to www.mta.info.

BOERUM HILL

Boundaries and Contiguous Areas: North: State Street; **East**: Third Avenue; **South**: Degraw Street; **West**: Court

East and slightly downhill from sedate Cobble Hill and just south of bustling downtown Brooklyn, Boerum Hill seems lighter and more spacious along its blocks of three- and four-story brick and brownstone homes. Stately sycamores shade quiet streets such as Bergen, where children play untended on sidewalks that line the flowering yards fronting set-back row houses. Ethnically more heterogeneous than its neighbors to the west, it is a community of families, who shop along commercial Smith and Court streets. Smith has also been dubbed the new "restaurant row" featuring French bistro-esque cafés. Nearby Atlantic Avenue is home to antique stores and Middle Eastern restaurants.

The Boerum Hill Historic District, bounded roughly by Hoyt and Nevins, Pacific and Wyckoff streets, contains an outstanding assemblage of pre–Civil

War Italianate and Greek Revival row houses, which constituted a fashionable district in the mid-19th century; the stretch of State Street between Hoyt and Smith has national landmark status. The neighborhood declined in later years, and today it is a monument to the efforts of new homeowners who, in the early 1960s, fought off a city effort to tear down the then-dispirited rooming houses to make way for urban renewal. Boerum Hill's turnaround—from near-slum to tight residential community—was achieved by a dedicated band of pioneers with enough foresight to see the area's potential. The neighborhood has a strong sense of community, and many keep close tabs on proposed development.

It was the construction of the Gowanus Canal and the draining of the swamps south of Warren Street beginning in 1845 that prompted the development of what are now Cobble Hill and Boerum Hill.

Rentals (when they can be found) in the handsome townhouses here are relatively affordable by New York City standards. Co-ops and condos can also be found. House prices are approaching the cost of comparable homes in Brooklyn Heights.

Slicing across Boerum Hill from the waterfront, noisy Atlantic Avenue is somewhat blighted by the presence of the grim Brooklyn House of Detention and its surroundings, but from Hoyt Street eastward its concentration of inviting antique and Victorian bric-a-brac shops attracts shoppers from all over the city.

Web Sites: www.southbrooklyn.net, www.brooklynonline.com, www.ibrooklyn.com, www.nyc.gov, www.boerumhillbrooklyn.org
Area Codes: 718, 347
Post Office: Times Plaza, 542 Atlantic Ave
Zip Code: 11217
Police Precinct: Seventy-sixth, 191 Union St between Hicks St and Henry St, 718-834-3211
Emergency Hospitals: Long Island College Hospital, 340 Henry St at Amity St, 718-780-1000; Brooklyn Hospital Center, 121 DeKalb Ave, 708-250-8000, www.tbh.org
Library: Pacific Branch, 25 Fourth Ave, 718-638-1531, www.brooklynpubliclibrary.org

Public School Education: School District #15 in region 8, 131 Livingston St, 718-935-4317, www.schools.nyc.gov

Adult Education: Brooklyn YWCA, 30 Third Ave, 718-875-1190, www.ywcabklyn. org, offers a health program plus a variety of adult classes.

Transportation—Subway: #2, #3, Hoyt St, Nevins St; #4, #5 Nevins St; F, Bergen St; G, Bergen St, Hoyt/Schermerhorn Sts; A to Hoyt/Schermerhorn Sts

Transportation—Bus: for a Brooklyn bus map and schedule call 718-330-3322, Monday through Friday from 9 a.m. to 5 p.m., or go to www.mta.info.

PARK SLOPE

Boundaries and Contiguous Areas: North: Flatbush Avenue; **East**: Prospect Park West; **South**: Windsor Place; **West**: Fifth Avenue

The mere mention of Park Slope to most New Yorkers conjures up images of armies of politically correct yuppie moms pushing their strollers about and trampling anyone inconsiderate to get in their way—one nickname is "Puke Slope" for the admittedly sometimes overwhelming baby carriage presence here. But it still remains one of the most heterogeneous—and handsome—of the up-and-coming Brooklyn neighborhoods, as well as the largest. But gentrification is full swing here, with income levels increasing up to 25% a decade, almost keeping up with the increase in restaurants. The one thing that hasn't changed is the 526-acre Prospect Park, designed by Central Park architects Frederick Law Olmsted and Calvert Vaux, and Park Slope's proximity to three of Brooklyn's cultural

bastions: the Brooklyn Museum, the Central Library at Grand Army Plaza, and the Brooklyn Botanic Garden. A recent addition to Prospect Park is the re-opened Wildlife Conservation Center, a state-of-the-art children's zoo with a restored 1912 carousel.

Park Slope's development paralleled that of Prospect Park in the 1880s. Sites with a park view were most highly prized, and small Victorian mansions line Prospect Park West. Proximity to the park and Grand Army Plaza determined the quality of the Victorian bow-fronted townhouses that march row upon stolid row down the west-sloping streets. North Slope, nearest Prospect Park West and the Plaza, is considered the classiest part of the neighborhood. South Slope, below 9th Street, is the less expensive, still-developing section. Old industrial properties, such as the Ansonia Clock factory complex on 12th Street (once the country's largest clock works and now deluxe condominiums) have been converted to apartments and co-ops. Seventh Avenue, the principal shopping street and scene of a hugely successful fair each spring, reflects neighborhood needs: boutiques, card shops, unisex hair cutters, twee gift shops and restaurants are everywhere. Think Berkeley, CA with an East Coast twist—there's even a popular food co-op (Park Slope Food Co-op, 782 Union Street, 718-622-0560, www.foodcoop.com) which provides fresh organic foods and household supplies at low prices to members who volunteer to work there. Since members do not have to be residents of Park Slope to join, folks come from all over Brooklyn.

Without qualification Park Slope, together with Brooklyn Heights, has arrived as a suitable address for middle-class professionals, especially those with families. P.S. 321, District 15's progressive, well-regarded elementary school, has served as an additional attraction to young families. But don't go looking for bargains; in real estate parlance, the neighborhood is "hot" (and has been for a while), especially along the park. Prices are lower down the slope and in adjoining **Windsor Terrace** and **Prospect Heights**, two communities nicely situated near Prospect Park. (For more on these, especially the proposed Atlantic Yards, see the section at the end of the chapter.) Down the slope west of Fifth Avenue around the Gowanus Canal, artists and crafters have established homes and studios in a neighborhood known now simply as **Gowanus**. Cleaned up, if not yet pristine, the canal twists through a somewhat gritty area where, as mentioned, some have even set up houseboats. Also, investigate the **Sunset Park/Green-Wood Cemetery** area, bounded by 65th Street on the south and Prospect Expressway on the north. This ethnically mixed community offers inexpensive rentals and fun neighborhood shopping and dining along Fifth Avenue. In the northeast corner is the hilly and inviting Green-Wood Cemetery (see **Greenspace and Beaches**). As you search for housing, pick up a copy of the *Park Slope Courier* (718-615-2500, www.yournabe.com), to enhance your feel for the neighborhood.

Web Sites: www.southbrooklyn.net, www.brooklyncb6.org, www.brooklynon-line.com, www.ibrooklyn.com, www.yournabe.com, www.nyc.gov

Area Codes: 718, 347

Post Offices: Van Brunt Station, 275 Ninth St; Park Slope Station, 198 Seventh Ave; Prospect Park West Station, 225 Prospect Park West

Zip Codes: 11215, 11217

Police Precinct: Seventy-eighth, 65 Sixth Ave between Sixth St and Bergen St, 718-636-6411

Emergency Hospital: Methodist Hospital, 506 Sixth St between Seventh Ave and Eighth Ave, 718 -780-5500, www.nym.org

Libraries: Brooklyn Central Library, Grand Army Plaza at Flatbush Ave, 718-230-2100; Park Slope Branch, Seventh Ave at Ninth St, 718-832-1853, www.brooklynpubliclibrary.org

Public School Education: School Districts #13 and #15 in region 8, 131 Livingston St., 718-935-4317, or for District 13, 335 Park Place, 718-935-3234 www.schools.nyc.gov

Adult Education: Brooklyn Museum Art School, 200 Eastern Pkwy, 718-638-5000, www.brooklynmuseum.org; Brooklyn Botanic Garden, 1000 Washington Ave, 718-623-7200, www.bbg.org, holds classes for plant enthusiasts; Brooklyn Conservatory of Music, 58 Seventh Ave, 718-622-3300, www.bqcm.com.

Community Resources: Brooklyn Museum, 200 Eastern Pkwy at Washington Ave, 718-638-5000; www.brooklynmuseum.org, behind the six Ionic columns of McKim, Mead and White's famed building are housed a number of exemplary collections as well as facilities for the cultural and educational programs sponsored daily by the museum; lectures and special programs are also offered; Brooklyn Arts Exchange, 421 Fifth Ave at Eighth St, 718-832-0018, www.bax.org; St. John's Recreation Center, 1251 Prospect Pl, 718-771-2787.

Transportation—Subway: with the exception of the A and C trains, subways stop near one part of Park Slope or the other. #2, #3, #4, #5 trains stop at Grand Army Plaza; F stops at Fourth Ave, Seventh Ave and 15th St; D stops at Seventh Ave and Atlantic Ave; B, M, N, R stop along Fourth Ave at Pacific St, Union St, 9th St, and Prospect Ave.

Transportation—Bus: for a Brooklyn bus map and schedule call 718-330-3322, Monday through Friday from 9 a.m. to 5 p.m., or go to www.mta.info.

FORT GREENE/CLINTON HILL

Boundaries and Contiguous Areas: North: Myrtle Avenue; **East**: Classon Avenue; **South**: Atlantic Avenue; **West**: Flatbush Avenue and Boerum Hill

"…Brooklyn's other fine residential district, the Hill…abounded in churches and middle-class houses, the majority of whose owners worked in New York." So wrote a Brooklyn historian of late 19th century Fort Greene and Clinton Hill. Despite a decline in the intervening years, that description is valid once again, except for the fringe areas to the north and east. What occasioned the turnabout? Historic designation and the brownstone revival, mainly.

Revival came late, in the 1970s, to **Fort Greene**. Even the once-elegant brownstones on the choice streets nearest Fort Greene Park had become dilapidated wino rows. But beneath the grime and neglect the original detailing remained, awaiting the attention of determined urban pioneers. Now, perfectly restored Anglo-Italianate brownstones line Washington Park, South Oxford Street, and South Portland Avenue. And sweeping 33-acre Fort Greene Park, the community's centerpiece designed by Olmsted and Vaux, has been restored to its rather English graciousness.

Once something of an Irish enclave (it was nicknamed "Young Dublin," not a compliment in the 1800s) Fort Greene is now integrated, both racially and socio-economically, and determined to stay that way. The throbbing cultural presence of the Brooklyn Academy of Music (BAM) helped stimulate the growth of a substantial community of African-American artists in Fort Greene. The area  around BAM continues to grow as a cultural enclave with dance troupes and artists moving into the neighborhood, as well as recently Williamsburg's renowned Galapagos art venue. The excellent Brooklyn Flea Market has opened in the area at Lafayette and Clermont (www.brownstoner.com) and for artists and entrepreneurs the nearby Navy Yards is an excellent resource for working spaces (the streets nearer the Yards are also where cheaper apartments can sometimes be found).

Clinton Hill, like Fort Greene, which it borders, contains an astonishing treasury of late 19th century urban architecture. The key name in this neighborhood is Pratt. Kerosene magnate Charles Pratt built several handsome mansions on Clinton Avenue including the present residence of the Bishop of Brooklyn, and also founded, built, and, until his death in 1891, ran Pratt Institute, the focal point and cultural center of the community. Now the students, grads, and faculty of Pratt (art, design, architecture, engineering, computers, and library sciences) fill the streets and much of the local housing.

Clinton Hill has a few high rises and lots of new quasi-industrial quasi-artist loft buildings going up, and therefore greater variety of housing than Fort Greene. But Clinton Hill has only one subway line, the sporadic G train (which is slated for further cuts), which means a transfer to reach Manhattan. Many find the five-minute bus ride to downtown Brooklyn with a free transfer to a variety of trains more convenient or a quick bike ride. Fort Greene, on the other hand, is well tended by the subway system (see below). Both neighborhoods offer easy on-street parking.

Both the Metrotech commercial development to the west on Flatbush Avenue and the Atlantic Center mixed-use development on the southeast edge of

Fort Greene have boosted the value and the cost of housing on the hill. Apartment hunting here is best done through a knowledgeable real estate agent.

Web Sites: www.fortgreenebrooklyn.com, www.brooklynonline.com, www.ibrooklyn.com, www.historicfortgreene.org, www.nyc.gov

Area Codes: 718, 347

Post Offices: Pratt Station, 524 Myrtle Ave; General Post Office, 271 Cadman Plaza East

Zip Codes: 11201, 11205, 11217, 11238

Police Precinct: Eighty-eighth, 298 Classon Ave, 718-636-6511

Emergency Hospital: Brooklyn Hospital, 121 DeKalb Ave, 718-250-8000, www.tbh.org; Interfaith Medical Center 1545 Atlantic Ave, 718-613-4000, www.interfaithmedical.com

Libraries: Clinton Hill Branch, 380 Washington Ave, 718-398-8713; Walt Whitman Branch, 93 St. Edwards St, 718-935-0244; Bedford Branch, 496 Franklin Ave, 718-623-0012; www.brooklynpubliclibrary.org

Public School Education: School District #13 in region 8, 335 Park Place, 718-935-3234, www.schools.nyc.gov

Adult Education: Pratt Institute, Continuing Education, 200 Willoughby Ave, 718-636-3779, www.pratt.edu; Medgar Evers Community College, 1150 Carroll St, 718-270-4900, www.mec.cuny.edu; St. Joseph's College, 245 Clinton Ave, 718-636-6868, www.sjcny.edu; Long Island University, 1 University Plaza, Flatbush Ave at DeKalb Ave, 718-488-1011, www.brooklyn.liu.edu

Community Resources: Brooklyn Academy of Music (BAM), the borough's premier cultural resource, founded in 1859, contains four theaters presenting a spectrum of performances by artists from all disciplines, 30 Lafayette Ave, 718-636-4100, www.bam.org; Brooklyn Children's Museum, splendidly renovated, at 145 Brooklyn Ave, Crown Heights, 718-735-4400, www.brooklynkids.org; Fort Greene Park, Brooklyn's first, 30 acres designed by Prospect Park and Central Park's Olmsted and Vaux, www.fortgreenepark.org; Clinton Hill Community Supported Agriculture, a nonprofit, volunteer-run organization that brings fresh, locally grown, organic produce to its members, 718-907-0616, www.clintonhillcsa.org; Museum of Contemporary African Diasporan Arts, contemporary art by black artists living in Brooklyn, 80 Hanson Pl, 718-230-0492, www.mocada.org.

Transportation—Subway: A, C, Lafayette Ave; B, D at DeKalb Ave; M, N, Q, R, DeKalb Ave; #2, #3, #4, #5 at Nevins St; G at Fulton St, Clinton/Washington Aves

Transportation—Bus: for a Brooklyn bus map and schedule call 718-330-3322, Monday through Friday from 9 a.m. to 5 p.m., or go to www.mta.info.

GREENPOINT

Boundaries and Contiguous Areas: North: Newtown Creek and Queens; **East**: Newtown Creek and the Brooklyn-Queens Expressway (BQE); **South**: North 12th Street and Williamsburg; **West**: East River

Set right next to the urban partyland of Williamsburg, Greenpoint—once known as "Little Poland"—can seem a world apart. Streets of colorfully sided tenements are lined with trees and the housewives in aprons chatting on the stoops are more likely to be speaking Polish than English. The northernmost tip, which borders Queens, is so cut off it feels like a country town—until you notice the Manhattan skyline across the river peeking over the rooftops

The one and only commercial drag is the two-lane Manhattan Ave. Dollar stores predominate and garlands of *kielbasa* sausages hang in most of the butcher shop windows. At least a half-dozen restaurants have Polish-language menus with specials like *pierogi* and *kasha*. But the flavor is changing. Thai and Jamaican restaurants are popping up—there's even a Starbucks—and the local health food store now offers everything from soy milk to tofu burgers. The neighborhood east of Manhattan Avenue, which borders a large industrial area, remains almost exclusively working-class Polish but the Greenpoint Historic District to the west, littered with the mansions of coffee and spice merchants of yore, has seen a flood of upscale professionals.

And more are on the way—20,000 new units are going up in riverfront high rises and while some moan about the loss of character, the buildings will finally make the riverfront, now lined with abandoned warehouses, accessible to everyone. These upcoming riverfront parks, plus beautiful Monsignor McGolrick Park with its weekend pony rides and recently revamped McCarren Park, with its running tracks and baseball diamonds, make the whole area extremely family friendly.

Two features, however, are likely to keep rents down. The northern area is only served by the erratic G subway line and the buses aren't much better (especially on weekends). In addition, the area sits on the largest oil spill in U.S. history. An estimated 17-30 million gallons of petroleum products were spilled near Newtown Creek in the 1940s and remain trapped beneath the neighborhood.

Although Greenpoint's drinking water is perfectly safe (it is piped in from upstate New York), the spill is currently the source of state litigation and there are recurrent concerns over health hazards posed by fumes rising from the soil. There's also a large sewage treatment facility in Greenpoint's northeastern corner that, while perfectly harmless, can get quite ripe when it rains.

Greenpoint is small enough to explore on foot and a day wandering about to get a feel for it is an excellent idea. Visit the local real estate offices you see, most of which have been in the area for decades (speaking Polish helps). You can find listings in the local Greenpoint Gazette (718-389-6067).

Web Sites: www.brooklynonline.com, www.ibrooklyn.com, hellobrooklyn.com, brooklyn-usa.org, freewilliamsburg.com, www.nyc.gov. For more info on the oil spill visit riverkeeper.org.

Area Codes: 718, 347

Post Offices: Greenpoint Station, 66 Meserole Ave; CPU 368, 94 Nassau Av.; Williamsburg Station, 263 South 4th St; CPU 369, 442 Lorimer St

Zip Code: 11222

Police Precinct: Ninety-fourth, 100 Meserole Ave, 718-383-3879

Emergency Hospital (nearest): Woodhull Medical and Mental Health Center, 760 Broadway, 718-963-800, nyc.gov; Brooklyn Hospital Center, 121 DeKalb Ave, 718-250-8000, www.tbh.org

Library: Greenpoint Branch, 107 Norman Ave, 718-349-8504, Leonard Branch, 81 Devoe St, 718-486-3365; Williamsburg Branch, 240 Division Ave, 718-302-3485; www.brooklynpubliclibrary.org

Public School Education: School District #14 in region 8, 131 Livingston St, 718-935-4299, www.nycenet.edu

Transportation— Subway: G, Greenpoint Ave, Nassau Ave

Transportation—Bus: Red Hook/Queens, via Manhattan Ave (B61); Williamsburg/Eastern Greenpoint via Nassau Ave (B48). For a complete Brooklyn bus map and schedule call 718-330-3322, Monday through Friday from 9 a.m. to 5 p.m., or go to www.mta.info.

WILLIAMSBURG/EAST WILLIAMSBURG

Boundaries and Contiguous Areas: *Williamsburg:* **North**: North Twelfth St and McCarren Park; **East**: Manhattan Avenue/Flushing Avenue and East Williamsburg; **South**: Kent Avenue and Clinton Hill; **West**: East River; *East Williamsburg:* **North**: Ridgewood/Maspeth (Queens); **East**: Bushwick; **South**: Broadway/Bedford-Stuyvesant; **West**: Maspeth Avenue/Manhattan Avenue and Williamsburg

Common lore has it that Williamsburg has more artists per capita than any other neighborhood in the United States. True or not, this former industrial wasteland, once one of the worst neighborhoods around, has undergone one of the most radical and fast moving transformations around, with many of its most recent newcomers arriving from western Europe. Williamsburg itself is considered an umbrella term describing four distinct neighborhoods. There is **Northside**, which lies northwest of the Brooklyn-Queens Expressway, with a fading Polish population; **Italian Williamsburg**, southeast of the same; there is **Southside**, south of Grand Street, with a heavier Puerto Rican population; and finally, the actual **Williamsburg**, a heavily concentrated Hasidic community near the Marcy and Hewes train stations. To the dismay of the families that have been living quietly here for generations, as well as the pioneering artists of the '90s, this entire area has exploded over the past decade, and shows no sign of slowing.

Once inexpensive and just a quick stop out of Manhattan on the L train, which is loved and loathed in equal measure by its riders (the L tracks have been undergoing an extensive retrofit, and service disruptions have been frequent and severe), in the mid 1990s Williamsburg became an annex to the boho East Village crowd, who loved its cheap rents and industrial ambiance. As vacancies in Williamsburg dried up and prices began to rise, the "second stop" and "third stop" out of Manhattan became the next best thing, and East Williamsburg began to absorb some of the growth. At this point the first stop (Bedford Ave) area has rents comparable to those in lower Manhattan and the crowds on any day and night (especially late night) can resemble the frat bar mobs that fill the Lower East Side bar scene. The most intense manifestation of this is on Bedford, between McCarren Park and Metropolitan Ave. It's a remarkably lively neighborhood, if lacking the gracious buildings and trees of other parts of Brooklyn: performance artists doing their thing on corners, impromptu sculptures, roving art exhibits and craft shows—even performance art snack trucks—are everyday events here.

It's been said you can walk from Warsaw to Puerto Rico to Israel if you traverse the 20-block-long stretch of this part of Bedford Ave and it's almost true. The Puerto Rican Southside is slowly gentrifying, with an interesting rich man's gulley along Broadway anchored by the luxury high-rise Schaefer Landing development and (soon) a huge new W Hotel. Beyond that is an area mixing Dominican and Hasidic residents, which at Division gives way to a completely Hasidic neighborhood. Rents are cheaper here but usually inaccessible to anyone who is not Hasidic.

As you go further inland things get rougher (particularly after the third Graham stop), with prices declining the farther you get from the L line.

The old meat-packing district near the waterfront is now full of restaurants serving sushi and other favorites, along with the new Williamsburg Music Hall and the bright yellow Brooklyn Brewery, complete with tours and a space for catering a party; much of this industrial area is currently being redeveloped, with whole blocks razed to become quasi-loft living and waterfront high-rises.

Numbered streets—declining from North 15th to Grand—cross Bedford Avenue, Northside's main street. To the east, traffic roars along the elevated Brooklyn-Queens Expressway.

After a $4.8 million restoration highlighting its rather Andalusian glory, the Metropolitan Pool and Bathhouse at Bedford and Metropolitan avenues is a fabulous neighborhood amenity. Accessible to the disabled, the pool and recreation center are operated by the parks department. A few blocks north, the 35 acres of McCarren Park have been given a huge uplift to match the new millionaire high-rises surrounding one side of it, including new ball fields, tennis courts, a running track, and a fitness course. The McCarren Pool, long abandoned and used for concerts, is now slated to return to its aquatic origins and become the largest pool in NYC. There are a few mini-parks along the river (slated to be joined into one long esplanade as development occurs) as well as a so-called "hipsters park" where North 11th meets the water.

The Brooklyn International Film Festival is centered in Williamsburg, with stated aims to discover, expose, and promote independent filmmakers while drawing worldwide attention to Brooklyn (www.wbff.org). Italian Williamsburg is host to the annual Festa del Giglio, a two-week (!) celebration of Italian culture, honoring St. Paulinus of Nola, www.olmcfeast.com.

It should be noted that there are probably more blogs devoted to Williamsburg than any other neighborhood in the entire tri-state area.

Web Sites: www.freewilliamsburg.com, www.11211magazine.com, www.wbff. com, www.brooklynonline.com, www.ibrooklyn.com, www.nyc.gov

Area Codes: 718, 347

Post Offices: Williamsburg Station, 263 S 4th St; CPU 369, 442 Lorimer St

Zip Codes: 11211, 11206

Police Precinct: Ninety-fourth, 100 Meserole Ave, 718-383-3879

Emergency Hospital (nearest): Brooklyn Hospital Center, 121 DeKalb Ave, 718-250-8000, www.tbh.org; Interfaith Medical Center 1545 Atlantic Ave, 718-613-4000, www.interfaithmedical.com; Wyckoff Heights Medical Center, 374 Stockholm St, 718-963-7272, www.wyckoffhospital.org

Library: Leonard Branch, 81 Devoe St, 718-486-3365; Williamsburg Branch, 240 Division Ave, 718-302-3485; www.brooklynpubliclibrary.org

Community Resources: McCarren Park, which forms a chunk of the boundary between Williamsburg and neighboring Greenpoint, has several ball fields and a recently resurfaced jogging track. It also contains the McCarren Park Pool, an enormous facility that closed as a pool in 1984 but has since become a staging ground for public art events and fairs—talk is that its concert days are over and it will soon become the largest public pool in NYC

Public School Education: School District #14 in region 8, 215 Heyward St, 718-302-7600, www.schools.nyc.gov

Transportation—Subway: L, Bedford Ave, Lorimer St, Grand Ave, Grant St, Montrose Ave, Morgan Ave; G, Nassau Ave, Metropolitan Ave, Broadway; J, M, Z, Marcy Ave, Hewes St, Lorimer St, Flushing Ave, Myrtle Ave

Transportation—Bus: for a Brooklyn bus map and schedule call 718-330-3322, Monday through Friday from 9 a.m. to 5 p.m., or go to www.mta.info

YOU MIGHT ALSO WANT TO CONSIDER...

- **Bay Ridge**, way out by the Verrazano Bridge and overlooking the Narrows, studded with parks and restaurants. This conservative community with a Scandinavian and Italian heritage is 50 minutes by subway from Manhattan. Community Board 10, 718-745-6827, www.bayridge.com.
- **Bushwick**, an inland area that adjoins Williamsburg, and has been relabeled Williamsburg by hopeful real estate agents. In a sense it is, albeit Williamsburg of the mid-1990s. The neighborhoods are rougher and the trendy mobs invisible, but there are growing pockets of younger artist types moving out here and the rents are definitely lower. Community Board 4, 718-628-8400.
- **Flatbush**, fairly vast and varied, geographically and psychologically the heart of Brooklyn. Its most appealing neighborhoods are Prospect Park South and Ditmas Park, both of which feature lovely old Victorian homes along stately, tree-lined streets, and strong community spirit. Prices are moderate, and the area is showing signs of new growth. Community Board 14, 718-859-6357.
- **Fort Hamilton**, just beyond Bay Ridge around the base of the Verrazano Bridge, has more co-ops and condos among its one-family houses, with a similar perch on the Narrows and about an hour by subway to Manhattan. Community Board 10, 718-745-6827.
- **Prospect Heights**, located uphill, but downscale in price, from Park Slope, Prospect Park, Brooklyn's major cultural institutions, and accessible transportation. Its handsome brownstones, greystones, and co-op apartments have attracted young, professional arrivals in recent years...and developers. The proposed Atlantic Yards project looms over Prospect Heights but whether this Gehry high-rise will raise its head remains in doubt at this point. Community Board 8, 718-467-5574.
- **Red Hook,** south of the Columbia Street Waterfront District on Upper New York Bay, is still for pioneers. The transportation situation remains difficult and although Ikea has opened its first NYC outpost here, it still remains off the beaten path for everyone but artisans and artists. Rows of small houses inter-

sperse the industrial landscape; the area features stunning views, a vast sky, and water edged by historic stone warehouses (as well as some of the largest and some say roughest housing projects NYC has to offer). Community Board 8, 718-467-5574.

- **Ridgewood**; arguably in Queens, this very quiet, traditionally German neighborhood has always considered itself part of Brooklyn and people still argue about it today. It's farther out on the L line but a number of Williamsburg refugees have started exploring the area, with its untouched 19th century streets and tree-lined avenues.
- **Stuyvesant Heights,** 12 landmarked blocks of exceptional brownstones along stately, tree-lined streets on the southern edge of Bedford-Stuyvesant, is home to a largely African-American professional community. Twenty-five subway minutes from Manhattan. Community Board 3, 718-622-6601.
- **Windsor Terrace**, a safe, old-fashioned community of small, detached houses, row houses, and apartments nicely sandwiched between Prospect Park and beautiful, park-like Green-Wood Cemetery. Quiet, except for the birds. Community Board 7, 718-854-0003.

QUEENS

"Queens is not New York!" exclaims a character in the film *Quiz Show*. And that is exactly what residents and lovers of Queens would have you believe. Being overlooked and underappreciated has protected Queens for decades from the madness of Manhattan that sent them (or keeps them) there in the first place.

Among the five boroughs, Queens is the acknowledged bastion of New York's middle class. As skyscrapers identify Manhattan and brownstones Brooklyn, so solid brick buildings—free-standing, Tudor-inspired houses, semi-detached, two-, three-, and four-family dwellings, and six-story apartment blocks—define a good part of the largest borough (in terms of land) in the city. And middle-class does not mean white by any means—according to the *New York Times*, in 2006 Queens became the only large-sized county in the country where African-American average income exceeded whites (by contrast, Manhattan has the largest income gap in the country between the two groups).

Until 1909 and the completion of the Queensborough Bridge, semi-rural Queens was a backwater connected to Manhattan only by ferry boat across the East River. But the bridge, followed almost immediately by train and then by subway service through new tunnels under the East River, opened the way for commuters and commerce. Developers snapped up great parcels of land, and 1908 saw the beginning of a building spree that continued, with few pauses, until World War II. While some communities are architecturally noteworthy—Forest Hills Gardens, a carefully designed 1909 enclave planned down to its English rustic street signs, and Malba, a charming mélange of lawns, leafy lanes, and

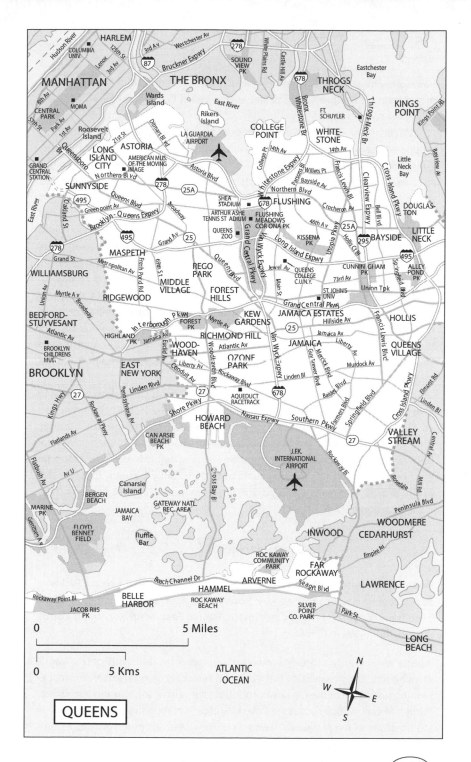

handsome, mostly 1920s homes nestled under the Whitestone Bridge—most of the housing is sturdy, unremarkable pre–World War II stock often laid out, suburban-style, in tracts.

While many Queens neighborhoods are identified with various ethnic groups—Greeks gravitate to Astoria, Latin Americans to Jackson Heights, Russians to Rego Park, Asians to Flushing—an international mix (over 125 languages are spoken by the borough's residents) of businessmen, engineers, and other professionals and their families continues to move into the area. Long Island City, just across the East River from Manhattan, is finally seeing its long-awaited development pick up steam. Astoria, situated north/northwest of Long Island City and Sunnyside, both equally accessible to Manhattan, has seen a rapid rise in rent as the middle class gets priced out of Manhattan. Within subway reach, Rego Park, Forest Hills, and Kew Gardens are popular established communities where one- and even two-bedroom apartments rent for about the same as a Manhattan studio. Further east, condominium units crowd every nook and cranny of Bayside with an endless sea of high-rises. Bayside has great appeal for those who prefer its quiet congestion to Manhattan's noise and immensity and who don't find the trip to Manhattan by express bus or Long Island Railroad too daunting.

Names of Queens real estate brokers will be found in **Finding a Place to Live**. The local publication, the *Queens Chronicle* (718-205-8000, www.queens chronicle.com), will provide real estate tips plus some insight into the borough itself. Craigs List (www.craigslist.com) has extensive listings, and is a first stop for both owners and brokers with listings. Remember that it is also a first stop for nearly everybody else, so refresh your browser constantly, be ready to call or visit as you browse, and read carefully: there are often misleading headers, and there is the occasional scam.

ASTORIA/LONG ISLAND CITY

Boundaries and Contiguous Areas: *Astoria*: **North**: Grand Central Parkway; **East**: Brooklyn-Queens Expressway; **South**: 35th Avenue and Sunnyside; **West**: Long Island City; *Long Island City*: **North**: Astoria; **East**: Steinway Street; **South**: Pulaski Bridge; **West**: East River

Astoria and Long Island City are technically separate, but with only a vague dividing line. Long Island City is the area immediately along the waterfront, beginning just south of the Queensborough Bridge (also known as the 59th Street Bridge—Feelin' Groovy?) and the Pulaski Bridge; Astoria is slightly inland, following the route of the N train to the north of the Queensborough Bridge. Astoria, with its many residents of Greek or Hispanic (or Italian or Yugoslavian or German) descent, offers a distinct old world feel. With and without belly dancers, the tavernas on Ditmars Boulevard and Broadway vibrate long and late to the keening of Greek dance music. Long a neighborhood of immigrant newcomers, the most recent wave has brought an infusion of Irish, South Americans, Slavs, and Asians. And more recently, a slew of urban professionals, many ex-Manhattanites, have discovered the apartments in the well-maintained two-story houses and small apartment buildings bordering Astoria's relatively safe streets. Check the area between Crescent and 35th Street, which is within walking distance of the N line and a 20-minute commute from Midtown. (A caveat: presumably Astorians have no problem with the improbably numbered streets, drives, and avenues here; outsiders find them nearly incomprehensible.) New York City's largest pool (over one acre in size), in spacious Astoria Park, just beneath the Triborough Bridge on the East River, is free, as is the uncrowded running space around the park. Condo living, with a health club and unobstructed view of the Manhattan skyline, came to Astoria with the opening of the 405-unit Shore Towers in 1990 at the southern end of the park.

Astoria was the home of Paramount Studios from 1919 until the 1930s, when the business moved—lock, stock, and W.C. Fields—to Hollywood. The movies are back, sharing with television the enormous, refurbished Kaufman Astoria Studios on 35th Avenue between 34th and 37th streets. The complex also houses the Museum of the Moving Image, a museum dedicated to movies, TV, and the interactive media. Several production facilities have sprouted nearby, as well as a 14-screen cinema near the Kaufman Astoria Studios.

Immediately across the river from Manhattan, and part and parcel of the film industry taking place in Astoria, new life is being breathed into **Long Island City**. Artists are coming, attracted by P.S. 1, a highly successful alternative art, dance, and theater space, along with filmmakers, actors, and designers, to the enormous film and television production facility Silver Cup Studios, the Eaves-Brooks Costume Company, and the gargantuan International Design Center, which contains more than 100 acres of showroom space. Also here is the renovated Isamu Noguchi Museum and Sculpture Garden located on Vernon Boulevard at 33rd

Road, and sculptor Mark Di Suvero has organized the Socrates Sculpture Park, with its changing display of monumental abstract works in a previously vacant East River lot. Putting Long Island City ever more on the map was the

marriage in 1999 between P.S. 1 and the prestigious Museum of Modern Art in Manhattan, creating MoMA QNS. Now that renovations of the Modern's old home are complete, the plan for MoMA QNS is to convert it into a storage and study center for the museum.

In late 2006 the city announced the purchase of 24 acres along Long Island City's waterfront, part of an enormous and ongoing effort by the city to revitalize a number of riverside sites that have fallen into disrepair and create a walkway all the way to the Williamsburg Bridge (excluding the Gowanus Canal river entry point). The city plans to build as many as 5,000 new rental units for middle-income families (annual incomes between $60,000 and $145,000 for a family of four, according to the *New York Times*). This will be the largest middle-income housing complex built in New York City in more than 30 years, and is the next and largest step in the ongoing development of this part of Queens, which includes almost half-a-dozen high rises on the river's edge.

Citibank's 50-story tower in southern Long Island City is the tallest building in Queens, and is soon to be joined by Court Square Two, a $200-million, 14-story "Little Brother" to the glass spire, and a centerpiece in what is meant to become a new central business district, although this is flagging behind residential interest. MetLife has moved hundreds of jobs from its former headquarters in the Flatiron district to a former carriage factory on Queens Plaza North. New housing options are springing up alongside these business developments. According to a recent *New York Times* article, gritty Queens Plaza's transformation is coming from several corners: in 2001 the Department of City Planning rezoned 37 blocks here and declared a Business Improvement District. The Queens Plaza, a 10-story, 66-unit building has just opened, featuring one-bedrooms with views of Manhattan priced at under half a million. The Crescent Street Tower is in planning stages, promising more condos. The Avalon Riverview (www.avalon-riverview.com) contains hundreds more rental apartments, ranging from studios to three-bedroom units. Along with all the big money developments, LIC has developed a thriving artist community with innumerable loft conversions, including the spectacularly grafittied palace known as 5 Pointz. LIC also has its own beach—Water Taxi Beach, complete with imported sand, volleyball courts and lots of barbecue (www.watertaxibeach.com) To get a further fix on life in Astoria and in greater Long Island City, go to www.licweb.com.

Web Sites: www.licweb.com, www.nyc.gov, www.licarts.org, www.astorialic.org
Area Codes: 718, 347
Post Offices: Astoria Station, 27-40 21st St, Astoria, Steinway Station, 43-04 Broadway, Astoria; Woolsey Station, 22-68 31st St, Astoria; Broadway Station, 21-17 Broadway, Astoria; Main Branch, 46-02 21st St, Long Island City; Plaza Station, 24-18 Queens Plaza South, Long Island City
Zip Codes: 11101, 11102, 11103, 11105, 11106

Police Precinct: One Hundred Fourteenth, 34-16 Astoria Blvd at 35th St, Astoria, 718-626-9311

Emergency Hospitals: Mt. Sinai Hospital of Queens, 25-10 30th Ave, Long Island City, 800-968-7637, www.mshq.org; Elmhurst Hospital Center, 79-01 Broadway, Elmhurst, 718-334-4000, www.nyc.gov

Libraries: Astoria Branch, 14-01 Astoria Blvd, Astoria, 718-278-2220; Steinway Branch, 21-45 31st St, Long Island City, 718-728-1965; Broadway Branch, 40-20 Broadway, Long Island City, 718-721-2462; www.queenslibrary.org

Public School Education: School District #30 in region 4, 28-11 Queens Plaza, 718-391-8323, http://schools.nyc.gov

Community Resources: Queens Chamber of Commerce, www.queenschamber.org; The Isamu Noguchi Museum and Sculpture Garden, 9-01 33rd Rd, 718-204-7088, www.noguchi.org; Socrates Sculpture Park, Broadway at Vernon Blvd, Astoria, 718-956-1819, www.socratessculpturepark.org; Museum of the Moving Image, 36-01 35th Ave, Astoria, 718-784-4520, Program Information, 718-784-0077, www.ammi.org; P.S. 1 Contemporary Art Center, 22-25 Jackson Ave, Long Island City, 718-784-2084, www.ps1.org;The Sculpture Center, 44 19 Purves Street, 718 361 1750. www.sculpture center.org

Transportation—Subway: N, W, Queensborough Plaza, 39th Ave, 36th Ave, Broadway, 30th Ave, Astoria Blvd-Hoyt Ave, Ditmars Blvd; E, G, V, 23rd St, Queens Plaza; G, R, V, E, Queens Plaza, 36th St, Steinway St and 46th St; F, 21st St/Queensbridge

Transportation—Bus: for a Queens bus map and schedule, stop by the College Point Bus Depot, 128-15 28th Ave, Flushing, or call 718-330-1234, or go to www.mta.info. The MTA also offers express service on several routes to midtown Manhattan for $5.

SUNNYSIDE

Boundaries and Contiguous Areas: North: Barnett Avenue and the Sunnyside Conrail Yards; **East**: 52nd Street and New Calvary Cemetery; **South**: Long Island Expressway; **West**: 36th Street and Long Island City

This traditionally blue-collar community bounded by railroad yards, industrial tracts, cemeteries, and the legendary LIE (the Long Island Expressway, also known as the world's longest parking lot) won't be the next "in" New York neighborhood. But, the sensible, mostly brick homes and apartments lining Sunnyside's residential streets, ten minutes by train from Manhattan, do attract young professionals, as well as immigrants, offering more space for lower-than-Manhattan rents.

Newcomers are especially drawn to **Sunnyside Gardens**. "The Gardens," the first US development to be modeled on the English garden community, occupies

55 leafy acres north of bustling Queens Boulevard. Towering London plane trees shade the 650 one-, two-, and three-family brick townhouses, which enclose long communal gardens. The effect is English village, with shrub-lined walks penetrating the landmarked blocks. "Like Greenwich Village and far more than Brooklyn Heights, it was a mixed community, in which one might mingle without undue intimacy with one's neighbors," recalls urban critic/historian Lewis Mumford, who lived in The Gardens from their inception in 1924 until 1936. They seem little changed and are likely to remain so, considering they were given landmark status in 2007.

There are private homes and rentals in greater Sunnyside as well, but most of the brick apartment blocks are non-rentable co-ops. The three main shopping thoroughfares are small-town Skillman Avenue at The Gardens' southern edge, Queens Boulevard in the shadow of the elevated IRT Flushing Line, and, running diagonally southwest from the Boulevard, Greenpoint Avenue, which leads directly into neighboring Brooklyn. There and on the side streets you can rent Korean movies, buy Irish imports, eat Italian, Middle European, or Chinese, or lift a pint at Moriarty's Pub Restaurant. The city's longest-established Spanish language theater, The Thalia on Greenpoint Avenue, plays to sellout crowds on weekends. There's a large and growing Orthodox Jewish community here as well.

Thanks in large part to the efforts of the Sunnyside Foundation, whose staff works on planning and preservation issues, Sunnyside is an appealingly cohesive community, for all its ethnic diversity. Stop by the foundation's office at 45-18 Skillman Ave or call 718-392-9139 for information, advice, and a free copy of the *Sunnyside Herald* if you're thinking of moving here.

Web Site: www.sunnysidechamber.org, www.nyc.gov, www.sunnysidenyc.com
Area Codes: 718, 347
Post Office: Sunnyside Station, 45-15 44th St, 718-729-7806
Zip Code: 11104
Police Precinct: One Hundred Eighth, 5-47 50th Ave, Long Island City, 718-784-5411
Emergency Hospital (nearest): Elmhurst Hospital Center, 79-01 Broadway, Elmhurst, 718-334-4000

Library: Sunnyside Branch, 43-06 Greenpoint Ave, 718-784-3033, www.queens
   library.org
Public School Education: School District #24 in region 4, 98-50 50th Ave, 718-
   592-3357, http://schools.nyc.gov
Community Resources: Museum for African Art, 36-01 43rd Ave at 36th St, Long
   Island City, 718-784-7700, www.africanart.org; Sunnyside Chamber of Com-
   merce, 718-784-7700, www.sunnysidechamber.org
Transportation—Subway: #7 to Manhattan, 40th St, 46th St, 52nd St
Transportation—Bus: for a Queens bus map and schedule, stop by the College
   Point Bus Depot, 128-15 28th Ave, Flushing, or call 718-330-1234, or go to
   www.mta.info. The MTA also offers express service on several routes to mid-
   town Manhattan for $5.
Transportation—LIRR: Woodside Station, Roosevelt Ave and 61st St

REGO PARK

Boundaries and Contiguous Areas: North: Queens Boulevard; **East**: Yellowstone Boulevard and Forest Hills; **Southwest**: Woodhaven Boulevard

Until 1920 only one thoroughfare wound through this vegetable farmland of western
Long Island, and that was a cow path. Within five years, the Real Good Construction
Company had purchased three of the farms and prudently named the area for itself
as Rego Park. A branch of the Long Island Railroad extended near the area, and development followed quickly; houses were purchased as soon as they were built, and
sometimes before they were finished.

Rego Park has long had a strong
Jewish community, with a growing
presence of Russian and Iranian families. Recent years have seen a rapid
influx of Asians, particularly South Koreans, and these and other cultures
mingle well in this middle- to upper-
class swath of land beside Forest Hills.
Three subway lines and several express
buses to and from Manhattan help
keep this diverse, low-crime neighborhood accessible. Also convenient are
the numerous businesses and shops
in the area, both along 63rd Drive—
that former cow path—as well as quick
access to the Queens Center (www.
shopqueenscenter.com), a mammoth

shopping complex anchored by Macy's, JC Penney, and H&M. Many of the independent businesses along 63rd Drive stand in the original buildings constructed in the twenties and thirties.

Running parallel to Queens Boulevard, the LIRR divides the commercial and residential interests in the area. Nearly two-thirds of the homes in Rego Park are rentals, but real estate prices have risen dramatically although they still remain about 25% less than most of Queens.

Area Codes: 718, 347
Post Office: Rego Park Station, 92-24 Queens Blvd
Zip Code: 11374
Police Precinct: One Hundred and Twelfth, 68-40 Austin St, Forest Hills, 718-520-9311
Emergency Hospital: St. John's Hospital, 90-02 Queens Blvd, Elmhurst, 718-558-1000, www.wyckoffhospital.org
Library: Rego Park Branch, 91-41 63rd Dr, 718-459-5140, www.queenslibrary.org
Public School Education: School District #28 in region 3 (see **Forest Hills**)
Adult Education: Queens College (see **Flushing**); St. John's University (see **Forest Hills**)
Community Resource: Queens Chamber of Commerce, 718-898-8500, www.queenschamber.org
Transportation—Subway: R, G, and V at 63rd Dr and 67th Ave
Transportation—Bus: for a Queens bus map and schedule, stop by the College Point Bus Depot, 128-15 28th Ave, Flushing, or call 718-330-1234, or go to www.mta.info. The MTA also offers express service on several routes to midtown Manhattan for $5.
Transportation—LIRR: Forest Hills Station, Austin St and 71st (Continental) Ave

FOREST HILLS

Boundaries and Contiguous Areas: North: Long Island Expressway; **East**: Grand Central Parkway and Corona Park; **South**: Union Turnpike and Kew Gardens; **West**: Yellowstone Boulevard and Rego Park

Practical Queens Boulevard, a major shopping thoroughfare that sensibly separates curbside businesses from through traffic with narrow concrete dividers, belies the charm of Forest Hills as it cuts through the heart of the neighborhood. To the north larger apartment buildings built by the Cord Meyer Development Co., which is still the largest landlord in the area, dominate. South a block just off

Austin, considered one of the most enticing shopping streets in Queens, lies "The Gardens." Forest Hills Gardens, designed in the eclectic tradition by an architect of the Beaux-Arts school and sponsored by the Russell Sage

Foundation, has few peers in the half-timbered world of Victorian Tudor. Brick-fronted Cotswoldian houses face curving drives and landscaped plots originally planned by Frederick Law Olmsted, Jr. The walled Gardens area is distinctively exclusive, being both gated and with private security. Shopping and noshing opportunities also add allure to the somewhat crowded Forest Hills neighborhood, as do the schools which perform on average about 30% better than most NYC schools. In addition to the attractive Austin Street spots, appealing cafés and craft and antique stores have cropped up on Metropolitan Avenue.

Old and established, Forest Hills is becoming increasingly cosmopolitan. (A local real estate agent reports a map of Forest Hills on sale in Tokyo bookstores.) And increasingly, its brick apartment buildings have gone co-op. The six- to ten-story, mostly red brick rental buildings congregating on either side of Queens Boulevard stretch across 108th Street and over to Forest Hills High School, standing prominently above the Grand Central Expressway, which borders the neighborhood from nearby Flushing Meadow Park. The IND/BMT subway lines, as well as major arteries like Ascan, Metropolitan, and 108th Street, are worth pursuing for their quality pre-war construction as well as convenience to public transportation and shopping. Semi-detached apartments and units in private homes may require a slightly longer walk but offer landscaped lots and winding streets as dividends. While a great number of Forest Hills' residents have been firmly entrenched for many years, rentals and co-ops occasionally do pop up; act quickly, they won't stay on the market long. Prices are on the upswing however, by some accounts increasing almost 15% a year. Count on $2 million for a large house and about $250,000 for a studio apartment (or about $1500 a month).

Web Sites: www.queensnewyork.com, www.nyc.gov
Area Codes: 718, 347
Post Office: Forest Hills Station, 106-28 Queens Blvd
Zip Code: 11375

Police Precinct: One Hundred and Twelfth, 68-40 Austin St, 718-520-9311

Emergency Hospitals: Forest Hills Hospital, 102-01 66th Rd, 718-830-4000, www.nslij.com

Libraries: Forest Hills Branch, 108-19 71st Ave, 718-268-7934; North Forest Park, 98-27 Metropolitan Ave, 718-261-5512; www.queenslibrary.org

Public School Education: School District #28 in region 3, 90-27 Sutphin Blvd, 718-557-2618, http://schools.nyc.gov

Adult Education: St. John's University, 8000 Utopia Pkwy, Jamaica, 888-9ST-JOHNS, www.stjohns.edu

Community Resources: Queens Chamber of Commerce, 718-898-8500, www.queenschamber.org; West Side Tennis Club, 1 Tennis Place (bounded by Burns and Dartmouth streets and 69th and 70th avenues), 718-268-2300, www.foresthillstennis.com; Forest Hills Jewish Center, 106-06 Queens Blvd, 718-263-7000, www.fhjc.org, offers a pool, gym, programs, classes, etc.

Transportation—Subway: E, F, G, and R, all to 71st (Continental) Ave

Transportation—Bus: for a Queens bus map and schedule, stop by the College Point Bus Depot, 128-15 28th Ave, Flushing, or call 718-330-1234, or go to www.mta.info. The MTA also offers express service on several routes to midtown Manhattan for $5.

Transportation—LIRR: Forest Hills Station, Austin St and 71st (Continental) Ave

KEW GARDENS

Boundaries and Contiguous Areas: Northeast: Queens Boulevard; **South**: Metropolitan Avenue and Forest Park; **West**: Union Turnpike and Forest Hills

Bracketed by LaGuardia Airport and John F. Kennedy International, Queens is home to thousands of airline employees. Kew Gardens, sitting nearly midway between the city's two prime airports, is particularly popular with flight crews, hence the nickname, "Crew Gardens." Real estate agents report more rentals available and more singles residing in Kew Gardens than in Forest Hills and Rego Park.

The neighborhood's oldest section dates to 1912, when the Kew Gardens Corporation was formed. The substantial Colonial and Tudor-accented private homes built on high, comparatively hilly ground between Maple Grove Cemetery and Forest Park have cachet even today. The blocks of red brick apartment buildings that ring Kew's center, the older ones especially, represent real value, though most are co-op. Austin Street and Metropolitan Avenue together with Lefferts and Queens boulevards make up Kew's main shopping area. There's a pleasingly small-town feel on Austin around the railroad station, and the 538-acre Forest Park (see **Greenspace and Beaches**) provides rustic peace and quiet, as well as horseback riding.

Nevertheless, with the infusion of recent immigrants, Kew Gardens has become a cosmopolitan community. Along Lefferts Boulevard a new Irish bar and restaurant, a Russian grocer, an Uzbekistan Cultural Center, and a Caribbean night-club suggest just a few of the ethnic components of this neighborhood. Good schools and easy accessibility to nearly all of the borough's main roads and highways make this a viable alternative to Forest Hills.

At its southeastern-most tip, Kew Gardens hosts not only the borough's newest commercial skyscraper, a tall, rectangular gray block with cutout circles at the corners, but also Queens Borough Hall just across the Van Wyck Expressway, a long bureaucratic brick and limestone structure usually filled with politicians and, occasionally, useful publications about the borough.

Web Site: www.nyc.gov, www.kewgardenshistory.com

Area Codes: 718, 347

Post Office: Kew Gardens Station, 83-30 Austin St

Zip Codes: 11415, 11375, 11365

Police Precinct: One Hundred and Second, 87-34 118th St, Richmond Hill, 718-805-3200

Emergency Hospital (nearest): Forest Hills Hospital, 102-01 66th Rd, Forest Hills, 718-830-4000, www.nslij.com

Libraries: Lefferts Branch, 103-34 Lefferts Blvd, Richmond Hill, 718-843-5950; Glen Oaks Branch, 256-04 Union Turnpike, Glen Oaks, 718-831-8636; www.queenslibrary.org

Public School Education: School District #28 in region 3 (see Forest Hills)

Adult Education (nearest): Queens College, 65-30 Kissena Blvd, Flushing, 718-997-5000, www.qc.cuny.edu

Community Resources: Queens Borough Hall, 120-55 Queens Blvd, Kew Gardens, 718-520-3220; Queens Chamber of Commerce, www.queenschamber.org

Transportation—Subway: E, F, Kew Gardens/Union Turnpike

Transportation—Bus: for a Queens bus map and schedule, stop by the College Point Bus Depot, 128-15 28th Ave, Flushing, or call 718-330-1234, or go to www.mta.info. The MTA also offers express service on several routes to midtown Manhattan for $5.

Transportation—LIRR: Kew Gardens Station, Lefferts Blvd and Austin St

FLUSHING

Boundaries and Contiguous Areas: North: Cross Island Parkway and Whitestone; **East**: Utopia Parkway and Francis Lewis Boulevard and Bayside; **South**: Union Turnpike; **West**: Grand Central Parkway and Forest Hills

Middle-class Flushing sprawls on either side of the Long Island Expressway, embraced by two great parks at the center of thriving northern Queens. The nexus of multiple bus routes, rail lines, and traffic arteries, downtown Flushing looks like the crossroads of the world. In recent years a strong influx of Asians—primarily Chinese and Koreans—has meant that the majority of residents are now Asian-American. It has New York's largest Chinatown (depending on who's counting), and the largest urban center in Queens. On weekends, the colorful Chinese fish-fruit-and-vegetable vendors, Korean gift stores, Muslim butchers, and sari shops along Main Street draw people from outside the area, and religious meeting places range from Protestant to Muslim to a number of Hindu temples. Toward the Long Island Expressway and surrounding Queens College is a less ethnically diverse area, where English is predominant and residents have lived for many years, some in red brick developments like Pomonok or Elechester, which were built for members of the electrical union.

Away from commercial Main Street, Union Turnpike, and Northern Boulevard, the grid of shady residential streets has changed little, except perhaps to

have become more presentable. The profusion of well-established trees, 2,000 varieties throughout Flushing, constitutes a treasure and a living remnant of the nursery industry that flourished here from pre-Revolutionary times until recently. Another survivor, its back turned to Northern Boulevard, the austere Friends' Meeting House has been a place of worship since 1694, except during the Revolutionary War when it was a British hospital, prison, and stable. The Bowne House Historical Society (37-01 Bowne Street), built nearby in 1661, was an earlier site of Quaker worship and of the struggle for religious freedom in what was then a Dutch settlement. Down Bowne Street, in a modest residential neighborhood, is an extraordinary Hindu temple covered with stone statues. That's Flushing.

Great tracts of green breathing space surround and bisect the neighborhood. Flushing Meadows–Corona Park contains within its 1,200 acres remnants of the 1939 and 1964 New York World's Fairs, two lakes, a marina, the Queens Zoo, a botanical garden, the Queens Museum, Theatre in the Park, the New York Hall of Science, and an indoor ice-skating rink. Adjacent is Shea Stadium, home of the New York Mets, and the USTA National Tennis Center, site of the annual US Open Tennis Championships. Tucked away within Flushing's borders is the more intimate and landscaped Kissena Park, which sits around a lake and contains an appealing nature center.

As might be expected, the presence of Queens College and Flushing's rich ethnic mix support an unusually vibrant cultural life: music, art, literary pursuits, and theater flourish here. The Flushing Branch of the Queens Borough Public Library on Main Street, handsomely rebuilt in 1998, is the busiest branch of the busiest library system in the nation. Open daily, its holdings include books, periodicals, videos, and CDs in some 30 languages, computer WorldLinQ in Chinese, Korean, Russian, Spanish, and French, an Adult Learning Center, and a unique International Resource Center. Renovation of the Main Street Flushing subway station nearby has been a boon to the 100,000 commuters who use it, many of them transferring from the web of bus routes that cross here.

Besides the convenience of transportation and the physical amenities, what Flushing has to offer is more space at less-than-Manhattan rents. For luxury condos look elsewhere, Bayside perhaps. High-rise apartments cluster near downtown Flushing. The rest is two-story brick apartment enclaves, one- and two-family houses, detached and semi-attached, all with on-street parking. Ads to sell or rent these properties are often placed in *Newsday* and the *New York Times* by their owners; consult these same pages and the list of realtors in **Finding a Place to Live** to find brokers who handle other properties.

Web Site: www.nyc.gov
Area Codes: 718, 347
Post Offices: CPU 60, 141-02 Northern Blvd; CPU 61, 40-02 Bowne St; Linden Hill, 29-50 Union St; Station A, 40-03 164th St; Kew Gardens Hills, 75-23 Main St
Zip Codes: 11354, 11355, 11358, 11365, 11366, 11367, 11368
Police Precincts: One Hundred and Ninth, 37-05 Union St, 718-321-2250; One Hundred and Seventh, 71-01 Parsons Blvd, 718-969-5100
Emergency Hospitals: New York Hospital Medical Center of Queens, 56-45 Main St, 718-670-1231, www.nyhq.org; Flushing Hospital Medical Center, 4500 Parsons Blvd, 718-670-5000, www.flushinghospital.org
Libraries: Flushing Main Branch, 41-17 Main St, 718-661-1200; Hillcrest Branch, 187-05 Union Turnpike, 718-454-2786; McGoldrick Branch, 155-06 Roosevelt Ave, 718-461-1616; Mitchell-Linden Branch, 29-42 Union St, 718-539-2330;

Pomonok Branch, 158-21 Jewel Ave, 718-591-4343; Queensborough Hill Branch, 60-05 Main St, 718-359-8332; www.queenslibrary.org; Benjamin S. Rosenthal Library, Queens College, 65-30 Kissena Blvd, 718-997-5000

Public School Education: School Districts #25 and #26 in region 3, 30-48 Linden Place, 718-281-7605 and 61-15 Oceania St., 718-631-6900, http://schools.nyc.gov

Adult Education: Queens College, 65-30 Kissena Blvd, 718-997-5000, www.qc.cuny.edu

Community Resources: Queens Historical Society, Kingsland House, 143-35 37th Ave, 718-939-0647, www.queenshistoricalsociety.org; Queens Chamber of Commerce, www.queenschamber.org; The Bowne House, 37-01 Bowne St, 718-359-0528; www.bownehouse.org; New York Hall of Science, 47-01 111th St, Flushing Meadows–Corona Park, 718-699-0005, www.nyscience.org, includes over 200 hands-on exhibits plus a science playground for children; Queens Museum of Art, New York City Building, Flushing Meadows–Corona Park, 718-592-9700, www.queensmuseum.org; Kupferberg Center for the Performing Arts, Queens College, Long Island Expressway and Kissena Blvd, 718-793-8080; www.kupferberger.org; Flushing Council on Culture and the Arts at Town Hall, 137-35 Northern Blvd, 718-463-7700, www.flushingtownhall.org; Kissena Park Nature Center, Rose Ave and Parsons Blvd, 718-699-4202; Queens Botanical Garden, 43-50 Main St, 718-886-3800, www.queensbotanical.org; Queens Theatre in the Park, Flushing Meadows–Corona Park, 718-760-0064, www.queenstheatre.org

Transportation—Subway: #7, Willets Point-Shea Stadium, Main St; E, F, Union Turnpike-Kew Gardens

Transportation—Bus: for a Queens bus map and schedule, stop by the College Point Bus Depot, 128-15 28th Ave, Flushing, or call 718-330-1234, or go to www.mta.info. The MTA also offers express service on several routes to midtown Manhattan for $5.

Transportation—LIRR: Main Street Station, Main St & 41st Ave

BAYSIDE

Boundaries and Contiguous Areas: North and **East**: Cross Island Parkway; **South**: Long Island Expressway; **West**: Francis Lewis Boulevard and Utopia Parkway

The bright barn-red Long Island Railroad station, white-trimmed and snappy, differentiates Bayside from other Queens stops. So does the concentration of pubs and restaurants—some dim and glitzy, others homey-comfortable with fireplaces—that surround the station. These places attract singles and have a bubbling atmosphere after work and on weekends more akin to Long Island than

New York. North of this Bell Boulevard and 41st Avenue junction, one- and two-family homes re-establish that urban/suburban quiet which typifies residential Queens, with gated Bayside Gables dominating the area, until you reach **Bay Terrace**.

Here, newer condominiums and co-op garden apartment buildings break the mold.

Bayside has been rated among the best places to live a number of times. While the older, free-standing homes contain rental apartments, condominium rentals in the pristine **Bay Club**, among other high-rises, are probably the biggest draw. The enormous development consists of 1,036 condominiums in two three-pronged towers, a glass-domed swim club, a health club, and five tennis courts. The **Bay Bridge** condo development nearby, with some 2,000 luxury townhouses, is a shorefront village in itself. From the Bay Club windows, and from those in the older co-ops, you can see how the community got its name—Bayside is bounded on two sides by Little Bay and Little Neck Bay. The Whitestone, Triborough, and Throgs Neck bridges connect Queens to The Bronx. Tucked within the densely populated high-rises that pack many a Bayside block are several town parks (including the 655-acre Alley Pond Park and the recently opened seaside Fort Totten), plenty of shopping, and excellent schools; these features, combined with the relative regularity of the LIRR schedule and the low crime rate, have made this family area a commuter favorite for decades, especially with NYC police and firefighters.

Bayside has water views but no direct subway connection to Manhattan. Commuters have three public transportation choices: the Long Island Railroad, express buses, or Queens buses to Flushing's Main Street Station and the #7 Flushing Line subway to 42nd street in Manhattan. The LIRR is typically the fastest route.

Web Sites: www.baysidequeens.com, www.nyc.gov
Area Codes: 718, 347
Post Offices: Bayside Station, 212-35 42nd Ave; Bayside Annex, 41-29 216th St; Bay Terrace, 212-71 26th Ave
Zip Codes: 11360, 11361, 11364, 11357
Police Precinct: One Hundred and Eleventh, 45-06 215th St, 718-279-5200

Emergency Hospital: St. Mary's Hospital for Children, 29-01 216th St, 718-281-8800, www.stmaryskids.org

Library: Bayside Branch, 214-20 Northern Blvd, 718-229-1834, www.queens library.org

Public School Education: School District #26 in region 3, 61-15 Oceania St, Bayside, 718-631-6900, http://schools.nyc.gov

Adult Education: Queensborough Community College, 222-05 56th Ave, 718-631-6262, www.qcc.cuny.edu

Community Resources: Crocheron Park, 33rd Ave and Little Neck Parkway, 718-762-5966, a 45-acre park; Queensborough Community College Gallery, 222-05 56th Ave, 718-631-6396, www.qcc.cuny.edu; Queens Chamber of Commerce, www.queenschamber.org

Transportation—Train: regular LIRR service

Transportation—Bus: for a Queens bus map and schedule, stop by the College Point Bus Depot, 128-15 28th Ave, Flushing, or call 718-330-1234, or go to www.mta.info. The MTA also offers express service on several routes to midtown Manhattan for $5.

Transportation—LIRR: Station: 213th St and 41st Ave

YOU MIGHT ALSO WANT TO CONSIDER...

- **Douglaston**, an upper middle-class community at the northeastern end of Queens bordering on Long Island, having mostly one- and two-family houses and co-ops, relatively low real estate taxes, and lower prices than upscale Great Neck (Long Island) to the east. A 25-minute commute to Manhattan on the Long Island Railroad. Community Board 11, 718-225-1054

- **Jamaica Estates**, with its winding roads, shady streets, Tudor houses, and English street names, is 45 minutes by the E or F train to Manhattan. Expensive homes in a small, rather exclusive community tucked away in mid to north Queens. Community Board 8, 718-264-7895 , www.queenscb.org

- **Middle Village is mid-Queens**, middle class, and relatively affordable, with tidy one- and two-family houses and a scattering of condos housing an old-fashioned "close-knit" community of civic-minded people and plenty of mom and pop stores. Amenities include Juniper Valley Park, from which the Manhattan skyline is visible, good schools, Italian specialty stores, and German bakeries. Community Board 5, 718-366-1834

- **Richmond Hill**, with Victorian houses, golf and tennis in Forest Park, and a variety of ethnic stores, but less expensive than neighboring Kew Gardens and Forest Hills, for the most part. An easy commute by train or subway. Community Board 9, 718-286-2686; Richmond Hill Historical Society, www. richmondhillhistory.org

- • **Ridgewood**, a half-hour from Grand Central by subway, boasts a German heritage still apparent in its shops and restaurants, solid row houses (some of them landmarked), and a strong neighborhood feeling. Especially prized are the harmonious yellow-brick houses along Stockholm St and two blocks of 69th Ave, between Fresh Pond Rd and 60th St. Community Board 5, 718-366-1834

- • **Whitestone**, between the Whitestone and Throgs Neck Bridges in northern Queens and 30 minutes on the #7 from Times Square (45 minutes by express bus). A highly residential, quiet, family neighborhood featuring some private homes plus many co-ops and condos—few rentals. Includes exclusive Malba (see the **introduction** to the **Queens** profile above) and Francis Lewis Park along the riverfront. Community Board 7, 718-359-2800

STATEN ISLAND

New York's least-populated borough is, for many, simply the turn-around point for New York's most beloved, and cheapest, boat ride, the Staten Island Ferry (it's free). Area residents would just as soon keep their 61-square-mile island off the coast of New Jersey to themselves. Dreams of remaining far from the maddening New York frenzy were conclusively shattered when the austerely beautiful Verrazano-Narrows Bridge connecting Staten Island with Brooklyn was opened in 1964. The island's semi-rural isolation ended once and for all—save for the three public golf courses and 15 parks—as Brooklynites flocked across the longest single-span bridge in the world to take up residence in dozens of new tract developments. And its population growth continues today. Not everyone agrees on the reasons or the impact. "Those who are coming want more to follow," says one realtor, meaning both residents and the businesses that serve them. "And those who are here want it to stop." That dark sentiment relates primarily to traffic, which is the first complaint on the lips of most who live here on "The Rock."

Giovanni da Verrazano discovered hillocky Staten Island in 1524 but, until the dedication of his namesake bridge 440 years later, the island remained something of a backwater. Henry Hudson claimed Staaten Eylandt for the Dutch East India Company in 1609; however, Britain acquired Staten Island when the British took over New Amsterdam in 1644. In 1687 the Duke of York offered the island as a prize in a sailing competition; the team from Manhattan won and has laid claim to the land mass ever since. By the mid-1800s, a railroad, trolley cars, and ferry service made the island's seashore and salubrious air accessible to the gentry.

The fickle fashionables had moved on though by the time Staten Island became part of New York City in 1898. Too bad, because the city improved the new borough's ferry service immeasurably: by 1904 there were a number of sturdy seaworthy boats running on schedule for the first time since young Cornelius Vanderbilt instituted ferry service to Manhattan around 1810. Today, 60,000 people a day brave the choppy waters between St. George and the Battery. Now,

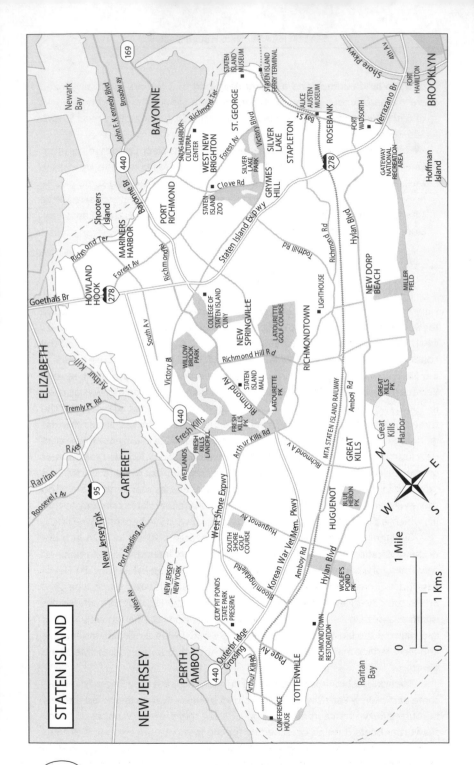

STATEN ISLAND

not only do tracts and shopping malls flourish south of the Staten Island Express-way, straining the island's over-taxed infrastructure, but a modest renaissance is also under way in communities within walking distance of the ferry landing. Wall Streeters cherish the office-to-ferry walk, as well as the uphill stroll home, almost as much as they cherish the fare: it's free. Traffic, however, continues to be a com-plaint, and is worsening as the borough's population increases.

Hills—precipitous slopes reminiscent of San Francisco—and stunning views from the craggy ridge that rises between St. George and Richmondtown charac-terize that portion of Staten Island nearest Manhattan. On leafy Todt, Emerson, and Grymes hills, multi-million-dollar homes look over the treetops to Brooklyn and Manhattan. Wood-frame Victorian houses, salted among the stucco mini-mansions and angular contemporary homes, are the darlings of homesteaders. You're more likely to find a rental apartment in a converted one- or two-family house than in an apartment building on Staten Island—although red brick apartment towers do exist , especially a half dozen new ones in St. George.

The Staten Island Chamber of Commerce (130 Bay Street, 718-727-1900, www.sichamber.com) sells an excellent street map and the MTA's Staten Island Bus Map (free at the Chamber) is equally useful. Rental classifieds in the *Staten Island Advance* (718-981-1234, www.statenislandadvance.com) are more numer-ous on Saturday and Sunday but this afternoon paper publishes real estate ads every day. In Manhattan, pick up a copy of the *Advance* at the newsstand located inside the ferry terminal.

The *Village Voice* has listings for Staten Island; craigslist.com and most of the websites listed within this chapter carry real estate ads as well.

ST. GEORGE

Boundaries and Contiguous Areas: North: Richmond Terrace and the Kill Van Kull; **East**: Bay Street; **South**: Victory Boulevard and Stapleton; **West**: Jersey Street and The Narrows

Flags aflutter, the beguiling limestone and brick Borough Hall caps a rise to the right of St. George's ferry terminal. To the left as you exit the terminal, a stunning structure, at once public sculpture, bridge, and lighthouse-like tower, crowns a plaza, inviting visitors to climb to its glassy top for a smashing view of the har-bor and lower Manhattan beyond. The two are symbolic of St. George's struggle against blight. The downtown sector, though quaint and historic, has defied gentrification, but uphill, within sight of the neo-Gothic spires of Curtis High School (between St. Mark's Place and Hamilton Avenue), you'll find restored Victorian, Tudor, and 1920s-stucco houses. Four formerly vacant apartment buildings there have been transformed into the Village on St. Marks with afford-able rentals suitable for commuters to the Financial District. And the Saturday

Greenmarket on St. Marks brings a village square feel to downtown St. George from May to December. In contrast to the maple-shaded period homes, the three converted grain and coffee warehouses that comprise Bay Street Landing are certainly up-to-date. Arguably the borough's trendiest housing, these waterside condominiums located a five-minute walk east of the ferry terminal are the first stage in a projected harborfront revival. Here, black pines and juniper separate the public marina, esplanade, and the glass-enclosed Landing Café from the access road—shades of Sausalito. New rentals, rare in Staten Island, are to be found in moderately priced waterfront mid-rises at Harbor View. Come spring, fishing enthusiasts flock to the charter boats tied up at the Landing's pristine docks. The Joseph L. Lyons Pool, one of Staten Island's four municipal swimming pools, and the George Cromwell Center, an indoor recreation center with tennis courts and a track situated on a pier, are both located near The Landing's complex. The new Richmond County Bank Ballpark is the home of exciting baseball action featuring the Staten Island Yankees (www.siyanks.com), a minor league affiliate of the Bronx Bombers.

Check the classifieds for rentals, and after filing off the ferry, walk through the gradually reviving community of St. George, which has recently put up a number of ten-story condo buildings near the water, where 1-bedrooms go for about $1,000 a month. This is also an area to look for new loft redos, now that the laws have changed.

Web Sites: www.statenislandusa.com, www.statenislandadvance.com, www.si-web.com, www.prodigalborough.com, www.silive.com, www.nyc.gov
Area Codes: 718, 347
Post Offices: St. George Station, 45 Bay St; Stapleton Station, 160 Tompkins Ave; CPU 503, 1300 Clove Rd
Zip Code: 10301
Police Precinct: One Hundred Twentieth, 78 Richmond Terr, 718-876-8500
Emergency Hospitals (nearest): St. Vincent's Medical Center of Richmond, 355 Bard Ave, 718-818-1234, www.svcmc.org
Library: St. George Library Center, 5 Central Ave, 718-442-8560, www.nypl.org

Public School Education: School District #31 in region 7, 715 Ocean Terr, 718-556-8350, www.nycenet.edu

Adult Education: CUNY: College of Staten Island, 2800 Victory Blvd, 718-982-2000, www csi.cuny.edu

Community Resources: Richmond County Bank Ballpark, 75 Richmond Terr, 718-720-9265; Snug Harbor Cultural Center, 1000 Richmond Terr, 718-448-2500, www.snug-harbor.org, is located in a clutch of handsome Greek Revival buildings on 80 tree-filled acres. Once a haven for indigent sailors, the colonnaded buildings are now the locus of Staten Island's cultural rebirth; concerts, art exhibits, and plays fill the high-ceilinged halls. Also on the grounds you'll find the Staten Island Botanical Garden, 718-273-8200, www.sibg.org, which contains the Chinese Scholar's Garden, 8 pavilions of peace and tranquility, www.sibg.org/cg; and the Staten Island Children's Museum, 718-273-2060. The nearby Staten Island Museum, 75 Stuyvesant Pl, 718-727-1135, www.statenislandmuseum.org, a museum offering tours and cultural events, and the Noble Maritime Collection, 718-447-6490, www.noblemaritime.org.

Transportation—Train: the Staten Island Railway, now run by the MTA, costs $2.00 one way and provides service between the St. George Ferry Terminal and Tottenville at the southern tip of the 13.9-mile-long island. The second stop, Tompkinsville Station, is used for Bay Street Landing. Call 718-330-1234 for information.

Transportation—Bus: local buses cost $2 one way. Express buses to Manhattan via the Verrazano Bridge and Brooklyn Battery Tunnel cost $5 one way. Call 718-330-1234, www.mta.info, for bus information.

Transportation—Ferry: free passenger ferries run every 15 or 20 minutes during rush hours, every half hour at other times, every hour from 11 p.m. to 6 a.m. Service is less frequent on holidays and weekends. Car service has been suspended on the ferry since September 11th, 2001. Call 718-330-1234 or visit www.siferry.com, for information.

STAPLETON

Boundaries and Contiguous Areas: North: Victory Boulevard and St. George; **East**: Bay Street and Upper New York Bay; **South**: Canal and Broad streets; **West**: Louis Street, Van Duzer Street and Grymes Hill

Bordering Bay Street, Stapleton boasts a batch of more-collectibles-than-antiques stores and a few somewhat upscale watering holes. These cafés, tarted up with Tiffany style lamps, polished brass, and old-fashioned bottle vases, point to the presence of newcomers in Stapleton's craggy hills.

Located only two subway stops from the ferry terminal, Stapleton for some time has attracted artists and young families looking for a third bedroom. Now, here

come bankers and stockbrokers from Lower Manhattan. Sturdy 19th-century homes characterize housing in **Stapleton Heights** and adjacent **Ward Hill**. Asphalt shingles sheath houses down on the flats near the gourmet takeout shops, the library, and handsome Tappan Park. The Mud Lane Society, a group of community boosters, promotes Stapleton with an annual house tour. An abandoned 6-acre military base on the shore is slated by the city for redevelopment into a 360-unit mix of retail and residential with a seaside walkway, although nothing has yet to materialize.

The area, still quaint and serene, has seen some modest growth on Beach and Van Duzer streets with the recent opening of new coffee shops, yoga schools, beauty salons, and Japanese restaurants. A new community center is in the works and a few townhouses have cropped up along Beach Street.

Web Sites: www.statenislandusa.com, www.si-web.com, www.silive.com, www. preservestatenisland.org, www.prodigalborough.com, www.nyc.gov

Area Codes: 718, 347

Post Offices: Stapleton Station, 160 Tompkins Ave; Rosebank Station, 567 Tompkins Ave

Zip Code: 10301

Police Precinct: One Hundred Twentieth, 78 Richmond Terr, 718-876-8500

Emergency Hospital (nearest): Staten Island University Hospital, 475 Seacrest Rd, 718-226-9140

Library: Stapleton Branch, 132 Canal St, 718-727-0427, www.nypl.org

Public School Education: School District #31 in region 7 (see **St. George**)

Adult Education (nearby): St. John's University, 300 Howard Ave, 718-390-4500, www.stjohns.edu

Community Resources (nearby): The Jacques Marchais Center of Tibetan Art houses Tibetan monastery artifacts at 338 Lighthouse Ave in Richmondtown, 718-987-3500, www.tibetanmuseum.com; the Richmondtown Restoration, a historic village comprised of 15 buildings operated by the Staten Island Historical Society at 441 Clarke Ave, 718-351-1611, www.historicrichmondtown. org; The Conference House, a pre-Revolutionary manor house, at 7455 Hylan Blvd, 718-984-2086, www.theconferencehouse.org; Alice Austen House Museum and Garden, 2 Hylan Blvd, 718-816-4506, www.aliceausten.org.

Transportation—Train: the Stapleton Station is the third stop on the SIRT train (details under **St. George**)

Transportation—Bus: the #74, #76, and #51 travel Bay St as far as Canal; the #78 runs along Van Duzer St and St. Paul's Ave in Stapleton Heights (details under **St. George**)

GRYMES HILL AND SILVER LAKE

Boundaries and Contiguous Areas: North: Louis Avenue; **East**: Stapleton, Van Duzer Street, and Richmond Road; **South**: Clove Road and the Staten Island Expressway; **West**: Victory Boulevard

On blustery autumn days, salty sea breezes rattle maple and birch branches, garnishing **Grymes Hill** with russet leaves. Save for the outline of Wall Street's mist-shrouded skyline, the place feels much more like Westchester. Interspersed with narrow blacktop lanes and imposing old houses, the hills of Staten Island radiate a rustic sub-urbanity.

The higher you climb any one of the island's myriad hills, the more imposing the homes become. Four-hundred-foot high **Todt Hill**, the tallest of Staten Island's peaks, is the toniest. Grymes Hill, nearer the ferry terminal, is the most intellectual: St. John's University and Wagner College cluster its slopes; the College of Staten Island lies in an adjacent valley, and the girl-only Notre Dame Academy occupies nine acres on the edge of town. Though 12-story Sunrise Tower is co-op, there are 475 two- and three-bedroom rental apartments in the Grymes Hill Apartments Complex, built by Donald Trump's father in the 1940s. In addition, rental apartments can be found in remodeled one-family homes and underneath it all is an old series of caves used to make beer during the Prohibition (now, alas, sealed up by a developer).

Silver Lake combines with Clove Lakes Park to form a sylvan greenbelt. There are tennis courts, bridle paths, an ice skating rink, and a municipal golf course laid out around the reservoir, and between Clove Road and Broadway a small, accessible zoo with a first-rate reptile collection.

Web Sites: www.statenislandusa.com, www.si-web.com, www.silive.com, www. nyc.gov

Area Codes: 718, 347, 917

Post Offices: St. George Station, 45 Bay St; Stapleton Station, 160 Tompkins Ave

Zip Codes: 10301, 10304

Police Precinct: 120th, 78 Richmond Terrace, 718-876-8500

Emergency Hospitals (nearest): Staten Island University Hospital, 475 Seacrest Rd, 718-226-9140; St. Vincent's Medical Center of Richmond, 355 Bard Ave, 718-818-1234, www.svmc.org

Library (nearest): Stapleton Branch, 132 Canal St, 718-727-0427, www.nypl.org

Public School Education: School District #31 in region 7 (see **St. George**)

Adult Education: College of Staten Island, 2800 Victory Blvd, 718-982-2000; St. John's University, 300 Howard Ave, 718-390-4500, www.stjohns.edu; Wagner College, 1 Campus Rd, near Howard Ave, 718-390-3100, www.wagner. edu; Notre Dame Academy, 76 Howard Ave, 718-273-9096, www.notredame academy.org

Community Resources: Staten Island Zoo, 614 Broadway, 718-442-3100, www. statenislandzoo.org (also see **Stapleton**)

Transportation—Train: A steep climb is required to reach Grymes Hill from Stapleton, the nearest stop on the SIRT line (details under **St. George**).

Transportation—Bus: the #74 bus traverses Van Duzer St along the base of Grymes Hill; the #61, #62, #66, and #67 traveling Victory Blvd connect with the #60 shuttle bus at Clove Rd. The shuttle follows Howard Ave as far as the St. John campus (details under **St. George**)

LIVINGSTON

Boundaries and Contiguous Areas: North: the Kill Van Kull; **East**: the Snug Harbor Cultural Center; **South**: Henderson Avenue; **West**: Bement Avenue

In fast-growing Staten Island, underdevelopment is a matter of some pride. This is readily apparent in Livingston, just a few miles west of bustling St. George on the North Shore in what is part of West New Brighton. Once an important stop on the Underground Railroad, the town, then called Elliotsville, was home to several prominent families, including that of Robert Gould Shaw, brought to modern-day fame by the film *Glory* as the leader of the first black regiment in the Civil War. The name Livingston came with the construction of a now-defunct railway station at Richmond Terrace and Bard Avenue, which was called Livingston Station, though no one knows why (no one knew then, either).

Livingston retains the wide streets and airy colonial homes of its auspicious history, and a great number of majestic elm and oak trees shade the sidewalks. The population of roughly 3,000 people is made up primarily of middle-class families that deeply appreciate the town's quiet, private feel, and take full advantage of the commercial options more readily available in nearby St. George.

Walker Park, near the north end of Bard Avenue, contains a number of tennis courts, and is home to the Staten Island Cricket Club; nearby Snug Harbor contains a wide array of activities (see **St. George**). For the privacy to

be found here, prices aren't bad: single-family homes, many of them built before 1900, range near half a million dollars. Two- family (and less historic) homes are also available, though pricier. Rentals run about less than half the cost of Manhattan apartments, with a roomy two-bedroom costing around $1,000. A 20-minute bus ride on the S40 will place you at the ferry terminal.

Web Sites: www.statenislandusa.com, www.si-web.com, www.silive.com, www.
     preservestatenisland.org, www.prodigalborough.com, www.nyc.gov
Area Codes: 718, 347
Post Office: West New Brighton Station, 1015 Castleton Ave
Zip Code: 10310
Police Precinct: 120th, 78 Richmond Terr, 718-876-8500
Emergency Hospitals (nearest): St. Vincent's Medical Center of Richmond, 355
     Bard Ave, 718-818-1234, www.svmc.org
Library (nearest): West New Brighton Branch, 976 Castleton Ave at North Bur-
     gher Ave, 718-442-1416, www.nypl.org
Public School Education: School District #31 in region 7 (see **St. George**)
Adult Education: St. John's University, 300 Howard Ave, 718-390-4545, www.
     stjohns.edu; Wagner College, 631 Howard Ave, 718-390-3100, www.wagner.
     edu
Community Resources: see **St. George**
Transportation—Bus: the S40 runs local along Richmond Terrace in the north,
     and is joined by the limited-stop S90. The local S44 and limited-stop S94
     run east-west along Henderson Ave. All four connect with the ferry at St.
     George.

YOU MIGHT ALSO WANT TO CONSIDER...

- **Port Richmond**, just south of West New Brighton on the Kill Van Kull, offers
  reasonably priced housing, much of it pre-war, one- and two-family homes,

and a 50-minute commute by express bus or bus/ferry from Manhattan. Community Board 1, 718-981-6900, or Staten Island Chamber of Commerce, 718-727-1900, www.sichamber.com.

- **Arden Heights, also known as Annadale,** is one of many South Shore neighborhoods that are being encroached upon by the rapid growth in the neighborhoods to the north. Centered on the Village Greens, one of New York's first planned urban developments, Arden Heights sports a number of homes and townhouses clustered on looped streets, which keep traffic at a minimum and ease the pain of parking suffered by other Staten Islanders. Two shopping centers, small parks, and a community center serve residents, and two Olympic-sized swimming pools lie in a 16-acre park.

- **Castleton Corners** was once called Four Corners, in reference to the intersection of Victory Boulevard and Manor Road, at the town's center. The intersection is now central to a commercial district, and the neighborhood around it, largely unaffected by the rapid growth that followed in the wake of the Verrazano Bridge, has become upscale.

- **Grasmere**; conveniently located on the self-named stop of the Staten Island MTA line, Grasmere has an unusually bucolic feel, even for Staten Island. The key feature of this tiny community is the 15-acre Brady's Pond, said to be the only swimmable freshwater pond in New York City, complete with lifeguards, beaches, rowboats and a bunch of irritable swans. The tiny hamlet's location near the Verrazano Bridge makes it an excellent nest for car commuters.

- **Mariners Harbor** is an old shipbuilding center with an interesting mix of traditional sea captain mansions and newer buildings. Quite popular with newer arrivals—including rumors of New York's first Wal-Mart—it's located on the northwest corner of the island with excellent views over Kill van Kull. It's not too far from the bizarre "Ships Graveyard" where dozens of half-sunken rotten hulls stick up out of the harbor in a fairy tale version of an urban-rot wonderland. Just ask around.

- **West New Brighton** is a stable community across the Kill van Kull from New Jersey and just southwest of the ferry. Here Victorian houses and apartments offer golf, tennis, and extensive parkland in Silver Lake Park and Clove Lakes Park, which includes the Staten Island Zoo. The Snug Harbor Cultural Center is nearby. Community Board 1, 718-981-6900, or Staten Island Chamber of Commerce, 718-727-1900, www.sichamber.com.

- **Rosebank** is located in the middle of the eastern part of the Island and claims to be where modern chewing gum was invented. This is a very quiet area with many older homes, but there are also some interesting old abandoned warehouses in the area that are being considered for renovation, now that the island's loft-conversion laws have changed.

NEW JERSEY

If you watched "The Sopranos," you'd think that New Jersey is known as "The Garden State" because of all the bodies found buried out back. In fact, most of them are dumped in the river. In real life, while there are still lots of Mafia types in some areas (or as realtors call them, "local color"), much of New Jersey is quite beautiful, and the area near Manhattan is especially ideal for young professionals who work in the city but prefer a more small-town feel after hours. Some of these quasi-bedroom communities have also been most affected by the economic meltdown of 2008 and in some cases serious bargains can be found—by some reports, just the last two weeks of November 2008 saw a 3% decrease in prices.

Below we list some of the major destinations for those who wish to live outside the city. A note about seeking homes: though the ever-popular Craigslist does have extensive listings for North Jersey, none of the towns there yet have ranked pages of their own within the site (although there is a page for those immediately around Manhattan). Personal visits and contacting locals and brokers will provide more detailed information. For those looking to buy, www.zillow.com is a useful resource for determining localized trends in housing costs, and for renters, www.rent.com has thorough and detailed New Jersey listings. Recently, state government has put in place a 211 phone service that helps residents connect with all its departments, as well as answer questions about what services are available.

FORT LEE AND EDGEWATER

Boundaries and Contiguous Areas: North: Englewood and Englewood Cliffs; **East**: Hudson River; **South**: Cliffside Park and West New York; **West**: Leonia and Palisades Park

Apartment towers in **Fort Lee** ride the Palisades above the Hudson like so many schooner masts making their way up the river. Beneath the rocky cliffs sits the small community of Edgewater, where George Washington and his Continental Army landed in November of 1776, after the battle of Washington Heights. General Charles Lee had supervised the fortifications on the site that bears his name, and their remnants are still to be found there. Fort Lee remained a sleepy little town with a ferry landing throughout most of the 19th century. Civil War gunboats used the volcanically formed Palisades for target practice, and these same cliffs provided the Belgian paving stones for the streets of Manhattan.

In the late 1800s a series of resorts and amusement centers flourished on The Bluffs, as they were known, only to dwindle away and be reborn as the country's movie making capital in the 1920s. For a while every major studio had lots here, only to get scared by the unpredictable weather and move to California. The area went into decline until the completion of the George Washington Bridge in

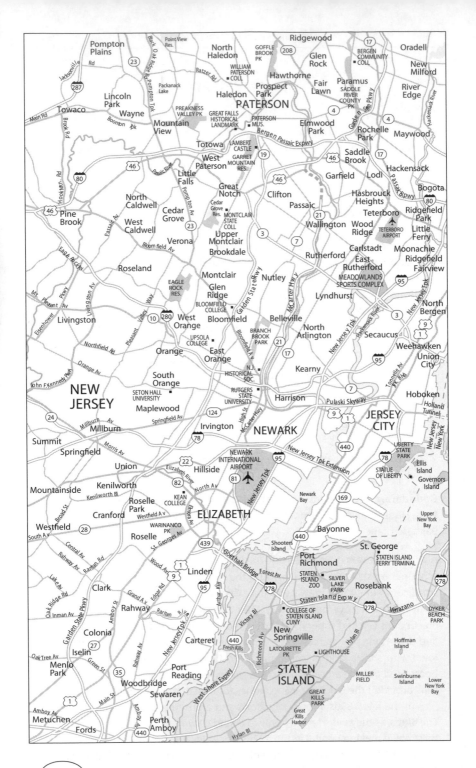

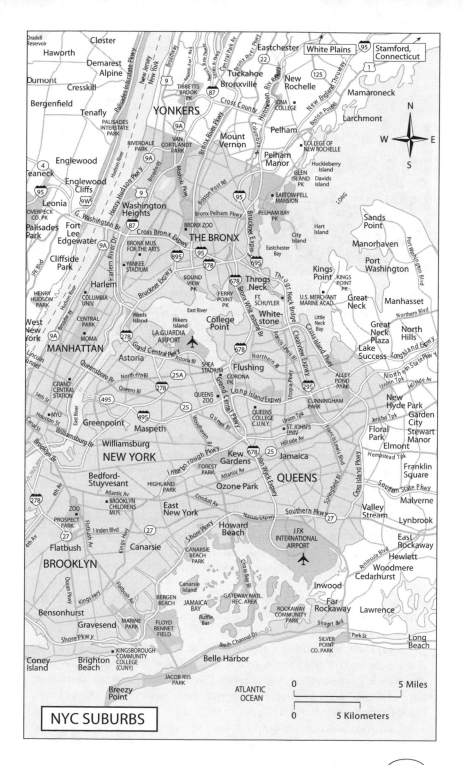

NYC SUBURBS

1931 gave Fort Lee a suburban future. The tallest high-rise in Bergen County rose in Fort Lee in 1972 and such buildings grew rapidly along Palisade Avenue. Fort Lee straddles the approach to the bridge—which can produce horrific traffic jams during rush hours—but the most sought-after housing lies south of the bridge. An estimated 80% of its approximately 35,000 inhabitants commute to jobs in the city, largely by Jersey Transit to the Port Authority Bus Terminal in Manhattan. In recent years there's also been a large influx of Asian inhabitants, some 30%, with a substantial Korean community.

Fort Lee has maintained a small-town feel, despite its having grown faster—and taller—than it could plan for. Along the quiet streets off Palisade Avenue, tidy homes nearly fill their lovingly manicured postage-stamp lots (they're expensive, nonetheless). It's the view—Manhattan afloat on the Hudson—that determines the price of real estate and rentals. Apartments with a view fetch near-Manhattan prices, whether they are co-ops, condos, or rentals, but you use the same pool and health club at a lower rent without the view. Away from the edge, garden apartments and two-family houses are less expensive.

At the eastern, river end of Main Street in 33-acre Fort Lee Historic Park, visitors trace the Revolutionary history of the area in the museum and discover the remnants of Continental Army dugouts. The park lies within the greater Palisades Interstate Park, a narrow strip of wooded land stretching for miles between the Hudson and the Palisades Interstate Parkway, with marinas, picnic areas, and a scenic drive. Known to few outside the immediate area, the park constitutes an extraordinary recreation asset for residents of Fort Lee and Edgewater. For the extremely energetic, this is also the starting point for The Long Path, a 330-mile hiking trail that goes all the way to Albany.

Main Street winds down the steep hill into River Road in **Edgewater**, one of the more unusual small towns in New Jersey. A blue-collar pocket only three streets wide, Edgewater hunches under the Palisades along steep, narrow streets, some of whose modest houses have recently been replaced by clutches of tidy condos. There's a somewhat funky feel to the town.

Construction of upscale, high- and low-rise condo and rental developments along the river side of River Road has brought a wave of affluent young professionals, and change, to Edgewater and the adjoining riverside towns directly to the south, North Bergen, West New York, and Weehawken (see below). Sprawling handsomely at water's edge, or suspended over it on piles, housing complexes with aquatic names such as Admiral's Walk, Mariner's Cove, and Jacob's Ferry offer all the amenities—tennis, pool, health club—and the view, at a price. Clustered about are cinemas, a supermarket, restaurants, a restaurant/club in a restored old Hoboken Ferry boat, and hotels; and Yaohan, a Japanese mall complete with a Japanese supermarket, restaurant, and specialty shops, attracts shoppers from throughout the tri-state area. Interspersed helter-skelter among these waterside centers are the occasional industrial site, a golf driving range, a tennis club, and marinas.

Edgewater is growing, with rental and condo projects proliferating, along with retail space and now a cineplex. Office complexes are being carved out of abandoned industrial sites. And with this critical mass, the megastores—Bed, Bath & Beyond, Barnes & Noble, Staples, etc.—have ventured in; Starbucks, too.

Although there is free commuter bus service to Edgewater ferry landing, a car is a necessity here in the relative isolation of Edgewater's narrow, winding River Road. It's advisable to drive around first to determine your proximity to the part of the city in which you work, as the commute to lower Manhattan can be longer than the view might suggest.

Web Sites: www.newjersey.com, www.fortleenj.org, www.edgewateronline.com

Area Code: 201

Post Offices: Main Branch, 229 Main St; Palisade Station, 1213 Anderson Ave, Fort Lee; Edgewater Station, River Rd and Russel Ave, Edgewater

Zip Codes: Fort Lee, 07024; Edgewater, 07020

Police Stations: Fort Lee Police Station, 1327 16th St, Fort Lee, 201-592-3700; Edgewater Police Station, 916 River Rd, Edgewater, 201-943-2200

Emergency Hospitals: Englewood Hospital and Medical Center, 350 Engle St, Englewood, 201-894-3000, www.englewoodhospital.com; Palisades Medical Center, 7600 River Rd, North Bergen, 201-854-5000, palisadesmedical.org

Libraries: Fort Lee Free Public Library, 320 Main St, 201-592-3614; Edgewater Free Public Library, 49 Hudson Ave, 201-224-6144; www.bccls.org

Public School Education: Fort Lee School District, 255 Whiteman St, Fort Lee, 201-585-4612, www.fortlee-boe.net; Edgewater Park Township School District, 25 Washington Ave, Edgewater Park, 609-877-2124, www.edgewaterpark.k12.nj.us

Transportation—Bus: call New Jersey Transit, 800-772-2222 or 212-564-8484 (Port Authority), for routes and schedules, or pick up same at the Port Authority Bus Terminal at Eighth Ave and 41st St in Manhattan. You can also go to www.njtransit.com.

Transportation—Ferry: Commuter-hour ferries run every half-hour from the piers at 983 River Rd to W 39th in midtown, with a bus to Port Authority (one-way $10; 10-trip pack, $93).

WEEHAWKEN

Boundaries and Contiguous Areas: North: West New York; **East**: Hudson River; **South**: Union City and Hoboken; **West**: Union City

Most housing secrets outside of Manhattan's madness are closely held and zealously guarded. Inevitably they are discovered and development follows, along with rising property values. Weehawken, a tiny little town along the Hudson River, is no exception. It can be roughly divided into three areas: **Boulevard East**, up above the Palisades, where multi-million-dollar homes share spectacular sweeping views of the Manhattan skyline, just across from midtown; **The Heights**, on the south side of the entrance to the Lincoln Tunnel (which provides rapid access to the city, when traffic is light); and the **Waterfront**, which has seen the most vigorous development.

The Dutch bought this site in the 17th century from the Lenni-Lenape Indians and modified its Indian name to suit Dutch tongues. Little had changed in 1804, when Aaron Burr killed Alexander Hamilton in a duel on a grassy plot near the shore here. Shipyards and industry along the shoreline came later, and with them, the mansions on the Heights. Frame, brick, and brownstone row houses were built along the side streets heading west from the cliffs and remain the chief source of prime housing in Weehawken. Most prized are houses in the tiny Bluffs section just south of Hamilton Park.

Rentals are primarily limited to one- and two-bedroom apartments that go for rates roughly two-thirds of comparable Manhattan spaces. Co-ops start

around a quarter of a million dollars, with luxury townhouses ranging from two to four million. Since there are a lot of Wall Street financial types in the area, the end of 2008 saw a markdown in prices of around 5% in the last few months of the year, accompanied by an increase in supply. Cars are owned by many residents, and parking is not good. As for nightlife, there's a constantly growing supply of restaurants and bars but with Manhattan only a quick bus/boat/train ride away most of the action is still heading to town. Cabs across the river are always expensive, no matter which direction you travel.

The housing stock in Weehawken is increasing by leaps and bounds thanks to a series of massive developments along the shoreline. The latest is Henley on Hudson, a planned "brownstone" community next to Port Imperial with every possible amenity and units up to $4 million. Literally right on the river and a quick walk from the ferry stop, it's a commuter's dream: private piers, riverside restaurants and gyms, immaculately manicured parks for the kids. It's also generated a fair amount of objections from long-time residents fearful of losing their river views.

Environmentally concerned residents should also be aware that much of this area was contaminated with hexavalent chromium, a carcinogen, the worst of which has been removed and the rest "capped" with topsoil and plastic sheeting.

NY Waterway offers continuous ferry service to Manhattan with connecting van service to midtown and the Wall Street area. (Two area ports also send ferries on 17-minute trips to destinations in lower and midtown Manhattan.) The Hudson-Bergen Light Rail also connects Weehawken with several other cities in North Jersey. Also planned is an 18.5-mile walkway along Weehawken's shore from the George Washington Bridge to Bayonne.

Many Weehawken properties are handled by Hoboken real estate brokers, or by their owners. Check the ads in the *Jersey Journal* (see **Jersey City**) and in the *Weehawken Reporter* (available locally in stores and apartment building lobbies).

Web Sites: www.weehawken-nj.us, www.newjersey.com
Area Codes: 201, 973
Post Office: Weehawken Substation, 4100 Park Ave, Suite 9
Zip Code: 07086, 07087
Police Station: 400 Park Ave, 201-863-7800
Emergency Hospital (nearest): Palisades Medical Center, 7600 River Rd, North Bergen, 201-854-5000
Library: Weehawken Free Public Library, 49 Hauxhurst Ave, 201-863-7823, www.bccls.org
Public School Education: Weehawken Board of Education, 53 Liberty Pl, 201-422-6125
Transportation—Bus: mini-buses troll Boulevard East for passengers to the Port Authority Bus Terminal in Manhattan continuously weekdays, less frequently on weekends. New Jersey Transit service is also 10 minutes to the terminal; call 800-772-2222 or 212-564-8484 for routes and schedules, or pick up same at the Port Authority Bus Terminal, Eighth Ave and 41st St in Manhattan. You can also go to www.njtransit.com.
Transportation—Ferry: service by NY Waterway between Port Imperial and Lincoln Harbor to midtown and lower Manhattan runs every 15 to 30 minutes on weekdays from 6 a.m. to 10 p.m. with a slightly different hourly schedule on weekends. Free shuttle buses work the main streets during rush hour. Call 800-533-3779 for information or go to www.nywaterway.com.

HOBOKEN

Boundaries and Contiguous Areas: North: Weehawken; **East**: Hudson River; **South**: Jersey City; **West**: Croxton

At the turn of the millennium, Hoboken was reinventing itself. Most of this tidy, small (population 40,000) "Mile Square City" sandwiched between the Hudson River and Jersey bluffs was built between 1860 and 1910. By 1900, Hoboken was famous as the first American port of call for tens of thousands of immigrants, many of whom stayed close by, finding jobs in the city's numerous light manufacturing plants. Industrious working- and middle-class citizens built the simple, unadorned brownstone and brick row houses that comprise most of Hoboken's real estate. These large families pushed Hoboken's population to 70,000 at its peak.

The patrician Stevens family, who bought what was to become Hoboken soon after the Revolution, lived in relative isolation and splendor in what is now the Stevens Institute of Technology.

Laid out in a grid that encompasses several pleasant, leafy squares, much of Hoboken retains a comfortable blue-collar feel. However, there is an increasingly massive presence of Manhattan refugees who are content to gaze back at a Manhattan skyline visually afloat on the river, gleaming in the afternoon sun and ablaze with lights at night. It began in the early 1970s when a tide of disaffected New Yorkers, many of them singles, were attracted to this community just ten minutes from Manhattan by subway (PATH). Artists and rock musicians as well as young professionals discovered Hoboken, and the row house renovations, the cafés, interesting shops, and galleries dotting the original downtown and Washington Street neighborhoods show it. Where homesteaders pioneer, serious developers almost always follow. Certainly, the conversion to condos of tenement blocks along Monroe, Adams, and the other "presidential" streets west of Washington, as well as the Curling Club, the Hudson Tea, and Hudson Park complexes, among other luxury rental developments on once-industrial land in the north-

west quadrant, bear witness to that fact. To the south, new brownstone lofts and luxury single-family brownstones stand occupied in formerly "undesirable" streets.

The latest and most valuable development is of the

city's mile-long waterfront. Long an industrial site that had fallen to ruin, it is now lined with new high rises like Shipyard's 1,100 apartments or the Vanguard, with indoor and outdoor children's play areas, a fitness center, easy access to the riverfront promenade, and a five-minute PATH train ride to Manhattan. The latest entry is a massive W Hotel on River Street topped with multiple floors of luxury condos with all W amenities (at only $4.5 million for the penthouse suite.) Interesting, despite the way this massive gentrification has increased the city's value (from $3 billion to $9 billion), the local government remains plagued with financial shortfalls. Hoboken was put under state protective order in 2008 over a $10 million budget deficit that may require a large local tax increase and local web sites routinely report rumors of corruption (one former mayor was sentenced to 30 months on federal corruption charges).

Meeting the needs of area residents, the Hoboken Ferry plies the Hudson from two Hoboken piers to Battery Park. The main terminal, which it shares with PATH and New Jersey Transit trains, is gloriously restored to its beaux-arts splendor, with Tiffany glass skylights, buff limestone, and ornamental plaster. Hoboken is now connected by electric trolleys along the 34-mile Hudson-Bergen Light Rail Transit System. The award-winning system provides a clean and efficient way for passengers to commute locally or to make major connections.

The *Hoboken Reporter* (201-798-7800, www.hobokenreporter.com), available in shops along Washington Street, is an excellent source of rentals, which tend to run 10% or more below comparable Manhattan dwellings and have dropped about 10% during the ongoing economic crisis. Condos are a little less than two-thirds the cost of comparable Manhattan apartments, with the median price for a home hovering around $650,000.

Web Sites: www.newjersey.com, www.hobokeni.com, www.hoboken411.com
Area Codes: 201, 973, 551
Post Offices: Main Office, 89 River St; Castle Point Station, 1 River Terrace; Uptown Station, 57 W 14th St; Washington St Station, 734 Washington St; West Side Station, 502 Grand St
Zip Code: 07030
Police Station: #1 Police Plaza, 106 Hudson St., 201-420-2100
Emergency Hospital: Hoboken University Medical Center, 308 Willow Ave, 201-418-1000, hobokenumc.com
Library: Hoboken Public Library, 500 Park Ave, 201-420-2280, www.hoboken.bccls.org
Public School Education: Hoboken Board of Education, 1115 Clinton St, 201-356-3613, www.hoboken.k12.nj.us
Community Resources: DeBaun Center for the Performing Arts (debaun.org; 201- 216-8937) has a rotating schedule of theater, music, and spoken word performances, or call the city's cultural affair coordinator at 201-420-2207 for a schedule of performances around town. Membership in the Hoboken-

North Hudson YMCA, with its tiled pool, workout rooms, and movement classes, is an inexpensive alternative to the pricey gyms proliferating here: 1301 Washington St, 201-963-4100. Even cheaper is the brand new sand beach at 12th and Sinatra, with free kayaking during the summer.

Transportation—PATH trains: 800-234-7284, shuttle between the Hoboken Station next to the Conrail (old Erie and Lackawanna Railroad) Terminal and Manhattan every 5 to 10 minutes from about 6:30 a.m. to 8:30 p.m., every 15 minutes between 8:30 p.m. and 11:45 p.m. and thereafter every 30 minutes until 6:30 a.m. Weekend times vary. A direct line runs between Hoboken and West 33rd St in Manhattan, also makes stops at Christopher near Hudson St, then at 9th, 14th, and 23rd Sts, all on Sixth Ave. The fare is $1.75 one way. For more details, go to www.pathrail.com.

Transportation—Bus: frequent commuter bus service on the #126 line operated by New Jersey Transit (njtransit.com for schedules); also provides connections from the Hoboken Terminal to Manhattan's Port Authority Bus Terminal at Eighth Ave and 42nd St.

Transportation—Ferry: service between Hoboken station at the 14th St Pier and NJ Transit Terminal to midtown's 39th St, Pier 11 at Wall St, or the World Financial Center in Manhattan. Tickets are $6 each way, or $199 to $242.50 for a monthly pass. Call 800-533-3779 for information or go to www. nywaterway.com.

JERSEY CITY

Boundaries and Contiguous Areas: North: Hoboken; **East**: Hudson River; **South**: Bayonne; **West**: Brunswick Street

Directly across the Hudson River from Lower Manhattan, New York's "sixth borough" is a small city with big-city amenities. And they're all new, from the glossy financial centers to the trim apartment towers rimming the Hudson, to the high-tech trolleys gliding between them. A resurgent economy in the late 1990s accelerated the expansion of relatively inexpensive commercial office space and rapidly proliferating housing to add to the city's stock of 19th-century brick and brownstone townhouses. All this within five minutes of Manhattan. Following September 11th, 2001, nearly 20,000 displaced workers found themselves commuting to work at new locations here. Many of the relocated companies are now back in Lower Manhattan but others have remained in Jersey City, taking advantage of local tax breaks.

New Jersey's second largest city—"settled in 1630" says the historical marker erected in **Paulus Hook**, the oldest section of town—was for the better part of three and a half centuries largely a working-class community. Like much of the

area, it started slipping into decline around the turn of the twentieth century and bottomed out in the 1950s and '60s, when a quarter of its now 250,000 inhabitants moved out and 10% of all jobs vanished. Then expatriate New Yorkers began buying and reclaiming townhouses in the historic districts bordering **Hamilton** and **Van Vorst parks**. Co-ops and condominium conversions sprang up in these neighborhoods and in the adjoining Paulus Hook historic district. And once Banker's Trust leased space at the vast Harborside Financial Center, it became clear that back-office operations of large Manhattan corporations would prove a boon to the local economy.

Now, gleaming skyscrapers soar along wide boulevards that connect Harborside with **Newport**, the enormous, $10-billion apartment, mall, business center, and townhouse-marina complex across the Hudson River from Manhattan's Battery Park City. Sears, J.C. Penney, and Macy's anchor the suburban-style shopping mall there. When the Lefrak Organization completes the planned 600-acre development around 2010, they expect to have 9,000 apartments on site and four landscaped parks, truly a city within a city. The size and energy of this project has driven development elsewhere in Jersey City. See www.newportwaterfrontassociation.org for more about this community.

South of Newport, the expanding **Avalon Cove** development (www.avaloncommunities.com) offers one- to four-bedroom rentals with tennis and racquetball courts, a swimming pool, and a riverfront walkway. **WALDO (Work And Live District Overlay)** is an eight-block area of rehabbed warehouses certified to rent space only to artists (availability is extremely limited). In the historic district at the foot of **Washington Street**, the Portside offers more luxury rentals with more upscale condo palaces at Port Liberté to the south. Less expensive condo options can be found to the west at **Society Hill**.

All this new construction is structured into six wards—Greenville, West Side, Journal Square, The Heights, Downtown, and Bergen/Lafayette—each of which contains smaller neighborhoods like Paulus Hook. The city heart is Journal Square, a traditional business district served by a web of local buses, while electric-powered trolleys connect the river area with the ferry and PATH tubes, as well as inland areas like Martin Luther King Drive and as far north as Port Imperial.

These 90-foot trains, winding among the city's mix of glass towers and historic brownstones, are expected to spur further growth in this rapidly changing city.

The *Jersey Journal* (www.thejerseyjournal.com) is the best source for Hoboken or Jersey City classified rental ads. In Manhattan, buy the *Journal* at newsstands at the 14th Street Downtown PATH station and outside the 33rd Street PATH station.

Web Sites: www.newjersey.com, www.cityofjerseycity.com

Area Codes: 201, 973

Post Offices: Main Branch (Downtown), 69 Montgomery St; Journal Square Station, 899 Bergen Ave; Five Corners Station, 645 Newark Ave; Gen. Lafayette Station, 322 Pacific Ave

Zip Codes: 07302 covers the downtown area; Port Liberté, 07305; Newport, 07310

Police Station: Headquarters, 8 Erie St, 201-547-5477

Emergency Hospital: Hoboken University Medical Center, 308 Willow Ave, Hoboken, 201-418-1000, hobokenumc.com

Library: Jersey City Public Library, 472 Jersey Ave, 201-547-4555, www.jclibrary. org

Public School Education: Jersey City Board of Education, 346 Claremont Ave Jersey City, 201-915-6000, www.jcboe.org

Adult Education: St. Peter's College, 2641 Kennedy Blvd, 888-SPC-9933, www. spc.edu; New Jersey City University, 2039 Kennedy Blvd, 201-200-2000, www. njcu.edu; Jersey City branch of Hudson County Community College, 168 Sip Ave, 201-714-7100, www.hccc.edu

Community Resources: The Jersey City Museum, 350 Montgomery St, at the corner of Monmouth, 201-413-0303, www.jerseycitymuseum.org; Liberty Science Center, 25 Phillip St, Liberty State Park, 201-200-1000, www.lsc.org.

Transportation—PATH trains: 800-234-7284; it takes 20 minutes at most from Journal Sq or Grove St to 33rd St in Manhattan (with stops at Sixth Ave and Christopher, 9th, 14th, and 23rd streets in between). PATH trains also run to Hoboken and Newark from all four Jersey City stations. Go to www.pathrail. com for more information.

Transportation—Bus: Coach USA, www.coachusa.com, operates frequent service between Jersey City and Wall St or the Port Authority Bus Terminal in Manhattan. New Jersey Transit runs multiple bus lines here (njtransit.com)

Transportation—Ferry: New York Waterway, 800-533-3779, www.nywaterway. com, operates passenger ferries from Paulus Hook, Liberty Harbor, and Port Liberté to midtown Manhattan, the World Financial Center and Pier 11 (approximately $57 per ten-ticket pack).

ADDITIONAL SUBURBS

NEW JERSEY SUBURBS

Check www.newjersey.com or www.nj.org for more about New Jersey communities.

- **Bayonne**; a working-class city of 62,000 south of Jersey City on Upper New York Bay, affordable and now just 20 minutes from Jersey City and the PATH tubes to Manhattan thanks to the Hudson-Bergen Light Rail system; www.bayonnenj.org.
- **Cliffside Park**, on the Palisades just south of Fort Lee, is an affordable family neighborhood of 25,000 with an ethnically mixed population; www.cliffsideparkonline.com.
- **Englewood**; cosmopolitan with its ethnically diverse population and housing that ranges from low-income to redone turn-of-the-century estates. Traditionally home to affluent business executives, it boasts good shopping and restaurants and a 30-minute bus commute to Manhattan. Chamber of Commerce, 201-567-2381, www.cityofenglewood.org.
- **Franklin Township**; named #5 among best places to live by *Money* magazine in 2008, this 46-square-mile municipality is only an hour from NYC and boasts the only primeval old-growth forest in the state, as well as a network of old canals, miles of country roads, an excellent public school district, and some of the lowest home prices in the area. Chamber of Commerce, 732-545-7044, www.franklintwpnj.org.
- **Leonia**, west of Fort Lee but less glitzy and not as high rise; middle-class with a significant Korean population and a village-like feel. Proximity to the George Washington Bridge makes it a quick commute by bus to the city. Borough Clerk, 201-592-5780, www.leonianj.gov.
- **Montclair**, cosmopolitan and affluent, enjoys a hilly perch from which Manhattan is visible at a distance to the east. Single-family housing is shaded by towering oaks. The bus commute takes about 30 minutes. Municipal Clerk, 973-509-4900, www.montclairnjusa.org.
- **Ridgewood**, a 60-minute commute northwest of the city, houses a homogeneous white-collar population of families along manicured, tree-shaded streets. Schools are excellent, taxes high, and the downtown shopping district seems not to have changed in 50 years. The Paramus malls nearby make up for that. Chamber of Commerce, 201-445-2600, www.ridgewoodnj.net.
- **South Orange**, with its downtown railroad station, is convenient and quaint, and one of the few places with old-fashioned gas street lights. Housing ranges from modest to upscale up the hill, and 60 acres of parkland with four town pools add to the comfort level. Chamber of Commerce, 973-762-4333, www.southorange.org.

- **Summit** is an affluent community of handsome homes along winding, hilly streets now just 50 minutes from Manhattan on the Midtown Direct train to Penn Station. On the web at www.cityofsummit.com.
- **Teaneck**, just west of Englewood and without the estates, is similarly hilly and tree-shaded, more middle-class, and proud of its ethnic diversity; a 30-40–minute commute. Chamber of Commerce, 201-801-0012; www.teaneck njgov.org.
- **Tenafly**, north of Englewood and a more homogeneous suburb, boasts a nice village center clustered around the railroad station and an excellent high school; also an easy commute. Borough Clerk, 201-568-6100, www.tenaflynj.org.
- **Westfield** nestles among the rolling Watchung hills of Union County, about an hour by bus or 50 minutes by train and PATH tubes from midtown. A strong sense of community, a quaint downtown, excellent schools, and extensive sports and recreation activities in three county-run parks make this culturally rich old town attractive to commuters. Chamber of Commerce, 908-233-3021; also on the web at www.westfieldnj.com.

LONG ISLAND SUBURBS

- **Garden City** was once a summer resort for the Morgans and Vanderbilts, and it's still expensive, tidy, and manicured. About 18 miles east of midtown Manhattan, it's an easy 40 minutes to Penn Station. Chamber of Commerce, 516-746-7724, www.gardencityny.net.
- **Great Neck**, just over the Queens border on the northern part of Long Island, is one of the jewels of the island. The quiet Village of Great Neck sports exclusive real estate and it's only a 40-minute commute to Manhattan. Chamber of Commerce, 516-487-2000, www.greatneckchamber.org.
- **Manhasset** residents enjoy the option of choosing between single-family homes and condos. The former are most attractively and expensively set around Manhasset Bay in Plandome to the north. Because of the department stores along Miracle Mile, real estate taxes are low here. About 35 minutes from Manhattan on the LIRR. Call North Hempstead Town Hall, public affairs office, 516-627-0590 for more details about the area; www.manhasset.org.
- **Old Westbury** once housed the North Shore estates of high society and still has 25 miles of horse trails and a polo club. Besides its rolling hills, the high cost of living here gets you good schools, three colleges, and Old Westbury Gardens. Village Clerk, 516-626-0800.
- **Port Washington**, formerly a glamorous summer resort on a peninsula in the Long Island Sound, is still attractive to boaters and boasts harbor events like the annual HarborFest. The 40-minute train commute is a relatively easy one. Chamber of Commerce, 516-883-6566; www.portwashington.org.
- **Rockville Centre** boasts an arts guild, eight parks, a thriving shopping center, and a variety of housing. But it is best known for its century-old municipal power

plant, which gives its residents the cheapest electricity on the island. About 35 minutes from Manhattan by the Long Island Railroad. Rockville Village Administrator's office, 516-678-9212; Rockville Centre web site, www.rvcny.us.

WESTCHESTER COUNTY (NY) SUBURBS

- **Bronxville**, on the city's northern border and hilly, feels rather English and looks rather Tudor. There are also co-ops and condos, quite elegant ones near the railroad station. Known for its good schools and 70 acres of parkland. Chamber of Commerce, 914-337-6040, www.villageofbronxville.com.
- **Dobbs Ferry,** on the Hudson just to the north, and about 40 minutes by Metro North's Hudson line from the city, also offers a variety of housing possibilities and a heterogeneous population. Appealing to academics and people in the arts. Village Clerk, 914-231-8500, www.dobbsferry.com.
- **Edgemont**, often called "Scarsdale lite," is a hamlet within the town of **Greenburgh** next to Scarsdale but more affordable. Its good schools have attracted a growing foreign-born population, especially Japanese. Houses are traditional in style; co-ops and condos are relatively plentiful and reasonable. Greenburgh Town Clerk, 914-993-1500.
- **Mamaroneck**, which includes **Larchmont**, houses a heterogeneous population just west of tony Rye on a neck of land in Long Island Sound. You'll find co-ops, condos, and single-family homes, with few rentals. Waterfront is what it's about, with good recreational facilities including boating and beaches on Harbor Island Park; a 35-minute commute. Town administrative offices, 914-381-7810, www.village.mamaroneck.ny.us.
- **Mt. Kisco** sports hilly terrain, good schools, a variety of restaurants, a town park, and a shopping area featuring Target, The Gap, Starbucks, and other chain favorites. Single-family homes, several condo developments, and apartment rentals can all be found in this northern Westchester hub. Chamber of Commerce, 914-666-7525, www.mtkisco.com.
- **New Rochelle** was mainly settled by French Huguenots in the late 17th century. Just 32 minutes from midtown on Metro North, it is a suburban city of 72,000, with an exceptional variety of housing choices, 9 miles of shoreline, and 35 parks, including one set on its own island; www.newrochelleny.com.
- **Pelham**, just over the Bronx County line and a 20-minute train ride north from the city, is cosmopolitan and relatively unknown. Fine old trees line its winding roads, and you can walk to everything, which includes beaches, a golf course, woodland hiking, and fishing. Taxes are high. Town Clerk, 914-738-0777, www.townofpelham.com.
- **Scarsdale**, rocky, wooded, and upscale, has few rentals or co-ops, but it does have beautiful homes along winding, wooded roads and lots of open land. Its highly competitive public schools attract a diverse population into this fam-

ily-friendly neighborhood. The commute to Manhattan is about 45 minutes. Chamber of Commerce, 914-725-1602; www.scarsdale.com.

- **Tarrytown** is part of Sleepy Hollow (yes, *that* Sleepy Hollow) near the Tappan Zee Bridge (which leads to Rockland County) and meanders above the Hudson River. This diverse white- and blue-collar town is rich with Revolutionary War history, including a number of battle sites. The commute is 45 minutes and housing runs the gamut from single-family homes to large condominium developments. Village Administrator, 914-631-1885; tarrytowngov.com.
- **White Plains**, 45 minutes from the city, offers a quick commute by train or express bus, good shopping, ethnic restaurants, a variety of housing choices, and relatively low taxes. Recreational facilities include a golf course, outdoor pools, tennis, and an ice skating rink. Chamber of Commerce, 914-422-1200; www.ci.white-plains.ny.us.

CONNECTICUT SUBURBS

- **Greenwich** (pronounced Gren'-itch), a 55-minute train commute from the city, offers genteel seclusion for the very wealthy along with upscale shopping and eateries, and excellent schools, beaches, and recreational facilities. Less expensive than the Greenwich "backcountry" is the downtown area, which includes some more moderate rentals. Nearby **Cos Cob**, **Byram**, and **Old Greenwich** are also somewhat more affordable; www.greenwichct.org.
- **Norwalk** is a diverse community and generally less expensive than surrounding towns. Partially redeveloped, south Norwalk, with its condos, galleries, and restaurants, appeals to a young crowd, many of whom work in nearby corporate offices. Boating, fishing, beaches, tennis, and paddle tennis are also a draw, as are its famous oysters. **Silvermine** to the west and **Rowaton** on the southwestern tip are more upscale; www.norwalkct.org.
- **Stamford**, 60 minutes from Grand Central on Metro North, is a city of 120,000 with a bustling downtown on the banks of the Mill River and the Long Island Sound. upscale housing abounds here, including sprawling estates to the north. Housing styles are varied, parks and beaches plentiful. City main line is 203-977-4140; www.ci.stamford.ct.us.
- **Westport** on Long Island Sound became a colony of artists and writers in the 1930s and it is still popular with the sophisticated set, more like New York City than the rest of Connecticut. There is a summer theater, and the arts are still a presence, as are pricey boutiques and good shopping in nearby Stamford. Water and woods, a variety of single-family homes, a few rentals and condos characterize the town. The train to New York takes over an hour. City main line is 203-341-1000; www.westportct.gov.

N EWCOMERS' SHOCK AT HOUSING PRICES IS NEARLY UNIVERSAL; living in New York City is expensive. And renting an apartment in New York City can be a daunting task. But you're not alone: according to the latest US Census, 67% of New York City residents rent rather than own.

> "In New York, real estate is a blood sport."
>
> –Craig Newmark (Craig's List), in the *New York Observer*, March, 2007

Over the last economic cycle rent increased dramatically in New York, even up through the middle of 2008 in many neighborhoods. Since the financial crisis began in October 2008, however, there have been signs that the historically tight housing and rental markets are slackening a bit, at least in Manhattan. Studios in Manhattan doorman buildings dropped their prices by almost 9% between January '08 and January '09, and non-doorman one- and two-bedrooms each dropped about 7% over that year. Savvy Manhattan landlords have responded to financial insecurities by—in many cases—paying tenants' broker fees (which are in some cases up to 12% of the annual rent), and even offering one, two, or three months' free rent. Overall vacancy rates remain low, however; it's hard to get the New Yorkers out of New York.

And whatever happens in the housing market, you will likely pay more for rent in New York City than you have ever paid before in your life, and you will likely get less in return. Rent prices are measured here in the thousands, not in the hundreds, even for studio apartments. It is likely that prospective tenants will enjoy a little more leverage over property owners than was previously true in New York, especially until the housing bubble stabilizes, but New York is still New York. Take advantage of special deals if they exist, but be prepared for a lot of competition, regardless. But take heart: in light of this perennially tough housing situation, New York has developed some of the most tenant-friendly renting laws in the country; for details, take a look at the NYC Rent Guidelines site at nychousing.com.

In Manhattan's most established neighborhoods, location doesn't influence price much. One rental expert estimates that in Greenwich Village and the neighborhoods between 15th Street and 96th Street (Chelsea, the Upper East and West Sides, Murray Hill, Gramercy Park), the price difference between comparable apartments is negligible. If cost is a serious concern you should expect a long, difficult hunt—consider subletting while you look—and should seriously consider the remoter reaches of upper Manhattan, over the bridges in Brooklyn, Queens, The Bronx, or Staten Island, or in the suburbs. Another option, especially attractive at the studio and one-bedroom level, is to purchase a condo or a co-op. At this writing, it's hard to say where mortgage rates will be, but with the income-tax deduction for mortgage interest factored in, these apartments may be less expensive than renting an equivalent space, plus you build equity. Some areas also have tax abatements that might ease the cost. To see what's involved in buying an apartment or a house, turn to **Buying** at the end of this chapter.

All that said, however, in return for the difficulty of finding housing you get all the riches the Big Apple has to offer, both tangible and intangible, including higher earnings (even now), incomparable cultural resources, dynamic street life, incredible social diversity, and unparalleled personal opportunity.

To compare cost of living analysis of US cities, visit www.bestplaces.net. Data cover quality of life, cost of living, and comparative salary information for 3,000 US cities.

APARTMENT HUNTING

First, renting—with fortitude and imagination, you can find an acceptable place to live in an appropriate neighborhood. Various strategies for doing so are listed below in order of conventionality and practicality. But to start, some golden generalities:

- **Don't panic**. Don't be immobilized by what you may have heard. Negativity will get you nowhere. If possible, start your search a couple of months before you expect to move. Through newspapers, rental agents, word of mouth, and posted "apartments for rent" signs, get an idea of which areas have the greatest turnover in rental apartments.
- **Be prepared for high rents**. In the long run, it may indeed be possible to find that charming, sun-drenched apartment in the neighborhood of your dreams for a reasonable sum, but such gems take time, contacts, more contacts, and a little luck, so brace yourself.
- **Be adventuresome but prudent**. The ever-ongoing housing squeeze and flight from luxury housing has intensified gentrification of neighborhoods throughout the city. Yesterday's marginal areas are meccas for today's trendsetters. One realtor notes that the hardest apartments to find are now the ones south of 14th Street, which was certainly not the case just a decade ago.

Behind dusty facades from the Bowery to upper Broadway lurk attractive apartments, but before getting too carried away, realize that not all areas are suitable, especially not for single women. If you are looking around Midtown or Wall Street, be sure to visit at night to see if these areas become too desolate after offices close. Visit the web site My Neighborhood at http://www.nyc.gov/ html/ops/html/mns/my_stats.shtml for a detailed block-by-block breakdown of everything from noise complaints to murder rates in any given area.

- **Inquire about a neighborhood.** Local police precincts (see listings under **Neighborhoods**) can supply valuable safety information about a particular neighborhood, street, or block within their boundaries. Stop by the precinct for candid and well-founded opinions about the characteristics and police problems of a particular area. Also, talk to store owners and doormen.

- **Consider subletting or sharing to start.** If you are in desperate need of a roof and have not discovered a feasible rental, seriously consider these alternatives. Subletting is a great way to get comfortable in the city while buying yourself time to find the optimum situation in the most suitable neighborhood. And, should you find a good roommate, sharing affords companionship and a more affordable start to life in the Big Apple.

Generalities out of the way, on to methods for finding your space…

ONLINE LISTINGS—APARTMENT HUNTING

In a fast world ever picking up speed, New York continues to move a half-step or more ahead of everyplace else, and this is most certainly the case when it comes to finding a home. Real estate listings are often posted and removed on the same day from many of the online sites that provide them. Of these sites, the current undisputed popularity champ is **Craig's List** (newyork.craigslist.org). With listings searchable by neighborhood, price range, size, and more, it isn't hard to find something that resembles what you're looking for. The trick that follows is getting your foot in the door. Have your phone at the ready, and refresh the page of your browser frequently, as listings are posted in real time. The *Village Voice*–sponsored **Backpage** (www.backpage.com) has a similar layout and is also very popular. Considering that anyone can list virtually anything at these sites, be wary of scams. Send no financial information online, and as tight as the market might be, see an apartment before you book it. **Rent.com** (www.rent. com), an eBay-owned site, has plentiful listings for those hunting apartments, roommates, sublets, and more. The newcomer to the crowd, and maybe the winner, is **StreetEasy.com,** an NYC-based service that aggregates all listings in an area, and places them into the context of pricing around the neighborhood— you can even find information about apartments that recently sold or rented in the same building, and how much they went for.

The *New York Times* online real estate service, www.newyorktimes.com/realestate, provides comprehensive coverage for those looking to rent, sublet, or buy an apartment in New York City and beyond. **New York City Realty** (www.cityrealty.com) offers detailed listings, photos, and floor plans of houses, co-ops, condos, and apartments for rent or sale in the city. They're updated hourly. You can search by location, price range, and size, with e-mail notification as properties in your categories come online. The site includes excellent, detailed neighborhood descriptions, and application forms. The computer-challenged can call 212-755-5544 for this site's information. It may also be worth your while to visit the web sites of some of the major rental agencies, such as **CitiHabitats** (www.citi-habitats.com) and **Halstead Property** (www.halstead.com) and large owner/management firms such as **Rockrose** (www.rockrosenyc.com), all to be found in the *Times* real estate ads. These sites are virtual data banks of each firm's entire listings. For apartment listings you might go to www.nyc-apartments.net. See also **No Fee Apartments Online**, below.

NEWSPAPER CLASSIFIED ADVERTISEMENTS

Newspapers do indeed still exist, and there is still housing to be found here, as well as a lot of contextual information in the Real Estate section that can give you up-to-date tips on what's happening in the market. Not all landlords or brokers list in craigslist.com, because of the high signal-to-noise ratio, so these can be good places to look for deals other people might not be seeing. Because individual landlords, and not just brokers, place ads, classifieds sometimes are a way to avoid brokerage commissions. Chances are, however, you will end up using a broker. The classifieds provide a good way of finding one and of discovering which brokers are active in a particular neighborhood.

- The **Sunday *New York Times'* Real Estate section** is printed Friday night and delivered to dealers sometime on Saturday. The *Times* actively discourages sale of the Sunday edition before the multi-sectioned paper is completed Saturday evening. However, many outlets sell the sections they have on hand (often for full newspaper price) Saturday morning. While far fewer in number, daily ads in the *Times* are also worth checking. But since the race is to the swift, you would do well to check the *Times'* web site, www.nytimes.com, where the Sunday ads appear before 5 a.m. Saturday morning, with daily updates.
- The ***Village Voice*** is a good source of rental listings for Manhattan as well as other boroughs. Newsstand deliveries are made around 5 a.m. Wednesdays; the newsstand on the island beside the Seventh Avenue IRT Uptown Christopher St subway entrance at Sheridan Square is one of the first places to receive delivery. Also, you can get early copies Tuesday night at the Village newsstand on Astor/Lafayette. Easier yet, the *Voice* listings are online, www.villagevoice.com, updated at 1 p.m. Tuesday, and 12:01 a.m. Wednesday–Saturday.

- The **Wall Street Journal**'s Friday edition lists apartments for rent in "The Mart" classified section.
- The **New York Post**'s rental classifieds are best consulted on Friday. The Friday edition is printed Thursday night and delivered to all-night newsstands in the mid-Manhattan area (try stands at Grand Central or Pennsylvania stations Thursday night around midnight). The *Post* is a particularly good source for apartments in Queens, Brooklyn, and The Bronx. The *Post*'s web site, www.nypost.com, is updated daily.
- **The Daily News'** Brooklyn and Queens editions carry numerous rental classifieds for those boroughs. Listings in the Manhattan edition are negligible. On the web at www.nydailynews.com.
- **Newsday**, published daily in Garden City, Long Island, and available in Manhattan, is the best source of listings in Queens and Long Island. On the web at www.newsday.com.
- **New York Press**, a somewhat offbeat free weekly, is distributed each Wednesday, and is a good source for sublets and shares. Look for it in restaurants, stores, and street boxes all over town. *Press* listings are online, www.nypress.com, at 10 a.m. Tuesday.
- **Jersey Journal**, published in Jersey City, Monday–Saturday, is the paper to consult for rentals in Hoboken and Jersey City. The *Journal* can be purchased at newsstands adjoining the 14th St and 33rd St PATH stations in Manhattan.
- New York City neighborhood newspapers—**The Villager**, **Chelsea Clinton News**, **The Spirit** (West Side), **Our Town** (East Side), **The Flatiron News**, **Tribeca Trib**, and others—occasionally carry a rental ad or two but are not prime sources.

REAL ESTATE BROKERS

Generally, New York City's real estate brokers focus on sales rather than rentals. However, some agencies specialize in rentals, and many have brokers who handle nothing else. Below, we've listed the names of real estate brokers as a service. Their presence in this book does not indicate an endorsement. Rather, firms and the neighborhoods they cover are given as possible starting points for your search.

Real estate agencies tend to concentrate their efforts on one or a series of contiguous neighborhoods, for example: the Upper East Side and Yorkville; Chelsea, the Village, and SoHo; Gramercy Park and Murray Hill. If your heart is set on one location, it is important to discover the savviest brokers in that area. If any neighborhood will do, make sure you list with several knowledgeable firms to get the coverage you need.

Count on spending some time and effort discovering a broker sympathetic to your needs and capable of showing you suitable places. In the long run, a broker may well be the best route to a decent apartment, and he or she can save you hours of calling and traipsing on your own. Broker commissions for unfurnished apartments currently run one month's rent or 15% of one year's rent, which you pay up front, but this may vary depending on the broker, landlord, neighborhood, availability, etc. Get some ground rules and ask how the commissions work before agreeing to work with someone. Sometimes there is no commission at all.

RECOMMENDATIONS FOR FINDING A REAL ESTATE BROKER:
- Ask friends, colleagues, your firm, and family for recommendations of brokers who are particularly helpful. As previously mentioned, not all capable agents with good lists advertise widely.
- Gather names from appealing classified listings.
- Do a web search for real estate brokers in your neighborhood(s) of choice.
- If your heart is set on one locale, try some of the smaller firms whose storefronts you'll notice while pounding the pavement. These firms seldom advertise but are often good sources for listings in the immediate vicinity.

As a start, we've compiled a list of brokers who handle rentals in Manhattan, parts of The Bronx, Brooklyn, Queens, Staten Island, and New Jersey. All addresses are in the broker-specializing borough or state; specific neighborhoods are included as appropriate. For a more complete listing of agents try sites like www.realestateyahoo.com, www.nysar.com, and www.nyrei.com.

MANHATTAN REAL ESTATE BROKERS

- **CitiHabitats**, 30 E 33rd St, 212-685-7777, and on the web at www.citi-habitats.com: all Manhattan
- **Coldwell Banker** has three Manhattan offices: 1200 Lexington Ave, 212-327-1200; 401 Sixth Ave, 212-255-4000; 329 Columbus Ave, 212-877-1300; 555 Madison Ave, 212-326-0300; www.cbhk.com: all Manhattan, Brooklyn is covered by their Brooklyn office at 155 7th Ave, 718-622-7600
- **Corcoran Group**, 660 Madison Ave, 212-355-5550, www.corcoran.com: all of Manhattan
- **Century 21, 575 Madison Ave**, 212-681-9200, c21nyc.com: all Manhattan
- **Eychner Associates Inc.**, 10 Christopher St, 212-807-0700, www.eychner.com: Greenwich Village and downtown
- **Green Real Estate**, 4310 Broadway, 212-795-0144: Washington Heights, Inwood, and North Harlem
- **Gumley-Haft-Klier**, Inc., 415 Madison, 212-371-2525, www.ghkrealty.com: luxury rentals, Upper East Side
- **Halstead Property**, 770 Lexington Ave (HQ), 212-253-9300, six Manhattan offices, www.halstead.com: handles all Manhattan
- **Hudson View Associates, Inc.**, 159-00 Riverside Dr West, 212-928-0508, www.hudsonview.com: Washington Heights

- **Kain Realty**, 37 W 84th St, 212-877-5100: Upper East and West Side and Midtown
- **Macklowe**, 515 E 72nd St, 212-265-5900, www.macklowe.com: all Manhattan
- **Alice F. Mason, Ltd.**, 635 Madison Ave, 212-832-8870, www.alicefmason.com: luxury rentals, primarily on the Upper East Side
- **Manhattan Apartments, Inc.**, rental office at 225 W 57th St, 212-378-2680; sales office at 1780 Broadway, 212-378-2360, www.manhattanapts.com: will provide corporate relocation services
- **New Heights Realty**, 634 W 207th St, 212-567-7200: primarily Inwood, some Washington Heights
- **Portrait Realty**, 144 W 19th St, 212-871-3070, www.portraitrealty.com, all Manhattan
- **Prudential Douglas Elliman, Rental and Relocation Division**, 3 E 54th St, 212-350-8500, 10 offices in the city, www.prudentialelliman.com: all of Manhattan
- **Salon Realty Co.**, 338 E 92nd St, 212-534-3131, www.salonrealty.com: Upper East Side
- **Sandra Greer Real Estate**, 201 E 77th St, 212-472-1878, www.sandragreerrealty.com: mostly Upper East Side
- **Simone Song Properties**, 241 Cabrini Blvd, 212-928-5100, www.simonesong.com: Washington Heights, especially Hudson Heights, Inwood, Northern Manhattan
- **Spencer Realty**, 353 Lexington Ave, 212-661-9440, www.spencerny.com: all Manhattan
- **Stein-Perry Real Estate**, 740 W 181st St, 212-928-3805, www.steinperry.com: Washington Heights
- **Stribling & Associates**, www.striblingny.com, 924 Madison Ave, 212-570-2440: Uptown, Tribeca, and Chelsea; 340 W 23rd St, 212-243-4000: all of Manhattan
- **Webb & Brooker Realty Inc.**, 2534 Adam Clayton Powell Blvd., 212-926-7100: Harlem

BRONX REAL ESTATE BROKERS

- **Belcut Corp**, 589 Prospect Ave, 718-993-7809
- **Susan Goldy Real Estate**, 5626 Mosholu Ave, 718-549-4116, www.susangoldy.com: Riverdale, Spuyten Duyvil
- **Robert E. Hill, Inc.**, 279 W 231st St, 718-884-2200, www.robertehill.com: Riverdale, Kingsbridge and Spuyten Duyvil
- **Spero Real Estate**, 33 South Broadway, 914-968-7862, westchesternyrealtors.com: Riverdale, Westchester County, and Putnam County

- **Trebach Realty Inc.**, 3801 Greystone Ave, Riverdale, 718-543-7174, www. TrebachRealty.com: Riverdale, Spuyten Duyvil, Fieldston, Kingsbridge, Van Cortlandt Village

BROOKLYN REAL ESTATE BROKERS

Try www.hellobrooklyn.com for a more extensive list of agents.
- **Apts and Lofts**, 171 Bedford Ave, 718-384-4022, aptsandlofts.com. Specializes in trendy digs in Williamsburg and surrounding area
- **Bedford Realty**, 307 Bedford Ave, 718-599-1321, www.bedfordrealtycorp.com
- **Coldwell Banker**, 155 7th Ave, 718-622-7600, www.cbhk.com
- **Corcoran Group**, with numerous Brooklyn offices, Main: 125 7th Ave, 718-499-3700, www.corcoran.com: Brooklyn Heights, Fort Greene, Cobble Hill, Williamsburg, and vicinity
- **Kenn Firpo Realty Corp.**, 04 Calyer St, 2nd Floor, 718-384-7000, www. kennfirpo.com: long-time realtor for Greenpoint and Williamsburg
- **King David Intl. Realty,** 107 Broadway, 718-599-0822, www.kingdavidintlrealty. com. One of the few realtors that has listings in the exclusively Hasidic part of Williamsburg
- **Flood Company**, 464 Bay Ridge Ave, 718-238-9800, www.floodcompany.com: Bay Ridge, Fort Hamilton, Dyker Heights, Bensonhurst, Sunset Park
- **Kline Realty**, 599 Lorimer St, 718-361-1776, www.klinerealestate.com: Greenpoint and Williamsburg
- **Frank Manzione Real Estate**, 223 Columbia St, 718-834-1440, www. manzionerealestate.com: South Brooklyn and Red Hook
- **William B. May Co.**, www.wbmay.com, 150 Montague St, 718-875-1289: Brooklyn Heights, Cobble Hill, Carroll Gardens; 100 7th Ave, 718-230-5500: Park Slope, Prospect Park
- **David Perlman**, 16 Court St, 718-855-8708: Brooklyn Heights, Park Slope, Cobble Hill, Boerum Hill, Carroll Gardens
- **Twyford Real Estate**, 389 Court St., 718-855 5650, www.twyfordrealestate. com: Boerum Hill, Cobble Hill
- **Renaissance Properties**, 71 Hoyt St, 718-875-5650, www.renaissanceproperty .com: primarily Boerum Hill

QUEENS REAL ESTATE BROKERS

- **Bay Benjamin**, 212-89 26th Ave, Bay Terrace Shopping Center, Bayside, 718-225-0800, www.baybenjamin.com and www.baybridgerealestate.com: Bayside
- **Castle Realty, Inc.**, 21-77 31st St, Astoria Blvd, Astoria, 718-545-7669, www. queensrealtymarket.com: Astoria, Long Island City
- **Century 21 Tri-Boro Realty**, 31-08 Astoria Blvd South, Astoria, 718-721-2700, www.c21triboro.com: Astoria

- **Dynasty Real Estate**, 34-16 30th Ave, 718-204-4800: Astoria, Woodside, Long Island City
- **Fresh Meadows Real Estate**, 61-43 186th St, Fresh Meadows, 718-886-2816, www.coldwellbankermoves.com: Flushing, Forest Hills, Kew Gardens, Rego Park, Bayside
- **Nu Place Realty**, 120-10 Queens Blvd, Kew Gardens, 718-793-9500: Forest Hills, Kew Gardens, Rego Park, Briarwood
- **Re/Max Today**, 32-75 Steinway St, Long Island City, 718-274-2400, www. seenyhomes.com: Astoria, Long Island City, Sunnyside
- **Terrace Realty**, 16 Station Square, Forest Hills, 718-268-1045, www. foresthillsrealestate.com: Greater Forest Hills, Rego Park, Kew Gardens
- **Welcome Home Real Estate**, 46-15 Skillman Ave, Sunnyside, 718-706-0957, www.welcomehomerealestate.biz: Sunnyside, Woodside, Astoria

STATEN ISLAND REAL ESTATE BROKERS

- **Robert DeFalco Realty**, 1678 Hylan Blvd, 718-987-7900, www.defalcorealty. com, all of Staten Island
- **Rachel Gannon Realty, Inc.**, 963 Post Ave, 718-273-9200, rachelgannon. homesandland.com: all Staten Island
- **Gateway Arms Realty**, 285 St. Marks Place, St. George, 718-273-3800, www. gatewayarmsrealty.com: St. George, Snug Harbor
- **Prudential Appleseed Realty**, 604 Forest Ave, New Springville, 718-981-0709: North Shore
- **Vitale-Sunshine Realty**, 1671 Hylan Blvd, 718-979-3333, www.vitalesunshine. com: all Staten Island

NEW JERSEY REAL ESTATE BROKERS

- **Action Agency**, 4301 Bergenline Ave, Union City, 201-348-8741: Fort Lee, Edgewater, Weehawken
- **Apartments & Homes of NJ, Fort Lee Inc.**, 214 Main St, Fort Lee, 201-947-6464: Fort Lee, Edgewater, Weehawken
- **Boyne Real Estate**, 303 Grove St, Jersey City, 201-451-0950, www. njbrownstone.com: Jersey City
- **Hoboken Brownstone Co.**, 1520 Willow Ave, Hoboken, 201-792-0100, www. hbrownstone.com: Hoboken, Weehawken, Jersey City
- **McAlear Cavalier Realtors**, GMAC, 327 Broad Ave, Leonia, 201-944-4660, www.mcrealtors.com: Leonia
- **Oppler-Ketive Realtors**, 2050 Center Ave, Fort Lee, 201-585-8080, www. classicrealtynj.com: eight offices throughout North Jersey
- **Severino Realty**, 830 Washington St, Hoboken, 201-653-1800: Hoboken
- **Singleton and Galmann**, 1106 Washington St, Hoboken, 201-656-5400, wwww.singletongalmannrealestate.com: Hoboken

- **Sky-Line Realty, Inc.**, 3506 Park Ave, Weehawken, 201-863-6090, www.sky-line realty.com: Weehawken

NO-FEE APARTMENTS ONLINE

You may have noticed, among the newspaper listings, ads for no-fee services, and if you're determined to avoid a broker's fee, one of these may help. Here's how they work: pay a flat fee, detail your specifications online, and receive a list of no-fee apartments being offered by management companies and private owners. Updates are daily or weekly, and you do the rest of the work. However, listings can be wrong or out-of-date. You'll find new lists advertised constantly on places like craigslist.com, but buyer beware. We mention seven services that may be useful:

- **Apartment Source**, www.apartmentsource.com, online only, lets you search their database for apartments according to price, size, location, and amenities, in addition to which you receive daily e-mail updates with new vacancies to meet your specifications. You may also occasionally find sublets and short-term rentals, and there is access to roommateclick.com, a roommate matching service. The site also offers a credit check.
- **Apartment Store**, www.nyaptstore.com, lets you search thousands of apartments. You can specify number of rooms, neighborhoods, etc. Moving services, insurance, and other services are also available. Membership is $49.99 and listings are updated frequently. You can elect to receive daily updates via fax or e-mail.
- **Backpage**, www.backpage.com is an extension of the *Village Voice* classifieds, in a style similar to Craig's List. The site offers listings in multiple cities, with extensive New York postings. No fee.
- **Citi Rent**, www.citirent.com; a clearinghouse of listings from management companies. Subscribers can search apartments by price and neighborhood. Price of subscription is determined by the number of buildings you apply to, averaging 99 cents per building.
- **Craig's List**, newyork.craigslist.org, is a national site with NYC listings; you can search vacancies provided by area landlords, or sublets, shared housing, or temporary accommodations as posted by individuals. No fee.
- **Metro List Xpress**, 212-220-4663, www.mlx.com, is a Manhattan-wide database with no-fee and fee listings. For $149, the subscriber receives an account number and a personal identification number for three months. Search specifications include desired location, apartment size, whether pets are allowed, maximum rent, etc. Members receive a list, by fax or e-mail, of all the apartments in the database fitting the requested specs, with updates on request for as long as necessary. You can change specifications to receive listings in other categories: different neighborhoods or rent limits, for example. A free membership gives access to more limited services. Included among the listings, which are

updated daily, are properties handled by some 200 brokerage companies—these would involve fees. Also included: co-ops, condos, and houses for sale by owners as well as brokers, photos.

- **Rent-Direct**, 1001 Fifth Ave, 4th Flr, 888-278-7111, www.rent-direct.com, has perhaps the deepest list of apartments in the city and New Jersey, as well as seven-day customer support and a walk-in office with computers for customer use. You pay $195 to access the service for 60 days or, if you are on a budget and seeking an apartment for $1200 per month or less, $165 for 60 days. Service includes access to their database of some 5,000 buildings, with photos of street panoramas and interior views. New apartment listings are provided via e-mail or, once you are an established user, you can go online to check out all listings.

A word about no-fee apartment guides sold in book form at bookstores and some newsstands. They tend to be unreliable and out-of-date.

NEW BUILDINGS

Renovated factories, warehouses, and other commercial buildings occasionally add new rental units to the city's supply. Apartments in reconstructed or totally new buildings command top dollar. However, it is often possible to avoid brokers' commissions in these buildings when landlords and managers pay on-site rental agents to fill the buildings as quickly as possible. You'll need to have the inside track to get on these buildings' short lists. Be sure to check that the unit is zoned for residential space as you may be denied renter's insurance if you live in a non-residentially zoned building and in rare cases, especially in Brooklyn, people have been evicted if the building is not kept up to code (or reasonably up to code).

DIRECT ACTION

In a town where single-minded apartment hunters have been known to read the obituary columns with as much intensity as the real estate classifieds, no one need feel self-conscious about approaching landlords, managing agents, superintendents, or local merchants in order to locate a place in a particular neighborhood or building.

Additional strategies include:

- **Call the managing agent of a likely building**. The firm's or agent's name is usually posted near a building's entrance. If no telephone number is given, check the phone book.
- **Speak with the superintendent directly**. To find him, check the building directory, buzzer listings, or, in the case of the smaller brownstones with shared part-time supers, your man could be the person sweeping the steps or put-

ting garbage cans out on the sidewalk. If an apartment is available, the super or manager will sometimes send you to a broker to gain access. If a vacant apartment is found through independent efforts, you are not liable for the broker's fee. However, since reasonable apartments are in short supply, need usually overrides the fine points of the legal situation; most people prefer to pay the commission rather than go without the apartment. Once secure in your nest, if you want redress, you can file a complaint with the Division of Licenses, New York Department of State, 123 Williams St, 19th Floor, NYC 10007, 212-417-5747, www.dos.state.ny.us/licensing. This might eventually result in a settlement.

- **Pavement pounding**, accompanied by incessant querying of merchants, stoop sitters, dog walkers, letter carriers—indeed anyone who looks like a resident of the neighborhood—can also yield results. Some hunters go building to building and strike up conversations with doormen.
- **Driving around** in the boroughs can give you the feel of a neighborhood (in Manhattan, walking is easier). You will likely see some rental signs on buildings. Take down phone numbers even if it is not a building or an area you are interested in. You never know what other buildings that rental agent or landlord can recommend.

WORD OF MOUTH

The grapevine approach—broadcasting your need through a network of local friends—is often an effective means to a desired apartment and certainly to a sublet or share that may get you into town and buy you several more months of happy hunting. However, when you're new to town the chances of having such a network are usually slim. Nonetheless, use any contacts available. Parents can call old college chums; who knows, their son or daughter may be leaving a desirable place. In any case, personal contacts are often a shot at the type of high-demand place that never makes it as far as the *Times* or a broker's office. In sublet situations, check to make sure the lease allows the tenant to sublet.

BULLETIN BOARDS

Certain neighborhoods, particularly the more homogeneous communities such as SoHo and Tribeca; some of the larger buildings; and some of the more "old-world neighborhoods" of Brooklyn and Queens have bulletin boards where an occasional apartment turns up among the sheets offering tutoring, a ride to California, or opportunities for self-improvement. Inquire locally to find out which café, supermarket, or grocery store serves this neighborhood function. Bulletin boards in university areas also include valuable information, notably New York University, Columbia, Cooper Union, and Hunter College. If you know someone in NYC in an apartment building, call ahead and ask him/her to check the building bulletin board for vacant apartments, sublets, or sharing options. If you are an ethnic minority, member of a religious group, or into biking or vegetarian ism or puppetry, you'll find a NY group that probably has an online presence where you can find off-the-radar rental opportunities. Sites like Craig's List have discussion listings where people looking for roommates with similar interests will advertise to prevent being swamped by responses. Many of these groups have email bulletins that sometimes include sublets or rooms. Some people don't even list apartments because they can't deal with the response—be sure to place listings describing yourself and what you are looking for and you just might get lucky.

HOUSE ORGANS

Many corporations and organizations publish newsletters or magazines or e-mail bulletins for their personnel that print employee advertisements. Sublets and the occasional rental turn up in these columns, and it is worth asking friends working for likely concerns to check their in-house publication for leads.

COLLEGE-RELATED ASSOCIATIONS

Some New York alumni associations try to address the difficulty graduates have settling or relocating in the city. Contact your alumni office or local group to see if they can help. Some university clubs also offer advice and an occasional lead. Alumni magazines and newsletters and internet academic discussion mailing groups may also offer sublet opportunities.

EMPLOYERS AND RELOCATION FIRMS

Frequently, large companies pay for the services of relocation firms to find suitable long- and short-term apartment rentals for their mid- and upper-level hires and to help solve the various problems associated with moving and settling in. The fortunate employee is saved money and headaches in the bargain. Presumably the company you are working for will inform you if it is prepared to offer help with your search for living quarters.

A variety of relocation services are also available to individuals through real estate firms, which are part of nationwide franchise networks such as Re/Max, Century 21, Prudential, and Coldwell Banker or networks of independent brokers such as Genesis, First Choice Real Estate, and Relo. While they exist primarily to service relocating homeowners or potential homeowners, these services are sometimes available to renters. Contact a broker near you affiliated with one of these networks before you move; they can help you sell your home and put you in touch with a realtor here. Particularly if you are new to NYC, having a relocation advisor is a good idea. He/she will take you in hand, provide you with local real estate information and show you communities that interest you, find you a place, get you pre-qualified for a mortgage, help you with insurance, get you a mover at a discount, help your spouse find a job, find a veterinarian for your cat, a painter for your bathroom, and a school for your children.

SUBLETS AND SHORT-TERM FURNISHED RENTALS

Even without the services of a relocation firm, you still have access to the same resources, but you're on your own. The vast majority of all sublets nowadays are being offered online. Craig's List dominates, but there are other major sites; you should definitely refer to the sites listed at the beginning of our neighborhood descriptions—almost all have classified sections. Many brokers also offer long-term sublets, furnished and unfurnished, and advertise them, together with regular rentals, in local newspapers and online; expect to pay a broker's fee. You may also find an un-brokered sublet offered among the classifieds by the owner or lessee. In recent years, ads have proliferated for short-term furnished rentals without broker's fees but at higher rental rates; these are not sublets, but are specifically marketed as short-term furnished rentals. Consider either of these useful interim measures, providing the time needed to discover the optimum rental apartment. Note: leaseholders of rent-stabilized or exceptionally reasonable apartments have been known to ask for fixture fees or key money in a sublet situation. While some people do pour money and energy into rehabilitating an inexpensive rental apartment and may deserve compensation for their efforts when they move, fixture fees that reflect no real value are tantamount to key money, which is illegal.

Prime sources for sublets and short-term furnished rentals include:

- **Craig's List,** newyork.craigslist.org, is, as always, the 20-foot monster of rentals. Check out the sublet/shared housing section for all manner of offers Move quickly, though—it's a popular site, and even 24 hours after a posting may be too late.
- The *Village Voice* with its special "Sublets" classified section, www.village voice.com; available at newsstands throughout the city.
- The *New York Times*, which lists sublets under "Apartments—Furnished" and "Apartments—Unfurnished," www.nytimes.com.
- *New York Press* is a free weekly distributed each Wednesday. Look for it in restaurants, stores, and street boxes all over town. Good source for sublets.
- **Brokers**: a number of sublet specialists advertise in the *Voice* and *New York Times*. Typically, commissions on furnished rentals run between one-half and one whole month's rent for periods of less than nine months. Most agencies charge 15% for longer sublets. Four brokers and one service currently specializing in sublets:
- **Apartment Placement Services**, 575 Lexington Ave, 4th Flr, 212-572-9609, specializes in short-term furnished sublets and unfurnished prime lease rentals for a fee; also places young professionals in shared apartments throughout the city. Call for an appointment.

- **Gamut Realty Group, Inc.**, 15 E 57th St, 800-437-8353 or 212-879-4229, on the web at www.gamutnyc.com.
- **New York Habitat**, 307 Seventh Ave, Ste 306, 212-255-8018, on the web at www.nyhabitat.com; specializes in sublets, short-term and long-term rentals, a no-fee service.
- **Prudential Douglas Elliman Rental and Relocation Division**, 3 E 54th St, 212-645-4040, www.elliman.com.
- **Senter Sublet**, 510 Madison Ave, 212-572-0762, www.sentersublets.com, call for appointment.
- **Bulletin boards** in large buildings, bars, or other neighborhood locations. Large apartment complexes have waiting lists for rental apartments the proverbial block long. However, leaseholders arrange sublets directly and occasionally post notices on community bulletin boards. Check with the management of these big units to see if they have a central sublet source.
- **In-house publications** tend to be a better source of sublets than of rentals.

SHARING

One of the best solutions to high housing costs, particularly for young, single people, is an apartment-share. But if you are just arriving in the city and don't know anyone, you may not have anyone to share with. If networking with old college buddies fails to turn up anything, your best bet is probably the newspapers or a roommate-finding service.

Again, the vast majority of all shares nowadays are being offered online. Definitely refer to the sites listed at the beginning of our neighborhood descriptions—almost all have classified sections. You should also check the *Times* ads under "Apartments to Share," and the *Voice's* "Shares." Some leaseholders prefer to have roommates pre-screened and list with agencies that arrange apartment shares for a flat fee up front. Reputations ebb and flow; we can't guarantee satisfaction. But if you want to investigate this option, two of the firms in Manhattan are:

- **Roommate Finders**, 253 W 72nd St, Ste 1711, 212-362-0162, www.roommatefinders.com; open Monday–Friday noon to 7:30 p.m., Saturday and Sunday noon to 6 p.m. For the $300 fee, the client, after filling out a registration sheet covering personal habits and preferences and discussing specifications in a half-hour interview, is given information sheets on prospective apartments and/or roommates. You can call daily for new listings for up to one year, and if you find your own roommate or apartment, you are entitled to a 50% refund. Listing is free.
- **New York Habitat**, 307 Seventh Ave, Ste 306, 212-255-8018, www.nyhabitat.com; open 9 a.m. to 6 p.m. This firm, which also handles sublets and rentals, charges the renter only when he/she agrees to rent an apartment share. The fee, a minimum of 30% of one month's rent, maximum of 15% of one year's rent, is based on length of stay.

Extremely popular is the national service, **Craig's List**, which features a wide range of roommate listings for numerous cities. The New York section includes a wealth of room shares with price and location. Click on the individual listing for more details. Then, through e-mail or in some cases by phone, you'll contact the individual. Craig's List also has extensive listings of apartments for rent. Keep in mind that anyone can post on Craig's List (meaning ads are not screened carefully, only categorized), so use some caution when following up leads. It's always a good idea to first meet with a prospective roommate or the person you will be subletting from in a public space, and bring along a friend to view the apartment.

CHECKING IT OUT

You've found what appears to be the perfect, sunny apartment in a pleasant neighborhood, and, best of all, you're the first person to see it! You want to shout, "I'll take it," but you should restrain yourself and spend a few minutes looking it over first. We suggest you bring a checklist of your musts and must-nots. In addition, you should make a quick inspection to make sure the apartment's beauty is not just skin deep. A little time and a few questions asked now can save you a lot of time, money, and headache later. Specifically, you may want to look for the following:

- Are the kitchen appliances clean and in working order? Do the stove's burners work? What about the oven? Is there enough counter and shelf space? Does it smell funny in the kitchen space—or anywhere else? Does the refrigerator work?
- Do the windows open, close, and lock? Do they open onto a noisy or potentially dangerous area?
- Are there enough closets and is there enough storage space?
- Are there enough electrical outlets for all your needs? Do the outlets work?
- What about laundry facilities, are they in the building or nearby?
- When was the apartment last painted? Is it lead-free paint? In the event you will stay longer than a year, who is responsible for painting the apartment?
- Do the bathroom fixtures work? Look for leaks under pipes.
- Is there a bug problem in the building? Look in the kitchen cabinets.
- Is the building wired for cable TV service? If not, what, if any, reception is there without cable, and can you have direct or satellite television installed?
- Is the superintendent easily accessible? Ask neighbors about the building staff. Are they helpful, trustworthy, competent, available?
- What about building security and cleanliness: check the building entry, lobby, and public areas.
- If you own a car, what is the parking situation like? Is there a long waiting list for garage space?
- Do you feel comfortable in the area? Will you feel safe here at night?

- What about public transportation and shopping? Is it nearby?
- How close is the nearest emergency hospital and police precinct?

Also, try to visit apartments during non-business hours when more people are home to get a feel for how noisy a unit will be. This will also give you a feel for the comings and goings of the building, specifically: is the front entrance locked, and is there a 24-hour doorman? Many New York apartments have astonishingly thin walls and floors so that even reasonable neighbors can be a real presence. If this might bother you, ask what the floors are made of—if it's just wood and sheet metal you should expect to hear everything your neighbors are up to. Ed Sacks' *Savvy Renter's Kit* contains a thorough renter's checklist for those interested in augmenting theirs.

If you have time you should use the NYC government sites to get a sense of the neighborhood and particular building. The site http://gis.nyc.gov/doitt/mp/Portal.do gives extremely detailed and up-to-date info on any building, ranging from the number of noise complaints filed by its residents, to rodent infestations to gang activity, as well as general info on nearby food programs and special education facilities. If you're drawn to an apartment because of its light and surrounding space, you might want to visit www.nyc.gov/html/dof/html/jump/acris.shtml to see when was the last time that vacant lot next to the window changed hands—there's nothing like moving into a new place and spending the next year listening to construction ten feet away.

If it all passes muster, be prepared to stake your claim without delay.

STAKING A CLAIM

It may seem to newcomers that securing an apartment, after having found one suitable, can be as difficult as gaining membership in an exclusive club. In a tight market, that's not far off the mark. You have to be found acceptable. For starters, arrive on time and be presentably dressed for appointments. Even in this city of "attitude," a little politeness goes a long way. Also, be sure to come armed with as many proofs of income as humanly possible, including the following:

- A certified check, bank check, or money order to cover a deposit equivalent to one to two months' rent. Without this, none of the rest will matter.
- Most recent W-2 form.
- Letter from current employer verifying that you are employed and, if possible, will continue to be; lacking that, your employer's business telephone number.
- Pay stubs showing a yearly income(s) equivalent to 40 to 50 times the monthly rent.
- A credit report or money to cover the fee for having a credit-check done. If you wish to know your own credit score, or to see what your brokers will be seeing, you may obtain your credit report for free once a year. Visit www.an-

nualcreditreport.com for statements from the Big Three: Equifax, TransUnion, and Experian.

- Reference letters (sometimes necessary), business and personal, and one from your current landlord stating you are prompt with rent payments.
- Recent statements from checking, savings, and investment accounts.
- A guarantor—parents, for example, in the case of youthful renters—with documents showing an income 80 to 100 times the monthly rent, if you do not have an income adequate to satisfy the landlord.
- Have the documents neatly arranged in a special folder—this gives the impression that you're organized and a low-maintenance tenant.

Having successfully navigated these shoals and been accepted, you are ready to sign a lease. First, a word of caution: there are fraudulent real estate and rental agents who take advantage of eager and unwary apartment seekers. To avoid them, meet real estate and rental agents only in an office, not on the street. Ask for a Department of State identification card and a photo ID. Give a deposit only to the landlord, and be wary of agents who can be reached only by cell phones.

TENANT/LANDLORD RELATIONSHIP, LEASES, SECURITY DEPOSITS

TENANT/LANDLORD OBLIGATIONS

Whether you are renting or subletting, before you sign a lease it's a good idea to investigate tenant/landlord obligations and rental restrictions. Specifics can be found at the **NYC Rent Guidelines Board** web site, www.housingnyc.com. The **New York Attorney General**'s Office, 120 Broadway, NYC 10271, 212-416-8000, has a comprehensive web site that addresses tenant rights, ordinances, and lease information: www.oag.state.ny.us. The state **Division of Housing and Community Renewal's** rent information line, 718-739-6400, can also provide information. A membership group called the **New Jersey Tenants Organization** (**NJTO**), www.njto.org, provides tenant-related information in that state. It assists with organizing local tenant associations in New Jersey, offers legal guidance to its members, and works for pro-tenant legislation. Individual membership is $22 a year. Ask about their publication, available for $21. The NJTO is located at 389 Main St, Hackensack, 201-342-3775. Also in New Jersey, the **New Jersey Department of Community Affairs**, **Office of Landlord Tenant Information**, 101 S Broad St, Trenton, NJ 08625, 609-292-6240, www.state.nj.us/dca, sets regulations for renters and landlords. Their "Truth in Renting" booklet ($1.50) is available at their office or you can send a check or money order to Treasurer, State of NJ, Office of Landlord Tenant Information, Truth in Renting, P.O. Box 805, Trenton, NJ 08625-0805. Finally, online you can go to the national site, www.

rentlaw.com, which provides renters with information regarding landlord/tenant law by state.

Additional resources include:

- **Metropolitan Council on Housing**, 212-979-6238, www.metcouncil.net, tenants union
- **New York City Rent Guidelines Board**, 212-385-2934, www.housingnyc.com
- **Rent Stabilization Association**, representing landlords and agents, 212-214-9200, www.rsanyc.org
- **TenantNet,** a web site dealing with tenants' rights, www.tenant.net

DEPOSITS

The first written check undoubtedly will be a deposit held by the broker or landlord while credit references are being researched. Some landlords require certified check or bank check rather than personal check, so inquire in advance. The first person to put down a deposit (customarily one month's rent) stands the best chance of signing the lease. The credit investigation should take no more than a couple of days if you have supplied the documentation outlined above. Once you are pronounced credit-worthy, the deposit check should be accepted as your first month's rent (some landlords require two months' rent in advance). The interest-earning security deposit, also generally one month's rent, will be refunded at the end of your lease, providing the apartment is left in the same condition in which it was found. (Now is the time to walk through with the landlord to record any existing damage.) If a real estate broker is involved, your third payment will be the broker's fee, which currently averages about 15% of the first year's rent. In some cases, the owner will pay all or part of the fee.

LEASES

Read the lease carefully *before* signing it or giving a security deposit. Married couples should have both names on the lease, especially if they go by different last names; unmarried couples should try to get both names on the lease, though the landlord is not legally obliged to do so. A standard form is customary. Be familiar with the content of the entire lease, but pay special attention to the end of the form where the qualifying clauses are printed. The document should specify any special arrangements made with the landlord about alterations, repairs, painting, and new appliances. Before signing is the time to ask questions or have uncertain terms clarified. Terms in leases can sometimes be negotiated, but be sure to get any such alterations in writing and initialed by the landlord. Ask about making alterations within the apartment, notification of moving, "quiet enjoyment" clauses, if pets are allowed, responsibility for repairs, and what, if any, responsibilities you have for public areas. Also, make sure to inquire about any extra fees, such as application fees for condo or co-op sub-leases or move-in/move-out deposits. Determine how the building is heated and who pays the bills. If the landlord is responsible, there must be a clause in the lease to this effect. Traditionally, especially in the pre-war buildings, landlords pay for steam heat and hot water so you only pay for gas (for cooking) and electricity. In newer buildings without boilers, tenants customarily pay for the more costly electrical heat.

Since 1982, smoke detectors, essentially one per sleeping area, have been mandatory in New York apartments. Tenants are responsible for the repair and maintenance of these alarms. Apartments with children are required by law to have window guards. And as of November 1, 2004, carbon monoxide alarms became legally required in all New York residences.

Your landlord is legally responsible for ridding your apartment of cockroaches. Some provide routine exterminator services; others simply take care of the matter as it crops up. Obviously, the ounce of prevention method is preferable and you should know in advance if regular service is included in your lease.

Check for a sublet clause. Subletting is allowed "with the landlord's permission." This means he or she can say no. To avoid permission being withheld capriciously, the clause should mention that the apartment can be sublet with written permission from the landlord and that "permission shall not be unreasonably withheld."

Conversely, if you are subletting an apartment from the original lessee, determine whether or not you have a legal right to be there. To address this and other questions, **Tenants & Neighbors,** 212-608-4320, 236 West 27th Street, 4th floor (tenantsandneighbors.org), offers useful information on your rights on their web site and in publications Call for information about membership ($35 per year, $10 for low-income). The **New York State Rent Guidelines** web site, www.housingnyc.com, is useful, and includes an online guide to renting. If you have questions about the propriety of a sub-tenancy and the apartment falls under city- or state-enforced guidelines, try calling one of the organizations listed below under **Additional Resources** (Rent Guidelines Board, the New York Loft Board, or the Office of the DHCR) with your concerns.

Subletting a cooperative apartment can be daunting. Not only is it necessary to prove yourself to the landlord but you must also pass the scrutiny of the building's board of directors. Unfortunately, the traditionally restrictive subletting practices of many cooperative buildings are still in effect. If you are very fortunate, you will meet with a rare co-op board that focuses on realistic concerns for their building and will consider a sublet situation. Keep in mind that if you sublet a co-op without the board's approval you could be evicted. Individually owned condominium apartments can typically be sublet at the owner's discretion.

Finally, for a comprehensive guide to the ins and outs of renting in the city, including housing laws, a list of agencies and resources for tenants, recent articles, and links to related sites, go to TenantNet, www.tenant.net.

RENT STABILIZATION AND RENT CONTROL

While municipal rent controls have been eliminated in most of the country, they have survived in New York City. Few if any of the **rent-controlled** apartments ever reach the market; they are either passed among qualifying members of one family like heirlooms or, once vacant, automatically become **rent stabilized** (apartments in large buildings) or decontrolled (apartments in buildings with five units or less). The Office of Rent Administration's web site states: "In New York City, rent control tenants are generally in buildings built before February 1, 1947, where the tenant is in continuous occupancy prior to July 1, 1971. Tenants who took occupancy after June 30, 1971, in buildings of six or more units built before January 1, 1974, are generally rent stabilized." Rents in condominiums and cooperative apartments are left to market forces. Under rent control guidelines, apartments in buildings with six or more units could only see limited increases (in 2008, rents increased 4.5% for one-year leases and 8.5% for two-year leases). After the $2,000 mark, apartments no longer qualify as rent-controlled units, and can be rented by the landlord at the market rate. To speed up this process, landlords are renovating many of the remaining low-rent apartments to push their value above $2,000, which allows these units to be taken off the rent control market. In short, rent control is becoming a thing of the past in New York City. The **Rent Stabilization Association** (the landlord group), 123 William Street, will answer questions about tenants' rights under rent stabilization. Call 212-214-9200 or go to www.rsanyc.org. If your apartment is rent controlled or rent stabilized, call the **Office of Rent Administration, State Division of Housing and Community Renewal** (**DHCR**) in your borough with any questions or problems: Upper Manhattan, above 110th Street, 163 West 125th Street, 212-961-8930; Lower Manhattan, below 110th Street, 25 Beaver Street, Fifth Floor, 212-480-6238; The Bronx, 1 Fordham Plaza, 718-563-5678; Brooklyn, 55 Hanson Place, Room 702, Brooklyn, 718-722-4778; Queens, 92-31 Union Hall Street, Jamaica, 718-739-6400; Staten Island, 60 Bay Street, Seventh Floor, Staten Island, 718-816-0278; web site, www.dhcr.state.ny.us.

LOFTS

During the 1960s, the trickle of hardy artists working and living illegally in industrial lofts located in manufacturing districts became a stream. Living in a vast, often high-ceilinged space *à la bohème* became a desirable alternative lifestyle. Add a few partitions, a restaurant gas stove, some antiques—instant chic.

Illegal loft tenancies proliferated throughout the 1970s, but an amendment to the state's Multiple Dwelling Law legalized loft living in manufacturing buildings (buildings with no residential Certificates of Occupancy) containing three or more rental units. Some areas of the city were exempted, but in Chelsea and lower Manhattan, in the Fulton Ferry area of Brooklyn, and Long Island City in Queens, loft dwellers breathed a legal sigh of relief.

The loft law did not, however, create complete order out of chaos, and the legality of some loft-living situations is still in doubt. Anyone considering renting or subletting a loft is well advised to check with the **New York City Loft Board**, 100 Gold Street, 2nd Floor, NYC 10038, 212-788-7610, before signing the lease. This is the city agency charged with overseeing the legalization of residential lofts.

Look for a Certificate of Occupancy for the building and check to see if you're signing a commercial or residential lease. Be sure to use the government sites listed in **Checking It Out** to see what kind of complaints and problems have been registered for the address. Converted industrial buildings are notorious for building and safety violations, so you might want to pop over to the New York Department of Buildings web site, www.nyc.gov/html/dob, where you can view any address's history going back at least 15 years.

ADDITIONAL RESOURCES—RENTERS

- **Gas or Electric** service shutoff hotline, 311
- **Housing Authority**, 250 Broadway, 212-306-3000, www.nyc.gov/nycha
- **Housing Discrimination for New York (and New Jersey)**: Fair Housing Hub, US Department of Housing and Urban Development, 26 Federal Plaza, Rm 3532, 800-496-4294; housing discrimination hotline, 800-669-9777 or www.hud.gov/complaints
- **Loft Board**, 100 Gold St, 2nd Flr, 212-788-7610, www.nyc.gov/html/loft
- **New York City Rent Guidelines Board**, 51 Chambers St, 212-385-2934, www.housingnyc.com
- **NYC Heat Hotline**, 311
- **NYC Urban League**, 204 W 136th St, 212-926-8000, www.nyul.org
- **Office of Rent Administration**, State Division of Housing and Community Renewal (DHCR): Upper Manhattan, above 110th St, 163 W 125th St, 212-961-8930; Lower Manhattan, below 110th St, 25 Beaver St, Fifth Flr, 212-480-6238 (see above under Rent Stabilization for additional borough listings), www.dhcr.state.ny.us
- **Rent Stabilization Association** (the landlord group), 212-214-9200 or go to www.rsanyc.org

If you're settling in the Lower East Side of Manhattan or the East Village, **GOLES** (stands for **Good Old Lower East Side**) is the tenant association, and is one of the best-run tenants groups in the city: 171 Avenue B, 212-533-2541, www.goles.org.

RENTER'S/HOMEOWNER'S INSURANCE

Your neighbor upstairs has a grease fire in his kitchen, which gets out of hand. There is no fire damage to your apartment, but smoke and water damage from extinguishing the fire have rendered your furniture unusable, your walls in need of new paint, and your television and computer are out of commission. The cost of replacing all this stuff is covered by the owner's building insurance, right? Wrong. You're out of pocket, unless you have renter's insurance.

While events such as this are relatively rare, when they occur they can be financially devastating. If your possessions are few, it may be worth the gamble to skip the insurance. However, your possessions can be insured against fire, water damage, and theft. Rates vary from company to company; be sure to shop around. It's a good idea to pay the additional cost for replacement coverage, and be sure your premiums provide personal liability coverage, protecting you and your family against lawsuits resulting from injuries to others, on or off the premises. If you own a dog, be sure the personal liability covers dog bites as well. Insurance is even more important for apartment owners, who will also need to be covered for structural improvements or alterations as well as loss of personal possessions in the event of a disaster. Some co-ops and condo buildings require such coverage. When seeking insurance from an insurance agent (Yellow Pages under "Insurance" or online under keywords "Renters Insurance" or at www.insure.com), it's a good idea to get quotes from at least three providers. One company will be more competitive than another in a specific neighborhood, or in rentals, say, than in condos. If you want to check your insurance record, contact **ChoicePoint Asset** (866-312-8076, www.choicetrust.com) to order your CLUE (Comprehensive Loss Underwriting Exchange) report. This national database of consumers' automobile and homeowner's insurance claims is used by insurers when determining rates or denying coverage. Contact ChoicePoint if you find any errors.

Some companies which sell renters/homeowners insurance in the metropolitan area:

- **Aetna Inc.**, 860-273-0123, www.aetna.com
- **Allstate**, 877-634-5317, www.allstate.com
- **Chubb**, 908-903-2000, www.chubb.com
- **Fireman's Fund**, 800-227-1700, www.firemansfund.com
- **The Hartford**, 860-547-5000, www.thehartford.com
- **Liberty Mutual Group**, 617-357-9500, www.libertymutual.com
- **Prudential** (homeowners insurance), www.prudential.com
- **Travelers**, 800-252-4633, www.travelers.com

For more information, or if you have a problem with your insurer, contact the **New York State Department of Insurance**, 212-480-6400, www.ins.state.ny.us; in New Jersey go to www.njdobi.org.

BUYING

In a city of renters, why buy? Real estate values have risen sharply since the late 1990s, but so have rents. When you factor in the income tax exemption for mortgage interest, which is highest in the early years of the mortgage, the cost of renting now can approach or even exceed the cost of buying, especially in the studio and one-bedroom apartment category. For many, the idea of having home equity, as opposed to paying rent to someone else, has a strong appeal. For others, it's the satisfaction and security of home ownership. Keep in mind, however, home ownership in New York City is quite different when compared to much of the US. The $400,000 that might buy a four-bedroom, three-bathroom house with plenty of greenery in parts of the US, in NYC may buy you a studio apartment with an alcove—if you're lucky.

That said, the newcomer to New York City would be well advised to rent or sublet for a year at least before buying: become comfortable in the city, familiar with some of its neighborhoods, and develop a sense of how you use the city. Furthermore, the case can be made that, given the expenses incidental to buying (described below) and the fact that real estate values tend to rise and fall in roughly ten-year cycles, it makes sense to buy only if you expect to spend at least ten years in the city. Even if the market goes soft for a while, New York real estate values will eventually rise again. New Yorkers whose parents bought brownstones in the 1940s or '50s for several thousand dollars can attest to that from their now inherited multimillion-dollar homes.

As with renting, the search for a condo, a co-op, or a house generally begins online or in the classified ads in the *New York Times*, the *Wall Street Journal*, or the *New York Observer*, a weekly newspaper distinctively pink in color and available at most newsstands. The ads lead the seeker to realtor web sites where one can browse through the images and specs. Web sites on the internet offering national real estate listings proliferate, many with virtual tours. Below, a few that may be useful:

- **Homes & Land Magazine**, www.homes.com
- **HomeGain**, www.homegain.com, free service that will help you locate a realtor, find the value of a home, find homes for sale or even apply for a mortgage
- **Owners.com**, www.owners.com, a "For Sale by Owners" site, excluding brokers, with area listings in New Jersey and Connecticut
- **Realtor.com** and **move.com** are affiliated sites controlled by the National Association of Realtors, a huge listing nationwide
- **RealtyGuide**, www.xmission.com/~realtor1, with links to broker web sites, lenders, for-sale-by-owner directories, and home-for-sale magazines
- **YahooRealestate**, http://realestate.yahoo.com/realestate, national real estate and rentals listings; relocation advice

- **Zillow.com**, a nationwide site that finds and compares value estimates of homes, provides maps, and shows housing trends in neighborhoods
- **ZipRealty**, www.ziprealty.com, a national site that combines internet service with the personal attention of an agent; no cost to register to view listings

Those looking online to buy a co-op, condo, or house in the city will probably be more successful at city-specific sites, most of which provide neighborhood profiles, comparative prices, and mortgage information:

- **MLX**, www.mlx.com, co-ops and condos as well as rentals, by neighborhood, primarily in Manhattan, with limited listings in the outer boroughs and New Jersey
- **New York City Real Estate Exchange**, www.cityrealty.com, with condos, co-ops, and houses in all boroughs

For those who are contemplating buying, a few considerations, now, which apply whether you are looking for a house, a co-op, or a condo. First, what can you afford to pay? The rule of thumb, and one that lenders use: it is safe to pay three or four times the buyer's yearly income, depending on a variety of factors. The required down payment will generally be 20% of the purchase price; it may go as low as 10%, in which case origination fees (points) to the bank will probably be higher. Be prepared for a thorough examination of your finances, your credit record, and your employment status. This, of course, assumes the buyer is not paying cash but will be obtaining a mortgage from a bank.

Know that the transaction you are about to make is going to cost more than the agreed-upon price. How much more? Generally, in New York, closing costs run 5 to 8% of the purchase price. This includes points, attorney's fees, title insurance, a title search, inspection and survey, recording tax, various fees, and the deposit of some real estate tax payments and homeowner's insurance premiums in escrow. The lender (bank or mortgage company) is required to give a good faith estimate of closing costs. In New York, the seller pays the broker's fee.

Whatever and wherever you are looking to buy, you'll need a good broker who listens to you, knows the neighborhoods, and can put you in touch with potential lenders and mortgage brokers. (See **Recommendations for finding a real estate broker**, above.) A buyer's broker, who represents only the buyer, is becoming common, particularly in the suburbs. It's a good idea to get pre-approved for a mortgage before looking; in today's market it can make the difference in your bid winning out against competing bids for a property. And in popular neighborhoods, you may need to act fast. Without being pre-approved, you can lose out on the apartment you want. You must also have a good real estate lawyer, whom you can find through the recommendations of friends, your own lawyer, or your broker. If you have no idea where to find an attorney who handles real estate transactions, call legal referral, 212-382-6600, at the **Association of the Bar of the City of New York**, 42 West 44th Street, www.nycbar.org.

If you are buying a **house**, you will do well to hire a building engineer to check the structure of the house, the heating and plumbing systems, fireplaces, etc.; a thorough inspection may save you thousands of dollars or prevent you from making a disastrous purchase. In New York City, there are lead paint disclosure forms that are to be filled out by the seller. In the case of a co-op, or condominium, it is important to check out the financial stability of the board of directors. In all buying scenarios, it is in the best interest of the buyer to have everything reviewed by a competent real estate attorney.

When you buy a **co-op** (cooperative apartment) you are buying shares in the ownership of a building, the other shareholders of which must approve your purchase through their board. And, should you choose to sell or rent your apartment later, the same approval process must be repeated, which can be a problem. In the most desirable buildings, approval may be more difficult than getting a mortgage, as shareholders attempt to guarantee the financial reliability and the "social acceptability" of their new partner. Your finances will be scrutinized, and your lifestyle may be considered. Try to get an idea about governing attitudes of the co-op board and check recent board decisions regarding upkeep and repair of the co-op before committing to an apartment. The wrong co-op board, with a list of onerous rules and regulations, can make life less than pleasant. Also, get a prospectus, minutes of the last meeting of the board, board/building rules, and a financial statement from the cooperative, and go over them with your broker and your lawyer. If your purchase is rejected, expect no explanation. Be aware that co-op size may affect your ability to get a mortgage; in co-ops with fewer than 12 units, lenders may be more likely to reject a mortgage application because the relatively small number of shareholders in such buildings raises the collective risk of default. Also, keep in mind that co-op maintenance fees (the cost of upkeep for everything outside the walls of your apartment) can be more than your mortgage, depending on the building, and only some of the maintenance fee (the portion of the fee that is allocated for property tax payments) is tax deductible. Forty to fifty percent is a ballpark figure.

In New York you will also run into low-income co-op arrangements, bearing in mind that low-income here might not be what you think. Run very much like a traditional co-op, these are designed to help people buy their own apartment by requiring at times little or nothing up front. You will need to prove your income (although some boards are very flexible in terms of what documentation they will accept) and you are usually restricted in terms of your re-selling price, i.e., you won't be able to re-sell for market value. The same caveats apply here as do to the more traditional co-ops.

The purchase of a **condo** involves fewer hurdles, though some condo management organizations request letters of recommendation from prospective buyers. Here you are buying an apartment outright, with the right to rent or re-sell when and as you choose. Of course, this means neither you nor the other residents have any control over who your neighbors are. In making this purchase you will also want your lawyer to examine a prospectus and financial statement on the building to avoid buying into a financially unstable property.

In either situation, condo or co-op, if you're the kind of person who likes to be left alone or has trouble getting along in a group with strict rules, purchasing a condominium or co-op could be a mistake. If such possible limitations are not an issue, then take the plunge.

Questions to ask about a co-op or condo:
- What percentage of the units are owner-occupied?
- How much are the association dues and projected assessments?
- What are the rules and regulations?
- Who manages the property?
- Have there been any lawsuits involving the association in the past five years?

These and many other issues are covered in the "Condominium/Townhome Guide," published by Re/Max Real Estate (800-878-8404). The guide provides information about different styles of housing, associations, and comprehensive checklists to use to evaluate developments.

Finally, a word about **mortgage brokers**. In the competition to win new clients, banks offer a confusing array of loans. Mortgage broker to the rescue! They function as a financial advisor who helps his/her client get a suitable mortgage. At no charge to you, he/she will examine your financial situation (age, income, assets, debt load, etc.) and the type of property you want to buy, and then recommend the most likely lender and the best type of mortgage for your needs. Given the mortgage broker's relationship with various banks, he/she can ease your way through the process, especially on co-op loans. If you're the ruggedly independent sort, keep in mind that in New York City your chances of getting a good mortgage are much higher with a qualified mortgage broker than without.

ADDITIONAL RESOURCES—HOMEBUYERS

You might check out the quasi-governmental agency **Fannie Mae** (800-732-6643, www.fanniemae.com) for credit counseling, assistance with finding low-cost mortgages, and advice for low-income and first-time buyers.

Once a New York City tenant, if necessary, you can contact the **Central Complaint Bureau** of the **New York City Department of Housing and Preservation**, 100 Gold Street, NYC 10038, by dialing 311 or by visiting www.nyc.gov/hpd.

Six books that we have found useful:
- *100 Questions Every First Time Homebuyer Should Ask: With Answers from Top Brokers From Around the Country*, 2nd edition (Three Rivers Press) by Ilyce R. Glink
- *The 106 Common Mistakes Homebuyers Make (And How to Avoid Them)*, 4th edition (Wiley) by Gary W. Eldred

- *The New York Co-Op Bible: Everything You Need to Know About Co-Ops and Condos: Getting In, Staying In, Surviving, Thriving* (Griffin) by Sylvia Shapiro
- *Opening the Door to a Home of Your Own*, a free pamphlet by the Fannie Mae Foundation, 800-834-3377
- *Your New House: the Alert Consumer's Guide to Buying and Building a Quality New Home*, 4th edition (Windsor Peak) by Alan and Denise Fields
- *The Ultimate Guide to Buying and Selling Coops and Condos in New York City*, 3rd edition (Nice Idea Publishing) by Neil J. Binder

The New York Public Library has a wealth of resources available in its branches and online. Go to www.nypl.org/research/sibl/realestate/print.html to find out more.

HAVING FOUND AND SECURED A PLACE TO LIVE, YOU NOW HAVE THE task of getting your stuff there and perhaps storing some of it because a New York apartment is not as big as it looks on TV.

TRUCK RENTALS

The first question you need to answer: am I going to move myself or will I have someone else do it for me? If you're used to doing everything yourself, you can rent a vehicle, load it up, and hit the road. Look in the Yellow Pages under "Movers/Moving" and call around and compare; also ask about any specials. (You can also check under "Automobile Rental" or "Truck Rental," or try looking for "truck rental" on the internet.) Below we list four national truck rental companies and their toll-free numbers and web sites. For the best information, you should call a local office. Note: most truck rental companies now offer one-way rentals as well as packing accessories and storage facilities. Of course, these extras are not free and if you're cost-conscious you may want to scavenge boxes in advance of your move and make sure you have a place to store your belongings upon arrival (see **Storage** below). Also, if you're planning to move during the peak moving months (May through September), call well in advance, at least a month ahead, of when you think you'll need the vehicle.

Once you're on the road, keep in mind that your rental truck may be a tempting target for thieves. If you must park it overnight or for an extended period (more than a couple of hours), try to find a safe place, preferably somewhere well-lit and easily observable by you, and do your best not to leave anything of particular value in the cab. Make sure you lock up and if possible use a steering wheel lock or other easy-to-purchase safety device. The back door of the truck should be padlocked.

Four national self-moving companies to consider:

- **Budget**, 800-428-7825, www.budget.com

- **Penske**, 800-222-0277, www.penske.com
- **Ryder**, 800-297-9337, www.ryder.com (now a Budget company, still operating under the Ryder name)
- **U-Haul**, 800-468-4285, www.uhaul.com

Not sure if you want to drive the truck yourself? Commercial freight carriers, such as ABF, 800-355-1696, www.upack.com, offer an in-between service; they deliver a 28-foot trailer or smaller pod to your home and you have a set number of days to pack and load as much of it as you need, and they drive the vehicle to your destination (often with some other freight filling the remaining space), and then you have another set number of days to unpack. Keep in mind though, if you have to share truck space with another customer you may arrive far ahead of your boxes—and bed. ABF also now offers ReloCubes, which are dropped off as a separate metal shipping container holding about one room's worth of furnishings (these can also be stored at a remote location for as long as you need and fit into most parking spaces). Try to estimate your needs beforehand and ask for your load's expected arrival date.. You can get an online estimate from some shippers, so you can compare rates. If you aren't moving an entire house and can't estimate how much truck space you will need, keep in mind this general guideline: two to three furnished rooms equal a 15-foot truck; four to five rooms, a 20-foot truck. Due to New York's narrow streets and overnight parking restrictions, self-moves may be best suited to those moving outside Manhattan.

MOVERS

INTERSTATE

First, the good news: moving can be affordable and problem-free. The bad news: if you're hiring a mover, the chances of it being so are much less. Probably the best way to find a mover is by personal recommendation. Absent a friend or relative who can recommend a trusted moving company, you can turn to what surveys show is the most popular method of finding a mover: the **Yellow Pages**. Then there's the internet: just type in "movers" on a search engine and you'll be directed to hundreds of more or less helpful moving-related sites.

You might ask a local realtor, who may be able to steer you towards a good mover, or at least tell you which ones to avoid. Members of the American Automobile Association have a valuable resource at hand in AAA's Consumer Relocation Services, which will assign the member a personal consultant to handle every detail of the move free of charge and which offers discounts with premier moving companies. Call 800-839-MOVE, www.aaa.com.

But beware! Since 1995, when the federal government eliminated the Interstate Commerce Commission, the interstate moving business has degenerated into a wild and mostly unregulated industry with thousands of unhappy, ripped-off customers annually. (There are so many reports of unscrupulous carriers that we no longer list movers in this book.) Since states do not have the authority to regulate interstate movers and the federal government has been slow to respond, you are pretty much on your own when it comes to finding an honest, hassle-free mover. That's why we can't emphasize enough the importance of carefully researching and choosing who will move you.

To aid your search for an honest and hassle-free interstate mover, we offer a few general recommendations. First get the names of a half-dozen movers and check to make sure they are licensed by the US Department of Transportation's Federal Motor Carrier Safety Administration (FMCSA). With the mover's Motor Carrier (MC) numbers in hand, call 888-368-7238 or go online to http://li-public. fmcsa.dot.gov, to see if the carrier is licensed and insured. If the company you're considering is federally licensed, your next step should be to check with the Better Business Bureau, www.bbb.org, in the state where the moving company is licensed as well as with that state's consumer protection board (in New York call 800-697-1220 or go to www.consumer.state.ny.us), or attorney general. Assuming there is no negative information, you can move on to the next step: asking for references. Particularly important are references from customers who did moves similar to yours. If a moving company is unable or unwilling to provide references or tells you they can't because their customers are all in the Federal Witness Protection Program, eliminate them from your list. Unscrupulous movers have even been known to give phony references that will falsely sing the mover's praises—so talk to more than one reference and ask questions. If something feels fishy, it probably is. One way to learn more about a prospective mover: ask them if they have a local office (they should) and then walk in and check it out.

Once you have at least three movers you feel reasonably comfortable with, it's time to ask for price quotes (always free). Best is a binding "not-to-exceed" quote, of course in writing. This will require an on-site visual inspection of what you are shipping. If you have any doubts about a prospective mover, drop them from your list before you invite a stranger into your home to catalog your belongings.

Recent regulations by FMCSA require movers to supply five documents to consumers before executing a contract. These include a brochure called "Your Rights and Responsibilities When You Move"; a concise and accurate written estimate of charges; a summary of the mover's arbitration program; the mover's customer complaint and inquiry handling procedure; and the mover's tariff containing rates, rules, regulations, classifications, etc. For more about FMCSA's role in the handling of household goods, you can go to their consumer page at www. protectyourmove.gov.

ADDITIONAL MOVING RECOMMENDATIONS:

- If someone recommends a mover to you, get names (the salesperson or estimator, the drivers, the loaders). To paraphrase the NRA, moving companies don't move people, people do. Likewise, if someone tells you he/she had a bad moving experience, note the name of the company and try to avoid it.

- Remember that price, while important, isn't everything, especially when you're entrusting all of your worldly possessions to strangers.
- Ask about the other end—subcontracting increases the chances that something could go wrong.
- Demand for moving equipment and services tends to be highest at the beginning, dead center and end of each month.
- In general, ask questions, and if you're concerned about something, ask for an explanation in writing. If you change your mind about a mover after you've signed on the dotted line, write them a letter explaining that you've changed your mind and that you won't be using their services. Better safe than sorry.
- Ask about insurance; the "basic" 60 cents per pound industry standard coverage is not enough. If you have homeowner's or renter's insurance, check to see if it will cover your belongings during transit. If not, ask your insurer if you can add that coverage for your move. Otherwise, consider purchasing "full replacement" or "full value" coverage from the carrier for the estimated value of your shipment. Though it's the most expensive type of coverage offered, it's probably worth it. Trucks get into accidents, they catch fire, they get stolen—if such insurance seems pricey to you, ask about a $250 or $500 deductible. This can reduce your cost substantially while still giving you much better protection in case of a catastrophic loss.
- Whatever you do, do not mislead a salesperson/estimator about how much and what you are moving. And make sure you tell a prospective mover about how far they'll have to transport your stuff to and from the truck as well as any stairs, driveways, obstacles or difficult vegetation, long paths or sidewalks, etc. Movers are particularly prickly about stairs and narrow hallway turns, a specialty of all New York apartments. The clearer you are with your mover, the better he or she will be able to serve you.
- Think about packing. If you plan to pack yourself, you can save some money, but if something is damaged because of your packing, you may not be able to file a claim for it. On the other hand, if you hire the mover to do the packing, they may not treat your belongings as well as you will. They will certainly do it faster, that's for sure. Depending on the size of your move and whether or not you are packing yourself, you may need a lot of boxes, tape, and packing material. Mover boxes, while not cheap, are usually sturdy and the right size. Sometimes a mover will give a customer used boxes free of charge. It doesn't hurt to ask. Also, don't wait to pack until the last minute. If you're doing the packing, give yourself at least a week to do the job; two or more is better. Be sure to ask the mover about any weight or size restrictions on boxes.
- You should personally transport all irreplaceable items such as jewelry, photographs, or key work documents. Do not put them in the moving van! For

less precious items that you do not want to put in the moving truck, consider sending them via the US Postal Service or by UPS.

- Ask your mover what is not permitted in the truck: usually anything flammable or combustible, as well as certain types of valuables.
- Although movers will put numbered labels on your possessions, you should make a numbered list of every box and item that is going in the truck. Detail box contents and photograph anything of particular value. Once the truck arrives on the other end, you can check off every piece and know for sure what did (or did not) make it. In case of claims, this list can be invaluable. Even after the move, keep the list; it can be surprisingly useful.
- Movers are required to issue you a "bill of lading"; do not hire a mover who does not use them.
- Consider keeping a log of every expense you incur for your move, e.g., phone calls, trips to New York, etc. In some instances, the IRS allows you to claim these types of expenses on your income taxes (See **Taxes** below.)
- Be aware that during the busy season (May through September), demand can exceed supply and moving may be more difficult and more expensive than during the rest of the year. If you must relocate during the peak moving months, call and book service well in advance (a month at least) of when you plan on moving. If you can reserve service way in advance, say four to six months early, you may be able to lock in a lower winter rate for your summer move.
- Listen to what the movers say; they are professionals and can give you expert advice about packing and preparing. Also, be ready for the truck on both ends—don't make them wait. Not only will it irritate your movers, but it may cost you. Understand, too, that things can happen on the road that are beyond a carrier's control (weather, accidents, etc.) and your belongings may not get to you at the time or on the day promised.
- Treat your movers well, especially the ones loading your stuff on and off the truck. Offer to buy them lunch, and tip them if they do a good job.
- Before moving pets, attach a tag to your pet's collar with your new address and phone number in case your furry friend accidentally wanders off in the confusion of moving. Your pet should travel with you and you should never plan on moving a pet inside a moving van. *The Pet-Moving Handbook*, published by **First Books** (www.firstbooks.com), also offers a wealth of practical information to help with pet relocation.
- Be prepared to pay the full moving bill upon delivery. Cash or bank/cashier's check may be required. Some carriers will take VISA and MasterCard but it is a good idea to get it in writing that you will be permitted to pay with a credit card since the delivering driver may not be aware of this and may demand cash. Unless you routinely keep thousands in greenbacks on you, you could have a problem getting your stuff off the truck. The State of New York allows movers to charge a 1% fuel surcharge fee whenever petrol goes over

$3.43 a gallon, with an additional 1% allowed for every 15-cent price increase thereafter.

INTRASTATE AND LOCAL MOVERS

According to Section 191 of the New York State Transportation Law, all companies involved in the moving business must be insured and hold a license that permits them to provide intrastate moving services within New York State. Licenses are issued by the **New York State Department of Transportation (DOT)**, www.dot. state.ny.us. To verify certification of your chosen mover, call 800-786-5368 and punch in the state license number listed on the mover's literature. Consumers can also call this number if they wish to file a complaint. According to the DOT, nearly 12,000 consumers use the service every year. New York's Better Business Bureau also estimates that three out of every ten moves into New York City each year result in the filing of a complaint; all the more reason to be careful about the company you hire.

CONSUMER COMPLAINTS—MOVERS

If a **move goes badly** and you blame the moving company, you should first file a written claim with the mover for loss or damage. If this doesn't work and it's an intrastate move, contact the **New York State DOT Carrier Certification Unit**, 47-40 21st Street, Long Island City, 11101, 718-482-4810, 800-786-5368 (complaints); also, New York State's **Motor Carrier Compliance Bureau**, 518-457-1016, can inform you of a mover's certification and can field complaints. Still not satisfied? Contact the **New York State Attorney General's Office**, locally at 55 Hansen Place, Brooklyn, NY 11217-1523, 718-722-3949, or the **New York State Consumer Protection Board**, 5 Empire State Plaza #2101, Albany, NY 12223-1556, 518-474-3514, www.consumer.state.ny.us, and you can call the Governor's **consumer hotline**, 800-697-122. For other questions within New York City, dial 311 to be directed to the appropriate office. Remember, for moves within the state of New York, the DOT can provide assistance only when you have used a licensed mover. Hire an unlicensed firm and you're on your own in case of damage or loss.

If your grievance is with an interstate carrier, your choices are limited. Interstate moves are regulated by the Federal Motor Carriers Safety Administration (FMCSA), www.fmcsa.dot.gov, an agency under the Department of Transportation, with whom you can file a complaint against a carrier. While their role in the regulation of interstate carriers historically has been concerned with safety issues rather than consumer issues, in response to the upsurge in unscrupulous movers and unhappy consumers, they have issued a recent set of rules "specifying how interstate household goods (HHG) carriers (movers) and brokers must assist their individual customers shipping household goods." According to their consumer page, carriers in violation of said rules can be fined, and repeat offenders may be barred from doing business. In terms of loss however, "FMCSA does not have statutory authority to resolve loss and damage of consumer complaints, settle disputes against a mover, or obtain reimbursement for consumers seeking payment for specific charges. Consumers are responsible for resolving disputes involving these household goods matters." They are not able to represent you in an arbitration dispute to recover damages for lost or destroyed property, nor enforce a court judgment. If you have a grievance, your best bet is to file a complaint against a mover with FMCSA (call 888-DOT-SAFT or go online to http://nccdb.fmcsa.dot.gov/HomePage.asp) and with the Better Business Bureau, www.bbb.org, in the state where the moving company is licensed, as well as with that state's attorney general or consumer protection office. To seek redress, hire an attorney.

STORAGE WAREHOUSES

Storage facilities may be required when you have to ship your furniture without an apartment to receive it or if your apartment is too small for all your belongings. If your mover maintains storage warehouse facilities in the city, as many do, you may want to store with them. Some even offer one month's free storage. Most warehouses are in Queens, Brooklyn, or New Jersey. Look in the Yellow Pages under "Storage Warehouses" and shop around for the best and most convenient deal. Below we list two major moving/storage companies. Listing here does not imply endorsement by First Books.

- **Approved Moving and Storage**, 718-622-2660, www.approvedmovers.com, has a fireproof warehouse in Brooklyn and mini-storage facilities on Long Island's South Shore. Estimates are based on the number of rooms of furniture and household goods to be stored.
- **Moishe's**, 800-536-6564, www.moishes.com, has warehousing in Brooklyn and in Queens, for goods hauled by their trucks and those of others.

The **New York City Department of Consumer Affairs** licenses storage—but not self-storage—warehouses. Dissatisfied? Call New York's Citizen's Service Center number, 311.

SELF-STORAGE

The ability to rent anything from 3' x 3' lockers to small storage rooms is a great boon to urban dwellers. Collectors, people with old clothes they can't bear to give away, and those with possessions that won't fit in a sublet or shared apartment all find mini-warehouses a solution to too-small living spaces.

Rates for space in Manhattan self-storage facilities are competitive: expect to pay at least $79 a month for a locker 4' x 4' x 7', $260 a month for an 8' x 10' x 8' space, and so on. Some offer free pick-up, otherwise you or your mover delivers the goods. If you're looking for lower rates, check the prices for storage units located in the suburbs and boroughs other than Manhattan.

As you shop around, you may want to check the facility for cleanliness and security. Does the building have sprinklers in case of fire? Do they have carts and hand trucks for moving in and out? Do they bill monthly, or will they automatically charge the bill to your credit card? Access should be 24-hour or nearly so, and some are air conditioned, an asset if you plan to visit your locker in the summer.

Finally, a word of warning: unless you no longer want your stored belongings, pay your storage bill and pay it on time. Storage companies may auction the contents of delinquent customers' lockers.

Here are a few area self-storage companies. For more options, check the Yellow Pages under "Storage."

- **Manhattan Mini Storage**, 1-800-STORAGE, www.manhattanministorage. com; with 17 locations including: 520 W 17th St, corner of Tenth Ave; 524 W 23rd St; 600 W 58th St, corner of Eleventh Ave; and 570 Riverside Dr, corner of 134th St, among others. Offers private storage rooms from 4' x 4' to 25' x 40' (larger than many NYC apartments).
- **Chelsea Mini Storage**, 626 W 28th St, Manhattan, 877-902-9751, www.chel-sea-mini-storage.com; also offers moving services.
- **Public Storage**, 800-447-8673, www.publicstorage.com; facilities in New Jersey and all boroughs but Manhattan.
- **Storage Deluxe**, 877-989-7867, www.storagedeluxe.com; ten Bronx storage locations, seven in Brooklyn and three in Queens, as well as Long Island and Connecticut.
- **Storage USA**, 800-895-5921,www.extraspace.com; eight facilities in and around Manhattan,.
- **U-haul Moving and Storage** has multiple mini-warehouses in the New York area, 800-468-4285, www.uhaul.com, with rooms around 3' x 4' x 4' for $52 and 6' x 10' x 8' for $339,.

CHILDREN

Studies show that moving, especially frequent moving, can be hard on children. According to an American Medical Association study, children who move often are more likely to suffer from such problems as depression, low self-esteem and aggression. Often their academic performance suffers as well. Aside from not moving more than is necessary, there are a few things you can do to help your children through this stressful time:

- Talk about the move with your kids. Be honest but positive. Listen to their concerns. To the extent possible, involve them in the process. Spend some time doing pre-moving research into activities so you can dive right in when you get to town, and have your children help out—they might even get positively enthusiastic for the move.

- Make sure children have their favorite possessions with them on the trip; don't pack "blankey" in the moving van.
- Make sure you have some social life planned on the other end. Your children may feel lonely in your new home, and such activities can ease the transition. If you move during the summer you might find a local camp (check with the YMHA or YMCA) in which they can sign up for a couple of weeks in August to make some new friends. Visit sites like www.parentsconnect.com or the kid activities/groups section of www.timeoutny.com.
- Keep in touch with family and loved ones as much as possible. Photos and phone calls are important ways of maintaining links to the important people you have left behind.
- If your children are school age, take the time to involve yourself in their new school and in their academic life. Don't let them fall through the cracks.
- Try to schedule a move during the summer so they can start the new school year at the beginning of the term.
- If possible, spend some time in the area prior to the move doing fun things, such visiting a local playground or playing ball in a local park or checking out the neighborhood stores with teenagers. With any luck they will meet some other kids their own age.

First Books (www.firstbooks.com) offers two helpful resources for children. For children ages 6–11, *The Moving Book: A Kids' Survival Guide* by Gabriel Davis is a wonderful gift, and younger children will appreciate *Max's Moving Adventure: A Coloring Book for Kids on the Move* by Danelle Till. For general guidance, read *Smart Moves: Your Guide Through the Emotional Maze of Relocation* by Nadia Jensen, Audrey McCollum, and Stuart Copans.

TAXES

If your move is work-related, some or all of your moving expenses may be tax-deductible—so you may want to keep those receipts. Though eligibility varies, depending, for example, on whether you have a job or are self-employed, generally, the cost of moving yourself, your family, and your belongings is tax deductible, even if you don't itemize. The criteria: in order to take the deduction your move must be employment-related, your new job must be more than 50 miles away from your current residence, and you must be at your new home for at least 39 weeks during the first 12 months after your arrival. If you take the deduction and then fail to meet the requirements, you will have to pay the IRS back, unless you were laid off through no fault of your own or transferred again by your employer. It's probably a good idea to consult a tax expert regarding

IRS rules related to moving. However, if you're a confident soul, get a copy of IRS Form 3903 (www.irs.gov) and do it yourself!

ADDITIONAL RELOCATION AND MOVING INFORMATION

- **www.firstbooks.com**; relocation resources and information on moving to Austin; Atlanta; Boston; Chicago; Dallas–Fort Worth; Houston; Los Angeles; Minneapolis–St. Paul; Portland, Oregon; San Francisco; Seattle; Washington, D.C.; London, England; plus a book for newcomers to the USA.
- **USA Today** has a comprehensive moving guide online, with everything from moving tips to mortgage quotes to national real estate listings. Visit www.usa-today.com/marketplace/realestate/front.htm
- **How to Move Handbook** by Clyde and Shari Steiner; an excellent general guidebook
- **http://realestate.msn.com**; online quotes
- **www.allamericanmovers.com**, 800-989-6683; online quotes
- **www.american-car-transport.com,** 866-322-3169; if you need help moving your car
- **www.erc.org**, the Employee Relocation Council, a professional organization, offers members specialized reports on the relocation and moving industries.
- **www.usps.com**, relocation information from the United States Postal Service.

A FTER FINDING YOUR NEW PLACE OF RESIDENCE, YOUR FIRST ORDER of business probably will be opening a bank account. The following information about personal savings and checking accounts, credit unions, and credit cards and credit resources should make the task less daunting. And, for your edification come April 15, we've included information about federal, state, and city income tax procedures, as well as details for those wanting to start or move a business.

BANK ACCOUNTS AND SERVICES

While most people tend to choose their bank for its location, other important determinants can be services, interest rates, and minimum balance requirements. If the services a bank offers are more important to you than location, particularly now that ATMs provide easy access to cash and account information outside the branch, be sure to shop around for the best deals for your banking needs. The city's two largest retail banks, Citibank and JP Morgan Chase & Co., operate more than 100 branches in Manhattan alone, plus more in the outer boroughs. However, fees at large interstate banks can be significantly higher than at smaller banks. The Yellow Pages contain some five pages of financial institutions. When deciding which one to choose, consider branch locations and hours of operation. Some banks are now open seven days a week. Below, we list eight banks with multiple branches.:

- **Apple Bank**, 914-902-2775, www.theapplebank.com
- **Bank of America**, 800-432-1000, www.bankofamerica.com
- **Bank of New York Mellon**, www.bnymellon.com, 1-888-LINKBNY
- **Citibank**, 212-627-3999, www.citibank.com
- **HSBC**, 800-975-4722, www.hsbc.com
- **JP Morgan Chase & Co.**, 800-CHASE-24, www.chase.com
- **North Fork Bank**, www.northforkbank.com, 1-877-694-9111

- **TD Bank**, 888-751-9000, www.tdbank.com
- **Valley National Bank** (formerly Merchants), 800-522-4100, www.valley nationalbank.com
- **Washington Mutual** (now acquired by **Chase**), 800-788-7000, www.wamu. com

Technology has transformed banking and continues to do so daily. All banks offer the option of banking via your home computer, although the majority of customers still feel more comfortable banking the old-fashioned way. What's more, traditional distinctions between commercial banks, savings banks, and brokerage houses have become blurred, although with the bank crisis unfolding as this book goes to press it seems likely those traditional boundaries will be strengthened. And financial software has crossed all these lines. In this fluid situation, "It's a consumer's market," says one bank officer.

Services offered by financial institutions include, but are not limited to, the following:

- **Checking**; take a completed application—two references are often required, usually the name of your current bank and that of your employer—to the branch where you intend to bank, together with two signed pieces of identification: driver's license, credit card, student ID with photo. One ID must have a photo. Some banks require a minimum start-up deposit. Your account can be opened immediately, but checks and deposit slips won't be issued until your signature is verified. "Regular" non-interest-bearing personal checking accounts typically carry no charges as long as a minimum daily balance is maintained. A certificate of deposit, money market or savings account linked to your regular checking account may also get you free checking. Institutions offering interest-earning NOW checking accounts charge a fee if the accounts fall below required minimum balances. **Debit cards** are issued automatically to new customers, many with a MasterCard or VISA imprint. Most can be used to make withdrawals through the nationwide network of CIRRUS and NYCE ATMs and can be used at retail outlets to pay for goods and services, debiting your checking account directly. You can arrange to have your paycheck go straight to your checking account via direct deposit. Be sure to inquire about fees and shop around before opening a checking account. If your address is uncertain or has problems receiving mail you can have checks and ATM cards mailed to your branch bank office.
- **Savings**; follow the procedures detailed above for checking accounts to apply for a "statement" savings account, which provides monthly statements of all transactions and can be linked to your checking account. Many banks require an average minimum balance of at least $1,500 to avoid maintenance charges. Again, inquire about fees.
- **Online banking**; Just as ATMs did not eliminate bank tellers, internet banking will not replace the brick-and-mortar branch. But the low operating costs

and convenience of online banking render the internet an optimal financial conduit. ING Direct, at www.ingdirect.com, is the leader in this area but almost all banks offer online services, and some banks exist exclusively online. Conventional services such as transfers and balance inquiries are standard, while some banks offer applications for loans and credit lines. Larger banks have tie-ins to investment accounts, and some sites even offer financial management tips and strategies. Some institutions offer incentives to those who make transactions online, ranging from waived fees to rewards on a point system. Security is paramount and, according to a *PCWorld* report, highly efficient: less than one percent of fraudulent bank activity occurs via online transactions. While banks will protect your information, you must also be attentive with your online account. Change your password regularly, and don't share it with anyone.

- **Banking by phone**; a touch-tone telephone gives access to all the banking services performed by an ATM, except deposits and cash withdrawals: you can check account balances and make transfers between accounts. For a small monthly charge (or free with a minimum combined balance of, say, $10,000) the bank will make scheduled bill payments such as rent, mortgage, or car payments, as well as payments on request to designated payees such as stores, credit card companies, and utilities. A year-end annual statement may be provided on request. Again, inquire about the latest refinements and fees, if any.

CREDIT UNIONS

According to the **National Credit Union Administration (NCUA)**, "A federal credit union is a nonprofit, cooperative financial institution owned and run by its members." Organized to serve, democratically controlled credit unions provide their members with a safe place to save and borrow at reasonable rates. Members pool their funds to make loans to one another. The volunteer board that runs each credit union is elected by the members. According to *American Banker's* annual survey, credit unions continually rank high in customer satisfaction. Because credit unions limit membership based on set criteria, you'll need to investigate a few for a match. Organizations such as employers, unions, professional associations, churches, and schools (alumni associations) typically provide membership. A few, such as the **Lower East Side Peoples' Federal Credit Union**, 37 Avenue B, 212-529-8197, www.lespeoples.org, have community charters enabling them to serve anyone who works or lives in that community. And some, such as the **Progressive Credit Union** at 370 Seventh Avenue, 212-695-8900, www.progressivecu.org, might contact your employer with an offer of free credit union services for company employees, which would qualify you. Credit unions lack the convenience of multiple branches but offer considerable financial benefit in exchange. For a complete list of local credit unions or information about them, you can visit the **National Association of Credit Union Service Organizations**, www.nacuso.org, or the **NCUA**, www.ncua.gov.

CONSUMER COMPLAINTS—BANKING

Federal and state governments regulate bank policies on discrimination, credit, anti-redlining, truth-in-lending, etc. If you have a problem, you should first attempt to resolve the issue directly with the bank. Should you need to **file a formal complaint** against your financial institution, you can do so through the Board of Governors of the **Federal Reserve System, Division of Consumer and Community Affairs**. For specifics, call 202-452-3693 or go to www.federalreserve.gov/pubs/consumerhdbk/complaint.htm. You can also pursue the issue with the following agencies:

- Nationally chartered commercial banks go through the **US Comptroller of the Currency**, Customer Assistance Group, 1301 McKinney St, Suite 3450, Houston, TX 77010, 800-613-6743, www.occ.treas.gov.
- **US Office of Thrift Supervision**, 1700 G St NW, Washington, DC 20552, 202-906-6000, www.ots.treas.gov; for thrift institutions insured by the Savings Association Insurance Fund and/or federally chartered (i.e., members of the Federal Home Loan Bank System).
- For federally chartered credit unions or state-chartered credit unions with federal insurance, contact the **National Credit Union Administration**, 9 Washington Square, Washington Avenue Extension, Albany, NY 12205, 518-862-7400, www.ncua.gov.

CREDIT CARDS

On the off chance that your mailbox hasn't been filled with credit card applications, you can call to request one. Many cards now offer various "rewards" as incentives to use them, the most common being frequent flyer miles. Shop around for the one that best suits your needs.

- **American Express**, 800-528-4800, www.americanexpress.com; once famous for issuing charge cards that must be paid off every month, American Express now offers nearly two dozen different cards, including credit cards and airline affinity cards that accumulate frequent-flyer miles. With the exception of a student card, all Amex cards have minimum income requirements, and most charge annual fees.
- **Diner's Club**, 800-234-6377, www.dinersclub.com; with annual fees and income requirements, the Diner's Club card is accepted mainly in travel and hospitality circles; cardholders have access to special amenities at most major airports.
- **Discover/Novus**, 800-347-2683, www.discovercard.com; Discover cards and affiliated Novus/Private Issue cards offer an annual rebate based on the

amount you charge, and some plans let you accumulate credit at various hotels or retail chains.

- **VISA** and **MasterCard** can be obtained from a variety of financial service organizations, usually banks. Interest rates vary, annual fees may even be waived,
and many cards offer frequent flyer miles. It pays to shop around, especially if
you don't pay off your balance every month.

- **Department store credit cards** can offer advantages over other forms of payment: advance notice of sales, mail or phone orders, no annual fee. Accounts
may be approved instantly upon application. Macy's and Bloomingdales cards
are popular among New York shoppers.

For a handy way to compare rates and to learn more about credit cards, visit
bankrate.com. **Cardweb.com** is an online directory of credit cards; search or
browse by interest rates, fees, special offers, or affinity features such as frequent-
flyer miles or charity donations based on the amount you charge. And finally,
you can visit the personal finance section of **www.epinions.com** for customer
reviews of specific institutions' credit cards.

BANKING AND CREDIT RESOURCES

For a list of articles about trends in banking and links to the Federal Trade Commission and other consumer protection agencies, visit the **National Institute
for Consumer Education** web site at www.nice.emich.edu. To look up current
interest rates on deposits, go to www.bankrate.com.

If you're buying a car or boat, renovating your new fixer-upper, or sending
the kids to college, you can still shop for loans the old-fashioned way, using the
Yellow Pages and the financial section of the newspaper, but the internet can
make the job a lot easier. Online loan calculators let you experiment with different payment plans. There are several loan calculators on bankrate.com but you
can look at other sites as well:

- **www.myfico.com**
- **Eloan,** www.eloan.com
- **Financial Power Tools**, www.financialpowertools.com
- **Women's Financial Network**, www.wfn.com
- **The Motley Fool**, www.fool.com (An excellent place to learn about money,
investing and banking. They offer online seminars, well-written articles, and
an active discussion board.)

Obtain copies of your **credit report** from the three major credit bureaus at
www.annualcreditreport.com. The national credit bureaus are:

- **Equifax**, P.O. Box 105873, Atlanta, GA 30348, 800-685-1111, www.equifax.
com

- **Experian**, P.O. Box 2104, Allen, TX 75002-2104, 888-397-3742, www.experian. com
- **TransUnion Corporation**, P.O. Box 390, Springfield, PA 19064-0390, 800-916-8800, www.transunion.com

INCOME TAXES

Heralded by freshly painted H&R Block signs and black-bordered boxes in the newspapers warning "Only 10 more days to file your income tax returns," April 15 arrives promptly every 365 days. In New York City, the Internal Revenue Service and New York Department of Taxation and Finance provide literature and taxpayer information services via telephone. In case you did not know it before moving here, the bad news is that New York City takes a yearly income tax bite out of your earnings, along with the state and federal government. The good news is that it is not the highest taxed state in the country.

- **Federal income tax** forms can be obtained by calling 800-829-3676; they are also available in most post offices and libraries at tax time. Call 800-829-1040 to obtain explanatory literature as well as answers to specific questions, such as which of the three tax forms—1040EZ, 1040A, or 1040—you should use. Many opt to visit the IRS's helpful web site, www.irs.gov, where you can find answers to tax questions as well as downloadable tax forms and information on filing electronically. The staff at the Internal Revenue Service office (hours are weekdays 7:30 a.m.–4:30 p.m.) downtown at 290 Broadway provides instruction in the fine art of calculating your federal income tax but won't do it for you.
- **New York State and New York City** use a combined income tax form. If you have not received forms by mail, call 800-462-8100 to order. If you use either IRS 1040EZ or 1040A, choose the IT 100, which you fill in and let the state tax people calculate for you, or the IT 200, which you calculate yourself. For those filing the Federal 1040 long form, you'll need the IT 201. The number for taxpayer assistance in New York State is 800-CALL-TAX. A number of federal forms are available at the IRS web site, www.irs.gov, and New York State tax forms can be downloaded from www.tax.state.ny.us/forms. Your federal adjusted gross income is the tax base for state and city taxes. New York State taxable income is calculated by adding and subtracting various New York State "modifications" and then the New York City resident's income tax is based on your state taxable income. New Jersey residents can get tax information and download state tax forms from www.state.nj.us/treasury/taxation.

ONLINE FILING AND ASSISTANCE

Filing your taxes online can save you time, especially if you already keep your personal financial records using compatible software such as Turbo, Quicken, or QuickBooks. Visit www.irs.gov/taxpros for details, including a list of companies that make tax software. For some, it may be advisable to get assistance in calculating and preparing your tax return. See the Yellow Pages under "Tax Returns" if you do not have a tax preparation firm recommendation from an acquaintance, or look up the nearest H & R Block location. Remember to keep all receipts, be prepared to spend some time, and don't show up on April 14th. Questions? Call the IRS helpline, 800-829-1040, to speak to an IRS representative. Automated information is available 24/7 at 800-829-4477; this is also the number to call to find out the status of your return if you have filed and have been waiting more than four weeks, or you can visit the IRS web site: www.irs.gov.

If you need help with a tax problem or are suffering some hardship due to the tax law, you can contact the **Taxpayer Advocate Service**, an independent agency within the IRS designed to help taxpayers resolve tax problems; contact them at www.irs.gov/advocate.

Taxpayer assistance in filing on paper or electronically is available for simple returns at no cost at Manhattan IRS offices: 290 Broadway, 110 West 44th Street, and 55 West 125th Street; Bronx IRS: 1200 Water Place; Brooklyn IRS: 625 Fulton Street; Queens office: 1 Lefrak City at 59-17 Junction Boulevard in Rego Park, Queens. No appointment is necessary at these sites, which are open Monday–Friday, 8:30 a.m.–4:30 p.m., but don't wait until April, unless you like standing in long lines. Assistance in preparing and filing returns, electronically at some sites, is provided by volunteers under the **VITA (Volunteer Income Tax Assistance)** program throughout the city and in New Jersey. To find the site nearest you call 800-829-1040 (customer assistance hotline).

For questions concerning New York State income tax call the **New York State Department of Taxation and Finance**, 800-225-5829.

STARTING OR MOVING A BUSINESS

According to the Tax Foundation, New York has the second highest state and local tax burden for businesses. Not to mention very high rents. But if proximity to power, money, and a diverse and deep talent pool is important to you, then New York City can't be beat as a place to locate a business.

If your business does not need to be based in Manhattan, you will find more space for your money in one of the other boroughs or in neighboring New Jersey.

You may choose to hire an attorney who is familiar with the process, but if you want to begin your research on your own, the following resources should help you get started:

- **Association of the Bar of the City of New York**, Legal Referral Service, 212-382-6600, www.abcny.org
- **Internal Revenue Service**, 800-829-1040, with whom you will need to talk to get an employer tax ID number.
- **New York City Department of Finance**, www.nyc.gov/finance

- **New York Department of State, Division of Corporations,** 41 State St, Albany, NY 12231, 518-473-2492, www.dos.state.ny.us; in order to incorporate in New York, you must first reserve a name here (do an advance name search). You can obtain information and fee schedules regarding filing for C Corporation, S Corporation, Limited Liability Company, or Limited Partnership status. Discuss your options first with your attorney and/or accountant.
- **US Small Business Administration**, www.sba.gov; from counseling and training to start-up guidelines to SBA loans, the SBA is ideal for finding small business information.

L ET'S SEE. YOU'VE SIGNED A LEASE OR MORTGAGE PAPERS AND OPENED a bank account. So now, keys in hand, it's time to have utilities connected, telephone installed, and to choose your cable and internet service providers. You can make yourself at home once you can cook and call, and really feel like a local once you possess a library card, are registered to vote, and have found a doctor. Here are some of the important how-to's (addresses are in Manhattan unless otherwise noted).

UTILITIES

CONSOLIDATED EDISON

Call **Consolidated Edison's** customer service to have gas and electricity turned on: 800-75-CON-ED. In New Jersey, call **PSE&G** (**Public Service Electric and Gas**), 800-436-7734, for service. A personal visit from either is not necessary unless the prior tenant's service was cut off for non-payment. Expect to wait at least one business day before service commences; note that PSE&G is open for new accounts Monday–Friday only. Deposits are no longer required for residential accounts unless a credit check indicates the need.

TELEPHONE

You have several choices for local and long distance phone service in New York City, and many of the companies that offer local service also offer long distance. Verizon (the largest local carrier), AT&T, Sprint, and RCN Communications (in Manhattan and Queens on a building-by-building basis) all offer local and long distance service and are among the many companies offering internet, cellular, and digital service. Cable television giants are also now offering telephone and internet service in the form of bundled telecommunications over their fiber optic cables. When calling to inquire about service, ask about weekday, evening, and weekend rates, specials, and the costs of installation. Whichever local phone service you choose, you will be offered a bouquet of extra features, each carrying an extra monthly fee, among them: Call Waiting (the most popular), Call Forwarding, Call Answering, Voice Dialing, Call Return, 3-Way Calling, and Caller ID. If you are looking to set up DSL service for your computer, inquire about the additional cost and ask about special deals.

In New York, widely used **long distance service providers** also provide local service. To institute new **local service** contact: **Verizon**, 212-890-2550, www.verizon.com; **AT&T**, 800-222-0300, www.att.com; **Sprint**, 800-877-7746, www.sprint.com; or **RCN**, 800-746-4726, www.rcn.com.

Verizon no longer requires a deposit from most customers; when required, the deposit accumulates interest and is refunded after a year. The set-up charges for all phone companies will vary depending on your needs. For example, if you need additional jacks you will pay more. It is advantageous to ask the superintendent or someone who works in the building where the phone lines come into the building. This will expedite the process of getting phone service.

For help comparing long distance calling plans see below. **Bundling** is the current buzzword in communications: i.e., charging one rate on one bill for two or more services, for example for long distance calls made from home phones and internet or cable television service. Other service plan variables include volume discounts, monthly minimums, and overseas service. Check around.

A word about **slamming**, being switched to a different long distance carrier without your knowledge or consent, or **cramming**, charges billed to you for calls you did not make: while these practices have been largely eliminated in recent years, should you notice such discrepancies on your bill you should contact your local service provider and report the problem. The next step is to report the offense to the FCC, should you wish to do so, at 888-225-5322. To inform the New York Public Service Commission, call 800-342-3377, or contact the New York State Consumer Protection Board at 800-NYS-1220, or better yet, consult their extensive web site, www.consumer.state.ny.us, an encyclopedically useful resource covering every conceivable consumer problem, including slamming and cramming. Web sites for the Federal Trade Commission, www.ftc.gov, and for the Federal Communications Commission, www.fcc.gov, have tips on combating cramming. (See **Rip-off Recourse** in **Helpful Services** for more on consumer protection.)

TELEPHONE DIRECTORIES

Most New Yorkers aren't aware of how much good information can be found in the city's telephone books. The **White Pages** includes extensive listings of community service numbers as well as government listings and an emergency care guide. The **Yellow Pages** is almost in itself a guide to doing business or getting whatever you need in New York City. Seek it as a reference for historical sites and landmarks, public transportation maps, a yearly calendar of events, and even sports stadiums and concert hall seating charts! The **Business to Business Yellow Pages**, which lists all wholesalers and manufacturers, is free of charge and can be obtained by calling your local telephone office.

In today's web-oriented world, **directory assistance** does not have to cost a lot of money. Numerous sites are dedicated to providing telephone listings and web sites, including:

- **www.bigbook.com** (Verizon's Super Pages)
- **www.anywho.com** (AT&T's site, includes searches for toll-free numbers)
- **www.superpages.com**
- **www.people.yahoo.com**
- **www.switchboard.com**
- **www.whowhere.lycos.com**
- **www.worldpages.com**
- **www.yellowpages.com**

Dialing 411 for directory assistance is très passé. Google's 1-800-GOOG-411 costs nothing, is faster (thanks to its superior voice recognition software and instant call through), and covers every place in the United States. It even has a sense of humor! If you insist on using 411, your nostalgia will cost you $1.25 plus tax (more for out-of-state directory assistance, and as much as $2.00 from some wireless providers). You can also call either 212-555-1212 or 718-555-1212; each call costs 80 cents. 800-FREE-411 provides directory assistance at no charge, but callers must listen to advertisements before receiving information. Information about city-related services is available by dialing 311 (outside New York City, 212-639-9675). Operators are ready to assist 24/7. The same 311 works for New Jersey.

AREA CODES

Until recently, all Manhattan was in area code 212, while the other boroughs were in area code 718. Now, new landline phones in Manhattan are given area code 646, and in Manhattan and the boroughs, area code 917 generally serves wireless phones and beepers. Boroughs previously reached at 718 have been extended to code 347; and 631 has been added to 516 on Long Island; in New Jersey, part of the 201 area, South Orange for example, has become 973; Westchester remains primarily 914. Until recently, you only needed to dial area codes when dialing between boroughs. Now, all calls within New York City require 11-digit dialing: "one," plus the area code, plus the seven-digit number.

CELL PHONES

Cell phone technology continues to change rapidly, and costs are falling, so much in fact, that some users have dispensed with landlines altogether. If you are considering a cell phone purchase, find out as much as possible before signing a contract. Better yet, try to find a service that does not require a long-term contract. And be sure to determine whether the cell phone you want to purchase is only operable if you subscribe to a particular service plan. The Better Business Bureau, www.bbb.org, has a page on their web site dedicated to complaints against cell phone service providers—a few of the larger providers are notorious for overbilling and aggressive collection practices.

Currently, five major companies provide cellular service in the metropolitan area:

- **AT&T**, 800-IMAGINE, www.wireless.att.com
- **MCI**, 800-444-2222, www.mci.com
- **Sprint** (now with **Nextel**), 800-480-4PCS, www.sprint.com, www.nextel.com
- **T-Mobile**, 800-937-8997, www.t-mobile.com
- **Verizon**, 800-256-4646, www.verizonwireless.com

If you want to compare long distance pricing, go to **SmartPrice** at www.smartprice.com for a free analysis of the carriers available in your area. Or contact **Telecommunications Research and Action Center (TRAC)**; unaffiliated with the communications industry, TRAC is a consumer organization that compares long distance and wireless calling plans and prices: www.trac.org, 202-263-2950.

INTERNET SERVICE PROVIDERS

Choices in internet service providers (ISPs) in the metro area are numerous, varied, and changing rapidly as technology advances. Newspaper ads occasionally offer deals.

When picking your provider, be sure to call around, as plans and pricing vary. Some ISPs currently available in the metropolitan area are:

- **America Online**, 800-827-6364, www.aol.com
- **AT&T WorldNet**, 800-967-5363, www.att.net
- **Compuserve**, 800-848-8990, www.compuserve.com
- **Earthlink**, 800-719-4332, www.earthlink.net
- **Juno**, 800-717-0453, www.juno.com
- **MSN**, 800-386-5550, www.msn.com
- **NetZero**, 877-665-9995, www.netzero.net
- **RCN**, 800-RING-RCN, www.rcn.com
- **Verizon**, 888-638-6100, www.verizon.com; also offers wireless internet coverage via their cell phone network.

Almost all of the above offer the older dial-up version as well as some form of **broadband**, high-speed connection via cable, telephone, or satellite. Dial-up goes for around $10 to $20 a month while cable/high-speed and DSL goes for from $30 to $50, depending on speed (plus the cost of installing the cable modem). Call **TimeWarner Cable**, 212-674-9100, or go to www.timewarnercable.com; other major providers include **Cablevision/Optimum**, www.optimumonline.com, at 718-617-3500 or 201-798-1134 in Jersey City, or **RCN**, 800-RING-RCN, www.rcn.com. If you don't want cable, **DSL** delivers a slightly slower form of high-speed internet connection over regular phone lines without disrupting simultaneous phone service. Where available, it costs around $30 per month usually with a one-time installation charge, but there may be a bundling advantage if you buy the service from your phone service provider. Go to www.dslreports.com to evaluate local plans. If this service is important to you, when looking for a place to live, be sure to inquire about which service is available in prospective apartments you are viewing. Where neither is available, satellite service may be the answer; for which, you will need to pay for the installation of a special dish antenna and receiver. Two-way satellite service is available through StarBand ("if you can see the southern sky, you can get StarBand"), 800-4Starband, www.starband.com. The other metropolitan area provider is **HughesNet** (formerly Direcway) at 866-347-3292, www.hughesnet.com.

CITY WATER

Considering the quantity of commercially bottled water consumed by its residents, you might think that New York City water is either unpalatable or unsafe. In fact, city water, which flows at a rate of over a billion gallons a day from vast supply systems north of the city in Westchester, the Catskills, and the Delaware River watershed, is both safe and exceptionally tasty when compared to water in other cities. Except in the infrequent years of extreme drought, the supply is ample and unrationed. Tenants are not charged for water but are encouraged to avoid water waste, especially in the summer months.

A slight rust-colored tint appears occasionally in water drawn from the Croton system (a small percentage of the total water supply), caused by a bloom of microorganisms, which are tasteless and harmless, if unappealing. Water in parts of Brooklyn appears milky white at first from suspended minerals, but this soon dissipates and is harmless. If the pipes have not been used for a while when you first move into your new apartment, let the water run for about ten minutes to clear out rust and the water will then be fine. Filtration of this water system, soon to be completed, should prevent discoloration. Questions about water quality or about the water system should be addressed to the **NYC Department of Environmental Protection**, Bureau of Public and Intergovernmental Affairs, 59-17 Junction Boulevard, Corona, NY 11368. Or contact the department's 24-hour Communications Center through the city's new 311 information line, where you can also address concerns about air quality, noise, hazardous materials, sewers, or any number of city-related problems. Visit the Department of Environmental Protection at www.nyc.gov/dep or contact them through the city's 311 call center.

Most of the eastern and northern parts of New Jersey, closest to New York City, are served by **United Water New Jersey**, www.unitedwater.com/uwnj. Problems/concerns are handled by their customer service center, 190 Moore Street, Hackensack, NJ 07601, 800-422-5987; emergencies: 888-770-6030.

For more on area water quality, go to the EPA's site, www.epa.gov, and read their guidelines on microbiological contaminants. Or call the **Safe Drinking Water Hotline**, 800-426-4791.

GARBAGE AND RECYCLING

Garbage service is provided by the city and is collected curbside in covered garbage cans or secured black plastic bags two to three times a week, depending on your location. Bulk trash, such as furniture and appliances, is picked up on the last day of regular garbage collection weekly. Garbage disposal for those living in large apartment buildings will most likely entail locating the trash chute in your hall. Some of the rougher loft conversions may try and charge you for trash pick-up, but it is the landlord's duty to arrange and pay for this service if the building is residential (commercial spaces must also recycle but it is not done through the NY governmental services). Check with your building super for any questions. To find out the pick-up days for your neighborhood call 311. (People in private homes in the boroughs, Westchester, and Long Island will need to supply their own trashcans and move them to the curb on specific pick-up days.)

Recycling is a part of life in New York City and, as with garbage collection, the service is provided by the city. Pick-up is weekly and is scheduled on one of your garbage collection days. Items to be recycled include paper: writing, copier, construction paper, glossy paper, envelopes, junk mail, postcards, smooth cardboard, wrapping paper, paperback books, and flattened boxes (no carbon paper, candy wrappers, take-out containers, napkins, paper towels, or hardcover books); glass; metal, including empty metal cans, aluminum foil trays, and general household items and appliances that are at least 50% metal; and number one and number two plastics (usually only bottles). FYI: returnable bottles and cans should be redeemed; in many neighborhoods they can be left neatly outside for the homeless to collect: often, it's their living. All recycled materials must be put in clear plastic bags. Paper products can also be put in special green-colored containers, while metal and plastics can go loose into special blue containers. Cardboard should be flattened and tied up in a bundle.

For drivers with a New York driver's license and registration, the sanitation department operates self-help bulk sites (for large items) in four boroughs; call 311 for locations and hours. The Sanitation Department's "Digest of Codes" outlines regulations, penalties, and procedures for trash disposal. For more specifics, visit the department's web site, www.nyc.gov/dsny. Fines for improper trash disposal range from $50 to over $250.

In New Jersey, garbage collection and recycling is provided municipally. The department to call for these services and the telephone number are listed here:

• **Edgewater**: Department of Public Works/Recycling, 201-943-1700
• **Fort Lee**: Department of Public Works, 201-592-3634
• **Hoboken**: Hoboken Environmental Services, 201-420-2385

- **Jersey City**: Waste Management, 201-435-1345
- **Weehawken**: Department of Recycling, 201-319-6070

CONSUMER COMPLAINTS—UTILITIES

If you have problems with a utility company (gas, electric, phones, water, steam, cable TV) you can contact the New York State Public Service Commission. By law, the commission is responsible for setting rates and ensuring that the public receives adequate service. You can file a complaint on the internet at www.dps. state.ny.us/complaintdept.html or by calling one of several hotlines including (contact New York Relay Service at 800-662-1220 for TDD assistance with these hotlines):

- **New York Public Service Commission**'s helpline: 888-697-7728; regulates telephone, cable TV, and energy utilities
- **Gas** or **Electric service shutoff hotline**: 800-342-3355

In New Jersey, contact **PSE&G** at 800-436-7734. If you have any questions about your rights as a consumer, you can also call the **New Jersey Board of Public Utilities** (**BPU**), which is responsible for regulating natural gas, water, telecommunications, and cable television, and for handling customer complaints: 800-624-0241.

PRINT AND BROADCAST MEDIA

New York is one of the last great multi-newspaper towns in the U.S, with not only multiple mainstream dailies going toe-to-toe, but a veritable tidal wave of ethnic, specialty, and religious rags—198 magazines and newspapers in 36 languages, with seven dailies in Chinese. What follows is only a partial listing. The smaller publications can be an excellent source of apartment listings that no one knows about, although it helps to be fluent in Tagalog.

MAJOR DAILIES

- *New York Post*, www.nypost.com; Rupert Murdoch's to-the-right entry into the Manhattan area has local news, opinion, gossip, sports, whose editors are in a daily battle for the most ingenious headline with their arch-rival…
- *New York Times*, www.nytimes.com; arguably the nation's premier source for national and world news as well as the latest on sports, technology, health, and science.
- *Newsday,* www.newsday.com; Long Island's top-rated daily also covers Queens and NY.
- The *New York Daily News*, www.nydailynews.com; which offers local New York news in the timeless Slash! Stab! Greed! Sex! Sex! Sex! tradition.
- *The Star-Ledger*, www.nj.com; New Jersey's largest daily paper.
- *The Wall Street Journal*, wsj.com; the bible of Wall Street.

OTHER PUBLICATIONS

- *11211*, www.11211.info; a sporadic glossy quasi-magazine with focus on local art and dining in Williamsburg, Brooklyn.
- *AMNY*, www.amny.com; this and its near twin (*Metro*, www,metro.us) are nearly identical free daily news digests scattered about town in newstands.
- *Brooklyn Daily Eagle*,www.brooklyneagle.com; once the most read newspaper in the country, this century-old institution is now the only Brooklyn daily.
- *The Brooklyn Downtown Star*, www.brooklyndowntownstar.com; focuses on Park Slope area and downtown Brooklyn
- *Brooklyn Rail*, www.brooklynrail.org; alternative monthly with arts focus and lots of essays and some reviews
- *Brooklyn Spectator*, www.brooklynspectator.com; another Brooklyn weekly
- *The Caribbean Voice*, caribvoice.org; covers news and events of the Caribbean
- *Carnarsie Courier*, canarsiecourier.com; Brooklyn's oldest weekly newspaper
- *Catholic New York*, www.cny.org; official newspaper of the Roman Catholic Archdiocese of New York
- *Columbia Spectator,* columbiaspectator.com; daily paper for Columbia University
- *Commentator Online*, www.yucommentator.com; newspaper of Yeshiva College
- *Crain's New York Business*, www.crainsny.com; daily financial news
- *El Diario*, www.impre.com/eldiariony; one of New York's Spanish language daily; the other is *Hoy*
- *The Forward*, www.forward.com; weekly with a focus on the Jewish community
- *Greek News*, www.greeknewsonline.com; self-explanatory, based in Queens and Astoria
- *Greenpoint Gazette*, www.greenpointnews.com; a very local weekly paper for Greenpoint, Brooklyn
- *Greenwich Village Gazette*, www.gvny.com; focus on Greenwich village news
- *India Tribune*, www.indiatribune.com; English language paper for the local India community
- *The Irish Echo*, www.irishecho.com; the nation's only Irish-American newspaper (or at least the largest)
- *The Jewish Post of New York*, www.jewishpost.com
- *The Jewish Week*, www.thejewishweek.com
- *The Journal of Commerce*, www.joc.com; specializes in trade and transportation news since the early 1800s
- *The L Magazine*, thelmagazine.com; a pocket-sized freebieall things relating or nearly relating to the L line community with lots of reviews
- *The New Sun*, www.newsun.com; the anti-NY rag, focuses on positive news
- *New York*, nymag.com; monthly arts and culture glossy, with extensive restaurant and bar guides, geared toward the young, media-obsessed, semi-ironic, and middle- to upper crust professional
- *The New York Amsterdam News*, www.amsterdamnews.com; weekly broadsheet focuses on African-American news.

- *The New York Law Journal*, www.nylj.com; a daily paper for NY's many, many lawyers
- *The New York Observer*, www.observer.com; this pink-toned weekly is terribly Manhattan, with an emphasis on Upper East Side gossip and media
- *The New York Press*; nypress.com; alt-weekly has a more hard-edged take on NY than the *Voice*
- *The New Yorker*, www.newyorker.com; better than ever under David Remnick, and now that you live here you can finally make solid, pragmatic use of those sterlingly belletristic "Tables for Two" reviews
- *New York Blade News*, www.nyblade.com; a weekly paper covering New York and national gay communities, with local arts and classifieds listings.
- *New York Waste*, www.newyorkwaste.com; nothing to do with garbage, this monthly focuses on the downtown art/punk scene
- *Queens Courier*, www.queenscourier.com; everything you wanted to know about Queens
- *The Onion*, www.theonion.com; NY's edition of this national humorous weekly newspaper.
- *The Queens Tribune*, www.queenstribune.com; another Queens weekly
- *Russian Bazaar*, www.russian-bazaar.com; weekly Russian language newspaper
- *Staten Island Advance*, www.silive.com; the borough's only daily paper, over a century old
- *TimeOut NY*, www.timeout.com/newyork; a comprehensive entertainment listing posing as a magazine
- *Times-Ledger Group*, yournabe.com; the web portal for almost 20 local papers
- *Tribeca Trib*, www.tribecatrib.com; only community newspaper covering Lower Manhattan, including Tribeca, Battery Park City, the Financial District, and the Seaport/Civic Center area
- *The Village Voice*, villagevoice.com; the left's long running classic free weekly has gone more mainstream but is as thick as ever
- *The Villager*, www.thevillager.com; small weekly focusing on the West Village

TELEVISION

LOCAL NETWORK CHANNELS

In Manhattan, you'll need cable to get any reception. No word by press time on how the switch to digital will affect this. In the boroughs, you can get away without cable, but reception will not be great although powered reception amplifiers can help. The major networks in New York City are: Channel 2–WCBS; Channel 4–WNBC; Channel 5–WNYW (Fox); Channel 7–WABC; Channel 9–WOR, the UPN Network during prime time hours (otherwise local programming); Channel 11–WPIX, offers the CW during prime time evening hours (otherwise local programming). Two PBS channels are available: Channel 13–WNET (Public Broadcasting System) and Channel 21–WLIW (Long Island's public network channel). They broadcast similar PBS programming but at different times.

You'll find weekly programs for the broadcast channels as well as cable channels (including HBO, Showtime, and the like) printed in *TV Guide* and the Sunday *New York Times'* "Television" section. This supplement also carries a complete "Station Guide" detailing the ownership and/or focus of broadcast and cable stations.

CABLE TELEVISION AND THE DISH

Expanded programming and famous skyscrapers make cable an attractive and often necessary option in New York City. Like the telecommunications industry, the cable industry is in the throes of change. Currently, service in Manhattan is provided by Time Warner and RCN, Cablevision and recently Verizon's FIOS service. The same companies cover much of Queens, Staten Island, Long Island, and Westchester. The eastern and northern portions of New Jersey, closest to New York, are handled primarily by Cablevision New Jersey and Comcast.

If your building isn't already wired, the owner or manager must request hookup, which has been known to take anywhere from several months to a year. In Manhattan, call **Time Warner Cable**, 212-674-9100 or go to www.timewarner-cable.com; for **RCN** service, dial 800-RING-RCN, or go to www.rcn.com. Queens and Brooklyn, call **Time Warner Cable** at 718-358-0900; The Bronx and Brooklyn, call **Cablevision** at 718-617-3500, www.cablevision.com.

If you want to avoid the uncertainties of digital broadcast reception and the tyranny of the cable companies, another option is **direct broadcast satellite** (**DBS**), more commonly known as "the dish." DBS provides the clearest reception available and hundreds of channels, now including the local channels, though only if you are in a position suitable for mounting an 18- to 36-inch dish outside your home, a difficult proposition for most Manhattanites. Basically, you'll need to own your building so you can use the roof—or have a southwest-facing balcony on which to mount the thing, and there can be no taller building to block the signal from the southwest. Clearly, TV junkies in the outer boroughs and the suburbs, where buildings are lower and spread out, have the advantage here. Currently two DBS signal providers compete in the metropolitan area: **DirecTV**, 800-347-3288, www.directv.com, and **Dish Network**, 800-333-3474, www.dishnetwork.com. You buy the receiver and dish, pay a one-time installation fee, and a monthly programming fee. Watch for occasional ads in the *Times* offering free installation with a one-year programming contract.

Along with pay cable networks such as HBO, Showtime, and Cinemax, plus numerous basic cable offerings, New York City has several of its own channels including New York One, which provides round-the-clock New York news, weather, and information for Time Warner customers, and the YES Network, owned and operated by the New York Yankees, among others. Public access also allows for several channels to be set aside for pay-as-you-go programming, most of which is less than mediocre and some of which is more than a bit risqué.

RADIO

RADIO STATIONS

Music lovers are best served by their FM dials; news and talk shows dominate the AM band. However, on either broadcast frequency most stations specialize further still, emphasizing one specific format. Check below to find your station. For program details, consult *Time Out New York*'s "Radio" page, which is particularly good; the *New York Times'* daily "Radio Highlights"; and "Radio Highlights" in *New York* magazine's "Cue" entertainment guide. If your reception is subpar many now broadcast over the internet.

AM STATIONS
- **AM news, sports, talk**: WCBS 880—"News Radio" and WINS 1010—two round-the-clock news stations plus sports, weather, traffic reports, etc. WCBS also carries the Yankees. WWRL 1600 is progressive talk radio; WABC 770 and WOR 710 are talk radio stations with popular talk radio personalities; WLIB 1190 religious and spiritual radio; WNYC 820 features cultural and consumer-oriented broadcasts, as well as National Public Radio's "All Things Considered"; WABC and WOR also carry Jets football.
- **AM Spanish news, talk, sports**: WADO 1280
- **AM Christian radio**: WMCA 570; WTHE 1520 for gospel
- **AM easy listening music**: WHLI 1100
- **AM sports**: WFAN 660 and ESPN sports radio 1050: both offer sports talk, WFAN is also home to the Mets, Knicks, Giants, and Rangers, while ESPN has Islanders hockey.
- **AM children**: WQEW "Radio Disney" 1560, pop favorites for children.

FM STATIONS
- **FM Caribbean**: WRTN 93.5
- **FM news/talk public affairs and NPR**: WNYC 93.9
- **FM urban**: WQHT "Hot 97" 97.1; WRKS "KISS-FM" 98.7; WWPR "Power 105.1" 105.1; WBLS 107.5; contemporary stations featuring hip-hop and R&B.
- **FM adult contemporary**: WLTW "Lite FM" 106.7; WFAS 103.9
- **FM classical**: WQXR 96.3, the *New York Times'* mostly classical music station
- **FM current hits**: WPLJ (Power 95) 95.5; WQHT 97.1; WHTZ "Z-100" 100.3; WKTU 103.5
- **FM jazz**: WBGO, "Jazz 88" 88.3 and WQCD 101.9
- **FM listener sponsored radio**: WBAI 99.5
- **FM oldies**: WCBS 101.1; hits from the 1960s and '70s; WKHL "Kool" 96.7
- **FM rock**: WAXQ 104.3

- **FM Spanish**: WPAT 93.1 and WCAA, 105.9 for Spanish contemporary hits; salsa and merengue: WSKQ "Mega" 97.9

In addition, nearly a dozen New York college radio stations between 88.1 and 90.9 on the FM dial offer a wide variety of musical styles and occasionally some interesting talk.

SATELLITE RADIO

After nearly a decade satellite radio has begun to make real headway among the general populace. The perks are nice: scores of commercial-free music channels, news and entertainment programs, sports broadcasts and more, including plans for streaming video, but it comes with a price tag. Users must purchase radio units, ranging from $30 to $400, and subscribe to a service, $12.95 a month and up. Two companies dominate the market, and both are aggressively expanding their reach. Howard Stern has moved his enormously popular program to Sirius from public broadcasting, and Oprah Winfrey has launched her own band on XM.

- **Sirius Satellite Radio**: 888-539-SIRIUS, www.sirius.com, nearly 70 music channels, plus programming from the NFL, NBA, Fox News, CNBC, C-SPAN, ESPN, NPR and more.
- **XM Satellite Radio**: 800-XM-RADIO, www.xmradio.com, over 70 music channels, a music-management partnership with Napster, and programming from Fox News, BBC World Service, PBS, Bloomberg, CNN , NASCAR and more.

OWNING A CAR IN NEW YORK

DRIVER'S LICENSES, AUTOMOBILE REGISTRATION (AND STATE IDS)

New residents with valid foreign or out-of-state licenses have 30 days to apply for a New York State driver's license and to register their cars and/or motorcycles. These exchanges are now handled by the DMV's License X-Press office, 300 West 34th Street between Eighth and Ninth avenues, open Monday–Friday, 8:30 a.m. to 4 p.m. Licenses and vehicle registrations are issued by the District Office of the New York State Department of Motor Vehicles, 141-155 Worth Street, corner Centre Street, NYC 10013, open Monday–Friday 8:30 a.m. to 4 p.m. Pick up a license application (which will have a convenient voter registration form attached), driver's manual and, if necessary, an automobile registration form at the District Office or have them sent by calling 212-645-5550 (if you can get through), or simply download the form from the DMV web site (see below). A valid out-of-state license exempts you from the road test, but you must pass the vision, road sign, and written tests, which means waiting on line at the DMV. You cannot drive in NYC with an out-of-town learner's permit.

If you are replacing an expired license, or acquiring a new one, you must make an appointment in advance to take the written test. You can stop by your borough's Preliminary Test Office of the Department of Motor Vehicles to schedule your test appointment or call the New York State Road Test Scheduling System at 518-486-6639, or go to www.nysdmv.com/roadtest. The written tests, based on the driver's manual, are given between 9 a.m. and 3 p.m. The best place for information on rules and regulations for obtaining a driver's license, plus motorcycle licenses, address changes, and more is at the **DMV web site**, www.nysdmv.com.

Tests are scored upon completion of your exam and, if you pass, you are issued a temporary license allowing you to drive immediately. Your official license, the one with the photograph, is mailed to you. On testing day, you must have the completed application form and your current license, and pay a fee of around $50 for renewals and $80 for a new one, which includes the written test fee, license validation fee, and picture (taken at the time your license is issued). New York State licenses are valid for eight years.

If your license has lapsed or this is your first, you'll need to pick up the materials and take the vision, road sign, and written tests noted above at the DMV, which also means waiting on line. You'll then be eligible for a learner's permit. With this in hand, after a five-hour course at a licensed driving school, it is possible to take the road test, the ultimate qualification for the New York Driver's License. Examiners can be finicky, but the most frustrating aspect of the road test is getting an appointment to take it. If you can arrange to take the test out of Manhattan, do so. If you make road test arrangements, pay $40, and then have to cancel, make sure you provide them with 72-hours notice or they will charge you another $40.

If you do not drive but wish to have a **state identification card**, visit any DMV office with at least two original identification documents, a combination of passport and Social Security card, for example, at least one of which must show date of birth and one with your signature. You can have your picture taken on site and receive a temporary ID. Yes, you'll wait on line. The permanent ID will arrive by mail in four to six weeks. For more details go to www.nysdmv.com.

To register your car or motorcycle you will need: a registration application or title (completely filled out), proof of ownership, proof of insurance, proof of vehicle inspection, sales tax clearance, and proof of your identity and birth. Read the back of the registration application to determine what "proofs" are acceptable. The registration fee depends on vehicle weight. New York State requires **liability insurance** on all automobiles, upon the purchase of which, from a licensed insurance company, you will be provided with an FS-20 card, which is your proof of insurance. New York is a no-fault insurance state. Auto emission tests are part of the annual inspection procedure necessary for operating a registered vehicle.

You may find it easier to do your DMV business at one of these offices (all can be reached at 212-645-5550 or 718-966-6155):

- 159 E 125th St, 3rd floor, 212-645-5550, Monday–Friday, 8:30 a.m. to 4:40 p.m., Thursday, 10 a.m. to 6 p.m.
- 625 Atlantic Ave, Brooklyn, Monday–Friday, 8:30 a.m. to 4 p.m.
- 2875 W 8th St, Brooklyn, Monday–Friday, 8:30 a.m. to 4 p.m., Thursday, 10 a.m. to 6 p.m.
- 696 E Fordham Rd, Bronx, Monday–Friday, 8:30 a.m. to 4 p.m., Thursday 8:30 a.m. to 6 p.m. No original license, permit, or non-driver ID transactions
- 1350 Commerce Ave, Bronx, Monday–Friday, 8:30 a.m. to 3:30 p.m. License or non-driver IDs only.
- 168-46 91st Ave, Jamaica, Queens, Monday–Friday, 8:30 a.m. to 4 p.m.
- 168-35 Rockaway Blvd, Jamaica, Queens, Monday–Friday, 8:30 a.m. to 4 p.m., Thursday, 10 a.m. to 6 p.m.
- 30-56 Whitestone Expressway, Flushing, Queens, Monday–Friday, 8:30 a.m. to 4 p.m., Thursday, 10 a.m. to 6 p.m.
- Showplace Bowling Center, 141 E Service Rd, Staten Island, Monday–Friday, 8:30 a.m. to 4 p.m., Thursday, 8:30 a.m. to 6 p.m.

Long lines are a Department of Motor Vehicles tradition. Best time to go is early in the week, but bring reading material along, *War & Peace* perhaps. Fridays are particularly busy. The last workday of any month can find the line spilling out onto the sidewalk and is to be avoided. Note: for a quickie (10-minute) renewal of your New York State driver's license or car registration, go to the DMV's License X-Press office. The fee for a renewal is $28 and is good for five years.

For information about the **New Jersey DMV**, go to www.nj.gov/nj/trans.

PARKING

Signs such as "Don't even think of parking here" give you an idea of how difficult it is to park in parts of New York City—particularly Manhattan. You can park legally on city streets if you are prepared to spend several hours a week switching parking spots to conform to the city's alternate-side-of-the-street parking laws. In addition, you will need a crash course in reading the complex street signs that regulate parking on every block—often you'll find several signs regulating various sections of the same block. Call 311 to find out what regulations are in effect on any given day or, better yet, get a free copy of the Department of Transportation's calendar showing the days your car doesn't have to be moved. Send a stamped, self-addressed envelope to Calendar, NYC Department of Transportation, 40 Worth Street, NYC 10013.

In the boroughs, you'll find street parking in residential areas much easier, and private homes generally have driveways and garages. Along main thoroughfares and in commercial shopping areas, such as Forest Hills in Queens, you may have to find garage space if you own a car. While many apartment buildings have garages, some have very long waiting lists. In Manhattan, monthly garage rates rival the price of monthly rent in other cities. There are alternatives, however, to be found in garages around the fringe of town, on the Lower East Side, south of Greenwich Village along and to the west of the West Side Highway, and north of Morningside Heights, although these are rapidly disappearing. **More Than Parking** (MTP) has relatively inexpensive indoor parking at 627 West 125th Street, 212-280-7487. Open lots are cheaper although some are better guarded than others. One good guide to cheap parking in New York is www.parkitguides.com.

Note: city residents are exempt from 8% of the 18.25% parking tax. To apply for the exemption go to www.nyc.gov and download the correct forms which are mailed to **New York City Department of Finance Parking, Tax Exemption Unit**, 59 Maiden Lane - 19th Floor, New York, NY 10038. You must send the name and license number of the lot or garage you use and proof of residence, which can be a copy of your car registration and driver's license. The process must be repeated yearly, but the savings make it worth the trouble.

If you use a car only occasionally, consider a private garage in a nearby community that is easily accessible by public transportation.

If you are frequenting Manhattan—other than midtown—for shopping or other purposes for a day or evening visit, you can usually find meters (outside of rush hours: 7 a.m. to 10 a.m. and 4 p.m. to 7 p.m.). Have plenty of quarters ready. Nighttime parking gets easier in many parts of the city where parking limits are not in effect between 7 p.m. and 7 a.m.

Many Manhattanites don't bother owning a car since lack of parking coupled with heavy traffic throughout Manhattan makes driving to and from the office stressful and inefficient. The cost of renting a car for the few times you really need one—such as taking a trip out of town—is cheaper than paying for parking, car insurance, taxes and fees, and maintenance. Using mass transit or taxis is the preferred method of getting around the city—especially on weekdays. See the **Transportation** chapter for information about car rentals, including **ZipCar**, an hourly car rental subscription service. For tips on auto services and repair, go to **Helpful Services**.

PARKING TICKETS AND TOWING

What's the price if you get caught? To help you decide whether to take that parking chance or not, keep in mind that parking tickets issued below 96th Street in Manhattan range from $65 to $180, depending on the violation. (Note: the web site for the New York City Department of Finance Parking Violations Operations, www.nyc.gov/html/dof, includes a wealth of parking information, including specifics about how to pay your ticket online, requesting a hearing, and information about towed vehicles.) Also, thanks to a little known and of course subject to change policy, challenging a parking ticket in person, online, or in writing can garner you a reduction for most fines if you agree to forgo a hearing.

Should you decide to take a chance and let your meter run over or block a crosswalk for a quick errand, you can be sure that a ticket will be waiting on your windshield. If you do get a ticket, you may pay by mail for the cost of a postage stamp; pay online at www.nyc.gov for $1.50 service charge; or pay by phone for $3 at 212-504-4041, using VISA, MasterCard, Discover, or American Express.

But tickets are only a part of the penalty. The real deterrent to joining the ranks of New York's parking scofflaws is the threat of having your automobile towed. It costs $185 to retrieve your car from the pound on Pier 76 (Twelfth Avenue and 38th Street) in Manhattan, plus $10 a day (which jumps to $15 a day on the third day) for storage, plus a fixed $70 "execution" fee. To retrieve your auto, you must produce the car's registration and your driver's license. If your name is on the registration papers, you can pay by check. Otherwise, or if you have accumulated traffic tickets, you must produce cash, certified check, or traveler's check for payment. The pound is open 7 a.m. to 11 p.m. on Mondays, and 24 hours a day from 7 a.m. Tuesday through 6 a.m. Sunday. Call 212-971-0773 to determine if your car has been towed. If it isn't in the pound (and you haven't misplaced it), your car has been stolen, and you should report it to the police. To find out if you have an accumulation of tickets (they sometimes blow off the windshield or are taken by other drivers who put them under their windshield wipers in order to fool the cops), all five boroughs have Help/Redemption Centers where you can get a free computer printout of your tickets or where you can pay to redeem a towed car: 150 Nassau Street, Manhattan; 1400 Williamsbridge Road, 1st floor, and 1932 Arthur Avenue, The Bronx; 144-06 94th Avenue, Jamaica, Queens; 210 Joralemon Street, 9th floor, Brooklyn; 350 St. Mark's Place, 3rd floor, Staten Island. Residents outside of New York City should check with their municipality for information regarding traffic/parking citations. In New Jersey, you can pay parking citations online by going to www.judiciary.state.nj.us/atswep/njmcdirectmain. To contact the New Jersey Motor Vehicle Commission, call 609-292-6500. For car safety, it is best not to leave any valuables in the car or any items in plain sight. A Chapman lock or the popular "Club" (a steering wheel lock) are also suggested. On quiet side streets, you are better off parking as close to a doorman building as possible, although such parking is generally limited.

KEEPING PETS

Can you bring your Portuguese water dog and your Burmese cat to New York? Will that pose a problem? Yes and maybe. The biggest hurdle to clear will be the first: finding an apartment that will accept pets (fish don't count). As a general rule, landlords and co-ops prohibit pets in their buildings, which means you may have to choose between the perfect apartment and the perfect pet. Be sure to inquire as you search for a pet-friendly home, and don't plan to sneak one in where they are prohibited. One web site, www.nycdoglife.com, is worth checking for its listing of pet-friendly rentals, condos, and co-ops, as well as other pet-related information. Dogs and cats being the most common city pets, we'll address their needs here. If yours is an exotic pet, say a miniature pig, you're on your own.

You will want to have a vet lined up before you need one. Start by calling the **Veterinary Medical Association of New York City**, 212-246-0057, for a list of accredited vets in your neighborhood. Visit the dog run, park, or vacant lot in your neighborhood frequented by dogs and their owners to glean information on local vets and the whole range of dog-owner concerns. Choosing a vet, like choosing a physician, is largely a subjective thing. Beyond the cleanliness and friendliness of the establishment, you and your pet will want to be comfortable with this vet. You may want to inquire to be sure your vet is available or covered after hours by an answering service. In case of a serious emergency after hours, the **Manhattan Veterinary Group**, a private animal hospital at 240 East 80th Street between Second and Third avenues, 212-988-1000, is open M–F 8 a.m. to 8 p.m., and 8 a.m. to 6 p.m. on weekends; the **Animal Medical Center** at 510 East 62nd Street at York Avenue, 212-838-8100, is open 24 hours and is one of the premier pet facilities in the city.

Dogs must be licensed by the city's Department of Health, 212-676-2120, for which you will need proof of rabies vaccination. Dogs must be leashed, except inside fenced dog runs; they may not enter playgrounds. Note: besides keeping your dog leashed, you must clean up after your dog.

Dogs typically need to be walked at least three times a day, not a problem if you work at home or someone is at home during the day. Being social animals they suffer more than cats from being left alone for long periods. Consider the proposition that two dogs are not much more bother than one, and both are happier together than one alone. In any case, if you are away for more than eight hours a day, you will probably need a **dog walker**, a person who has your keys and who will come in and take your dog out for 15 to 60 minutes. Expensive? Yes. To find a reliable walker check with other dog owners and your vet for recommendations. Some of the better pet-care establishments keep a list of walkers whose credentials they can vouch for. Some dog walkers will also pet-sit when you are away, either staying in your home to care for your pets and plants or visiting three times a day to feed, water, play with, and walk your pet. The price? Currently a minimum of $22 a day for cats, $25–$35 a day for dogs, more in some neighborhoods. There are kennels in the city, at least one without pens; those out of town, most of which will pick up and deliver your dog, tend to be roomier and less expensive. You may also want to look into doggie day care; more and more providers appear on the internet frequently, and www.urbanhound.com, also referenced below, is a good place to start.

Dog runs, fenced-in enclosures in which dogs can play off-leash, have proliferated in the city in recent years; at this writing there are 49 in the five boroughs. Most, such as those in Riverside Park, are open to all non-aggressive dogs that are not in heat. Others, such as the run at West Houston and Mercer Streets in the Village, are by membership only and often have a waiting list to get in.

Carl Shurz Park on the Upper East Side has the city's only small-dog enclosure, in addition to space for large dogs. To find a dog run in your neighborhood go to www.urbanhound.com/houndplay, which also has useful information on dog-friendly getaways, transportation with dogs, and links to other canine sites.

If you're looking to **acquire a dog or cat** you might consult the classified ads in the Sunday "Sports" section of the *New York Times*. There are purebred rescue groups in the city for most breeds; they find homes for animals of a particular breed that need to be placed, usually at less cost than from a breeder. Of course, if you adopt a pet from the **Center for Animal Care and Control** (**CACC**), the largest animal adoption organization in the city, you are saving it from almost certain euthanasia. For about $75 to $100 you can adopt a mixed breed dog ($150 for purebreds) or a cat, complete with vaccinations and spaying/neutering, at any of the CACC adoption centers in the five boroughs. In Manhattan the shelter is at 326 East 110th Street, 212-788-4000, open for adoptions daily, 11 a.m. to 6 p.m. Call 212-442-2076 for the location and hours of the other four shelters or visit their web site at www.nycacc.org; with links to petfinder.org it allows you to search other shelters in the metropolitan area. The **ASPCA Shelter and Adoption Center**, 424 East 92nd Street at First Avenue, 212-876-7700, www.aspca.org, also offers animals for adoption. The **Bide-A-Wee Manhattan Shelter** at 410 East 38th Street east of First Avenue, 212-532-4455, www.bideawee.org, does not destroy animals and offers dogs and cats for adoption at minimal cost.

Now available is the pet HMO, Pet Assure, which offers members 25% off all medical care and supplies for pets using participating veterinarians and 10% to 50% off the cost of pet foods, supplies, training, grooming, and boarding at participating establishments in the five boroughs, Manhattan especially. Call 888-789-PETS, www.petassure.com. Or, for straight medical coverage try Veterinary Pet Insurance, 800-872-7387, www.petinsurance.com.

Dog owners may find useful information, training advice, and links to other dog-related web sites at www.canine.org and www.urbanhound.com.

FINDING A PHYSICIAN

"What about how to find a doctor?" a plaintive reader inquires, adding, "It's been tough." Indeed. They're out there, more than 13,000 of them in Manhattan alone, but choosing a personal physician is more like choosing a mate than buying a car. You're looking for a doctor who has graduated from an excellent medical school, done residency in a good teaching hospital, is board-certified, has practiced long enough to know what he/she is doing but not so long as to be out of touch with the latest research and technology, and has just the right professional manner—concerned, straightforward, a listener with, perhaps, a good sense of humor. In short, you want a doctor you can rely on. If you put it off until you need one, you're apt to wind up sitting miserably in the nearest emergency room, followed by a big bill.

If you are enrolled in an HMO through your employer or independently, you are probably limited in your choice of physicians to those listed by that HMO. This makes choosing somewhat easier, but the criteria for choosing remain the same. More about HMOs below.

You may choose a physician as many do, on the basis of the recommendation of friends, which can be a good start. Question your friend closely on what exactly he/she does and does not like about a doctor. Or, if you had a physician you liked before moving here, he may be able to recommend a colleague here who will suit you.

Conventional wisdom says that one should have a doctor who is on staff or is an attending physician at one of the **teaching hospitals**. These physicians have been carefully screened and their credentials certified, the reasoning goes, and the teaching hospitals tend to offer a wider range of services and sophisticated procedures than do the smaller community hospitals. Bear in mind also, that as a patient in a teaching hospital, you may be poked and probed by students and residents, and some care may be provided by residents without additional supervision. Many of these hospitals also have student clinics which offer low-cost care, sometimes with financial aid, although this is on a case-by-case basis. In any case, these hospitals have referral services, which is one place to start your search. Referrals are based on medical specialty and location. The major academic hospitals in Manhattan, with their physician referral lines, are:

- **Beth Israel-St. Luke's-Roosevelt**, First Ave at 16th St, 888-445-0338
- **Columbia-Presbyterian Medical Center**, 622 W 168th St, 800-227-CPMC
- **Mount Sinai Medical Center**, Fifth Ave at 100th St, 800-MD-SINAI
- **NY Presbyterian Hospital-Cornell Medical Center**, 525 E 68th St, 800-822-2NYH
- **NYU Medical Center**, 550 First Ave, 888-7-NYU-MED
- **St. Luke's-Roosevelt Hospital Center**, 1000 Tenth Ave, 888-445-0338
- **St. Vincent's Hospital and Medical Center**, 153 W 11th St, 888-478-4362

Some of these hospitals also have treatment centers elsewhere, and their doctors practice throughout the metropolitan area. See the Yellow Pages for more hospitals in Manhattan and in the other boroughs.

Another source of referrals is the county medical society, which in Manhattan (NY County Medical Society, 12 East 41st Street, NYC 10016, 212-684-4670, www.nycms.org) has some 6,000 members. The caller can specify the area of choice, hospital of choice, specialty, sex, and be given three names. Note: you can also check on the credentials, training, and board specialties of a physician.

Referral(s) in hand, call the specific doctor's office to ask about an introductory visit. Inquire about office hours and their procedure for an introductory interview, which may be by phone or in person, and what the charge will be. Is the office staff helpful? Before talking with the physician have your questions written down: in which hospital does he/she practice, who covers for him/her when he/she is unavailable, can he/she be reached by phone after hours if need be, what are his/her billing procedures, etc. You may also want to discuss such sensitive issues as his/her views on abortion and life support. If you are satisfied so far, you'll probably make an appointment for a physical exam and some tests to establish a baseline profile. Ask about that and what it will cost. If you are not satisfied, go elsewhere.

A word about **HMOs**; if you are not covered by some form of health insurance and are not in an HMO connected with your place of employment, you can join one directly yourself on a "direct pay" basis. That means you pay, and it isn't cheap, at least until you consider the alternative, should you or a family member become ill or injured. Competition between HMOs is intense, and the field is rapidly changing. It's a good idea to request information from a number of organizations in order to determine what is available and what best suits your situation and your pocketbook. Some unions and associations that you may belong to also have HMO plans, which will be less costly for members than if you joined one as an individual.

To assist in this and/or in the choice of a physician, look into *New York* magazine's annual "Best Doctors in the City" issue, in which you can gather names of physicians in various fields of medicine.

Should you have a **serious complaint**, which you cannot resolve with your physician, contact the **NY State Board for Professional Medical Conduct**, NY State Department of Health, Office of Professional Medical Conduct, 433 River Street, Suite 303, Troy, NY 12180, 518-402-0855, www.health.state.ny.us. In New Jersey, contact the **NJ State Board of Medical Examiners**, 140 East Front Street, Second Floor, Trenton, NJ 08608, 609-826-7100, www.state.nj.us/lps/ca/medical.htm.

VOTER REGISTRATION

Registering to vote is as simple as calling the New York State Board of Elections voter registration hotline, 800-FOR-VOTE, to request a voter application. You can also call the **Manhattan Board of Elections** at 212-868-3692, www.vote.nyc.ny.us, for an Application for Registration and Enrollment by mail. Complete this form and return it to the board. If you live in another borough, the Manhattan Board will pass the completed application along to the appropriate borough board: Bronx, 718-299-9017; Brooklyn, 718-797-8800; Manhattan, 212-886-2100; Queens, 718-730-6730; and Staten Island, 718-876-0079. Pre-stamped applications are also available in post offices, libraries, and some public agencies. If you enroll in a political party, the form must be received by the Board of Elections 25 days before the primary or general election. You can also register in person at Election Board headquarters, 32 Broadway.

For information on voter registration in New Jersey, start with the League of Women Voters of New Jersey, 204 West State Street, Trenton, NJ 08608, 609-394-3303, http://www.lwvnj.org.

LIBRARY CARDS

The New York Public Library, www.nypl.org, with four stellar but non-circulating research libraries, numerous special divisions for various disciplines, famous reference collections, and over 79 branches in Manhattan, The Bronx, and Staten Island, is one of the city's great treasures. Residents of Brooklyn and Queens, however, aren't bookless: the Brooklyn Public Library has 59 branches, the Queens Borough Public Library, 60. Neighborhood branch libraries are listed at the end of each neighborhood profile in the **Neighborhoods** section.

Library cards are free and entitle you to borrow or request circulating books from any branch in the system. To obtain a card, give your name, address, and proof of residence to the librarian at the return desk of the nearest branch library. In New York City, call 212-661-7220 for library hours—which vary widely from branch to branch.

A wonderful resource is New York Public's **Telephone Reference Service**, 212-340-0849. Library researchers try to answer all possible questions and, if they cannot, will refer you to the department most likely to have the required data. If the Manhattan number is busy, try the Brooklyn number, 718-230-2100, or Queens, 718-990-0714. You can also renew books over the phone by dialing 212-262-7444 or online by going to the www.nypl.org website.

In New Jersey, library information is available at the New Jersey Library Association's web site: www.njla.org/resources, or try one of the following contacts:
- **Edgewater Public Library**, 49 Hudson Ave, Edgewater, NJ 07020, 201-224-6144, www.bccls.org/edgewater
- **Fort Lee Public Library**, 320 Main St, Fort Lee, NJ 07703, 201-592-3615, www.bccls.org/fortlee
- **Hoboken Public Library**, 500 Park Ave, Hoboken, NJ 07030, 201-420-2280, www.hoboken.bccls.org
- **Jersey City Public Library**, 472 Jersey Ave, Jersey City, NJ 07302, 201-547-4500, www.jclibrary.org
- **Weehawken Public Library**, 49 Hauxhurst Ave, Weehawken, NJ 07087, 201-863-7823, www.library.weehawken-nj.us

For more on New York's fabulous literary traditions and opportunities, see **Literary Life** in the **Cultural Life** chapter.

PASSPORTS

Whether you are applying for a passport for the first time or renewing, do not wait until just before your summer or Christmas vacation to do so. Apply early and relax. First, call New York City **Passport Agency** at 212-206-3500 for recorded passport application information and to schedule an appointment. For detailed information and to download the proper mail-in forms, you can visit the **US Department of State Bureau of Consular Affairs'** link: www.travel.state. gov, or call them at 877-487-2778, TDD 888-874-7793, Monday–Friday 8 a.m. to 8 p.m. EST. General travel information and advisories are also available at the site.

If you are applying for a passport for the first time, you must have (1) proof of citizenship: an original or copy of your birth certificate with a raised seal, or naturalization papers, and (2) proof of your identity: a driver's license or other ID with a photograph and signature. (If you don't have these papers, call the number above for alternatives.) You will need two passport photos (which can be made while you wait in most neighborhood photo shops) and $100 ($75 if by mail) if you are age 16 or older, $85 ($60 by mail) for those under age 16; renewals are $70. For expedited service, add $60. New applications for passports use form DS-11, and for minors under age 14 an additional consent form, DS-3053. You will find the necessary forms at many post offices and libraries, at the county court offices (listed below), or online at the State Bureau of Consular Affairs (www.travel.state.gov/passport/). You must appear in person to get your first passport; this includes minors. To **renew a passport**, pick up form **DS-82** at the address listed above and mail it as directed with two passport pictures, and your expired/expiring passport. Allow four to six weeks, more if you're applying in high summer season, or mention the date of your departure on the form; passports are processed on the basis of departure date. A passport is good for ten years and can be renewed within two years after expiration.

Visit the New York City Passport Agency for passport processing only if you have an appointment for a priority passport (see below). These government centers can process your application:

- **New York State Supreme Court County Offices**: New York County Clerk, Supreme Courthouse, 60 Centre St, Manhattan; Kings County Clerk, Supreme Court Building, 360 Adams St, Brooklyn; Bronx County Clerk, Supreme Courthouse, 851 Grand Concourse, The Bronx; Queens County Clerk, Supreme Courthouse, 88-11 Sutphin Blvd, Jamaica, Queens; Richmond County Clerk, 130 Stuyvesant Place, Staten Island

Many **Post Offices** have passport acceptance services; call the USPS, 800-275-8777, or go to www.passportinfo.com/Local/NY.htm (New York) and www. passportinfo.com/Local/NJ.htm (New Jersey) to locate a passport acceptance facility.

If you must leave the country in a hurry, it is possible to obtain or renew a passport in three days by calling 877-487-2778 from a touch-tone phone to make an appointment at the **New York City Passport Agency**, 376 Hudson Street, 10th floor, at West Houston Street, open 7:30 a.m. to 3:30 p.m. You will punch in your Social Security number, the date of your travel ticket, and other information, and be given a choice of three appointments. To your appointment, bring your ticket and other necessary papers and cash or check for the full fee, plus extra cash for priority handling fees, and be prepared to return for your passport. In high season (April through June, just before Christmas, Easter, and other school holidays) an applicant with an appointment made by phone is likely to need two hours to get to the head of the line.

Suppose you've got to go to Botswana on short notice, you don't even know what documents and shots you need, and you're too busy to get it together. What to do? For a fee (up to $200 for a same-day passport renewal) the knowledgeable staff at **Passport Plus**, 20 East 49th Street, 212-759-5540, www.passportplus.net, will handle it for you.

BUILDING STAFF

New Yorkers rely on the staff of their buildings in ways that are unique to the city—and they reward their staff in an equally unique manner.

Most multi-unit residences have a superintendent (the "super") who is responsible for the maintenance and day-to-day operation of the building. Some superintendents may be assisted by porters and hallmen. There are also doormen (and today, the occasional doorwoman) in many buildings, and in luxury buildings, perhaps a concierge who runs the building's wine cellar and will bring you up your bottle, not to mention in-house massage therapists.

Because many New Yorkers do not rely on their cars to accomplish their daily tasks, goods and services are delivered by businesses to the consumer's home even when they are not there, hence the importance of the building staff. Other staff duties may include hailing cabs, supplying important building information, directing repair people, door holding and—in some buildings—even mail delivery. Most of all, your staff, particularly the doorman, is the first line of security in your building, making certain that anyone who seeks entrance truly belongs there.

In addition to the generally higher rents found in staffed buildings, there is an unspoken cost associated with the extra service. It is widely expected that a building's residents tip the staff at Christmas-time for general services rendered throughout the year. (Anything beyond a general service, such as pet-walking or heavy lifting, is best attended to at the time the service is performed.) The tip is by no means mandatory but individual service has been known to decline precipitously for those tight-fisted residents. The custom varies widely from building to building both in terms of cost and how the money is dispersed. It is a good idea to find out what is customary in your building and budget for the holiday season accordingly.

CITY SAFETY

The incidence of violent crime in New York City has declined significantly in the last decade. In fact, according to a recent FBI Uniform Crime Report, New York City had the lowest overall crime rate of large cities in the US (cities with more than one million people). Despite this good news, it is still prudent to pay attention to your surroundings and be cautious, particularly for those new to an urban environment. Consider the following:

- Always remain alert to what is around you (in front and in back); if you don't pay attention to your surroundings, you make yourself a target for crime.
- Trust your instincts; they are usually right.
- Stay clear of deserted areas such as empty streets, uninhabited subway cars or platforms, and lonely automatic teller machines.
- If you must take the subway late at night, always get in the car that houses the brakeman (generally one of the middle cars). Typically, there is a black and white "zebra" sign marking the spot where the brakeman's car stops.
- Look for children playing outside or women walking on their own as signs that an area is safe.
- If you do find yourself on an ominous-looking block, avoid the sidewalk and walk directly in the street to be in view of traffic.
- If you feel you are being followed, walk into the nearest restaurant or store, or flag a cab.
- Conceal your valuables, and if you wear a diamond ring turn it around so only the band is showing. Cover watches and necklaces or put jewelry away when riding the subway.
- Hold your handbag close to you, wearing the strap across your chest, keeping the bag in front of you. Don't hang a purse on a restaurant chair or restroom hook. Men, don't put your wallet in your back pocket.
- Do not count your money in public or use big bills. Tuck your money in a safe place before leaving an ATM vestibule.
- If you're walking alone, or even as a pair, avoid crowds of teens (or any groups) congregated or hanging out on street corners. Cross the street and walk on the other side.
- Beware of operators working as a team: someone who tells you she just dropped her contact lens might well have a friend who is reaching in your handbag.
- Do not hold or open doors that are supposed to be locked in your apartment building for anyone you do not know.
- Remember: you do not owe a response to anyone who asks for one. This may seem callous but it is better to err on the side of bad manners rather than bad judgment. Go with your instincts.

The New York City Police Department publishes free brochures on safety. These booklets include safety precautions addressed to men, women, children, and the elderly—even to runners. Brochure topics also include how to safeguard your apartment, car, and small business. See the final section of this book for emergency phone numbers. Residents outside of New York City should contact their local police station for similar pamphlets and safety initiatives.

Police officers, being human, can err, and unfortunately, sometimes these are errors of judgment. If you witness or experience inappropriate behavior or actions by an officer and wish to register a complaint, you may do so by contacting the Civilian Complaint Review Board at 40 Rector Street, 2nd Floor, Monday through Friday from 8 a.m. through 6 p.m. You may also submit a complaint online, at www.nyc.gov/html/ccrb/html/complaint.html. For CCRB inquiries (and inquiries only, you can *not* file a complaint on the phone) call 212-442-8833.

If your security desires can only be satisfied by high-tech gadgetry, you may want to pay a visit to the Counter Spy Shop at 444 Madison Avenue or in the lobby of the Waldorf-Astoria.

Finally, become involved in your neighborhood. All over town, people organize block associations to monitor crime and make stronger communities by helping out and working together. To find out if a block association exists in your neighborhood, or to set one up, call **Citizen's Committee for NYC** at 212-989-0909, www.citizensnyc.org.

Contrary to popular belief, when it comes to the good of the common cause, New Yorkers have shown a remarkable ability to go above and beyond. In numerous instances, including the citywide power outage in 2003, during transit strikes, paralyzing snowstorms, and of course the tragedy of September 11, 2001, New Yorkers pull together and help each other.

I T SHOULD COME AS NO SURPRISE THAT THE INTERNATIONAL SERVICE capital is as energetic in supplying the needs of New Yorkers as it is of those the world over. Multitudinous talents and supremely innovative minds combine to provide a mind-boggling array of services, for individuals as well as for industry. Local magazines and newspapers seldom let an issue go by without feature articles about umbrella repair specialists, third-generation tapestry re-weavers, or the pair of clever Upper East Side women available to organize your closets and your life. We'll leave these summaries of the city's more *recherché* services to the press and provide instead the names of a few representative firms and organizations that supply basics such as house cleaning, mail and shipping services, auto or computer repair, as well as organizations to contact for consumer protection, or that address the concerns of the lesbian and gay communities, the needs of senior citizens, people with disabilities, and immigrant newcomers.

Note: listing in this book is merely informational and is not an endorsement or recommendation by First Books. Addresses are in Manhattan unless otherwise noted.

HOUSE CLEANING

Word of mouth is your best bet for finding a cleaning person (women have no monopoly on the profession here). Ask friends and neighbors if they know of someone with a few hours available. If this doesn't work, you might try one of the services listed below. The hourly rates typically include dusting, changing linens, mopping, vacuuming, laundry, cleaning bathrooms, and washing dishes. The same firms provide specialists to handle floor waxing, washing walls, and other heavy-duty jobs at higher fees. For more help with domestic concerns refer to the listings under **Au Pairs and Nannies** and **Babysitters** in **Childcare and Education**. The *Irish Echo*'s classifieds, published in the city and available at newsstands throughout the city, are a good place to look for house-cleaning personnel.

- **Lend-A-Hand, Inc.**, 350 5th Ave, Suite 3304, 212-614-9118, www.lahny.com; housecleaning is one of the many services provided by this agency's actors, musicians, and dancers. They also offer party services, clerical services, and childcare.
- **Maid in NY**, 200 Park Ave S, 212-777-6000, www.maidinnewyork.com; homes as well as industrial sites and business offices are serviced by some 100 employees. Times and schedules are arranged to suit the client: weekly, bi-weekly, or just once for a thorough spring cleaning. Provides online estimates. Fully insured and bonded.
- **Maids Unlimited**, Flatiron Services, 230 E 93rd St, 212-369-9100, www.flat-ironcleaning.com; founded in 1893, it's the first cleaning agency in New York. For regular service, the same person will be sent when possible. One or two days' notice required. Help is bonded. Maids use your supplies. Provides online estimates.

MAIL AND SHIPPING SERVICES

The General Post Office has sat prominently at 421 Eighth Avenue between 31st and 33rd streets since 1913. It is open 24 hours a day, seven days a week (be advised that last collection is 10 p.m., Monday through Saturday). Addresses for neighborhood post offices are listed in the information provided following each neighborhood description; the telephone number and web site are 1-800-ASK-USPS (1-800-275-8777) and www.usps.com. Post boxes rent from about $82 (including tax and $10 key deposit) for a standard size box for four months. To snag a box at a high-occupancy station line up early on the 15th of the month, when leases expire. If you need more than just a box, a mail service center, which will also forward mail and typically offer fax and copy service, may be your best bet. Such services have even been known to accept dry cleaning and flowers for their customers. The UPS Store (formerly Mail Boxes Etc.) is the most prolific chain in the city. Check the Yellow Pages under "Mail Receiving Services" for a comprehensive list. Less expensive are the neighborhood businesses that take in mail and offer no services beyond renting boxes and notifying their occupants of package arrival.

Need to send a set of golf clubs to your brother in Kansas? Then you need a shipping service. The Yellow Pages under "Delivery Service" lists a host of them, from local to national and overseas shipping services. National package delivery services include:

- **Craters & Freighters**, 800-736-3335, www.cratersandfreighters.com; for especially heavy or bulky items they claim they're the best. Locations in New York City and New Jersey.
- **FedEx, and FedEx Ground**, 800-238-5355, www.fedex.com

- **United Parcel Service (UPS)**, 800-742-5877, www.ups.com
- **US Postal Service Express Mail**, 800-222-1811, www.usps.com

JUNK MAIL

Junk mail will surely follow you to your new locale. In order to curtail this kind of unwanted mail we suggest you send a written note, including name and address, asking to be removed from the **Direct Marketing Association**'s list (Direct Marketing Association's Mail Preference Service, PO Box 282, Carmel, NY 10512). Some catalogue companies will need to be contacted directly with a purge request. For **junk e-mail**, you may also go to their web site, www.dmaconsumers.org, and request an opt-out service for your e-mail address. The service will accept three non-business e-mail addresses at a time. This should reduce the amount of e-mail you receive from national e-mail lists. Another option is to call the "opt-out" line at 888-567-8688, and request that the main credit bureaus not release your name and address to interested marketing companies. (**Curb phone solicitations** by going to the government's do not call registry, www.donotcall.gov, and registering your phone number—or call 800-382-1222, TTY 866-290-4236.)

AUTOMOBILE SERVICES AND REPAIR

There are hundreds of auto repair shops throughout the city, and many of them are competent and honest. Which ones? Alas, there is no consumer rating system for auto repair shops. Talk to friends and colleagues for their recommendations before you have a problem; you may find a gem of a repairman. If so, try to establish a good rapport—they're often just as valuable as a good doctor. Recommendation in hand, before taking your car in, it's still a good idea to check with the Better Business Bureau to see if any complaints have been filed against a repair shop. Membership in AAA (American Automobile Association), $58 for the first year, $48 thereafter, is probably the best investment you can make in your car in the city. The emergency road service alone, with free battery charge and free towing within a three-mile radius to an AAA-affiliated service station, is worth the price of admission. Their list of affiliated stations is a valuable starting point. Members also receive free maps, trip-planning services, trip interruption insurance, the service of AAA travel agents, travel discounts, and a host of products and services highlighted in their monthly magazine, *Car and Travel*. Drop in to their Manhattan branch at 1881 Broadway at 62nd Street or call 212-586-1166. In Brooklyn, AAA has an office at 2334 Ralph Avenue between avenues M and N, 718-279-7272; in Queens, 186-06 Hillside Avenue, Jamaica, 718-279-7272. They are open from Monday to Friday 8:45 a.m. to 5:30 p.m., Saturday from 9 a.m. to 5 p.m. They're also on the web at www.aaany.com. When all else fails, try calling "Car Talk," 888-CAR-TALK, NPR's popular radio show where the entertaining Click and Clack brothers (Tom and Ray) try to diagnose your car's problems and then offer advice. On their web site, www.cartalk.com, they have a useful "find a mechanic" section.

COMPUTER REPAIRS

Of course, you should always back up your files. So when the crash comes…well, you know. But that won't save you from unscrupulous computer repair shops. Stories abound, but in fact there are reliable repair shops out there—usually found by word of mouth. We list one that *New York* magazine rated highly. First, a few guidelines: if you have a problem with your computer and you are still under your manufacturer's warranty, call the company directly to see if they can help. If that doesn't work, call a repair shop and describe the problem; a good shop may be able to talk you through a diagnosis and self-repair. Before taking the computer in, ask if the shop stocks spare parts for your system, how long repairs typically take, if there is a diagnostic fee and if that fee will be applied toward any work they do to fix the computer. Be sure to get an estimate and make them understand that they are not to do any work until it has been authorized by you. If the technician seems vague or intimidating, call someone else. As with auto repair shops, be sure to check with the Better Business Bureau to see if any complaints have been filed against a particular shop before you take your computer in for repairs.

- **Tekserve**, 155 W 23rd St, 212-929-3645, www.tekserve.com, Macintosh only

CONSUMER PROTECTION—RIP-OFF RECOURSE

It goes without saying that the best defense against fraud and consumer victimization is to avoid it. You read all contracts down to the smallest print, save your receipts and canceled checks, get the name of telephone sales and service people with whom you deal, check a contractor's license number with the Department of Consumer Affairs for complaints. But you've been stung. A dry cleaner returns your blue suit, but now it's purple and he shrugs. A shop refuses to give you a refund as promised on the expensive gift that didn't suit your mother. Your landlord fails to return your security deposit when you move. After $733 in repairs to your automobile's engine, the car now vibrates wildly, and the mechanic claims innocence. Negotiations, documents in hand, fail. You're angry, and embarrassed because you've been had. *There is something you can do*:

- File a complaint with the **New York State Consumer Protection Board**, 800-NYS-1220, www.oag.state.ny.us, or the NY State Consumer Frauds and Protection Bureau, Office of the Attorney General, 120 Broadway, NYC 10271. You may want to call the bureau's complaint line, 212-416-8000, first for advice or a complaint form. Or go in to the office in person, third floor, open Monday–Friday 9:30 a.m.–4:30 p.m. Again, have all your documentation organized and in hand.

- Call the **NYC Department of Consumer Affairs**, Complaints Department, 212-487-4444, for information on filing a complaint; have all your information organized before calling, and be prepared to spend some time on the phone. Better yet, file a complaint online at www.nyc.gov.
- File suit for relief, up to $3,000, in **small claims court**. You do not need a lawyer, and some 60,000 New Yorkers use this resource annually. There are six small claims locations in the city, two of them in Manhattan, all open one evening until 10 p.m. For details, call New York City's civil information line, 212-791-6000; ask for two excellent booklets, *A Guide to Small Claims Court* and *Preparing for the Collection of a Small Claims Judgment*. Be advised that winning in small claims court is much easier than ever collecting on a judgment.
- In New Jersey, file a complaint with the **New Jersey State Office of Consumer Protection**, 124 Halsey St, Newark, NJ 07102, 973-504-6200, www.njconsumeraffairs.gov

Before doing any of the above, inform your adversary of your intentions, politely but firmly. You may force a settlement, thereby saving yourself the trouble of following through.

IMMIGRANT NEWCOMERS

Multinational New York City has been a doorway—and homestead—for immigrants since its very founding. It is probably easier here than anywhere else for transplanted citizens to find one another. According to the 2000 census, 36% of the city's populace is foreign-born. But New York is still very much an American city, and navigating its bureaucracies, legalities, and idiosyncrasies can be baffling. For advice and legal matters, your best first resource may be your embassy or consulate, many of which are listed below (check http://gonyc.about.com/od/foreignvisitorstonyc/a/foreign_consula.htm). To better understand the ins and outs of everything from American states to American business etiquette, consult the *Newcomer's Guide for Moving to and Living in the USA* by Mike Livingston, published by **First Books**. Call 503-968-6777 or visit www.firstbooks.com.

CONSULATES

There are over 20 consulates in New York City. Here are a few:
- **Consulate General of Australia**, 150 E 42nd St, 34th floor, NYC 10017, 212-351-6500, www.australianyc.org
- **Consulate General of Brazil**, 1185 Ave of the Americas, 21st floor, NYC 10036, 917-777-7777, www.brasilny.org
- **Consulate General of Canada**, 1251 Ave of the Americas, NYC 10020, 212-596-1628, http://canada-ny.org
- **Consulate General of China**, 520 12th Ave, NYC 10036, 212-244-9456, http://www.nyconsulate.prchina.org/eng

- **Consulate General of the Federal Republic of Germany**, 871 United Nations Plaza, NYC 10017, 212-610-9700, www.germany.info/newyork
- **Consulate General of France**, 934 Fifth Ave, NYC 10021, 212-606-3600, www.consulfrance-newyork.org
- **Consulate General of Great Britain**, 845 Third Ave, NYC 10022, 212-745-0200, www.britainusa.com/ny
- **Consulate General of Italy**, 690 Park Ave, NYC 10021, 212-737-9100, www.consnewyork.esteri.it
- **Consulate General of Japan**, 299 Park Ave, 18th floor, NYC 10171, 212-371-8222, www.ny.us.emb-japan.go.jp
- **Consulate General of Mexico**, 27 E 39th St, NYC 10016, 212-217-6400, www.sre.gob.mx/nuevayork
- **Consulate General of New Zealand**, 222 E 41st St, Suite 2510, NYC 10017, 212-832-4038, www.nzmissionny.org
- **Consulate General of Poland**, 233 Madison Ave, NYC 10016, 212-561-8160, www.polandconsulateny.com
- **Consulate General of Russia**, 9 E 91st St, NYC 10128, 212-682-8592, www.ruscon.com
- **Consulate General of Spain**, 150 E 58th St, NYC 10155, 212-355-4080, http://www.maec.es/subwebs/consulados/nuevayork/es/home/Paginas/Home.aspx
- **Consulate General of Taiwan**, 1 E 42nd St, 4th floor, NYC 10016, 212-486-0088, www.taiwanembassy.org/US/NYC/

IMMIGRATION AND NATURALIZATION SERVICE

US Citizenship and Immigration Services (**CIS**) for New York City is in lower Manhattan: USCIS New York City District Office, Jacob Javits Federal Building, 26 Federal Plaza, 3rd floor, NYC 10278, 800-375-5283, www.uscis.gov.

IMMIGRATION RESOURCES

- **Bureau of Immigration and Customs Enforcement**, www.ice.immigration.gov
- **Customs & Border Protection**, www.cbp.gov
- **Department of Homeland Security**, www.dhs.gov
- **General Government Questions**, 800-688-9889, www.usa.gov
- **International Center in New York**, 50 West 23rd St, 7th floor, NYC 10010, 212-255-9555, www.intlcenter.org; English conversation and American culture for immigrant newcomers
- **Social Security Administration**, 800-772-1213, www.ssa.gov
- **US Bureau of Consular Affairs**, www.travel.state.gov
- **US Department of State, Visa Services**, www.travel.state.gov/visa/visa

- **US Immigration Online: Green Cards, Visas, Government Forms,** www.uscis.gov

PUBLICATIONS

"America is too rich in contradictions for any definition of it to be possible." This quote from British economist John Gray opens the ***Newcomer's Handbook for Moving to and Living in the USA*** by Mike Livingston (First Books), and fittingly. A wealth of information in a compact volume, this handbook is an excellent reference for everything from currency to street signs to the public education system. It will help you sort through the nuances (and oddities) of American culture and behavior. Visit **www.firstbooks.com**.

MOVING PETS TO THE US

- ***The Pet Moving Handbook*** (First Books) covers domestic and international moves, via car, airplane ferry, etc. Primary focus is on cats and dogs.
- **Cosmopolitan Canine Carriers**, based in Connecticut, 800-243-9105, www.caninecarriers.com, has been shipping dogs and cats all over the world for over 25 years. Contact them with questions or concerns regarding air transportation arrangements, vaccinations, and quarantine times.

LESBIAN AND GAY CONCERNS

In a city with large and established lesbian and gay communities, there are many organizations, businesses, and publications that address their various needs and interests—too many to detail here. We mention one important umbrella organization and five other resources as starting points. All are in Manhattan.

- **The Lesbian, Gay, Bisexual and Transgender Community Services Center**, 208 W 13th St, 212-620-7310, www.gaycenter.org; is just that, and it offers numerous services seven days a week in a newly renovated, 150-year-old former schoolhouse in Greenwich Village. Besides social, cultural, and recreational offerings and events galore there are alcohol and substance abuse counseling; adoption and parenting support; a gender identity project; a variety of HIV/AIDS-related services, counseling and bereavement support; couples mediation; and public policy programs, among others. Center orientation provides newcomers to the city with "a map of New York's organized lesbian and gay community"; it offers a monthly open house known as the "Orientation Welcome Wagon" and a "Welcome Packet" for gay, lesbian, bisexual, and transgender tourists, which includes entertainment guides listing gay bars, clubs, and restaurants; fliers on cultural programs; and a monthly calendar of events. The center's web site is updated daily and hyper-linked with most New York City and national gay organizations, and contains a daily calendar of events and a bi-monthly newsletter.

- **Callen-Lorde Community Health Center**, 356 W 18th St, 212-271-7200, www.callen-lorde.org, is the largest primary health care center in the country devoted to lesbians, bisexuals, gay men, and transgenders. Patients pay on a sliding scale, according to their income.
- **Gay Women's Focus** at Beth Israel Medical Center, 10 Union Square East, Suite 2B, 212-844-8500, is a full-service internal medical practice with links to OB-GYN, psychiatric, and social work specialists.
- **Rainbow Roommates**, 124 W 60th St, 212-627-8612, www.rainbowroom-mates.com, is an apartment share referral service for the gay and lesbian community throughout the city and in New Jersey.
- **Senior Action in a Gay Environment** (**SAGE**), 305 7th Ave, 16th floor, 212-741-2247, www.sageusa.org, is a non-profit community support agency that offers workshops, discussion groups, and day trips for gay seniors, many of them for free. With an annual membership one receives a monthly newsletter, information on lectures, day trips, and excursions, plus extensive social services for GLBT seniors.

RESOURCES AND SERVICES FOR PEOPLE WITH DISABILITIES

Living in New York City with a disability has never been easy, but after passage of the federal Americans with Disabilities Act (ADA) in 1990 it became easier as the city began to address the needs of the disabled more seriously. Increasingly, street curbs and public buildings were modified to become wheelchair accessible. Following are some New York services, organizations, and resources that make life safer, easier, and more pleasant for people with disabilities. (In New Jersey, call 888-285-3036 or go to the **New Jersey Department of Human Services**, Disabilities Services section: www.state.nj.us/humanservices/disable/index.html.)

GETTING AROUND

- **Buses**: all buses operated by the Metropolitan Transit Authority (MTA) are wheelchair-accessible, with lifts at the rear door. If you have a qualifying disability or are 65 years of age or older, you are eligible for reduced fare travel on MTA buses and subways. To get the reduced fare card and for more information, call 718-243-4999, TTY 718-596-8273, or go to www.mta.info.
- **Subway**: there are *Accessible Transfer Points* within the New York City subway; a pamphlet of the MTA lists all the subway stations and transfer points in the system which are wheelchair-accessible by elevator, with a map of the system. Reduced fare as described above also applies to the city's subway system and to the Long Island and Metro-North Railroads, except at peak morning hours. The pamphlet, also in large type and on audiotape, is available from customer assistance, MTA NYC Transit, 370 Jay Street, 8th floor, Brooklyn 11201, or by calling the MTA customer service line, 718-330-3322.

- **CITY ACCESS** is a city program that contracts with private carriers to provide rides for customers who are unable to use city bus or subway service for some or all of their trips. For more information, go to www.nyc.gov.
- **Parking Permits for People with Disabilities** (**PPPD**): the city Department of Transportation issues two types of permits for citizens with disabilities: the New York State permit, which allows the driver to park in spaces marked by the International Symbol of Access, which in the city are all off-street in parking lots; and the NYC permit, which allows the driver to park on city streets in all "no parking" and "restricted parking" zones. For more information and to request an application for either or both permits write: Parking Permits for People with Disabilities (PPPD), NYC Department of Transportation, 28-11 Queens Plaza North, 8th floor, Long Island City, NY 11101-4008, or call 718-433-3100; TTY 718-433-3111.

COMMUNICATION

The **Verizon Communications Center for People with Disabilities** offers information, services, and a variety of adaptive communications equipment necessary or useful to people with various disabilities. Some of these devices, such as enlarged number rings, are free; others, such as Weak Speech Handsets, may be rented, leased, or purchased. The Teletypewriter Device for the Deaf, alternately referred to as TTY or TDD and available at cost through Verizon, sends typed words over the phone lines to the New York Relay Center, from which special operators relay conversations verbally 24 hours a day. The service is confidential and free of charge, except for the cost of the call. Hearing callers to TTY users reverse the process, calling a number (below) from which a special relay operator types the message to the TTY recipient, etc.

- **Verizon Communication Center for People with Disabilities**, 890-0550 from any NYC area code for Voice and TTY calls. Include the area code when dialing.
- **New York Relay Center**, TTY 800-662-1220; others 800-421-1220.

OTHER RESOURCES

- **Andrew Heiskell Library for the Blind and Physically Handicapped**, 40 W 20th St, 212-206-5400, TTY 212-206-5458, talkingbooks.nypl.org; wheelchair accessible, offers books in Braille and recorded books, an extensive collection of large-print books, print and non-print materials on disabilities. Also here, a collection of community information services on resources for people with disabilities, as well as recreational, cultural, and service-oriented programming for and about people with disabilities. Materials are for use on site or by postage-free mail to those who are homebound, 212-621-0564, TTY 212-621-0553.

- **Associated Blind**, 135 W 23rd St, (212) 620-9109, operates 205 apartments for the blind and wheelchair bound at this address, but there is a long waiting list. Non-resident blind also have access to social workers, recreation, and the fitness center here.
- **Con Edison Concern Program** for the hearing-impaired and sight-impaired, 800-872-8846, TTY 800-642-2308, www.conedison.com.
- *Exceptional Parent Magazine*, 800-372-7368, www.eparent.com, is a guide for parents of children and young adults with disabilities or health problems. Also publishes an annual resource guide available in bookstores or through the magazine.
- **Goodwill Industries International**, 4-21 27th Ave, Astoria, Queens, 718-728-5400, www.goodwill.org, offers a host of job training and computer classes for people with physical and mental disabilities.
- **Hospital Audiences Inc**. (**HAI**), 548 Broadway, 3rd floor, 212-575-7676, www.hospitalaudiences.org/, provides access to the arts for New Yorkers with disabilities. They also provide the indispensable *Access for All: A Guide to New York City Cultural Institutions for People with Disabilities*, which lists 300 cultural venues accessible to the handicapped, including major galleries and historical monuments; available online at no charge.
- **International Center for the Disabled** (**ICD**), 340 E 24th St, 212-585-6000, TTY 212-585-6060, www.icdnyc.org, provides primary medical care, vocational evaluation, job training and placement for learning and physically disabled.
- **League for the Hard of Hearing**, 50 Broadway, 6th floor, 917-305-7700, www.lhh.com, provides a range of services including hearing rehabilitation. Call for their resource manual or get information on their programs and services from their web site.
- **Learning Disabilities Helpline**, 212-645-6730, operated by the Learning Disabilities Association of New York, 27 W 20th St, Suite 303, provides information and referrals in English and Spanish from their database of resources for the learning disabled.
- **The Lighthouse, Inc.**, 111 E 59th St, 212-821-9200 or 800-829-0500, www.lighthouse.org, provides vision rehabilitation and other services to the visually impaired. Services include readers, mobility training, computer training, career services, a child development center, and adaptive skills classes.
- **Mayor's Office for People with Disabilities**, 100 Gold St, 2nd floor, 212-788-2830, TTY 212-788-2838, www.nyc.gov/html/mopd; for information and referrals.
- **Metropolitan Museum of Art**, 1000 Fifth Ave at 81st St, 212-535-7710, TTY 212-570-3828, www.metmuseum.org, is wheelchair accessible and has programs with sign language interpretation for the hearing impaired; guides by appointment only for the visually impaired; tours and programs for the developmentally disabled.

- **National Center for Learning Disabilities**, 381 Park Ave S, Suite 1401, 212-545-7510, www.ncld.org; provides information and referrals concerning learning disabilities in children and adults at 888-575-7373, and on their web site, which has links to related organizations and resources, publications, and recent events. Their concerns include dyslexia and adult literacy.
- *Able*, a monthly newspaper "Positively For, By and About the Disabled," with news, commentary, a calendar of events, and ads of interest to people with disabilities. Write P.O. Box 395, Old Bethpage, NY 11804, or call 516-939-2253, 718-792-3533 or 201-836-5785. Visit www.ablenews.com.
- **New York Public Library Branches** (see also Andrew Heiskell Library above). Most Manhattan, Bronx, Queens, and Staten Island libraries are wheelchair accessible as are more than a dozen Brooklyn libraries with more upgrading under way. Call the local branch first and ask, or go to www.nypl.org. Included on the list are the Library for the Performing Arts, 40 Lincoln Center Plaza at 65th St, 212-870-1630; Mid-Manhattan Library, 455 Fifth Ave at 40th St, 212-340-0833; Science, Industry, and Business Library, 188 Madison Ave at 34th St, 212-592-7000; the Fordham Library Center, 310 E Kingsbridge Rd, The Bronx, 718-579-4244; and St. George Library Center, 5 Central Ave, St. George, SI, 718-442-8560, among others. Project ACCESS, by appointment at the Mid-Manhattan, St. George, and Fordham branches, uses Kurzweil Personal Readers to give sight-impaired readers access to the full range of the library services and materials. Other helpful technology, such as Braille writers, is available here and at some other branches. For information about these and other services call 212-340-0843, TTY 212-340-0931.
- **New York Society for the Deaf**, available through F.E.G.S., 315 Hudson St, 212-366-0066, www.fegs.org/deaf; provides multiple services for the deaf.
- **Resources for Children With Special Needs**, 116 E 16th St, 212-677-4650, www.resourcesnyc.org
- **Rusk Institute of Rehabilitation Medicine's** driver training program, 400 E 34th St, Room RR312, 212-263-6028; offers technicians to evaluate the particular needs of prospective drivers with physical handicaps, adapting each car with special devices, and train the driver to operate the adapted car.
- **Technology Resource Center**, operated by United Cerebral Palsy of New York City, 122 E 23rd St, www.ucpnyc.org 212-979-9700. Come here to the demonstration center to view, learn about, and try a range of adaptive products and get information about others through a resource specialist and catalogues. Products range from adapted toys to augmentative communication devices, computers, home products, and accessibility modifications.
- **TAP, Theater Access Project of the Theatre Development Fund**, 1501 Broadway, 21st floor, 212-221-1103, TTY 212-719-4537, www.tdf.org, offers signed performances of selected shows and discounted tickets for people with physical disabilities.

- **Visions Services for the Blind and Visually Impaired**, 500 Greenwich St, 3rd floor, 212-625-1616, www.visionsvcb.org; offers free and low-cost rehabilitation and social services to the blind and multi-handicapped, including those who are non-English speaking. Self-help audio guides at cost teach life skills, and there are peer support groups and recreation year-round at Vacation Camp for the Blind in Rockland County, transportation provided.
- **Walter Reade Theater**, 70 Lincoln Center Plaza at 67th St, 212-875-5600, www.filmlinc.com, shows first-run features with open captions for the deaf once a month. Call 212-876-5610 after 2 p.m. for details.

RESOURCES AND SERVICES FOR SENIORS

If you are or are soon to be a senior and living in New York City get yourself a copy of *Take Charge! A Complete Guide to Senior Living in New York City* by John Vinton (New York University Press), a comprehensive reference to services, resources, and some practical advice you didn't know you'd need. It includes guidance on avoiding rip-offs in home repair and other areas in which seniors are targeted, where to get help with financial/estate planning, resources for long-term care, end-of-life concerns such as hospice, assisted death, and burial. Another good resource for young seniors is *Retire in New York City—Even If You're Not Rich* by Janet Hays (Bonus Books).

The prime source of services and assistance for seniors here is the city's **Department for the Aging** (**DFTA**), whose web site, www.nyc.gov/aging, is useful in discovering and accessing these services. Call 311 for information.

The Department for the Aging also operates 335 senior centers throughout the boroughs, where meals are served, cultural trips originate, and outreach gives access to other services. The department offers guidance on government benefits and referral to community services; provides transportation for health care, social services and necessities; arranges home care for the qualified; helps victims of elder abuse; offers job training for the employable unemployed; subsidizes part-time employment; offers computer training and customer service skills and placement in jobs in private industry; arranges legal assistance to those in need; and more.

Some useful numbers:

- **Alzheimer's and Long Term Care Services**, 212-442-3086, offers counseling and referrals for families of seniors with Alzheimer's disease.
- **Elder Pharmaceutical Insurance Coverage** (**EPIC**), 800-332-3742, www.health.state.ny.us/health_care/epic, offers savings on the cost of drugs for qualified individuals.
- **Health insurance information and counseling**, www.ins.state.ny.us
- **Housing**, for the department's *Alternatives in Senior Housing: A Comprehensive Guide for New York City*, call 212-442-1384. In recent years complexes for senior

"assisted living" at market prices have sprung up throughout the city and in the greater metropolitan area; see ads in the *New York Times*.

- **Legal assistance**: Call the Manhattan office at 212-426-3000 and ask for information regarding Queens and The Bronx; in Brooklyn, call 718-645-3111; Staten Island, 718-273-6677.
- **Reduced fare** for seniors: people with disabilities and those 65 and older can purchase a MetroCard at half-price. Write MTA, Reduced Fare, P.O. Box 023158, Brooklyn 11202-0064, or call the reduced fare line at 718-243-4999, TTY 718-596-8273. You may also visit the office at 3 Stone Street, NYC.
- **Senior Citizen Rent Increase Exemption** (**SCRIE**) is for those over 62 whose income falls below $20,000; this is a city subsidy. Call 311 for more information or visit www.nyc.gov.
- **State School Tax Relief** (**STAR**) offers reduced school property taxes for homeowners (condos and co-ops included) on limited incomes. Write STAR Program, Office of Real Property Services, 16 Sheridan Ave, Albany, NY 12210, or call 518-474-2982 (www.orps.state.ny.us/star).

Under state law **new rental housing** in the city is frequently classified **80/20**, which means that 20% of the apartments are reserved for seniors at below-market rents. Applicants are chosen by lottery, and the waiting list is long. Get on the list before you need the apartment. To find out if you are eligible and to get on line, call the **New York State Housing Finance Agency** (**HFA**), 212-688-4000.

The city abounds in culture at a discount for seniors. Museums, movie theaters, and some theaters discount admission for seniors, and state parks and historic sites are free to seniors who present a photo ID that includes date of birth.

Exercise programs for seniors, free or at low cost, are widely available. Exercise classes, stress management, and walking clubs are located in many of the senior centers. Call **Health Promotion Services** (**HPS**), 212-442-0954, to find out more. The Parks and Recreation Department operates 25 recreation centers in the city (membership, $10 annually for seniors, $50–75 for adults), some of which offer senior aerobics and other classes. The Parks Department also sponsors concerts in the parks and other activities. For all parks information call the citywide information line 311 or visit www.nycparks.org. And, finally, there are exercise programs for seniors at many YMCAs and YMHAs (see **Health Clubs, YMCAs, YWCAs, and YMHAs** in the **Sports and Recreation** chapter).

Access to college courses on a "space available" basis is offered to seniors at a discount by most of the major universities and colleges in the city. To name some:

- **Brooklyn College**, "Institute for Retired Professionals and Executives," 718-951-5647

- **City University of New York**, "Quest" Program, 212-925-6625, www.cuny.edu, offering free course auditing to those 60 and older in the four-year colleges, enrollment courses (for credit) in the community colleges.
- **College of Staten Island**, "Options for Older Adults," 718-982-2182, www.csi. cuny.edu
- **Columbia University**, "Life Long Learners," 212-854-2820, www.columbia. edu
- **Fordham University**, "College at 60," 212-636-6374, www.fordham.edu
- **New School**, "Institute for Retired Professionals," 212-229-5682, www.new school.edu
- **NYU School of Continuing Education**, 212-998-7080, www.nyu.edu
- **Pace University**, "Adult Resource Center," 212-346-1288, www.pace.edu
- **Queens College**, "Center for Unlimited Enrichment," 718-997-3635, www. qc.edu
- **St. John's University**, Queens, 718-990-6161, www.stjohns.edu

A host of volunteer opportunities are available to seniors (see **Getting Involved** chapter) and some of the resources detailed above (**Resources and Services for People with Disabilities**) are valuable for seniors as well. A few other resources are worth noting:

- **Alzheimer's Association**, 1-800-272-3900, www.alz.org; useful for those who are diagnosed with the disease and for their families.
- **Con Edison**, 800-872-8846, in their "Concern" program for seniors age 62 and older, provides a newsletter and advice on bill payments, financial assistance, a Home Energy Assistance Program (HEAP), and turn-off protection for seniors who are blind or disabled.
- **New York Foundation for Senior Citizens**, www.nyfsc.org, 212-962-7559, offers a free home safety audit to homeowners (condos and co-ops included) 60 and older. They also have a home repair program, providing minor electrical, plumbing, masonry, and carpentry repairs.
- **SAGE, Senior Action in a Gay Environment**, is a non-profit community support agency described above under **Lesbian and Gay Concerns**, 212-741-2247, www.sageusa.org.

R AISING CHILDREN IN NEW YORK CITY, LONG FAMOUS FOR NOT BEING child-friendly, has become much more common. Streets are crowded with strollers and the now clean and (relatively) safe parks are crowded with families and nannies. It is of course still a challenge to raise children here. But it is also richly rewarding, for child and parent alike. In fact, it isn't so much difficult as it is just different here in the Big Apple. This chapter attempts to make it a little easier by describing the available options in childcare, nursery schools, primary and high schools—public, private, and parochial—with information to help parents choose between them. We begin with babysitters and infant care and wind up with high schools, followed by a brief look at some of the opportunities for higher education in the city. For a more in-depth look at raising kids in the city, you may want to read *The Grownups' Guide to Living with Kids in Manhattan* by Diane Chernoff-Rosen.

Please note: listing in this book is merely informational and is *not* an endorsement or a recommendation. Always be careful when entrusting your child with strangers. Addresses given are in Manhattan unless otherwise indicated.

CHILDCARE

Quality daycare, now typically called childcare, can be hard to find and is usually more expensive in New York than anywhere else in the country, thanks to the tremendous cost of real estate and the need for stringent standards governing the operation of daycare centers. Asked what is required to open a daycare center here, Frances Alston, former program director of the not-for-profit Day Care Council, says, "First thing is, rob a bank. You can't start a daycare center in New York for less than a quarter million dollars." According to the National Association of Childcare Resources (www.naccrra.org) in 2004, daycare and preschool costs in New York City averaged over $9300 annually, the most expensive relative to income in any American city.

High prices aside, there are many options, and not all are with such high price tags; some take into consideration your financial situation and childcare needs. Non-profit agencies, which act as go-betweens for parents and daycare providers, are proliferating. We list some below under **Information Sources**. Your employer may have daycare information and some even offer on-premises facilities.

Also below, you'll find thumbnail descriptions of the kinds of preschool care (and education) available in New York City. Arranged chronologically by ages covered—from birth through six years—these categories are followed by the names of organizations that provide specific daycare recommendations.

New York State establishes the eligibility requirements for publicly funded daycare, be it family daycare in a private home or group care at a center. To be eligible, a family must meet established maximum income requirements. Almost all those entitled to assistance still pay something; currently fees range from a low of $1 per week, per child, up to $99 per week.

The US Department of Education provides a useful source of parenting information covering such topics as children's television viewing habits, sleep problems, childcare, and behavioral issues, with a library of articles and book abstracts and links to special interest organizations; visit www.ed.gov, or call 800-USA-LEARN. KinderStart's web site at www.kinderstart.com has a handy "childcare locator," which can help you find childcare in your neighborhood. For a daycare safety-hazard checklist and safety recalls, you can call the Consumer Product Safety Commission, 800-638-2772 or go to www.cpsc.gov. Available free in school lobbies, pediatricians' offices, and laundromats, a variety of monthly parent magazines, the most ubiquitous of which is *Big Apple Parent* (as well as *Queens Parent* and *Westchester Parent*), offer useful advice and information on everything from nutrition to single parenting, daycare, schools, and child health and recreation. *BigApple's* web site, www.parentsknow.com, has links to current and past articles, an extensive monthly calendar of events for parents and children, and a bulletin board worth checking for babysitters, nannies, playgroups, Spanish classes for children…the list goes on. Another useful site is www.nymetroparents.com.

AU PAIRS AND NANNIES

When it comes to sitters, New York's no different than the suburbs. Neighborhoods are filled with reliable teenagers looking for jobs. But it takes time to meet them. As with many personal services, the best sources for good babysitters or nannies are recommendations from friends, relatives, or colleagues. You can also stop by a crowded playground and talk to the many nannies that you'll find watching the neighborhood children. Naturally, before hiring anyone to watch your children, you should carefully screen applicants and check all references. In case networking fails, we've listed a number of alternatives. Some of the agencies also provide full-time, sleep-in or day only help.

Au pairs are young women (between 18 and 25), usually European, who provide a year of in-home childcare and light housekeeping in exchange for airfare, room and board, and a small stipend ($110 to $150 per week). Less expensive than nannies, they are also less experienced, may be less mature, and are gone in a year. The program is certainly valuable for the cultural exchange it offers the host family and the au pair. The US Information Agency oversees and approves the organizations that place au pairs. Either of the national agencies listed below will connect you with a local coordinator who will match up your family with a suitable au pair:

• **Au Pair in America**, 800-928-7247, www.aupairinamerica.com
• **Au Pair USA**, 800-AU-PAIRS, www.aupairusa.org

Good fortune is having a friend who passes on to you her excellent **nanny**, her children having outgrown the need, just when you need one. Failing that, there are want ads, the internet, and nanny agencies to fall back on. An invaluable source of full- and part-time nannies, both live-in and out, as well as house-cleaning personnel, is the classified ad section in the *Irish Echo*, published in the city and available at newsstands throughout the city. Those seeking positions are not necessarily Irish, and some of the ads under "situations wanted" are placed by the satisfied employers of nannies whose services they no longer need. On the internet, www.4nannies.com carries classified nanny listings allowing you to avoid agency fees, which can run $800 to $3,000. You simply pay the application fee. The site has links to firms that do background checks and some that provide nanny tax advice and/or service. According to press reports, New York City area nannies make about $660 a week with a range of $250–$1000. Live-outs work, on average, 48 hours a week, and make $777 with a salary range of $500–$1600. There are, of course, huge variations.

An agency, on the other hand, will have checked the nanny's background, perhaps by detective, her Social Security record, driving record, credit record, and so far as possible, any chance of criminal record. Note that there are no national criminal records available to investigators. But the agency will also have interviewed the nanny, in person or by phone, and will have checked her references. The agency can inform you about necessary nanny tax procedures and insurance and should provide a detailed contract. The **International Nanny Association** maintains a useful web site, www.nanny.org, which provides information about nanny agencies and the nanny selection process. Another site, which is advertiser supported, www.nannynetwork.com, contains a database of nanny placement agencies and referral services, nanny insurance services, and background verification services as well as a library of articles.

However you find your nanny, be sure to check at least two of the prospective nanny's references, questioning them carefully, and repeatedly, if necessary. You will also want to interview the nanny in your home if possible in order to ensure a good fit.

NANNY AGENCIES

- **Best Domestic**, a national agency at 10 E 39th St, #1108, 212-683-3060, www.bestdomestic.com, handles nannies, live-in or -out, as well as housekeepers and other domestic help. Weekly wage for a nanny runs $450 to $600, with a two-month guarantee, and an agency fee of 12% of one year's salary, paid one week after the nanny starts work.
- **Fox Agency**, 30 E 60th St, 212-753-2686, providing baby nurses and nannies since 1936. Rates are hourly, daily, or weekly. Nannies, screened by the agency, run $400 and up weekly, higher for living in (the rate may or may not include the legally mandated Social Security taxes and unemployment insurance).
- **Irish Agency**, 10 E 39th St, 212-IRELAND (473-5263), and PO Box 205, Old Greenwich, CT, provides full-time nannies throughout the metropolitan area, living in or out, for between $600 and $800 per week, with an agency fee of five weeks' salary. As their nannies, not necessarily Irish, have been with them for some time, they do not do a background check unless it is requested; however, they do check references.
- **NY Nanny Center, Inc.**, 250 W 57th St, New York, NY 10107, 212-265-3354, www.nynanny.com, has both live-in and -out nannies in the tri-state area. The nannies are evaluated by the director, a former social worker. Nannies in this program attend a monthly support meeting. Weekly wages start at $500, with an agency fee of four weeks' salary starting at $2,000 and a 60-day guarantee.
- **Pavillion Agency, Inc.**, 15 E 40th St, 212-889-6609, www.pavillionagency.com, one of the larger companies, specializes in nannies (as well as butlers, domestics and chauffeurs) who negotiate their rates depending on the needs of their clients. Currently nannies, living in or out, cost $500 and up weekly, plus Social Security taxes and unemployment insurance. The agency fee is 15% of the annual salary. Pavilion includes a 30-day trial period, during which clients do not pay, and performs both background and motor vehicle checks (where appropriate).

BABYSITTERS

AGENCIES

Most babysitting is via word of mouth; short of that, try:
- **Baby Sitters' Guild**, 60 E 42nd St, 212-682-0227, www.babysittersguild.com; hourly fee for one child starts at $25 plus transportation costs ($4.50 before midnight, $10 if leaving after), with higher rates for more children. With

enough advance notice, a sitter with a nursing background is provided for children under one year. There is a four-hour minimum plus travel pay, which varies depending on time of day. The guild can provide a babysitter fluent in one of 16 languages for an additional fee. All fees include the agency's commission. Call between 9 a.m. and 9 p.m. seven days a week. While requests made the same day can usually be filled, it is better to call a day prior. The guild was established in 1940.

- **Pinch Sitters**, www.nypinchsitters.com, 799 Broadway, 212-260-6005; babysitters, on short notice if necessary, starting at $20 per hour, plus transportation at night, four-hour minimum. There is a transportation fee, depending on the hour. Call Monday–Friday, 8 a.m.–5 p.m.. Hours change seasonally.

NON-PROFIT

- **Parents League**, 115 E 82nd St, 212-737-7385, www.parentsleague.org; the league's babysitting service is just one of several benefits included in the $125 annual membership fee. Sitters are students, ages 13 to 18, who attend league member schools or who are the children of members. Riffle through the sitter files, arranged by neighborhood, in the league's office between 9 a.m. and 4 p.m., Monday–Wednesday, 9 a.m. to 7 p.m. on Thursday, and until noon on Friday. The league also provides plenty of information on city schools; see **Nursery Schools** below.

SCHOOLS

- **Barnard College Babysitting Service**, 49 Claremont Ave, 212-854-2035, www.eclipse.barnard.columbia.edu/~bbsitter/; to preregister, call in your name, address, phone number and name of your pediatrician. Once you are in their file, call Monday or Friday, 10 a.m. to 4 p.m., or Tuesday through Thursday from 10 a.m. to 3 p.m., two days in advance of your needs. A student will call you back. Rates start at around $10 per hour but most parents pay more in this competitive market. There is also a $20 annual fee.

FAMILY DAYCARE

More and more middle-class parents are electing family care for their toddlers. Here in New York City the Health Department and/or other agencies involved in the field certify and supervise individuals caring for infants and toddlers in their apartments. These "providers," often mothers of young children drawn to childcare as a means of remaining at home with their own youngsters, are allowed to oversee up to six children—no more than two of whom can be infants—in their dwelling at one time. Typically, parents who do not qualify for assistance pay between $40 and $50 per child for a six- to eight-hour day, approximately 25% less than the more traditional daycare centers. To obtain a list of licensed daycare facilities in New York City, write to NYC Department of Health, Bureau of Daycare, 2 Lafayette Street, 22nd floor, New York, NY 10048, or call 212-676-2444. The city site, www.nyc.gov, has a link to the bureau if you type in "day care." The bureau also has a complaint hotline at 311.

GROUP DAYCARE CENTERS

These city-licensed facilities, be they in the private or public sector, offer educational as well as care-taking programs for groups of children primarily, but not exclusively, between the ages of two and six years for an extended (beyond normal nursery school hours) or a full eight-hour day.

- **Publicly funded daycare centers** are usually found in, or contiguous to, neighborhoods with the greatest economic need. Even with an income above the maximum allowed by the state, parents proving "social" need—those working full-time qualify—can apply to publicly funded daycare centers, if they are prepared to pay the full cost for their child's care. Depending on the facility, full-time care now runs approximately $13,000 a year for an infant and $10,000 a year for a four-year-old (or about three times the national average).
- **Private centers** tend to be either nursery schools, which have added full-day care to the regular school curriculum, or centers established to supply childcare, which also offer education. Private daycare centers in New York City can run up to $30,000 a year, depending on facilities and educational component.

Contact the city's **Agency for Child Development** through the city information line, 311, during business hours or the **Department of Health, Bureau of Day Care**, 212-676-2444, for a list of publicly funded daycare centers. Ads for private centers and for the occasional playgroup will be found in parent magazines such as *Big Apple Parent*, which are distributed free in school lobbies, as well as various user groups on the web like www.meetup.com, www.nyc.babyzone.com, and www.nyc.parentzone.com.

INFANT CARE

Formal programs for the two-month-old to two-year-old set are almost all publicly funded and appended to daycare centers. Call the New York City Health Department's Bureau of Day Care, 212-676-2444, for the names of city-licensed facilities. Infants can also be placed in family daycare homes; costs are around $8,000 a year full-time.

PLAY GROUPS

Neighborhood parents often band together informally, usually in cooperative fashion, to care for a small group of preschoolers for a half-day or so, one, two or three times a week. Do some networking, a little research, and use your best judgment about such existing groups, or start your own. Sites like www.meetup.com, www.nyc.babyzone.com, and www.nyc.parentzone.com, are just one place to start.

INFORMATION SOURCES

Who Knew Raising Kids in New York Could Be This Easy by Heidi Arthur (St. Martin's Press) covers everything from sneakers to strollers, playgrounds to preschools, and all that falls in between. Several non-profit organizations as well as the Agency for Child Development, jointly sponsored by the city, state and federal governments, provide information about local facilities. To determine the most suitable daycare solution for your family's needs, consult these sources while pursuing the other leads suggested below.

- **Agency for Child Development**, 30 Main St, Brooklyn; dial 311 for preschool information and referrals from the ACD's Vacancy Information Service. Their staff provides names and addresses of private as well as publicly funded and Head Start childcare facilities located in the five boroughs. This information is supplied to ACD by the Department of Health's Bureau of Day Care, 212-676-2444, the group charged with licensing preschool facilities. Their "Directory of Day Care Services in New York City" is available by mail free of charge.
- **Day Care Council of New York, Inc.**, 12 W 21st St, 212-206-7818, www.dc-cnyinc.org, has 50 years' experience as a non-profit providing free information, counseling, and referrals on all types of childcare, including babysitters, nannies, and daycare throughout the five boroughs.
- **The New York Public Library's Early Childhood Resource Center at Mid-Manhattan Library**, 455 Fifth Ave (at 40th St), (212) 340-0833, www.nypl.org, devotes a section to resource materials for parents and caregivers, along with a playroom for kids, open Tuesday–Saturday afternoons.
- **The Parents League of New York**, 115 E 82nd St, 212-737-7385, www.parentsleague.org, provides parenting help, support, babysitting, after-school activities, tutors, and special workshops and programs for a $125 annual membership fee.

OTHER LEADS

Check out some of the following resources for referrals in your particular neighborhood: **churches** and **temples**, large and small; old-fashioned, wall-mounted **bulletin boards**, most often found in the larger supermarkets; **private schools**, ask the admissions director for the names of feeder schools, daycare centers, or playgroups; **pediatricians**; **hospitals**, talk with the administrative officer in charge of residents and interns; and, last but perhaps most accessible and knowledgeable of all, **playgrounds** and **neighborhood parents**.

SCHOOLS

NURSERY SCHOOLS

It is at this point, typically, that parental anxiety sets in. And it needn't. In Manhattan alone there are more than 175 privately run preschool programs, generally geared to three-, four-, and five-year-olds, often including toddlers' groups and sometimes all-day care as well. They vary widely in educational philosophy and style, and admission to none of them is essential to a child's later success at Harvard—although some cost almost as much. *The Manhattan Directory of Private Nursery Schools* by Victoria Goldman and Catherine Hausman (SoHo Press) is a detailed listing of more than 150 nursery and all-day programs plus other useful information. It's a good place to start. Meanwhile, talk with mothers in the parks you frequent and with parents of children in neighborhood nursery schools. The search process typically begins just after Labor Day preceding application, and many schools will have open houses; this is also the time to request information from the schools you might wish to consider. And finally, in helping you decide what might be the best school for your child (and for you), the two sources below should be helpful:

- **The Independent Schools Admissions Association of Greater New York** (ISAAGNY, www.isaagny.org), 212-737-738, has a searchable database of more than 120 private member schools, from preschool through high school. Nursery schools and toddler groups, as well as numerous elementary and secondary schools, along with preschool groups, are listed.
- **Parents League of New York, Inc.**, 115 E 82nd St, www.parentsleague.org, 212-737-7385; with 106 member schools, mainly in Manhattan, the Parents League is an excellent source of private school information. One counseling session with a specialist from their School Advisory Service—for example, their expert on toddlers' groups and nursery schools—is well worth the league's annual $125 membership fee. A panoply of other child-related services, not the least of which is their reliable Baby Sitter-Young Helper listing, a great boon to any newcomer with kids, also comes with league membership, as does their "Toddler Activities Directory."

GRADE SCHOOLS

Here, decision-making can become more difficult because there are so many options. To begin with, there is the choice among public, private, and parochial schools. For some it is a choice easily made; they know they want one or the other, or they can't afford private school. A word to the undecided: know that there are some excellent public schools in the city, just as there are some dreadful ones.

Those opting for a **private school** will find the resources above under **Nursery Schools** helpful. The *Manhattan Family Guide to Private Schools* by Victoria Goldman and Catherine Hausman (SoHo Press) offers an independent evaluation of the specific schools; however the focus is distinctly uptown, giving scant attention to some excellent downtown schools. They do provide useful information and advice on navigating the admissions process. When trying to determine which school is right for your child—public or private—it is possible to do a lot of research on your own. For starters, you can go to each school's web site, which will offer quite a bit of preliminary information. Ask parents whose children attend area schools. Contact schools directly and arrange a time to visit, and be sure to ask the administrators and staff about school philosophy, structure, and performance indicators. Read the school literature carefully. Examine the physical facility. Observe the relationships between children, staff, and administration. Consider the program, in theory and in practice. Finally, what is your gut reaction? Remember, you and your child may spend the next eight to twelve years here, and no decision is irrevocable. Just hard. In the case of private schools, school advisors are available, for a fee.

Catholic **parochial schools**, which cost considerably less than many of the city's private schools, have found favor in recent years with non-Catholics as well as Catholics as an attractive alternative to public schools. The Archdiocese of New York, www.ny-archdiocese.org, 212-371-1000, operates 144 elementary and 39 high schools in Manhattan, The Bronx, and Staten Island. The Roman Catholic Diocese of Brooklyn and Queens operates 156 elementary schools and 22 high schools. Contact the Superintendent's office (718-399-5900, www.dioceseofbrooklyn.org) for more information. There is no source of comparative evaluation of the parochial schools, which are independently run, so interested parents are left to make their own evaluation on a school-by-school basis.

Parents considering **public school** should begin by contacting the community school board in their district (see **Neighborhoods**) for a list of schools and to find out in which school zone they reside. Many school boards have brochures from which it is possible to get a sense both of the character of the district and its schools. When visiting schools, try to get a grasp of teacher-student interaction, school safety, PTA involvement, class size, and the overall feel of the school. Apparently, some Manhattan parents even hide out in the bathroom to eavesdrop on middle-schoolers' conversations and get the real scoop on goings-on at the school. You likely needn't go this far. But do ask questions.

It is often possible to send a child to a school outside of his/her zone, space permitting, and if the process is begun early enough. One reason to do this is if your workplace is in a different district; inquire with that district about the required variance procedure.

In recent years several grade groupings have evolved among the city's schools, making choice more complicated. And within these groupings are schools with varying focus. The most common configurations below the high school level are:

- **Early childhood schools**, pre-kindergarten to second or third grade, popular for their focus on the needs of young children.
- **Elementary schools**, K–fifth or –sixth grade, are the most common configurations. Many districts are now shifting sixth grade to middle schools to avoid crowding.
- **Grammar schools**, K–8, are very rare but can serve as an alternative to middle school.
- **Middle schools or intermediate schools**, containing sixth through eighth grades or, sometimes, seventh and eighth. Some of these are theme schools, focusing on a particular subject area, such as the performing arts or technology; some require entry exams. These are the most common schools following K–5 and have essentially replaced the junior high school. Middle school is often where crowding, social issues, and transportation issues (children taking buses and even subways to get to school) begin. It is, therefore, a time when some families head for the boroughs or the suburbs, or opt for private schooling for their kids. This is not to say there aren't good public middle schools. It just takes perseverance to find the right one.

For further guidance and encouragement in choosing public schools for your child, you can turn to three books from SoHo Press written by Clara Hemphill, a researcher at the Public Education Association. In *New York City's Best Public Elementary Schools: A Parents' Guide* (updated in 2005), she profiles the top 200 elementary schools in the city. In *New York City's Best Public Middle Schools: A Parents' Guide* (updated in 2008), and *New York City's Best Public High Schools: A Parents' Guide* (updated in 2003), she takes a similar look at middle and high schools, providing excellent descriptions and ratings of schools in each district of the city. You can also find much of this information on the web site of Advocates for Children (www.advocatesforchildren.org), which includes digests on more than 50 schools and a complete list of programs for gifted children and their admissions criteria. The Chancellor's office now grades all New York public schools and you can get the latest ratings at his website, http://schools.nyc.gov.

HIGH SCHOOLS

Decisions at this level, however fraught with anxiety, are made somewhat easier by the guidance procedures at your child's current school, as well as by the fact that your about-to-be-a-high-schooler will participate in the decision. Again, public or private? Information sources for the private schools are as noted above.

Admission to many of the public high schools is citywide, a trend that is increasing as theme schools proliferate at this level. Parents and students often find themselves in a mad scramble for entry into the "best school." Competition can be fierce, as the number of good high schools—particularly in Manhattan—is limited. Depending on the high school and the specific program, students may be selected by audition (for performing arts programs), by test scores, middle school grade averages, or a combination thereof. If not applying to a specific school, students are selected by lottery or in some cases (generally in the boroughs outside of Manhattan) they attend the school nearest them. Typically, parents of Manhattan middle school students start scouting high schools much in the manner of college selections. Key concerns are safe transportation to and from the school, special programs, and how the school rates both academically and in terms of student safety. According to the *Times*, in 2004 about 34% of students were assigned to their first school choice.

The various categories of high school include the following major groupings:

- **Audition schools**, such as Fiorello LaGuardia High School of Music and Art and the Performing Arts, and High School of Art and Design, to which the student must be recommended and must audition or present a portfolio for admission.
- **Competitive schools,** to which admission is by competitive exam; Bronx High School of Science, Brooklyn Tech, Hunter High School, and Stuyvesant are the most well known and desirable schools in this group.
- **District schools**, which range from abysmal to excellent.
- **Special interest schools** include the School of Fashion Industries and the New York School of Printing, among others.

INFORMATION SOURCES

The annual public school options fair, with workshops and guides to schools in several Manhattan districts, at the 92nd Street YMHA (212-996-1100), is worth a visit. The Parenting Center there has a variety of seminars on public and private schools, and one need not be a member to attend. Call the center for particulars.

- **New York City Department of Education**, 52 Chambers St, 718-935-2000, http://schools.nyc.gov; contact them for a free "Public High School Directory."
- **The Division of Assessment and Accountability of the Board of Education**, 52 Chambers St, Rooms 309 & 310, 212-374-3990, http://schools.nyc.gov/daa, publishes an annual report, commonly known as the "Report Card," which describes each of the public schools statistically for the previous year. It's a source of information on enrollment, ethnic composition, reading scores, etc.
- **SchoolMatch**, www.schoolmatch.com, 800-992-5323, is a private organization that provides information about schools, public or private, which best suit your requirements as determined by a questionnaire.

COLLEGES AND UNIVERSITIES

New York City offers a wide variety of higher education opportunities, many of which are listed below. In addition to graduate degrees and an inviting array of evening courses, these schools also offer lectures and workshops of interest, not to mention musical and theatrical performances. You can also visit some of these institutions on their web sites via links at www.ny.com/academia/colleges.html.

MANHATTAN AND THE BRONX

- **Bank Street College of Education**, 610 W 112th St, 212-875-4400, www.bnkst.edu
- **Barnard College**, 3009 Broadway, 212-854-5262, www.barnard.edu
- **Baruch College of Continuing and Professional Studies**, 17 Lexington Ave, 212-802-5600, www.baruch.cuny.edu
- **City College**, CUNY, 138th St and Convent Ave, 212-650-7000, www.ccny.cuny.edu
- **City University of NY Graduate School and University Center**, 365 Fifth Ave, NYC 212-817-7000, www.gc.cuny.edu
- **Columbia University**, Broadway at 116th St, 212-854-1754, www.columbia.edu
- **Cooper Union**, 30 Cooper Square, 212- 353-4120, www.cooper.edu
- **Fordham University**, 113 W 60th Street, 800-FORDHAM or 212-636-6000, www.fordham.edu
- **Hebrew-Union College-Jewish Institute of Religion**, One W 4th St, 212-674-5300, www.huc.edu
- **Hunter College**, 695 Park Ave at 68th St, 212-772-4000, www.hunter.cuny.edu
- **Jewish Theological Seminary**, 3080 Broadway, 212-678-8000, www.jtsa.edu
- **Manhattan College**, Riverdale, 718-862-8000, www.manhattan.edu
- **Marymount Manhattan College**, 221 E 71st St, 212-517-0430, www.mmm.edu
- **New School University**, 66 W 12th St, 212-229-5600, www.newschool.edu
- **New York University**, 25 W 4th St, 212-443-4700, www.nyu.edu
- **Pace University**, 1 Pace Plaza and 535 Fifth, 866-772-3338, www.pace.edu
- **Parsons School of Design**, 66 Fifth Ave, 212-229-8900, www.parsons.edu; part of NYU
- **Pratt Manhattan**, 144 W 14th St, 212-647-7775, www.pratt.edu
- **Union Theological Seminary**, 3041 Broadway at 121st St, 212-662-7100, www.uts.columbia.edu
- **Yeshiva University**, 500 W 185th St, 212-960-5400, www.yu.edu

BROOKLYN

- **Brooklyn College**, 2900 Bedford Ave, 718-951-5000, www.brooklyn.cuny.edu
- **Pratt Institute**, 200 Willoughby Ave, 718-636-3600, www.pratt.edu
- **St. Joseph's College**, 245 Clinton Ave, 718-636-6800, www.sjcny.edu

QUEENS

- **Queens College**, 65-30 Kissena Blvd, Flushing 718-997-5000, www.qc.cuny.edu
- **Queensborough Community College**, 222-05 56th St, Bayside 718-631-6262, www.qcc.cuny.edu
- **St. John's University**, 8000 Utopia Pkwy, Jamaica, 888-9-STJOHNS, www.stjohns.edu

STATEN ISLAND

- **College of Staten Island**, CUNY, 2800 Victory Blvd, 718-982-2000, www.csi.cuny.edu
- **St. John's University**, 300 Howard Ave, 718-390-4500, www.stjohns.edu
- **Wagner College**, 631 Howard Ave, 718-390-3100, www.wagner.edu

BIG CITY LIVING ENCOURAGES IDIOSYNCRATIC LIFESTYLES. AND NEW Yorkers pursue their interests and goals singularly unencumbered by considerations as to "what the neighbors might think." Home decoration is a striking case in point. Anything (within the terms of the lease) goes, and when it comes to providing all the goods and services necessary for us to feather our wildly divergent, albeit mainly minuscule, nests, the city really comes through for its residents. Generally speaking, there are at least three approaches to shopping in Manhattan: (1) largish, fairly priced, standard sources; (2) famous signature shops and upscale boutiques; and (3) discounters, warehouse-style superstores, and/or alternative resources such as wholesale districts and sample sales.

Note from the shopping strategies department: unless you are literally sitting and sleeping on the floor of your new apartment, it pays to wait until winter for the annual, city-wide furniture and housewares sales to make those major purchases. In both department stores and specialty shops, the savings in January and February are considerable, 20% to 50% off. Watch for the ads in the *Times*. And it's worth noting, especially if you anticipate making a major purchase, the **sales tax** in New York City is 8.38%, but the tax bite in New Jersey is 7% and most clothing items are exempt. Depending on the "spree," the savings in New Jersey may more than pay for the toll to cross the Hudson.

While most stores are open on Sundays, except in Paramus, New Jersey, where blue laws are still in effect, store hours will vary, with many stores cutting hours during the summer and staying open late as the end-of-year holiday season approaches. Many run specials during Memorial Day, President's Day, Independence Day, etc.—check ads and call stores for hours and sales. In some cases you can get on their e-mail or mailing lists to find out about sales and other happenings. In the sections below, addresses are in Manhattan unless otherwise indicated.

235

FULL-SERVICE DEPARTMENT STORES

As designer sections fragment the more traditional uniform displays of merchandise, one-stop shopping at full-service department stores has lost some of its cohesiveness. Still, it beats 15 stops in a 20-block neighborhood. Although more difficult than it once was, it's comforting to take a 15-item list—electronic organizer through silk sheets—and pass the afternoon under one roof. So, we lead off with the royalty of New York's department store scene:

- **Bloomingdale's**, at 59th St and Lexington Ave, 212-705-2000, and 504 Broadway, 212-729-5900, and other locations, www.bloomingdales.com; for all the zap and glitter, Bloomie's has a sturdy core: you can leave your watch for repair, order Christmas cards, shop the best white sales in town—January and August—buy a TV, a mattress, and sweat socks, as well as try out glittery shoes to a funky beat, or nosh the food of the moment at one of several chic cafés. The main floor offers a full array of make-up and makeovers, plus exquisite jewelry and other top-of-the line items. Once above the initial frenzy of the main floor, you'll find designer clothing and much more in calmer environs. Services include At Your Service personal shoppers, 212-705-3135, translators, a bridal registry, decorators, dining, and 24-hour telephone order service.
- **Century 21**, 22 Cortlandt St, 212-227-9092; 472 86th St, Bay Ridge, Brooklyn, 718-748-3266, www.c21stores.com; not the nationwide real estate broker but something that is unique to New York City—a full-service department store where nearly everything is discounted. There are many bargains here and the service is pleasant and no-nonsense. Beware: the Manhattan store can be a zoo around Christmas-time.
- **Daffy's**, 5th Ave & 18th St, 212-529-4477; Madison Ave & 44th St, 212-557-4422; Broadway & 34th St, 212-736-4477; 57th between Park & Lexington, 212-376-4477; Broadway & Grand St, 212-334-7444; www.daffys.com; this citywide fashion-focused discount chain emphasizes European styles with on-and-off success. Some of the lowest prices in the city although many do not like the communal changing rooms (separated by gender, of course).
- **Filene's Basement**, 620 Ave of the Americas (Sixth Ave) between West 18th and 19th streets, 212-620-3100; other locations at 2222 Broadway at 79th St, 212-873-8000, and 187-04 Horace Harding Expy in Fresh Meadows, 718-479-7711, and 4 Union Square South, 212-58-0169 www.filenesbasement.com. Some good bargains at busy locations. Don't expect a lot, or any, personal attention.
- **Kmart**, 770 Broadway at 8th St, 212-673-1540, www.kmart.com; essentially the antithesis of Bloomingdale's, the big "K" offers practical goods at reasonable prices. Fairly comprehensive, including even a houseplants department as well as clothing, furniture, housewares, and appliances, not to mention Martha Stewart linens, paints and furniture. Another Kmart at 250 W 34th St

between 7th and 8th avenues, 212-760-1188, is much smaller, not really a department store in the true sense.

- **Lord and Taylor**, 424 Fifth Ave, 212-391-3344, www.lordandtaylor.com; wide selection and helpful sales staff. Lots of women's clothing including formal wear and smart business suits.
- **Macy's**, Broadway at 34th St, 212-695-4400, www.macys.com; enormous! Complete! The crown jewel of New York City department stores. And, yes, it can be overwhelming! First-timers take advantage of the multilingual assistance and location maps at the first floor information booths. Others might opt for Macy's By Appointment, the personal shopping service, and the 24-hour telephone ordering service, 212-494-4181. Included are special events and a bridal registry. A total revamp of the beloved behemoth began at the basement level with the creation of the superb Cellar, a bazaar-like warren of individual food and housewares shops, and moved skyward as each floor was completely redone with pizzazz and flair: a merchandising tour de force. Even if you're not setting out with a specific shopping goal, Macy's is a great place to browse and browse and browse...
- **Macy's** at 422 Fulton St, Brooklyn, 718-875-7200, www.macys.com; talk about full service! Lucky Brooklyn residents need travel no further than the Hoyt Street stop on the #2 or #3 train for practically any nicety or necessity. Macy's has both an optometrist and a podiatrist on duty and a fur storage and restyling service. From TVs, furniture, and electronics on the lower level to fabric on six, this rather reserved, no-nonsense institution also heeds the latest fashions with up-to-the-minute styles from leading designers on three.
- **Macy's**, 90-01 Queens Blvd, Elmhurst, 718-271-7200, www.macys.com; not as vast as Herald Square, but it provides full service and is convenient to the entire borough from a Queens Boulevard location.
- **Saks Fifth Avenue**, 611 Fifth Ave at Rockefeller Center, 212-753-4000, www.saksfifthavenue.com; carefully coifed customers, calm and self-assured, and elaborate bouquets that cascade nonchalantly into the glowing, wood-paneled aisles characterize Saks Fifth Avenue. So do the most refined escalators in New York. They float you silently past eight well-lit shopping floors against a backdrop of perfectly placed plants, mirrors, and pinky-beige marble. Luxurious Saks exudes well-being from every tasteful counter. Departments are stylish and help is generally available. Saks also harbors a useful set of shops along 49th and 50th streets. Housewares, luggage, bathing suits, and sportswear, the bath and linen shop, and the art gallery all have private entrances. Recently, the store has made a fetish of personalized service. The Fifth Avenue Club, on the third floor, shelters five personal shopping services, among them the Executive Service for women executives.
- **Sears**, Cross County Pkwy and Route 87, Yonkers, 914-377-2100, www.sears. com; other Sears stores at 50 Mall Dr W in the Newport Mall, Jersey City, NJ, 201-420-5300; 2307 Beverly Rd, Brooklyn, 718-826-5800; 96-05 Queens Blvd,

Rego Park, Queens, 718-830-5900; 5200 Kings Plaza, Brooklyn, 718-677-2100, call for hours. For those with wheels this reliable old standby represents convenience and good value with plenty of selection. Parking is free, and in the New Jersey store just outside the Holland Tunnel the sales tax bite is less painful.

- **T.J. Maxx**, 620 Ave of the Americas (Sixth Ave) between West 18th and 19th streets, 212-229-0875, www.tjmaxx.com; again, not one of the grand old department store dames, but it's more than just off-price clothing. You'll find housewares and some small furniture items. The location upstairs over Filene's Basement (clothing only) doesn't hurt.
- **Target**, 135-05 20th Ave, College Point, Queens, 718-661-4346; 139 Flatbush Ave, Brooklyn, 718-290-1109; 543 River Rd, Edgewater, NJ, 201-402-0253, www.target.com; new to the metropolitan area in 1998, this popular department store, nestled in a shopping center among other national chain giants, lacks only full furniture and hardware departments. Everything else, from clothes to appliances and their exclusive line of household products for the garden, kitchen, and living room, designed by architect Michael Graves, is here; check their cryptic newspaper ads.

The city is full of stores that specialize in any and every type of product you might want. Some of these stores provide savings and offer minimal customer service while others will practically hold your hand through the purchase— of course you'll spend a little more. Either way, you can find a vast selection of goods throughout the city, so don't settle—shop around and get what you want. Most stores also have web sites so you can go online to view and even make purchases.

APPLIANCES, ELECTRONICS, CAMERAS

These three categories have been lumped together because many of the stores listed below cross merchandise lines.

- **Macy's**, see **Full-Service Department Stores**, above.
- **Sears**, see **Full-Service Department Stores**, above.
- **Olden Camera**, 1263 Broadway Suite 4, at 32nd St, 2nd Floor, 212-725-1234, www.oldencameralens.com; lots of camera and even computer equipment.
- **Willoughby's Konica Imaging**, 298 Fifth Ave, 800-378-1898 or 212-564-1600, www.willoughbys.com; offers phone quotes. Complete rental and service departments complement the most extensive new and used photographic stock in the city. Willoughby's also has a computer department.

SPECIALTY SHOPS

- **Alkit Image Express**, 227 E 45th St (between 2nd and 3rd avenues on the second floor), 212-674-1515, www.alkit.com; full video and stereo line but fame rests on the quality and quantity of the professional and amateur cameras and other photographic equipment offered, along with Alkit's custom order department, rental, and repair services.

- **Innovative Audio**, 150 E 58th St between Lexington and Third avenues, 212-634-4444, www.innovativeaudiovideo.com; perhaps a bit higher-end, but they offer a full range of quality equipment. They are noted for their helpful sales staff.
- **Lyric High Fidelity**, 1221 Lexington Ave at 83rd St, 212-439-1900, www.lyricusa.com; "Only the finest stereo components." A good selection of speakers.
- **Sound by Singer**, 18 E 16th St, 212-924-8600, www.soundbysinger.com; full range of audio equipment, quiet listening rooms, and an extremely knowledgeable sales staff. Specializes in American brands.
- **Stereo Exchange**, 627 Broadway at Houston St, 212-505-1111; this established sound emporium specializes in home theater, audiophile stereo, and new components. Used high-end components, expertly repaired in-house and sold at 60% to 70% off what they might cost new, are a real draw.

DISCOUNT STORES

The Lower East Side doesn't have a monopoly on good buys any longer. Appliances and electronics are sold all over the city at less than retail. A few of the many discounters in Manhattan:

- **Adorama**, 42 W 18th St near Sixth Ave, 800-223-2500; mail order: 212-741-0052, www.adoramacamera.com, is a favorite of professional photographers and filmmakers. Carries a staggering array of cameras, accessories, video equipment, lighting, lenses, VCRs, and more. Call for their specialty catalog or drop by for one.
- **B&H Photo-Video-Pro Audio**, 420 Ninth Ave at 34th St, 800-606-6969, 212-444-6670, www.bhphotovideo.com; whether you need an English-made Billingham photographer's vest, a point-and-shoot, or a Hasselblad, professional lighting and movie equipment, or camcorder, you'll find it in this sprawling audio-video bazaar with knowledgeable sales staff, a large professional clientele, and an encyclopedic catalog. Biggest price breaks are on professional equipment.
- **Bondy Export**, formerly ABC Trading Co., 40 Canal St, 212-925-7785; call for hours. Offers photographic equipment, small as well as major appliances, audio equipment and supplies, TVs, and DVD players.
- **J&R Music World**, 31 Park Row across from City Hall for audio-video hardware, and 27 Park Row for kitchen and small personal appliances and fitness equipment, 212-238-9000, www.jandr.com. It's definitely not all music, though their stereo selection is perhaps the best among the discounters. This string of outlets along Park Row also draws shoppers from all over for CDs, cameras, camcorders, cellular phones, television and video equipment, home office equipment, computer hardware and software (see **Computers** below).

- **P.C. Richard & Son**, 120 E 14th St between Third and Fourth avenues, 212-979-2600; 205 E 86th St between Second and Third avenues, 212-348-1287, www.pcrichard.com; also at more than 40 other locations in Brooklyn, Queens, Westchester, Long Island, and New Jersey. Home appliances, digital cameras, DVDs, and video games.
- **Vendome Trading Corp.**, 247 W 37th St, 212-279-3333; offers phone quotes. A member of a cooperative buying group that has its own warehouse, Vendome sells air conditioners, washing machines, and other major, as well as small, appliances, computers, TVs, and stereos.

BEDS, BEDDING, AND BATH

Department stores can take care of all your bedding needs under one roof. Lay in supplies during January and August, traditional white sale months. Bloomingdale's becomes particularly generous at these times, stocking irregular Martex towels and name brand sheets at great savings.

SPECIALTY SHOPS

- **Bed, Bath & Beyond**, 620 Sixth Ave at 18th St, 212-255-3550; 410 E 61st St at First Ave, 646-215-4702; 96-05 Queens Blvd, Rego Park, Queens, 718-459-0868; 459 Gateway Dr, Brooklyn, 718-235-2049; Edgewater Commons Mall at 489 River Rd, Edgewater, NJ, 201-840-8808, www.bedbathandbeyond.com; this popular and affordable chain store has almost everything for your household needs. Helpful service, too. The Manhattan store boasts wide aisles, plenty of departments, easy checkout, and a special escalator for your shopping cart.
- **Dixie Foam**, 113 W 25th St, 212-645-8999, www.dixiefoam.com; in this factory/showroom, 4" and 5 1/2" thick foam mattresses are the forte. Choose standard sizes or have irregular sizes cut and covered to order. Closed Sundays.
- **Gracious Home**, 1220 Third Ave between 70th and 71st streets, 212-517-6300, www.gracioushome.com; imported linens for the Upper East Side, bathware, fabrics, stationery, and giftware. Free gift-wrapping and delivery in Manhattan, not to mention phone orders.
- **Laytner's Linen & Home**, 2270 Broadway at 81st St, 212-724-0180, 237 E 86th St, 212-996-4439, www.laytners.com; outfit your bedroom and bath here, and then some. Besides a limited selection of handsome cotton drapes, you'll find bedding, feather beds, duvets, spreads, towels and bathroom and closet supplies, tablecloths, chenille throws and scatter pillows, but none of it in overwhelming quantities. Scattered among these soft goods are items of Mission-style furniture, also for sale.
- **Sleepy's**, 962 Third Ave at 58th St, 212-755-8210; huge chain offering beds, beds, beds of all kinds; frames and headboards; and mattresses as well. Call 800-SLEEPYS or go to www.sleepys.com for a location near you.

ALTERNATIVE SOURCES

Household linens on the **Lower East Side** are squashed into two blocks on Grand Street between Allen and Forsyth. An uptown look has intruded on the cram-jammed bargain basement fustiness always considered *de rigueur* in the city's most raffish bazaar area. The uninitiated will find comparatively sleek **Harris Levy**, 98 Forsyth at Grand Street, 212-226-3102, a satisfying shopping opportunity with goods from Laura Ashley, Marimekko, Martex, Wamsutta, Cannon, and Stevens, in addition to the scores of other stores along Grand. All closed Saturday, open Sunday. Department store white-sale prices match those you're likely to find on the Lower East Side but, if you avoid the Sunday crush, you'll discover sales personnel often more knowledgeable and helpful than their uptown counterparts.

- **ABC Carpet & Home, 881 and 888 Broadway at E 19th St, 212-473-3000**; 1055 Bronx River Pkwy, Bronx (warehouse outlet), 718-842-8770; www.abchome.com; it's certainly not just carpets anymore. Imported- and domestic designer lines, spreads, and towels, along with a fetching array of country furniture, folk art objects, decorative pieces, and scatter pillows. Now there's crystal, earthenware, Limoges, bone china, and flatware as well. Sink into the Pipa Restaurant and refuel when energy flags, or try Le Pain Quotidien, which has some of the best pastries and bread in town (and some of worst, or weakest, coffee).

- **Dial-A-Mattress, showroom at 4–29 31st Place, Long Island City, 718-472-1200, www.mattress.com**; but you don't need to go there unless you want to personally try out a mattress or look at their bedding, sofa beds, frames, or accessories. Simply dial, 24 hours a day, and a bedding consultant will help you choose among discounted Sealy, Simmons, Serta, or Spring Air mattresses according to size, firmness, and price range. Delivery is within 24 hours, on approval, with a 36-day comfort exchange (softer or firmer). It's hard to beat if you're busy and want a mattress for that aching back in a hurry.

CARPETS AND RUGS

For an overview, check the department stores, in particular Macy's for broadlooms and Bloomingdale's for imports.

- **ABC Carpets**, 881 and 888 Broadway at E 19th St, 212-473-3000; just across from the main store is this carpet only emporium occupying four floors. Expensive but high quality

- **Einstein Moomjy Inc.**, 155 E 56th St between Third and Lexington avenues, 212-758-0900, www.einsteinmoomjy.com; also New Jersey locations. At this self-described "Rug Department Store" located in the Architects and Designers Building, the very best broadlooms share floor space with luminous Orientals as well as domestic and imported carpets of all kinds. Don't worry about missing an Einstein Moomjy sale: newspapers and the television are flooded with ads.

- **Safavieh**, 238 E 59th St, 212-888-0626; 902 Broadway at 20th St, 212-477-1234; 153 Madison Ave, 212-683-8399, and other city locations, www.safavieh. com. They sell a variety of handmade Oriental rugs new and antique, silk and wool, and an assortment of Aubusson weaves. Watch for their sales. See their web site for stores in Connecticut, Long Island, and New Jersey, some of which also sell antique reproduction furniture.

ALTERNATIVE SOURCES

Carpets and rugs also turn up at thrift shops, auctions, and flea markets. See **Furniture** for details.

COMPUTERS AND SOFTWARE

A number of the big computer stores have decamped but personal computers can be bought in a variety of places, from comparatively cozy neighborhood centers to barn-like discount warehouses. Many outlets offer courses as well as literature on the subject. For an overview of current prices and trends, check the "Circuits" section of the Thursday *New York Times*, where the weekly computer columns are flanked by ads for hardware, software, and allied services.

- **The Apple Store**, 103 Prince St, SoHo, 212-226-3126; lovely store in which to browse the newest and coolest Macs. Classes available. Also at 767 Fifth Ave, 212-336-1440; equally *moderne*.
- **J&R Computer World**, 15 Park Row across from City Hall, 212-238-9100, www. jr.com; a knowledgeable sales staff and a showroom with all the major computer hardware lines available to try out, in stock and discounted, have made this the largest single (non-chain, that is) computer store in the country. They'll install your upgrades for you or repair your old PC. Call for a catalogue, and if you know what you want, order by phone at 800-221-8180.
- **RCS Computer Experience**, 575 Madison Ave at 56th St, 212-949-6935, www. rcsnet.com; an experienced sales staff at these service-oriented stores handles the major computer lines, Apple included; desktop and notebook as well as accessories, peripherals, software and digital cameras are available at competitive prices. The bonus is a service staff prepared to make home and office calls and telephone help technicians to talk you out of digital blind alleys.
- **Staples**, 488-92 Broadway at Broome, 212-219-1299; 5-9 Union Square at W 14th St, 212-929-6323; 425 Park Ave at 56th St, 212-753-9640; 1280 Lexington Ave at 86th St, 212-426-6190; 2248 Broadway at 81st St, 212-712-9617, www. staples.com; and at many other locations. Everything for the (home) office, including computers, peripherals, and software.

FABRIC—DECORATING

Ringed around the **Decoration & Design Building**, 979 Third Ave between 59th and 60th streets, wholesale fabric showrooms marked "To The Trade Only" usually require shoppers to be accompanied by a decorator or to possess a decorator's card. No entrée? Try the department stores or the retail fabric importers or discount merchants listed below, all of whom stock dress goods as well as slipcover, curtain, and upholstery fabrics. For more information, call 212-759-5408 or go to www.ddbuilding.com.

DISCOUNT STORES

- **Baranzelli/Silk Surplus**, 1127 Second Ave between 59th and 60th streets, 212-753-6511, www.baranzelli.com; while noted for Scalamandré seconds, heavy embroideries and other elegant coverings, including silks, are stocked here, along with some traditional furniture. Closed Sundays.
- **Beckenstein Home Fabrics**, entrance at 4 W 20th St, 212-366-5142, www. beckensteinfabrics.com; for over 80 years the place to go on Orchard Street, this former Lower East Side bastion of discount fabric has now moved uptown and is somewhat upscale. With fabric now on racks and some furniture as well, the selection in decorating fabric remains broad and the prices still represent a savings over the uptown boutiques.
- **Long Island Fabric**, 406 Broadway at Canal St, 212-925-4488; right in the heart of the fabric wholesale district between SoHo and City Hall, this ramshackle three-story outlet houses notable bargains.
- **Martin Albert Interiors**, 9 E 19th St, 212-673-8000, www.martinalbert.com; formerly located on Grand St, this discounter still sells uptown fabric at downtown prices.

ALTERNATIVE SOURCES

Long a mecca to home decorators and seamstresses, the Lower East Side fabric shops clustered on **Grand Street** at the Eldridge Street intersection (between Forsyth and Allen), like the household linen outlets adjacent, are open Sunday–Friday, closed on Saturday. But just as uptown shops are moving downtown, so Lower East Side is moving uptown. Three of the major fabric discounters have decamped for uptown locations. The remaining grand old man, **Harry Zarin Home**, 314 Grand Street, 212-925-6112, holds the fabric fort. Prices for the curtain, upholstery, and slipcover fabrics in stock are almost always a better bargain than materials you select from the sample books. But these too are discounted. You'll find stellar names printed on the selvages of velvets, embroideries, cottons, and tapestries: Brunschwig & Fils, Givenchy, Schumacher, and Stroheim & Roman among them.

FURNITURE

Antique furniture dealerships tend to cluster. Rare pieces from the 17th, 18th, and 19th centuries, of the quality found at the Winter Antiques Show held late each January at the Seventh Regiment Armory, are most likely to be found in elegant shops along Madison Avenue north of 67th Street. Increasingly, retail outlets for less prestigious pieces are infiltrating the wholesale "to the trade only" antique district located in the quadrant formed by University Place, Broadway, East 9th, and East 11th streets in the Village. Art deco dealers and those specializing in the Depression era, in retro furniture, and in the now-fashionable Fifties clump together in SoHo and NoHo. A handful of good sources can also be found in Greenwich Village. The more upscale antique stores, dealing mostly in Early American and French country furniture, line Bleecker west of Seventh Avenue.

Look for furniture sales post-Christmas. Those held by New York department stores at their warehouses in the boroughs and suburbs offer especially large savings for anyone with a car and enough stamina to brave the stampede.

- **Carlyle Custom Convertibles**, main store 1056 Third Ave near 62nd St, 212-838-1525; clearance at 122 W 18th St between Sixth and Seventh avenues, 212-675-3212, www.carlylesofa.com; offers quality custom-made sofas in a variety of fairly conservative styles and fabrics. Allow four to six weeks for delivery.
- **Crate & Barrel**, 650 Madison Ave, 212-308-0011, and 611 Broadway, 212-780-0004, www.crateandbarrel.com; somewhat incongruously located at the base of a sleek office tower, this emporium of handsome, countryish furniture, dish- and cookware, decorative items, and linens is theme-decorated in natural pine. The earth tones are muted, and the selection of reasonably priced glassware is extensive. It's affordable and stylish one-stop home furnishing.
- **The Door Store**, 10 area locations including 1 Park Ave at 33rd St, 212-679-9700; 969 Third Ave at 58th St, 212-421-5271; 123 W 17th St west of Sixth Ave, 212-627-1515; www.doorstorefurniture.com; an excellent source of reasonably priced contemporary furniture, especially desks, computer tables, wall units, chairs, and tables in oak, teak, and pine—but no doors. Their sales are well worth the wait.
- **Ethan Allen**, 192 Lexington Ave at 32nd St, 212-213-0600; 103 West End Ave, 212-201-9840; 1107 Third Ave at 65th St, 212-308-7703; 2275 Richmond Ave, Staten Island, 718-983-0100, among other locations, www.ethanallen.com. Handsome, well-made traditional furniture for the whole house. Watch the Times for their sales.
- **George Smith**, 73 Spring St in SoHo, 212-226-4747, www.georgesmith.com; it's quiet here in two vast rooms just steps from the bustle of lower Broadway, perhaps because all the large sofas, chairs and stools are down/feather filled, which muffles sound. This is high-end, meticulously English-made furniture in the classic style, and requires space most city apartments haven't got. Up-

holstered to order in your fabric or theirs, in cotton brocades, florals, checks, antique kilim, or leather, they'd all look splendid in a paneled home library. Custom orders take 10 to 12 weeks, or you can buy off the floor.

- **Ikea**, One Beard Street in Red Hook Brooklyn, 718-246-IKEA; 1000 Ikea Dr, Elizabeth, NJ, 908-289-4488; Broadway Mall, Hicksville, Long Island, 516-681-4532, www.ikea.com; worth the trip from the city for excellent deals. Take the LIRR from Penn Station to the Hicksville station, or better, bring a car to stock up. Selections range from inexpensive pine dressers to kitchen tables, beds, and living room furniture, all designed Swedish-style with clean lines and natural materials. Pick up sheets, glasses, wallpaper, lamps and more—for less. At the Jersey and Red Hook stores, have a Swedish meatball lunch for less than $5 in the spacious, clean (if slightly antiseptic) cafeteria, also open for breakfast and dinner. Delivery is available and there are free buses on the weekend (and sometimes ferries to the Red Hook outlet).

- **Jennifer Convertibles**, 111 Third Ave, 212-260-0522; 373 Third Ave, 212-696-1353; 965 Third Avenue, 212-752-2078; 902 Broadway, 212-677-6862; 1757 Broadway, 212-581-1559; 893 Broadway, 212-674-1338, leather only; plus stores in Brooklyn, the Bronx, Queens, Staten Island and Long Island· www jenniferfurniture.com. No question, stores in this chain, which bills itself "America's largest sofa bed specialist," have the city's widest selection of relatively inexpensive convertible sofas, including Sealy and Simmons models.

- **Jensen-Lewis**, 89 Seventh Ave at 15th St, 212-929-4880, www.jensen-lewis. com; famous for deck chairs, satchels, backpacks, and other canvas products in lots of zippy colors. In big, bright quarters puffy sofas and easy chairs, beds, and an expanding housewares department fill the showroom.

- **Maurice Villency**, 949 Third Ave, corner of 57th St, 212-725-4840, www.mauricevillency.com; If sleek and modern, embellished with glass and brass, is the look you favor, then head for this sparkling showroom, where furniture lines exclusive to Maurice Villency are displayed.

- **Pottery Barn**, 600 Broadway at W Houston St, 212-219-2420, 1965 Broadway at 67th St, 212-579-8477, 127 E 59th St, 917-369-0050, www.potterybarn.com; where's the pottery? Mostly gone now. This former emporium of tableware has evolved into a design studio and catalogue operation focusing on home furnishings in a fairly country mode. Reasonably priced sofas and chairs often covered in tough cotton, rugs, dining and occasional furniture, drapes, and decorative items fill their catalogs and the stores. There's also a selection of inexpensive to moderately priced imported glassware, china, and table settings, augmented by quality cookware, sometimes below list price, and occasional gourmet items. Their periodic sales of specific merchandise are worth catching.

- **Restoration Hardware**, 935 Broadway at 22nd St, 212-260-9479, plus stores in New Jersey and Long Island, www.restorationhardware.com. Hardware? In fact, there are some drawer pulls, some bathroom hardware, and fireplace and cleaning supplies, but these spacious showrooms, part of a nationwide chain, are furniture and housewares emporia. You can buy sturdy garden furniture and the garden clogs and tin floral buckets to go with it, along with rugs, picture frames, and the like, but the draw here is the mission-style furniture with its clean lines and sturdy oak construction.

ALTERNATIVE SOURCES

- **Art & Antiques Magazine** can be helpful. Pick up their magazine at newsstands or check out their web site, www.artandantiques.net, for a list of New York City antique dealers.
- **Atlantic Avenue**, Brooklyn; the *Village Voice* describes this as the best strip in the five boroughs for vintage furniture above the junk category. Beware of pricey delivery costs, the *Voice* warns, and think about renting a van. Atlantic Avenue between Nevins and Bond streets.
- **Auction houses**: diverting, and occasionally rewarding, auctions are another way to obtain basic necessities such as mattresses, as well as moth-eaten moose heads, which, in fact, make poor hat-racks. Check the auction pages at the back of the "Arts and Leisure" section of the Sunday *Times* for sale descriptions and viewing hours. The big three: **Christie's**, 20 Rockefeller Plaza, 212-636-2000, www.christies.com; **Phillips, de Pury & Luxembourg**, 450 W 15th St, 212-940-1200; and **Sotheby's**, 1334 York Ave, 212-606-7000, www.sothebys.com, hold specialty auctions of interest to collectors and connoisseurs (and voyeurs) once or twice a week in season. The second tier, including **Christie's East**, 219 E 67th St, 212-606-0400 (weekly); **William Doyle Galleries**, 175 E 87th St, 212-427-2730, www.doylenewyork.com (every other Wednesday); and **Sotheby's Arcade Auctions**, 1334 York Ave, 212-606-7000, usually auction off a varied selection of household goods in a single session. These are typically not places for the price-conscious consumer. Designers prowl the tag-sale operation where Doyle's disposes of high-class flotsam from the adjacent gallery, 8:30 a.m. to 4:30 p.m., Monday–Friday, 10 a.m. to 5 p.m., Saturday; you can too. For erratic quality, more fun, and lower prices try **Swann Galleries**, 104 E 25th St, 212-254-4710, www.swanngalleries.com, and **Tepper Galleries**, 110 E 25th St, 212-677-5300, www.teppergalleries.com.
- **Flea markets**—this raffish country custom is almost extinct in New York City. The venerable Garage Market at 26th St and 6th is reputedly closing up in 2009, which leaves two small ones on 25th St between 5th and 6th Aves and a miniscule remnant at 6th Ave and 17th St. There are still lots of smaller ones that come and go depending on the weather or the availability of a vacant lot, but if you want a real flea you now have to go to Fort Green at Lafayette and Vanderbilt, where as of 2008 the Brooklyn Flea was up and running with over 150 vendors and some great food. A fair amount is craft-driven, but there lots of hand-me-downs to be had. There's also a new Hell's Kitchen flea where many

of the Chelsea refugees sometimes set up shop, at 123 W 18th St, www.hell-skitchenfleamarket.com.

- **Housing Works Thrift Shops**: 143 W 17th St at 7th Ave, 212-366-0820; 202 E 77th St between Second and Third avenues, 212-772-8461; 306 Columbus Ave between 74th and 75th streets, 212-579-7566, and 157 E 23rd St, 212-529-5955, www.housingworks.org; they sell clothes, books, records, bicycles, and whatever, but furniture is the best buy here, where proceeds go to house and service homeless people with AIDS/HIV. Come at 10 a.m. for the best buys. There are three higher quality but unrelated thrift stores on 17th St between 5th Ave and 7th Ave.

- **Public school PTAs** sometimes sponsor flea markets on school grounds in order to raise funds. These are rain-or-shine affairs; sometimes they take place on Saturdays and Sundays and sometimes they don't. The most consistent markets include the one in the Greenwich Avenue school yard of P.S. 41 between Seventh Ave and 10th St; in the P.S. 183 yard on E 67th St between York and First avenues—also indoor in the cafeteria where jewelry dealers abound with good prices; and in the Columbus Avenue yard of Intermediate School 44, between 76th and 77th streets.

- **Salvation Army**, main store: 536 W 46th St between Tenth and Eleventh avenues, 212-757-2311, www.thesalvationarmy.org, and seven other outlets. Credit cards accepted for purchases over $10. For those of humbler means, the two huge warehouse floors on 46th St contain everything a homemaker needs to set up housekeeping. Some fine bargains and clothes, too. Closed Sunday.

- **The street**: a *New York Times* "Home" section featured the apartment of a dedicated young middle-class scrounger who furnished his two rooms with street finds. The comfortable living room looked just like home in the heartlands: traditional, with overstuffed chairs, a coffee table, and standing lamp. Resourcefulness, a strong back, and willing cabbies are all that's required for street shopping—well, that and a knowledge of the Sanitation Department's collection days for whatever area you're combing. It's legal to put large items on the sidewalk after dark on the evening before any regular collection day. The Upper East Side tends to be fertile territory for found furniture, so if that's your game, Sunday, Tuesday, and Thursday evenings after 8 p.m. are the time to canvas. For other neighborhood collection days, consult the Sanitation Department via the city service number, 311, and navigate the menus. Be careful, though. If an item has been sitting outside on the street for more than a few hours it may not be something you want to bring into your home...or touch for that matter.

- **Thrift shops**: charities and hospital research programs benefit from the proceeds of these stores, just as donors benefit from the tax deductions and buyers benefit from the bargains on everything from designer clothes to silver pitchers and down sofas. Head to Third Ave between 80th and 86th streets and east to Second Ave for new and gently used goods. **Spence-Chapin Corner Shop**, 1850 Second Ave between 95th and 96th streets, 212-426-7643; and **Memorial Sloan-Kettering Cancer Center Thrift Shop**, 1440 Third Ave at 82nd St, 212-535-1250, are just a couple of the many thrift stores concentrated in this neighborhood.

HARDWARE, PAINTS AND WALLPAPER

On Saturdays, slow-moving lines make local hardware stores as good a way of meeting people as local bars later that night. But once you've made new friends along with those seemingly endless purchases, you may require more than the good old, all-purpose neighborhood reliable to fill decorating needs. Some specialty resources, then (the behemoth **Home Depot** is listed below under **Superstores**):

- **Gracious Home**, 1217 & 1220 Third Ave at 70th St, 212-517-6300, and 1992 Broadway at 67th St, 212-231-7800; www.gracioushome.com; the sprawling hardware/houseware/home-furnishings center for the Upper East Side, and its slightly smaller Upper West Side version, are both well organized and staffed. From screws to decorative bathroom fixtures, paints, electrical fixtures, and power tools, to glassware and hard-to find-vacuum cleaners.
- **Janovic**, 20 area locations including 1150 Third Ave at 67th St, 212-772-1400; 2680 Broadway at 102nd St, 212-531-2300; 1555 Third Ave at 87th St, 212-289-6300; 771 Ninth Ave at 52nd St, 212-245-3241; 215 Seventh Ave between 22nd and 23rd streets, 212-645-5454; 80 Fourth Ave at 10th Street, 212-477-6930; 292 Third Ave at 23rd St, 212-777-3030; and 136 Church St in Tribeca, 212-349-0001, www.janovic.com; the Bloomingdale's of the paint-and-wallpaper scene, Janovic's image is as glossy as its enamels and printed foil papers. For the latest colors and trends, as well as an overall view of what's available, Janovic can't be beat.
- **Kraft Hardware**, 316 E 62nd St between First and Second avenues, 212-838-2214, www.kraft-hardware.com; just the place to find those special pewter or bronze drawer pulls, mahogany switch plates, elegant hinges and door knobs, fluted porcelain sinks, and the like.
- **Simon's Hardware and Bath**, 421 Third Ave near 30th St, 212-532-9220, www.simons-hardware.com; join the inevitable throng of contractors and decorators shopping Simon's first-rate stock of brass, bronze, pewter, plastic, wood, steel—whatever!—decorative hardware. They've recently expanded to include tile, bath fixtures and lighting as well.

ALTERNATIVE SOURCES

Hardware and plastics—nuts and bolts made dingy by neighboring bright, bouncing baubles—overflow rows of cut-down cardboard boxes that alternate with the racks of surplus and flea market clothing lining Canal Street between

West Broadway and Broadway. Most of this sidewalk hardware and pretty plastic bric-a-brac is useful only to the professional handyman or collage artist, but inside, generalists revel in complete selections of quality merchandise at exceptionally fair prices. Try any of the stores sitting side by gray dilapidated side on Canal, west of Broadway.

- **Pearl Paint Co.**, 308 Canal Street, 212-431-7932, www.pearlpaint.com; listed here because of the discounted house paints, including Benjamin Moore. Pearl Paint is in fact renowned for art-related materials and accessories, and its four upper floors are usually swamped with an international array of fine artists.

HOUSEWARES

Of course, any department store or furniture store will offer scads of traditional and funky housewares, particularly Crate & Barrel, the Pottery Barn, Ikea, as well as Target, Kmart, and the list goes on (see above). Those specializing in housewares include:

- **Design Within Reach**, 142 Wooster St, 212-475-0001; 408 West 14th St, 212-242-9449; 76 Montague St, Brooklyn, 718-643-1015; www.dwr.com
- **Jonathan Adler New York**, 47 Greene St and 465 Broome St, 212-941-8950; contemporary home furnishings.
- **Moss**, 146 Greene St, 212-204-7100, www.mossonline.com; cool, sleek designs for every room of the house.
- **Pier One Imports** 1550 Third Ave, 212-987-1746; 71 Fifth Ave, 212-206-1911; and other locations, www.pier1.com; glassware, crystal, housewares, plenty of gift items and even some furniture at reasonable prices.
- **Zabar's**, 2245 Broadway at 80th St, 212-787-2000, www.zabars.com; housewares department on the mezzanine. Expansive Zabar's, mecca to millions for unequaled edibles, houses an equally esteemed and often bargain-priced selection of supplies for the home and kitchen in four rooms on the mezzanine. Try to avoid weekend forays there.

SPECIALTY SHOPS

- **Bridge Kitchenware**, 711 Third Ave, 212-688-4220, www.bridgekitchenware. com; purveyors of durable, professional-quality kitchen equipment to the city's food establishment and serious cooks the world over—you'll find, for example, the chrome-topped glass shakers found on every luncheonette counter worth its salt, an enviable selection of French tin-lined copper pots, and huge Hobart dough mixers.
- **Broadway Panhandler**, 65 E 8th St, 212-966-3434, www.broadwaypanhandler.com; discounted cookware (Calphalon, All-Clad, Le Creuset) and quality kitchen tools for the serious cook.
- **The Container Store**, 725 Lexington Ave, 212-366-4200; 629 Sixth Ave, 212-366-4200; 370 Route 17 North, Paramus, NJ, 201-265-9004; 145 Westchester

Avenue, White Plains, NY, 914-946-4767, www.containerstore.com; organize your closets, your kitchen, your drawers, your desk, your life! This is the last word in containers: garment bags, shelving, shoe holders, drawer dividers, wicker boxes, closet accessories.

- **Fishs Eddy**, 889 Broadway at 19th St, 212-420-9020, and 122 Montague St, Brooklyn, 718-797-3990, www.fishseddy.com; offers surplus restaurant china where you can buy just one piece. Everything guaranteed chip- and crack-free.
- **Hammacher Schlemmer**, 147 E 57th St, 212-421-9000, www.hammacher.com; a department store of sorts for the eclectic, has plenty of off-beat luxury items, gadgets, electronic toys, and a premier collection of quality kitchen- and barware. They tend to carry the best of any given machine and its worth visiting just to get an idea of what's quality.
- **S. Feldman Housewares, Inc.**, 1304 Madison Ave near 93rd St, 212-289-7367, www.wares2u.com; upscale cookware, including Calphalon, LeCreuset, and All-Clad, as well as the popular Miele vacuum cleaners. Watch for their sales.
- **Tiffany and Co.**, 727 Fifth Ave at 57th St, 212-755-8000, www.tiffanys.com; stand up straight, speak softly, and be on your best behavior when entering the hallowed halls of the famous high end department store. The main-floor jewelry draws oohs and ahs from a multitude of tourists, but if you ask the elevator operator for "three please," you'll find shimmering ivory walls and plates by Picasso nudging Royal Crown Derby place settings. The selection of fine china and glassware is exquisite. Tired of jelly glasses? Crystal's to your right. And if you're getting married, for many this is *the* place to register.
- **Williams-Sonoma**, 110 Seventh Ave, 212-633-2203; 121 E 59th St, 917-369-1131; 1175 Madison Ave, 212-289-6832, www.williams-sonoma.com; known through their appealing catalogue to serious cooks nationwide, this California-based firm specializes in quality cookware, handsome glassware, and mostly imported country-style tableware. The familiar pieces, and then some, are available here, along with gourmet food items and cookbooks. For lovers of blue and color-coordinated kitchens, it's a treasure trove.

ALTERNATIVE SOURCES

- **The Restaurant Supply District**: as the use of professional kitchenware in the home increases, the wholesale restaurant strip along the section of Bowery between West Houston and Broome streets has become an accepted destination for retail shoppers. Pots, pans, butcher block, Robot Coupes, Garland ranges, bar ware and thick, nigh on to unbreakable dishes are available from most stores at less than uptown retail. Outlets include **Bari Restaurant Equipment Corp.**, 240 Bowery, 212-925-3786, for a grand assortment of pots, pans, strainers, stirrers and such must-haves as pizza ovens and gigantic wooden pizza spatulas; and **Chef Restaurant Supply**, 294 Bowery, 212-254-6644, "unbelievably cheap" and favored by uptown chefs. It's also well worth checking out the cookware available in Chinatown, which can be outrageously cheap.

- **Secaucus Outlet Center**, Secaucus and Flemington, NJ; don't visit during the Christmas rush without full armor plate. At other times, values obtained in these two discount giants may well be worth the schlep. To get to Secaucus, located about 15 minutes from the Lincoln Tunnel, follow signs to Route 3 West continuing about six miles to the "Meadowlands Parking" exit, take the down ramp to the light, then hang a left and continue past two more sets of lights to American Way, take another left and you will be confronted by a number of warehouses. Bring boxes for your gleanings and a companion to watch them as you gather. From the first warehouse, get a booklet containing a map and brand names listed by merchandise category. Mikasa and Copco both have large outlets here. While you're at it, if you've the stamina, load up on discount Gucci shoes, Liz Claiborne goodies, Oleg Cassini, and the like.

LAMPS AND LIGHT FIXTURES

You can't beat the department stores for variety and choice; wait for the winter sales if you can. But if you want better prices or the newest imports, shop some of the sources below.

SPECIALTY SHOPS

- **Gracious Home** (see above listing under **Beds, Bedding, and Bath**)
- **Just Bulbs Ltd.**, 5 E 16th St, 212-228-7820; an eclectic and funky mix of bulbs (and more bulbs!). Can make you a little "light" headed.
- **The Lighting Center**, 1111 2nd Ave at 59th St, 212-888-8383; although a large selection of mainly American contemporary lighting fixtures crams the center's small, gray-walled retail shop, the specialty is track lighting. Have a system custom designed or choose from the Halo, Lightolier, Lighting Services, or Altalite lines already on hand. Not for the bargain conscious. Closed Sundays.
- **Lightforms**, 142 West 26th St, 212-255-4664; 509 Amsterdam Ave, 212-875-0407; interesting, moderate-to-expensive contemporary light fixtures.
- **Oriental Lampshade Company**, 816 Lexington Ave near 62nd St, 212-832-8190, www.orientallampshade.com; hand-made shades to order and less expensive ready-mades in a great variety of colors, shapes and styles. Lamp repair too.
- **Lighting Plus**, 680 Broadway, 212-979-2000; a wide variety of lighting fixtures along traditional lines, at reasonable prices makes this a source worth investigating.

ALTERNATIVE SOURCES

The Lamp and Light Fixture District concentrated on The Bowery between Broome and Canal streets abuts wholesale restaurant supply stores that begin at Broome and end a few blocks north at Houston. If you know what you want, don't be daunted by lurid window displays of fantasy fixtures. Push on past high kitsch, find a salesman, and describe your product. Chances are the fixture can be ordered or will be in stock at less than retail. But don't count on tender loving care. That's reserved for large wholesale buyers. Try **Bowery Lighting Corp.**, 132 Bowery, 212-941-8244, one of the largest stores in the district, or **Just Shades**, 21 Spring Street, 212-966-2757, which covers the gamut from burlaps to fine pleated ivory silks in all sizes.

SUPERSTORES

Well established in the suburbs and rural areas across the country, big box stores such as Home Depot arrived in the outer boroughs in the late 1990s, and now even inhabit Manhattan. The cost of space and community resistance to their establishment poses the ultimate challenge to these warehouse-style behemoths. For those who have the stamina to roam their vast aisles and the storage space at home for, say, 32 rolls of toilet paper, they represent real savings, though some require yearly membership fees. Note: a car is a definite asset, if not a necessity, when shopping these outlets.

- **BJ's Wholesale Club**, 137-05 20th Ave, College Point, Queens, 718-359-9703, 396 Marin Blvd, Jersey City, 201-798-0500, www.bjs.com; sells everything from tires to oven mitts to peanut butter—in the gigantic family size. Bring some muscle to carry everything to and from the car (or van, or rental truck, or blimp). Members pay $40 annually for access.
- **Costco**, 32-50 Vernon Blvd, Long Island City, Queens, 718-267-5500; 2975 Richmond Ave, Staten Island, 718-982-9000; 976 Third Ave, Brooklyn, 718-965-7600; also at four New Jersey locations: www.costco.com. Vast stores housing books, jewelry, computers, cameras, hardware, the list goes on. Membership is $50 per year.
- **Home Depot**, 40 West 23rd St, 212-929-9571; 980 Third Ave, 212-888-1512; 585 DeKalb Ave, Brooklyn, 718-230-0833; 50-10 Northern Blvd, Long Island City, 718-278-9031, 550 Hamilton Ave, Brooklyn, 718-832-8553; 131-135 Avery Ave, Flushing, Queens, 718-358-9600; 112-20 Rockaway Blvd, Jamaica, Queens, 718-641-5500; 124-04 31st Ave, Flushing, 718-661-4608; plus numerous stores in the Bronx, New Jersey and elsewhere; www.homedepot.com. This mecca for do-it-yourselfers has finally opened two long-awaited locations in Manhattan. Home Depot offers clinics on how to build it, paper it, paint it, wire or plumb it, and plant it; and they stock everything you'll need to do it from nuts and bolts to toilets and hot tubs. Make a list before you go.

SAMPLE SALES

These are special sales of a designer's leftover inventory (from jewelry to furniture to upscale bathroom fixtures), and they offer considerable savings for the determined shopper. Typically, designers do not advertise their sample sales, but predominant sale months are November, December, April, and May. Scan *New York* magazine's "Sales & Bargains" section for some sale times and locations. Better yet, subscribe to the **S&B Report**, 877-579-0222, a monthly publication stating every major designer showroom sale in the city. A one-year subscription is $124 ($75 for the online subscription); www.lazarshopping.com.

FOOD

New York eats, but in ways that take some getting used to. The city is host to some of the finest and some of the most expensive restaurants in the world, as well as hundreds of excellent eateries of every ethnic and national persuasion, large and small. For this you're on your own to explore the city's restaurant riches as far as your pocketbook permits, and with perhaps a *Zagat's Restaurant Guide* or the "Food" section of the *New York Times* in hand. You're also on your own to explore the possibilities of take-out, which has become a ubiquitous part of the city's food life. It seems you're never more than a block away from a source of take-out; many New Yorkers depend on it. And the host of corner delis throughout the city providing late night sandwiches, coffee, milk, beer, and snack food, needs no chronicling. You have one in your immediate neighborhood. Chances are, you also have an open-air fruit and vegetable stand operated nearly round-the-clock and stocked with beautifully displayed, fresh but somewhat pricey produce. These islands of color, almost invariably operated by Korean-Americans, brighten the city streets while also offering convenience and a sense of neighborhood. New York is sometimes referred to as "the city that never sleeps" perhaps because New Yorkers have too much fine food available 24 hours a day.

Sooner or later, though, you'll need that jar of spaghetti sauce, steak, box of rice, or shaker salt, not to mention some toilet paper. Thanks to the high cost of space here, the city is not supermarket-proud. They're scarce in some neighborhoods, lackluster in others. The best of them are clean but crowded, with narrow aisles and often selections that run dry much faster than their sprawling suburban counterparts. Depending on where you live, specialty shops may provide the best selection for fresh meats and produce, and summer finds many New Yorkers shopping for the freshest fruits and vegetables at sidewalk carts. If stocking up suits you, but you don't have access to a car, consider signing up with the online grocery delivery service **Fresh Direct** at www.freshdirect.com. More reasonably priced than you might imagine, this company delivers to much of Manhattan and has plans to begin service to Queens and Brooklyn.

As far as **local grocery chains** go, we begin with **D'Agostino's**, www.dagnyc.com, which is perhaps the best in terms of cleanliness, quality of selection, and consumer friendliness. Additionally, we list the main chains that operate multiple supermarkets in the city. Within these chains, some outlets are better than others:

- **Associated Food Stores and Supermarkets**, www.afstores.com
- **Food Emporium**, www.thefoodemporium.com
- **Gristede's**, www.gristedes.com
- **Met Food**, www.metfoods.com
- **Pioneer**, www.pioneerspmkt.com

You want some good French or Italian bread, a decent paté, fresh smoked salmon, and some frisée for Sunday brunch? Manhattan especially is well served by excellent bread bakers in just about every neighborhood, and by gourmet shops, which carry good breads and every other imaginable edible—at a price. Listed in the Yellow Pages under "Gourmet Shops," you'll find some of the finest shops in the world offering any tasty delicacy you have in mind. Here are just a few:

- **Agata & Valentina**, 1505 First Ave at 79th St, 212-452-0690
- **Balducci's**, 155 W 66th St, 212-653-8320
- **Citarella**, 2135 Broadway at 75th St and 1313 Third Ave at 75th St, 212-874-0383
- **Dean & Deluca**, 560 Broadway at Prince St, 212-226-6800; 1150 Madison Ave, 212-717-0800; 235 W 46th St, 212-869-6890; 75 University Pl, 212-473-1908; www.deandeluca.com
- **E A T Gourmet Foods**, 1064 Madison Ave between 80th and 81st streets, 212-772-0022
- **Fairway**, 2127 Broadway at 74th St, 212-595-1888; and 2328 12th Avenue at 132nd Street, 212-234-3883; also a huge store in Red Hook, Brooklyn.
- **Garden of Eden Farmers Market**, 162 W 23rd St, 212-675-6300
- **Gourmet Garage**, 117 Seventh Ave S at Christopher, 212-414-5910; 453 Broome St at Mercer, 212-941-5850; 301 E 64th St between First and Second Aves, 212-535-6271; and 2567 Broadway between 96th and 97th streets, 212-663-0656, www.gourmetgarage.com
- **Grace's Marketplace**, 1237 Third Ave at 71st St, 212-737-0600
- **Jefferson Market**, 450 Sixth Avenue between 10th and 11th streets, 212-533-3377
- **Todaro Brothers**, 555 Second Ave at 30th St, 212-532-0633
- **Trader Joe's**, 142 E. 14th at 2nd Ave, 212-529-4612; California's ubiquitous cut-rate gourmet chain has finally bitten the Big Apple and it's a huge success. Lines can be absolutely absurd, but then so can the prices. They also have a discount wine outlet just down the street.
- **The Vinegar Factory**, 431 E 91st St, 212-987-0885
- **Whole Foods Market**, 250 Seventh Ave at 24th St, 212-924-5969; 10 Columbus Circle, 212-823-9600; 40 East 14th St at Union Square, 212-673-5388; www.

wholefoods.com. These enormous stores have become enormously popular. Always crowded, but lines move efficiently.
- **Zabar's**, 2245 Broadway at 80th St, 212-787-2000, www.zabars.com

Vegetarians and those in search of organic foods find the farmers' markets a good source, and the better gourmet stores have organic sections as well as good selections of soy and grain products. But there are also stores catering to this market. They can be found in the Yellow Pages under "Health and Diet Food Products—Retail." Some of the better-known health food stores are listed here:
- **Commodities Natural Market**, 165 First Ave between 10th and 11th streets, 212-260-2600
- **Gary Nulls Whole Foods**, 2421 Broadway at 89th St, 212-874-4000
- **Integral Yoga**, 229 W 13th St between 8th and 9th avenues, 212-243-2642
- **LifeThyme**, 410 Sixth Ave at 8th St, 212-420-9099
- **Park Slope Food Co-op**, 782 Union St, Brooklyn, NY 11215, 718-622-0560, www.foodcoop.com; provides fresh organic foods and household supplies to community members, who now number over 6,000. Each member pays a one-time $25 joining fee and then contributes a $100 investment to the co-op (returnable when the member leaves the co-op), and each member must do a minimal work share. The co-op buys food and sells it to members for much less than competing grocery stores.
- **Westerly Natural Market**, 911 Eighth Ave at 54th St, 212-586-5262

ETHNIC FOODS

The ongoing immigration history of New York is displayed in the sidewalk stalls and food markets of its ethnic neighborhoods. For every conceivable item of **Chinese** vegetable, ingredient, and condiment, not to mention fish, and **Korean**, **Japanese**, **Thai**, and **Malaysian** food items, all very reasonably priced, New Yorkers go to Chinatown on either side of Canal Street downtown, or to Flushing on either side of Main Street, or to Sunset Park in Brooklyn. For the ultimate in Japanese food shopping, Yaohan on River Road in Edgewater, NJ, is the place to go. Little **Italy**, just north of Chinatown, isn't the only place to buy Italian food items; it just feels more authentic. In fact there are pockets of Italian specialty stores in the Village, on Ninth Avenue in the Thirties, and along legendary Arthur Avenue in The Bronx. Pungent **Indian** spices scent the air along Lexington Avenue between 23rd and 28th streets. **Polish** and **Ukrainian** foods hold their ground among other ethnic outlets along First and Second Avenues between 14th and Houston streets, but Greenpoint, Brooklyn, is the Polish food capital of the city. **Latino** food specialties are to be found throughout the city, especially in East Harlem along 116th Street, along Broadway in Washington Heights, and in Jackson Heights, Queens. No city outside Israel has more to offer in the way of **Jewish** foods than New York, in parts of The Bronx, Brooklyn, and Queens. In Manhattan, aficionados go to Broadway on the Upper West Side, East Houston Street near

Orchard, and elsewhere in the Lower East Side especially for "the best" bagels, lox, pastrami, smoked whitefish, stuffed derma, etc. It's Brighton Beach, Brooklyn, no question about it, for **Russian** food (and some more Jewish, as well).

GREENMARKETS/FARMER'S MARKETS

One of the surprises and joys of New York shopping has been the great success of the many greenmarkets that now take place throughout the city. The **Council of the Environment of New York City**, 212-788-7900, www.cenyc.org, sponsors these affairs by arranging for farmers and bakers from the tri-state area to sell their produce and goods at various outdoor locations within the five boroughs. In addition to fruit and vegetable growers, the council invites suppliers of beef, pork, lamb, poultry, eggs, honey, dairy, breads, wine, flowers, maple syrup, and other delectable items. Prices are competitive and the quality and freshness are superior to anything else in the city. All this and a general air of festivity is the reason why so many urbane New Yorkers—as well as some of the city's top chefs—have made greenmarkets a regular part of their shopping routine, especially at Union Square, the mother of all greenmarkets. (Personal tours may be arranged of the Union Square greenmarket on Wednesdays, Fridays, and Saturdays; a tour takes about 90 minutes. Call the council for more information.) Because the produce does come from the tri-state area, the warmer months are the most bountiful time to shop the markets. Market hours typically start at 8 a.m. and end anywhere from 2 p.m. to 6 p.m. Check the council's web site for a comprehensive list of greenmarket locations and an accompanying map.

A couple to start out with:

- **Essex Street Market**, 120 Essex St (at Delancey St), www.essexstreetmarket.com; since 1940, this roofed collective has been bringing low-cost produce, fish, cheese, and what-not to the LES community. It still has some of the least expensive fish and produce in the city, as well as a recent infusion of more upscale stands selling local cheeses, as well as some nice little eateries.
- **The Chelsea Market**, 9th Ave and 15th St, www.chelseamarket.com; the best covered marketplace in NYC, with wine cellars, excellent cafés and restaurants, the best fish and produce providers, and even the Food Network upstairs! All done in a fab industrial rehab complete with a rusted-pipe waterfall.

THE INCREDIBLE DIVERSITY AND DEPTH OF THE CITY'S CULTURAL, intellectual, and artistic life is a magnet for many. Nowhere else can such an enormous range of interests and avocations be accommodated on so many levels. While it is impossible to cover all the opportunities New York offers, we can help the newcomer, young and old alike, access this cultural smorgasbord by providing a compilation of ticket, subscription, and membership information for leading opera companies, symphony orchestras, dance companies, theatrical repertory groups, and museums. We've also included cultural opportunities for children as well as a section called **Literary Life** that focuses on libraries and bookstores. Addresses provided are in Manhattan unless otherwise noted. For more cultural life and opportunities see the community resources that are listed at the end of each neighborhood profile at the beginning of the book, and also check out offerings of the many colleges and universities (see **Higher Education** at the end of the **Childcare and Education** chapter).

First, what is showing, where, and when? Two particularly useful sites for tracking down event details are the *New York Times'* www.nytoday.com or www.nytimes.com, and the extensive web site of the Alliance for the Arts, **NYC Arts On Line** at www.allianceforarts.org. The latter comprehensive compendium lists concert halls, galleries, museums, theaters, historical structures, monuments, and parks throughout the five boroughs, with links to web sites, information about hours and admissions, timely articles, performance calendars, and a culture guide for children. Area publications offering **event information** include:

- "**Weekend**," two sections in the *New York Times'* Friday edition, features reviews, articles, and tips on the endless arts and entertainment possibilities for Friday, Saturday, and Sunday. The "Performing Arts" section also contains an up-to-the-minute "movie clock," useful in a town where movie schedules are notoriously unreliable.

257

- "**Arts and Leisure**," *New York Times'* Sunday edition, besides reviews and critical articles on current trends and upcoming events in the arts, includes listings for the arts with thumbnail reviews.
- *The New Yorker*, on the stands Wednesday, includes not just plays, opera, and museums in its comprehensive "Goings on About Town," but also poetry readings, sporting events, and nightlife. Most listings include abbreviated reviews. www.newyorker.com
- *New York* **magazine**, on the stands Monday, incorporates Cue, "A Complete Guide to Entertainment, the Arts, and Dining for the Week." Included are brief movie and theater reviews. Comprehensive. www.newyorkmag.com
- *Time Out New York*, on the stands Wednesday, offers comprehensive listings and reviews in all aspects of entertainment and the arts, as well as gay and lesbian features, and listings of events for children. www.timeoutny.com
- The *Village Voice*, free on the street Wednesday, is filled with entertainment ads and carries a "Listings" column of weekly free events. Particularly good for alternative events. www.villagevoice.com
- *New York Press* is distributed free in restaurants, stores, and in street boxes below 28th St; sparsely uptown. A favorite with downtowners as a reference for what's going on in the arts and music, the weekly also includes restaurant reviews and feature stories. Attitude at no extra cost. www.nypress.com
- *Club freeTime*, a monthly sold at a dozen Manhattan newsstands and by subscription, is indispensable for the culturally active but financially challenged New Yorker, listing as it does a host of free and cut-rate lectures, dance, and theater performances, concerts, walking tours, film screenings, poetry readings, street festivals, and the like, mostly in Manhattan. Just goes to prove you can pig out culturally in the city for free. You can join Club freeTime on their web site at www.clubfreetime.com or subscribe for $20 a year by calling 212-545-8900.

If you don't know which show you want to see or you want to buy a block of seats to a musical, call the **Broadway Show Line**, operated by the League of American Theatres and Producers, 888-292-9669, for descriptions of Broadway and off-Broadway shows, performance schedules, seat locations, and group sales information. You can also order tickets here, with service charges the same as from Telecharge. For New York Theater listings you can also check out Theatermania at www.theatermania.com, or the Theater Development Fund at www.tdf.org.

ELECTRONIC RESOURCES

There is a huge range of curated e-mail listings that give subscribers (almost always free) an insight into unusual events in New York. Many are just for a particular organization, some focus on a discipline or media, but they're excellent ways to find out about offbeat events. You go to the list's website to sign up and then receive weekly emails of listings. Here are a few of the larger ones.

- **Flavorpill**, flavorpill.com; this curated weekly listing is emailed out to subscribers with a listing of what the editors think are exciting performances/events, with an emphasis on alternative-type events. It's actually an international service, but with a NY franchise. Free.

- **Nonsense NYC**, www.nonsensenyc.com; this low-key and very personal entertainment listing specializes in guerrilla and homemade entertainment (along with occasional listings for rooms). It's one of the older homespun mailing lists in NYC and a good source of alternate events.

TICKETS

How can you buy tickets to New York's plays, concerts, ballets, operas, and special mega-events? Let us describe the ways.

BOX OFFICE

To get the best seats for the day you want, go to the appropriate box office in person well in advance of the performance desired, cash or charge card in hand. Not only can you check the theater's seating diagram (usually posted near the ticket window), you won't pay a handling fee. When ordering by telephone or mail, you have no control over the exact row or seat issued because orders are filled automatically on a "best available" basis. Box offices are usually open from 10 or 11 a.m. until the evening performance. Note: sometimes producers, directors, or actors release their personal tickets and these go back to the box office for sale at the last minute, making it possible for the persistent to see a hot show that has officially sold out.

TELEPHONE ORDERS

Most theaters list a special number to call for reservations. Billed to credit cards, tickets are mailed if time allows; otherwise pick them up at the theater the day of the performance. **Telecharge.com**, 212-239-6200, represents some 20 Schubert Theaters in New York City and adds $5.50 per off-Broadway ticket and $6.50 per Broadway ticket to your bill plus a $2.50 handling charge for the entire order. **Ticketmaster**, 212-307-7171, www.ticketmaster.com, now handles theater productions as well, collecting $4 to $6 per ticket plus a handling fee of $2.50. It all adds up. While usually not at all convenient, the theater box office is much cheaper if you're buying more than one ticket to an event.

ONLINE ORDERS

Individual tickets and subscriptions to most major concert series, operas, dance programs, and the like can be ordered online from their web sites using a major credit card. Likewise, tickets to plays, sporting events, and popular entertainment generally can be ordered through www.telecharge.com or www.ticketmaster.com.

TICKETMASTER

Promoters determine how tickets to their events will be sold: at Ticketmaster outlets, by calling Ticketmaster, or both. First call 212-307-7171 or go to www. ticketmaster.com to find out what performances they are offering and whether tickets can be ordered by phone and charged to a credit card (fees range, depending on the venue and type of ticket) or whether they must be picked up in person and paid for in cash at one of Ticketmaster's 2,200 outlets in the US and Canada. There are 160 outlets in the tri-state area.

BROKERS

Unless you have a friend with a personal broker or an "in" with a hotel concierge, don't expect to walk into a ticket agency and get front row center for the town's hottest musical the day of the performance. These seats are held for valued clients. However, for most people, events brokers, who usually handle only orchestra, mezzanine, and box seats, are still probably the easiest way to get into a show or sporting event in a hurry. Expect to pay 20% to 50% over the total price for their service. Note: deal only with licensed brokers in the city; out-of-town brokers operating with 800 numbers are not regulated, and you can get burned. See "Ticket Sales—Entertainment and Sports" in the Yellow Pages for names, among whom American Tickets and Continental Guests Services, operating out of major hotels, are large and well established. Scalping is illegal, so think twice before buying from the guy hawking tickets in the street. For seating charts of several major New York City venues check the Yellow Pages.

ALTERNATIVE SOURCES

At the **Times Square Information Center**, a flashy complex on 7th Avenue between 46th and 47th Street, 212-869-1890, www.timessquarenyc.org, open daily 8 a.m. to 8 p.m., you can buy same-day and advance sale tickets to Broadway and off-Broadway shows at box office prices (subject to availability) plus a per-ticket service charge of up to $5. The center, in a renovated old movie theater, also sells MetroCards and tickets to sightseeing tours and airport shuttles, and provides free internet access, multilingual tourist counselors, theater seats in which to rest, as well as clean, handicap-accessible public restrooms.

Tickets to sports events, tours, and other entertainment, as well as theater tickets, can be bought at the city's super-futuristic **Official NYC Information Center**, 810 Seventh Avenue at 53rd Street, 212-397-8200, www.nycgo.com, Monday–Friday, 8:30 a.m. to 6 p.m., and Saturday and Sunday, 9 a.m. to 5 p.m. There is a service charge for these tickets. Also available here is the CityPass, a steeply discounted ticket to six major tourist attractions good for nine days, plus maps, brochures, and multilingual tourist counselors.

Suppose you've just got to have tickets to that hot show now, and cost is no object. Call the **Actors' Fund of America**, 212-221-7301, or **Broadway Cares/ Equity Fights AIDS**, 212-840-0770, www.broadwaycares.org, for the best seats at hard-to-get shows. The tariff? You'll pay twice the box office price, but half of that is tax-deductible.

DISCOUNTS

- **TKTS** is one of the city's great bargains, and a rite of passage for the theater-bound. The Theatre Development Fund operates two outlets for half-price and 25%-off day-of-performance tickets to Broadway and off-Broadway shows. Availability information is posted on large boards near ticket sales booths, and a small fee—currently $4—is charged for each ticket; cash or traveler's check only. Note: ticket selection is better and lines shorter early in the week. For a list of discounted tickets available that night go to www.newyork.citysearch. com or www.nytoday.com after 4 p.m.
- **TKTS Times Square**, W 47th St and Broadway, sells Broadway, off-Broadway, dance, and music event tickets for evening performances from 3 p.m. to 8 p.m., Monday–Saturday, and 11 a.m. to 7:30 p.m. on Sundays. Matinee tickets go on sale on Wednesdays and Saturdays only, starting at 10 a.m. They accept credit cards, cash, and traveler's checks. For more information go to the Theatre Development Fund web site at www.tdf.org or write: Theatre Development Fund, 1501 Broadway, 21st floor, New York, NY 10036-5652.
- **TKTS South Street Seaport**, on the corner of Front St and John St (the rear of the building at 199 Water St), has the same tickets available as the Times Square location, and usually with a shorter line. Also, tickets for matinees are available the day before, a service not provided at the midtown location.
- **TKTS Downtown Brooklyn Booth, at 1 Metro Tech Center (Jay and Myrtle),** sells tickets to evening shows on the day of the performance, and, like the South Street Seaport location, sells matinee tickets on the previous day; it also sells tickets to Brooklyn performing arts events.
- **Twofers** resemble theater tickets but are, in fact, passes. When exchanged at Broadway (and some off-Broadway) box offices, twofers entitle the bearer to two tickets for little more than the price of one. A convenient way to keep a show open after bad reviews or at the end of a long run, twofers can be found all over town. Try: restaurant cash registers, the city's official Visitor Information Center at 810 Seventh Ave at 53rd St, in college dorms, or hotels.
- **The Theatre Development Fund**, 1501 Broadway, 21st floor, Attention: TDF Membership, NYC 10036, 212-912-9770, www.tdf.org; offers tickets to a variety of plays, musicals, dance, and jazz performances at reduced prices, typically less than $36 for a Broadway play or musical and under $25 for off-

Broadway productions. Memberships are available to seniors (62 or older), students, teachers, performing arts professionals, union members, staff members of a non-profit organization, and members of the clergy or armed forces. Download the application from the TDF web site and mail it in. The annual membership fee is $27.50.

- **Audience Extras**, 61 Lexington Ave, Suite 1A, 212-686-1966, www.audience-extras.com, provides free tickets to plays in preview and post opening (whose producers wish to "paper" the house, i.e., fill it with freebies to stimulate word-of-mouth) to its members in the theater industry. For $115 you get a one-year membership card, renewable for $85, with a reserve fund against which a $3 service charge per ticket is charged as well as access to their 24-hour hotline, which lists available shows. There is no limit on free shows.
- **Quicktix**; a small allotment of seats for each of the various performances at the New York Shakespeare Festival's Public Theater on Lafayette St (see **Theater** section) go on sale at 5:30 p.m. on the day of performance, for about half the price of regular tickets. You need to be a **Public Theater** member. Call 212-260-2400 after 1 p.m. for information. The Public Theater is online at www.publictheater.org.
- **Ask.** Many theaters offer rush tickets, often at discounts, that are made available only hours before a performance. Typically, rush tickets are reserved for students or seniors, or are assigned through a lottery (usually two to three hours before a show). Limited-view seats are also discounted, and are more likely to be found at the box office than through a second- or third-party vendor. Contact the theater for specific details.
- **Hit Show Club**, 212-581-4211, www.hitshowclub.com; free membership offers savings and discounts to a range of shows both Broadway and off-, as well as restaurant/show packages.
- **StubHub,** 1440 Broadway, 866-788-2482, www.stubhub.com; this new service is the E-bay of tickets—sporting, Broadway, what have you. It's scalping by another name, but here it is guaranteed because the auctions are online and everyone selling has to register a credit card. Even better, they have an office at Broadway and 40th St where you can pick up your tickets last minute.

Student tickets at half price or less are often available to those holding bona fide student IDs as follows:

- **New York Philharmonic** at Avery Fisher Hall, Lincoln Center, has two arrangements. They sell $16 tickets for rehearsals about a month before the actual date. For shows with high availability, students and seniors can receive Rush tickets for $12 (call 212-875-5656 on day of show, or go to Avery Fisher Hall box office; students may also phone to reserve tickets up to 10 days before the performance). For more information, go to www.nyphil.org.
- **New York City Opera**, also at Lincoln Center, www.nycopera.com, sometimes has student tickets for those who line up at the theater by 10 a.m. on

the morning of a performance, 11:30 a.m. on Sunday. Tickets, if available, are $16. Call the box office, 212-870-5570, for more information. Students may also buy half-price tickets in the week before the show, throuch CenterCharge, 212-721-6500.

- **Carnegie Hall** sells $10 tickets, when available, on a first-come, first-served basis, to select events. You can call 212-247-7800 on the day of the concert starting at noon to see if tickets will be available. Day-of tickets are available at the box office from noon until one hour before the performance.
- **Grace Rainey Rogers Auditorium** at the Metropolitan Museum of Art sells standing-room tickets for half price on the day of a concert. Call the box office at 212-570-3949 to check on availability.

High school students have access to the best deal of all on tickets to music, theater, museums, dance, and more through **High 5 Tickets to the Arts**. Students 13 to 18 years old can get $5 tickets to weekend (Friday–Sunday) performances, two for $5 for weekday performances by presenting school ID at any Ticketmaster outlet, including HMV, Tower Records, and other stores in the city and in much of New Jersey, at least a day before the performance. Museum admission is two for $5 any day, with ID, at the museum. Free catalogs of High 5 events are available at participating Ticketmaster outlets, public libraries, and at High 5's office, 1 East 53rd Street. Call 212-750-0555 for information or visit www.highfivetix.org. The School Theater Ticket Program also offers discount vouchers for Broadway, Off-Broadway, and Lincoln Center events. Visit www.schooltix.com.

A few of the smaller to mid-size Manhattan theaters (generally off-Broadway and off-off-Broadway) will exchange admission for volunteer ushering, a boon to the theater devotee who is light of wallet. Call around for participating theaters.

If you are a frequent theater-goer, sports fan, or classical music enthusiast, you might want to pick up **STUBS**, a paperback that publishes the seating plan of every concert hall, opera house, stadium, arena, and theater in town. STUBS in hand, you can immediately locate the seats being offered by TKTS booths, brokers, Ticketmaster outlets and others that have no seating diagrams available for ticket purchasers. The book sells for $12.95 and can be ordered on www.amazon.com or found in New York bookstores.

SUBSCRIPTIONS

Common practice dictates that new subscriptions to any series—symphonic, operatic, dance, theatrical—must wait to be filled until the previous season's subscribers are given an opportunity to renew. Once the renewal deadline is past, new subscriptions are processed on a first-come, first-served basis. The initial announcement of each new season's schedule is sent to everyone on the mailing list anywhere from six weeks to six months before performances are scheduled to begin. To assure a position near the beginning of the line, call whatever institution interests you well in advance of its season and ask to be put on the mailing list. Upon receipt of the announcement schedule, choose your series and return the coupon and a check quickly. Often this can be done online at the appropriate web site. Full-page ads in the *New York Times* Sunday "Arts and Leisure" section herald symphonic, operatic, and dance seasons five to six months before performances begin, but usually a week or two after the first public subscription mailers have been sent out.

Incidentally, certain nights are traditionally more popular than others. If good seats are more important than sitting next to the right people, find out which night or series has the best tickets available.

One great bargain:

- **People's Symphony Concert Series**, www.pscny.org; this series of a half dozen classical performances each year has some of the world's greatest ensembles—but tickets can be as low as $7 if you buy a subscription. They have three different series every year.

GRAND OPERA

- **Metropolitan Opera**, Metropolitan Opera House, Lincoln Center, 212-362-6000, http://www.metoperafamily.org; subscriptions range from $120 for an eight-opera series high up in the Family Circle to $1,360 for an eight-opera series in the Center Orchestra. The Met charges $35 per subscription for handling. Renewal notices are mailed to current subscribers, and once these orders are processed in the spring, new subscriptions are filled. The Met's season is broken into three periods for the sale of individual seats: fall, winter, and spring. Subscribers are given first crack, then seats for single performances are offered to the public, first through a mailing, then via newspaper ads about a month and a half before each of the three seasons begins. Standing room goes on sale the Sunday before performance. You might also catch the Met during their free concert series in the parks during the summer. They visit each of the five boroughs. Check their web site for a schedule as the summer approaches.
- **New York City Opera**, New York State Theater, Lincoln Center, subscriptions, 212-496-0600 or 212-870-5580; box office, 212-870-5570; www.nycopera. com. The New York City Opera offers numerous two- to four-opera series for performances September–April. There are several different plans; ticket prices vary.
- **Opera Orchestra of New York**, 239 W 72nd St, 212-799-1982, www.operaorchestrany.org; under the musical direction of Eve Queler, performs three non-staged (that is, concert style) operas per season at Carnegie Hall. Performed by singers of the first rank but not super-stars, these are usually operas by major composers that are rarely staged. Subscriptions to the 2006–2007

season ranged from $75 for a seat in the rear balcony to $375 for parquet center and first tier, plus a suggested donation ranging from $20 to $85.

CLASSICAL MUSIC

- **New York Philharmonic**, Avery Fisher Hall, Lincoln Center, 212-875-5656, www.nyphilharmonic.org; numerous series are available for a September–June season. Easiest to obtain are subscriptions to the three-concert mini-series. Fall schedules are announced in late February/early March.
- **Carnegie Hall**, 57th St and Seventh Ave, 212-247-7800, www.carnegiehall. org; 115 years old and still counting, Carnegie, featuring splendid acoustics, is still the concert hall preferred by many performers, and it continues to host programs by a variety of virtuosos and orchestras, plus popular superstars and even chamber music, with age-given grace. Call Carnegie Hall for subscriber information.

CHAMBER MUSIC

Several halls traditionally host the extraordinarily popular chamber music groups that perform here regularly. The Guarneri Quartet, the Juilliard Quartet, and the Beaux Arts Trio might give three or more New York concerts during any given year, each at a different location. Only the Lincoln Center Chamber Music Society has a hall—Alice Tully Hall in Lincoln Center—that it can call home. Good seats go fast once the *Times* advertisements appear, so it's important to get on each group's mailing list. The following spaces are most likely to host chamber music performances. Call them or keep your eyes on the "Arts and Leisure" section of the Sunday *New York Times* in late spring and summer.

- **Abraham Goodman House**, Merkin Concert Hall, 129 W 67th St between Broadway and Amsterdam Ave, box office, 212-501-3330, www.kaufman-center.org
- **Alice Tully Hall**, Lincoln Center, 212-721-6500, www.lincolncenter.org; concerts by the Lincoln Center Chamber Music Society as well as other groups
- **Brooklyn Academy of Music (BAM)**, 30 Lafayette Ave, Brooklyn, 718-636-4100, www.bam.org
- **Metropolitan Museum of Art**, Grace Rainey Rogers Auditorium, 83rd St and Fifth Ave, 212-570-3949, www.metmuseum.org
- **92nd Street Y (YM-YWHA)**, Kaufmann Concert Hall, 1395 Lexington Ave, 212-427-6000, www.92y.org

DANCE

It could be argued that New York is the dance capital of the world. Certainly it is possible to see a performance of some form of dance—ballet, modern, jazz, ethnic, avant-garde—just about any night of the week somewhere in the city. Dance enthusiasts watch the publications above to catch visiting troupes and local groups at alternative sites. Among the latter, for example, are **Dance Theatre Workshop** at 219 West 19th Street, 212-924-0077, www.dancetheatreworkshop. org; **Danspace Project** at St. Mark's Church, 131 East 10th Street,866-811-4111, www.danspaceproject.org; **Performance Space 122**, 150 First Avenue at Ninth Street, 212-477-5288, www.ps122.org; **Joyce SoHo**, 155 Mercer Street, south of Houston Street, 212-431-9233, www.joyce.org; and **Theater of the Riverside Church**, 91 Claremont Avenue at 120th Street, 212-870-6784, www.theriver-sidechurchny.org; Below we've listed the established troupes and theaters to which one can subscribe. Get yourself on one mailing list and others are likely to find you.

- **American Ballet Theater**, 890 Broadway, third floor, 212-477-3030, www.abt. org; subscription series are offered for the ABT's spring season at the Metropolitan Opera House, April–June. The first announcement, mailed to friends in late December, is followed shortly by a new subscriber mailing, then a week or so later by the traditional January *New York Times* ad. Subscriptions for seats vary. Individual tickets at the box office and by phone from the Met Ticket Service go on sale in March.

- **New York City Ballet**, New York State Theater, Lincoln Center, 212-870-5580 for subscriptions or 212-870-5570 for performance information, www.nycballet. com; Two seasons provide balletomanes the opportunity of feasting on dancing by Balanchine's company. Both the winter season, November–February, and the spring season, April–June, have sixteen four-performance series, and good seats are easiest to come by for weekend matinees. First announcements go out nine weeks before the season begins. A tip for *Nutcracker* ballet fanciers: first orders for single, non-subscription performances of the *Nutcracker* are accepted in late October and tickets go fast for this seasonal family favorite. Call 212-870-5500 for prices and dates, and if certain seats for special performances are important, make your order several weeks before that time.

- **The Joyce Theater**, 175 Eighth Ave at 19th St, 212-242-0800, www.joyce.org; celebrating dance of all kinds—ballet, modern, flamenco—the Joyce is an elegantly revamped former Art Deco movie house in Chelsea. Your reward for buying tickets to performances by four different dance groups during the fall or spring season is a membership that entitles you to 40% off on all tickets purchased subsequently. Your membership card also entitles you to priority seating and various discounts at fifteen Chelsea restaurants located between 14th and 23rd streets and Sixth and Tenth avenues.

- **The City Center Theater**, 131 W 55th St, 212-581-1212, www.nycitycenter.org; dance companies once dominated the City Center's performance schedule; today they vie with a variety of musical comedy performances. The following **dance troupes** are among the major groups performing here regularly:
  - **Martha Graham**, 316 E 63rd St, 212-521-3611, www.marthagrahamdance. org

- **Alvin Ailey American Dance Theater**, 405 West 55th Street, 212-405-9000, www.alvinailey.org
- **Paul Taylor Dance Company**, 552 Broadway, 212-431-5562, www.ptdc. org
- **Dance Theatre of Harlem**, 466 W 152nd St, 212-690-2800, www. dancetheatreofharlem.com
- **American Ballet Theater**, 890 Broadway, third floor, 212-477-3030, www. abt.org
- **Mark Morris Dance Group**, 3 Lafayette Ave, Brooklyn 718-624-8400, www. mmdg.org

As with the chamber music ensembles, it is best to get on each company's mailing list. Call the company direct or City Center's Subscription Department. Prices vary for each series.

THEATER

Broadway, besides designating Manhattan's longest avenue, refers to the mid-town theater district on and around "the Great White Way," home to the greatest theatrical productions in the nation, ranging from grand musicals and comedies to classic dramas. It's the big time and a magnet for theater-lovers everywhere. But a high percentage of the most critically acclaimed plays and musicals pro-duced in any given year originate off-Broadway, more often than not in theaters that offer subscriptions as a means of financing productions. Season tickets not only ensure exposure to new artists, playwrights, and directors, but in most cases save money as well. A few of the most established groups are mentioned here, but please don't be limited by this list. Many more experimental but no less rewarding companies exist and should be explored.

- **Circle in the Square Theatre School**, 1633 Broadway at 50th St, 212-307-0388, www.circlesquare.org; professional conservatory and acting and musical the-ater. Beginning in the 1950s in the Village, plays by Tennessee Williams and Eugene O'Neill premiered at Circle in the Square with such young actors as Jason Robards and George C. Scott. Uptown now, the theater continues to stage some of the best contemporary drama and comedy with first-rate actors and directors.
- **CSC Repertory Theater**, 136 E 13th St, 212-352-3101, www.classicstage.org; founded in 1967, CSC has been performing Ibsen, Strindberg, Brecht, and other mostly contemporary classics in this comfortably intimate theater since then. It's not a resident company, but three or four plays are performed in rep-ertory throughout the season, with an occasional lecture bonus.
- **Joseph Papp Public Theater**, 425 Lafayette St south of E 8th St, www.pub-lictheater.org; members call 212-539-8650 for tickets; non-members call 212-967-7555. Joseph Papp, who died in 1992, was perhaps the single most important figure in the post-WWII American theater. This venue, complete

with the New York Shakespeare Festival's Public Theater and the cabaret, Joe's Pub, offers events that are hailed for their diversity as well as their excellence. A membership package plan allows the public inexpensive access to productions and flexibility in choosing which of the season's productions one wishes to see. A small allotment of the seats for any performance at The Public are held for same-day sale at a discount. The tickets, called Quicktix (see **Discounts** section), go on sale at 6 p.m. for about half the price of regular tickets.

- **Lincoln Center Theater**, 150 W 65th St, 212-239-6200, www.lct.org; members in this innovative theater program have access to a potpourri of presentations from Shakespeare to Mamet, with an occasional first-rate musical thrown in, be it at Lincoln Center on Broadway or off-off-Broadway at the experimental LaMama. The $40 membership fee buys one year's access to Lincoln Center Theater plays already in progress around town and first crack at six new productions a year as they come up. Popular productions with outstanding casts have included *Our Town*, *Waiting for Godot*, and *Anything Goes*. For tickets call Telecharge, 212-239-6200.
- **Manhattan Theatre Club**, 311 W 43rd St, 212-399-3030, www.mtc-nyc.org, has been producing critically acclaimed plays since its founding on the Upper East Side in 1970. After some years with one foot at City Center on W 55th St, MTC has settled in there, at 299-seat Stage I and at 150-seat Stage II. Productions that prove to be especially successful typically move to larger Broadway or off-Broadway venues. Single tickets can also be purchased through City Tix: 212-581-1212.
- **Pearl Theatre Co.**, 80 St. Marks Place, 212-598-9802, www.pearltheatre.org; a repertory theater company, it mounts regular productions of theater classics such as Ibsen, Chekhov, and Shakespeare for a loyal audience in an intimate East Village theater. Various subscription plans for three to five performances range from $105 to $150.
- **Roundabout Theatre Company**, 231 W 39th St, Suite 1200, 212-719-1300, www.roundabouttheatre.org; with a subscription base of some 20,000, this not-for-profit theater company is obviously doing something right. What that involves is presenting revivals such as Pinter's *Betrayal* and O'Neill's *Anna Christie*, along with musicals such as *Cabaret*, with such stars as Natasha Richardson, Nathan Lane, Laura Linney, and Alan Cumming in their handsome home, The American Airlines Theater, 227 W 42nd St, while also staging off-Broadway performances of new plays by established writers.

ALL OF THE ABOVE

- **Brooklyn Academy of Music**, 30 Lafayette Ave, Brooklyn, 718-636-4100, www.bam.org; is a center for all the performing arts. Best known for its Next Wave Festival, which takes place September to December, BAM (as it is popularly known) is a prime showcase for cutting-edge dance, theater, music, and opera. From the intimate LeClerq Space to the magnificent Opera House and the rejuvenated Majestic Theater, BAM presents everything from small chamber performances to alternative new age music. With several series taking place year-round, it is best to call and get on the mailing list in order to have a shot at getting tickets. Subscriptions represent a real value here, and if you become a Friend of BAM you'll get priority seating.

- **Queens Theatre in the Park**, Flushing Meadow Corona Park, Flushing, 718-760-0064, www.queenstheatre.org; brings major dance companies, off-Broadway plays, and children's theater to its two theaters located in the Philip Johnson–designed New York Pavilion of the 1964–65 World's Fair. From *Charlie and the Chocolate Factory* to *Dames at Sea* to laser vaudeville to the Latino Culture Festival, Queens Theatre offers a variety of performances for a wide range of tastes.

FILM

New York is a movie buff's paradise. Screening of new filmmakers' works is a constant at the **Whitney Museum of American Art**, 945 Madison Avenue, 212-570-3676, www.whitney.org, and at the **Guggenheim Museum**, 1071 Fifth Avenue 212-423-3500, www.guggenheim.org, as well as at most of those all-encompassing, art-encouraging alternative spaces sprinkled throughout New York. **New School University**, 66 West 12th Street, 212-229-5600, www.newschool. edu, and the **Cinema Department of New York University**, 721 Broadway, 6th floor, 212-998-1600, www.cinema.tisch.nyu.edu, explore movies in depth through numerous seminars and courses and, almost every semester, sponsor a film series or two as well.

Some of Manhattan's remaining revival and art film showcases include: **Angelika Film Center and Café**, 18 West Houston Street, 212-995-2000, www. angelikafilmcenter.com; **Anthology Film Archives**, 32 Second Avenue at Second Street, 212-505-5181; **Cinema Village**, 12th Street east of Fifth Avenue, 212-924-3363; **Film Forum**, 209 West Houston, 212-727-8110; Landmark Sunshine Theater, 143 E. Houston (near 1st Ave) 212-330-8182; and the **Walter Reade Theater**, 165 West 65th Street at Broadway, 212-875-5600. Weekly schedules for these theaters are found in the "Arts and Leisure" section of the Sunday *Times* and the *New Yorker*. More comprehensive yet and including films shown in truly alternative venues is *Time Out New York's* "Film, Alternatives and Revivals" section.

Additional film societies and museums include:

- **The American Museum of the Moving Image**, 36-01 35th Ave at 36th St, Astoria 718-784-0077, www.movingimage.us, is a continuous movie, animation, and video art retrospective with exhibits, speaker series, symposia, celebrity appearances, and film series throughout the year to quicken the pulse of the true movie maven. Membership, $65 for individual, $100 for family, gives you admission, reservation privileges for screenings, a subscription to the Quarterly Guide, a 15% discount at the museum shop, and reduced admission to special programs and celebrity appearances. You need not be a member to visit; day rates available.

- **The Film Society of Lincoln Center**, 140 W 65th St, 212-875-5600, www.filmlinc.com, presents the New York Film Festival each fall (late September through October) at the Walter Reade Theater (see above) as well as the New Directors/New Films series in conjunction with the Museum of Modern Art each spring. Established in 1963, the Film Festival presents some 20 films during its annual run. A $75 membership in the Film Society provides the following perks: the right to buy two twelve-film subscriptions to the New York Film Festival and first crack at certain other festival tickets, discounts on tickets for New Directors/New Films at the Museum of Modern Art, and a free subscription to the society's bi-monthly magazine, *Film Comment*. If you're not interested in membership, it's a good idea to get on the society's mailing list before the Film Festival's program is announced the last week in August, in order to obtain the schedule before it appears in the papers. The box office for performances at **Alice Tully Hall** is at 1941 Broadway at 65th St, 212-875-5050. It opens the Sunday after Labor Day for single-ticket sales to the public.
- **Tribeca Film Institute**, 375 Greenwich St, 212-941-3890, www.tribecafilminstitute.org, offers year-round cultural events, including comedy, film, music, and theater, as well as the annual Tribeca Film Festival held each spring. Established by Robert De Niro and Jane Rosenthal in an effort to make Lower Manhattan a "centerpiece for culture and the arts."

Of course, there are plenty of movie theaters around the city showing the latest in Hollywood's big-screen hits. Theaters range from the small screens and tight seating in the multiplex theaters to the more spacious and comfortable Beekman on 66th and Second Avenue in Manhattan, where you might just catch a star-studded opening night. The IMAX Theater on Broadway and 68th Street with a four-story screen is worth checking out, especially with children. New Yorkers love to get out to the movies so expect to find lines for the hottest new flicks. Call the **movie phone**, 777-FILM, or go to www.moviefone.com or fandango.com to find out what is playing in your neighborhood and when.

BROADCASTING

The Paley Center for Media (formerly the The Museum of Television and Radio), 25 West 52nd Street, 212-621-6800, www.paleycenter.org, shouldn't be missed as a chance to revisit your childhood and to experience American culture in video and audiotape form. "...The Shadow knows," Fred Allen on radio, *All in the Family, I Love Lucy*—it's all there. The museum offers 96 video monitors for individual viewing of any television program in their collection. Call for schedule listings of special screening events. Annual memberships vary with special prices for students, which allow admission to the museum's theaters and screening and listening rooms. Membership also gives you a discount on museum seminars and magazines as well as all gift shop items.

MUSEUM MEMBERSHIPS

The benefits to be reaped by joining any of the city's myriad non-profit institutions are really quite amazing. There seem to be museums and societies for every possible interest, so if you're an aficionado of a particular discipline, seek out the institution that best reflects your avocation and join. You'll be inundated with free literature, offered perquisites of many kinds, and probably be invited to teas, cocktail parties, and even banquets if your contribution is big enough. For the generalist, membership in one or two of the city's established cultural citadels is a wonderful way of obtaining well-researched information on any number of subjects. As an indication of the kind of benefits memberships provide, we've noted below details for a few of New York's major institutions:

- **American Folk Art Museum**, 45 W 53rd St, 212-265-1040, www.folkartmuseum.org; a wide array of folk art from weathervanes to textiles is found depicting America's history from the 18th century to the present. Membership ranges from $65 annually for an individual to $85 for a family and includes free admission to the museum, discounts on gift shop purchases, a subscription to the museum's newsletter, access to the museum's library and other perks.
- **American Museum of Natural History**, Central Park West at 79th St, 212-769-5100, www.amnh.org; an associate membership here entitles you to as many visits to the dinosaurs as you wish, to say nothing of the Rose Center for Earth and Space, a subscription to *Natural History* magazine and a 10% discount in the store. A family membership adds a monthly newsletter and calendar, 25% discount on Hayden Planetarium tickets, and invitations to previews of the exhibitions. You also receive a 10% discount on most educational programs at the museum and a hefty discount at the IMAX Theater with its oversized retractable screen and a dizzying IMAX projector.
- **The Bronx Zoo** (its official name: **New York Zoological Society International Wildlife Conservation Park**), Fordham Road and Bronx River Parkway, The Bronx, 718-367-1010, is the largest zoo in the five boroughs and, stretching over 265 acres, the largest urban zoo in the world. Membership includes admission to this zoo as well as to the **Central Park Zoo**, Central Park, E 64th St and Fifth Ave, 212-439-6500; the **New York Aquarium**, Surf Ave and W 8th St, Coney Island, Brooklyn, 718-265-3474; the **Queens Wildlife Center**, 718-271-1500, and **Children's Farm**, 111th St at 54th Ave, Corona Park, Flushing, Queens. Bronx Zoo membership also includes four free parking passes and discounts at gift shops, certain zoo restaurants, and on educational classes.

These organizations are all part of the Wildlife Conservation Society, online at www.wcs.org.

- **Frick Collection**, 1 E 70th St, 212-288-0700, www.frick.org; membership in Friends of the Frick entitles you to unlimited admission to the collection, a subscription to the new *Frick Members' Magazine* with information on special exhibits, lectures, and concerts, and a 10% discount in the museum shop.
- **Guggenheim Museum**, 1071 Fifth Ave, downtown at 575 Broadway at Prince, 212-423-3500, www.guggenheim.org; even the basic individual membership confers an architectural bonus, providing free admission to the justifiably famous Frank Lloyd Wright spiral uptown and the Peggy Guggenheim Collection in her palazzo on the Grand Canal in Venice. In addition, members get invitations to parties, private viewings, book signings, and discounts at Guggenheim stores and the Guggenheim café.
- **The Jewish Museum**, 1109 Fifth Ave at 92nd St, 212-423-3200, www.jewishmuseum.org; Jewish culture is represented in 28,000 objects including fine arts, Judaica, and through the broadcast media. The permanent collection, Culture & Continuity: The Jewish Journey, depicts 4,000 years of Jewish history, including ancient times in Egypt, the Holocaust, and the formation of the State of Israel to the present. Membership includes unlimited admission, invitations to special previews of new exhibitions, discounts in the museum store and the Weissman Café, guest passes, invitations to the Family Hanukkah Party, and various other perks.
- **Metropolitan Museum of Art**, Fifth Ave at 82nd St, 212-879-5500, www.metmuseum.org; the sumptuous *Bulletin* published quarterly by the Met, filled with high-quality color photographs and illuminating texts of catalog caliber, comes free with the museum's $95 individual membership. Other bonuses include the bi-monthly *Calendar News*, free admission to the museum and the Cloisters, invitations to previews and private viewings of two exhibitions a year, and copies of the Met's Christmas and spring catalogues illustrating the museum's publications and glamorous reproductions of everything from Chinese scarves to early American pewter pitchers, which, as a member, you can buy at a 10% discount. But probably the biggest bonus you'll receive is the program and exhibition information, which will impel you to get over to the Met more often than you might otherwise.
- **Museum for African Art**, 36-01 43rd Ave, Long Island City, Queens, 718-784-7700, www.africanart.org; the Queens-based museum is widely recognized as housing the pre-eminent exhibition of African art. (Completion of their permanent home on 110th St in Manhattan is expected at some time in the future.) Membership includes admission to public programs, a subscription to the newsletter, discounts in the museum store and on birthday party packages, plus invitations to holiday receptions and the annual gala dinner.
- **The Museum of Modern Art (MoMA)**, 11 W 53rd St, 212-708-9500, www.moma.org; completely redone, MoMA now offers an unparalleled collection

of 20th century art in its six-story gallery building and eight-story Education and Research Center, with the top floors dedicated to the expanded library and archives; the renovated lobby offers views of the sculpture garden. Entry-level memberships receive a 10% discount at the museum store and on catalog and online merchandise, as well as admission to the galleries and daily film programs, and invitations to exhibition previews and special events. It also houses one of the city's top restaurants and an excellent communal table café.

- **The New Museum of Contemporary Art**, 236 Bowery, 212-219-1222, www. newmuseum.org; known for its distinctive architecture—it's a stack of offset, aluminum-shelled boxes—this museum showcases an über-modern collection of the latest of the latest and supposedly the greatest. Four floors, with a pretty comprehensive collection of the cutting edge in visual arts of all kinds
- **South Street Seaport Museum**, 207 Front St, 212-748-8600, www.southstseaport.org; encompasses the new Fulton Market with its intriguing stores and jolly restaurants, restored Schermerhorn Row's handsome brick houses, and the Museum Block with old shops and new walkways. Membership tends to be a youngish crowd, drawn as much by the ambiance and the idea of the museum as by the perks, which include free admission to the museums, galleries, and ships at the Seaport Gallery, invitations to gallery openings and educational programs, a subscription to *Seaport: New York's History Magazine*, plus discounts in several stores at the seaport.
- **Whitney Museum of American Art**, 945 Madison Ave at 75th St, 212-570-3676, www.whitney.org; membership benefits its holder with museum admission for two, discounts on classes and lectures, discounts at the museum store, invitations to exhibition opening receptions, and a free museum publication, as well as a calendar of events. If American art or experimental film interests you particularly, it is worth belonging to the Whitney to have ready access to its excellent series of large and small exhibitions and also to the works presented by the museum's New American Filmmakers series in some 25 to 30 different programs every year.

CULTURE FOR KIDS

Perhaps the greatest asset in raising children in the city is the astonishing wealth of theater, film, museums, and programs designed for them. It goes without saying that all of the institutions and organizations above are accessible to and appropriate sooner or later for children: the New York City Ballet's exquisite *Nutcracker*, the popular armor collection at the Metropolitan Museum, so much of the Museum of Natural History including the famed dinosaurs, the Bronx Zoo, children's museums in Manhattan and Brooklyn, to name just a few. Many of them design exhibits and programs specifically for children. And there are institutions and groups that exist specifically for the younger population.

How to find it all? You'll pick up a lot about what's going on where from school bulletin boards, from other parents, and from the parent magazines distributed free in school lobbies and libraries. Neighborhood weeklies such as *The Villager* often include events for children in their weekly listings. The comprehensive *Kids Culture Catalog*, compiled and published by the **Alliance for the Arts**, 330 West 42nd Street, #1701, 212-947-6340, www.allianceforarts.org, offers brief descriptions of and directions to scores of local institutions and attractions—from historic houses and botanical gardens to alternative art spaces and zoos. Their excellent *New York City Kids Arts Culture Calendar* is published twice yearly, and there is an annual **NYC Arts Calendar** available in June. Pick up either at the Alliance for the Arts office, New York's Visitor Center, or at area cultural institutions and libraries, or go to www.nyc-arts.org.

Other resources include:

- **New York magazine,** in the Cue section, has a "Kids" page that carries listings of children's events and attractions, with free events marked and including times, prices, and telephone numbers.
- **The *New York Times,*** in Friday's "Weekend" sections, carries extensive descriptions of theater, museum, and zoo events for children in the "Spare Times for Children" column, further descriptions of special events under "Family Fare," and reviews of new movies from the perspective of their suitability for children.
- *Time Out New York*, www.timeoutny.com, is a good source of information for child-friendly events going on around town.

THEATER FOR CHILDREN

Venues offering theater for children include the following:

- **Asphalt Green's Mazur Theater**, 555 E 90th St, 212-369-8890, www.asphaltgreen.org; puppet theater that runs during the school year.
- **Brooklyn Academy of Music**, 30 Lafayette Ave, Brooklyn, 718-636-4100, www.bam.org
- **Brooklyn Arts Exchange**, 421 Fifth Ave at 8th St in Park Slope, 718-832-0018, www.bax.org; also has classes for kids in theater, dance, and choreography.
- **Brooklyn YWCA**, The Shadow Box Theatre, 30 Third Ave between State and Atlantic Ave, Brooklyn, 212-724-0677, www.shadowboxtheatre.org
- **Henry Street Settlement, Abrons Art Center**, 466 Grand St, Lower East Side, 212-598-0400, www.henrystreet.org
- **New Victory Theater**, 209 W 42nd St, 646-223-3020, www.newvictory.org; revamped with a grand staircase rising to a jewel-box theater and family friendly. Engaging programming ranges from the pleasingly silly to the avant-garde but remains respectful of the audience's age and maturity.
- **Theatreworks USA**, 2162 Broadway at 76th St, 212-647-1100, www.theatreworksusa.org

- **South Street Seaport Museum and Marketplace**, South and Fulton streets, Lower Manhattan, 212-748-8600, www.southstseaport.org
- **Swedish Cottage Marionette Theater**, Central Park, 212-988-9093
- **Symphony Space**, 2537 Broadway at 95th St, 212-864-5400, www.symphonyspace.org
- **Thirteenth Street Repertory Company**, 50 W 13th St, 212-675-6677, www.13thstreetrep.org

If you want to really inspire your kids, go to a performance of the **Broadway Kids**. Since 1994, this rotating troupe, comprising children who have been in Broadway shows, has been wowing audiences at various venues around the city. For an upcoming schedule of performances, visit their web site at www.broadwaykids.com.

MUSEUMS AND LIBRARIES FOR CHILDREN

Many of the major museums and libraries host events and exhibitions specifically for children; others are dedicated entirely to kids.

- **American Museum of Natural History**, 79th St and Central Park West, 212-769-5100, www.amnh.org; a must, naturally.
- **Brooklyn Children's Museum**, 145 Brooklyn Ave at St. Mark's Place, Crown Heights, 718-735-4400, www.brooklynkids.org; wonderfully hands-on and inventive.
- **Brooklyn Museum of Art**, 200 Eastern Pkwy at Prospect Park, 718-638-5000, www.brooklynmuseum.org
- **Children's Museum of the Arts**, 182 Lafayette St near Broome St, 212-274-0986, www.cmany.org
- **Children's Museum of Manhattan**, 212 W 83rd St, 212-721-1234, www.cmom.org; fun for adults, too.
- **Historic Richmondtown**, Staten Island Historical Society, 441 Clarke Ave, Richmondtown, Staten Island, 718-351-1611, www.historicrichmondtown.org
- **Intrepid Sea Air Space Museum**, Pier 86, W 46th St at 12th Ave, 212-245-0072, www.intrepidmuseum.org
- **Madame Tussaud's Wax Museum**, 234 W 42nd St, 800-246-8872, www.nycwax.com; pricey but fun.
- **Museum of the City of New York**, Fifth Ave at 103rd St, 212-534-1672, www.mcny.org
- **New York City Fire Museum**, 278 Spring St, SoHo, 212-691-1303, www.nycfiremuseum.org; little ones love this place.
- **New York Hall of Science**, 47-01 111th St, Flushing, Queens, 718-699-0005, www.nyscience.org; highly regarded and recently expanded, this hands-on technology center is popular with budding young scientists.
- **New York Public Library**, various branches, 212-340-0849, www.nypl.org

- **Queens Museum of Art**, Flushing Meadow Corona Park, 718-592-9700, www. queensmuseum.org; home to the most amazing miniature panorama of the city with some 800,000 buildings capturing almost every structure in the five boroughs—a must see to believe.
- **Queens Public Library**, various branches, 718-990-0700, www.queenslibrary. org
- **Staten Island Children's Museum** at Snug Harbor Cultural Center, 1000 Richmond Terrace, Livingston, Staten Island, 718-273-2060, www.statenislandkids. org

FILM FOR CHILDREN

The **Museum of Modern Art** (see above) screens movies for children, some of them about art, some artful, in their Roy and Niuta Titus Theater, 11 West 53rd Street, 212-408-6663. Children and their parents who attend the annual **New York International Children's Film Festival** at NYU's Cantor Film Center, 36 East 8th Street, 212-998-1212, in February choose the grand prize winners; www. gkids.com describes the films and gives show times.

MUSIC AND DANCE FOR CHILDREN

Many of the major venues for music and dance in the city present special programs for children. Among them:

- **Alice Tully Hall, Jazz for Young People**, Lincoln Center, Broadway at 65th St; for tickets call 212-721-6500.
- **Carnegie Hall**, family concerts, 57th St and 7th Ave, 212-247-7800, www. carnegiehall.org
- **Florence Gould Hall, Little Orchestra Society**, 55 E 59th St, 212-971-9500, www.littleorchestra.org
- **Brooklyn Arts Exchange**, 421 Fifth Ave at 8th St in Park Slope, Brooklyn, 718-832-0018, www.bax.org
- **Joyce Theater, Eliot Feld Kids Dance**, 175 Eighth Ave at 19th St, 212-242-0800
- **Symphony Space**, 2537 Broadway at 95th St, 212-864-5400, www. symphonyspace.org
- **The Town Hall**, 123 W 43rd St, 212-840-2824, www.the-townhall-nyc.org

PARKS

The city's parks and botanical gardens are hopping with children's programs and activities year-round. To name just several:

- **Central Park**, the park always has a variety of activities for children including the Swedish Marionette Theater, Belvedere Castle, and the Charles A. Dana Discovery Center, 110th St near Fifth Ave, 212-860-1370, www.centralparknyc. org, which offers free activities and nature programs for children most weekends. Registration required. The Central Park Zoo, East 64th St at Fifth Ave, 718-220-5100, and Children's Zoo are perennial favorites and more accessible than the Bronx Zoo, although much smaller.

- **New York Botanical Garden**, 200th St and Kazimiroff Blvd in The Bronx, 718-817-8700, www.nybg.org; has a Children's Adventure Garden in addition to occasional programs for children, and the wonderful Christmastime miniature train extravaganza.
- **Prospect Park** on Flatbush Ave in Brooklyn hosts a small zoo near Empire Avenue with sheep, chickens, rabbits, and a friendly snake, as well as activities for children, 718-399-7339, www.wcs.org. The Lefferts Homestead Children's Museum in the park along Flatbush Ave near the zoo offers demonstrations and activities, 718-789-2822.

Not to be forgotten, of course, are the **Bronx Zoo**, the **New York Aquarium**, and the **Queens Wildlife Center and Children's Farm**, which sits adjacent to the Hall of Science.

LITERARY LIFE

Given that New York is home to many of the largest publishing houses in the world, it's no surprise that New Yorkers love to read. From breakfast over the Book Section of the Sunday *New York Times* to lunch hours spent browsing the pages of new best sellers at a Barnes & Noble superstore, New Yorkers enjoy their literature.

Just over 200 public libraries can be found in the five boroughs, and several private membership libraries still survive, some dating back to the 18th century. In addition, several of the city's museums have libraries and nearly all have well-stocked book sections in their gift shops.

PUBLIC SPECIALTY LIBRARIES

Along with the neighborhood branches (see the list of resources following the neighborhood profiles at the beginning of the book), New York City is home to several public premier research libraries pertaining to specific areas of interest:

- **The New York Public Library: Center For the Humanities**, Fifth Ave, between 40th and 42nd Streets, 212-661-7220; exhibitions and programs, 212-869-8089; research, 212-930-0830; www.nypl.org/research/cyhss. Beyond the spectacular floor-to-ceiling marble entranceway you'll find an amazing collection of nearly 40 million items in the form of books, periodicals, newspapers, manuscripts, microfilm, maps, paintings, ephemera, and CDs. All are tucked away within this magnificent structure guarded by two larger than life stone lions flanking the grand Fifth Avenue entrance. Built over a ten-year period from 1901 through 1911, at a cost of nine million dollars, this world-famous library is home to the first five folios of Shakespeare's plays, ancient Torah scrolls, a Gutenberg Bible, and many other historic literary items. Free tours meet at the front entrance between 11 a.m. and 2 p.m. Monday–Saturdays. Note: this is not a lending library.

- **New York Public Library for the Performing Arts: Dorothy and Lewis B. Cullman Center**, 40 Lincoln Center Plaza, 212-870-1630, www.nypl.org/research/lpa; located in Lincoln Center, this newly renovated library features an extensive collection items related to the arts: posters, correspondence, sheet music, scripts, press clippings, periodicals, books, and recordings. Patrons include many budding performers, playwrights, choreographers, and musicians.
- **Science, Industry, and Business Library**, 188 Madison Ave, 212-592-7000, www.nypl.org/research/sibl; opened in 1996 at the price of $100 million dollars, this state-of-the-art facility is devoted to science, technology, economics, and business. Features over 60,000 volumes of reference materials, 50,000 circulating titles, and over 100,000 periodicals. Membership includes discounts at the library shops and an informative newsletter/calendar.
- **Schomburg Center for Research in Black Culture**, 515 Malcolm X Blvd, 212-491-2200, www.nypl.org/research/sc; featuring a vast array of resources collected by Arthur Schomburg, the library is part of the larger exhibit space, which displays African-American culture. The Jean Blackwell Hutson General Research and Reference Division includes rare books and writings available in text and electronic formats.

MEMBERSHIP LIBRARIES

Before there were public libraries, there were private membership libraries, three of which survive in New York, a clubby step back in time and a haven for the book lover.

- **The New York Society Library**, 53 E 79th St, 212-288-6900, www.nysoclib.org; the oldest library in the city, founded in 1754. Offers members the opportunity to search extensive holdings and even borrow some of the titles. Membership costs $200 per year or $150 for six months per household.
- **The Mercantile Library**, 17 E 47th St, 212-755-6710, www.mercantilelibrary.org; formed in 1820 and houses only fiction. Is noted for its lively panel discussions. Individual membership is $100. Check their calendar for upcoming events.
- **The General Society Library**, 20 W 44th St, 212-840-1840, www.generalsociety.org; founded in 1820, it seems little changed over the last century. More than 150,000 volumes can be found on its old wooden shelves, including a special collection of the works of Gilbert & Sullivan. Membership starts at $50 per year.

BOOKSTORES

Bibliophiles are amply served in New York City, although more recently there has been a real dearth of smaller stores, and larger chains like Barnes & Noble have recently closed key stores. Today's chains are more than just shelves of titles; they offer steaming lattés and scones in the far corner, as well as poetry readings and evening acoustical performances. But there are times when you don't know just what book you want, perhaps for your mother, or when you want Donald Westlake's latest and don't know what it is, or who was that Polish Nobel Prize–winning poet you meant to read? At such times, a particular bookstore with a knowledgeable staff and the cozy feel of a traditional small bookshop is what you want. There are still some smaller bookstores left in Manhattan. You'll find descriptions of the best in *New York's 50 Best Bookstores for Book Lovers*, a paperback by Eve Claxton. We list a few of Manhattan's more notable ones:

- **Argosy Book Store**, 116 E 59th St, between Lexington and Park avenues, 212-753-4455, www.argosybooks.com; rare books, antique maps, photos, and documents.
- **Bank Street Bookstore**, 610 W 112th St, at Broadway, Bank Street College, 212-678-1654, www.bankstreetbooks.com; offers books for and about children.
- **Books of Wonder**, 18 W 18th St, 800-207-6968, www.booksofwonder.net; offers a lovely selection of children's books, readings, and events.
- **Complete Traveler Bookstore**, 199 Madison Ave (at 35th), 212-685-9007; everything an aspiring traveler could want to plan their wanderings.
- **Housing Works Used Book Cafe**, 126 Crosby St, 212-334-3324, www.housingworks.org/usedbookcafe; sip espresso, browse books and pick up a used couch, proceeds go to house the homeless with HIV/AIDS.
- **Hue-Man Bookstore & Café**, 2319 Frederick Douglass Blvd, 212-665-7400, www.huemanbookstore.com; large selection of African-American literature and books.
- **Kitchen Arts & Letters**, 1435 Lexington Ave at 93rd St, 212-876-5550, www.kitchenartsandletters.com; new and hard-to-find books on food and wine.
- **Book Culture**, 536 W 112th St between Broadway and Amsterdam Ave, 212-865-1588, www.bookculture.com; university press, and scholarly books and journals.
- **Murder Ink**, 2486 Broadway and W 92nd St, 212-362-8905; where you'll find that Donald Westlake title.
- **Posman Books**, 9 Grand Central Terminal, 212-983-1111, www.posmanbooks.com; offers an eclectic selection of books and frequent author readings.
- **Rizzoli Bookstore**, 31 W 57th St, 212-759-2424, www.rizzoliusa.com; great selection of exquisite art books.
- **Ruby's Books Sale**, 119 Chambers St, 212-732-8676; lots of dusty used titles at low prices.

- **Shakespeare & Co.**, 716 Broadway at Washington Place, 212-529-1330; 939 Lexington Ave at 69th St, 212-570-0201; 137 E 23rd St at Lexington Ave, 212-505-2021; also one Brooklyn location at 14 Hillel Place, 718-434-5326; www.shakeandco.com
- **Strand Bookstore Inc.**, 828 Broadway at 12th St, main store, 212-473-1452, and 95 Fulton St, 212-732-6070, www.strandbooks.com; the world's largest used bookstore, they say ("18 miles of books"), and mind-boggling.
- **Urban Center Books**, 457 Madison Ave, 212-935-3595, www.mas.org; urban history and architecture.

I N NEW YORK YOU CAN ROOT, ROOT, ROOT FOR THE HOME TEAM, CANTER along Central Park's cinder track, join a pickup basketball game, swim laps after work, or sit spellbound at the US Open Tennis Championships. The city hosts events for every season and activities for every appetite. To help you sort out the teams you wish to follow and the activities you wish to pursue, details about the area's major teams are listed below, followed by a section devoted to **Participant Sports**. For specifics about ticket sales see also **Tickets** in the **Cultural Life** chapter. Locations are in Manhattan unless otherwise specified.

PROFESSIONAL SPORTS

For weekly specifics on leading amateur and professional sporting events, check "This Week in Sports" in the "Sports" section of the Sunday *New York Times* and *Time Out New York*'s "Sports" section.

BASEBALL

The season begins at the end of March and lasts until early October (or longer, as is often the case for the Yankees). Tickets range from $12 for bleacher seats to $110 for boxes that are generally long sold out. There are also special $5 ticket nights: see the team schedule available at the box office or at www.yankees. mlb.com. Mets tickets range from $12 to $400, depending on the location of the seats and which team they are playing. You can purchase tickets for Mets or Yankees games through Ticketmaster, 212-307-7171 or www.ticketmaster.com; charge tickets to a credit card and have them sent, or pick them up at one of 20 locations in Manhattan. Note: as with theater tickets, there is a service charge tacked on to the price of each ticket purchased through Ticketmaster, which can be costly. To save some money, you can purchase tickets at the stadium box office. Mets tickets are also available at the Mets Clubhouse shops: 1275 Broadway (in the Manhattan Mall) and 11 West 42nd Street, both in Manhattan. For Yankees tickets, go to the Yankee Clubhouse stores at 110 East 59th Street, 393 Fifth Avenue, 8 Fulton Street, 745 7th Avenue, and 294 West 42nd Street in Manhattan. Schedules for upcoming Mets or Yankees games are always easy to find in the newspapers or at www.mlb.com, the official site of Major League Baseball.

- **New York Mets** (National League), Citi Field, 126th St and Roosevelt Ave, Flushing, NY 11368; 718-507-METS for information; box office: 718-507-8499, www.mets.com. Along with season tickets, the Mets have innumerable subscription plans, and buying single-game tickets in advance is generally not difficult as they typically only sell out a few times a year. There are plenty of fun promotional days for kids, with giveaway items. You can drive to Citi Field on the Grand Central Parkway and park for a fee in the stadium lot or take the #7 train, which takes about 50 minutes from midtown and brings you right to the stadium. One caveat—Citi Field might not be the name of the new stadium (which replaces the old Shea Stadium) by the time you read this book, depending on what happens with its failing namesake, Citibank. But the address will be the same.
- **New York Yankees** (American League), Yankee Stadium, 161st St and River Ave, Bronx, NY 10451, 718-293-6000, www.yankees.com; the Yankees have several ticket subscription plans ranging from season tickets to several games. Games against top teams will sell out, but generally, tickets for weeknight games—and certainly weekday games—are usually available on game day. The new Yankee Stadium (or the house that Ruth built) replaces the classic ballpark from the 1920s and a great place to watch a ballgame. Monument Park just over the centerfield fence pays tribute to classic Yankee teams and is a great place to explore prior to the game. There are also tours offered of the stadium, starting at $14 for adults and $7 for children and seniors. You can drive to Yankee Stadium, which is just off the Major Deegan Expressway, and park in one of several lots (for a fee) or take the #4 train from Manhattan—it's about 25 minutes from midtown and an easy trip as the subway stops right behind the bleachers.

BASKETBALL

The NBA basketball season begins when baseball leaves off, around late October, and continues through mid-April or into May or even June if the teams are in the playoffs. Knicks' home games are played in Madison Square Garden; the Nets play at the Meadowlands. Single seats for the Nets and the Knicks range between $25 and $1,500. Call Ticketmaster, 212-307-7171, to order tickets, or visit a Ticketmaster outlet to pick up your tickets.

- • **New York Knickerbockers** (NBA), Madison Square Garden, 33rd St between Seventh and Eighth avenues, NYC 10001, 212-465-5867 or 877-NYK-DUNK, www.nba.com/knicks; season plans cost several thousand dollars but there are some limited plans available. Individual tickets go on sale in early September and can be purchased at Ticketmaster outlets, 212-307-7171, as well as at the Garden Box Office. Seats are not easy to get so plan to purchase well in advance. To get to Madison Square Garden it's best to take the subway—1, 2, 3, 9, A, C, E trains—or the Long Island Railroad, which stops at Penn Station under the Garden. If you drive, your best bet is parking after 7 p.m. on side streets (24th through 29th streets), otherwise you'll end up in costly lots waiting for up to an hour to get your car after the game.

- **New Jersey Nets** (NBA) play in the Continental Airlines Arena in the Meadowlands Sports Complex in East Rutherford, NJ 07073, six miles west of the Lincoln Tunnel; call 800-7NJ-NETS or go to www.njnets.com for ticket information. Ticket plans range from season tickets for the 41-game home season, plus exhibition games, to short plans of six to ten games. You can always purchase single game tickets in advance and usually on game night. There is plenty of parking in the arena lot.

- **New York Liberty** (WNBA), Madison Square Garden, 33rd St between Seventh and Eighth avenues, NYC 10001, 212-465-6073, www.wnba.com/liberty, is professional women's basketball at its best. Tickets can be purchased at the Madison Square Garden Box Office or at Ticketmaster outlets, 212-307-7171. Tickets are easy to get. The season runs from May through August.

FOOTBALL

The popularity of Jets and Giants games during the pro football season, September–December, is clearly demonstrated by ticket scarcity.

- **Giants** (NFL), Giants Stadium, Meadowlands Sports Complex, East Rutherford, NJ 07073, 201-935-8222, www.giants.com; regular season tickets are sold out years in advance. Your best bet: become chums with a season ticket holder or buy through a ticket broker.

- **New York Jets** (NFL) also play at the Giants Stadium in the Meadowlands Sports Complex. Call 516-560-8200 for ticket information, www.newyorkjets.com. Renewals for season tickets to the eight home-game season are filled by May 15. New subscriptions are then issued from the fairly long waiting list on a first-come, first-served basis in early June. Good luck.

HOCKEY

The New York Rangers, Islanders, and New Jersey Devils play NHL hockey starting at the end of September and going into the spring.

- **New York Rangers** (NHL), Madison Square Garden, 33rd St between Seventh and Eighth avenues, NYC 10001. Call Ticketmaster to order tickets by phone, 212-307-7171. Whether the Rangers are playing well or not, tickets are very hard to come by as most season ticket holders keep their seats for years. Be on-line at the box office when tickets go on sale for the season or sign up in advance for a mini-plan if any are still available. Get ticket information at the team web site, www.newyorkrangers.com. For information on Madison Square Garden see above.

- **New York Islanders** (NHL), Nassau Coliseum in Uniondale, Long Island, NY 11553, 516-501-6700, ticket hotline, 800-882-ISLES, www.islanders.nhl.com; tickets also available through Ticketmaster. Islander tickets are easier to get than Ranger tickets. In fact if you want to see a Rangers game, this is one way to do it—just don't let on that you're a Rangers fan while at the Coliseum—or for that matter if you're an Islander fan, be quiet at the Garden.
- **New Jersey Devils** (NHL), Continental Airlines Arena, Meadowlands Sports Complex, East Rutherford, NJ, six miles west of the Lincoln Tunnel, 800-NJ-DEVIL, www.devils.nhl.com; they've won three Stanley Cups since 1995, making them the area's most successful hockey team and making tickets harder to get. The Devils are expected to move into a new arena, currently under construction near Newark Penn Station in Newark, in time for the 2007-2008 season.

RACING: HARNESS AND THOROUGHBRED

All the local tracks are easily reached by public transportation. For those who enjoy betting but do not feel the need to be at the racetrack, the city features numerous off-track betting locations. More information can be found at the New York Racing Association's web site, www.nyra.com. Call the numbers listed below for directions.

- **Aqueduct**, Jamaica, Queens, 718-641-4700, www.nyra.com; the track is open from October until May for thoroughbred races starting at 12:30 p.m. daily except Mondays and Tuesdays.
- **Belmont Park**, Elmont, Long Island, 516-488-6000, www.nyra.com; thoroughbred races May–July and September–October.
- **Saratoga**, Saratoga Springs, NY, 518-584-6200, www.nyra.com; home of the Travers Stake, America's oldest thoroughbred race. Season runs from the end of July through early October; post time 1:00 p.m.
- **Meadowlands Racetrack**, Meadowlands Sports Complex, East Rutherford, NJ, 201-843-2446, www.thebigm.com; open at 6 p.m. nightly Tuesday–Saturday. December–August harness racing; thoroughbreds run October–November.
- **Monmouth Park**, Oceanport, NJ, 732-222-5100, www.monmouthpark. com, thoroughbred races daily Wednesday–Sunday at 12:55 p.m., late May–September.
- **Yonkers Raceway**, Yonkers, NY, 914-968-4200, www.yonkersraceway.com; the post time is 7:40 p.m. Daily schedule varies as the track is sometimes used for festivals and other events, so call in advance.

TENNIS

The biggest tournament held in the New York area is the US Open. The West Side Tennis Club at Forest Hills (once the site of the US Open) hosts the Tournament of Champions for men in May.

- **United States Open Tennis Championships**, United States Tennis Center, Flushing Meadow Park, Queens, NY 11365; for ticket information call 866-OPEN-TIX. The nation's premier tennis tournament, the US Open, consists of 13 days of afternoon and evening matches held in late August and early September. The finals take place the weekend after Labor Day. Individual tickets for the finals and semifinals are sold as soon as the first mailing goes out in late March or early April. Tickets for matches earlier in the tournament aren't as hard to come by and are sold at Ticketmaster outlets as well as the Tennis Center. If you drive, there is parking in lots for a fee. If the Mets are also playing that day, the area gets more congested, as Citi Field (formerly Shea Stadium) is practically across the street. You can also take the #7 train from Manhattan.

PARTICIPANT SPORTS

Swimming pools, tennis, squash and racquetball courts, bowling alleys, and billiard parlors, as well as roller and ice skating rinks dot the island for your sporting pleasure, and practically any outdoor recreation you want can be found in New York City, and especially in Central Park. It's not just a super place to ride bikes or listen to classical performances on summer evenings; you can also schedule football and softball games, play tennis, or row a boat around the Lake. Flanked by Central Park West and Fifth Avenue to the east, the park covers some 750 acres between 59th and 110th streets and is Manhattan's prime outdoor recreation area. So, before listing information about sports citywide, as well as multipurpose facilities such as health clubs and YMCAs, we've detailed opportunities to be found in the park, sport by sport. To learn more about the park itself, see the chapter on **Greenspace and Beaches**. For information about city parks you can call the **NYC Department of Parks & Recreation** at 212-360-3456 or visit their web site at www.nycgovparks.org.

CENTRAL PARK

The park's **Visitor Information Center** is located at the Dairy, 65th Street between the zoo and the carousel. The Arsenal, 830 Fifth Avenue at East 64th Street in front of the zoo, is the park's administrative hub. For event and park information, call the **Central Parks Conservancy**, which runs the park under contract from the city, 212-310-6600, or go to www.centralparknyc.org.

- **Ball: Baseball, Softball, Football, Rugby**, and **Soccer** fields are located in the North Meadow, at the Great Lawn and Heckscher Playground. Call 212-408-0226 for permits.
- **Bicycling** is popular when the park drives (but not the sunken cross-town transverses) are closed to motorized traffic on weekends from 7 p.m. Friday until 6 a.m. Monday (all day on holidays), and from 10 a.m. to 3 p.m. and 7 p.m. to 10 p.m. weekdays, from April through October. For rentals, see **Bicycling** below for names of bicycle shops near the park.
- **Boating**; the Loeb Boathouse, near East 74th St, 212-517-2233, rents rowboats for outings on the Lake, from 10 a.m. until between 4 and 6 p.m. You can also glide beneath Bow Bridge in a black Venetian gondola, complete with a gondolier. Armchair sailors can enjoy the comfort and cuisine of lunch and brunch in the glass-enclosed Boathouse Café. Evening dining is offered from the end of March through the first of November.
- **Horseback Riding**; the Claremont Riding Academy, 175 West 89th Street, 212-724-5100, rents mounts to experienced riders for rides along the six miles of bridle paths that circle the park. You must reserve in advance.
- **Ice Skating**; the park boasts two beautiful main rinks: Wollman Memorial on the East Side near 62nd St, 212-439-6900, and Lasker Memorial at Lenox Ave at 110th St, 212-534-7639. Wollman is open September–April. Of the two, Lasker is less crowded. At both rinks, mornings and weekdays offer the best ice time: i.e., fewer skaters.
- **Paddleball and Handball**; you can use the ten courts located near the North Meadow at West 97th St and Transverse Rd on a first-come, first-served basis.
- **Roller/In-line Skating**; in-line skaters and old-fashioned roller skaters can be found strutting their stuff (or falling down) throughout the park, but the road west of the Sheep Meadow near 69th Street is designated specifically for blading and skating. Skates can be rented for use at Wollman Memorial, 212-439-6900, April–November. Call for hours and admission.
- **Running**; joggers traditionally work out on the 1.58-mile cinder track girdling the Reservoir between East 85th and 96th streets, but running isn't limited to that patch. The **New York Road Runners Club**, 9 East 89th St, 212-860-4455, www.nyrrc.org, sponsors races and clinics during the season. (See **A New York City Year** at the end of the book for specifics on New York Road Runners' New Year's Eve midnight run.) The 97th Street Field House contains lockers and showers for men and women.
- **Sledding**; the park has hills for all levels of experience. For children or timid sledders, a perfect spot is Pilgrim Hill by the 72nd St and Fifth Ave entrance closest to the pilgrim statue. For more of a challenge, try Cedar Hill close to the Belvedere Castle at the 77th Street entrance off Central Park West.
- **Tennis**; twenty-six clay and four all-weather courts, open from 7 a.m. to dusk, are located on the west side of the park near 95th Street. In season, play necessitates a seasonal tennis permit, which in turn requires a completed ap-

plication, photo ID (service provided at the time of application), and $100 (no personal checks). Permits can be obtained by mail or in person at the Arsenal Building, Fifth Ave and 64th St, NYC 10021, between 9 a.m. and 4 p.m., weekdays. Permit holders can reserve a court by going to the Tennis House adjacent to the 95th Street Courts and paying a small fee. Call 212-360-8131 for permit information. You can also purchase single play tennis tickets at $7 for one hour of court time, which are issued at the courts on 93rd Street on a first-come, first-served basis. Tennis center daily information: 212-280-0205.

BEYOND CENTRAL PARK

The New York City **Department of Parks and Recreation (DPR)** directs and maintains baseball fields, basketball court, and more throughout the city. The best resource is their website at www.nycgovparks.org, but you can also call the following numbers (although you won't always get an answer).

- **Bronx**, 718-430-1840/4
- **Brooklyn**, 718-965-8941
- **Manhattan**, 212-408-0226
- **Queens**, 718-393-7272
- **Staten Island**, 718-667-3545

BASEBALL

Most of Manhattan's more than two dozen diamonds (seven of which are located in Central Park) are under the direction of the **DPR**. Call 212-408-0226 or visit www.nycgovparks.org. Fields can be difficult to get onto in the spring due to corporate softball leagues.

BASKETBALL

The **DPR**, www.nycgovparks.org, maintains more than 1,000 courts throughout the city in gyms (see **Swimming** below) as well as in city parks, large and small. Some of the health clubs and YMCAs have basketball courts, and the **Chelsea Piers Sports and Entertainment** complex, www.chelseapiers.com, includes two new courts with electronic scoreboards used in league basketball which is open to players of all skill levels for a fee.

BICYCLING

In the last few years New York has made significant progress in making the city bike-friendly. Separated paths run up the major avenues and green-painted bike lanes are popping up everywhere. It still has miles to go—people still drive like maniacs and taxi passengers are lethal—but more and more commute on two wheels. In addition, in 2007, Manhattan opened its first mountain bike trail, the Highbridge Trail, in Highbridge Park in Inwood, with cross-country, free-ride, and

BMX/dirt-jump trails. You can find up-to-date bike maps at www.nycbikemaps. com, or visit the mountain-biking association at www.nycmtb.com.

- **Century Road Club Association**, P.O. Box 20412, Greeley Square Station, NYC 10001, www.crca.net, is a racing club, which provides coaching clinics for beginners and sponsors friendly competitions for kids of all ages.
- **Five Borough Bicycle Club**, 891 Amsterdam Ave, 212-932-BIKE (2453), www. bikenewyork.org, organizes bicycling events, rides, and courses.
- **Fast and Fabulous Cycling Club**, 212-567-7160, www.fastnfab.org, is a gay and lesbian bicycle club affiliated with Front Runners New York (see **Running** below). They organize training, morning rides in city parks, and road trips.
- **Hostelling International New York**, 891 Amsterdam Ave, 212-932-2300, www.hinewyork.org, the city's largest cycling organization, sponsors Bike New York, the Great Five Borough Bicycle Race, which bumps and winds its way through all five boroughs each spring. Hostelling International New York also promotes a number of day rides as well as weekend trips for enthusiasts.
- **New York Cycle Club**, P.O. Box 20541, Columbus Circle Station, NYC 10023, 212-828-5711, www.nycc.org, sponsors rides in and around the city, offers training, and its members receive discounts from a handful of bike shops in the city.

If you don't own a bike, you may well want to rent one on a beautiful spring day. At least half of Manhattan's bike dealers rent bikes. Rates average $8 to $10 an hour and about $30 a day. You'll have to leave money, or a driver's license or major credit card behind as a deposit, although you might hesitate to do that with some of the street operators who operate at Columbus Circle. A handful of the many bike rental outfits include:

- **Bicycles Plus**, 1400 Third Ave, 212-794-2929, 1690 Second Ave at 87th St, 212-722-2201
- **Central Park Bicycle Tours and Rentals**, 5 W 63rd St at the YMCA, 212-541-8759, offer bike rentals ($20 for an hour, $65 for all day), and bike tours of Central Park.
- **Gotham Bikes**, 112 W Broadway, 212-732-2453, offer rentals from Spring to Fall.
- **Metro Bicycles: 1311 Lexington Ave at 88th St**, 212-427-4450; 360 W 47th St, 212-581-4500; 231 W 96th St, 212-663-7531; 332 E 14th St, 212-228-4344; 417 Canal St, 212-334-8000; and 546 Ave of the Americas at 15th St, 212-255-5100
- **Pedal Pusher Bike Shop**, 1306 Second Ave at 69th Street, 212-288-5592
- **Toga Bike Shop,** 110 West End Ave, 212-799-9625
- **Tread Bike Shop**, 250 Dyckman St, 212-544-7055, www.treadbikeshop.com; along with basic bike rentals, this shop offers demos/rentals of über-expensive specialized FSR suspension bikes. Near to the Highbridge bike trail, for best testing.

BILLIARDS

There are more than two dozen pool halls in New York City, and no doubt, Minnesota Fats would still be comfortable at many of them. Others, with clubby ambiances that are different from the hustler hangouts of yore, have attracted women to the traditionally male pastime of pocket pool, billiards, and snooker, and have brightened the sport's image in the process.

- **Amsterdam Billiards & Bar**, 212-995-0333, 110 E 11th Street; an old stalwart that recently moved, it still boasts over 20 tables with a full-service bar.
- **Brownstone Billiards**, 308 Flatbush Ave at Seventh Ave, Brooklyn, 718-857-5555; open noon to 1 a.m., to 4 a.m. Friday and Saturday. With 32 tables, six ping-pong tables, air hockey, and video games, Brownstone has positioned itself as a family entertainment center.
- **Eastside Amusements**, 163 E 86th St between Lexington and Third avenues, 212-831-7665; features billiards, an arcade, and a party space for as many as 250 of your closest friends.
- **Slate Billiards**, 54 W 21st St west of Fifth Ave, 212-989-0096; a two-floor all-in-one restaurant/lounge/ping pong room/pool parlor, complete with 25 pool tables. Yet, you might still have to wait for a table, Friday nights especially. Best times are mornings and Sunday daytime. There is a room with two tables for private parties.

BIRD WATCHING

"Oh! A winter wren," warbles naturalist Sarah Elliott as she leads a group of bird-watching enthusiasts through the Ramble in Central Park. Unlikely as it may seem, **Central Park** is a mecca for birders. Encircled in concrete, from the sky the park appears as an oasis in which to land, rest, and refuel. The city's outer parks also offer prime sites for dedicated birders. Below are a few organized groups and walks. For a greater selection, turn to *New York's 50 Best Places to Go Birding in and Around the Big Apple* by John Thaxton and Alan Messer.

- **The American Museum of Natural History**, 212-769-5700 (discovery tours), www.amnh.org; the **Brooklyn Botanical Garden**, 718-623-7200, www.bbg.org; and the **New York Botanical Garden** (Bronx Park), 718-817-8700, www.nybg.org, make the guidebooks as good bird-watching areas. **Rare Bird Alert**, 212-979-3070, provides recorded information on interesting sightings in the New York City area.
- **Brooklyn Bird Club**, www.brooklynbirdclub.org, founded in 1909, hosts lectures, monthly meetings, and weekly field trips, open to both non-members and members (membership $20) alike. Their attractive web site includes detailed maps and descriptions of some 15 excellent bird locations in Brooklyn and Queens, directions, some history, and lists of the species one is likely to find at each site.
- **New York City Audubon Society**, 212-691-7483, www.nycaudubon.org

- **Sarah Elliott** has become a noted fixture, a movable one, in Central Park, with her Wednesday and Sunday morning walks, spring and fall. She teaches bird-watching basics and leads her pack on their quest for the indigo bunting, the grackle, and the pileated woodpecker. The walks leave at 9 a.m. in spring and fall, Wednesdays from Fifth Avenue and 76th Street, and Sundays from the Loeb Boat House. The fee is $10; call 212-689-2763 for more information. For a year's subscription to the bi-monthly "Elliott Newsletter: Nature Notes from Central Park," send a check for $25 to her at 333 East 34th Street, #17D, NYC 10016.
- **The Urban Park Rangers** sponsor a variety of bird walks, such as the fall hawk watch, in all five boroughs, not to mention courses in animal tracking and survival. For times and meeting places call 212-628-2345 for more information, or visit www.nycgovparks.org.

BOWLING

Check the Yellow Pages for the alley nearest you. Here are a couple:
- **AMF Chelsea Piers Bowling**, Pier 60, West Side Hwy at 23rd St, 212-835-2695, www.chelseapiers.com, 40 lanes, open seven days. There's a bar and restaurant on site, a pro shop, and arcade with video games to keep the kids occupied. Thursday, Friday, and Saturday nights they offer "extreme bowling" (glow-in-the-dark bowling). League bowling and lessons are also available. Call for lane availability and/or to reserve. Be forewarned: bowling here ain't cheap at $8.00 per game per person plus $6.00 for shoe rental evenings and weekends, or $84 for a family of four (or two couples) to bowl just two games.
- **Bowlmor Lanes**, 110 University Place (btw. 12th & 13th sts), 212-255-8188, www.bowlmor.com; can bowling really be this trendy? Still, the cocktails are good and where else can you get a wasabi burger and a lane? Costs range around $5 a game.
- **Gil Hodges Lanes**, 6161 Strickland Ave, Brooklyn, 718-763-6800, is named after the famed Brooklyn Dodgers first baseman. This 68-lane alley is the biggest in the five boroughs.

BOXING

- **Church Street Boxing Gym**, 25 Park Place off Church St, Downtown, 212-571-1333, www.nyboxinggym.com; bills itself as "New York's last authentic boxing gym" (translate: Manhattan's). It's not a health club or fitness center; it's about boxing. The 8,000-square-foot gym has two full-size rings and co-ed membership classes in boxing, kick-boxing, and Thai boxing. Membership is by the month, quarter, or year. It's probably also the best place in the city to watch boxing; enthusiastic crowds pack the occasional Friday night fights.
- **Gleason's Gym**, 77 Front St at the foot of the Brooklyn Bridge in Brooklyn, 718-797-2872, www.gleasonsgym.net; going strong since 1937, it boasts sev-

en world champions among its past or present membership, Riddick Bowe included. Women also work out here in this old-style boxing gym. Get lean and mean working up a sweat on the equipment or work with one of 62 trainers for an hourly fee. Closed Sunday.

CHESS

Though it's not a "sport," enthusiasts pursue chess with the intensity of an athletic competition. New York City, with its huge immigrant community, has a large and active chess community. If you're looking for information about where to play or compete, try the following leads (or head to Washington Square Park, where "pick-up" games of speed chess are ongoing at the chess tables):

- **The Chess Forum**, 219 Thompson St, 212-475-2369, www.chessforum.com
- **US Chess Federation**, 3054 NYS Route 9W, New Windsor, NY, 914-562-8350; their web site, www.uschess.org, contains a great list of places to play.
- **The Village Chess Shop**, 230 Thompson St, 212-475-9580, www.chess-shop. com

FENCING

- **Blade Fencing**, 245 W 29th St, 800-828-5661, www.blade-fencing.com, arms and dresses the duelist for competition with a full range of foils, épées and sabers
- **New Amsterdam Fencing Academy**, 2726 Broadway, 2nd floor, 212-662-3362, www.nyfencing.com; there are private and group classes for children through adults, beginner through Olympian, Monday through Saturday.

FOOTBALL

Most playing fields fall under the **Department of Parks and Recreation**; call 212-408-0226 for information and permits. Eighteen football fields, some of which are suitable also for soccer, are located in Manhattan.

GAMES AND GAMING

From RPGs to LANs, whether you seek to buy board games or conquer animated nations, you can get your gaming fix at one of these locations:

- **Game Time Nation**, 111 E 12th St, 212-228-4260, www.gametimenation.com; provides real time gaming for PS2 and Xbox in their Gaming Lounge.
- **Kings Games**, 1685 E 15th Street, Brooklyn, 888-33-KINGS, www.kingsgames. com; an RPG/TCG (trading card game) room and separate LAN center, tournament hosting and league play.
- **Web2Zone Cyber Center**, 54 Cooper Square, 212-614-7300, www.web2zone. com; repeatedly voted one of New York City's best for gaming, holds tournaments and game events for PC, Xbox, PS2, and GameCube. Party room and packages also available.

GOLF

Manhattan boasts no 18-hole golf courses (a 17-acre course on Randall's Island has been in planning stages for years), but you'll find several city-owned public courses in the outer boroughs. A permit, which can be purchased at any of the New York City Courses or from the parks department, will get you onto the city courses where 18 holes will cost less than $20. There are also nine-hole rates and twilight rates, plus discounts for juniors and seniors. Non-residents or city residents without a permit can also play for a few dollars more. Courses are popular during the spring and summer, so get there early and prepare to wait…or go at 4 p.m. and take advantage of the longer daylight hours. Reservations can be made for several city courses by calling 718-225-4653. There are also plenty of even nicer public clubs on Long Island and in Westchester. Higher fees are the norm at suburban courses and you'll need to reserve tee times well in advance. Perhaps the nicest courses closest to NYC are those at Bethpage State Park at 99 Quaker Meeting House Road in Farmingdale, Long Island, 516-249-0700. These three award-winning courses have attracted top tournaments, top players, and garnered high ratings in the golf world.

New York City **public courses** include:

- **Mosholu Golf Course**, 3700 Jerome Ave, The Bronx, 718-655-9164; also features a driving range.
- **Pelham/Split Rock Golf Course**, 870 Shore Rd, north of Bartow Circle, The Bronx, near City Island, 718-885-1258
- **Van Cortlandt Park Golf Course**, Van Cortlandt Park at Bailey Ave, The Bronx, 718-543-4595; a marvelous 100+ year old course that has seen everyone from Babe Ruth to the Three Stooges to presidents and diplomats tee off.
- **Dyker Beach Golf Course**, Seventh Ave and 86th St, Brooklyn, 718-836-9722
- **Marine Park Golf Course**, 2880 Flatbush Ave, near the Belt Parkway, Brooklyn, 718-338-7149
- **Clearview Golf Course**, 202-12 Willets Point Blvd, Queens, 718-229-2570
- **Douglaston Golf Course**, 63-20 Marathon Pkwy, Queens, 718-428-1617; if you like hills.
- **Forest Park Golf Course**, 101 Forest Park Dr off Woodhaven Blvd, Queens, 718-296-0999; bring plenty of extra balls.
- **Kissena Park Golf Course**, 164-15 Booth Memorial Ave, Queens, 718-939-4594
- **LaTourette Golf Course**, 1001 Richmond Hill Rd, Staten Island, 718-351-1889; also has a driving range.
- **Silver Lake Golf Course**, 915 Victory Blvd, near Forest Ave, Staten Island, 718-447-5686
- **South Shore Golf Course**, 200 Huguenot Ave, Staten Island, 718-984-0101

Miniature golf courses can also be found in the outer boroughs. Among the city's other **driving ranges** are:

- **The Golf Club at Chelsea Piers**, Hudson River at 17th St, 212-336-6400, www. chelseapiers.com; this golf club, with its white shingled clubhouse entrance, pro shop, putting green, and golf academy has, as its *pièce de résistance*, 52 heated, weather-protected driving stalls with Japanese-designed, computerized automatic ball returns and tee-ups in four tiers fronting a 200-yard, net-enclosed artificial turf fairway with four target greens, overlooking the Hudson River...No you can't aim at passing boats. Pay according to the number of balls used.
- **Randall's Island Driving Range**, Randall's Island, north of Downing Stadium, 212-427-5689

HANDBALL

A city sport in which two or four players hit a rubber ball with their hands against a cement wall, volleying furiously for points, handball is played on outdoor courts all over the city. And at many sites it is also a spectator sport. Among the many handball courts in the city, two stand out as shrines:

- **Surf Avenue** at W Fifth St, Coney Island, on whose six courts the Nationals are played. Attracts a colorful crowd of betting spectators.
- **"The Cage"** at W Fourth St and Sixth Ave, the Village; the action on the adjacent basketball court is equally spectacular.

To learn more about one of the world's oldest games go to www.ushandball.org.

HORSEBACK RIDING

Horseback riding in Central Park vanished as of 2007 with the closing of Claremont Riding Academy. But there are lots of options outside the city.

- **Bronx Equestrian Center**, 9 Shore Rd, Bronx, 718-885-0551, www.bronxequestriancenter.com; open daily 8 a.m. until dusk, but call ahead for a guided trail ride, Western only, through the woods by the Split Rock Golf Course and Pelham Bay. Lessons, English or Western, are offered individually or as a group. Reachable by car from the New England Thruway. Alternatively, take the #6 train to the last stop and walk east, or take the City Island Bus, number 29, which stops across the street from the stable.
- **Jamaica Bay Riding Academy**, Belt Parkway East between exits 11 (King's Plaza) and 13 (Rockaway Parkway), Marine Park, Brooklyn, 718-531-8949, www. horsebackride.com; located on some 300 acres of prime real estate, they offer a riding shop, lessons, wooded trails, and can accommodate birthday parties. You need no appointment for a guided trail ride along Jamaica Bay beach, open year round. Bring your own helmet.
- **Kensington Stables**, 51 Caton Place at Coney Island Ave, Brooklyn, 718-972-4588, www.kensingtonstables.com; operates guided trail rides, English or

Western, in lovely Prospect Park. Private and group lessons offered. Call ahead. Take the F train to Ft. Hamilton Pkwy.

- **Lynne's Riding School**, 88-03 70th Rd, Forest Hills, 718-261-7679, www.lynnes riding.com; you can take public transportation—the F train and then the Q23 bus—to Queens, where Lynne's offers riders a choice between Eastern or Western tack. Private lessons are available, as are pony rides and boarding.
- **Riverdale Riding Centre**, W 254th St and Broadway, inside Van Cortlandt Park, 718-548-4848, www.riverdaleriding.com; four riding rings and an indoor Olympic-sized arena. Rabbits, raccoons, and other wildlife are a bonus on the guided trail rides in this large city park. Pony rides are available for children and pony parties can be arranged. All rides by appointment. To get there by public transportation take the #1 train to 242nd St (last stop) and the #9 bus (262nd St); ask to get off at the stables. Or take the Liberty Line Bx-M3 bus, which goes up Madison Ave, stopping every 10 blocks, and drops you at the stable door; 20 minutes from the Upper East Side.

ICE SKATING

In addition to the Wollman and Lasker rinks in Central Park (see above), and the Sailboat Pond at 73rd St when it freezes, New York City boasts many fine places to skate.

- **Kate Wollman Rink**, sister to Central Park's Wollman Rink, is located on the east side of Prospect Park, off the Parkside and Ocean Ave entrance, in Brooklyn, 718-287-6431. November–March.
- **Polar Rink**, Natural History Museum (at 79 Street And Central Park West, www. amnh.org. The museum has also just opened its smallish ring of synthetic ice (open November–February).
- **The Pond**, 866-221-5157, www.thepondatbryantpark.com; there is also now a lovely part-time and free rink at Bryant Park that runs late October through January.
- **Riverbank State Park**, 145th St and Riverside Dr, 212-694-3642; skate outdoors just above the Hudson River in this beautiful 28-acre park. Skate rentals available. Roller-skating here during the summer.
- **Rockefeller Center Rink**, 50th Street off Fifth Avenue, 212-332-7654; open daily and evenings in season. Skate rentals available. One of the country's most famous skating rinks sits adjacent to a lovely café and, in December, below the massive Rockefeller Center Christmas tree. Plenty of onlookers, so brush up on your skating skills. October–April.
- **Skyrink at Chelsea Piers**, Pier 61 at Hudson River and 22nd St, 212-336-6100, www.chelseapiers.com; with two indoor rinks in use some 20 hours a day, this facility offers public skating, figure skating, and hockey instruction for adults and children, league hockey, a skating club, and ice theater. Rentals and a skate shop are on site, as well as audience seating for 1,600, including two

skyboxes for special events, and a snack bar. You can even hold a birthday party here. Year round.

- **World's Fair Skating Rink** (sometimes referred to as Flushing Meadow Skate Rink), 111th St, Corona, Queens, in Flushing Meadow Park, 718-271-1996. You can walk to this large, indoor rink from the Citi Field stadium–111th Street subway stop on the #7 train. Skate rentals and weekend lessons available. Year round.

LACROSSE

Chelsea Piers Field House, 23rd St and the Hudson River, 212-336-6500, www. chelseapiers.com; offers lacrosse. Open to individuals and complete teams, men and women, for indoor, adult lacrosse league play on a variety of skill levels. Teams play one night a week for a season of 8 to 12 games and league playoffs. Games consist of two 25-minute halves.For league information in New York and New Jersey, go to www.eteamz.com/lacrosse.

RACQUETBALL

Devotees of this popular sport can burn calories at two of the Ys we mention below—the West Side YMCA at 5 W 63rd St and the 92nd St YMHA at Lexington Avenue (three practice courts only)—as well as:

- **New York Health and Racquet Club**, 110 W 56th St, 212-541-7200; 24 E 13th St, 212-924-4600; 132 E 45th St, 212-986-3100; 20 E 50th St, 212-593-1500; 115 E 57th St, 212-826-9650; 39 Whitehall St, 212-269-9800; 1433 York Ave, 212-737-6666, 62 Cooper Square, 212-904-0400; www.hrcbest.com; with ten locations in the city, one in Long Island, and still adding. They've taken charge of the racquetball scene in New York City.
- **Printing House Fitness and Racquet Club**, 421 Hudson St in Greenwich Village, 212-243-7600, www.phfrc.com; is a membership club with five racquetball and four squash courts on the first floor. Membership rates depend on how much of the club the member intends to use. Call for specifics.

ROLLER/IN-LINE SKATING/SKATE BOARDING

For exhilarating outdoor fun, try **Central Park** for blade action. Roller disco, though passé, also still has some followers. Other in-line skating hot-spots: **Union Square**, **Battery Park City**, "the banks" under the Manhattan side of the **Brooklyn Bridge**, and Brooklyn's **Prospect Park**. In fact, now you can skate (walk or bike) along the Hudson River from Gansevoort Street to Battery Park City. If you plan to rent, bring a credit card for a deposit on the equipment.

- **Blades Board and Skate**, 156 W 72nd St, 212-787-3911; 901 Sixth Ave, Lower Level II, 212-733-2738; Pier 61, Chelsea Piers, 212-336-6199; 659 Broadway in the Village, 212-477-7350; www.blades.com. With the help of the friendly staffers at any of these locations, you too can join the fun. Rollerblades, the best-known brand, can be rented for the day with wrist guards and kneepads included. You can also buy skates, equipment, and gear.

- **Chelsea Piers Skate Park and Roller Rinks**, 23rd St and Hudson River, 212-336-6200, www.chelseapiers.com; besides general skating in two outdoor, regulation-sized in-line and roller rinks, there are classes at various levels: from basic technique to hip-hop to aggressive, as well as league hockey games for adults and youths. Also, two half-pipes with 11- and 6-foot walls respectively. Or you can just watch.
- **Lezly Skate School**, 212-777-3232, www.skateguru.com; offers skating instruction for every skill level in four-week sessions, both indoor and out. Classes are at the Roxy at 515 W 18th St or in Central Park and other locations. Skate rentals available for classes only.

RUGBY

- **Gaelic Park**, 718-548-9568, in The Bronx, is the center of rugby play in New York City. The park is located at Broadway and W 240th St.
- **The New York Rugby Club**, www.newyorkrugby.com, supports rugby for men, women, boys, girls, and masters. It is billed as the oldest rugby club in the USA, having been originally formed in 1929.

RUNNING

- **Front Runners**, NY, www.frny.org, is the hyperactive local branch of Front Runners International, which organizes running, walking, cycling, and triathlon events for lesbians, gay men, and supportive non-gays. Their weekly "fun runs" take place in Central Park and Prospect Park in Brooklyn. Participants gather after the runs for a snack or a meal. The organization also offers coaching and training, events for cyclists and walkers, and competitions for runners and triathletes. Visit their web site for a schedule of runs.
- **Hash House Harriers**, 212-427-4692, www.hashhouseharriers.com, is a group of not-totally-serious joggers who meet at various locations throughout the city and in Westchester to follow a flour-marked trail looping four to five miles and winding up at a bar for post-run analysis fueled by food and copious quantities of beer. Runners are called "hashers" and the trails are set by "hares." You need only running shoes and about $15 in "hash cash" to join in. Some call it "the drinking club with a running problem." Hashing originated in 1938 in Kuala Lumpur and is now international, so you can hash away from home. Global information is on the web at www.gthhh.com.
- **The New York Road Runners Club**, with over 25,000 members "the world's largest running club," maintains an "International Running Center" at 9 E 89th St, 212-860-4455, www.nyrrc.org. The Road Runners Club sponsors the New York Marathon and more than 150 other races a year.

SAILING

If you want to bound over Long Island Sound, City Island in The Bronx is an accessible starting point. Take the #2 (Seventh Avenue) or #6 (Lexington Avenue) train to Pelham Parkway and transfer to The Bronx #12 City Island bus. This and some other watery options are listed here:

- **Manhattan Sailing School**, 393 South End Ave in Battery Park City, 212-786-0400, www.sailmanhattan.com; sail out of classy North Cove Yacht Harbor in front of the World Financial Center. Beginners can take a 20-hour basic sailing course and continue on to basic coastal cruising, also 20 hours, in J-24 sailboats. Private lessons available.
- **New York City Community Sailing Association**, 1500 Harbor Blvd, Weehawken, NJ, 212-400-1668, www.sailny.org; operating with nine 22- to 24-foot keel sloops, five of which are Solings, out of Lincoln Harbor Marina in Weehawken, NJ. This non-profit organization was founded in 1996 with the idea that sailing ought to be easy and affordable. Basic membership is $25 a year, and their ASA Basic Keelboat 101 course is a bargain at $325. You must be a member to participate in recreational sailing and races. Call or check their web site for more information.
- **New York City Downtown Boathouse**, 646-613-0375, 646-613-0740 (daily status line), www.downtownboathouse.org, is an "all-volunteer organization dedicated to providing access to the Hudson River." Boathouse locations in Tribeca, Chelsea, and Uptown. Contact them about sailing or kayaking lessons.
- **New York Sailing Center & Yacht Club**, 140 City Island Avenue (at Consolidated Yachts), City Island, The Bronx, 718-885-3309, www.startsailing.com, is a sailing school, yacht club, boat rental, boat storage, and more.
- **The New York Sailing School**, 22 Pelham Rd, New Rochelle, Westchester, 914-235-6052, www.nyss.com, offers sailing courses, programs, boat rental, and more.
- **North Cove Sailing School & Club**, 393 South End Ave, 201-915-4398; shares the North Cove Yacht Harbor with the Manhattan Sailing School. $1,000 memberships for individual crew members. Basic sailing courses start at $498.
- **Offshore Sailing School**, 62 Chelsea Piers, 800-221-4326, www.offshore-sailing.com; take the Learn to Sail course from this national sailing school, then stop back at Chelsea Piers for a relaxing dinner or to hit a bucket of balls.

SCUBA

While no one's suggesting dives to the murky depths of the Hudson, you can take certification courses in local pools in preparation for a plunge into the Caribbean's turquoise waters.

- **PanAqua Diving**, 460 W 43rd St between 9th and 10th avenues, 212-736-3483, www.panaquadiving.com; in addition to selling and repairing equipment, they organize group and individual diving travel and run certification courses evenings and weekends. Courses, held variously at the West Side Y, Vanderbilt Y, 92nd Street Y, and Manhattan Plaza, range from one-weekend intensive to five weeks of evenings. The open water dive required for certification is extra.

SEA KAYAKING

That's right—sea kayaking. For those who seek watery adventure in and out of the city, the **Metropolitan Association of Sea Kayakers**, www.seacanoe.org, unites groups of paddlers who plan trips up and down the East Coast as well as to locations as far north as Greenland and Alaska. Two or three trips around the island of Manhattan each summer, light and currents permitting, start and end in Liberty State Park (New Jersey) and take about 11 hours. Membership includes a published schedule, a quarterly newsletter, and a guide to coastal launch sites along the East Coast. Contact Capt. Al Ysaguirre at the Metropolitan Association of Sea Kayakers, 195 Prince Street, basement, NYC 10012, or visit their web site. Also, check with the **New York City Downtown Boathouse** (see **Sailing** above) about kayaking lessons.

SKIING

You won't schuss downhill in New York City, but cross country skiers take to the gentle slopes of Central Park and, in the boroughs, Van Cortlandt Park, Split Rock Golf Course in Pelham Bay Park in The Bronx, Prospect Park in Brooklyn, and Flushing Meadow Park in Queens. No official trail grooming, so break your own, or follow trails carved out by fellow skiers.

Downhill skiers take to the slopes two hours north of the city in the Catskills or at Bear Mountain, 909-866-5766, www.bearmountain.com, in northern West-chester. Lake Placid, www.lakeplacid.com, home of the 1980 Winter Olympics, is also a skiing destination. Vernon Valley/Great Gorge, 201-827-2000, www.skislopes.net, across the George Washington Bridge in New Jersey, is another popular ski destination for city dwellers. Check local sporting goods stores for day or weekend ski rental packages.

SOCCER

The **Cosmopolitan Soccer League**, 201-943-3390, www.cslny.com, represents amateur and semi-pro clubs from New York, New Jersey, and Connecticut. The League has one semi-pro and two amateur divisions consisting of about 20 clubs each. You don't have to join a club to play on a team, but club facilities are limited to members. Coaches are available for training; all age groups are welcome.

Indoor league play is available now in the field house at **Chelsea Piers**, 23rd Street at the Hudson River, 212-336-6500, http://www.chelseapiers.com/fhSoc. htm. Teams accommodating men and women at various skill levels play one night a week on an Astroturf indoor field. A season consists of 8 or 12 games, consisting of two 25-minute halves, and league playoffs.

Some city parks also have soccer fields. For permit information in New York, contact the NYC Department of Parks and Recreation, 212-408-8226, www.nycgovparks.org.

SQUASH

When you consider that a tennis court takes up about ten times as much space as a squash court, it is easy to understand the great attraction squash holds for sports club operators as well as for a population determined to exercise, but at the lowest cost possible. See **Health Clubs** and **Ys** for other locations with courts.

- **New York Sports Clubs**, www.nysc.com; 61 W 62nd St, 212-265-0995; 151 E 86th St, 212-860-8630; 575 Lexington Ave, 212-317-9400; and 110 Boerum Place (Cobble Hill), 718-643-4400
- **Printing House Fitness and Racquet Club**, 421 Hudson St at Leroy St in Greenwich Village, 212-243-7600, www.phfrc.com; is a membership club with five international squash courts on the first floor. Membership rates depend on how much of the facility the member wishes to use. Call for specifics.

SURFING

It may not be Oahu, but New York City surfers need not abandon their beloved boards; a stretch of Rockaway Beach in Queens has been designated the city's sole "Surf Only" beach. Surfing at other city beaches may get you a summons, so unless you want to make the long haul to southern Jersey's Ocean City, Rockaway is your best (and cheapest) bet. Surfing is also permitted at a number of beaches on Long Island.

- **Rockaway Beach**, near Beach 90th St, Rockaway, Queens, 718-318-4000; take the A train out to Rockaway, and transfer to the S train. Check www.newyorksurf.com for more information, and www.northeastsurfing.com for extensive listings of conditions.

SWIMMING—POOLS

The Department of Parks and Recreation, www.nycgovparks.org, maintains a number of indoor and outdoor pools throughout the city with inexpensive admission. In the heat of summer, the outdoor pools are more for play and cooling off than serious lap swimming. The swimming is easier during off-hours in winter. Winter indoor pool hours are generally 3 p.m. to 10 p.m. weekdays, 10 a.m. to 5 p.m. Saturday, closed Sunday. Summer hours for the outdoor pools vary, and indoor pools are closed. Most of the pools require a membership or registration fee—pay by money order or credit card. In 2006, the permit fee was $75 for adults (annually), $10 for seniors (age 55 and older), and free for children 17 and under accompanied by an adult. Shower before and after using city pools. For saltwater swimming at city beaches see the chapter on **Greenspace and Beaches**. Check the DPR's web site for a complete list of public pools. Here are a few (with gyms attached) to get you started:

- **Asser Levy Pool**, 23rd St, between First Ave and FDR Dr, 212-447-2020; built in 1906 as a public bath modeled on the Roman baths, this granite gem with a marble lobby and 20-foot ceilings re-opened in 1990 after extensive renovations. The indoor pool is open until late June when it closes on behalf of the outdoor pool, which is open until around Labor Day.
- **Carmine Street Gymnasium and Pool**, Clarkson St and Seventh Ave S (Greenwich Village), 212-242-5228, offers a 20' by 70' indoor pool and a 50' by 100' outdoor pool. Two upstairs gyms and a running track. Annual membership.
- **Hansborough Recreational Center**, 35 W 134th St, 212-234-9603, in Harlem has an indoor pool and gym with dance and aerobic classes.
- **Metropolitan Pool and Fitness Center**, 261 Bedford Ave, Greenpoint, Brooklyn, 718-599-5707, recently renovated, is probably the most beautiful of the pools operated by the city. Light pours through a copper-framed skylight into the somewhat Andalusian pool area, which is handicap-accessible. Best to avoid early evenings and Saturdays. Mornings from 7 to 9:30 are quiet.
- **West 59th Street Gymnasium and Pool**, W 59th St and West End Ave, 212-397-3166 or 3159, offers a 34' by 60' indoor pool and a 75' by 100' outdoor pool. The gym has basketball and paddleball courts.

Health clubs and Ys with pools are described at the end of this chapter. Dedicated swimmers might wish also to check out other swimming locations such as:

- **Brooklyn Floating Pool**, locations vary but this is the latest addition to the NYC Parks summer cool-off program—an enormous outdoor pool that floats in the East River during the summer (filtered water, of course). Locations vary somewhat but its usually near Brooklyn Heights. Check the Parks Dept site for more details
- **Coles Sports and Recreation Center**, 181 Mercer St at Houston, 212-998-2020; New York University's sports facility, with racquet ball and squash courts, a weight room, and a 25-meter pool with six lanes beneath frosted glass windows is available to residents from 14th to Canal streets, Fourth to Eleventh avenues, and students, faculty, and staff affiliated with NYU.
- **Manhattan Plaza Swim and Health Club**, 482 W 43rd St at Tenth Ave, 212-563-7001; the handsome, verdant, glass-enclosed 40' by 75' pool with four lap lanes is the main lure here, but there is also a gym and sauna. Of course, you'll need an annual membership and to get one, or to just get pricing information, you must first schedule an appointment for a personal consultation with one of the club's consultants.

- **Metropolitan Masters**, www.metroswim.org; call or visit their web site for a list of places where club members can swim in and around New York City. Options include several YMCAs, Chelsea Piers, and the New York Athletic Club.
- **Riverbank State Park**, 679 Riverside Dr at 145th St, 212-694-3600; this glorious facility atop a waste treatment plant over the Hudson River is a treasure for Uptowners who pay a couple of dollars to go for a swim in its indoor Olympic-sized pool (50 meters)—no membership "or consultation" needed. There are a host of water classes and activities between sessions, and there is an outdoor pool open in the summer. Call for hours.
- **Trinity School Swim Club**, 139 91st St, between Columbus and Amsterdam avenues, 212-873-1650; the 45' by 75' pool is available to members for swimming six nights a week. Membership is for a summer session and for a winter session that corresponds to the academic year (and therefore includes fall and spring). Currently, there's a long waiting list.

TENNIS

The Department of Parks Permit Office in each borough issues tennis permits for city courts. Manhattan permit particulars are detailed above under Central Park—Tennis. Of the city's 535 public courts, more than 100 are located in Manhattan at nine sites. The largest single concentration, 30 courts, is in Central Park off 96th Street. Seven of the other locations are north of 96th Street, and the eighth is at East River Park at Broome Street on the Lower East Side. In Manhattan, the phone is 212-360-8131

In Brooklyn, permits are sold at the Brooklyn Borough Parks Department office in Litchfield Mansion, 95 Prospect Park West off Fifth Street, 718-965-8914, Monday–Friday 9 a.m. to 4 p.m. Call for annual permit fees. The ten city courts located at the Parade Grounds, Coney Island and Parkside avenues, open from April to November, are probably those most popular with tennis permit holders. The same courts are covered with a bubble and run as a concession in the winter.

Five private clubs with four or more courts in Manhattan, Roosevelt Island, and across the East River in Queens are listed below. Check the Yellow Pages for other facilities near you.

- **Manhattan Plaza Racquet Club**, 450 W 43rd St, 212-594-0554; membership, hourly and seasonal rates.
- **Midtown Tennis Club**, 341 Eighth Ave at 27th St, 212-989-8572, www.midtowntennis.com; hourly and seasonal rates.
- **Roosevelt Island Racquet Club**, 281 Main St, Roosevelt Island, 212-935-0250, www.rirctennis.com; clay courts indoors, league play, a seniors' club, babysitting, membership, hourly rates.
- **West Side Tennis Club**, 1 Tennis Place, Forest Hills, Queens, 718-268-2300, http://www.foresthillstennis.com, has 43 outdoor courts, including grass, clay, Deco-Turf, and four Har Tru courts under a bubble in cold weather. A member-

ship club on the former site of the US Open and home to some 800 members, West Side hosts a variety of tennis programs and tournaments and includes on the premises a fitness room, platform tennis, basketball, and a new outdoor pool complex. Membership dues vary depending on age and family status. Lessons with a pro are available at extra charge.

Of course, if you really want to play where the pros play, you can rent a court at the **Billie Jean King National Tennis Center**, which is open to the public almost all year (closed for Thanksgiving, Christmas, and for two weeks in late August/early September for a little tournament called the US Open). Located in Flushing Meadow Park, Queens—across from Citi Field stadium (take the #7 train). For rates and information call 718-760-6200 or visit the USTA web site at www.usta.com. Junior and adult training programs plus junior summer camps are also available.

TRAPEZE

Yes indeed, you too can planche and whip, execute twisting layouts, or pull off a double pirouette return. Of course, it will take time, practice and instruction, and there is no better place than Trapeze School New York. Established in 2001, the TSNY has seen explosive growth, especially after exposure from *Sex in the City* and the *Today Show*. The school, located just north of Pier 26 on the Hudson, caters to all levels, with special focus on beginners. Classes range from $47 to $65, with discounts for purchasing blocks of five or more classes. Visit www.trapezeschool.com for more information, or call 917-797-1872. Truly, this town has everything.

YOGA

Not a sport really, but universal at all many health and fitness clubs. It's the unsport in sports. Listed below are just some of the many sites other than health clubs where yoga, in one form or another, is taught and practiced.

- **Dharma Yoga Center**, 297 Third Ave at 23rd St, 212-889-8160, www.dharmayogacenter.com, offers classical yoga, meditation, breathing classes, and posture classes for different levels.
- **Integral Yoga Institute**, 227 W 13th St between 7th and 8th avenues, 212-929-0586, www.integralyogaofnewyork.org; classes on the Upper West Side and Lower East Side. The main location offers open classes in Hatha I, beginners, intermediate, and advanced Hatha, prenatal and postpartum classes, Hatha in Spanish and for persons with HIV. They operate an adjacent health food store and a vitamin store nearby. The Integral Yoga Teaching Center at 200 W 72nd St and Broadway, 212-721-0400, offers a similar roster of classes as well as yoga for mobility and private lessons in yoga and meditation.

- **Om Yoga Center**, 826 Broadway, 6th floor, 212-254-9642, www.omyoga.com; with Hatha yoga classes at all levels, partner yoga, a breathing workshop, and meditation courses.
- **Prana Studio**, 5 W 19th St between 5th and 6th avenues, 212-666-5816, www. thepranastudio.com, specializes in Ashtanga yoga.
- **Sivananda Yoga Vedanta Center**, 243 W 24th St between 7th and 8th avenues, 212-255-4560, offering multi-level yoga for all ages, courses and one-day workshops on meditation, philosophy, and vegetarian cooking. They also offer yoga retreats at their ranch in the Catskills.
- **White Street Center**, 43 White St between Broadway and Church St downtown, 212-966-9005; yoga classes, personal trainers, body work, and massage therapy.
- **Yoga Studio**, 351 E 89th St, 212-988-9474; private one-on-one classes by appointment only.

HEALTH CLUBS, YMCAS, YWCAS, AND YMHAS

HEALTH CLUBS

Beyond offering personal trainers and customized fitness regimens, most health clubs offer various classes, ranging from kick-boxing and spinning to yoga and fencing. Facilities go from bare-bones weight rooms to ubiquitous all-purpose spas where you set your own pace using the most appealing facilities. These often include a pool (varying from postage stamp to Olympic in size), exercise equipment (aerobic and weight), steam-rooms, whirlpools, and saunas. Hospitals have gotten into the act as well by offering low-key but well-equipped exercise facilities for patients and others affiliated with the hospital; contact the hospital nearest you to find out what may be available. To indicate the amenities offered, a few of the dozens of health facilities located in the city are described here.

Get a tour, and if possible a free pass or two, before signing on the dotted line—you may decide that the reality of exercising to skull-pounding music is not so healthful after all. When you're told that the club you're visiting is having a "sale," take it with several grains of salt; with few fixed prices, words like "special" and "discount" are next to meaningless in the fitness business. The person on the treadmill next to you may have paid double or half what you paid. Ask at your place of work if they offer an employer-sponsored program. Finally, don't let yourself be pressured into signing up for a long-term commitment—unless you're *really* sure you want that multi-year membership. One excellent way to get a feel for what's available is the New York Fitness Passbook, which gives you passes to 150 private gyms and clubs in the area. The cost is around $75, and there are also yoga and other fitness passbooks available from the same company, The American Health and Fitness Alliance, 212-808-0765, www.health-fitness.org.

- **Asphalt Green**, 1750 York Ave at 90th St, 212-369-8890; www.asphaltgreen. org; two gyms, indoor and outdoor running tracks, state-of-the-art cardiovascular and weight-training equipment at this community-oriented, not-for-profit 5.5-acre sports and fitness complex. But the centerpiece is its AquaCenter, a spectacular 50-meter Olympic-standard pool. Membership is on a monthly, semi-annual, or annual basis. Non-members can purchase a day pass for full access to the facility.
- **Bally's Total Fitness Clubs**, www.ballyfitness.com; this nationwide club has a number of New York area locations including 45 E 55th St, 212-688-6630; 335 Madison Ave, Bank of America Plaza, 212-983-5320; 350 W 50th St, Worldwide Plaza, 212-265-9400; 1915 Third Ave, 212-369-3063; 641 Ave of the Americas, 212-645-4565; and 139 W 32nd St, 212-465-1750; and clubs in Queens, Riverdale, and New Jersey. Aqua fitness, step training, athletic training, dance fitness, conditioning, mind-body training, circuit training, yoga, spinning, and plenty of other classes are offered in the membership plans. Personal training is also available. Be sure to tour the club you will use most, as the clientele and facility vary greatly from place to place.
- **Battery Park Swim & Fitness Club**, 375 South End Ave, 212-321-1117; swim in a glass-enclosed pool with a patio that opens out onto the Hudson River in summer. Swim classes and "aquacize" are offered, as well as free weights, Cybex and Nautilus, StairMasters, treadmills, and Lifecycles. A host of classes, whirlpool, saunas, and steam rooms complete the facility. Membership.
- **Crunch Fitness**, www.crunch.com, is proliferating, with 10 Manhattan locations including 25 Broadway, 212-269-1067; 404 Lafayette St, 212-614-0120; 1109 Second Ave between 58th and 59th streets, 212-758-3434; 54 E 13th St near Fifth Ave, 212-475-2018; 144 W 38th St, 212-869-7788; 555 W 42nd St, 212-594-8050; and 162 W 83rd St, 212-875-1902; plus two in Brooklyn and one on Long Island. Crunch packs 'em in with catchy ads and fairly outlandish exercise classes, which appeal to a mostly young crowd. Call it entertainment fitness. Amenities vary at the different clubs but include personal training, boxing, rock climbing walls, steam rooms, pools, saunas, and even tanning. Membership.
- **Dolphin Fitness Clubs**, www.dolphinfitnessclubs.com; in Manhattan at 94 E Fourth St, 212-387-9500 and 18 Ave B, 212-777-1001. There are nine clubs total in The Bronx, Brooklyn, Queens, and Staten Island. Provides all the basics including muscle toning and aerobic classes, Nautilus equipment, personal trainers, weight training, cardiovascular equipment and pools and racquetball courts at some locations. Membership.
- **Equinox Fitness Club**, www.equinoxnyc.com, 16 Manhattan locations including 897 Broadway at 19th St, 212-780-9300; 344 Amsterdam Ave at W 76th St, 212-721-4200; 2465 Broadway at 92nd St, 212-799-1818; 140 E 63rd St at Lexington Ave, 212-750-4900; 205 E 85th St, 212-439-8500; 54 Murray St, 212-566-6555; 97 Greenwich Ave, 212-620-0103; 14 Wall St at Nassau, 212-

964-6688, plus 7 more in the surrounding area. Certified personal trainers and some 200 classes, from high- and low-impact aerobics to Aerobox, pre- and postnatal exercise to yoga and meditation. Besides up-to-date equipment, the club boasts boxing circuit training, one-on-one boxing (for women too), and cardio/theater television with the cardiovascular workout equipment. In addition, you'll find childcare, a juice bar, shopping and more at these health emporiums. A nutritionist supervises personal weight-loss programs. At the Amsterdam Avenue location a physiology lab offers comprehensive metabolic testing for a fee to non-members as well as members. No boxing uptown. Membership.

- **Lucille Roberts**, 800-USA-LUCILLE, www.lucilleroberts.com, operates at several Manhattan locations: 143 Fulton St, 212-267-3730; 300 W 40th St, 212-268-4199; 505 W 125th St, 212-222-2522; 80 Fifth Ave at 14th St, 212-255-3999; and 1387 St Nicholas Ave, 212-927-8376; plus more gyms in Brooklyn, Queens, The Bronx, and New Jersey. Forget the sauna and the personal trainers, and bring your own towel. Classes are the draw, including one called "butt and gut." In some neighborhoods, there are classes in Spanish. The cost of membership, comparatively low, varies by location, as do hours. Individual gyms have occasional sales promotions, when it's cheaper to join; they're worth checking out.

- **New York Health & Racquet Club**, www.hrcbest.com, 212-797-1500, has several locations (plus a yacht club on 23rd St if you want to take a sea cruise). Rates go down considerably in the summer (watch for ads offering discounts, and ask about corporate discounts). Membership includes use (for a fee) of the club's tennis court in the Village and admission to any of its locations. Most locations have pools, saunas, and racquetball courts.

- **New York Sports Clubs**, www.nysc.com, over 20 locations, among them: 575 Lexington Ave at 51st, 212-317-9400; 1637 Third Ave, 212-987-7200; 61 W 62nd St, 212-265-0995; and 113 E 23rd St, 212-982-4400. Eagle and Nautilus circuits, Lifecycles, StairMasters, Gravitron, and other equipment available in all clubs. Most have one-on-one training, pools, squash courts, whirlpools, and saunas. Membership includes entrance to all clubs and access to tennis courts in Brooklyn (additional court fee). Fees vary by location. This is one of the few clubs that does not require payment for a full year upfront, but will bill you monthly.

- **The Printing House Fitness and Center**, 421 Hudson St at Leroy, www.phfrc.com, 212-243-7600; on the first floor are five squash courts, on the ninth floor are machines, treadmills, locker rooms, and a sauna, steam room, and whirlpool, as well as a cardiovascular fitness center, two dance studios, and a full-service salon. On the roof above is a seasonal 20' by 30' heated outdoor pool. There are three different membership rates here, depending on whether you want to use just the squash courts, just the gym, or everything. Call for specifics.

- **Reebok Sports Club/NY**, 160 Columbus Avenue at 67th Street, 212-362-6800, www.reeboksportsclubny.com, is an upscale, landscaped urban country club. This state-of-the-art 140,000-square foot facility on six floors features a 45-foot climbing wall, a rooftop in-line skating and running track, full basketball and volleyball courts, swimming pool with underwater sound, sauna, a virtual reality sports simulator for skiing, wind-surfing, and golf, a bar, health food café, and a bistro. They even have a dry cleaning service.
- **Sports Center at Chelsea Piers**, 23rd St and Hudson River, 212-336-6000, www.chelseapiers.com; this 150,000-square-foot pier houses a four-lane, 1/4-mile running track; competition track; three basketball courts; a 100-foot climbing wall and a bouldering wall; a six-lane, 25-yard swimming pool; two outdoor sun decks; cardiovascular, circuit, and strength training equipment; a boxing ring; aerobic studios; and an infield for volleyball, sand volleyball, and touch football. Also training, sports medicine, spa facilities, and a physiology lab available. Members have the use of all the other Pier facilities at a 10% discount. Membership or day passes. Popular for kids' parties.
- **The Sports Club/LA**, 330 East 61st Street, 212-355-5100. www.thesports clubla.com, is that glamorous seven-story building you see when entering Manhattan on the 59th Street Bridge from Queens: lots of tinted glass, gleaming chrome, and lithe-looking figures back-lit and working out. The big club accommodates a 20' by 40' pool, exercise machines, five international squash courts, sun deck, restaurant, and juice bar, among other amenities. The club also features classes in Tae Kwon Do, yoga, and boxing. Other location: 45 Rockefeller Plaza, 212-218-8600.

YMCAS, YWCAS, AND YMHAS

- **92nd Street YMHA** (Young Men's and Women's Hebrew Association), 1395 Lexington Ave, 212-415-5500, www.92y.org; annual athletic membership entitles you to participate in many programs including indoor jogging, weight training, volleyball, and handball as well as fitness programs and use of the 50' by 75' pool.
- **Brooklyn YWCA**, 30 Third Ave between State St and Atlantic Ave, Brooklyn, 718-875-1190; for a reasonably priced athletic membership plus a Y membership, both men and women can work out on the Universal machines, punching bags, the large basketball court, jogging track, and in the 20' by 60' swimming pool, and relax in the sauna.
- **Harlem YMCA**, 180-181 W 135th St by Lenox Ave, 212-281-4100, www.ymcan-yc.org, offers two pools (for adults and children), Nautilus and weights, a track, basketball courts, table tennis, aerobics, yoga and karate classes, and personal trainers. Athletic membership (for men and women) plus initiation fee.
- **McBurney YMCA**, 225 W 14th St, 212-741-9210, www.ymcanyc.org; this Y has a carefully developed children's after-school program as well as adult gym-

nastics, adult lap and recreational swimming, full-court basketball, indoor jogging track, fencing, handball, volleyball, and a weight lifting room. Annual adult membership plus joiner's fee for the first year. Excellent new facilities.

- **Vanderbilt YMCA**, 224 E 47th St, 212-756-9600, www.ymcanyc.org, has an after-school program (with escorts from certain neighborhood schools) plus yoga, handball, and paddleball, along with swimming, basketball, volleyball, indoor jogging, Nautilus, and aerobics. Regular membership plus joiner's fee includes use of the gym, 20' by 60' swimming pool, a 40' by 75' lap pool, and other sports facilities. Annual dues for the Businessman's Club and the men's Athletic Club are higher.

- **The West Side YMCA**, 5 W 63rd St, 212-875-4100, www.ymcanyc.org, is justifiably proud of its Sports Fitness Department, which keeps both men and women members in the very best of shape. The seven-story building houses two pools, a wrestling room, indoor running track, handball, squash, and racquetball courts, universal exercise machines, and numerous other facilities. Annual adult membership plus initiation fee.

NESTLED AMONG THE CONCRETE, STEEL, AND GLASS OF NEW YORK'S riotous urban landscape are pockets of greenery and nature so lush and rich that even the most hard-nosed New Yorkers cannot help but forget their customary brusqueness and the madcap rush of the city itself. Though the buildings and blocks may be densely packed, it is the parks that New Yorkers truly share with one other. From the smallest community garden on a vacant lot in a dense neighborhood, where neighbors lovingly tend an iris bed and riotous morning glories, to green bands streaked with runners, bladers, and cyclists along watery borders, to Manhattan's great lush centerpiece, Central Park, and its sister, Prospect Park, in Brooklyn, New Yorkers use and cherish their parks. Beyond these groomed and cultivated parks familiar to most, there are about 9,000 acres of urban wilderness in the domain of the city's parks department, where the nature lover can wander wooded paths, meadows, and marshlands alone and silent among swans, egrets, herons, turtles, muskrats, and rabbits. For the price of a subway ride, one can spend the day in a national park, Gateway National Recreation Area, a birders' paradise, parts of which are within the city. And the city's beaches, seaside parks of a sort, guarantee sandy access to the Atlantic Ocean and Long Island Sound.

There are more than 1,700 parks and playgrounds throughout the 28,000 acres maintained by the Department of Parks and Recreation in the five boroughs. These range from vest-pocket neighborhood playgrounds to the 2,700-acre Pelham Bay Park in The Bronx. Suffice it to say we can't describe or even list them all. Rather, this chapter focuses on the major parks in each borough, with brief descriptive mention of some others and, finally, a look at the city's beaches. For further information about parks in general or a particular park call 311 within New York City, 212-NEW YORK outside the city, or go online to www.nycgovparks.org.

Open from dawn to 1 a.m., all city parks are free and accessible by public transportation. Statistically speaking, the parks are very safe. That said, it is good to remember these are urban parks; common sense tells you it's not a good idea to stroll or jog through a wooded park area alone, day or night—there are plenty of trails in wide-open spaces. Unless you're watching one of the special concerts in the park, or visiting some other crowded park event, avoid the parks after dark. Dogs must be on leashes, and you are expected to clean up after your dog. It's the law.

PARKS

MANHATTAN

In 1858 Frederick Law Olmsted and Calvert Vaux won a design competition for the construction of the first public park to be built in America. It was to occupy swampy land inhabited by poor squatters, bone-boiling mills, and swill mills, an area described in one report as "a pestilential spot where miasmic odors taint every breath of air." The inhabitants were removed, buildings torn down, swamps drained, tons of earth moved, and Manhattan schist blasted away. Following plans for a picturesque landscape of glades alternating with copses, water, and outcroppings, and threaded with drives, footpaths, and bridle paths, over a period of 20 years the park emerged from wasteland. What Olmsted and Vaux had named Greensward became **Central Park**, 840 acres of man-made romantic landscape stretching rectangularly from 59th Street north to 110th Street, and from Fifth Avenue west to Central Park West (Eighth Avenue): the green jewel in the middle of Manhattan.

Today the park is managed, under contract with the city, by the **Central Park Conservancy** (www.centralparknyc.org), a non-profit organization responsible for extensive restoration of the park. The most heavily visited area is the southern portion of the park, especially the area around the ever-popular **Central Park Zoo** (www.centralparkzoo.com), which includes the revamped Children's Zoo. The northern portion beyond the Reservoir, with its heavily used jogging track, contains the wildest terrain, including the Ravine area with its waterfall and the 1814 Blockhouse, as well as the only formal garden in the park, the elegant **Conservatory Garden** at 105th Street and Fifth Avenue. The **Charles A. Dana Discovery Center**, 212-860-1370, in the northeast corner of the park, features ecologically oriented exhibits and programs for all ages on a regular basis, and has fishing poles for use at the adjacent Harlem Meer. The Conservancy offers free seasonal events throughout the park, including bird-watching walks and ecological activities. Pick up the Conservancy's excellent Central Park Map and Guide at the Dairy, just north of Wollman Rink near the 65th Street Transverse, open Tuesday–Sunday, 10 a.m.–5 p.m.

New Yorkers use Central Park: for sports, from croquet to horseback rid-ing to league softball (see the chapter on **Sports and Recreation**); for cultural events such as Shakespeare in the Park and outdoor performances by the Met-ropolitan Opera and the New York Philharmonic; for children's recreation in its numerous playgrounds; for storytelling sessions, kite-flying, and carousel riding, and organized nature activities; for sunbathing on its rocky outcroppings or on bucolic Sheep Meadow; for bird-watching in the Ramble, especially during the annual spring warbler migration; for boating in the Lake or floating beneath Bow Bridge in a Venetian gondola; for sailing toy boats in the Lake; for weddings; and even for films, many of which have been shot in or around the massive park—the musical *Hair*, for example was primarily shot in Central Park. And it's used for daydreaming or reading a good book. In fact, sometimes just knowing it is there is enough.

Central Park is open from a half-hour before dawn to 1 a.m. As in the other large city parks, it is best visited in daylight or at night in the well-lighted areas along the edges and with companions. Check www.centralparknyc.org for an invigorating virtual visit and plenty of information. This excellent, non-official web site offers a colorful virtual tour, park history, sporting events, a listing of park events, and links to other park-related sites.

Having completed Central Park, Olmsted and Vaux focused their attention on the banks of the Hudson River and designed most of what is now **Riverside Park**. This elongated ribbon of green, stretching along the river from 72nd Street to 152nd Street and bisected lengthwise by the Henry Hudson Parkway, is par-ticularly beautiful in the spring when daffodils dot the grassy banks and swarms of flowering trees create a haze of pink and white. Riverside Drive winds among great trees along the upper terrace, and the mighty Hudson, nearly a mile wide here, sweeps along past cyclists and joggers on the riverfront promenade. Sail-boats and a few houseboats at the 79th Street boat basin bob at anchor, and in good weather reasonably priced sailing lessons are to be had here (see **Sports and Recreation**). Tennis, handball, soccer, and volleyball are played here, and a facility for bladers and boarders, with ramps and half-pipes at 108th Street, draws youthful enthusiasts. Soaring Riverside Church and Grant's Tomb add to the ap-peal of Riverside Park. For more information call the park administrator's office at 212-408-0264 or visit www.riversideparkfund.org. Further along at 145th Street and Riverside Drive an iron gate gives access to **Riverbank State Park**, 212-694-3600, built atop a waste treatment plant, where ice skating, swimming, and other athletic activities can be pursued at way-below-health-club rates.

Fort Tryon Park in Washington Heights stands atop a ridge of Manhat-tan schist at the island's highest natural point. The site of one of the earliest Revolutionary War battles (we lost), this land was purchased in 1917 by John D. Rockefeller, Jr. He hired Frederick Law Olmsted, Jr., to design a park here, reserv-ing four acres at the northern end of the 67 acres for a museum of medieval art, The Cloisters—a fortuitous pairing, those juniors. Taking advantage of the sweeping Hudson view at this 250-foot elevation, Olmsted designed a series of terraces with stone parapets and retaining walls, the whole threaded with eight miles of paths. The centerpiece of the park is the three-acre Heather Garden, with heaths, brooms, and thousands of bulbs, which bloom from January through autumn. Further along the Promenade are leafy Linden Terrace and The Cloisters, with its three medieval gardens. Bring a picnic lunch. For more information call Fort Tryon Park, 212-408-0100, or The Cloisters, 212-795-1388 (www. metmuseum.org for a schedule of exhibitions).

Just north of Fort Tryon Park at the very top of Manhattan, little-known **Inwood Hill Park** contains the last remaining natural woodland in Manhattan, not to mention arresting views of the Hudson River and the Jersey Palisades beyond. Interesting geology on the wooded ridge, which is criss-crossed with paved and graveled paths, includes glacial potholes and cliffs with a hodge-podge of blocky gray rocks, the Indian Rock Shelters, which once sheltered Algonquin Indians. From these rocky cliffs, paths descend to playing fields, grassy parkland, and marshland along swift Spuyten Duyvil Creek, across which the Henry Hudson Bridge soars to The Bronx. There is an excellent **Urban Ecology Center** here staffed by Urban Park Rangers. They lead occasional walks and canoe trips into the Hudson. For information call 212-304-2365.

South of Central Park, greenspace is measured out in much smaller portions. **Bryant Park** behind the Beaux Arts main branch of the New York Public Library at 42nd Street, between Fifth and Sixth avenues, for example, is too small to encourage sports much more strenuous than chess. It is now greenspace with a rather European feel, and those who work in the neighborhood are grateful for it. During the summer months it hosts concerts and private parties (www. bryantpark.org). **Union Square Park** is a 3½-acre rectangle south of the Flatiron District. Serving as a gateway into downtown Manhattan, the park is heavily trafficked and open 24 hours. There are dog runs, and a new upscale restaurant at the north end for dining al fresco, but the limited greenspaces within are made available only occasionally. The square has a long history as a meeting place for rallies, protests, and artisans, and in the winter hosts a labyrinthine complex of merchants housed in candy cane–striped kiosks. One of the city's best greenmarkets is found here (see **Greenmarkets** in the **Shopping for the Home** section), and the park is surrounded by shops, restaurants, theatres, and schools (www. unionsquarenyc.org). Not a place to picnic, but the people watching is fantastic. Further downtown at the foot of Fifth Avenue, **Washington Square Park** provides greenspace for Greenwich Village and SoHo, where people-watching and attending the annual art show are the sports of choice. Nearly surrounded by New York University, which threatens to engulf it entirely, Washington Square Park has managed to retain a sense of its history, which has included being a potter's field, the site of the hangman's tree, a military parade ground, and an elegant park for the wealthy. Its Village location and the presence of college students keep it youthful and colorful. To the east, **Tompkins Square Park**, truly a people's park with an English provenance and great old trees that have always made it a shady haven in the summer for a working-class population, is the front yard for the East Village. Gentrification has brought more young professionals and families to the area, and the park is often crowded. There are several dog runs there, including a "Small Dog Area" exclusively for dogs under 23 pounds. Way downtown you'll find a series of small parks connected by a sinuous, elegant **Esplanade** spacious enough to accommodate joggers, cyclists, bladers, walkers, and baby strollers moving at their own pace within sight of the Statue of Liberty and Ellis Island. Students from nearby Stuyvesant High School toss frisbees in the offshore breeze, and children romp and climb in a fanciful playground. The landscape at the south end was designed to resemble the original shoreline. Just to the south, at the very foot of the island, is **Battery Park**, once part of New York Harbor, with Castle Clinton surrounded by water rather than grass. This inviting, grassy stretch looks out on the harbor, the statue, and Staten Island, and invites a hop onto the free Staten Island Ferry. This is just the downtown end of the Manhattan Waterfront Greenway, a 32-mile stretch of car free pedestrian/biker paradise that almost encircles the entire island (the 10 blocks around the Queensborough Bridge remains un-green, as of yet). It is taboo to all motorized traffic, but anything else is a go. Combined with the new crosstown bike lanes it's an excellent way for two-wheel commuters to avoid traffic.

Saving the smallest for last, don't forget the Green Thumb Community Gardens, throughout the Lower East Side area, www.greenthumbnyc.org; one of the more inspiring urban movements of late, the Green Thumbs program began as a way for the crime-wracked Lower East Side community to take control of hundreds of trash-filled vacant lots in the 1970s. These lots—saved in part by a donation from singer Bette Midler—have been turned into hundreds of teeny community-run gardens that provide much needed relief from NYC congestion. Some are astonishing paradises of plants and flowers and sculpture, some have stayed closer to their roots as vacant lots but they're one of the most beloved movements in this part of town. The best ones are well worth a visit (check for what hours they're open to the public, usually weekend afternoons).

GOVERNOR'S ISLAND

Governor's Island, www.govisland.com, accessible by ferry from 10 South Street, 212-440-2200; almost lost to commercial development, this military base (closed in 1996) was instead sold to the people of New York for one dollar in 2003. It now is one of the more popular summer greenspace destinations, with a number of 18th-century forts and hundreds of acres of forest and waterfront with lovely views of the Statue of Liberty. Bring your own bicycle, or rent one, and explore this car-free island. It's become an immensely popular day trip for Manhattanites.

BROOKLYN

Who but Calvert Vaux and Frederick Law Olmsted could have designed **Prospect Park**, sister to Central Park and younger by just a few years? In fact, its designers considered it their masterpiece. Free of Manhattan's grid, it is irregularly shaped in a somewhat elongated ovoid, smaller at 526 acres, and unlike Central Park, it is undisturbed by criss-crossing traffic. Prospect Park was designed for strolling along a network of paths: on vast Long Meadow, the park's magnificent centerpiece, around Prospect Lake and the Lullwater, through The Ravine and the Midwood Forest, and by The Pools. Sounds English? It is. Olmsted and Vaux incorporated the natural terrain into their design, including water, magnificent old trees and geological features such as glacial kettle ponds, one of which became the charming Vale of Cashmere. To these features they added rustic bridges, a waterfall, and lakes, the final effect of which is vistas, surprising nooks and glades, and hilltop prospects. There's even a Quaker cemetery, among whose residents is the actor Montgomery Clift, and an elegant, Palladian-style boathouse. This is not to say that strolling is the sole Prospect Park activity. **Wollman Rink** is here for ice-skating; birding is excellent in the park; jogging, tennis, softball, kite flying, and soccer flourish here; and on summer weekends the Bandshell at 9th Street and Prospect Park West features music, from calypso to jazz, klezmer, and new urban Latin grooves. For more information and for upcoming events in the park visit www.prospectpark.org. The park is bounded by Ocean Avenue, Flatbush Avenue, Prospect Park SW, Prospect Park West, and Parkside Avenue.

Across Flatbush Avenue from Prospect Park, and behind the Brooklyn Central Library and the Brooklyn Museum, the **Brooklyn Botanic Garden**, 1000 Washington Boulevard, 718-623-7200, www.bbg.org, has extended an open invitation to Brooklynites and visitors since 1912. Within its compact 52 acres it contains an extraordinary variety of greenery and flora, beautifully landscaped so as never to seem crowded. The Cherry Esplanade, said to be the finest in America, draws crowds in May when the cherry trees are in exquisite bloom. Don't miss it, but come early and on a weekday if possible. There's a rock garden, water-lily ponds, and a lilac collection, offering intoxicating blooms each spring. An herb garden is arranged as an Elizabethan knot, and the stunning Japanese garden is a perennial favorite. Year-round, the gently undulating terrain invites wandering, beginning in February, when the witch hazel blooms and the snowdrops begin to come up. Call it mid-winter botanical balm. Before you bliss out, don't miss the original Palm House. You may decide to get married there, as many have.

Green-Wood Cemetery, with its main entrance on Fifth Avenue at 25th Street, is at once a cemetery and one of the most beautiful, not to mention unusual, parks in the city. This is an active cemetery, so you will not play soccer here, and jogging its winding, hilly drives would be a challenge. What you can do, if not on a cemetery-related mission, is walk, bird watch, identify exotic trees, of which there are many, and look for the graves of the once-famous, including

Lola Montez, Boss Tweed, Peter Cooper, and Samuel F.B. Morse, to name but a few. Opened in 1840, before Prospect Park was conceived, on 478 acres of glacial terminal moraine, and overlooking New York Harbor from the highest point in Brooklyn, it was promoted by its developers as an idyllic spot for strolling among the hills, ponds, superb vistas, and plantings. It was, de facto, the city's first park. The extraordinary mausoleums, obelisks, temples, pyramids, and rustic grave markers make it something of a museum of Victoriana and a draw for occasional guided tours. The main gate building, designed by Richard Upjohn, is a Gothic Revival extravaganza, housing the office where you pick up a pass, brochure, and a map of the cemetery. The office is open Monday–Friday, 8 a.m.–4 p.m., 718-768-7300, www.green-wood.com. If you wish to roam the cemetery on the weekend you should pick up a pass in advance.

Stepping out of the car at the **Marine Park** parking lot on Avenue U, just west of Flatbush Avenue, you'll find yourself in a landscape of salt marsh and meadow somewhat reminiscent of Holland. This 798-acre park, most of it saltwater wetlands surrounding Marine Park Creek, north of Sheepshead Bay, contains playing fields, tennis courts, a running track, and a golf course, in addition to a watery urban wilderness. From the parking lot you can hike the Gerritson Creek Nature Trail for about a mile, through grasses, sedges, and reeds with glimpses, perhaps, of diamond-back terrapin, horseshoe crabs, cottontails, marsh hens, myrtle warblers, cormorants, and peregrine falcons. It's hard to believe you're in New York City. For more information, call the Brooklyn Borough Office of the Department of Parks and Recreation at 718-965-8900. There's also the **Salt Marsh Nature Center** at 33rd Street and Avenue U, 718-421-2021, www.saltmarshalliance.org.

Even more unbelievable, and not known to many New Yorkers, is the presence of a 26,000-acre national park, **Gateway National Recreation Area**, www.nps.gov/gate, which encompasses most of Jamaica Bay in Brooklyn and Queens, and part of the Rockaways in Queens, a long stretch of the southern shore of Staten Island, and parts of the Jersey shore. Besides Jacob Riis Park, an ocean beach with a boardwalk (see **Beaches**, below), the best known point of interest in the area is the **Jamaica Bay Wildlife Refuge**, 718-318-4340, a prime birding preserve with salt water marshes, upland fields, and woods, where land and shore birds stop during migration. After obtaining a permit at the visitor center on Crossbay Boulevard in Broad Channel, Queens, visitors can explore diverse habitats by hiking an extensive trail system. Insect repellent in summer is strongly advised. Rangers give interpretive talks and lead nature walks; evening walks, workshops, and other programs are offered on a seasonal basis. Fishing can also be done for the cost of a permit. **Floyd Bennett Field**, 718-338-3799, the city's first municipal airfield, contains the North 40 Nature Trail, miles of runways for cycling or blading, and Hangar Row, where outdoor concerts and special events are held. Across Flatbush Avenue from the Field, **Dead Horse Bay** is a popular fishing area with a nature trail. **Canarsie Pier** just off the Beltway in Brooklyn is the site of summer concerts, excellent fishing, a children's playground, and a restaurant. Fishing is also popular, along with bird watching, at **Breezy Point Tip** on the Rockaway Peninsula and at **Fort Tilden**, 718-318-4300, www.nyharborparks.org, a 317-acre former Army base, where visitors can also hike and explore a military past, participate in organized athletics, or attend special events. On the south shore of Staten Island, **Great Kills Park**, 718-980-6130, offers ocean beaches, nature trails, a model airplane field, and fishing areas. Ranger walks at **Miller Field**, 718-351-6970, a former Army Air Corps defense station, and at **Fort Wadsworth**, 718-354-4500, dating from the 18th century, appeal to military buffs and children.

Admission to all portions of Gateway, except Sandy Point, N.J., is free. For the latest information on concerts, special programs, and ranger-led activities, visit Gateway on the web at www.nps.gov/gate. Or contact the National Park Service, Gateway National Recreation Area, Floyd Bennett Field, Building 69, Brooklyn 11234, 718-338-3799, for a seasonal program guide, which includes transportation directions to all parts of the area.

QUEENS

At long last **Flushing Meadows-Corona Park**, 718-760-6562, is coming into its own, becoming the grand park originally envisioned when the 1939 World's Fair was held there, and again at the time of the 1964 World's Fair. Built on what was once a garbage heap on Northern Boulevard, between Grand Central Parkway and the Van Wyck Expressway, both fairs were to pay for park construction, but neither made money, and the great park limped along with World Fair leftovers and a neighboring baseball stadium, Shea. The Unisphere, the signature attraction of the 1,255-acre park, and its grassy surrounds have been renovated, and extensive landscaping and plantings have beautified the central portion of the park, which also hosts the New York Hall of Science, Science Playground, and the Queens Museum, which is undergoing extensive and long-overdue renovations. It is expected that soon the park's entire waterfront along Flushing Bay will be distinguished by an elegant promenade with shade and ornamental trees, shrubs, and flowers along a curved railing. From reproduction cast iron benches visitors will be able to view the crowds and gaze at the flowerbeds or the boats bobbing in the World's Fair Marina. Elsewhere in the park are the Queens Theatre, the Queens Zoo, the US Tennis Association's Arthur Ashe Stadium and Tennis Center, an ice-skating rink, a par three pitch-and-putt golf course, running trails, and two large lakes lying to the south of the Long Island Expressway, one, Meadow Lake, with a boathouse.

Alley Pond Park sprawls and meanders south from Little Neck Bay to Union Turnpike. Despite being sliced by numerous parkways, it encompasses forests, meadows, salt marshes, and wetlands, making it an ideal environment for a network of nature trails from which one can observe muskrats, bullfrogs, salamanders, and hawks. Up on the northern end near Alley Creek, an environmental center offers a variety of educational classes and workshops: 718-229-4000.

Along Woodhaven Boulevard en route to the Rockaways, the beach, and JFK International Airport, you'll find **Forest Park**, 718-235-4100. It offers a public golf course, playing fields, and a magnificent 150-year-old oak forest honeycombed with picturesque nature trails. Summer concerts and other events take place at the bandshell. Call for information.

In the heart of Flushing, within cheering distance of Shea Stadium and the US Tennis Center, **Kissena Park Corridor** contains the **Queens Botanical Gardens and Arboretum** and connects up with greater Kissena Park, a gracious greenspace surrounding a lake and meandering stream. There's also a bicycle track and a public golf course: 718-886-3800, www.queensbotanical.org

To the east, adjacent to Cross Island Parkway and Hempstead Turnpike, **Belmont Park** is famous for its exceedingly beautiful racetrack, where thoroughbreds compete annually for the Belmont Cup. But you don't have to be a horse-lover to enjoy the park.

Nearing Long Island, in the eastern part of Queens, is **Cunningham Park**. This small but busy park on Union Turnpike in Fresh Meadows has several tennis courts, baseball fields, and even bocce courts, as well as plenty of picnic locations. The Big Apple Circus pays an annual visit.

And finally, Queens is home to much of **Gateway National Park**, bordering Brooklyn and described above.

THE BRONX

Up in the northeast corner of The Bronx, sprawling alongside and into Long Island Sound, is the city's largest park, 2,700 acres of it. **Pelham Bay Park**, 718-430-1890, has it all: a city beach, a golf course, miniature golf and a driving range, a stable, tennis courts, baseball diamonds, picnic grounds, and a historic mansion-museum, not to mention a range of habitats—the most diverse of any of the city parks. Just offshore and connected to the park by a bridge, City Island dangles like a fish on a line. The largest portion of the park lies on the north side of the Hutchinson River and Eastchester Bay, with Split Rock Golf Course and Pelham Bay Golf Course (see **Sports and Recreation**) scenically occupying the northernmost part. Also on Shore Road are Pelham Bay Riding (again, see **Sports and Recreation**) and extensive bridle trails. Nearby is the **Thomas Pell Wildlife Refuge and Sanctuary**, home to a variety of owls, wild turkeys, and deer. Just to the north and east, off Shore Road, is the Barton-Pell Mansion and Museum; dating from 1675 and with alterations done in the 19th century, it is the single manor house remaining of 28 country estates that once comprised the park area. It is well worth a visit. Orchard Beach (see **Beaches** below) cuts a great sandy arc on Long Island Sound. At its far end is the **Environmental Center**, where you can pick up literature and a guide booklet to the Kazimiroff Nature Trail, which winds through the adjoining Hunter Island Sanctuary, perhaps the most beautiful section of the park. Mature woodlands give way to salt marsh, where a profusion of water birds can be spotted year round, plus migrating hawks and ospreys in the fall. The great rounded boulders off-shore in the sound are glacial erratics, and the gray bedrock visible here is the southernmost extension of the ancient bedrock that forms most of the New England coast.

Directly to the west, abutting Riverdale and Yonkers, **Van Cortlandt Park**, 718-430-1890, also contains playing fields, two golf courses, a riding stable and trails, and a historic mansion-museum. Heavily used for recreation and once the site of an extensive Native American village, the Parade Ground is also home to weekend cricket competitions by largely West Indian teams. Nearby, you can visit the Van Cortlandt Mansion and Museum, 718-543-3344, the oldest house in The Bronx (1748) and a lovely example of vernacular Georgian architecture. To the north, where the Henry Hudson Parkway crosses Broadway and slices through the park, the **Riverdale Equestrian Centre** (www.riverdaleriding.com) rents horses for trail rides and offers lessons (see **Sports and Recreation**). The **Van Cortlandt Golf Course**, the oldest municipal course in the country, surrounds much of long, narrow Van Cortlandt Lake, while the **Mosholu Golf Course** lies in the southeast corner of the park (see **Sports and Recreation** for both). Birders and nature lovers seek out two popular trails: the forested **Cass Gallagher Trail** with its dramatic rock outcroppings in the northwest portion of the park, and the **John Kieran Nature Trail** in the southern portion. The latter, which skirts freshwater wetlands and the Tibbetts Brook area, esteemed by bird watchers, follows a former rail corridor, where deer, wild turkeys, and coyotes are seen occasionally, and swings down along the lake, where egrets and great blue herons are to be found. The **Urban Forest Ecology Center**, 718-548-0912, offers restrooms and information at the southern end of the Parade Ground. Urban Park Rangers offer nature walks and programs out of this facility throughout the year.

Bronx Park in the center of the north Bronx is comprised entirely of the **New York Botanical Garden** and the **International Wildlife Conservation Park** (Bronx Zoo), neither of which, properly speaking, is a park. Separated by Fordham Road and each bisected by the scenic Bronx River, they bear mentioning here because of their natural beauty, their accessibility, and their popularity. The **Botanical Garden**, 718-817-8700, www.nybg.org, on the north, is at once an internationally recognized botanical research facility and an extraordinary Victorian conservatory, with gardens and educational programs on 250 acres of geologically interesting virgin forest and a variety of landscaped gardens, all accessible by pathways and tram. Two cafés and picnic areas make it possible to spend the day here. Leave the dogs home and please don't pick the daisies. Note: the Botanical Garden operates a shuttle between it and the American Museum of Natural History and the Metropolitan Museum of Art in Manhattan weekends and Monday holidays, March–November. The **Bronx Zoo**, 718-367-1010, www.bronxzoo.com, on similar wooded terrain with rock outcroppings and wonderfully varied flora, would be a great place to spend the day even without the animals. But it is, of course, a world-class zoo, where you can wander out of the northeast woods into a rainforest, a savanna, or a Himalayan mountain enclave. Avoid holiday weekends, and during warm weather, parking is easier on weekdays.

Another greenspace that bears mention, though it is not a park at all, is **Woodlawn Cemetery**, 718-920-0500, www.thewoodlawncemetery.org, just east of Van Cortlandt Park, between the Bronx River and Jerome Avenue. Less spectacular in terrain than Green-Wood in Brooklyn, Woodlawn is nevertheless a splendiferous array of mausoleums, memorials, and tombstones in a richly planted, peaceful setting. Stop by the office at the Webster Avenue entrance at 233rd Street for a map and brochure. You can drive or walk around the terminal mansions of Jay Gould, the Woolworths, Herman Melville, and Fiorello ("The Little Flower") LaGuardia, whose modest tombstone bears a simply carved little flower. The cemetery is open daily, 9 a.m.–4:30 p.m.

STATEN ISLAND

Well into the middle of the 20th century, most of Staten Island remained something of a sleepy backwater of woods, meadows, and farms. Unbridled suburban sprawl threatened to sweep that away until community action resulted in the preservation of significant chunks of remaining natural lands in the center of the island, now designated the **Staten Island Greenbelt**. Twelve individual parks strung together by narrow corridors form the 2,500-acre greenbelt, encompassing five distinct vegetative zones and an astonishing variety of terrain. The Wisconsin glacier stopped here some 10,000 years ago, which accounts for the rocky ridges and kettle ponds. Two trails traverse the area: the 8.5-mile **Blue Trail**, running roughly east-west, and the 4-mile **White Trail**, running roughly north-south—the two cross at Bucks Hollow in Latourette Park. And don't forget the bizarre Ship Graveyard on the northern end of the island where dozens of wrecks pop out of the waves—hardly a natural site, but it makes for fantastic afternoon kayaking. Ask locals for directions.

One of the parks in the Greenbelt, **High Rock Park** on Todt Hill, 718-667-2165, happens to be the highest coastal point in the East south of Acadia National Park in Maine. Trails crisscross the 90-acre park, which was once a Girl Scout campground, winding in and out of woods, along the **Richmond Country Club** golf course and freshwater wetlands, and down steep slopes to glacial kettle holes. It's a bird watcher's paradise, with woodcock, indigo buntings, northern orioles, and other birds that generally shun urban areas. From the highest point on a clear day one can see the Atlantic Ocean.

Clay Pit Ponds State Park Preserve, 718-967-1976, near the southwest shore of the island, is the only state park preserve in the city, and its 260 acres perpetuate a remnant of Staten Island's rural past, its bogs, meadows, ponds, sand barrens, woodlands, and swamps. Some 160 acres are designated state freshwater wetlands and unique natural areas, and as such are closed to visitors. But the remainder has much to offer. Two interesting walking trails, with bridges and boardwalks through the wet areas, are easily hiked, even for children, who will marvel at the amphibians to be glimpsed along the way: black racer snakes, box turtles, frogs, lizards, and red-backed salamanders. One trail goes through part of one of the designated natural areas. A former pasture is now a meadow full of wildflowers and butterflies. An observation platform overlooks Abraham's Pond, a former clay pit abandoned in the 1920s. Look for muskrats, red-winged blackbirds, and painted turtles here. The park is free, open daily from dawn to dusk; the headquarters and restrooms are open weekdays, 9 a.m.–5 p.m. No pets allowed.

And, of course, there's **Miller Field** and **Great Kills Park**, Staten Island's share of Gateway National Recreation Area described above under **Brooklyn**; call 718-351-6970.

BEACHES

The air seems to bake in the concrete corridors of the city. The pungent aroma of the subway becomes nearly asphyxiating. You find yourself ducking into stores just to cool down. Then, on the train, you notice something odd: an assortment of men, women, and children in beach wear, carrying coolers and beach bags and towels. Summer-mad residents? Self-deluded European tourists? No: beach-savvy New Yorkers. There are city-run saltwater beaches in every borough but Manhattan, all one fare away—except for Jones Beach on Long Island, which is not a city beach but is included here because it is wonderful and many prefer it to the more crowded city beaches. If you venture to Jones or any other city beach by car on those really hot summer weekends, prepare for a significant amount of beach traffic and make sure your a/c is working. City beaches are free and parking is usually in the $5 to $10 range, unless you get lucky and find street parking.

City strands traditionally open on Memorial Day and close the day after Labor Day. Managed by national, state, and city park departments, all the beaches mentioned below are staffed by lifeguards. For information on beaches open to the general public, as opposed to residents with permits in Nassau and Suffolk counties, call the Long Island Convention & Visitors Bureau, 631-951-3440, or visit www.licvb.com for specific beach and park information. We begin with the northernmost beach, in The Bronx, and wind up on Long Island:

- **Orchard Beach**, 718-885-3273, on a long, sandy crescent on Long Island Sound in The Bronx with all of Pelham Bay Park at its back, is exceptionally popular, so much so you'll need to get there early on weekends if you're driving. Parking can be difficult.
- **Coney Island**, 718-372-5159, www.coneyislandusa.com, Coney Island Avenue and West 8th Street, is more than just a beach, it's a state of mind and

an icon. The vast sandy beach and the long boardwalk reaching from near the tip of the "island" to the Esplanade at Manhattan Beach is a scene for sure on summer weekends. You've seen the pictures, now try the beach. While you're there, don't miss the excellent New York Aquarium, the legendary Cyclone roll-ercoaster, and Astroland, another scene unto itself although by all reports not for long—the area is set for major redevelopment (on hold while the econo-my recovers). You might also catch a Cyclones game (the Mets class "A" minor league baseball team) at Keyspan Park. If nothing else, you should certainly stop by the original Nathan's for one of their world famous hot dogs.

- **Brighton Beach**, 718-946-1350, at Brighton Court and Brighton Second Street, in the heart of heavily Russian Little Odessa, makes for exotic people watch-ing along the long, broad boardwalk. Stock up on Russian gourmet specialties and incredibly cheap produce at the stands along Brighton Beach Avenue be-fore taking the subway home. For more about the beach and the area you can go to www.brightonbeach.com.

- **Manhattan Beach**, 718-946-1373, just east of Brighton Beach off Oriental Boulevard in Brooklyn, is a forty-acre public park and beach area with parking, a sandy beach, ballfield, and concession stand; a favorite with families. Best reached by car. After a day in the water you can eat at one of Sheepshead Bay's popular restaurants and perhaps catch an outdoor concert at nearby Kings-borough Community College.

- **Jacob Riis Park**, 718-318-4300, in the Gateway National Recreation Area on the Rockaway Peninsula in Queens, has a 13,000-car parking lot, a mile of wide, sandy beach with a boardwalk, and handsome, WPA-era buildings. It is perhaps the preeminent city beach. Until recent years, it was the only city beach where visitors could parade about in the all-together. Now, attire is re-quired. Besides swimming and tanning, there's handball, paddle tennis, and shuffleboard. It is here that famous Polar Bear Club members take their winter water frolics in January. Lifeguards come on duty here in mid-June.

- **Great Kills Park**, 718-987-6790, in the Gateway National Recreation Area on Staten Island's south shore, boasts miles of trails for jogging and walking, a model airplane field, athletic fields, a fishing area and marina as well as the guarded beach.

- **Jones Beach State Park**, 516-785-1600, is six and a half miles long and beau-tiful, well worth the drive, the bus ride from the Port Authority Bus Terminal, or the train from Penn Station to Freeport, where there's a shuttle bus to the beach. Field six, the most popular, attracts a peaceful mix of seniors, families, and couples gay and straight, but on summer weekends the parking lot fills up early. Field five is sheltered from waves, good for kids. West End two al-lows fishing and surfing and is the most peaceful. Weekend traffic on the Long Island Expressway is daunting, to say the least. Easily accessible from all five boroughs, Jones is the most popular public beach. Also here, a pitch-putt golf course, a pool, and a much-loved summer concert series at the outdoor Marine Theater featuring familiar name acts.

- **Robert Moses State Park**, Babylon, Long Island, 631-669-0470; just beyond Jones Beach, over two bridges on the Robert Moses Causeway, you'll find five more miles of beach; less well known than Jones, but along the same Atlantic Ocean. There's a per-car fee and you can enjoy the beach or visit the picnic area until the sun goes down. You'll also find a pitch-putt golf course, playgrounds, a day-use boat basin and more…just 48 miles from Manhattan, or about 90 minutes when you factor in traffic.
- **Rockaway Beach**, Beach 9th Street to 149th Street, Rockaway, Queens, 718-318-4000; on the south shore of Long Island, though technically within city limits, Rockaway is an extremely long beach, with numerous handball courts and high, heaving waves. The weekend scene is dominated by families that live on the outer rim of Queens. Five hundred yards near Beach 90th Street are devoted to surfers alone, the only chunk of city beach so designated.

For information or travel directions to any of these beaches, call your preferred beach directly or the Transit Authority, 718-330-1234, for directions.

NEW YORK SEEMS LIKE THE LEAST GREEN CITY IN THE WORLD—THE average New Yorker creates four pounds of waste daily, more per capita than any other city in the world and totaling 24 million pounds of trash every day of the week. You see it everywhere, in the four-foot high piles of garbage bags on the pavement, the overflowing city garbage containers, and the rancid smelly waters of the Gowanus Canal. But looks deceive. Thanks to its density and mass transit system, New York is also one of the most energy-efficient places in the world per capita per square foot. And now that green has become the new black, fashion-conscious Manhattanites have taken to zero-footprint living with a vengeance (if often more in image than fact).

Being green in NYC requires a little more effort than dragging around that $15 "I Feed Ten" shopping bag available at Whole Foods (although that's a start).

GREENING YOUR HOME

A green home or apartment is well-insulated and energy-efficient, incorporates nontoxic and sustainably produced materials, and/or has sustainable features like solar-assisted hot-water heating. Unfortunately, green materials and features tend to cost more upfront (sometimes significantly more) than non-green. Sometimes, depending on the feature, the savings gained over the lifespan of the efficiency product will recoup the premium paid in the beginning; other times, a clearer conscience is the primary reward. However, the cost gap between the idealistic and practical is rapidly closing as green technology continues to advance. Whether social consciousness or financial savvy motivates a homeowner, there are many features one can add to an existing home to make it greener.

GREEN REMODELING

Unless you own your apartment or building, traditional remodeling is not really an option in NYC. However, there has been of late a huge increase in greener building design, ranging from high-end, high-tech, entirely green-designed apartment complexes, to programs to put a lawn on everyone's roof. The New York City Department of Design and Construction has placed a priority on identifying and implementing cost-effective ways to promote greater environmental responsibility in building design, and its "High Performance Building Guidelines" (www.nyc.gov/html/ddc/downloads/pdf/guidelines.pdf) is one of the key works on minimizing a building's effect on the environment. As of 2008, there are almost 60 new green buildings under construction, including the Freedom Tower being built on the site of the World Trade Center, which will include solar panels and a wind farm (there's quite a breeze at 1,776 feet) that are expected to provide up to 20% of the building's expected energy demand. Battery Park is another high-profile green complex; its features include the recycling of its own wastewater in order to water the garden roofs. Another leader in this area is the Green Building Council, which offers a national Leadership in Energy and Environmental Design (LEED) rating system. Under NYC's 2006 Green City Buildings Act, any nonresidential project costing $2 million or more must meet LEED standards. Ask your realtor if your prospective new home meets these standards.

For smaller remodeling projects, there's a whole host of tools and services. The city's **Department of Design and Construction** (www.nyc.gov/html/ddc) has a variety of publications for green remodeling on its website. The **Community Environmental Center**, 43-10 11th Street, Long Island City, 718-784-1444, www.cecenter.org, is a non-profit group that helps smaller home-owners meet LEED standards and go as green as possible. Going green doesn't just mean microwindmills. Some 70 million tons of building materials are thrown onto the streets of New York every day and using scavenged/recycled materials has a huge impact on the environment. **Build It Green!** at 3-17 26th Ave at 4th St in Queens, 718-777-0132, www.bignyc.org/frontpage, has 75 tons of salvaged building materials, making this non-profit is the area's leader in in low cost eco-firendly salvage. There's also **Rebuilders Resource Co-op**, 461 Timpson Place in the Bronx, 718-742-1111, www.rebuilderssource.coop. **Moon River Chattel**, 62 Grand St, Brooklyn, 718 388 1121, www.moonriverchattel.com, has a smaller but beautifully edited salvage operation across the street from its main store. It also specializes in antique, remilled floorings. Low-emission paints are now available in every serious hardware and paint store, but for more interesting possibilities, both in terms or recyled composite woods and paints, try Williamsburg's **Bettencourt Green Building**, 75 Freeman Street, Brooklyn, 718-218-6737, www.bettencourtwood.com, which has an impressive array of composite eco-friendly woods and paints, including the ultra-organic American Clay line. Brooklyn's **Green Depot**, 1 Ivy Hill Road, 718-782-2991, offers a large range of eco-products, ranging from home mold-testing kits to low-flow showerheads. It's set to open a Manhattan branch on Bowery between Prince and Spring streets sometime in 2009. The **Council on the Environment of NYC (CENYC)**, 51 Chambers Street #228, 212-788-7900, is a hands-on non-profit dedicated to green the city and promoting waste prevention and recycling.

If you're thinking of making your building go solar (cost after tax incentives and rebates, $10,000-20,000) one recommended consultant is **Bright Power**, 11 Hanover Square, 15th floor, 212-803-5868, www.brightpower.biz.

ENERGY EFFICIENCY

Even if you're not able to build a 90-story green skyscraper or fund a million-dollar remodeling job, there are a number of small steps you can take to make your apartment more energy efficient without giving your landlord an excuse to evict you. The city's main website, www.nyc.gov, has a host of suggestions that are well worth looking at. Be sure to use energy-efficient appliances with the **Energy Star** label on it. Their website, www.energystar.gov, offers a store-locator engine for finding Energy Star–rated products. For smaller projects, contact **GreenHomeNYC**, www.greenhomenyc.org, a non-profit NYC organization that helps apartment dwellers and smaller buildings become environmentally friendly. **Con Edison**, the main electricity supplier of New York, has a number of tips on its website, *www.coned.com*. They also list rebates and incentives to assist with energy-saving improvements for your home

The following are typical recommendations for boosting your home's energy efficiency:

- **Insulate and weatherize your home**. Poorly insulated walls, ceilings, and floors allow heated or cooled air to escape from your house, needlessly raising your energy use (and energy bill). In apartments, poorly sealed doors and windows can allow in huge amounts of cold air during the winter, so seal or caulk leaks around doors, windows, pipes, and vents. Replace leaky old windows with insulated windows.
- Many older apartments have central steam heaters controlled by the landlord, but this invariably means you need supplemental heat. Be sure to investigate an energy-efficient mode of heating—the differences can be up to 50%, in both energy use and energy bills. The same is true for air-conditioning units. For summer, utility companies suggest setting the thermostat for 78 or higher, and in the winter setting it to 68 or cooler.
- **Upgrade inefficient appliances**. Replacing old, inefficient washing machines, dishwashers, water heaters, and especially refrigerators with more efficient models can have a major effect on your energy consumption (and, in the case of washing machines and dishwashers, on your water consumption, too). Forgo using the appliance entirely, if possible: let washed dishes and clothes air dry instead of using the dishwasher or clothes dryer.
- **Install efficient lighting**. Compact fluorescent light bulbs use 75% less energy and last up to ten times longer than standard incandescent bulbs. They also generate less heat. For an assurance of quality, choose ENERGY STAR° bulbs. (As mentioned at the beginning of this chapter, CFL bulbs do contain

mercury and require special handling if they break. The state requires you to dispose of these bulbs at hazardous waste collection centers.)

- **Turn off appliances when not in use**. Many home electronics such as the TV, DVD player, computer printer, and microwave oven are actually in standby mode and continue to draw a small amount of power even when "off." Plug these appliances into a power strip and turn off the power strip when not in use to completely cut off the drain. Recharging devices continue to use energy even when not in use, so unplug them or attach them to a power strip and turn it off.
- **Go solar**; sure, its pretty hard in a place like New York, but if you're determined there are now innumerable small-scale solar rechargers for everything from fans to cell phones.

Going green is not cheap (although it can pay for itself in the long run). But New York State has a variety of green-building tax credits, as well as ones for using solar and wind energy that can be applied to various business and personal income taxes. The Green Building Tax Credit provides for tax credits to owners and tenants of eligible buildings and tenant spaces which meet certain "green" standards—talk to your accountant for more details. Federal tax credits are also available; visit the federal government's **Energy Star** web site (www.energystar. gov) or the **Tax Incentives Assistance Project** (www.energytaxincentives.org) to review homeowner incentives.

RENEWABLE ENERGY

Consider buying green power from your utility. **Con Ed,** 800-752-6633, gives consumer the option of buying only wind or solar produced energy for their home, thus increasing demand and lowering costs. Visit /www.conedsolutions.com for more details. Alternately, there's **ECONergy**, 800-895-8586, www.econergy.com. These are the only two licensed suppliers at the moment, but the New York State Public Service Commission constantly updates its list of green supplies on its website, www.askpsc.com.

Exhaustive water conservation advice, like washing full loads of laundry and taking shorter showers, can be found at www.bewaterwise.com as well as at www. nyc.gov. There are tax rebates for installing high-efficiency clothes washers, showers and ultra-low-flush toilets (or convert your own by putting a full liter bottle of water in the tank). The **Department of Environmental Protection** offers free water-conservation seminars on a regular basis, and will even send out inspectors to your home to check for water efficiency (you'll also get free faucet aerators and low-flow showerheads). You can call **311** to set up an appointment.

LANDSCAPING

The idea of landscaping in NYC might seem ridiculous, but a growing number of people with roof access are turning their roofs into cooling and heat conserving gardens. The state of New York recently even passed an up to $100,000 tax credit for people who install a roof garden covering at least 50 percent of available rooftop space. One place to contact is **Sustainable South Bronx** at www.ssbx. org. Larger new buildings are now required to have a minimal amount of green covering on their roofs.

RECYCLING

In recovery from the dark ages of 2002, when the Bloomberg administration essentially canceled the city's recycling program, New York now has a comprehensive and extensive program for recycling its residents' endless supply of garbage. Metal, plastic, paper, and cardboard are included, and you can get a free chart detailing precisely what goes where by simply calling 311 and asking for it. You can get even more detailed information and printouts, as well as a schedule for pickups of unusual materials, by going to the website of the **NYC Department of Sanitation** at www.nyc.gov/html/dsny.

ENVIRONMENTALLY FRIENDLY PRODUCTS AND SERVICES

The best way to encourage the proliferation of environmentally friendly products and services is to support them. For businesses concerned about the bottom line, customer demand is the most compelling motivation to change. Here are a few resources for finding green products and services.

- *The Big Green Apple: Your Guide to Eco-Friendly Living in New York City* by Ben Jervey
- *Greenopia, New York City: The Definitive Guide to More Than 1,300 Eco-Friendly Businesses and Resources* describes sustainable products and services from New York-based business; visit www.greenopia.com.
- **New York Eco Spaces**, www.nyecospaces.com, offers up-to-the minute news on living Green in the Big Apple
- **The Consumers Union guide to environmental labeling** is online at www.eco-labels.org; the site includes a report card for various environmental claims, and labels and assesses whether the claim is meaningful and/or verified.
- *Consumer Reports* maintains a web site that assesses the environmental soundness of various products: visit www.greenerchoices.org.

FOOD

New York has traditionally had some of the worst, most environmentally unfriendly produce in the country. On the positive side, it was also the most expensive. Actually, it still *is* the most expensive, but the the quality has increased enormously and, thanks to GreenMarkets and the locavore movement, as well as the arrival of the Whole Foods chain, it is becoming increasingly environmentally friendly.

For those concerned with eating locally, the hugely popular GreenMarket movement has been a blessing. Not only are products in these roving markets

all produced locallly, their quality is usually infinitely superior to anything available in stores. The **Council on the Environment of NYC** (CENYC), 51 Chambers
Street #228, 212-788-7900, is a hands-on non-profit dedicated to running what
is now the largest farmers' market program in the country. Visit their site (www.
cenyc.org) for market locations and times, but the one at Union Square is not to
be missed, if only for the people watching.

Many grocery stores in New York have an organic produce section. In
addition to seeking out organic labels, certifications such as **Salmon Safe**
(www.salmonsafe.org) will assure that the source farm or vineyard uses wa-
tershed-friendly practices; the **Marine Stewardship Council** (www.msc.org)
certifies seafood as being from sustainable fisheries; and the **Food Alliance** (www.
foodalliance.org) certifies farms and ranches for sustainable and humane practices. Make sure the product actually says Certified Organic; the word "natural"
means almost nothing.

Finally, because livestock production is resource intensive and can result
in their mistreatment, the earth conscious and animal compassionate suggest
reducing the amount of meat in your diet.

GREEN MONEY

Some banks, including large national banks, are making efforts to become
greener in their operations and lending practices. **Bank of America** and **Citi**
have promised to invest millions of dollars to go green. But the simplest way for
consumers to conserve paper and fuel is to do all of their banking online.

For those looking to invest their money in a socially conscious manner, start
your research with **GreenMoneyJournal** (www.greenmoneyjournal.com) or
The Progressive Investor (www.sustainablebusiness.com/progressiveinvestor).
And don't forget the Working Assets Visa, which donates a percentage of every
purchase done with the card to causes of your choosing.

GREENER TRANSPORTATION

This is the one area that New York excels at. With millions of people riding the
MTA everyday, the car pollution problems of Los Angeles or Houston are virtually
non-existent. It does, however, have its own particular form of pollution—noise.
Decibel levels in the limbic netherland of the MTA can reach the level of an
airplane taking off. This kind of constant noise has been associated with hy-
pertension, exhaustion and hearing problems. Some people wear earplugs to
alleviate the noise. Others simply listen to Anthrax on their I-Pods at full blast,
although the health benefit of this approach is in doubt.

If you can't beat the spending over an hour ever day in the netherworld
of the New York subway system, there's biking. New York is small enough to be
covered on two wheels, and the city has made enormous strides to making this
a viable alternative for commuters, with new bike lanes with barriers popping

up on a number of major avenues and a new TK miles of bike ways through-out the city. Go to www.nycbikemaps.com to see if biking makes sense for you commute.

If you have to drive, consider owning a more fuel-efficient vehicle. The most popular and efficient mass-production cars are gas-electric hybrids like the Toy-ota Prius or the Honda Civic hybrid. A hybrid car consumes less fuel, and you may be entitled to up to a $2,000 federal tax credits if you buy one, as well as a $2,000 New York state tax credit, plus a partial refund of your sales tax.

No matter what car you own, routine maintenance ensures that the engine runs as efficiently as possible. The nation's only environmentally friendly auto club, **Better World Club** (866-238-1137, www.betterworldclub.com), can pro-vide roadside assistance and travel advice. They offer the full menu of auto-club services, along with discounts on hybrid rentals, bicycle roadside assistance, and an electronic newsletter.

GREEN RESOURCES

The following are just a fraction of the available resources on sustainability and environmental protection:

- **Green Brooklyn**, www.greenbrooklyn.com, a local website that keeps fans abreast of the latest green developments in Brooklyn and NYC in general, as well as providing a list of eco-friendly suppliers
- **EcoGeek**, www.ecogeek.org; web site analyzes earth-friendly technology.
- **Carbon offsets** relies on the theory that you can neutralize the carbon di-oxide you generate by funding anti-CO_2 measures. Carbon offsets funds projects that store carbon or reduce carbon emissions from other sources, such as tree-planting projects, energy-efficiency projects, and alternative-en-ergy investments. You can calculate how much CO_2 you're producing at www.LiveNeutral.org. Offsets are available from sources like Terra Pass (877-210-9581, TerraPass.com), Green Tags (503-248-1905, www.greentagsUSA.org) and My Climate (www.myclimate.org).
- **The City of New York's Department of Environmental Protection**, 311, www.nyc.gov/dep, offers information and seminars for local sustainability re-sources and environmental affairs.
- **The New York State Department of Environmental Conservation**, 625 Broadway, Albany, New York 12233-0001, or Hunter's Point Plaza 47-40, 21st Street, Long Island City, NY 11101-5407, 718-482-4900, www.dec.ny.gov/, oversees a wide range of environmental topics that affect New York residents.
- The **United States Department of Energy**'s Energy Efficiency and Renewable Energy web site, www.eere.energy.gov, informs consumers about renewable energy.

D ESPITE THE CITY'S RAPID PACE AND ANONYMITY, OR PERHAPS because of it, New Yorkers by the thousands volunteer their services to hundreds of worthy causes. Motivations are as varied as the tasks. So are the rewards.

VOLUNTEERING

A mind-boggling array of public, private, and non-profit organizations will gladly put to use whatever talents or interests you have. Experience is not necessarily required; most institutions provide training. What kinds of jobs are available where? The single best way to connect with the right group is the www.volunteernyc.org website. It has up-to-date listings of all of New York's infinite groups and their current needs; just plug in your locations, choose from among the various categories sush as Homeless or Gay, and you will be presented with probably dozens of organizations looking for every skill imaginable. Another good resource is the Get Involved section of TimeOut New York, which lists a dozen volunteer opportunities every week.

Below are the names of agencies that refer volunteers to other organizations or who are seeking help themselves. Addresses are in Manhattan unless otherwise noted.

AREA CAUSES

THE HUNGRY AND THE HOMELESS

Scores of volunteers concern themselves with shelter for the city's homeless. Jobs include monitoring and organizing the shelters; providing legal help; ministering to psychiatric, medical, and social needs; raising money; manning phones; and caring for children in the shelters. Many people solicit, organize, cook, and serve food to the destitute at sites throughout the city. Still others deliver meals to the homeless and the homebound.

CHILDREN

If involvement with children is especially appealing, you can tutor in and out of schools, be a big brother or sister, teach music and sports in shelters or at local community centers, run activities in the parks, entertain children in hospitals, and accompany kids on weekend outings. Schools, libraries, community associations, hospitals, and other facilities providing activities and guidance for children are all worth exploring.

HOSPITALS

The need for volunteers in both city-run and private hospitals is manifold: from interpreters to laboratory personnel to admitting and nursing aides, many volunteers are required. Assistants in crisis medical areas—emergency rooms, intensive care units, and the like—are wanted if you have the skills, as are volunteers to work with victims of sexual abuse. If you just want to be helpful, you might assist in food delivery or work in the gift shop. Most city hospitals are large and busy, and many are in need of help.

THE DISABLED AND THE ELDERLY

You can read to the blind, help teach the deaf, work to prevent birth defects, help the retarded and developmentally disabled, among others. You can also make regular visits to the homebound elderly, bring hot meals to their homes, and teach everything from nutrition to arts and crafts in senior centers and nursing homes.

EXTREME CARE SITUATIONS

Helping with suicide prevention, Alzheimer's and AIDS patients, rape victims, and abused children is a special category demanding a high level of commitment—not to mention emotional reserves and, in many cases, special skills.

THE CULTURE SCENE

There are museums all over the city in need of volunteers to lead tours or lend a hand in any number of ways. Libraries, theater groups, and ballet companies have plenty of tasks that need to be done. Fundraising efforts also require many volunteers to stuff envelopes and/or make phone calls. The Public Broadcasting Service (PBS) is a good example. Their large volunteer staff raises money for their stations through extensive on-air fundraising campaigns that include collecting pledges.

THE COMMUNITY

Work in your neighborhood. Block associations and community gardens are run strictly by volunteers. You can help out at the local school, nursing home, settlement house, or animal shelter.

WHERE YOU CAN HELP

SPECIFIC-NEED ORGANIZATIONS

The organizations in New York City that address a major disease, disability, or social problem are legion. For example, there's the Memorial Sloan-Kettering Cancer Center, The Coalition for the Homeless, Volunteer Services for Children, New York Association for the Blind (The Lighthouse), Literacy Volunteers of New York, Volunteers in the Schools, the Gay Men's Health Alliance, Women in Need, and City Harvest, which collects and distributes food to the hungry.

INSTITUTIONS

New York's health, education, and—some would say—its very civilization rest upon the city's institutions. Hospitals, museums, libraries, schools, animal shelters, opera and ballet companies are mostly under-funded and rely on a veritable army of volunteers to survive.

THE RELIGIOUS CONNECTION

Individual churches and synagogues (in particular, those serving the homeless and the needy), and church federations such as the Federation of Protestant Welfare Agencies, the Catholic Charities, Lutheran Social Services, and the UJA-Federation of Jewish Philanthropies, use volunteers for a variety of activities.

THE COMMUNITY

More than 5,000 block associations and neighborhood-wide organizations, such as Greenwich House in the Village and Yorkville's Civic Council, can use your talents. Citywide there is a need for volunteers in the schools, parks, and shelters, as well as in consumer affairs. The Natural Resources Defense Council, located in New York, www.nrdc.org, is a national organization dedicated to improving city centers and deterring urban sprawl.

MULTI-SERVICE ORGANIZATIONS

Don't forget such well-known groups as the Salvation Army, American Red Cross, March of Dimes, United Way, and Visiting Nurse Service (you don't have to be a nurse).

THE CORPORATE CONNECTION

Corporations encourage employee volunteerism through company-supported projects such as literacy programs, pro-bono work, and management aid to non-profit groups. Check with the company personnel or public relations department to see if your firm is involved in any specific project. Many corporations have set up programs with the United Way.

REFERRAL SERVICES

If you don't know which way to turn, try one of several umbrella organizations that find volunteers for affiliated agencies. At these referral services, staff members will help you determine the tasks you would be interested in doing, where and when. Your interviewer will make specific suggestions and appointments at the places that sound appealing. Interview at several sites if you wish, and return to the referral agency until you find something you want to undertake.

- **Catholic Charities of New York**, 1011 First Ave, 11th Floor, 212-371-1000, www.catholiccharitiesny.org; are affiliated with more than 100 different agencies dealing with shelters, food kitchens, and the homeless. An interview may be requested.
- **The Federation of Protestant Welfare Agencies**, 281 Park Ave S, 212-777-4800, www.fpwa.org, open 8:30 a.m. to 5 p.m., Monday–Friday; this ecumenical group, with connections to hundreds of agencies in the metropolitan area, finds jobs for volunteers of any religious persuasion.
- **The Mayor's Volunteer Center of New York City**, 1 Centre St, 12th floor, 212-251-4016, www.volunteernyc.org; the center's mission: "to bridge individuals, corporations, government agencies, and non-profit organizations in order to connect people with meaningful volunteer opportunities that significantly improve the quality of life in New York City." As mentioned earlier, this enormous clearinghouse can place just about anyone in a useful job, especially in the human services, educational, and cultural areas.
- **New York Cares**, 214 W 29th St, 5th floor, 212-228-5000, www.ny.cares.org, is a favorite volunteer organization among busy young professionals who are discouraged by the time commitments required by other organizations. New York Cares lets its 8,000 volunteers choose from a monthly calendar of events set up with the more than fifty not-for-profit organizations they serve. These projects include reading with homeless children, serving brunch at soup kitchens, cleaning public parks, and visiting elderly homebound. Call to attend one of three weekly orientation meetings.
- **The United Jewish Appeal–Federation of Jewish Philanthropies**, 130 E 59th St, 212-980-1000, www.ujafedny.org; the Jewish Information Referral Service helps match volunteers with one of many volunteer projects. Programs

include revitalizing old neighborhoods and synagogues as well as working with children, immigrants, the elderly, and the homeless.

- **The Volunteer Referral Center**, 161 Madison Ave, 212-889-4805, www.volunteer-referral.com; interviews by appointment. The center places adult and student volunteers at some 250 not-for-profit agencies throughout the city.

OTHER CONNECTIONS

- **Check bulletin boards** at your office, church, neighborhood grocery store, Laundromat, and school.
- Walk into local churches, temples, community organizations, and/or libraries.
- The **Yellow Pages**, under "Social and Human Services," contains more than five pages of organizations and institutions—in categories from "Abortion Alternatives Counseling" to "Youth Services"—many of which welcome volunteers. It's a great source of ideas, as well as a tool for follow-through.
- **www.bigsnyc.org**, Big Brothers/Big Sisters of New York City
- **www.heartsandminds.org/linksnyc**, for volunteering or donations.
- **www.volunteermatch.org**, offers a searchable database of volunteer options.

What follows is a far-from-exhaustive listing of some of the main community, national and international groups, broken down by category.

HUMAN RIGHTS

- **The Osborne Association**, 809 Westchester Ave, 718-707-2660, http://www.osborneny.org; specializes in reforming the criminal system and aiding defendants.
- **American Civil Liberties Union**, ACLU, 125 Broad St, 18th Floor, 212-344-3005, www.aclu.org; specializes in constitutional, legal, and human rights.
- **The Legal Aid Society of New York**, 199 Water St, 212-577-3346, www.legal-aid.org; helps underrepresented defendants and does research to reform the legal system.
- **The Brennan Center for Justice**, 161 Ave of the Americas, 12th floor, 212-998-6730, www.brennancenter.org; non-profit focused on constitutional issues and human rights.

SUBSTANCE ABUSE

- **Alcoholics Anonymous of New York**, 307 Seventh Ave (W 28th St), Room 201, 212-647-1680, www.nyintergroup.org; the Manhattan central organization for Alcoholics Anonymous.
- **Phoenix House,** 1-800-Drug-HELP; national organization with NY centers specializing in drug abuse, especially among the youth.
- **El Regress Foundation Drug Abuse Treatment**, 189-191 South 2nd St, 718-384-6400; specializes in substance abuse among the Hispanic population.

- **Alcoholism Council of New York, Inc.**, 2 Washington St, 7th Floor, 212-252-7001, www.alcoholism.org
- **Cocaine Anonymous of NY**, 48 West 21st St, 9th Floor, www.ca-ny.org
- **Narcotics Anonymous, Inc.**, 154 Christopher St Suite 1A, 212-929-711, www.newyorkna.net

MENTORING

- **Mentoring USA**, 5 Hanover Square,212-400-8294, www.helpusa.org; a national organization that will hook up anyone with a mentoring opportunity.
- **Imentor**, 212-461-4330, ext 55, www.imentor.org; specializes in arranging mentoring over the Internet.
- **Catholic Big Sisters and Big Brothers**, 212-475-3291 x208, www.csbb.org; Catholic-run group that has been working with children for over a century.
- **Big Brothers and Sisters of New York,** 223 E 30th St, (212) 686-2042, www.bigsnyc.org; local branch of this national organization.

SENIORS

- **New York Foundation for Senior Citizens**, 212-962-7559, www.nyfsc.org
- **Jewish Association for Services for the Aged (JASA)**, 132 West 31st St, 10th Floor, 212-273-5291, www.jasa.org; an organization that provides multiple services with a focus on the Jewish Community. One such program is JASA Pets, which finds suitable animals for the aged.
- **SAGE**, 305 7th Ave, 6th Floor, 212-741-2247, www.sageusa.org; specializes in senior services for the gay, lesbian, and transgendered communities.

CULTURE AND THE ARTS

- **New York Philharmonic**, Avry Fisher Hall, 10 Lincoln Center Plaza 212-875-5900, nyphil.org/support/volunteer.cfm; this august ensemble needs everything from volunteer ushers to backstage geeks.
- **The American Airlines Theater, The Roundabout Theatre Company**, 227 W 42nd St.; 212-719-9393, roundabouttheatre.org
- **Astor Place Theater**, 434 Lafayette St., 212-254-4370, blueman.com
- **Century Center Theater**, 111 E 15th St., 212-982-6782, ext. 11
- **The Cherry Lane Theatre**, 38 Commerce St., 212-989-2020, cherrylanetheatre.com
- **The Joyce Theater**, 175 Eighth Ave.; 646-792-8355, joyce.org
- **Lucille Lortel Theater**, 322 Eighth Ave., 21st Floor, 212-924-2817; lortel.org
- **Manhattan Theatre Club**, W 55th St., 212-247-0430, mtc-nyc.org
- **New York Theatre Workshop (NYTW)**, 79 E 4th St., 212-780-9037, nytw.org
- **Second Stage Theatre**, 307 W 43rd St.; 212-787-8302, ext. 216; secondstagetheatre.com

- **The Signature Theatre Company**, 555 W 42nd St., 212-244-7529; www. signaturetheatre.org

GAY ISSUES

- **Gay Men's Health Crisis Inc**, 119 W 24th St, 212-367-1030, www.gmhc.org; one of New York's oldest health organizations service the gay, lesbian, bisexual and transgender community.
- **Positive Health Project**, 301 West 37th St N, 212-465-8304, www.positive healthproject.org; specializes in health outreach to the transgendered community.
- **International Gay & Lesbian Human Rights Commission**, 350 5th Ave, 212-268-8040, www.iglhrc.org; focuses on international and national human rights issues pertaining to the gay community
- **Harlem United Community AIDS Center**, 123-125 W 124th St, 212-531-1300
- **SAGE**, 305 7th Ave, 6th Floor, 212-741-2247, www.sageusa.org; specializes in senior services for the gay, lesbian, and transgendered communities.

ANIMAL RIGHTS

- **Jewish Association for Services for the Aged (JASA)**, 132 West 31st St, 10th Floor, 212-273-5291, www.jasa.org; an organization that provides multiple services with a focus on the Jewish Community. One such program is JASA Pets, which finds suitable animals for the aged.
- **ASPCA, American Society for the Prevention of Cruelty to Animals**, 212-876 -7700, www.aspca.org

LITERACY

- **Little Sisters of the Assumption Family Health Service**, 333 East 115th St, 646-672-0434, www.lsafhs.org; working in East Harlem, this group offers a number of services, specializing in children and education.
- **Community Impact at Columbia University,** 2980 Broadway, 105 Earl Hall 212-854-9621, www.columbia.edu/cu/ci; serves the communities near Columbia University.

HOUSING AND THE HOMELESS

Scores of volunteers concern themselves with shelter for the city's homeless. Jobs include monitoring and organizing the shelters; providing legal help; ministering to psychiatric, medical, and social needs; raising money; and organizing, cooking, and serving food to the destitute at sites throughout the city. Still others deliver meals to the homeless and the homebound, or spend one night a month bedded down in a homeless shelter to make sure it runs smoothly. Many soup kitchens tend to be overwhelmed with well-meaning volunteers during the winter holidays, when they can use help year round. So consider pitching in "off season." The list of shelters following the general organizations are actively seeking volunteers.

- **Broadway Housing Communities**, 583 Riverside Dr., 212-568-2030 ext. 210, www.broadwayhousing.org; specializes in finding affordable housing for the homeless, including their own temporary apt. complex.
- **Gospel Assembly Shelter** (c/o Bethel Gospel Assembly), 2-26 East 120th St, 212-860-1510
- **Red Cross Shelter** (Bowery Mission), 227 Bowery, 212-674-3456
- **Grand Central Neighborhood Social Services Corporation (GCNSSC)**, 152 E. 44th St, 212-818-1220
- **Holy Apostles Soup Kitchen**, 296 9th Ave, 212-924-0167
- **Homes for the Homeless**, 36 Cooper Square 6th Floor, 212-529-5252
- **New York City Rescue Mission**, 90 Lafayette St, 212-226-6214
- **Sanctuary for Families**, 105 Chamber St Suite 5A, 212-349-6009
- **Shelter and Food for the Homeless Inc.**, 602 E 9th St, 212-228-5254
- **St. Paul's House**, 335 West 51st St, 212-265-5433
- **Part of the Solution**, 2763 Webster Ave Bronx, NY, 718-220-4892
- **New York City Department of Homeless Services**, 33 Beaver St, 212-361-7955, http://www.nyc.gov/dhs; umbrella group for official and unofficial homeless service groups.
- **Food Bank for New York City**, 90 John St Suite 702, 212-566-7855, www.food-banknyc.org; a key central resource for a variety of homeless organizations.

WOMEN AND CHILDREN

- **Center Against Domestic Violence**, 25 Chapel St Suite 904, 718-254-9134; counseling and placement for victims of domestic abuse
- **Neighbors Together Corporation**, 2094 Fulton St, Brooklyn, NY, 71-498-7256; soup kitchen that provides social services.
- **Providence House**, 703 Lexington Ave, NY, 718-455-0197; women and children only
- **Child Development Support Corporation**, 352 Classon Ave, Brooklyn, 718-398-2050, www.cdscnyc.org; specializes in children affected by domestic abuse situations
- **A Caring Hand,** The Billy Esposito Foundation, 1375 Broadway, 3rd Floor, 646-278-6737, www.acaringhand.org; helps people, especially children, deal with grief.
- **SCO Family of Services/Independence Inn II**, 400 Grant Ave, Brooklyn, NY, 718-827-8465, www.sco.org; a national organization that works to strengthen families.
- **Grace Institute,**1233 Second Ave, 212-832-7605, www.graceinstitute.org; national organization whose mission is to empower uneducated women.

N EW YORK CITY TEEMS WITH PEOPLE, WITH FAITHS, AND WITH PLACES in which those people may practice those faiths and in many cases devote themselves to one of the many social problems listed above. Whether you seek the orthodox, the scholarly, the ecumenical, the activist, or an approach to faith beyond your previous experience, you can find a community here. There are an estimated 2,300 churches (not counting storefront Pentecostals) and some 650 synagogues in New York City. You'll find some, but by no means all, of them listed by denomination in the Yellow Pages. Finding a suitable church or synagogue may be as simple as following the suggestion of an acquaintance. Or it may be as intensely personal and complex as choosing a spouse. The houses of worship listed below alphabetically were chosen specifically for their possible appeal to newcomers. It's a place to start. (Addresses are in Manhattan unless otherwise noted.)

BAHÁ'Í

- **Bahá'í Faith**, 53 E 11th St, 212-674-8998, www.bahainyc.org, conducts devotions and discussion Sunday at 11 a.m.

BUDDHIST

- **New York Buddhist Church**, 331-332 Riverside Dr at 105th St, 212-678-0305, www.newyorkbuddhistchurch.org; a stunning bronze statue of Shinran-Shonin in front of this landmarked building marks the presence of this Shin Buddhist Temple. Regular Dharma service in English at 11:30 a.m. Sunday is occasionally preceded by a service in Japanese. In addition, there are regularly scheduled Dharma study classes for adults and for children, meditation sessions, and other classes offered in various subjects.

- **Soka Gakkai International—USA**, 7 E 15th St, 212-727-7715, www.sgi-usa. org; with lectures, discussions, and group chants for some 5,000 area members who practice the Buddhism of Nichiren Daishonin. It's a warm and accepting community in a harmonious Romanesque Revival building.

CHRISTIAN

ROMAN CATHOLIC CHURCHES

Most Catholics attend Mass near their home or office. But there are a few churches that, for one reason or another, attract worshipers from beyond the parish confines. One of these may suit you. Contact the Archdiocese of New York, 212-371-1000, or the Archdiocese of Brooklyn (also handles Queens), 718-399-5900, for your local parish. Or go to www.ny-archdiocese.org.

- **Cathedral-Basilica of St. James**, 250 Cathedral Pl (at Jay St near Tillary St), Brooklyn Heights, www. brooklyncathedral.net, 718-852-4002, was built in 1822 and restored in recent years to a Georgian brick elegance befitting its prominence. St. James is Brooklyn's cathedral, a bishop's church, but it is also a non-territorial parish, and is especially popular among young professionals in the area, for whom the daily business communion at 12:10 is a special convenience. Mass here is traditional, and the music quite wonderful.
- **Church of the Epiphany**, 239 E 21st St (Second Ave and 22nd St), 212-475-1966, is at once striking and modest, an unusually successful modern structure of rounded verticals in brown brick. It's a family church, with a traditional Mass at 11:15 a.m. and a popular family mass to guitar accompaniment at 10 a.m. But there's a difference, for one thing, altar girls. Nuns are involved in work traditionally done by priests, and women's issues are addressed. The church is popular with young professionals in the community, and there is a social action group.
- **Church of St. Agnes**, 143 E 43rd St at Lexington Ave, 212-682-5722, is convenient to Grand Central Station and offers multiple daily masses including a Latin Mass, Sundays at 11 a.m.
- **Church of St. Thomas More**, 65 E 89th St between Park and Lexington Avnues, 212-876-7718; stone Victorian Gothic, was built as an Episcopal Church and still feels a bit like one, with its intimately peaceful, fragrant interior beneath a timbered ceiling. Ever so decorous. You can linger for coffee after 10 o'clock Mass.
- **Holy Trinity Chapel**, 58 Washington Square South, 212-674-7236, is the Catholic chapel at New York University, but its congregants are by no means all students. A moderately liberal intellectual approach and active social life attract a committed band of Catholics from the surrounding Village and beyond to this modest but appealing modern brick structure. An active out-

reach program includes tutoring as well as providing a soup kitchen and other neighborhood services. There are sessions of silent Christian meditation.

- **St. Francis Xavier**, 46 W 16th St, 212-627-2100; this hulking, gray stone Jesuit presence dominates the block between Fifth and Sixth Avenues. The style here is rather less formal than you might expect, perhaps because the congregation covers such a broad social spectrum: Hispanics, knowledgeable Catholic activists, and young professionals. Actively involved in the community, the church shelters the homeless and serves 800 meals a week. It's equally busy on the spiritual front, with lay spirituality group retreats, healing Masses, and discussion groups for a fiercely devoted following.

- **St. Ignatius Loyola**, Park Ave at 84th St, 212-288-3588; this solidly limestone Italian Baroque structure is definitely high church and upscale: incense, ornate vestments, and a fine professional choir at the traditionally sung morning High Mass. But the rigorous Jesuit approach is apparent in a strongly social and economic outlook from the pulpit. At 11 a.m. you can attend a folk Mass in the undercroft (Wallace Hall) and linger over coffee. The church is also known for its series of formal musical programs featuring the fine choir and organist as well as visiting musicians. Contemporary music Sundays at 7:30 p.m.

- **St. John the Baptist**, 210 W 31st St, 212-564-9070, as a distinct sideline to its normal parish activities, is host to the Catholic charismatic movement in Manhattan. There are seminars, prayer meetings, and a monthly charismatic Mass.

- **St. Joseph's**, 371 Ave of the Americas at Washington Place, 212-741-1274; in the heart of Greenwich Village, appeals to a variety of Catholics in the neighborhood and even outside the city. At once a bustling family church and an aesthetic experience, with professional musicians performing at traditional Masses and at evening concerts; distinctly high church. The lovely stone and stucco Greek Revival structure, resplendent inside with creamy plaster, crystal chandeliers and wide, carved balconies, is the oldest Catholic Church in the city (1833), and the first to open a shelter for homeless men.

- **St. Patrick's Cathedral**, 14 E 51st St, 212-753-2261, www.ny-archdiocese.org; this looming Gothic-style cathedral is the seat of the Archbishop of New York.

GREEK ORTHODOX CHURCHES

- **Cathedral of the Holy Trinity**, 319 E 74th St, 212-288-3215, www.thecathedral.goarch.org; tucked away among the modern buildings on the Upper East Side of Manhattan, this church has stood since the 1890s when it was originally built as a Protestant church. Today the church includes a full parochial school program, nursery through eighth grade, as well as afternoon language classes and Sunday school classes. Cultural and human services programs can also be found.

- **St. Demetrios Cathedral**, 30-11 30th Dr, Astoria, Queens, 718-728-1718; just over the Queensborough Bridge from Manhattan stand two expansive cathedrals that help serve the city's largest Greek Orthodox community, St.

Demetrios and St. Irene. The more majestic of the two, St. Demetrios was built in 1927 and features the architectural stylings of the Byzantine cathedrals of Athens. Adult Greek language courses and Sunday school classes are offered.

- **St. Irene Chrysovalantou**, 36-07 23rd Ave, Astoria, Queens, www.stirene.org 718-626-6225; newer, and slightly larger than nearby St. Demetrios', St. Irene's is a large converted Protestant church with a grand and elaborate interior design. A full complement of elementary and junior high school programs is offered, plus many youth and teen activities. A daycare center is also available weekdays from 9 a.m. to 5 p.m.

PROTESTANT CHURCHES

BAPTIST

- **Calvary Baptist Church**, 123 W 57th St between Sixth and Seventh Avenues, 212-975-0170, www.cbcnyc.org, across from Carnegie Hall, is probably the largest Baptist Church in Manhattan. You might begin a typical Sunday at the 9:30 a.m. contemporary praise and worship service, followed by a Young Professionals' topical Bible study and fellowship at 11 a.m., and then coffee. Traditional worship service is at 11 a.m. Young Adult Ministries offers occasional weekend retreats, and there are outreach programs to the prison population, the poor, and welfare hotel children.

EPISCOPAL

- **Cathedral of St. John the Divine**, 1047 Amsterdam Ave at 112th St, 212-316-7540, www.stjohndivine.org, dwarfs its surroundings even as it awaits the (hopeful) completion of its stone towers. One of the largest cathedrals in the world—at once Byzantine, Romanesque, and Gothic—it is truly awesome, especially inside, where spectacular stained glass windows light the vast dark vaults and music echoes ethereally. It is also a bustling and exciting community church, a leader in the movement to feed and house the poor. And the performing arts flourish here almost around the clock. Don't miss the blessing of the animals on the first Sunday of October in honor of St. Francis.
- **Church of the Ascension**, 12 W 11th St, 212-254-8620, www.ascensionnyc.org; its communicants find this church especially pleasing aesthetically. A LaFarge altar fresco and a St. Gaudens altar relief enliven the quietly tasteful interior, and liturgical music of the highest quality in special evening concerts is a welcome treat.
- **Church of the Heavenly Rest**, 2 E 90th St at Fifth Ave, 212-289-3400, www.heavenlyrest.org, sits confidently but unostentatiously—in stripped contemporary Gothic in pale gray stone—facing Central Park. It's an upscale neighborhood family church, where the congregants stay for coffee after the morning service while the children play decorously about the door.

- **Grace Church**, 802 Broadway at E 10th St, 212-254-2000, www.gracechurchnyc. org, despite its rather patrician, lacy English Gothic elegance, is relatively low-church. Worship is traditional, however, with wonderful music, especially on holy days. The congregation runs to young families and a variety of students and artists. Pastoral counseling is available as well as adult classes on a variety of topics. Also: outreach groups to college students and victims of HIV/AIDS, programs for children and families, and the popular Bach at Noon program, an open service for prayer and meditation.
- **St. Bartholomew's**, 109 E 50th St, 212-378-0200; this landmarked Roman-esque-Byzantine church houses a friendly, welcoming community numbering about 1,000 worshipers each Sunday. Lay participation in all aspects of church life is encouraged. Sundays feature a stimulating Rector's Forum and Sunday School, in addition to several services, and Bible studies are offered during the week. Several adult social clubs offer a variety of social, athletic, and theatrical activities. Communicants and non-members alike volunteer at the homeless shelter and the feeding program operated by the church.
- **St. James'**, 865 Madison Ave at 71st St, 212-774-4200; distinctly Upper East Side, this trim brownstone is a warm, neighborhood family church that is also decidedly activist in the community and beyond: feeding, mentoring, sup-porting, and sometimes even demonstrating. Despite its rather liberal bent, St. James' is moderately high church. Its education programs for adults and children are worthy of note.
- **Trinity Church**, 74 Trinity Place, 212-602-0800, www.trinitywallst.org; this Neo-Gothic church dominated New York's skyline when it was finished in 1846. Now a bit more tucked away, it offers a peaceful respite to bustling low-er Manhattan. Daily services, community outreach, and fellowship are all part of Trinity's ministry. This was one of the key bases for relief work during the 2001 WTC attack.

INTERDENOMINATIONAL

- **Judson Memorial (Baptist-United Church of Christ)**, 55 Washington Square S, www.judson.org, 212-477-0351; worldly young adults and seminarians are attracted to this ornate Romanesque church designed by Stanford White and its fairly traditional Protestant liturgy with progressive elements, including a monthly Agape Meal. There is a consumer health library and support for peo-ple with AIDS.
- **Riverside**, 490 Riverside Dr at 120th St, 212-870-6700, www.theriversidechurchny. org; this towering Gothic gift of John D. Rockefeller, Jr., dominates the heights overlooking the Hudson River. Inspired by Chartres, it boasts spectacular stained glass and beautifully carved stone in the large but simple nave and chancel, and about the entrance. Rev. Dr. Brad R. Braxton has recently taken over as minister of a congregation widely known for activism and political

debate; there are also plentiful opportunities for involvement in musical, intellectual, and social, not to mention spiritual activities.

- **Chelsea Community Church**, 346 W 20th St, 212-886-5463, www.chelseachurch. org, is a nondenominational Christian church welcoming "persons of all faiths and of uncertain faith" at its lay-led Sunday services at 11:45 a.m. in historic St. Peter's Church.

LATTER-DAY SAINTS/MORMON

- **The Church of Jesus Christ of Latter-Day Saints**; in Manhattan, the newly renovated Mormon temple is located at 125 Columbus Ave at 65th St (across from Lincoln Center), 917-441-8220, www.lds.org; several different congregations (called "wards" and "branches") conduct worship services every Sunday in three-hour blocks, beginning at 9 a.m. These include English-speaking "family" wards, an English-speaking ward for single adults, Spanish-speaking wards, and a deaf branch. Also, each congregation offers social and musical activities during the week.

LUTHERAN

- **Holy Trinity**, Central Park at 3 W 65th St, 212-877-6815, www.holytrinitynyc. org; offers challenging preaching at traditional, rigorously Lutheran services. But it is music, at the regular services and at the Sunday vespers, featuring Bach cantatas with professional musicians for which Holy Trinity is widely known (go to www.bachvespersnyc.org for more information). The sturdy Gothic Revival church is the setting for frequent evening concerts as well.
- **St. Peter's**, 619 Lexington Ave at 54th St, 212-935-2200; sleek and angular like a modern stone tent, St. Peter's is nestled beneath the towering Citicorp Center. A large Louise Nevelson sculpture punctuates the stark, light interior, scene of a sung Mass with traditional liturgy in the morning and Jazz Vespers with jazz as the sermon Sunday afternoons. Classical and jazz concerts, often free, theater, and provocative adult-forum lectures attract an ecumenical following, to say the least.

METHODIST

- **Christ Church**, 520 Park Ave at 60th St, 212-838-3036, is sedately Byzantine outside, dazzlingly so inside, every inch covered with mosaics in blazing blues, greens, and gold. It's a wonderful setting for the religious music-dramas occasionally performed here. The congregation, though relatively small, supports a weekly soup kitchen and excellent pastoral counseling.
- **John Street**, 44 John St between Nassau and William St, 212-269-0014; to step into this landmarked little Italianate brownstone church (1841) among the towering monoliths of the financial district is to step out of place and time into a peaceful haven of creamy modest proportions and brass sconces. It's

the oldest Methodist society in the US, and few know about it. Inquire about the occasional Wednesday noon hymn-sings.

- **Park Ave**, 106 East 86th St, 212-427-5421, www.parkavemethodist.org; a mixed and growing congregation, mostly young families and singles, is attracted by the moderately liberal approach and active social scene at this smallish, restfully intimate, Moorish-looking church. Adult Bible study precedes and a coffee hour follows the traditional Sunday service with volunteer choir.
- **Church of St. Paul and St. Andrew**, 263 W 86th St, 212 362 3179, www.sp sanyc.org; with a large children's program, extensive outreach, and a devotion to the arts, this 110-year old Romanesque church is home to many: the sanctuary is shared with B'nai Jeshurun, a Conservative Jewish Congregation; the Gay Gotham Chorus has made their residency here since 1993; and the West End Theatre on the second floor houses five professional companies. The West Side Campaign Against Hunger was founded here in 1979, and helps provide a million meals annually to the hungry.

PRESBYTERIAN

- **Brick Church**, 62 E 92nd St, between Park and Madison, 212-289-4400, www. brickchurch.org; staid neo-Georgian with a rather ornate interior, is distinctly Park Ave. But the welcome is friendly, including a popular coffee hour after the Sunday service. The church's day school is prestigious.
- **Fifth Avenue**, 7 West 55th St, 212-247-0490, www.fapc.org; the city's largest Presbyterian Church has a warm, woody interior behind its otherwise undistinguished brownstone facade. A variety of social fellowship groups attract large numbers to the traditional services. Activities of these groups may include Sunday night church suppers, after-church brunch, movies, and ski retreats, as well as dinner meetings with outside speakers at the Women's Roundtable (for businesswomen) and the Men's Fellowship. Also here, a Center for Christian Studies. Fees are minimal and non-members are welcome.
- **Madison Avenue**, 921 Madison Ave at 73rd St, 212-288-8920, www.mapc. com, has a cozy, Scottish feel, with its Gothic-timbered white walls, carved pews, and galleries. The music program is strong, including a volunteer choir and frequent Sunday afternoon concerts. You'll also find an adult education program and young adult fellowship group that meets for Bible study, discussion, and socializing.
- **Redeemer Presbyterian**, church office at 1359 Broadway, 4th floor, 212-808-4460; this recently organized and rapidly growing congregation holds three Sunday services in the Hunter College Auditorium, 69th St between Park and Lexington Avenues. The scripture-based emphasis is on preaching, which is intellectually engaging, and there is an array of spiritual, social, and outreach activities.

UNITARIAN

- **All Souls**, 1157 Lexington Ave at 80th St, 212-535-5530, www.allsoulsnyc.org; New England simple and elegant, from 1891, this Federal-style brick church looks Unitarian. As might be expected here, the busy church calendar tends toward activism on a variety of fronts including running a soup kitchen and tutoring children. A fairly intellectual approach to adult education features book groups, films, and lectures. Music is stressed. Social activities are many and varied, including a Career Networking Group.

ETHICAL SOCIETIES

Ethical societies offer a meeting place and fellowship to members and visitors. Their "focus is on core ethical values that people have in common." Acknowledging that humans are both individualistic and social in nature, the society explores what it means to understand the inner workings of self and how to relate to each other in a respectful/ethical/moralistic way. For more information go to www.aeu.org.

- **Brooklyn Society for Ethical Culture**, 53 Prospect Park W, Brooklyn, 718-768-2972, www.bsec.org
- **New York Society for Ethical Culture**, 2 West 64th St, 212-874-5210, www.nysec.org
- **Riverdale-Yonkers Society for Ethical Culture**, 4450 Fieldston Rd, The Bronx, 718-548-4445, www.ethicsny.org

HINDU

- **Ramakrishna Vivekananda Center**, 17 E 94th St, 212-534-9445, www.ramakrishna.org, is a Vedanta Hindu Temple of universal worship with a Sunday lecture service at 11 a.m. Tuesday evenings at 8 are devoted to the reading and discussion of the gospel of Sri Ramakrishna.
- **Vedanta Society**, 34 W 71st St, 212-877-9197, www.vedanta-newyork.org, is affiliated with the Ramakrishna Math and Mission in India. The shrine room is open for meditation daily from 9 a.m. to 6 p.m. There is a lecture Sunday at 11 a.m. and classes Tuesday and Friday evenings.

ISLAM

MOSQUES

- **The Mosque of New York**, in the Islamic Cultural Center, 1711 Third Ave, 212-722-5234; this imposing structure, the gift of a group of Islamic countries, houses the largest of some 80 mosques in the city. The design is modern, with numerous references to traditional elements of Muslim architecture. The effect is at once peaceful and spiritual. In addition to the weekly congregational prayer service, the Mosque is open for daily prayer at the five prescribed times. There are classes for children and adults, which cover a range of Islamic topics. There are Saturday classes for women only.

- **The Muslim Center of New York**, 137-58 Geranium Ave off Kissena Blvd, Flushing, 718-460-3000, www.muslimcenter.org, serves the growing Muslim community in Queens and Long Island. In a modest neighborhood an octagonal minaret rises from the polished rose quartz structure. Congregational prayers Friday at 1:15 p.m. are followed by Koranic studies. There are Sunday school and weekday afternoon religious school for children. Call for hours.

JEWISH

REFORM SYNAGOGUES

- **Brooklyn Heights Synagogue**, 131 Remsen St, Brooklyn, 718-522-2070, www.bhsbrooklyn.org, moved up the St from its brownstone home of 20 years to the larger brownstone formerly housing the Brooklyn Club, in order to accommodate its after-school religious education for children and extensive adult education classes. Preschool is also now available. Services here are characterized by a greater use of Hebrew and more congregational singing than is generally found in reform synagogues. The warmth and friendliness of this relatively small congregation and their purposeful inclusiveness makes this a particularly appealing synagogue for newcomers. Congregants come from all the boroughs; numbers swell sufficiently on the high holy days that these services are held in a church nearby.
- **Central**, 652 Lexington Ave, 212-838-5122, www.centralsynagogue.org, is the oldest Jewish house of worship (1872) in continuous use in New York. The Moorish brownstone structure with its interior richly stenciled in red, blue, and gold suffered extensive damage from a fire in 1998. Restoration is now complete and the traditionally oriented synagogue tends to the manifold interests, worldly as well as spiritual, of its 1,400-member congregation in groups and classes ranging from Hebrew and Yiddish to Bible to bridge, teens' and singles' groups. Hebrew school.
- **Temple Emanu-El**, 1 E 65th St, corner of Fifth Ave, 212-744-1400, www.emanuelnyc.org, is perhaps a little less traditional, nevertheless classical Reform in approach, and it is the largest reform temple in the US, with over 3,000 members. The landmarked limestone Moorish-Romanesque temple facing Central Park seats 2,500 beneath a high, colorfully painted wood ceiling and stunning stained glass windows. The temple has a large staff to run its many facilities, classes, and community outreach programs, as well as a large religious school. Services are broadcast every Friday evening at 5:30 over WQXR (96.3 FM).

CONSERVATIVE SYNAGOGUES

- **Ansche Chesed**, 251 W 100th St at West End Ave, 212-865-0600, www.anschechesed.org, houses four separate congregations, each with a different approach to Conservative Judaism, in one medium-sized, squat, brick building. Alternatives within a framework of Jewish tradition are stressed at this much-talked-about West Side synagogue, which offers an adult beginners' service, courses on a wide range of Jewish topics, and social action projects.
- **Baith Israel Anschei Emes/Kane St**, 236 Kane St at Tompkins Place in Cobble Hill, Brooklyn 718-875-1550, has grown considerably in recent years, partly, perhaps, because of the emphasis on egalitarianism in its observances. Vibrant and involved, with challenging study groups, it is regularly packed with congregants, mainly young, from Cobble Hill and nearby Brooklyn Heights.
- **B'nai Jeshurun**, 257 W 88th St between Broadway and West End Ave, www.bj.org, 212-787-7600; under the charismatic leadership of the late Rabbi Marshall Meyer, "BJ," as it is affectionately known, burst its ornately Byzantine/Romanesque seams. Emphasis is on study, with a variety of adult courses and lectures as well as a Hebrew school for children. And the diverse congregation thinks of itself as a community, with a strong commitment to social action, Tikkun Olam, in the wider Jewish and non-Jewish community beyond. Plan to come early for services, which tend to fill up fast; non-members will want to call about high holy days.
- **Brotherhood**, 28 Gramercy Park S, on E 20th St, www.brotherhoodsynagogue.org, 212-674-5750, occupies a landmarked (1859) Friends' Meeting House, starkly beautiful in Italianate brownstone and overlooking lovely Gramercy Park. About its courtyards are housed a shelter for the homeless, a religious school, adult education, and an educational program for the developmentally disabled.
- **Park Ave**, 50 E 87th St at Madison Ave, www.pasyn.org, 212-369-2600, is the city's largest Conservative temple and an East Side Moorish landmark in carved golden stone. The rich interior boasts fine stained glass, sculpture, and paintings, and the traditional services are distinctly formal, with organ and choir. There are programs for children and a food pantry for the neighborhood's hungry.
- **Shaare Zedek**, 212 W 93rd St between Broadway and Amsterdam Ave, www.sznyc.org, 212-874-7005; this congregation, founded 160 years ago on the Lower East Side and housed now in a gray stone Greek Revival temple, has experienced a revival in the mid-1990s with an infusion of college students and young professionals. Friday evening services, usually downstairs in the social halls, can be especially busy. Special events fill out the social calendar.
- **Tifereth Israel/Town and Village**, 334 E 14th St between First and Second Avenues, www.tandv.org, 212-677-8090, stresses sexual egalitarianism in its informally innovative, traditional services and attracts an involved family con-

gregation, largely from the adjacent community, including Stuyvesant Town and Peter Cooper Village. Adult education and a young married group are both popular. The Sol Goldman YW-YMHA of the Educational Alliance next door, with whom it shares a Hebrew school, offers members the advantages of a social center with a pool, gym, and classes.

- **United Synagogue of Hoboken**, 115 Park Ave, Hoboken, NJ, 201-659-4000, www.hobokensynagogue.org; Friday evening and Sabbath services are in the converted Victorian brownstone Hudson St temple, the last of many serving the predominantly German Jewish community here at the turn of the century. The small but growing egalitarian congregation is youngish and welcoming. Extensive adult education courses include Hebrew reading and Jewish history, a Hebrew discussion group, a book club, Jewish women's and men's discussion groups, karate, and adult bar and bat mitzvah instruction. There is also a Hebrew School for children.

ORTHODOX SYNAGOGUES

- **Civic Center**, 49 White St, west of Broadway, 212-966-7141, occupies a small, award-winning, modern structure scrunched among cast iron manufacturing lofts and loading docks. Its flame-shaped interior houses a membership of about 100 families with about 1,000 supporters, including elderly members of long standing as well as artists and young professionals from surrounding Tribeca, Independence Plaza, and Battery Park. There are both Hebrew and adult education classes, as well as parenting sessions conducted by Educational Alliance West.
- **Kehilath Jeshurun**, 125 E 85th St between Lexington and Park Avenues, www.ckj.org, 212-774-8000; though old and rich and housed in classical Romanesque gray stone, this is probably the most progressive of the Orthodox congregations. Its size makes possible a host of activities for singles, couples, and children, recreational facilities, and an educational program including the Ramaz School. Emphasis is placed on outreach to beginners and singles, with classes, special services, and Friday night dinners for them.
- **Lincoln Square**, 200 Amsterdam Ave at 69th St, 212-874-6100, www.lss.org, sometimes referred to as "the hip synagogue," might be described physically as synagogue-modern. Its nickname and popularity among the young professionals who pack four Saturday services is due in large part to the charm and zealous outreach efforts of Rabbi Ephraim Buchwald, who hosts the 9:15 "Learners' Minyan," which is followed by wine and cookies and, if you like, lunch with an experienced family. Senior Rabbi Shaul Robinson is overseeing a move of the entire congregation to new facilities a block away in 2007.
- **Shearith Israel**, 8 West 70th St at Central Park West, 212-873-0300, known as the Spanish and Portuguese synagogue, is the oldest Jewish congregation in the US, dating from 1655, when a group of Sephardic Jews arrived from

Brazil. In the formal sanctuary scholarly rabbis conduct formal services, which offer the best opportunity to observe Sephardic tradition and music. Excellent adult education explores Sephardic and Ashkenazi culture and tradition, with visiting scholars leading seminars. There are special educational and social events for young adults.

OTHER

- **Congregation Beth Simchat Torah**, 57 Bethune St in the Westbeth complex, 212-929-9498, www.cbst.org; at about 800 members the largest gay and lesbian Jewish congregation in the world, it celebrated its 25th anniversary in 1999. The rabbi is Reconstructionist, the community liberal, and the services traditional, with egalitarian minyans rotating among traditional, liberal, tot shabbat, junior congregation, family minyan, and Hebrew egalitarian; Saturdays at 10 a.m. Friday evening services are so heavily attended the congregation moves to the Church of the Holy Apostles on Ninth Ave at 28th St.
- **Society for the Advancement of Judaism**, 15 West 86th St off Central Park West, 212-724-7000, www.thesaj.org; known as the SAJ, this is the original Reconstructionist synagogue. Reconstructionism, which attempts to reconcile traditional Conservatism with modern life, views Judaism as evolving rather than divinely inspired. The Torah is observed, and services are largely traditional but egalitarian. The approach here is distinctly intellectual, not social.
- **West End Synagogue**, 190 Amsterdam Ave at 69th St, www.westendsynagogue.org, 212-579-0777, is a popular Reconstructionist congregation flourishing with a slightly more emotional, interpersonal emphasis and monthly Shabbat dinners as well as concerts, debates, and social action programs. Also a Hebrew school.
- **The 16th Street Synagogue** (formerly Young Israel), 421 Hudson St, www.sixteenthstsynagogue.or 212-255-4826, is one of three such temples in Manhattan. Young Israel can be defined as modern Orthodoxy, observing all the Orthodox forms, including separate seating of the sexes, but emphasizing programs serving the entire family. This includes communal singing and participation, youth and singles programs, outreach, adult education, and attention to community needs.

LAST BUT NOT LEAST

- **The Church of Satan**, P.O. Box 499, Radio City Station, www.churchofsatan.com; the self-appointed official church of Lucifer does not accept phone calls nor allow personal visits by the uninitiated, but it is happily ensconced in Sin City.

GETTING AROUND

BY SUBWAY

P EOPLE ARE THE LIFEBLOOD OF NEW YORK CITY, AND THE SUBWAY IS the circulatory system in which they travel. It is also the great equalizer: all manner of people, from the wealthy broker to the night time porter, from the lowly tourist to Mayor Bloomberg himself vie for the same seats, inhale the same pungent odors, and curse the same just-missed train. It is the quickest way around town, and one of the cheapest. Its 800-plus miles of track and the trains that run on them are managed by the Metropolitan Transit Authority (MTA), who, in conjunction with the NYPD, has managed to substantially decrease crime. One should of course remain aware of one's surroundings and use common sense.

As intimidating as the system will be at first, it will be a short matter of time before you wonder why you had fretted. There are numerous resources that will help you better understand the subway system, including the maps that are posted in every car and station (free maps are also available at station booths), and the MTA web page, www.mta.info, but your most ubiquitous resource for help will be your fellow citizens. Don't be shy about asking for help; everyone, even veteran New Yorkers, sometimes needs a little guidance when on unfamiliar lines.

Transfers, express trains, partial-service lines…and that's before getting into weekend construction and late-night redirections. How does one navigate this tangled web? Start with color. You will notice that the trains are grouped by color, and then separated by letter or number. The 4, 5, and 6 trains are all green, and run along Lexington Avenue in Manhattan. On the Upper East Side, you will see that while the 6 stops at 59th, 68th, 77th, and 86th streets, the 4 and the 5 stop only at 59th and 86th streets. This indicates that the 4 and the 5 are express trains, skipping local stops for a faster ride. You'll quickly become aware of which stations serve as express stops. Stations shared by local and express trains typically have easy transfers between them.

Transfers are also available at stations that serve more than one train line, and sometimes are available between separate stations. 14th Street/Union Square serves the Lexington lines as well as the Broadway lines (the yellow N, R, Q, and W), and also the crosstown L, which is gray. Moving between separate lines often means moving from one platform to another, and there are plenty of signs to direct you. Transfers between stations typically involve long walks in the city's underbelly, marked on the maps by a thin black line. The 42nd Street/ Times Square stop is connected to the 42nd Street/Port Authority stop in this manner, connecting the Eighth Avenue lines (blue A, C, and E) to the nine trains that stop in Times Square. Such treks can be a drag, but they can be a blessing on a rainy day!

A little more confusing are the partial-service lines. The orange trains on Sixth Avenue, B, D, F, and V all run together at certain points and separate at others (this is true of most lines), but the B is different: it runs only on weekdays, and even then only from 6:30 a.m. until 9:00 p.m. For someone who lives near Central Park West and depends on this line, this means that in the B train's off-hours, another train will serve (in this case, the C train). This too is only a small example of what happens to the system at large at nights and on weekends, when service changes are most likely to take place. Express trains may run local, trains may be diverted, and lines might even be replaced with shuttle buses in the event of construction. Keep an eye out for signs posted in your station, check the MTA web page, or call 718-330-1234 for service changes. And of course bear in mind that this all changes on a regular basis; as we go to press, budget problems are causing the MTA to consider cutting down on the G and M lines and eliminating the Z and W. To help soften the pain of these service cuts, however, MTA's leaders plan to raise the fares 25% (the same percentage they raised it 18 months earlier). If you plan to ride an unfamiliar line, consult the Subway Service Guide at the base of the MTA map. The schedule for each line is broken down by day of the week and hour of the day.

Start with one line, and build from there. If you are closest to the 1 train (red, Seventh Avenue), start there, and gradually work your way into the 2 and the 3. Eventually you will find yourself exploring other lines that connect, and inevitably you will make a mistake and end up in unfamiliar territory. Fear not: this is a rite of passage. Don't get discouraged, either; there will come a day when the unexpected will occur (sudden diversion, poorly marked service change, train stuck in a station or tunnel) and you can vent all your frustration at the vast, faceless machine that is the MTA.

Although, it's not nearly as faceless as it used to be. The station attendants are now required to wander the station in a burgundy vest instead of sitting with

Buddha-like expressions in the mini-fortress booths of yore. If you'd rather go the faceless route, though, the MTA has established a service advisory e-mail notification program, available at www.mta.info. When you sign up, you can select whichever lines you frequent, and you will be informed of any coming changes in service. If you are entirely vexed and want to take action or simply seek additional information, contact the Straphanger's Campaign, a transit advocacy group that has been campaigning for riders' rights since 1979, 212-349-6460, www.straphangers.org.

New York's infamous subway tokens are long gone and in its place is the MetroCard. The card, available at vending machines (accepting credit and debit cards) in subway stations, is to be used on all subway lines and on all city buses (though coins may still be used on buses). At press time, two MetroCard options were available at the following prices (recent news reports indicate a fare increase is likely any day now). The pay-per-ride card works like a debit card; when the card is empty you deposit more money (putting $7 or more on your card gets you 15% bonus). A single ride is $2 ($5 for express buses). To use, swipe the card through the turnstile slot, and one fare is subtracted. A more economical option is the unlimited usage pass: one-day, weekly, or monthly. A one-day pass is $7.50, the seven-day pass is $25, and a 30-day MetroCard is $81—good if you ride the subway frequently. Weekly and monthly passes purchased with a credit or debit card are insured against loss by the MTA and if you want your money back you can theoretically just mail it in and get a refund on the remaining value. You can also link it to your credit card and have it automatically refilled every month. Seniors and people with disabilities are eligible for half-fare cards, while turnstile jumpers get a 100% discount, minus the occasional fine. Reduced fare information is available at 718-243-4999. Children under 44 inches in height travel free (although they have to sit on their guardians' lap on express buses). School children are issued free passes if they attend a public or private school that is a specified distance from their home. Two-zone transfers means riders with the MetroCard can move from subway to a bus (and vice versa) without paying another fare, although this is only applicable in certain areas. For general MetroCard information call 212-METRO-CARD.

Subway trains operate 24 hours a day, but service slows appreciably after 11 p.m. At night, wait for trains near the subway booth or the turnstiles where transit cops seem to hang out. Be alert on subways or platforms and never leave personal items unattended. If you've come to New York to start a career in crime, you should know that the chip in your MetroCard actually keeps a record of where it was used—the police have solved several crimes using this bit of info.

BY PATH

The PATH (for Port Authority Trans-Hudson) tubes provide clean and efficient service connecting Manhattan with Hoboken, Jersey City, and Newark for $1.75

around the clock. Unlimited 30-day cards are $54. Trains leaving 33rd Street at Avenue of the Americas (Sixth Avenue) go to Hoboken or Jersey City, with stops along the way at 23rd, 14th, 9th and Christopher streets. Schedules are available in most stations, or call 800-234-7284.

BY BUS

Independent bus lines found mainly in boroughs other than Manhattan co-exist with those run by the MTA. Call 718-330-1234 for Transit Authority information as well as telephone numbers for the independents. Also, you can now get up-to-date transit information on the MTA web site: www.mta.info. Maps are sometimes available from drivers but are always stocked at the information booths mentioned under **Subways** above. Buses cost $2 (express buses are $5). Transfers to other buses are free. Use the MetroCard or exact change.

Call 212-564-8484 (Port Authority) for bus routes and schedules, or pick up a map at the Port Authority Bus Terminal at Eighth Avenue and 41st Street in Manhattan. You can also go to www.njtransit.com.

BY FERRY

There was, before the advent of the auto, a time when some 125 passenger-boats plied 50 different routes across the Hudson and East rivers. With the closing of the Hoboken Ferry in 1967, only the Staten Island Ferry remained, both a commuter necessity for Staten Islanders and an excursion delight for Manhattanites and tourists alike.

The water commute is once again a reality thanks to a dozen privately operated routes connecting Manhattan with New Jersey, Brooklyn, and Queens. And the Hoboken Ferry is back, faster than ever, docking at a floating terminal with a canvas marquee in Battery Park City. These ferries cruise at 35 miles per hour, twice as fast as the Staten Island Ferry. In increasing numbers, commuters are choosing this alternative to traffic gridlock, exorbitant parking fees, and expressway dementia, especially during the oppressive heat of summer. As more passengers take to the water, increased service comes on line.

- **Staten Island Ferry**, free, and certainly one of New York's best deals in transportation (and entertainment). Taking 25 minutes, the ferry leaves the South Ferry Terminal at Whitehall in Lower Manhattan for St. George, Staten Island, every 20 to 30 minutes daily, less frequently at night. Car service is available. Call 311 for information or go to www.statenislandferry.com.
- **NY Water Taxi**, 212-742-1969, www.nywatertaxi.com; service every 25 minutes from Brooklyn Army Terminal to Pier 11 in Manhattan during commuter hours and makes several other Brooklyn-Manhattan-Queens excursions daily from the Fulton Ferry Landing to Battery Park, Battery Park City, Chelsea, Midtown, and Queens. Fares vary and some lines don't run during the coldest months. The **Mets Express** shuttle was suspended for the 2008 baseball sea-

son (with 2009 in limbo as of press time), but there is a free shuttle available between Pier 11 in Manhattan and the Brooklyn IKEA store.

- New Jersey passenger ferries are dominated by **NY Waterway**, 800-53-FERRY, www.nywaterway.com, which operates the Hoboken Ferry, running weekdays every six to ten minutes during rush hours between 6:15 a.m. and 10 p.m., and every 15 minutes off-peak. Service is every half-hour on weekends, 10 a.m. to 9 p.m.. The firm also operates service to Pier 11 from Liberty Harbor, Port Liberté, Newport, Harborside, Colgate, Weehawken, and Belford. Sightseeing cruises (known as the "booze cruise") and theater packages are also offered. You can purchase monthly passes on the NY Waterway web site. Parking in New Jersey costs extra; parking passes are available at the web site as well.
- **Seastreak**, 800-BOAT-RIDE, www.seastreak.com, operates commuter ferries from Highlands and Atlantic Highlands, NJ and from South Amboy in Middlesex County, NJ, to Pier 11 at the foot of Wall Street, and to 35th Street on the East River. Hours are weekdays between 5:30 a.m. and 9:30 p.m. Fares are around $23 one way and $40 for round trip depending on the hour. Call or visit the web site for schedules.
- **Yankee Clipper**, operated by NY Waterway, 800-53-FERRY, www.nywaterway. com; departs Weehawken, Pier 11, East 34th Street, and East 90th Street for night games and weekend day games at Yankee Stadium; service to Shea Stadium, weekends only. Round trip costs $22 from any point (except Belford) to either stadium.

BY BIKE

The city government has mounted a serious campaign to get out-of-shape New Yorkers to bike, and it's actually working to some extent—they claim bike trafic is up 35% in 2006 and the growing numbers of bike lanes has become obvious to everyone (in particular, the irate taxi drivers). There was even an attempt to imitate Paris's hugely successul free downtown bike rental program (albeit with 300 bikes instead of Paris's 20,000). The virtues of the bicycle are obvious: speed and economy. The downside? Vulnerability in city traffic. In addition to alert, defensive riding, there are also a number of **city laws** governing bicyclists that contribute to their safety:

- Bicycles are allowed on all city streets, but not on highways unless signs permit.
- Always ride with traffic and never on sidewalks.
- Traffic rules apply to bicycles as well as to cars. Riders must use hand signals.
- Bicycles must use bike lanes where they are provided.
- Bicycles must be equipped with a bell or horn, brakes, a headlight, and tail light.
- Accidents resulting in injury must be reported to the police.
- A rider may not wear more than one earphone to an audio player.

• Common sense mandates the wearing of a bicycle helmet.

Bicycles are permitted on subways, but a few gates limit entry/exit. MetroNorth and the Long Island Railroad require a one-time purchase of a permit to carry a bike on a train, except during rush hours and on weekends, when they are not allowed. Call MTA/Metro North Railroad at 212-532-4900 and speak to a customer service representative or go to Window 27 in Grand Central Station to purchase a permit. For the LIRR call 718-558-8228 or check www.mta.info. Jersey Transit requires no permit on its trains, but bicycles are not allowed during rush hours or on weekends. The same rules apply on the PATH tubes.

There are 119 miles of bike lanes in the city streets and 75 miles of greenway. **The Bicycle Network Development**, a city project that aims to create an immense, 1800 mile network of bicycling paths and facilities, is entering its second phase of development with the creation of almost 200 miles of new bike paths, including separated paths on 8th and 6th Ave. Maps for the five boroughs are available at the **Department of City Planning**, 22 Reade Street, NYC 10007-1216, 212-720-3300, and online at www.nyc.gov or www.nycbikemaps. com. City biking laws and safe riding tips are outlined on the city's Department of Transportation page: go to www.nyc.gov and click on "residents" and then "transportation."

Transportation Alternatives, 127 W. 26th Street, Suite 1002, 212-629-8080, is a member-supported non-profit citizens' group for the promotion of biking and public transportation. Their encyclopedic web site, www.transalt.org, provides up-to-date news of interest to bikers and hikers, links to biking organizations in the metropolitan area, lists of shops offering discounts to members and information on the annual September Bike Tour, as well as other tour rides which they sponsor. There's also **Critical Mass**, times-up.org, which attempts to raise consciousness about the virtues of biking by holding riding rallies on the last Friday of every month. They tend to take over an entire street and are not very popular with the police.

For more concerning biking in the city, see Bicycling in the Sports and Recreation chapter.

BY CAR

For the most part, New Yorkers don't get around Manhattan by car, except when they're in a cab. Why? Because on-street parking is so limited and off-street parking so expensive. So who are all those cars causing the periodic gridlock? Cabs, car services, and we did say "for the most part." Those living in Manhattan may own a car or rent a car occasionally. Those in the other boroughs typically own at least one car, and many drive into Manhattan, adding to the major rush-hour delays. We'll continue with a few things you need to know about driving in and out of the city. (See also **Parking** and **Parking Tickets and Towing** in the **Getting Settled** chapter and **Auto Services and Repair** in **Helpful Services**.) For those who don't want to deal with the fuss and muss of owning a car, but still want to have one readily available, you can join **Zipcar** (www.zipcar.com, 866-4ZIPCAR), an hourly car rental subscription service.

New York drivers are aggressive, cabbies especially. Get used to it. In an odd balance, almost like playing "chicken," New York pedestrians do not follow the rules either: they cross against the light and mid-block when they feel like it; watch out for them. Also, keep your eye out for bike messengers who defy all traffic rules as they weave in and out of traffic.

Gridlock is a way of life here, at least on weekdays. "Don't block the box," means don't enter the intersection unless you are sure you can cross it before the light changes. Failure to heed this command causes gridlock and can cost you points on your license. If you can, avoid entering or leaving the city during rush hour traffic (roughly 7 a.m. to 10 a.m. and 4 p.m. to 7 p.m.). Friday and Sunday evenings are especially bad. In New York, street signs are everywhere, so pay attention for bus lanes and turning-only lanes. Unlike much of the country, right turns are NOT permitted on a red light in New York City, unless indicated by a rare sign.

Nonetheless, because of the logical street grid covering most of the island and because traffic is so slow, driving in Manhattan is easier than you might think. The north-south avenues for the most part are one-way, generally in an alternating pattern: hence, First Avenue runs uptown, and Second Avenue runs downtown. Park Avenue is two-way, as are portions of Third Avenue. The east-west streets are, for the most part, one-way, with the even-numbered streets running east (remember, even-east), and odd-numbered streets running west; the exceptions are typically major cross-town streets: Canal, Houston, 14th, 23rd, 34th, 42nd, and 57th streets, for example, which are two-way. Left turns are rarely permitted during the day, so watch signs closely. For driving in the other boroughs you'll need a map: AAA members get them free; Hagstrom maps are sold at bookstores and newspaper/magazine shops all over the city. A good selection of maps is available at www.firstbooks.com.

Manhattan is bracketed by two major north-south arteries, the West Side Highway/Henry Hudson Parkway (Rte. 9A) along the Hudson River on the west side, and Harlem River/FDR Drive along the East River on the east side. At the southernmost tip of the island the Brooklyn Battery Tunnel (toll) runs under the harbor to Brooklyn, where it connects to the Brooklyn-Queens Expressway (BQE), Rte. 278, which arcs around the Brooklyn shoreline and into Queens on either end. The BQE also connects with the Verrazano Bridge (toll) to the Staten Island Expressway across the Goethals Bridge to New Jersey.

On the FDR Drive, three bridges cross the East River to Brooklyn: south to north, the Brooklyn Bridge, the Manhattan Bridge, and the Williamsburg Bridge. At 34th Street, the Queens Midtown Tunnel (toll) shoots under the river to Queens and the Long Island Expressway running east to Long Island. The Queensborough Bridge crosses from 59th Street into Long Island City for free (be prepared for construction, which seems continual on this stretch), and the Triborough Bridge (toll) at 125th Street crosses into either Queens or The Bronx (watch the signs carefully). The Willis Avenue Bridge also takes you across the East River from the FDR to the Bronx (no toll) and connects with the Major Deagan Expressway, a north/south highway that passes Yankee Stadium.

From the West Side Highway the Holland Tunnel (toll) at Canal Street goes under the Hudson to Jersey City, and the Lincoln Tunnel (toll) at 38th Street crosses to Weehawken, both connecting to the Jersey Turnpike (I-95) and routes 78 and 22 west into New Jersey and the Garden State Parkway. Further north, the George Washington Bridge (toll) sweeps across the Hudson River on two levels to connect with the Palisades Parkway (I-9), which runs north along the west bank of the Hudson, the New Jersey Turnpike and I-80, which heads west straight across New Jersey. The Cross Bronx Expressway, which runs onto the bridge, also runs (crawls is sometimes more like it) east, connecting with I-95 north into Connecticut, I-87 north into Yonkers and Upstate New York, and the Bronx River Parkway north. From the northernmost tip of Manhattan the Henry Hudson Bridge (toll) soars into Riverdale north on the Henry Hudson Parkway to Rte. 87 and other routes north into Westchester and on to New England.

Tolls on the bridges and tunnels range from $3 to $10 and there's now talk of adding tolls on the East River bridges going into Brooklyn. But drivers with the E-Z Pass can save money. The pass also saves time, as it doesn't require counting money and more lanes are open for pass holders. To get the E-Z Pass, which also works on the New York State Thruway and in neighboring states, go to www.e-zpassny.com and apply online, or call 800-333-TOLL for an application. The pass works like a debit card, subtracting the toll from your balance with each use; you can pay to keep the pass filled by check or money order, but if you pay by credit card the pass is automatically filled as necessary. Your monthly statement will tally your toll spending.

TAXI AND CAR SERVICES

All car services in New York City, unlicensed as well as licensed, come under the jurisdiction of the Taxi and Limousine Commission (TLC). Call the commission with questions, complaints, or for the lost and found, 212-227-0700, or go to www.nyc.gov/taxi.

Licensed cabs in New York City tend to be reliable and safe, although in 1994, for the first time, the TLC required licensed cabs to install Plexiglas shields between driver and passenger. This is intended more for the driver's safety, however. The TLC licenses chauffeur-driven stretch limos as well as three types of cabs:

- **Yellow cabs**, or "medallion" cabs—for the emblem affixed to the hood—are the only taxis authorized to pick up passengers on the street. A licensed cab (the ones you should get into) will have a photo license of the driver displayed on the right side of the dashboard. There are more than 12,000 of these charging $2.50 upon entry and 40¢ for each 1/5th of a mile, and 40¢ for each 120 seconds waiting time. A 50¢ surcharge is collected between 8 p.m. and 6 a.m. No legal surcharge for luggage. Tips in the 15% to 20% range are expected. If you are crossing a toll bridge or tunnel you are responsible for paying the tolls. Most Manhattan cabs now take credit cards. If you're going cross-town, though, especially mid-day in the crush of midtown traffic, it pays to take a cross-town bus. Better yet, walk; it's faster. Outer borough dwellers should know that cabbies are legally required to take you as a fare, even if they hate going to Queens. If you're having a run of refusals, threatening to report them can work wonders.

- **Black cars**, the trade term for those high-quality, (near-luxury) radio-dispatched fleet sedans you see around, aren't licensed to stop for street hails. Corporations and private charges account for most of the "black car" business. In theory, these meterless "voucher cabs" (which charge by zone or by mileage registered on the odometer) will respond to telephone requests from "charge-accountless" individuals. If a driver sees you hailing a cab and offers to pick you up, he's doing so illegally and you are taking a risk.

- **Car services** are licensed to work only from a telephone base and can't legally pick up passengers on the street. The vehicles, of which there are some 36,000 licensed, range from the less-than-lovely to the pristine-upscale, but they are never yellow. Each vehicle, as proof of licensing, must display the blue decal of the Taxi and Limousine Commission on the passenger side of the front windshield. Especially useful to residents of the outer boroughs, where cabs rarely cruise, and to baggage-laden wayfarers, these for-hire vehicles charge flat rates per trip, sometimes less than the cost of a metered cab. This is the way to go when you need to get home from the boroughs at night—share with a couple of people if possible.

It pays to shop around by phone. Some rides can be reserved immediately before departure, others require a day's notice. Rates and features vary; you may wish to pay a few dollars extra for a mini van or for a Lincoln Town Car, and you may wish to arrange to have the car wait for you for the return trip, for which some services charge only half fare. In any case, be sure the service is licensed, and if you're shopping around, don't hesitate to ask how much liability insurance they carry for passenger injury; they should carry a minimum of $1 million.

The car lurching to your side looks a wreck, and there's no decal? Then it's probably an unlicensed gypsy cab, in which you'll ride at your own risk without recourse in case of bad service. Avoid them.

LIMOUSINE SERVICE

For those occasions when you wish to ride in style or have a car and driver at your beck and call, consider hiring a limousine. Many car services also operate limousines; rates are usually on a per hour basis, although some firms set flat rates for trips to airports or for dinner-and-theater evenings. White, 40-foot-long stretch Hummers, such as those operated by **Amex Limousine Service**, 800-804-7456, are the current ultimate. These block-long beauties carry up to 30 people, and some models even have an open-air jacuzzi; the garden-variety limos offer stereos, color TV, and a stocked bar with ice for five or six. One day's notice is usually required, though cars (but not necessarily your first choice) are sometimes available on short notice. Most firms accept major credit cards, but check when you call. Add 15% to 20% gratuity for the driver. Several companies deal primarily with corporate accounts.

- **All-State Car and Limousine Service, Inc.**, 163 Eighth Avenue, 212-333-3333, www.allstatelimo.com ; this service requires a two-hour minimum plus gratuity when you rent a sedan or a stretch limo. All-State also offers good rates to LaGuardia, JFK and Newark airports. Rates vary depending on the neighborhood you are traveling to/from. Call for more information.
- **Carey International**, 62-07 Woodside Avenue, Woodside, Queens, 800-336-4646, www.carey.com; call for rates.
- **Dav-El Livery**, 212-645-4242, www.davel.com; all trips are charged a two-hour minimum. Call for rates.
- **Fugazy International Corp.**, 212-661-0100; call for rates. Sedans and stretch limos available.
- **London Towne Cars**, Long Island City, 800-221-4009; call for rates, sedans and limousines available.
- **Tel Aviv Car and Limousine Service**, 139 First Avenue near Eighth Street, 800-222-9888, www.telavivlimo.com; New York magazine called Tel Aviv "the best ride in town."

CAR RENTALS

If you let your fingers do the walking through the 19 yellow pages of car rental firms in the Manhattan Telephone Directory, you will undoubtedly come up with the best rate for your particular needs. National and local companies rent everything from the latest model cars in all sizes to sub-compacts, mini vans, and "oldies." Prices vary widely from firm to firm, and special rates (for a weekend or even midweek) are common; call around for cost comparisons. Keep in mind that companies located just outside the city may offer rates low enough to more than make up for the hassle of getting there. In White Plains, NY, for example—a half hour by train from Grand Central—the Hertz office by the train station offers rates lower than what can be found at Hertz offices in Manhattan.

Be sure to ask if there is a charge for leaving the car at another location, if that is your plan. Some other helpful hints: Manhattan car rental companies run out of availability quickly, especially on holiday weekends. Do not wait until the last minute to try to reserve a car, and calling early may also get you a better discount. Check with your employer as well, who may have a corporate account that can get you a reduced rate. When you book your reservation, ask for a confirmation number, which will help get the rate you were quoted when you reserved the car. It's also a good idea to arrive early to pick up your car.

Finally, becoming a member of New York City's AAA, 212-757-2000, www. aaany.com even if you do not own a car, is a good idea. Benefits include discounts on car rentals, free travelers' checks, maps, travel guides, trip planning service, travel discounts, and travel agents. At $58 to join and $48 annually thereafter, it's a good deal.

Here are some of the largest car rental companies. All have several Manhattan locations and with the exception of Thrifty, all have locations at the three major area airports.

- **Avis: In New York City call 212-308-2727 for information and reservations; elsewhere call 800-331-1212**, www.avis.com.
- **Budget**, 800-527-0700, www.drivebudget.com
- **Dollar**, 800-800-4000, www.dollar.com
- **Hertz**, 800-654-3131, www.hertz.com
- **National**, 800-227-7368, www.nationalcar.com
- **Thrifty**, 800-THRIFTY, www.thrifty.com

COMMUTER AND NATIONAL RAIL SERVICE

Pennsylvania Station, between 31st and 33rd streets and Seventh and Eighth avenues, with the Long Island Railroad Station adjacent, between 33rd and 34th streets, and Grand Central Station at 42nd Street, between Vanderbilt and Lexington avenues at Park, are the railroad hubs in New York City. Grand Central has been restored to its former glory, its gray stone walls cleaned and the spectacular azure vaulted ceiling with gilded constellations uncovered. It is once again truly a destination worthy of its calling. The once dim and dirty passageways now house a spiffy mall: a seductive food court, fine restaurants, Godiva, Starbucks, and more. The Oyster Bar downstairs, unbelievably, is one of New York's best restaurants. Penn Station, on the other hand, remains a work in progress and plans to restore it to its former greatness seem eternally stalled.

- **Amtrak** trains, 800-872-7245 for information and reservations, or go to www. amtrak.com. Leave Pennsylvania Station for the Northeast Corridor—between Washington and Boston—and for destinations throughout most of the country and to Canada. Amtrak's high-speed Acela Express service with a sleek bullet train shooting along the Northeast Corridor between Boston and New York and on to Washington D.C. at speeds peaking at 150 mph, cutting travel time by a third.. Both Acela Express and the less expensive, and slower, Acela Regional come in two classes, first and business. Metroliner service between New York and Washington is also available. Look for "rail sale" entries online, where discounts on long-distance coach train tickets may be available.

- **Metro-North** trains, 212-532-4900, www.mta.info, leave from Grand Central Station and include the Hudson Line to Poughkeepsie, NY; the Harlem Line to Brewster, NY; and the New Haven Line to New Haven, CT. Find up-to-date Metro-North information on the MTA web site.
- The **New Jersey Transit Information Center**, 800-772-2222, is the place to call for Penn Station-New Jersey train schedules. Also, check www.njtransit. com.
- **Long Island Railroad** (LIRR) trains, 718-217-5477, TTY 718-558-3022, www. mta.info, leave from the LIRR station, right next to Penn Station. You'll find up-to-date LIRR information on the MTA web site.
- **Staten Island Rapid Transit**, 718-966-SIRT, www.mta.info, runs between St. George and Tottenville stations 24/7. At the St. George Station, riders can make connections with the Staten Island Ferry.

COMMUTER AND NATIONAL BUS SERVICE

- **The Port Authority Bus Terminal**, between 40th and 42nd streets and Eighth and Ninth avenues, 212-564-8484, www.panynj.gov; slightly modernized and enlarged, is the center for almost all inter-city bus traffic. The exceptions are inter-borough expresses, which have designated pickup points at certain Manhattan intersections, and buses, mostly from New Jersey, that arrive and leave from the Port Authority Bus Station at the George Washington Bridge. Call the "Customer Connection" at 800-221-9903 for more specifics.
- **Greyhound Bus Lines**, 800-231-2222, www.greyhound.com, has its principal ticket offices in the Port Authority Terminal, and its buses arrive and depart from the Lower Level of the North Wing with entrances on both 41st and 42nd streets.
- **Peter Pan Trailways**, 800-343-9999, www.peterpanbus.com; uses Adirondack Trailways as its local ticket agent in the Port Authority Terminal. Its buses also arrive at and depart from the Lower Level of the North Wing.

AIRLINES

The Port Authority of New York and New Jersey manages John F. Kennedy, LaGuardia, and Newark airports, and strives mightily to upgrade airport transportation and services and to disseminate information to the public about the facilities. To this end, they distribute particularly helpful materials and staff several telephone information numbers.

Since deregulation, the 80-plus airlines serving the three airports seem to be perpetually changing flight schedules, destinations, and names, to say nothing of fares. To order this chaos, the Port Authority publishes the International and Domestic Consolidated Airline Schedule, a pocket-sized quarterly useful for finding the flight to fit one's needs.

The Port Authority web site, airport section, www.panynj.gov/aviation.html, provides information on each of the three major New York City airports. For a menu of recorded information, including details about ground transportation and parking information, call 800-A-I-R-R-I-D-E.

AIRPORT TRANSPORTATION

The cheapest route (and one of the slowest) to JFK is the A train ($2, destination Rockaways, not Lefferts Blvd.) to the Howard Beach station; from there, connect with AirTrain ($5) for all stops at JFK. Allow an hour and a half or more. Call 800-247-7433 for Howard Beach Station departure times.

You can, of course, drive to the airport and park there for up to 30 days at Kennedy International, LaGuardia, or Newark (costly at $250+). Short-term parking is available at all airports. Day rates vary from $10 to nearly $50, depending on the airport and the proximity to the terminal. Also, keep in mind that on Fridays and during holiday periods the lots fill up quickly. Business travelers fill short-term lots on Wednesdays. Arrive at the lot before 3 p.m. most days to be sure of a parking spot, and don't expect to find a space at LaGuardia Sunday night.

For up-to-date information on transportation to any of the three airports go online to the Port Authority's web site, www.panynj.gov, or call the individual airport, below.

Every half-hour, between 6:30 a.m. and 9:30 p.m., New York Airport Service Express, 718-875-8200, www.nyairportservice.com, offers Inter-Airport Service, a shuttle bus that loops between the passenger terminals at Kennedy to LaGuardia, with service to Manhattan hotels, Penn Station, Grand Central Station, and the LIRR. Check the web site for schedules and rates—online discount rates may be available.

If you are traveling with a companion, or can find someone to share with, it is probably worth taking a taxi to and from any of the major airports. Get taxis only at taxi stands and do not follow someone who claims to be a driver to his "parked" cab somewhere in an airport lot, unless you're hoping to get mugged. More on airport transportation under each airport listing below.

JOHN F. KENNEDY INTERNATIONAL AIRPORT (JFK)

JFK, which has been shedding its various skins for a few years now, is expected to finish rebuilding itself handsomely by 2006. A new light rail system, **AirTrain**, is now in place, looping the eight terminals and linking up with the Long Island Railroad, subways, and buses at Jamaica Station and at Howard Beach. Travelers can now zip from midtown to JFK in 45 minutes. For more information about AirTrain, call 877-535-2478 or go to www.panynj.com. Security at JFK is tight, so you need to give yourself additional time and be patient. It should go without saying, but do not leave your bags unattended. Call 718-244-4444 for **airport**

information, 718-244-4225 for lost and found, and 718-244-4168 for **parking**; online, go to www.kennedyairport.com.

- **Taxis to Manhattan** cost a flat fee of $45, plus tolls and tip. If there is a second person going beyond the first stop in Manhattan, the meter is started after the first stop and this passenger pays the metered rate. From destinations in the other four boroughs, taxis will typically run from $20 (Queens) to $45 for Staten Island. Allow 45-90 minutes from Manhattan, depending on time of day, with rush hour being the longest commute. Remember, when leaving JFK get taxis only at taxi stands.

- **New York Airport Service Express Bus**, 718-875-8200, www.nyairportservice. com; buses leave from Grand Central, Penn Station, Bryant Park, and the Port Authority Bus Terminal every 30 minutes. The trip from downtown takes 45 to 60 minutes or more, depending on time of day, and the one-way fare to or from Manhattan destinations is between $12 and $15. See the web site for schedules and rates. Discounts may be available if you purchase tickets online.

- **SuperShuttle (Blue Van)**, 800-BLUE-VAN, www.supershuttle.com; operates 24/7, shuttling passengers from all destinations in Manhattan to each of the three major airports. Call ahead and make reservations, which are required. You will be notified at the time of your reservation if delays of more than 15 minutes are expected. When arriving at JFK you can go to the ground transport desk located by the baggage claim area to reserve pick up. You can expect about a 15-minute wait. Fares range from $13 to $30, depending on your destination.

- **Bus or subway**; if you're looking to save money but not time, you can take the E or F train from Manhattan, or the Q60 bus from 60th Street and Second Avenue to the Union Square/Kew Gardens Station and transfer there to the Q10 to Kennedy, where it circles the airport, stopping at each airline terminal; one fare. The A train from 59th Street and Columbus Circle in Manhattan is the fastest route by subway. You will need to board either the Far Rockaway or Rockaway Park trains (not Lefferts Blvd.). At the final stop (Far Rockaway) are free shuttle buses to the airport. The A train cuts through lower Manhattan, Brooklyn and the Rockaway section of Queens.

LAGUARDIA AIRPORT

Call 718-533-3400 for airport information; 718-533-3988 for lost and found; and 718-533-3850 for parking. Online, you can visit www.panynj.gov.

- **Taxis** to and from midtown cost about $19 to $26, plus tolls and tip. If you can find a friendly fellow Manhattan (or wherever you are going) bound traveler you can split the fare.

- **New York Airport Service Express Bus**, 718-875-8200, www.nyairportservice. com; buses leave from Penn Station, Port Authority, Bryant Park, and Grand Central Terminal every 30 minutes. The trip from downtown takes about 40 minutes, more during rush hours, and costs between $12 and $15, depending on the stop. Discounts may be available if you purchase online.

- **SuperShuttle (Blue Van)**, call 800-BLUE-VAN, www.supershuttle.com. They bought out Express Shuttle USA (Grey Line) and now operate 24/7 shuttling passengers from all destinations in Manhattan to each of the three major airports. You will be notified at the time of your reservation if van delays of more than 15 minutes are expected. Fares range from $13 to $23.
- **Public subway and bus**; call the Transit Authority, 718-335-1000, for information. Take the E or F train to the Roosevelt Station in Queens and change to the Q33 bus, which runs to LaGuardia every 15 minutes 24 hours a day. Total cost: $2 one way using a MetroCard (or coins on the bus). If you're leaving from the Upper West Side and have 45-60 minutes to spare, take the M60 bus from Broadway and 116th Street, or anywhere along Broadway north to 125th Street to Second Avenue before midnight. It goes to LaGuardia for one fare. The M60 connects with the 1, 2, 3, 4, 5, 6, A, C, N and W trains.

NEWARK LIBERTY INTERNATIONAL AIRPORT

Call 973-961-6000 for airport information; 973-961-6243 for lost and found; and 888-397-4636, then press 22, to receive parking information. Online, visit www.newarkairport.com.

The Port Authority, which runs all three New York City area airports, supervises efficient, inexpensive transportation to and from Newark.

- **Taxis**, the trip from midtown to Newark Airport costs between $40 and $50 plus tolls. In addition, taxis can add a $15 surcharge. Returning to Manhattan, New Jersey cabs are limited to fixed fares determined by location. "Share and save" rates for groups of up to four passengers cut costs by almost half and are available between 8 a.m. and midnight. Check with the dispatcher at the terminal's hack stand.
- **Newark Airport Express by Coach USA, 877-8-NEWARK**, www.coachusa.com; service between Newark Airport and Manhattan (across 42nd Street from Grand Central Station) for $15 (one way) or $25 (round trip). Comfy ride. Other drop-off points available. Contact Coach USA for more specifics.
- **SuperShuttle (Blue Van)**, call 212-258-3826 on day of departure; from out of town or to reserve before day of departure, call 800-BLUEVAN, www.supershuttle.com. Operates 24 hours a day shuttling passengers from home, office, or hotel to the three major airports. Call and make reservations, which are required. When arriving at Newark Airport, you can go to the ground transport desk in the baggage claim area and order a Blue Van pick up. There will typically be about a 15-minute wait until the van picks you up. The fare is $21.
- **Rail: NJ Transit**, 800-772-2222, www.njtransit.com; PATH, 800-234-PATH, www.pathrail.com; Amtrak 800-USA-RAIL, www.amtrak.com: trains operate from Penn Station in Manhattan to and from Newark Penn Station between 5

a.m. and 2 a.m. AirTrain is the new light rail system that whisks you between the train station and the airport terminals: 888-397-4636, www.panynj.com.

SATELLITE AIRPORTS

Three airports outside the city offer an attractive alternative to the JFK-LaGuardia-Newark axis: un-crowded access roads, easy parking, and fewer delays all around for domestic flights.

- **MacArthur Airport**, 100 Arrivals Avenue in Islip, Long Island, 631-467-3210, www.macarthurairport.com. Served by several major airlines, including Delta Express, Continental Express, Southwest, and US Airways. Access is easiest via the LIRR. Ride to Ronkonkoma (about 90 minutes) and catch a $5 shuttle to the airport.
- **Stewart Airport**, 1180 Windsor, New Winston, New York; 845-564-2100, www.stewartintlairport.com; a former Air Force base 60 miles north of the city in Newburgh, NY, at the juncture of I-87 and I-84, opened for commercial service in 1990. Airlines include: Conair/Delta Connection, American Eagle, Southeast, and US Airways Express.
- **Westchester County Airport** on Airport Road in White Plains, 914-995-4850, www.westchestergov.com/airport, is served by Air Canada, American, Continental Express, USAir, and United. The airport boasts a new terminal, completed in 1995, and ample parking in a three-story lot. Lacking a car, take the Harlem Line out of Grand Central to White Plains, and the Bee Line #12.

FLIGHT DELAYS

Information about flight delays can be checked online on your airline's web site, or at www.fly.faa.gov. Similarly, the site www.flightarrivals.com offers real-time arrival, departure, and delay details for commercial flights.

CONSUMER COMPLAINTS—AIRLINES

To register a complaint against an airline, the Department of Transportation is the place to call or write: 202-366-2220, Aviation Consumer Protection Division, C-75 Room 4107, 400 7th Street SW, Washington, D.C. 20590.

WHEN YOU FIND YOURSELF FLYING DOWN THE SIDEWALK— shoulder bag or briefcase in tow, feet sore, elbows jostling, grinding teeth ready to chew up the slowpokes in front of you—take heed: that pounding in your head is not a war drum, it's a warning. It is time to get out of the city. Like all great things, New York City is better appreciated when experienced with some moderation. It is infectious, but it is also exhausting, especially in the dog days of August. You'll be glad you left once you're gone, and you'll be glad you're back when you return.

By virtue of its location, its size, and the multitude of transit systems that pass through New York City, entire volumes could be devoted to getting out of town, and every magazine runs lists of seasonal getaway trips ranging from bucolic swimming spots to places you can eat foie gras naked—of course, if it was in last week's *New York* magazine, you'll end up squeezing in with the rest of the city, so you might want to peruse *last* summer's recommendations instead. And don't forget all-day escapes like Governor's Island or Fire Island! Here we point you in the direction of some good resources, with a few trips suggested as well. The tri-state area is rich with destinations for a day trip, and the Northeast provides ample opportunity to get away for a weekend. Friends and co-workers will doubtless have a number of favorite spots (and suggestions on how to get there). And don't be afraid to venture out on your own. How fun, how 1950s, to simply board a train and ride until something grabs your fancy?

MODES OF TRANSPORTATION

TRAINS

- **Metro-North**, the MTA's regional rail service, offers numerous "One-Day Getaways" to upstate villages, Connecticut casinos, biking regions, hiking trails, rafting purveyors and more; "Manhattan Getaways" are package deals for travel to some of New York's better destinations. Visit www.mta.info for more, or call 212-532-4900.

- **Long Island Railroad**, the key for the car-less to Long Island, provides year-round service to destinations deemed best for the season: beaches and fishing villages in the summer, for example, and orchards in the fall; they also have packages for the hobby photographer, the gambler, and the oenophile. www. mta.info/lirr, or call 718-217-LIRR, 1-516-822-*LIRR*, or 1-631-231-*LIRR*.
- **Amtrak**; perhaps you'd like to visit Boston or Philly or DC for a day, or maybe you're eyeing a long weekend in Montreal. Amtrak can get you there, and though it is more expensive than many other options, the ride is comfortable and the booking fees for short notice travel beat flying every time. See www. amtrakvacations.com for packages and deals, or call 800-268-7252.

BUSES

- **Greyhound Bus** frequently offers discounted fares to nearby cities, and occasionally puts forth promotional packages of its own. Check www.greyhound. com, or call 800-231-2222.
- **Chinatown Bus**; a long-held secret has been spilled. There are numerous privately owned bus lines that offer express service between the Chinatowns of various East Coast cities: New York, Boston, Philadelphia, DC, and so on. These services vary widely in terms of reliability, cleanliness, and safety, but they are indisputably cheap. Thorough reviews and info can be found at www.staticleap.com/chinatownbus, 202-370-7958.

CAR RENTAL

If you'd like to escape and set your own pace, or have a destination in mind that isn't served by train or bus, you may wish to rent a car. For a short trip on short notice, ZipCar (866-4ZIP-CAR, www.zipcar.com) is your best option. But be aware of your mileage: beyond 180 you pay $.45 to $.55 per mile.

STATE RESOURCES

The tri-state area is not shy about self-promotion, and with good cause. There is plenty to see and do, and the variety of options are dazzling. Below is information pertaining to these three beautiful states.

- **New York**: www.iloveny.co is the state's enthusiastic and thorough official tourism website, rife with plans, packages, destinations, and deals—from "Culinary Adventures" to "Girlfriend Getaways." Additional info at 800-CALL-NYS.
- **New Jersey**: www.state.nj.us/travel is a somewhat dry site that seems more geared to school field trips than day trips, essentially an online version of the brochure racks that clog the entryways to roadside service station. The

information is reliable, though, and the Calendar of Events is excellent. Call 1-800-VISITNJ for more.

- **Connecticut**: www.ctvisit.com is simple, clean and straightforward, with numerous packages and promotions. New events are posted for each approaching weekend, and be sure to check out the "52 Great Getaways." Also call 888-CT-VISIT.

WEB RESOURCES

Online you will find a cavalcade of tourism sites, promotions, charters, and more. Here are some of the best.

- **About.com's Easy Day Trips** from New York City, www.gonyc.about.com/od/daytrips, has a rotating list of activities ranging from the decadent (drinking, gambling) to the special interest (renaissance fairs, tours of the military academy). .

- **Fun New Jersey**, www.funnewjersey.com, from which the state-run site could learn a lesson, has more thorough listings for the Garden State. Make sure you've got your internet Flash plug-in updated, however, or the site will kick you unceremoniously away.

- **GORP.com**, gorp.away.com, named for the infamous trail mix combination, has an extensive listing of day trip ideas ranging from fall foliage guides to day hikes to river rafting, most of which are self-guided. Free registration required.

- **North Jersey Day Trips for Kids**, www.fmfcorp.com/familyspot/trips.html, contains a comprehensive listing of events and destinations in North Jersey, with a focus on the family.

- **USA Today**, destinations.usatoday.com/newyork/day_trips, has a useful, no-frills online travel guide with day-trip suggestions and links to various sites, accommodations, and other resources.

- **Mommy Poppins**, www.mommypoppins.com; a friendly little website that focuses on fun day trips for kids or without a car, as well as local overnighters like the kid sleepover in the Museum of Natural History.

UMMER ACCOMMODATIONS IN UNIVERSITY DORMS, YS, CHURCH-run women's residences, hotels, and even B&Bs provide temporary shelter en route to a permanent living situation. Later, there may be the occasional visiting aunt and uncle whom you cannot squeeze into your cramped one bedroom. Descriptions of these varied lodgings are offered, together with a selection of hotels categorized by price and location. Addresses are in Manhattan unless otherwise noted.

A few generalizations: rates are often negotiable and vary depending on time of the year; weekends and the summer months offer the best opportunity for lodging bargains; holidays and the fall months are usually the priciest times to stay in the city. To avoid sticker shock at checkout, note that New York hotel rooms are subject to 13.375% in city and state taxes, plus a room occupancy tax of $3.50 (higher for multiple-room suites). Interestingly, this is at the low end of the national scale.

SUMMER ONLY

Dorm accommodations and other special situations include:

- **International House New York** (near Columbia University), 500 Riverside Dr at 123rd St, 212-316-8400, www.ihouse-nyc.org; you don't have to matriculate at Columbia to be eligible for one of the approximately 700 dorm rooms and suites available to students, interns, and other visitors from late May to mid-August on a first-come, first-served basis. Rooms can be had at $60 per night for short term stays (max 20 days). Monthly stays are for students only. These bargain accommodations are sometimes available during the school year as well, but not often.
- **New York University Dormitories**, c/o New York University, Office of Summer Housing, 14A Washington Place, 212-998-4621, www.nyu.edu/summer/housing; there is a three-week minimum stay requirement at the NYU dorms,

which are open to other students, age 17 or older (and June graduates), from mid-May through early August. Priority is given to enrolled summer students, whose rates begin at only $80/week for a dorm-type setting. Non-student rates start at $160/week, and go up to $350/week for an apartment-like setting. The lower, dorm rates require the purchase of a $100-$110 meal plan. You may apply for housing online; minimum three weeks' payment required upon application.

See also **Sublets and Sharing** in the **Finding a Place to Live** chapter.

TRANSIENT YMCAS

Two Ys in Manhattan, one in Brooklyn and one in Queens, offer accommodations for both men and women; all rent rooms on a day-to-day basis only. To obtain reservations at the four YMCAs listed below, either contact each Y individually or go online to www.hostels.com. Rates vary ($95 for a single and $120 for a double at the Vanderbilt in Manhattan, or $48/$68 for a small/large single in Greenpoint, Brooklyn). In all cases the room rates include use of all athletic facilities on the premises (see YMCAs in Sports and Recreation). Note that you will be sharing a bathroom with your hallmates.

- **Vanderbilt YMCA**, 224 E 47th St, 212-912-2500; 370 rooms
- **West Side YMCA**, 5 W 63rd St, 212-875-4100; 530 rooms
- **Flushing YMCA**, 138-46 Northern Blvd, Flushing, 718-961-6880; 127 rooms
- **Greenpoint YMCA**, 99 Meserole Ave, Brooklyn, 718-389-3700; 100 rooms

TEMPORARY RESIDENCES

Daily transients are not accepted by any of the residences noted below, which, with the exception of the 92nd Street YM-YWHA, are for women only. Weekly rates are the norm and many include two meals a day in the price. Full occupancy is the rule at most of these places, as is the requirement for a personal interview, and you should therefore make arrangements for a room well in advance of arrival. Some have special house rules, such as curfews, so inquire about these before booking.

- **92nd Street YM-YWHA**, de Hirsch Residence, 1395 Lexington Ave, 212-415-5650, http://www.92y.org/content/de_hirsch_residence.asp; co-ed, for men and women ages 18 and older, with 225 rooms, minimum stay one month (by application only); rates for single rooms start at $1,550, shared double rooms are also available for around $1200 a person, depending on size. Must be working full time or going to school. Apply several months in advance. Rooms are adjacent to the Buttenwieser Library, which offers internet access. Occupants also receive reduced or free admission to concerts and lectures, plus discounted rates for the gym and pool.

- **Brandon Residence for Women**, 340 W 85th St between Riverside Dr and West End Ave, 212-496-6901, www.thebrandon.org; with 120 single rooms, shared baths, a handsome lobby, and 24-hour security. Applicants who will be working or students must apply in advance, with approval pending an interview. Rates range from $1,023 to $1,218 a month, breakfast and dinner included.

- **Markle Evangeline Residence** (Salvation Army), 123 W 13th St, 212-242-2400, www.themarkle.org; private room and bath, includes two meals a day. Christian focus. Weekly rates $350–470. Monthly rates for singles run about $1,360, doubles from $1,100-$1,500.

- **St. Mary's Residence** (Daughters of the Divine Charity), 225 E 72nd St, 212-249-6850; with three-month commitment, $196/week for private rooms with shared baths and facilities. Otherwise, $225 a week with two-week minimum stay. Women only.

- **Webster Apartments**, 419 W 34th St between Ninth and Tenth Aves, 212-967-9000, www.websterapartments.org; call well in advance to reserve for a minimum of four weeks at this attractive establishment, which features gardens and a library. An interview is required of applicants in the area; out-of-towners write directly for an application. Current weekly rates range from $250 to $268; there are occasional short-term rooms for $75 a night (three-day minimum, breakfast included). You must provide proof of enrollment in a school, a letter of proof of internship, or proof of employment. Many residents here stay for months at a time, so if you're moving to the city and your place isn't quite ready, or if you're looking for the right place, this is a good option for women.

BED AND BREAKFASTS

In Manhattan? Yes! Many a resourceful New Yorker has let out that extra room and thrown a continental breakfast into the bargain. It's even possible to have the whole apartment, in a charming brownstone or a high-tech high-rise, to yourself, which is to say un-hosted. In any case, it will be cheaper than comparable digs in a hotel, but the visitor may give up something in privacy, service, or convenience. However, don't look for hand-lettered shingles advertising availability because owners require anonymity and an agency acts as intermediary.

This cottage industry is unregulated, though reputable agencies inspect the properties they represent and attempt to monitor the quality of service and accommodations on an ongoing basis through visitor critique cards. Shop around by phone; be as specific as you can be about preferred location, likes and dislikes, allergies, and other restrictions. There is usually a two-night minimum stay, but there may be exceptions off-season. For the best choice, book well in advance (reasonable B&Bs have gotten as scarce as affordable hotel rooms) and expect to pay at least a 25% deposit (some charge 50%). The commission is included in the fee. A sales tax, which varies, is charged above the room price. Many accept credit cards. Many people also rent out their entire apartments on a weekly/monthly basis to supplement their incomes. Check craigslist.com for listings, but buyer beware.

- **1871 House**, 130 E 62nd St, 212-756-8823, www.1871house.com; want to stay in a historic brownstone on the fashionable Upper East Side, just two blocks from Bloomingdale's? Now you can. High ceilings, oriental rugs, cozy sitting areas, fireplaces, and plenty of antiques (no, this isn't the place for the kids). Seven spacious apartments, including two suites, with plenty of first-class amenities. Check availability and rates on the web site.

- **Abode Bed and Breakfast**, P.O. Box 20022, NYC 10021, 212-472-2000 (800-835-8880 for out-of-state callers only), www.abodenyc.com, represents about 50 un-hosted apartments, all in Manhattan, some long-term locations. They request business references from guests. Four-night minimum, rates vary. Most rooms non-smoking.

- **Bed and Breakfast Network of New York**, 130 Barrow St, NYC 10014, 212-645-8134, 800-900-8134, www.bedandbreakfastnetny.com, lists 200 places, hosted and un-hosted, and suggests a few weeks' advance notice. There is a two-night minimum in most cases. Call to order a brochure.

- **City Lights Bed and Breakfast and Short Term Apartment Rental**, 212-737-7049, www.citylightsnewyork.com, lists several hundred rooms and apartments, hosted and un-hosted, all in Manhattan. Rates vary depending on the accommodation; three-night minimum.

- **Manhattan Lodgings, Inc.**, 70 E 10th St, NYC 10003, 212-677-7616, www.manhattanlodgings.com, offers a wide range of furnished, short-stay apartments in Manhattan. Five-night minimum; rates range from around $150 per night to $6,000 per month.

EXTENDED STAY HOTELS

A number of hotels, particularly smaller neighborhood properties equipped with kitchenettes, quote weekly and monthly as well as daily rates. You'll find several listed below under **Inexpensive Hotels**. The late 1990s saw the proliferation of high-end, all-suite hotels for extended stays only, sometimes in apartment buildings, sometimes within transient hotels, but all designed primarily for the businessperson, offering hotel services and amenities along with fax machines and multi-line telephones. You can go to the NYC's official visitors' site, www.nycgo.com, for some ideas. Here are a few of our own:

- **Affinia Hospitality**, 866-246-2203, www.affinia.com; formerly Manhattan East Suites Hotels, it represents eight prime properties in Manhattan including The Shelburne (Murray Hill), Eastgate Tower (fringes of Murray Hill), and the Surrey (Upper East Side). Extended-stay reservations available only by phone. Rates for small studios can be as low as $5,500, but expect to pay $7,000 a month or more for these luxury accommodations.

- **Marmara-Manhattan,** 301 E 94th St, 212-427-3100, www.marmara-manhattan .com, has 108 apartments that were formerly condominiums. Amenities include an exercise room and a daily buffet breakfast (charged as extra). From $4,500 to $13,000 monthly; studios, one-, two-, and three-bedroom units available.

- **The Phillips Club**, 155 W 66th St, 212-835-8800, www.phillipsclub.com; at the high end and designed for the corporate traveler, contemporary apartments in a sleek 32-floor building just north of Lincoln Center, a few short blocks from Central Park. From overnight stays to extended stays to owning a piece of Manhattan real estate, you can enjoy luxurious surroundings at this corporate minded hotel. From $8,000 to $22,000 a month. Fully equipped kitchens.

HOTELS

There are over 63,000 hotel rooms in New York City. Prices and occupancy rates fluctuate seasonally depending on location. The friendly, and sometimes frenetic, first-class commercial establishments along Central Park West and Lexington and Park avenues in the East 40s and 50s are impossibly full on weekdays in the fall, winter, and spring, but both occupancy and prices languish during the dog days of summer. Typically, the in-season rates in New York City begin in the fall and extend through the holiday season. The most affordable deals can be had during the summer months when many New Yorkers head for the Hamptons and other beach locales. Additionally, there is significantly less business travel to the city during the summer and hotels are looking to fill their rooms, so many will offer amenities as part of a package.

Weekend rates are almost always lower than prices charged during the week. However, glossy "weekend packages" with champagne, flowers, and free brunches for two won't represent the best value. Ask about the no-frills prices available Friday, Saturday, and sometimes Sunday nights. Weekend rates are, in effect, contingency plans to fill the house as corporate weeknight visitors depart. If full occupancy looms, off they go.

One place to look for deals is at the web site of the **New York Convention and Visitors Bureau**, www.nycitytourist.com, www.nycgo.com; Go there, or drop in at their Visitors Information Center (810 Seventh Avenue at 53rd Street, 212-397-8200), for an extensive listing of discounted hotel rooms. This useful site includes pictures, hotel descriptions, and ratings listed by date of availability, number of nights, number of beds, and online booking. There is also a listing of special summer rates for members of American Express, which sponsors the site.

Hotel discounters buy blocks of rooms from hotels at volume discounts and pass savings, some as high as 60%, on to consumers. Visit their web site or call for specifics. Generally, cancellations must be made 24 to 72 hours in advance; be sure to check in advance on their cancellation policy. Keep in mind, unless you know the city, you should inquire about the location of the hotel. A discounted room in a less desirable neighborhood may not be worth the savings. **Reservation services** include:

* **Central Reservation Services**, 800-548-3311, www.crshotels.com; especially good at getting mid-to low-priced rooms in New York and in about a dozen other cities.
* **Quikbook Hotels**, 800-789-9887, or 212-779-7666 from outside the U.S., www.quikbook.com; will connect you with a reservation agent who can reserve rooms at dozens of moderate to deluxe hotels all over Manhattan (and more than 30 other cities).

Additionally, you can check with the following:

* **Expedia.com**, 800-397-3342, www.expedia.com
* **Hotels.com**, 800-964-6835, www.hotels.com
* **Hotwire.com**, 866-468-9473, www.hotwire.com
* **Priceline.com**, www.priceline.com

INEXPENSIVE HOTELS

Doubles for less than $300 a night, not including tax, may not seem cheap, but that's the range that more or less separates New York's bargain hotel category from the rest of the flock. Options on the lower cusp of $200 (and under) can also be found.

* **Best Western Seaport Inn**, 33 Peck Slip, 212-766-6600, www.seaportinn.com; pleasingly restored 19th century building one block from the waterfront at the very lower tip of Manhattan. Rooms are a bargain, especially if you get one of the upper floor rooms with great views of the Brooklyn Bridge.
* **Chelsea Savoy Hotel**, 204 W 23rd St, 212-929-9353, www.chelseasavoynyc. com; good location in Chelsea, small (90 rooms), and reasonable prices.
* **Clarion Hotel Fifth Avenue**, 3 E 40th St between Fifth and Madison avenues, 877-424-6423, www.clarioninn.com; reasonably priced and centrally located, this midtown newcomer offers spacious, no-frills comfort. You can walk to Grand Central Station and the glorious Morgan Library.
* **Excelsior**, 45 W 81st St, 212-362-9200, www.excelsiorhotelny.com; a landmark building in a great location facing the Museum of Natural History and Central Park. Rates vary by season and range from very reasonably priced standard rooms to suites. Health club and concierge.
* **Gershwin Hotel**, 7 E 27th St, 212-545-8000, www.gershwinhotel.com; east side hotel, within walking distance of Gramercy Park, the Village, and Chelsea.
* **Habitat Hotel**, 130 E 57th St, 212-753-8841, www.hotel57.com; recently renovated, the Habitat is well situated in a prime location. Despite no-frills and basic small rooms, the place is often full.

- **Hampton Inn**, 108 W 24th St, 800-hampton, www.hamptoninn.com; located in Chelsea, it prides itself on offering stylish contemporary rooms at reasonable rates.
- **Herald Square**, 19 W 31st St, 800-727-1888, 212-279-4017, www.herald squarehotel.com; with a handsome beaux-arts façade, it's a favorite with European travelers looking for a good value. Good location, especially if you want to shop at Macy's.
- **Holiday Inn**, 138 Lafayette St, 212-966-8898, www.hidowntown-nyc.com; near Chinatown and Little Italy.
- **Hotel Wolcott**, 4 W 31st St, 212-268-2900, www.wolcott.com; near the Empire State Building and about 10 blocks from the theater district.
- **Hudson**, 356 W 58th St, 212-554-6000, www.hudsonhotel.com, opened in 2000 with 1,000 small rooms behind a bland brick façade. Inside, however, hotelier Ian Schrager and designer Philippe Starck have fashioned a fascinating interior, which includes a public library with a pool table, a lobby-as-townsquare, and a witty garden.
- **Off SoHo Suites**, 11 Rivington St, off the Bowery, and 212 E 12th St, 800-633-7646, www.offsoho.com; two locations, walking distance to SoHo, Chinatown, Alphabet City and NoLiTa. The accommodations are clean and comfortable, and a bargain especially for a family or a group of four. On Rivington there are 38 suites plus a café on site, and 24-hour parking (fee). At 12th St there are furnished 1-, 2-, and 3-bedrooms available.
- **Paramount**, 235 W 46th St, 212-764-5500, www.nycparamount.com; the designer of the avant-garde Royalton, Philippe Starck, turned his charms on a lower-priced venue. This whimsical effort aimed at the young and hip includes an on-site restaurant and a fitness room. Ask about special weekend rates.
- **Pod Hotel**, 230 E 51st St between Second and Third avenues, 212-355-0300, www.thepodhotel.com; Formerly The Pickwick, this has been completely redone into 100s of teeny but minimally hip little crash pads that is proving enormously popular, both for its style and its just over $100 a bed price. East 50s location.
- **Washington Square Hotel**, 103 Waverly Place, 212-777-9515, www.wshotel.com; some rooms with views of the historic Washington Square Park.

WEST SIDE TOURIST HOTELS

The cheapest rates for reliable, if far from classy, rooms are found in the tourist hotels along Eighth Avenue and in the West 40s surrounding the theater district. Better deals are offered here in the winter than in the summer.

- **Hotel Edison**, 228 W 47th St, 212-840-5000, www.edisonhotelnyc.com; 770 rooms in this old standard from 1931, convenient to the theater and reasonably priced.

- **Hampton Inn North Times Square**, 851 Eighth Ave and 51st St, 212-581-4100; Formerly Howard Johnson's, the Hampton Inn is clean, decent, and reasonably priced, with parking available for $26 per day.
- **Milford Plaza Hotel**, Eighth Ave and 45th St, 212-869-3600 www.milford plaza.com, is big, basic, and sometimes exceedingly reasonable. Call for rates.

FIRST-CLASS COMMERCIAL OR DELUXE HOTELS

Manhattan is known for its grand and luxurious hotels, a handful of which are legendary: the Pierre, the Plaza, the Carlyle, the Plaza Athenée, the Waldorf Astoria, Four Seasons, RIGHA Royal Hotels' The London NYC, and the Peninsula, to name but several—deluxe hotels all. We've chosen to list a few which are perhaps less well-known, on the basis of glamour and singularity as well as fair prices, when they can be found. Discounts and good weekend values in these hotels are generally available only in the summertime. Typically rates in these hotels will be in the $600+ (some quite considerably +) range, with occasional off-season discounts.

Since rates change often and there are frequent special deals, you should call hotel reservations for rates or look online for special offers. The finer in-room amenities including cable television and mini-bars are typically offered, and most hotels have a concierge and various services available, including babysitting.

- **Omni Berkshire Place**, 21 E 52nd St at Madison Ave, 1-800-444-OMNI, www. omnihotels.com; carefully created bouquets frame the elegant marble lobby and provide a backdrop for the classy tea-and-cocktail area on the far side of the flowers. An accommodating concierge caters to clients with dispatch in this bijou hotel, where the only major drawbacks are the smallish rooms. Fitness center on site.
- **Grand Hyatt New York**, 42nd St and Lexington Ave at Grand Central Station, 212-883-1234, www.grandnewyork.hyatt.com; fast-paced and glitzy with a terrific lobby, especially when the fountains are splashing, and a dramatic bar cantilevered over 42nd St. Rooms and lobby recently renovated. The penthouse health club and other features appeal to business travelers. Weekend specials sometimes available. Commodore Grill, Sky Bar, and Lobby Café are all on the premises for dining.
- **LES Thompson**, 190 Allen St, 212-460-5300, www.thompsonhotels.com; one of the hip new hi-rise hotels pimpling out of the Lower East Side, complete with minimalist tongue-in-cheek boutique, and trendy restaurant with cut-out black-plastic chandeliers.
- **The Mandarin Oriental**, 80 Columbus Circle at 60th Street, 212-805-8800 or 866-801-8880, www.mandarinoriental.com. Your Frette linens are attended to twice daily in this "most sophisticated" Central Park hotel. Dining includes the best and most expensive European and Asian restaurants in New York City, Per Se and Masa. Health club on site.

- **Michelangelo**, at the Equitable Center, 152 W 51st St at Seventh Ave, 212-765-1900, www.michelangelohotel.com; this is the old Taft Hotel resurrected in Euro-style "neoclassical" elegance to which well-designed rooms and great baths attract a glitzy crowd. Bring the kids. Summer rates are particularly good, and weekend packages may be available.
- **Helmsley Middletowne**, 148 E 48th St near Third Ave, 212-755-3000, www.helmsleyhotels.com; one-, two-, and three-room suites all with kitchenettes and cheerful flowered decor. A favorite of UN personnel when the General Assembly is in session.
- **Millenium Hilton**, 55 Church St, 212-693-2001; www.hilton.com; classy and convenient (if you're visiting Wall Street), the Millenium offers stunning views as well as first-class amenities such as computers and a health club with an attractive pool. Service is also top-notch. Call for rates. All rooms are discounted on weekends.
- **Millennium UN Plaza**, 1 UN Plaza at 44th St, 212-758-1234, www.unplaza-hotel.com; superior service and sensational views from every room because they begin on the 28th floor. A good-sized pool, health club, tennis court, and free limousine rides to Wall Street make this classically modern hotel unique. Great location.
- **Morgan's**, 237 Madison Ave between 37th and 38th streets, 212-686-0300, www.morganshotel.com; an upstart on New York's rather traditional hotel scene, this narrow, vertical little place around the corner from the Morgan Library has been redecorated and toned down from its original sleek look to a more muted, design-conscious feel. Small but nicely appointed rooms.
- **Royalton**, 44 W 44th St off Fifth Ave, 212-869-4400, www.royaltonhotel.com; with mahogany beds, Danish faucets, French and Italian furniture, Ian Schrager has fashioned a swinging silk purse out of a sow's ear. Good location, especially if you love the theater.
- **San Carlos**, 150 E 50th St, between Lexington and Third Aves, 212-755-1800, www.sancarloshotel.com; quiet, small hotel with pleasantly spacious rooms and kitchenettes. Good location. Rooms renovated in 2003.
- **SoHo Grand**, 310 W Broadway between Grand and Canal Sts, 212-965-3000, www.sohogrand.com; until recently the only hotel in SoHo, offers 369 rooms with amenities to suit the businessman as well as tourists. Located in the midst of the art galleries, boutiques, and cafés that fill the formerly industrial buildings of this landmarked cast-iron district. Check out the Grand Bar & Lounge. Rates vary almost daily.
- **St. Regis**, 2 E 55th St at Fifth Ave, 212-753-4500; http://www.starwoodhotels.com/stregis/index.html; this *grande dame* of Fifth Avenue reopened in all her Beaux Arts glory, and then some, after a multi-million-dollar restoration in 1991. A continental hotel in the old style with no modern convenience overlooked. And, yes, you can still dance on the St. Regis roof.

- **W Square**, 201 Park Avenue South , 212 253-9119, www.starwoodhotels.com/whotel, one of the half dozen W hotels in NYC, this is one of the most prominent, right on up-and-coming Union Square in lower Manhattan.

SOME FAVORITES

Small, charming, personal-feeling hotels are not the city's forte, but we list six fairly priced, medium-sized hotels in other Manhattan areas that deserve special mention (the hotels mentioned here reflect a purely personal taste and are not meant to be an all-city catalog of lodgings):

- **Algonquin**, 59 W 44th St, 212-840-6800, 888-304-2047 www.algonquinhotel.com; completely refurbished in 2004 in muted rose, green, and burnished wood, the famous lobby bar combines with anachronistic elevators and smallish, genteel rooms to make you feel welcome, secure, and part of a pleasantly elite and talented group. Enjoy cocktails in the Blue Bar or dinner and cabaret in the Oak Room. Call for rates and ask about specials, particularly in the summer.
- **Doubletree Guest Suites**, 1568 Broadway, 212-719-1600, doubletree1.hilton.com; overlooking Times Square, Doubletree rents suites (sitting room and bedroom) rather than single rooms, at reasonable rates. Now part of the Hilton Group.
- **Hotel Chelsea**, 222 W 23rd St, 212-243-3700, www.hotelchelsea.com; where colorful eccentrics like Sid Vicious and Virgil Thompson like to stay. In Chelsea. Great art. Relatively affordable rooms.
- **Hotel Wales**, 1295 Madison Ave corner of 92nd St, 212-876-6000, www.waleshotel.com; clean and cheerful little 86-room hotel, the Wales represents good value in tastefully renovated rooms. Terrific location for Museum Mile along Fifth Ave.
- **Lowell**, 28 E 63rd St, 212-838-1400, www.lowellhotel.com, is a small 65-room European-style hotel with plenty of amenities, on a quiet Upper East Side street. The more-attractive-than-ever art deco hotel remains intimate and friendly. Great location. Ask about specials.
- **Salisbury**, 123 W 57th St, 212-246-1300, or 888-692-5757 from out of town, www.nycsalisbury.com; pleasant, pastel rooms in a relatively intimate setting attract a high percentage of women travelers. Large rooms, good prices.

NEW YORK CITY FAIRLY CRACKLES WITH EVENTS: PARADES, FESTIVALS, celebrations, ethnic holidays, shows, feasts, and tournaments. Imperceptible at first, there is, in fact, a rhythm to this endless round of activity; many of these events occur annually at about the same time, and New Yorkers look forward to them. The calendar below lists them by month. Check out the *New York Times*, *New York* magazine, *Time Out New York*, or the *New Yorker* for specific dates and details. Or stop by the **New York Convention & Visitors Bureau** at 810 Seventh Avenue at 53rd Street, 212-484-1200, to pick up brochures and a complete seasonal calendar of events, or go to their website at www.nycgo.com. For more information on the web, you can also check the following sites: www.cityguidemagazine.com, or www.allianceforarts.org.

The following is just a fraction of what the Big Apple has to offer.

JANUARY

- **Big Apple Circus**, Lincoln Center, www.bigapplecircus.org
- **NY National Boat Show** at the Jacob Javits Center, www.newyorkboatshow.com
- **Outsider Art Fair**, www.sanfordsmith.com
- **Three Kings Parade**, Fifth Avenue, 104th to 116th streets, www.elmuseo.org
- **Winter Antiques Show** at the Seventh Regiment Armory, www.winterantiquesshow.com
- **Winter Festival**, Central Park, www.centralparknyc.org
- **Winter Restaurant Week**, various restaurants in Manhattan, nycgo.com/restaurantweek
- **Antiques Show Armory**, www.winterantiquesshow.com

FEBRUARY

- **Black History Month**, citywide events

- **Chinese New Year celebrations**, Chinatown and elsewhere
- **NY International Children's Film Festival,** www.gkids.com
- **Valentine's Day**, 24-hour Marriage Marathon at the Empire State Building, www.esbnyc.com
- **Westminster Kennel Club Dog Show**, Madison Square Garden, www.west minsterkennelclub.org

MARCH

- **Elephant Walk** to Madison Square Garden, www.madisonsquaregarden.com
- **Greek Independence Day Parade**, Fifth Avenue, www.greekparade.org
- **International Cat Show**, Madison Square Garden, www.madisonsquaregarden.com
- **New York Flower Show** at the Jacob Javits Center, www.javitscenter.com
- **New York Underground Film Festival,** www.nyuff.com
- **Ringling Brothers & Barnum & Bailey Circus,** Madison Square Garden
- **St. Patrick's Day Parade**, Fifth Avenue, www.saintpatricksdayparade.com
- **Triple Pier Antiques Show**, multiple pier locations 212-255-0020

APRIL

- **Annual Egg Rolling contest**, Central Park
- **Cherry Blossom Festival**, Brooklyn Botanic Garden, www.bbg.org
- **Easter Parade**, Fifth Avenue near 50th Street
- **Greater NY International Auto Show,** Jacob Javits Center, www.javitscenter.com
- **Mets and Yankees** baseball season begins
- **Tribeca Film Festival**, www.tribecafilmfestival.com

MAY

- **9th Avenue International Food Festival**, 37th to 57th streets
- **New York Bike Week**: The Five Boro Bike Tour, www.newyorkbikeweek.com
- **Broadway Spring Festival**
- **Fleet Week**, Manhattan west side docks
- **Lower East Side Festival of the Arts,** www.theaterforthenewcity.net
- **Promenade Art Show**, Brooklyn Heights
- **Washington Square Outdoor Art Exhibit**, LaGuardia Place, University Place, and adjacent side streets
- **Marijuana March,** globalmarijuanamarch.org

JUNE

- **Annual Lesbian and Gay Pride March,** www.nycpride.org
- **The Belmont Stakes**, Belmont Park, www.nyra.com
- **Brooklyn Pride Festival and Parade**, www.brooklynpride.org

- **Bryant Park Summer Film Festival**, www.bryantpark.org
- **Feast of St. Anthony of Padua**, Sullivan Street below Houston
- **Hudson River Park** summer events, including the popular "Take Me to the River" film series on the pier. www.hudsonriverpark.org
- **Mermaid Parade**, Coney Island, Brooklyn, www.coneyisland.com
- **Museum Mile Festival**, Fifth Avenue, www.museummilefestival.org
- **New York Jazz Festival ,** www.festivalnetwork.com
- **Puerto Rican Day Parade**, Fifth Avenue, www.nationalpuertoricandayparade.org
- **Queens Festival**, Flushing Meadows-Corona Park
- **Restaurant Week**, various restaurants in Manhattan
- **Salute to Israel Parade**, Fifth Avenue, www.salutetoisrael.com
- **Summer Stage** concerts begin, Central Park, www.summerstage.org
- **Welcome Back to Brooklyn Festival**, Grand Army Plaza

JULY

- **Bryant Park Summer Film Festival**, Monday nights,www.bryantpark.org
- **Free Shakespeare In Central Park**, Delacorte Theatre, www.publictheater org
- **Macy's 4th of July Fireworks**, Lower Hudson River
- **Midsummer Nights Swing** at Lincoln Center, www.lincolncenter.org
- **Festa de Giglio**, Williamsburg, Brooklyn, www.olmcfeast.com

AUGUST

- **African-American & Hispanic Harlem Week**, Harlem, www.harlemweek. com
- **Bronx Puerto Rican Day Parade**, East Tremont Avenue to East 161st Street
- **Brooklyn Puerto Rican Day Parade**, Lindsay Park in Williamsburg
- **Fringe Festival**, theater, music, dance and whatever from outside the mainstream, throughout the Lower East Side, www.fringenyc.org
- **HOWL! Festival**, celebrating LES's counterculture heyday over one long weekend, www.howlfestival.com
- **Mostly Mozart Festival**, Lincoln Center, www.lincolncenter.org
- **Summer Streets**, closing of NYC main streets to cars on assorted weekends, www.nyc.gov/summerstreets
- **US Open Tennis Tournament**, Flushing, Queens, www.usopen.org

SEPTEMBER

- **African-American Day Parade**, Adam Clayton Powell Blvd., 111th to 142nd Street to Fifth Avenue, www.africanamericandayparade.org
- **African-American/Caribbean Parade**, Bronx, Tremont Avenue to 161st Street

- **BAM Next Wave Festival**, www.bam.org
- **Brooklyn Book Festival**, www.brooklynbookfestival.org
- **Feast of San Gennaro**, Mulberry Street, Little Italy, www.sangennaro.org
- **Greenwich Village Jazz Festival**, around the Village and in Washington Square Park
- **Labor Day Parade**, Fifth Avenue, 33rd to 72nd streets
- **Lincoln Center Out-of-Doors Festival**, www.lincolncenter.org
- **Metropolitan Opera season** begins, Lincoln Center, www.metoperafamily.org
- **NY Film Festival**, Lincoln Center, www.filmlinc.com
- **NY Giants** and **NY Jets Football Season** opens, Meadowlands, New Jersey
- **NYC Underground Comedy Film Festival**, www.nycundergroundcomedy.com
- **Van Steuben Day Parade**, Fifth Avenue, 61st to 86th streets
- **Washington Square Outdoor Art Exhibit,** LaGuardia Place, University Place, and adjacent side streets
- **West Indian Carnival,** www.wiadca.com
- **Wigstock**, Pier 54, 13th Street and Hudson River, www.wigstock.nu

OCTOBER

- **Columbus Day Parade**, Fifth Avenue, 44th to 86th streets
- **Feast of St. Francis**, pets and animals from goldfish to horses come to church in the thousands to be blessed, www.stjohndivine.org
- **Greenwich Village Halloween Parade**, 6th Avenue, www.halloween-nyc.com
- **Hispanic Day Parade**, Fifth Avenue, 44th to 72nd streets
- **New York Rangers hockey season** begins, Madison Square Garden, www.madisonsquaregarden.com
- **Next Wave Festival**, Brooklyn Academy of Music, www.bam.org
- **Promenade Art Show**, Brooklyn Heights
- **Pulaski Day Parade**, Fifth Avenue, www.pulaskiparade.com

NOVEMBER

- **Christmas Spectacular stage show**, Radio City Music Hall, www.radiocity.com
- **Christmas Tree Lighting**, Rockefeller Center, www.rockefellercenter.com
- **New York City Marathon**, www.nycmarathon.org; all five boroughs
- **New York Knicks basketball season begins**, Madison Square Garden
- **NY City Ballet**, winter season, Lincoln Center, www.nycballet.com
- **Macy's Thanksgiving Day Parade**, 77th Street to Herald Square
- **Queens International Film Festival**, www.queensfilmfestival.com

- **Skating Season**, free and not so free rinks open throughout the city, www. bryantpark.org, www.wollmanskatingrink.com, www.rockefellercenter.com, www.amnh.org
- **Veterans Day Parade**, Fifth Avenue, 39th to 24th streets

DECEMBER

- **Fireworks**, South Street Seaport; Grand Army Plaza, Brooklyn
- **First Night, events throughout city**
- **Lighting of the Hanukkah Menorah**, the world's largest, natch; Grand Army Plaza
- **New York Road Runners Club Midnight Run**, Central Park, www.nyrrc.org
- **New Year's Eve Celebration**, Times Square
- **New Year's Eve Concert**, NY Philharmonic, Lincoln Center

B ELOW, WE LIST A FEW BOOKS THAT THE NEWCOMER MAY FIND helpful, enlightening, or just entertaining.

GUIDES

- *AIA Guide to New York City* edited by Elliot Willensky and Norval White (Three Rivers Press); the guide and reference book for anyone interested in New York City architecture. Includes maps, drawings, and directions to neighborhoods throughout the five boroughs. Encyclopedic and fascinating.
- *The Cheap Bastard's Guide to New York City* by Rob Grader (Globe Pequot Press); tips on leading the good life in the city…for pennies.
- *The Grownup's Guide to Living with Kids in Manhattan* (Grownup's Guide Publishing) by Diane Chernoff-Rosen
- *Nature Walks In and Around New York City* by Sheila Buff (Appalachian Mountain Club Books); just the thing to get you out of the apartment for a walk in the woods, the fields, the wetlands—all in New York City.
- *New York: 15 Walking Tours* by Gerard Wolfe (McGraw-Hill Professional); The most mainstream of the many walking tour guides. Consider getting it in audiobook format.
- *New York Tenants' Rights* by Mary Ann Hallenborg (Nolo Press)
- *New York Times Guide to New York City Restaurants* by William Grimes & Eric Asimov (*New York Times*); reviews some 1,000 of the city's restaurants.
- *New York's 50 Best Places to Go Birding In and Around the Big Apple* by John Thaxton and Alan Messer (now out of print, but if birding is your thing try to track down a copy).
- *New York's 100 Best Little Places to Shop* by Eve Claxton (City & Co.)
- *Nosh New York: The Food Lover's Guide to New York City's Most Delicious Neighborhoods* by Myra Alperson (St. Martin's Press)

- *Queer New York City; The Annual Guide To Gay & Lesbian NYC* edited by Martin J. Quinn (On Your Own Publications); from bars to bookstores.
- *Retire in New York City—Even If You're Not Rich* by Janet Hays (Bonus Books)
- *Take Charge! The Complete Guide to Senior Living in New York City* by John Vinton (New York University Press); encyclopedic how-to manual for seniors and gonna-bes.
- *Where to Go: A Guide to Manhattan's Toilets* by Vicki Rovere (published by Vicki Rovere); don't laugh! In a city with a dearth of public toilets, this can be a life-saver. Now updated.

ZAGAT SURVEY GUIDES
- *Zagat Survey: New York City Restaurants*
- *Zagat Survey: New York City Marketplace*
- *Zagat Survey: New York City Nightlife*
- *Zagat Survey: New York City Shopping*

PETS

- *The Dog Lover's Companion to New York City* by Joanna Downey (Avalon Travel Publishing); offers the inside scoop on where to take your dog.
- *The Great New York Dog Book; The Indispensable Canine Resource Guide for New York City Dogs and Their Owners* by Deborah Loven (Harper Perennial Library); you can keep a dog here, and here's how.

NEW YORK CITY HISTORY

- *Central Park, an American Masterpiece: a Comprehensive History of the Nation's First Urban Park* by Sara Cedar Miller (Harry N. Abrams)
- *Discovering Black New York: A Guide to the City's Most Important African American Landmarks, Restaurants, Museums, Historical Sites, and More*, by Linda Tarrant Reid (Citadel Books); most of the restaurant material is dated, but the history remains a good guide.
- *The Encyclopedia of New York City* edited by Kenneth T. Jackson (Yale University Press); from A&P to Zukofsky, this unwieldy literary monument will delight any Gotham-lover.
- *Gotham: A History of New York City to 1898* by Edwin G. Burrows and Mike Wallace (Oxford Press); the best and most comprehensive history, with volume two yet to come.
- *Literary Landmarks of New York City: The Book Lover's Guide to the Homes and Haunts of World Famous Writers* by Bill Morgan (Rizzoli); provides a unique look at the city through the city's great scribes from Poe to Mailer.

- *New York for New Yorkers: A Historical Treasury and Guide to the Buildings and Monuments of Manhattan* by Liza M. Greene (W.W. Norton & Co.)
- *New York Streetscapes: Tales of Manhattan's Significant Buildings and Landmarks* by S. Christopher and Braley Gray (Harry N. Abrams)
- *The WPA Guide to New York City: The Federal Writers' Project Guide to the 1930s New York by William Whyte—Federal Writers Project* (Pantheon Books); mapped, photographed, illustrated and described in this classic. Among the writers, the young John Cheever.

PARENTS/STUDENTS

- *City Baby: The Ultimate Guide for New York City Parents from Pregnancy to Preschool* by Kelly Ashton and Pamela Weinberg (Universal Books); everything from nannies to playgrounds.
- *Cool Parent's Guide to All of New York* by Alfred Gringold and Helen Rogan (Universal Books)
- *The Grownup's Guide to Living with Kids in Manhattan* by Diane Chernoff-Rosen and Lisa Levinson (Resource Marketing Group); comprehensive guide and resource book for parents of kids ages one to twelve.
- *Manhattan Family Guide to Private Schools* by Victoria Goldman and Catherine Hausman (Soho Press)
- *New York City's Best Public Elementary Schools: A Parent's Guide* by Clara Hemphill (Teachers College Press); the last word on the city's public schools—how to choose and get into good ones.
- *New York City's Best Public Middle Schools: A Parent's Guide (second edition 2004)* by Clara Hemphill (Teachers College Press); the sequel to the above, with descriptions and ratings of middle schools, district by district.
- *A Parent's Guide to New York City* by Judith Mahoney Pasternak (Mars Publishing); suggests child-friendly places to go and itineraries.

W HILE THERE IS CLEARLY NO SUBSTITUTE FOR CONDUCTING MOST newcomer business in person, a significant portion of preparatory work can be done by phone or online. Whether it is researching available apartment rentals, determining the nearest library in your neighborhood, or discovering which train to take from your friend's apartment in Brooklyn to your office on the first day on the job, much of the information you need may be gathered even before you arrive.

What follows is a partial listing of phone numbers and web sites that cover a variety of services. In addition, there are many others embedded throughout the book. Check in your section of interest for additional listings.

A great number of city services and agencies are now available through two principal conduits: **311** is the city's 24-hour, all-purpose information line, with live operators prepared to connect you to virtually any city service, from reporting leaking fire hydrants to finding a towed car; **www. nyc.gov** is the umbrella homepage for what had once been a disjointed web of many city sites. Between the two, 311 is a faster and more efficient path to answers, while www.nyc.gov will give you more information and a better overview of the topics you seek to explore.

> # 311
> is the city's
> 24-hour,
> all-purpose
> information line.

ALCOHOL AND DRUG DEPENDENCY

- **Alcoholics Anonymous**, 212-647-1680, www.nyintergroup.org
- **Alcoholism Council of New York, Inc.**, 212-252-7001, www.alcoholism.org
- **Cocaine Anonymous**, 212-929-7300, www.ca-ny.org
- **Narcotics Anonymous, Inc.**, 212-929-7117, www.newyorkna.org
- **National Council on Alcoholism and Drug Dependency**, 212-269-7797, www.ncadd.org

- **The Watershed**, 212-431-4640, www.thewatershed.com, a referral service for addiction to alcohol and drugs and 24-hour help line.

ANIMALS

- **ASPCA**, American Society for the Prevention of Cruelty to Animals, 212-876-7700, www.aspca.org
- **Animal Bites**, Bureau of Veterinary Public Health Services, 212-676-2483
- **Bobst Hospital/Animal Medical Center**, 212-838-8100, www.amcny.org; open 24 hours; phone calls 9 a.m. to 11 p.m.
- **Center for Animal Care and Control** (**CACC**), Manhattan Shelter and Adoption Center, 212-788-4000, www.nycacc.org; **Animal Rescue Service**, 311

BIRTH/DEATH CERTIFICATES

- **New York City Department of Health, Vital Records**, 311, www.nyc.gov/records

CABLE TELEVISION AND THE DISH

CABLE

MANHATTAN

- **Time Warner Cable**, 212-674-9100, www.timewarnercable.com
- **RCN**, 800-RING-RCN, www.rcn.com

QUEENS AND BROOKLYN

- **Time Warner Cable**, 718-358-0900, www.timewarnercable.com

THE BRONX AND BROOKLYN

- **Cablevision**, 718-617-3500, www.cablevision.com

NEW JERSEY

- **Cablevision New Jersey**
- **Comcast**

DISH

- **DirecTV**, 800-347-3288, www.directv.com
- **Dish Network**, 800-333-3474, www.dishnetwork.com

CONSUMER COMPLAINTS AND SERVICES

- **Better Business Bureau**, 212-533-6200, www.newyork.bbb.org
- **Federal Trade Commission**, 212-607-2829, www.ftc.gov
- **NJ Attorney General's Consumer Protection Hotline**, 800-242-5846
- **New York City Department of Consumer Affairs**, 311, www.nyc.gov/consumers

- **NY State Attorney General's Consumer Help Line**, 800-771-7755, www.oag. state.ny.us
- **NY State Consumer Protection Board**, 518-474-3514, www.consumer.state. ny.us
- **NY State Department of Insurance, Consumer Services Bureau**, complaints and inquiries, 212-480-6400, 9 a.m. to 5 p.m., Monday through Friday, www. ins.state.ny.us
- **New York State Department of Transportation**, 800-786-5368, www. nysdot.gov
- **New York State Governor's Consumer Hotline**, 800-697-1220, www. nysconsumer.gov
- **Public Service Commission's Call Center**, 800-342-3377, www.dps.state. ny.us/help.html
- **US Consumer Product Safety Commission Hotline**, 800-638-2772, www. cpsc.gov

CRIME/CRISIS

- **Crime in Progress**, 911
- **Precinct Referrals,** dial 311 or 212-NEW-YORK
- **Suspicious Behavior/Unattended Packages**, 800-828-7273 for Port Authority, 888-NYC-SAFE for MTA

CRISIS HOTLINES

- **Ambulance**, 911
- **Arson Hotline**, 718-722-3600
- **Girls & Boys Town National Hotline**, 800-448-3000, www.boystown.org
- **New Jersey School Safety Hotline**, 877-624-8082
- **Rape/Battered Persons Crisis Center Hotline**, 800-621-4673
- **Sex Crimes Unit**, Police Department, 212-267-7273, 24-hour service staffed by female NYPD detectives
- **Samaritans of New York Suicide Hotline**, 212-673-3000, www.samaritansnyc.org

CHILD ABUSE & FAMILY VIOLENCE

- **Abducted, Abused, and Exploited Children**, 800-248-8020
- **Battered Women Domestic Violence Program**, 800-621-4673, 24-hour
- **New York State Child Abuse and Maltreatment Register**, 800-342-3720, TDD 800-638-5163
- **Emergency Children's Services**, 212-966-8000

CULTURAL LIFE

- **Alliance for the Arts**, 212-947-6340, www.allianceforarts.org

- **City Search**, www.newyork.citysearch.com
- **Curator's Choice**, www.nymuseums.com
- **NYC/OnStage**, 212-912-9770, www.tdf.org
- **New York City & Company**, Convention and Visitors Bureau, 212-484-1200, www.nycgo.com
- *New York* **magazine and New York Metro**, www.nymag.com, customer service, 800-678-0900
- *New York Times*, www.nytimes.com
- **Tele-Charge**, 212-239-6200, www.telecharge.com
- **Ticketmaster**, 212-307-7171, www.ticketmaster.com
- *Time Out New York,* www.timeoutny.com
- **Times Square Visitor's Center**, www.timessquarenyc.org; business improvement district
- *Village Voice*, www.villagevoice.com

DISCRIMINATION

- **New Jersey Division of Civil Rights**, 609-292-4605, www.state.nj.us/oag/dcr/commission.html
- **New York City Commission on Human Rights**, 212-306-7450, www.nyc.gov/cchr
- **US Department of Fair Housing & Discrimination Hotline**, 800-669-9777, www.hud.gov/complaints

EDUCATION

- **New Jersey Department of Education**, 609-292-4469, www.nj.gov/education
- **New York City Department of Education**, 311, http://schools.nyc.gov

ELECTIONS

- **Board of Elections**, 866-VOTE-NYC, TDD 212-487-5496, 9 a.m. to 5 p.m., Monday to Friday, www.vote.nyc.ny.us

EMERGENCY

- **FEMA Disaster Assistance Information**, 800-621-FEMA, TTY 800-462-7585, www.fema.gov
- **Fire, police, medical**, 911
- **Poison Control Center**, 800-222-1222, TDD 212-689-9014, 24-hour service, www.aapcc.org

GOVERNMENT

State and local government listings for all profiled communities are on the net at www.statelocalgov.net.

NEW YORK CITY
- **Bronx Borough President**, 718-590-3500, www.bronxboropres.nyc.gov
- **Brooklyn Borough President**, 718-802-3700, www.brooklyn-usa.org
- **City Council**, 212-788-7210, www.council.nyc.gov
- **Manhattan Borough President**, 212-669-8300, www.mbpo.org
- **New York Mayor's Office/City Hall**, 311, www.nyc.gov
- **Official New York City Web Site**, www.nyc.gov
- **Public Advocate**, 212-669-7200, www.pubadvocate.nyc.gov
- **Queens Borough President**, 718-286-3000, www.queensbp.org
- **Staten Island Borough President**, 718-816-2000, www.statenislandusa.com

NEW YORK STATE
- **Attorney General**, 212-416-8000, TTY 800-788-9898, www.oag.state.ny.us
- **Governor's Office**, 518-474-8390, www.ny.gov/governor
- **State Assembly**, www.assembly.state.ny.us
- **State Senate**, www.senate.state.ny.us

STATE OF NEW JERSEY
- **Attorney General**, 609-292-4925, www.state.nj.us/lps
- **Governor's Office**, 609-292-6000, www.state.nj.us
- **New Jersey Legislature Office of Legislative Services**, 609-292-4840, www.njleg.state.nj.us

FEDERAL
- **Federal Citizen Information Center**, 800-333-4636, www.usa.gov/
- **Social Security Administration**, 800-772-1213, 7 a.m. to 7 p.m., Monday to Friday, www.ssa.gov

HEALTH AND MEDICAL CARE
- **Ambulance Emergency Number**, 911
- **Dental Emergencies**, New York County Dental Society, 212-573-8500, www.nycdentalsociety.org
- **Doctors-on-Call** (private group), 718-745-5900; 24-hour house-call service
- **Lead Poisoning Prevention Program**, 311, www.nyc.gov
- **National Health Information Center** (**NHIC**), US Department of Health and Human Services, 800-336-4797, www.health.gov/nhic
- **New York County Medical Society** (**AMA**), 212-684-4670, www.nycms.org
- **New York Public Advocate**, 212-669-7200, www.pubadvocate.nyc.gov

- **NJ State Board of Medical Examiners**, 609-826-7100, www.state.nj.us/lps/ca/medical.htm
- **NY State Department of Health**, Office of Professional Medical Conduct, 518-402-0855, www.health.state.ny.us
- **Poison Control Center**, 800-222-1222, TDD 212-689-9014
- **US Department of Health and Human Services**, 877-696-6775, www.hhs.gov

HOSPITALS

- **Bellevue Hospital Center**, 212-562-3015, www.nyc.gov/hhc
- **Beth Israel Medical Center**, 212-420-2000, www.wehealny.org
- **Calvary Hospital**, Bronx, 718-518-2300, www.calvaryhospital.org
- **Coler-Goldwater Hospital**, 1 Main St, 212-318-8000, www.ny.gov
- **Columbia-Presbyterian Medical Center**, 212-305-2500, www.cumc.columbia.edu
- **Harlem Hospital Center**, 212-939-1000, www.nyc.gov
- **Jacobi Medical Center**, Bronx, 718-918-5000, www.nyc.gov/hhc
- **Jamaica Hospital and Medical Center**, Queens, 718-206-6000, www.jamaicahospital.org
- **Kings County Hospital Center**, Brooklyn, 718-245-3131, www.nyc.gov/hhc
- **Lenox Hill Hospital**, 212-434-2000, www.lenoxhillhospital.org
- **Metropolitan Hospital Center**, 212-423-6262, www.nyc.gov
- **Manhattan Eye, Ear and Throat Hospital**, 212-838-9200, www.nymeeth.org
- **Mount Sinai Hospital**, 212-241-6500, www.mountsinai.org
- **New York Presbyterian Hospital-Cornell Medical Center**, 212-746-5454, www.nyp.org
- **New York Downtown Hospital**, 212-312-5000, www.downtownhospital.org
- **New York Eye and Ear Infirmary**, 310 E 14th St, 212-979-4000, www.nyee.edu
- **New York-Langone Medical Center**, , 212-263-7300, www.med.nyu.edu
- **New York University Medical Center**, 212-263-7300, www.med.nyu.edu
- **St. Luke's Roosevelt Hospital Center**, 212-523-4000, www.wehealny.org
- **St. Vincent's Catholic Medical Center**, 212-604-7000, www.svcmc.org
- **St. Vincent's Medical Center of Richmond**, Staten Island, 718-818-1234, www.svcmc.org
- **Staten Island University Hospital**, Staten Island, 718-226-9140
- **Woodhull Medical Center**, Brooklyn, 718-963-8000, www.nyc.gov/hhc

HOUSING RESOURCES

- **Department of Environmental Protection**, 311, www.nyc.gov/dep
- **Division of Housing & Community Renewal**, 212-480-6700, rent information line 718-739-6400, www.dhcr.state.ny.us
- **Gas or Electric service shutoff hotline**, 800-342-3355

- **Housing Authority**, 212-306-3000, www.nyc.gov/nycha
- **Housing Discrimination** for New York (and New Jersey): Fair Housing Hub, US Department of Housing and Urban Development, 212-264-9610 or 800-496-4294; housing discrimination hotline, 800-669-9777, www.hud.gov/complaints
- **Metropolitan Council on Housing**, 212-979-6238, www.metcouncil.net; tenants union
- **New Jersey Landlord Tenant Information Service**, 609-292-4174, www.state.nj.us/dca
- **New Jersey Tenants Organization (NJTO)**, 201-342-3775, www.njto.org
- **New York City Loft Board**, 212-788-7610, www.nyc.gov/html/loft
- **New York City Rent Guidelines Board**, 212-385-2934, www.housingnyc.com
- **NYC Heat Hotline**, 311
- **NYC Urban League**, 212-926-8000, www.nyul.org
- **Office of Rent Administration**, State Division of Housing and Community Renewal (DHCR), 866-275-3427, www.dhcr.state.ny.us
- **Rent Stabilization Association**, 212-214-9200, www.rsanyc.org
- **TenantNet**, www.tenant.net
- **Tenants & Neighbors**, 212-608-4320
- **US Department of Fair Housing and Anti-predatory Hotline**, 800-477-5977, www.fairhousing.com

INFORMATION LINES

- **New York's "311" line** (212-NEW-YORK outside New York City) is the general information line for all city agencies and related services. Operators will transfer calls to appropriate agency departments based on your specific needs.
- **411, 212-555-1212, 718-555-1212**, are general information lines that can be used for locating either commercial businesses or personal phone numbers of anyone or any business listed in the New York City telephone directories. There is a charge of $1.25 to dial 411, and $.80 for the other numbers. Calls to 411 from a mobile phone can cost as much as $3.49. Far better is Google's new computerized assistance at 800-GOOG-411. All calls are free and they connect you through free of charge; the only drawback is there is no live operator available (their new VOR software, however, is excellent, not to mention humorous).

INTERNET SERVICE PROVIDERS

- **America Online**, 800-827-6364, www.aol.com
- **AT&T WorldNet**, 800-967-5363, www.att.net
- **Compuserve**, 800-848-8990, www.compuserve.com
- **Earthlink**, 800-719-4332, www.earthlink.net

- **Juno**, 800-717-0453, www.juno.com
- **MSN**, 800-386-5550, www.msn.com
- **NetZero**, 877-665-9995, www.netzero.net
- **RCN**, 800-RING-RCN, www.rcn.com
- **Verizon**, 888-638-6100, www.verizon.com

LIBRARIES

See **Literary Life** in the **Cultural Life** chapter for descriptions of area libraries.
- **Bronx Library Center**, 718-579-4244, www.nypl.org
- **Brooklyn Central Library**, 718-230-2100, www.brooklynpubliclibrary.org
- **New York Public Library Central Branch**, 212-340-0833, www.nypl.org
- **Staten Island, St. George Central Library**, 718-442-8560, www.nypl.org
- **Queens Public Central Library**, 718-990-0700, www.queenslibrary.org
- **Branch libraries**: see listings following Neighborhood Profiles.

MARRIAGE LICENSES

- **NYC Marriage License Bureau**, 212-669-2400, www.nycmarriagebureau.com

MOTOR VEHICLES/PARKING

- **American Automobile Association**, 212-757-2000, www.aaany.com
- **Automobile Dealer (used) Complaints**, 212-487-4444
- **Licenses and Registration Information**, New York State Department of Motor Vehicles, 212-645-5550, 8 a.m. to 4 p.m., www.nysdmv.com
- **New Jersey Motor Vehicle Commission**, 609-292-6500, www.state.nj.us/mvc
- **NYPD Towing** (towed cars), 311
- **Parking Violations Hotline**, NYC Department of Transportation automated help line, 212-504-4041, 8 a.m. to 5 p.m., Monday to Friday, www.pubadvocate.nyc.gov
- **State Department of Motor Vehicles**, 212- 645-5550, www.nysdmv.com

PARKS AND RECREATION

- **General information**, including special events, 888-NY-PARKS, www.nycgovparks.org
- See **Sports and Recreation** and **Greenspace and Beaches** chapters.

POLICE

See **Neighborhoods** chapter for precinct stations.
- **New Jersey State Police**, 609-882-2000, www.njsp.org
- **New York State Police Troop**, NYC, 917-492-7100, www.troopers.state.ny.us
- **Police Emergencies** dial 911

POST OFFICE

- **US Postal Service**, 800-275-8777, www.usps.com

SANITATION AND GARBAGE

- **NYC Department of Sanitation**, dial 311 or 212-NEW-YORK, www.nyc.gov/dsny

SENIORS

- **NYC Department for the Aging**, 311, www.nyc.gov/aging
- **New York Foundation for Senior Citizens**, 212-962-7559, www.nyfsc.org
- **Social Security and Medicare Eligibility Information**, 800-772-1213, TTY 800-325-0778, 7 a.m. to 7 p.m., Monday to Friday, www.ssa.gov

SPORTS

PARTICIPANT SPORTS AND ACTIVITIES

- **Bronx**, 718-430-1858
- **Brooklyn**, 718-965-8900
- **Central Park Conservancy**, 212-310-6600, www.centralparknyc.org
- **Gateway National Recreation Area**, 718-338-3799, www.nps.gov/gate
- **Manhattan**, 212-408-0205
- **New York City Parks and Recreation**, www.nycgovparks.org
- **Queens**, 718-520-5936
- **Staten Island**, 718-390-8000

PROFESSIONAL

- **New Jersey Devils**, 800-NJ-DEVIL, www.devils.nhl.com
- **New Jersey Nets**, 800-7NJ-NETS, www.njnets.com
- **New York Giants**, 201-935-8222, www.giants.org
- **New York Islanders**, 800-882-ISLES, www.islanders.nhl.com
- **New York Jets**, 516-560-8200, www.newyorkjets.com
- **New York Knicks**, 212-465-5867, 877-NYK-DUNK, www.nba.com/knicks
- **New York Liberty**, 212-465-6073, www.wnba.com/liberty
- **New York Mets**, 718-507-METS, www.mets.com
- **New York Rangers**, 212-307-7171, www.newyorkrangers.com
- **New York Yankees**, 212-307-7171, www.yankees.mlb.com

STREET MAINTENANCE

- **Potholes**, NYC Bureau of Highways, 311
- **Streetlights**, 311
- **Water mains and sewers**, NYC Department of Environmental Protection, 311

TAXES

CITY
- **NYC Department of Finance**, 311, www.nyc.gov/dof

FEDERAL
- **Internal Revenue Service**, 800-829-4477, www.irs.gov

STATE
- **NYS Department of Taxation and Revenue**, 800-225-5829, TTY 800-634-2110, www.state.ny.us
- **New Jersey Division of Taxation: Taxpayer Customer Service Center**, 609-292-6400, www.state.nj.us/treasury/taxation

TELEPHONE (LAND LINES)

- **AT&T**, 800-222-0300, www.att.net
- **MCI**, 800-444-3333, www.mci.com
- **RCN**, 800-746-4726, www.rcn.com
- **Sprint**, 800-877-7746, www.sprint.com
- **Verizon**, 212-890-2550, www.verizon.com

TRANSPORTATION

- **AirTrain**, 800-247-7433, www.panynj.gov
- **FMCSA**, 888-368-7238, www.fmcsa.dot.gov
- **NJ State Department of Transportation**, 609-530-2000, www.njdot.nj.gov
- **NY State Department of Transportation**, 718-482-4594, 800-786-5368, www.nysdot.gov
- **Port Authority of New York & New Jersey**, 212-564-8484, 800-221-9903, www.panynj.gov
- **US Department of Transportation**, 866-377-8642, www.dot.gov

AIRPORTS
- **John F. Kennedy International**, 718-244-4444 for airport information, 718-244-4225 for lost and found, and 718-244-4168 for parking; www.kennedyairport.com.
- **LaGuardia International Airport**, Call 718-533-3400 for airport information; 718-533-3988 for lost and found; and 718-533-3850 for parking; www.panynj.gov.
- **Newark Liberty International Airport**, 973-961-6000 for airport information; 973-961-6243 for lost and found; and 888-397-4636, then press 22, to receive parking information; www.newarkairport.com.
- **Port Authority of New York & New Jersey**, 212-435-7000, 800-221-9903, www.panynj.gov

BUSES

- **Port Authority Bus Terminal Information**, 212-564-8484, 800-221-9903, www.panynj.gov
- **Greyhound Bus Lines**, 800-231-2222, www.greyhound.com
- **Peter Pan Trailways**, 800-343-9999, www.peterpanbus.com

FERRIES

- **NY Water Taxi**, 212-742-1969, www.nywatertaxi.com
- **New York Waterway**, 800-53-FERRY, www.nywaterway.com
- **Seastreak**, 800-BOAT-RIDE, www.seastreak.com
- **Staten Island Ferry**, 311, www.statenislandferry.com

RAIL

- **Amtrak** (Penn Station), 800-872-7245, www.amtrak.com
- **Long Island Railroad** (Penn Station), 718-217-5477, TTY 718-558-3022, www.mta.info
- **Metro-North,** 212-532-4900, TTY 800-724-3322, www.mta.info
- **New Jersey Transit** (Penn Station), 800 772 2222, 800 772 2222, www.njtransit.com
- **Staten Island Rapid Transit**, 718-966-SIRT, www.mta.info

SUBWAYS AND CITY BUSES

- **Lost and Found** (NYC Transit Authority), 212-712-4500, www.mta.info
- **MTA Customer Service**, 718-330-1234, www.mta.info
- **Metro Card**, 212-METRO-CARD
- **PATH service to New Jersey**, 800-234-7284, www.panynj.gov
- **Subway and Bus Schedules** (NYC Transit Authority automated system for fares, routes, schedules), 718-330-1234, www.mta.info

TAXIS, LIMOUSINES

- **Taxi and Limousine Commission**, 212-NYC-TAXI, www.nyc.gov/taxi

TOURISM AND TRAVEL

- **National Park Service**, www.nps.gov
- **New York & Company** (The Convention and Visitors Bureau), 212-484-1200, www.nycgov.com
- **New York State Travel Information Center**, 800-CALL-NYS, www.iloveny.com
- **New Jersey Department of Travel & Tourism**, 800-847-4865, www.state.nj.us/travel
- **New York Passport Agency, Automated Appointment Number**, 877-487-2778, www.travel.state.gov

UTILITY EMERGENCIES

- **Electrical emergencies or gas leaks**, Con Edison, 800-752-6633, www.conedison.com
- **Gas or Electric service shutoff hotline**, 800-342-3355

ZIP CODE INFORMATION

- **USPS zip codes request**, 800-275-8777, www.usps.com

The Newcomer's Handbook for New York City was first published in 1980 by Jennifer Cecil. For many years, a key contributor was Belden Merims. The 21st edition was updated by Jack Finnegan.

The most recent update was done by Stewart Lee Allen, who describes himself as follows:

STEWART LEE ALLEN lives in a derelict toy factory in Williamsburg, Brooklyn. His books on travel, food, drugs and religion have been translated into 15 languages.

INDEX

READER RESPONSE

We would appreciate your comments regarding this fifth edition of the *Newcomer's Handbook® for Moving to and Living in Los Angeles.* If you've found any mistakes or omissions or if you would just like to express your opinion about the guide, please let us know. We will consider any suggestions for possible inclusion in our next edition, and if we use your comments, we'll send you a free copy of our next edition. Please e-mail us at readerresponse@firstbooks.com, or mail or fax this response form to:

Reader Response Department
First Books
6750 SW Franklin, Suite A
Portland, OR 97223-2542
Fax: 503.968.6779

Comments: _____

_____

_____

_____

_____

_____

_____

_____

_____

Name: _____

Address: _____

_____

_____

Telephone: ( ) _____

Email: _____

6750 SW Franklin, Suite A
Portland, OR 97223-2542
USA
P: 503.968.6777
www.firstbooks.com

RELOCATION RESOURCES

Utilizing an innovative grid and "static" reusable adhesive sticker format, *Furniture Placement and Room Planning Guide...Moving Made Easy* provides a functional and practical solution to all your space planning and furniture placement needs.

MOVING WITH KIDS?

Look into *The Moving Book: A Kids' Survival Guide*.

Divided into three sections (before, during, and after the move), it's a handbook, a journal, and a scrapbook all in one. Includes address book, colorful change-of-address cards, and a useful section for parents.

Children's Book of the Month Club "Featured Selection"; American Bookseller's "Pick of the List"; Winner of the Family Channel's "Seal of Quality" Award

And for your younger children, ease their transition with our brand-new title just for them, *Max's Moving Adventure: A Coloring Book for Kids on the Move*. A complete story book featuring activities as well as pictures that children can color; designed to help children cope with the stresses of small or large moves.

NEWCOMERSWEB.COM

Based on the award-winning *Newcomer's Handbooks*, **NewcomersWeb.com** offers the highest quality neighborhood and community information in a one-of-a-kind searchable online database. The following areas are covered: Atlanta, Austin, Boston, Chicago, Dallas–Fort Worth, Houston, Los Angeles, Ninneapolis–St. Paul, New York City, Portland (Oregon), San Francisco, Seattle, Washington DC, and the USA.

NEWCOMER'S HANDBOOKS®

Regularly revised and updated, these popular guides are now available for Atlanta, Boston, Chicago, China, London, Los Angeles, Minneapolis–St. Paul, New York City, Portland, San Francisco Bay Area, Seattle, Texas and Washington DC.

"Invaluable ...highly recommended" – Library Journal

If you're coming from another country, don't miss the *Newcomer's Handbook® for Moving to and Living in the USA* by Mike Livingston, termed "a fascinating book for newcomers and residents alike" by the *Chicago Tribune*.

F8 FIRST BOOKS

6750 SW Franklin Street
Portland, Oregon 97223-2542
Phone 503.968.6777 • Fax 503.968.6779
www.firstbooks.com

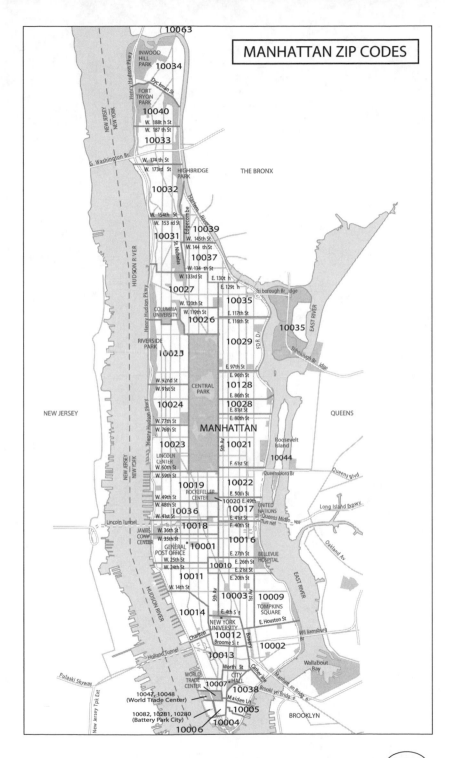

MANHATTAN ZIP CODES

10063

INWOOD HILL PARK

10034

FORT TRYON PARK

10040

W. 188th St
W. 187th St

10033

G. Washington Br.

W. 174th St
W. 173rd St   HIGHBRIDGE PARK

THE BRONX

10032

W. 154th St
W. 153rd St

10039
W. 145th St

10031   W. 144 th St

10037
W. 134 th St
W. 133rd St   E. 130th

E. 129 th

10027
W. 120th St   Triborough Br. idge

COLUMBIA UNIVERSITY   W. 119th St   10035
E. 117th St

10026   E. 116th St

RIVERSIDE PARK   10029

10023   E. 97th St
EAST RIVER

W. 92nd St   E. 96th St   10128
W. 91st St   CENTRAL PARK   E. 86th St

10024   E. 81st St   10028
W. 77th St   E. 80th St
W. 76th St   MANHATTAN

QUEENS

10023   5th Av   10021
LINCOLN CENTER
W. 60th St   Roosevelt Island
W. 59th St   E. 61st St   10044

10019   Queensboro Br.   Queens Blvd
ROCKEFELLER CENTER   10022
W. 49th St   E. 50th St   Long Island Expwy
W. 48th St   10020 E. 49th
10036   10017
UNITED NATIONS
W. 41st St   E. 41st St   Queens Midto
10018   E. 40th St   Queens Midtown Tun nel   Oakland Av
JAVITS CONV. CENTER   W. 36th St
W. 35th St   10016
GENERAL POST OFFICE   10001
W. 25th St   E. 27th St   BELLEVUE HOSPITAL
W. 24th St   10010   E. 26th St
E. 21st St
10011   E. 20th St
W. 14th St   EAST RIVER

5th Av   10003   10009
10014   TOMPKINS SQUARE
E. 4th S
NEW YORK UNIVERSITY   E. Houston St
10012   Williamsburg Br
Broome St   Bowery
10013   10002
Wallabout Bay
Holland Tunnel   Worth St
Canther Ave   Manha tt an Bridg e
WORLD TRADE CENTER   CITY HALL   10038
10007   Brookl yn Bridg e
10047, 10048   Maiden Ln   BROOKLYN
(World Trade Center)   10005
10082, 10281, 10280
(Battery Park City)   10004
10006

NEW JERSEY

HUDSON RIVER

Henry Hudson Pkwy

NEW JERSEY
NEW YORK

Lincoln Tunnel

HUDSON RIVER

Pulaski Skyway

New Jersey Tpk Ext

Dyckman St

Henry Hudson Pkwy

Edgecombe

Harlem River

St. Nicholas

FDR Dr.

Triborough Br. idge

421